TORT LAW AND ECONOMIC INTERESTS

Tort Law and Economic Interests
Second Edition

PETER CANE

Corpus Christi College, Oxford

CLARENDON PRESS · OXFORD
1996

Oxford University Press, Walton Street, Oxford OX2 6DP
Oxford New York
Athens Auckland Bangkok Bombay
Calcutta Cape Town Dar es Salaam Delhi
Florence Hong Kong Istanbul Karachi
Kuala Lumpur Madras Madrid Melbourne
Mexico City Nairobi Paris Singapore
Taipei Tokyo Toronto
and associated companies in
Berlin Ibadan

Oxford is a trade mark of Oxford University Press

Published in the United States
by Oxford University Press Inc., New York

British Library Cataloguing in Publication Data
Data available

Library of Congress Cataloging in Publication Data
Cane, Peter, 1950–
Tort law and economic interests / Peter Cane. — 2. ed.
p. cm.
Includes index.
1. Torts—Economic aspects.   2. Liability (Law)—Economic aspects.
3. Interest (Ownership rights)—Economic aspects.   I. Title.
K923.C36 1995   346.03—dc20   [342.63]   95–46834
ISBN 0–19–876430–8   ISBN 0–19–876429–4 (Pbk)

Typeset by Hope Services (Abingdon) Ltd.
Printed in Great Britain
on acid-free paper by
Biddles Ltd., Guildford and King's Lynn

Preface

In his review of the first edition of the book ((1992) 12 OJLS 558) John Fleming said that for 'tort scholars accustomed to view the subject primarily through the lens of personal injuries, getting into [the] book is an experience somewhat like Alice's crossing through the Looking Glass'. I was very glad of this reaction because my prime aim in originally writing this book was to provide a radically fresh perspective on the subject. I am very grateful to Richard Hart of OUP for giving me the opportunity to update and improve upon my first attempt.

Fleming also thought that the book was overwhelmingly detailed and that it lacked an overarching theory to explain what was going on in Wonderland. I have not significantly reduced the amount of detail, although I have pruned the footnotes significantly. I still feel that in order to justify my approach to the subject I need to do more than rearrange and supplement the table of contents of the traditional tort text. I also need to show how the new organization is rooted in the legal materials and this requires that certain topics be dealt with in some detail. Many others which are discussed at length in most tort books are here either passed over lightly or totally ignored. In this edition I have, however, tried to provide rather more signposts and to make more explicit the conclusions which I believe my analysis supports and the insights which I think my approach yields. This should enable readers to pass over details in which they are not interested without losing the main thread of the analysis. As for an overarching theory, I have nailed my colours to the mast in the conclusion to Chapter 10—I do not believe that there is such a theory to explain this or any other large area of the law.

There have been very many relevant changes in common and statute law in the past five years or so, and I hope that I have identified all the important ones. Some sections of the book have been radically rewritten, but the basic structure is unchanged. Jane Stapleton read the entire manuscript of this edition and made many fundamental and penetrating comments and criticisms which have helped me make various minor and some very major improvements. The usual caveats apply. The typescript was substantially completed in mid-August 1995.

Oxford, August 1995   P.F.C.

Contents

Table of Cases

Table of Legislation

STATUTES

UNITED KINGDOM

STATUTORY INSTRUMENTS

Abbreviations

Birks	P. Birks, *An Introduction to the Law of Restitution*, rev. repr. (Oxford, 1989)
Burrows	A. Burrows, *Remedies for Torts and Breach of Contract*, 2nd edn. (London, 1994)
CDPA	Copyright, Designs and Patents Act 1988
Cornish	W. R. Cornish, *Intellectual Property: Patents, Trade Marks and Allied Rights*, 2nd edn. (London, 1989)
D	defendant
Fleming	J. G. Fleming, *The Law of Torts* , 8th edn. (Sydney, 1992)
Goff and Jones	Lord Goff of Chieveley and G. Jones, *The Law of Restitution*, 4th edn. (London, 1993)
Goode	R. M. Goode, *Commercial Law* (London, 1982)
Gray	K. Gray, *Elements of Land Law*, 2nd edn. (London, 1993)
Hanbury and Maudsley	H. G. Hanbury and R. H. Maudsley, *Modern Equity*, 14th edn., J. Martin (ed.) (London, 1993)
Harris	D. R. Harris, *Remedies in Contract and Tort* (London, 1988)
Harvey and Parry	B. W. Harvey and D. L. Parry, *The Law of Consumer Protection and Fair Trading*, 4th edn. (London, 1992)
Megarry and Wade	Sir R. Megarry and H. W. R. Wade, *The Law of Real Property*, 5th edn. (London, 1984)
P	plaintiff
Phillips and Firth	J. Phillips and A. Firth, *Introduction to Intellectual Property Law*, 3rd edn. (London, 1995)
Salmond	R. F. V. Heuston and R. A. Buckley, *Salmond and Heuston on the Law of Torts*, 20th edn. (London, 1992)
TMA	Trade Marks Act 1994
TULCRA	Trade Unions and Labour Relations (Consolidation) Act 1992
Treitel	G. H. Treitel, *The Law of Contract*, 9th edn. (London, 1995)
UCTA	Unfair Contract Terms Act 1977
UTCCR	Unfair Terms in Consumer Contracts Regulations 1994
Wedderburn	Lord Wedderburn of Charlton, *The Worker and the Law* (London, 1986)
Whish	R. Whish, *Competition Law*, 3rd edn. (London, 1993)

PART I

Introduction

1

Foundations

Preliminary Matters

This book is about the way the law of tort deals with 'economic interests',
by which (as I shall explain in more detail later) I mean interests for the invasion of which a finite sum of money can provide complete recompense. A
number of themes run through the book. One concerns the province of tort
law: it is commonly thought that the protection of economic interests is the
focus of the law of contract, trusts and restitution whereas the focus of tort
law is personal injury and damage to tangible property. I hope to convince
the reader that the protection of economic interests is in fact a major function of tort law as well. A second theme concerns the relationship between
tort law and other legal categories. Although the primary focus will be on
areas of the law which can justifiably be treated as part of the law of tort, it
is, in my view, impossible fully to understand the way tort law protects economic interests without considering the relationship between rules and principles of tort law and other areas of the law such as the law of contract,
property, trusts, and restitution which also play a part in protecting economic
interests.

A third theme concerns the relationship between the common law of tort
and relevant statute law: once we think of the law of tort in terms of a set of
techniques for protecting economic interests rather than as a set of causes of
action (such as trespass, negligence, nuisance, and so) which have been
invented by the courts, the distinction between the common law and statute
becomes relatively insignificant. For instance, the legal techniques underlying
the statutory protection of intellectual property are essentially similar to those
found at work in the tort of trespass. Throughout the book I will seek to inte-
grate common law and statutory causes of action in tort by reference to the
interests they protect and the legal techniques by which they provide that protection.

The phrase 'economic interests' needs explanation. In the first place, it is
worth noting some nuances in the use of the word 'interest'. When we speak
of someone having, for instance, a 'property interest', we mean that the person has some sort of claim over or right in some tangible or intangible thing;
and when we speak of someone having a 'contractual interest' we mean that

the person has some claim or right by reason of a contract. In such instances the word 'interest' is more or less synonymous with the words 'right' or 'claim'. An interest in this sense relates to (or is 'in' or 'over') some tangible or intangible thing such as property or a contract. A useful general term to describe the subject matter of interests is 'assets'. This book is primarily about economic interests in assets. On the other hand, we often speak of a person's interests or of the public interest in a broader sense to mean simply objectives or states of affairs which are, or would be, to the person's or the public's advantage: for example, the public interest in the due administration of justice, thought to be furthered by the barrister's immunity from suit in respect of negligence in the conduct of litigation in court; or the interest in free competition recognized in the defence of justification in the tort of conspiracy. This sense of the word 'interest' comes into play particularly in Chapter 5. While it is clear that both types of interest may be 'legal' in the sense of 'recognized and protected by law', interests of the former type are, on the whole, better protected than those of the latter type, at least in the sense that interests of the former type often constitute legal 'swords', whereas those of the latter type are often only effective as 'shields'.

A second point to make about economic interests is this: it is sometimes said that the *only* interests which the law of tort protects are economic, because the only form of compensation which the law can provide is monetary. However, this proposition is only superficially attractive. The law of tort does sometimes award non-monetary remedies: injunctions and orders for the return of specific goods; and such remedies are awarded sometimes, at least, exactly because the plaintiff's interest in the subject matter of the action is *not* solely economic: a person may want to enjoy their garden in quietness, not to be paid to put up with noise; or a person may want a particular piece of property back, not its value in money.

More importantly, we should distinguish between that which is protected—a person's interest, and the means for protecting it—the remedy. The law of tort protects a variety of non-economic interests: for example, an interest in physical health and bodily wholeness (recognized by the rules allowing damages for pain and suffering and loss of amenities); an interest in mental and psychological health and well-being (recognized by the rules allowing recovery for nervous shock, distress and inconvenience); an interest in the enjoyment of one's land (recognized by the rules allowing damages for interference with the enjoyment of land); an interest in good repute (recognized by the rules allowing damages for lowering of reputation). Of course, each of these non-economic interests can have an economic dimension: injuries to body or mind can reduce earnings and generate expenses; one's reputation or the amenities of one's land may be a source of wealth. In other words, non-economic interests and economic interests may exist side-by-side in a given set of circumstances. When the remedy awarded for interference with a non-economic interest is money damages it is, at best, only a poor sort of recompense; in many cases, the injured party would still feel a sense of loss no matter how generous the damages awarded. On the other hand, a remedy of money damages is a wholly adequate one for interference with an economic interest. This fact marks the essential difference between economic and non-economic interests.

In some instances the law is prepared to assume the existence of non-economic interests: damages for loss of the amenities of life can be awarded in accordance with a tariff to all victims of personal injuries without inquiry into, and regardless of, their personal habits and circumstances, and even if the victim is permanently unconscious.[1] In other instances the claimant must positively establish the existence of a non-economic interest: for example, where property is tortiously damaged and the cost of repair exceeds the diminution in the value of the property resulting from the tort, a claimant who seeks an award of the cost of repair will have to establish that there is a genuine (non-economic) interest in repair which would justify the award of damages greater than the diminution in value.[2] By contrast, the law *always* requires the plaintiff to prove the existence of an economic interest and the extent of the financial loss flowing from interference with it.

Definition of 'Economic Interest'

An economic interest, then, in the sense in which the term is used in this book, is an interest for the invasion of which a finite sum of money can provide complete recompense—*restitutio in integrum* in the fullest sense. A party whose economic interests have been injured should feel no further sense of loss, having received a sum of money which accurately reflects the value of what has been lost. If the party does feel a sense of unsatisfied loss then his or her interest is not purely economic; or, more accurately, the party has some non-economic interest in addition to the economic interest. Economic interests are capable of objective valuation: if something has additional subjective value for its 'owner' then that person's interest is not just economic.[3]

In this sense, economic interests are interests based on exchange: if there is no market in what a person has lost, then his or her interest is not (in my sense) economic, and the loss is not economic.[4] Accuracy in valuing economic interests and losses is defined in market terms, and it is the impossibility of valuing non-economic interests and losses accurately in such terms which leads us to view damages for the invasion of such interests as essentially arbitrary and inadequate, in the sense that they are more in the nature of solace

[1] Burrows, 188–90.   [2] See 92 below.

[3] For a similar distinction drawn in terms of types of compensation rather than types of interest, see R. E. Goodin (1989) 9 *OJLS* 56.

[4] Note that this exchange definition relates to the interest, not the asset which is the subject matter of the interest. So, for instance, in our society there are no (lawful) markets in bodily parts, but most adults have an economic interest in at least some of the parts of their bodies.

than of recompense. This is not to say that assessing value in market terms is always a straightforward exercise.[5] For example, the value of the shares in a company may be calculated in different ways, and it may not be immediately obvious which way of valuing them the law ought to adopt in a particular context.[6] Nor does it follow that the law always adopts the market value of what has been damaged or lost as the appropriate measure of monetary compensation. For example, by virtue of the requirement that losses be mitigated, a commonly adopted measure of damages for physical harm to property is the cost of repair as opposed to reduction in the market value of the property caused by the damage.[7] But none of this challenges the basic definition of an economic interest: in the case of shares, the 'takeover bid value' is based on the market in buying and selling shares, and the 'true asset value' is based on the market in buying and selling assets of the type the company owns. In the case of damaged property, the cost-of-repair measure is based on the market in buying and selling the services and materials needed for repair.

The justification for limiting the scope of this book to economic interests so defined is that there is an important conceptual (and practical) distinction between things which can be objectively valued and things which cannot; or, put more accurately, between interests (in things) which can be objectively valued and interests which cannot. Whether, and to what extent, the law should protect particular economic interests thus defined raises rather different issues from whether, and to what extent, it should protect particular non-economic interests.

Qualifications to the Definition

Interests and Losses

This definition of economic interests needs to be glossed in at least two ways. First, it is couched in terms of economic 'interests', not in terms of economic 'loss'. This emphasis on interests illuminates important issues. For example, even though the focus of the tort of negligence is on loss caused by negligent conduct,[8] one consequence of the refusal of courts to recognize a general principle of liability for negligently caused economic loss[9] has sometimes been an emphasis on the plaintiff's allegedly invaded interest as a criterion for drawing the line between actionability and non-actionability. An example is provided by the rule that economic loss is recoverable in some contexts only if

[5] See e.g. *Smith, Kline & French Laboratories Ltd* v. *Long* [1989] 1 WLR 1.
[6] See further P. Cane [1982] *JBL* 79.   [7] See 92 below.
[8] See Cane, 'Economic Loss and Products Liability' in C. J. Miller (ed.), *Comparative Product Liability* (London, 1987), 47.
[9] See e.g. *Yuen Kun Yeu* v. *A-G of Hong Kong* [1988] AC 175.

it is a causal consequence of damage to the plaintiff's property. More importantly, economic loss is of essentially the same nature in every case—the loss
of money or money's worth. If we look at situations in terms of the interest
which was invaded we may be able to identify relevant differences between
cases involving economic loss and be able to explain why such loss is recoverable in some cases but not in others.[10]

On the other hand, the emphasis on interests might be thought unsatisfactory because some people might not recognize simple diminution of wealth,
which is the subject of many tort claims, as invasion of an economic interest.
For example, it might be said that in *Ministry of Housing and Local
Government* v. *Sharp*[11] the plaintiff's complaint was not that the defendant
had invaded some interest of its but rather that, as a result of the defendant's
negligence, it was poorer in monetary terms than it would have been if the
tort had not been committed. On this view, whereas in some tort cases the
complaint is that the defendant has invaded or interfered with some property
or contractual or other interest, in other cases the complaint is that the defendant has reduced (or, more rarely, failed to increase) monetary wealth.[12]

In my view, it is useful to think of tortious diminution in wealth as invasion of an economic interest; and so the first gloss to be put on the above
definition of economic interests is that it includes an 'interest' in the preservation of one's monetary wealth. The main forms of monetary wealth are
currency, negotiable instruments, and bank accounts.[13] The stipulation that
economic interests are based on exchange applies *ex hypothesi* to monetary
wealth. Monetary wealth is a form of property, but it differs from other
forms of property in that it is predominantly a universal medium of exchange
rather than the subject of exchange transactions. It is necessary to say 'predominantly' because of the fact that currency and negotiable instruments are
themselves bought and sold; but the primary function of money is as a
medium of exchange.

Treating actionable diminution of wealth as invasion of an economic interest alerts us to an important point about the relationship between interests
and remedies. It is helpful to draw a distinction between 'constitutive rules'
which state how legal interests, such as interests in property and contractual
interests, may be created, and 'protective rules' which state the causes of
action and the remedies which are available to provide redress for invasions

---

[10] Of course, a focus on interests will not explain everything. For instance, the plaintiff's interest in *Hedley Byrne & Co. Ltd* v. *Heller & Partners Ltd* [1964] AC 465 was the same as that of
the plaintiffs in *Caparo Industries PLC* v. *Dickman* [1990] 2 AC 605; but in the former case it
was held that a duty of care could arise, and in the latter that no duty could arise.

[11] [1970] 2 QB 223.

[12] I am using 'money' in the way an economist might in the abstract sense of 'purchasing
power', rather than in a strict legal sense: see generally F. A. Mann, *The Legal Aspect of Money*
(London, 1982), ch. 1.

[13] The second and third differ from the first because, in strict legal terms, they consist of contractual rights. However, for the purposes of the law of tort they can be treated as monetary
wealth: see Salmond, 105–6.

of legal interests. Some of the economic interests for invasion of which the law of tort provides redress, such as property rights and rights under contracts, are the product of constitutive rules of the law of property and the law of contract respectively. However, we can only fully understand what we mean by an economic interest in property or in a contract if we can give an account of the ways in which the law of tort remedies invasions of such interests. The ways in which it remedies invasions of economic interests in property and in contracts are part of what we refer to when we speak of such interests as being legal interests. Furthermore, there are some economic interests protected by the law of tort, such as that in monetary wealth, which are defined solely in terms of the causes of action and the remedies which are provided by the law to protect them. There is no body of legal rules constitutive of the interest in monetary wealth as such. For this reason, the link between such interests and the tort actions and remedies which are available for interference with them is much closer than that between tort remedies and economic interests in property and in contracts, for instance. It is a pervasive theme of this book that we can only fully understand what we mean by economic interests when we have given an account of the causes of action and the remedies which the law of tort makes available to provide redress for interferences with them.

Use Value and Exchange Value

The second way in which the definition of economic interests needs to be glossed is this: a distinction can be drawn between the use value and the exchange value of things.[14] Although I have defined economic interests as interests based on exchange, the term does not apply only to interests in things which are valued for exchange rather than for use. A person can have an economic interest in a thing valued for use because the use of a thing (such as a car or a building) can itself have market value. Moreover, even if the owner of property values it solely for personal use (as is often the case with cars, for instance) the owner's interest in it may be economic in the sense that were the property, for example, damaged or destroyed the owner would be completely satisfied with a remedy which enabled it to be repaired or replaced and which provided compensation for any financial loss consequent upon the thing not being available for use. On the other hand, a person may have a non-economic interest in using a thing such as a dwelling. A person deprived of the use of a dwelling may not be satisfied with receiving as recompense the full cost of the use of another house.

---

[14] B. Rudden draws a related but different distinction between 'things as thing and things as wealth': (1994) 14 *OJLS* 81 esp. at 93.

2. PERSONAL INJURIES

This book does not contain any systematic discussion of the law relating to personal injuries or death.[15] This is not because the infliction of personal injuries or death never involves invasion of economic interests in the sense in which I have defined them. Indeed, the individual's interest in maintaining his or her earning power is the most important economic interest most people have. This is why, in theory at least, the law does compensate in full for loss of wages or financial support and for expenses which have been, or will in the future be, generated by personal injuries.[16] Further, a person who is fully compensated for his or her economic losses should, *in respect of those losses*, feel no unsatisfied sense of economic deprivation. However, there are several reasons why such economic interests associated with the interest in bodily and mental health have been excluded from this book. The first arises from the fact that victims of serious personal injuries which have permanent adverse effects on their health or capacities tend to feel that they would rather not have been injured, even if they have been fully compensated for their economic losses and generously compensated for their non-economic losses. It is obvious why most people who were formerly whole in mind and body would rather still be whole, no matter how generously they had been recompensed in money for their non-pecuniary losses. But it is surely also true that most people who have been partly or wholly disabled from work (whether paid or unpaid) would rather be able still to work, even if their lost income is fully made up or damages are awarded to enable their unpaid services to be replaced. Similarly, normally the dependants of a deceased person would strongly prefer to have the relative alive.

It might be objected that this sort of argument does not apply to people who have suffered only minor personal injuries which leave no (or only very minor) permanent effects. Indeed, it may be argued that the tort system is too generous towards such people[17] in the sense that it provides them with relatively large amounts of compensation for non-pecuniary loss against which people normally do not and cannot insure themselves. At the time they get their compensation (which will usually be some considerable time after the injuries were sufffered), such victims may feel that they have been made

---

[15] Suppose a solicitor negligently fails to commence an action for personal injuries before the expiry of the limitation period. Any damages received by the client from the solicitor will, as against the solicitor, represent compensation for economic loss; but they will also, for the client, represent damages for personal injuries. Their claim for inclusion in this book resides in the fact that the solicitor, by negligence, has deprived the client of financial compensation—the solicitor has not inflicted personal injuries on the client. But in reality, such damages compensate the client for the personal injuries.

[16] Indeed, Lord Reid in *Baker* v. *Willoughby* [1970] AC 467, 492 asserted that a claim for personal injuries causing economic loss is not a claim in respect of the injuries themselves but one in respect of consequential economic (and other) loss.

[17] P. Cane, *Atiyah's Accidents, Compensation and the Law*, 5th edn. (London, 1993), 236.

better off by it than they were before they suffered their injuries. But it is unlikely that such people, if questioned immediately after the accident, would say that a generous award of damages to be received at some time in the future would make the suffering of the injuries worthwhile.[18] This fact makes personal injuries different from other types of injury and loss[19] and provides a justification for leaving them out of a book concerned with the way the law of tort treats economic interests.

A second reason for excluding personal injuries and death from the discussion is that in policy debates about tort law, personal injuries law is often treated separately and as a candidate for hiving off from the rest of the law of tort, as has already happened to a greater or lesser extent in a number of jurisdictions in the common law world. But even if it is not hived off, the principles and policies underlying protection of the economic interest in one's body (or that of another, in the case of fatal accidents) are so heavily affected by the fact that these particular economic interests are associated with the interest in bodily and mental health that they do not easily fit into the scheme of this book.

3. AIMS AND STARTING POINTS

Concentration on Plaintiff's Interests

The basic aim of this book is to examine the law of tort to see in what ways and under what circumstances it protects and vindicates economic interests. This project involves a number of unorthodox moves. First, it involves abandoning the expository division of torts into intentional torts, torts requiring negligence, and torts of strict liability. The motive for doing this is that the tripartite division hinders proper examination of the way the law deals with economic interests by focussing on the conduct of the defendant.[20] By so doing it tends to hide the deeper structure of the law; for example, the fact that the property torts (trespass, conversion, and so on) focus on the rights of the plaintiff rather than on the conduct of the defendant. Again, an important element in discussions of recovery for economic loss in the tort of negligence is concerned with defining the sorts of interests which the law ought to

---

[18] This is not to deny that there may be circumstances in which people would agree to undergo physical 'injury' in return for money. Even apart from certain sexual practices, free markets in human blood and bodily organs such as kidneys, are not unknown. But here we are concerned with unintentional injury inflicted for no purpose which serves to make it acceptable to the sufferer.

[19] Cf. P. S. Atiyah (1986) 49 *Law and Contemp. Problems* 288, 292–3.

[20] Cf. P. S. Atiyah and R. S. Summers, *Form and Substance in Anglo-American Law* (Oxford, 1987), 394–5. For an argument against this approach see *Clerk and Lindsell on Tort* 16th edn. (London, 1989), 13–14: for me, the fact that classification according to interests 'presents the material in an unfamiliar light' is a positive advantage.

protect. We have little difficulty justifying legal concern for bodily health and safety, but we find legal protection of economic interests against negligent interference much more problematic. It is worthwhile to examine the law of negligence in terms of the types of economic interests it does protect and those it does not.

Secondly, the approach taken in this book involves abandonment of the expository division of the law into discrete torts. This is not an entirely novel move. Classification of the law of tort in terms of broad categories of invaded interest has often been laid on top of the division into discrete torts, although never very satisfactorily because most torts can be seen as protecting more than one interest. More significantly, the 'imperialism' of the tort of negligence has led to its expository division according to the different types of injury for which damages can or cannot be recovered. As the requirement of negligent conduct has become easier for the plaintiff to prove, control devices (duty principles) based on the interests of the plaintiff have become more important as tools for restricting the incidence of negligence liability. Compulsory motor and employer insurance against liability for personal injuries has contributed to the already-noted fact that personal injuries law has come to be seen as separate and self-contained by policy makers, and as concerned at least as much with the interests of the plaintiff as with questions about the nature and basis of the defendant's liability. More relevantly for present purposes, the unwillingness of the courts to develop a general principle of liability for economic loss in negligence has led modern writers to give more attention to the position and interests of the plaintiff and less to the nature of the defendant's conduct. So in a number of ways, partial attempts have been made to explore the law of tort from the plaintiff's point of view. This book attempts to pursue this project systematically in relation to one of the types of interests (that is, economic interests) which the law of tort protects.

In saying 'one of the types of interest', I do not mean to imply that there are no relevant distinctions between different types of economic interest. Indeed, as we will see in due course, important distinctions exist within the law of tort between five types of economic interest: property interests and certain other interests akin to property interests (which are dealt with in Chapter 2), contractual interests (which are the subject of Chapter 3), contractual expectancies, non-contractual expectancies, and the interest in the preservation of monetary wealth (all of which are dealt with in Chapter 4). Property interests can be further divided into interests in tangible property and interests in intangible property. A contractual interest I define as a right under an existing contract, while a contractual expectancy I define as an interest in entering an advantageous contract in the future.[21] A non-contractual expectancy is an expectation of making a future gain otherwise than by a

---

[21] For further discussion of these definitions see 107 and 150 below.

contractual transaction (for example, under a will). The interest in preserving existing monetary wealth is residual in that it embraces economic interests which do not fall into any of the other categories.

It does not follow from this expository or organizational emphasis on the plaintiff's interests at the expense of the nature and quality of the defendant's conduct that the law can be adequately understood without paying careful attention to the nature of actionable interferences with economic interests. It is essential, for example, to examine which economic interests are protected only against intentional interference and which only against negligent interference. The relevance of the defendant's motives also needs to be examined. Moreover, it is also necessary to specify in more detail the nature of the interference. Five types of interference are identifiable: (1) deprivation; (2) appropriation; (3) exploitation or use; (4) interference with use, enjoyment or exercise; (5) damage or destruction. Not all of these modes of interference are applicable to every type of interest; but most are applicable to more than one type.

Something needs to be said about the difference between deprivation and appropriation. Both involve a reduction in the plaintiff's assets; but they differ in that appropriation implies a benefit to the defendant—the defendant appropriates some asset of the plaintiff, in fact or in effect, to him or herself; whereas deprivation implies no such benefit to the defendant. Deprivation only applies to money as where, for example, a person makes a bad investment as a result of reliance on a negligent misstatement by another. On the other hand, money may be appropriated by an investment adviser—for example, by conversion of a cheque; or by the supplying of substandard goods.

Damage to Tangible Property

The third slightly unorthodox move made in this book is to treat physical damage to tangible property *prima facie* as invasion of an economic interest. For many purposes the law brackets physical damage to tangible property with personal injury; and in some contexts, the law erects an unbridgeable chasm between physical damage to property and economic loss consequent upon it on the one hand, and economic loss not consequent upon it to the plaintiff's property on the other. But I will systematically treat physical damage to tangible property *prima facie* as a form of economic loss.[22] The reasons for the law's attitude are probably the fact that the common law has traditionally placed high value on property interests, and, more recently, the fact that, as in the case of personal injury, the extent of the damage to

---

[22] There is some judicial support for such an approach: e.g. *Leigh & Sillavan Ltd* v. *Aliakmon Shipping Co. Ltd* [1985] QB 350, 379 *per* Oliver LJ.

tangible property likely to be caused by any one act of negligence tends to be limited by its physical nature.[23]

The theoretical justification for treating physical damage to tangible property *prima facie* as a form of economic loss is straightforward: tangible property is very often treated by its owner simply as a commodity or an investment. Of course, this is not always so, especially in the case of dwellings, for instance. The law recognizes this latter fact in a number of ways: aggravated damages, which go beyond compensating the plaintiff for financial loss but which are recognized as different from exemplary damages, may be awarded for trespass to land, for example.[24] Similarly, damages for distress can be awarded for invasion of property rights.[25] Again, damages may be recoverable for nervous shock resulting from unintentional damage to or destruction of property;[26] and the return of specific converted goods may be ordered instead of damages if the goods have some special value to the owner. Still, it seems more realistic to start with an assumption that physical damage to tangible property represents only invasion of an economic interest and to modify this assumption in appropriate cases rather than to assume that tangible property normally has non-economic value for its owner. Indeed, the law of tort normally assumes that tangible property has only economic value and requires proof that it also has non-economic value.

There are, however, two important attacks on this approach which need to be mentioned now. The first is to argue that redress for physical damage to property ought to be excluded altogether from the ambit of the law of tort.[27] In its most developed form, the case for exclusion rests on three grounds: first, there are moral and political arguments based ultimately on the fact that property is unevenly distributed throughout society; secondly, there are arguments based on the availability, prevalence and advantages of first party (loss) insurance as a means of protecting against physical damage to property; and thirdly, there is an argument about the unclear and unsatisfactory state of the law relating to property damage.[28]

On reflection, it appears that this attack is not relevant to the treatment of physical damage to property as invasion of an economic interest. Rather, its proponents are in favour of a greater or lesser reduction of the territory

[23] R. Stevens (1973) 23 *U. Tor. LJ* 431, 454–5.

[24] Salmond, 517–8; Harris, 228–9.

[25] e.g. *Reed* v. *Madon* [1989] Ch. 408 (trespassory use of a burial plot).

[26] *Attia* v. *British Gas PLC* [1988] QB 304; *Graham* v. *Voigt* (1989) 95 FLR 146 (conversion of a stamp collection).

[27] R. L. Abel in M. Furmston (ed.), *The Law of Tort* (London, 1986); P. S. Atiyah in T. Simos (ed.), *Negligence and the Economic Torts* (Sydney, 1980). Abel is concerned only with 'accidental' damage, whereas Atiyah includes intentional damage. Abel includes within his definition of 'property damage' some economic loss not consequential upon physical damage to property; but here I am concerned only with property damage and loss consequential upon it. In addition, Abel includes loss of wages in his definition of property damage, but this aspect of his argument is beyond the scope of this book.

[28] The first and third arguments are Abel's.

occupied by the law of tort: the first ground for exclusion arguably applies to all economic assets protected by the law of tort (including the individual's earning capacity), because all such assets are unevenly distributed throughout society; and the second (insurability) ground arguably applies to some interests in addition to that in the physical integrity of property. So we should defer further discussion of the attack until later. All three grounds will be examined in Chapter 10; the second ground will also be examined at various other points throughout this book.

The second attack does relate exactly to the assimilation of physical damage to tangible property with 'mere financial interests'. The argument is that damage to physical property should be analogised to personal injury, and that the law of tort should be concerned more with people than with commercial or business entities:

Senses can be gratified only by people and things; things can appeal to the senses in a way in which disembodied wealth—stocks and shares and bank balances and future inheritances and so on—simply cannot . . . I . . . most strongly opppose the nameless current perversion which holds that things are worth only what they can fetch in the market . . . This occlusion of human values by business values I find very ominous. It is happening because most litigants are not humans at all, but businesses . . . companies, unlike human beings, have no senses. Accordingly, they cannot, except for accounting purposes, distinguish between stock-in-trade and accounts receivable: they are both just assets.[29]

According to this approach, tangible property has non-economic value merely by virtue of being tangible and should not be treated merely as a financial asset.

A number of comments seem apposite. First, why should we give such primacy to physical senses? Many people find their emotions gratified by intangible wealth and, conversely, suffer emotional distress if their intangible assets are unexpectedly depleted;[30] why should the law not recognize this, too? Indeed, it does to some extent. In *Archer* v. *Brown*,[31] for example, damages for mental distress were awarded to a person who was induced by a fraudulent misrepresentation to buy shares from a person who did not own them. In *Perry* v. *Sidney Phillips & Son*[32] damages were awarded for mental distress caused by the physical inconvenience of having to live in a house with defects which the defendant surveyor had failed to report, and for anxiety about when repairs would be done. Although this latter case concerned tan-

---

[29] J. A. Weir (1974) *City of London LR* 15; see also (1972–3) 12 *JSPTL* 171, 185.

[30] In 1989 it was reported in the press that administrative inefficiency had led to a number of cases of people not having life assurance cover which they thought they had bought. One couple was reported to have suffered 'apoplexy' when they discovered, after the event, that they had been without cover for four months. Financial institutions responsible reportedly paid compensation: see articles in the *Independent*, 8 Apr. 1989, 23 and 16 Apr. 1989, 25. Various allegations were made in the wake of the large underwriting losses incurred by Lloyds of London in the early 1990s that some Names had committed suicide as a result of their financial difficulties: *Financial Times*, 19 Feb. 1994.

[31] [1985] QB 401.   [32] [1982] 1 WLR 1297.

gible property, the plaintiff's distress is unlikely to have been 'sensually' based (or, at least, entirely so). Furthermore, when people are attached to physical objects, this attachment often transcends the sensible qualities of the object, as when we speak of something having 'sentimental value'.

Secondly, the argument depends for some of its force on assuming that people always value their tangible possessions as more than articles of commerce. In a world of mass production and planned obsolescence this assumption, as a generalization, is insupportable. People often do have non-economic as well as economic interests in their physical assets, and the law recognizes this in some circumstances. But there seems no point in pretending that physical assets are always the object of non-economic interest.

Thirdly, the argument rests on too sharp a distinction between commercial entities and people. Not all commercial entities are multi-national corporations—businesses consist of business *people*; all businesses are of interest, both financial and emotional, to some person or persons. Besides, the question whether tangible property ought to be better protected than intangible property is quite different from that whether people ought to be better protected from interference with their property interests than other legal entities.

The approach in this book is to recognize that tangible property is often seen by those with interests in it as just an item of commerce; to the extent that this is true, it seems reasonable to treat physical damage to tangible property as invasion of an economic interest. People (and other legal entities, for that matter) also sometimes have non-economic interests in property (whether tangible or intangible); whether, and to what extent, the law should protect such interests is not a focus of direct attention in this book. The question whether people should be better protected than other legal entities is a separate one which will arise at various points in the course of this book.

Tort Law in Context

A proper understanding of the role of the law of tort in protecting economic interests requires consideration of the relationship between tort law and other means of protecting economic interests. Another aim of this book is, therefore, to place tort law in a wider context by considering issues such as the relationship between insurance and tort liability; the relationship between tort law and other bodies of law which protect economic interests; and non-judicial means of protecting such interests.

4. ECONOMIC INTERESTS IN THE WIDER CONTEXT OF TORT LAW

As already stated, the law of tort protects a variety of different interests. If we assume, for present purposes, that the law relating to personal injuries can be treated as separate and self-contained, it is worthwhile at this stage to note the main types of non-economic interests protected by the rest of the law of tort which are not, by definition, dealt with in this book. First, there are what might be called 'dignitary interests'. The main dignitary interests are reputation and privacy. The former is clearly within the law of tort as traditionally defined; the latter is not recognized as such, but it is to some extent indirectly protected, for example, by the tort of trespass to land and by the law of breach of confidence (although whether the latter is 'properly' treated as part of the law of tort is a matter of dispute).[33] The law of tort also protects the public's interest in social peace and order (the torts of trespass and nuisance can be used for this purpose); and, conversely, the individual's interest in being free of unwanted physical interference is protected by the tort of trespass to the person.

The important point to emphasize is that each of these non-economic interests might be accompanied, in any given situation, by an economic interest. For example, an individual might have both a non-economic and an economic interest in his or her reputation. Another way of putting this is to say that any particular tort may protect more than one interest in any given case. This is one of the main reasons why I have abandoned exposition of the law in terms of discrete torts in order to examine more closely the circumstances under which and the principles according to which the different economic interests are protected.

5. FINANCIAL CONSEQUENCES OF INTERFERENCE WITH ECONOMIC INTERESTS

There is another set of distinctions which needs to be introduced at this stage. It cuts across the distinctions between different types of economic interests and different modes of interference with them. It is a classification of the financial consequences of interference with economic interests. We must first distinguish between loss to the plaintiff and gain to the defendant. Tortious interference by D with an economic interest of P may inflict financial loss on P or generate a financial gain for D, or both. In other words, as a result of tortious conduct by D, P may suffer financial loss which does not corrrespond to a financial gain by D; or P may suffer financial loss which corresponds to a financial gain by D; or D may make a financial gain which does not correspond to a financial loss suffered by P.[34]

Financial loss flowing from interference with or invasion of economic interests may consist in reduction of (the value of) existing assets, for example, loss resulting from damage to physical property or from the making of pay-

---

[33] See 107 below.

[34] e.g. a claim for mesne profits can be made in an action for possession of land, and a claim for the hire value of chattels in an action for conversion, even if the property owner could not have let the property to anyone else; see Birks, 23–4 and 41 and 45 below.

ments to another. Or it may consist in the interruption of a stream of income which the plaintiff expected would continue uninterrupted: earnings or profits are the typical examples. Such interruption may or may not be consequential upon physical damage to property. For example, in *Spartan Steel & Alloys Ltd* v. *Martin & Co. (Contractors) Ltd*[35] the plaintiff claimed damages for loss of profits consequent upon damage to metal which was being processed when the defendant negligently cut off the electricity supply to its factory, and loss of profits consequent merely upon the cutting off of the supply. Financial 'loss' may also consist in failure to realize or obtain some increase in one's assets which was expected to materialize in the future: for example, failure to obtain an expected legacy under a will; this type of loss is often referred to as the 'loss of an expectation'.

There are also relevant distinctions to be drawn between the measures of monetary recompense which may be awarded in a tort action. Where the plaintiff has suffered actionable loss, the law of tort will *compensate* for that loss. Where P's actionable loss corresponds to a gain made by D, we may want to focus on D's gain rather than P's loss; if so, we may say that the law *restores* D's gain to P. If, as a result of tortious conduct, D makes an actionable gain which does not correspond to a loss suffered by P, we may say that the law requires D to *disgorge* that gain. Finally, in certain circumstances the law of tort may require D to pay a 'civil fine' to P in the form of 'punitive' or 'exemplary' damages. Thus, the law of tort recognizes four types of monetary recompense: compensation, restoration, disgorgement, and fine. However, in cases where P suffers a loss which corresponds to a gain made by D, compensation and restoration are just two sides of the same coin.

There may be a temptation to treat the law dealing with gains made (as opposed to losses suffered) as a result of tortious conduct as part of the law of restitution rather than the law of tort. This temptation should be resisted if the full range of the law's responses to interferences with economic interests is to be properly understood.

[35] [1973] QB 27.

PART II

Tort Doctrine

2
Property and Quasi-Property Interests

The protection of property has always been one of the prime functions of the law of tort. This Chapter is concerned with the ways in which the law of tort protects property interests and what I call 'quasi-property interests'. The latter are interests in things which have certain of the legal characteristics possessed by property such as land and chattels. A good example is the interest in reputation which is, of course, protected by the tort of defamation. Questions which I shall seek to answer in this Chapter include: what is a property interest? What interests does the law of tort recognize as property or quasi-property interests? What forms of interference with property and quasi-property interests does the law of tort provide protection against? In what ways and by what techniques does the law of tort protect property and quasi-property interests? What remedies does the law of tort provide for interference with property interests? What respective roles do statute law and the common law play in protecting property and quasi-property interests?

The first section explores what is meant in law by 'property'. The rest of the Chapter considers the various forms of interference with property and quasi-property interests for which the law of tort provides remedies, namely appropriation (section 2), exploitation falling short of appropriation (section 3), interference with the use and enjoyment of property (section 4) and damage to property (section 5). In the final section some pervasive threads are drawn together.

1. THE NOTION OF PROPERTY

The common law's earliest concern was with land and chattels, for the obvious reason that these were the main forms of property in medieval society. It is a notable feature of the English law of tort that it is concerned not only with damage to and destruction and loss of tangible property, but also with disputes about title to such property. For example, the modern action for possession of real property (formerly called the 'ejectment' action) had its origins in the action of trespass which, for complex reasons, replaced the older 'real actions' (that is, actions designed to protect proprietary interests in real property) as a means of settling disputes about title,[1] although its main function today is as a means of recovering possession from trespassers and overstaying tenants who do not dispute title.[2] The essence of the modern tort of conversion is interference with the right to possession.[3] The old 'personal action' of detinue, which protected the right to possession and which was finally supplanted by actions on the case for conversion in the early seventeenth century, was not seen as part of the law of obligations but as part of the law of personal property; although, when it was revived in the nineteenth century, detinue was treated as a tort.[4] Nuisance began life as an adjunct to the real actions, but the shortcomings of the real actions (which it shared) led to its being supplanted by actions on the case (part of the law of obligations).[5]

This use of the law of obligations to perform functions which might more properly be thought to belong to the law of property had a fundamental impact on the structure of the law of tort, which contains within itself two quite different conceptual orientations—one towards the compensation of losses, and the other towards the protection of rights. This can be seen very clearly in the tort of nuisance: although, as already noted, nuisance is defined in terms of the plaintiff's rights, P must nevertheless normally prove damage to establish a cause of action.[6] Indeed, one of the difficulties in using the law of obligations for the protection of rights in property was that the it was concerned with providing monetary compensation, whereas specific remedies are needed for the full protection of title (in order to vindicate my right to have what is mine). Of course, specific remedies were developed, the prime modern example being the order for possession of land. But in relation to chattels, protection of title is subordinated to compensation in the rule that an order for specific return of a chattel (with or without the option of paying its value in lieu) will normally be made only if the property has some peculiar value to the plaintiff which could not adequately be captured in an award of monetary compensation. The use of the law of tort to protect property interests has generated a number of other peculiar rules which will be discussed in due course.

One important feature of the modern law of tort is that it is not a means of protecting interests in particular types of property but of protecting 'property interests' in an abstract sense. Once the notion of property interests achieves abstract status independent of any particular things which are the subject of property interests, the possibility arises of extending protection to new 'forms of property'. Before this can be done, it is necessary to have some definition of 'property' in its abstract sense by reference to which it is possible to identify new forms of property. One way of approaching the

---

[1] J. H. Baker, *Introduction to English Legal History*, 3rd edn. (London, 1990), 341–3.

[2] The main reason why actions for possession are now very rarely used to resolve disputes about title is that title is now much easier to prove than it was when the ejectment action was developed.

[3] Baker, *Introduction to English Legal History*, 451.   [4] *Ibid.*

[5] *Ibid.*, 478–83.   [6] R. A. Buckley, *Law of Nuisance* (London, 1981), 105–6.

formulation of a definition is to list the incidents of ownership, which is the largest interest in property which the law recognizes: the right to possess, the right to use, the right to manage, the right to the income, the right to the capital, the right to security, transmissibility, indefinite duration; and, negatively, a prohibition on using the property in such a way as to harm others, and liability to seizure to meet legal liabilities.[7] These incidents of ownership might be said to give us a definition of what can be called 'the full concept of property'. It is, of course, possible to have interests in property less than ownership, and such interests would consist of some, but not all, of these incidents. Further, we might be prepared to attach the name 'property' to things in which the largest interest recognized by the law did not possess all of these incidents. But this list of incidents would at least give us a benchmark against which to test attributions of the name 'property'. What I have called 'quasi-property interests' have one or more of these incidents, at least in a metaphorical sense.

In the case of the paradigms of property—land and chattels—the law of tort plays some part in protecting most of the positive incidents from interference. It protects the right to possess (this will be dealt with under the heading 'appropriation'), the rights to use and to the income (these will be dealt with under the heading 'exploitation short of appropriation'), the right to the capital (this will be dealt with under the headings of 'appropriation' and 'damage', which includes 'destruction'), and the right to security (this may be interfered with by appropriation or destruction). The law of tort is also important in securing the negative incident of prohibition of harmful use, chiefly through the law of nuisance (dealt with mainly under the heading 'interference with use and enjoyment'), and negligence (dealt with mainly under the heading 'damage'). However, the prohibition on harmful use is not a universal one, and cases in which a person is allowed to use property regardless of the possibility of injury or damage to another are dealt with in Chapter 5.

The obvious difficulty with this approach to the identification of property[8] is that it defines it in terms of the forms of legal protection of (or, in other words, the legally protected incidents of), and the legal limitations on the use of, things which we call 'property'; but it does not help us in deciding which things have (or ought to have) any or all of these incidents. It is this latter

[7] This list is A. M. Honore's: 'Ownership' in A. G. Guest (ed.), *Oxford Essays in Jurisprudence Series I* (Oxford, 1961). Property can be both a source of wealth and, via wealth, a source of power. Property is also a source of power in a more direct way because it gives power over things and, through that, over people. There are many external restraints on the exercise of property rights; property power is far from being absolute power. My main concern in this book is with property as wealth; but property may be used as a tool for exercising power over people without regard to its value as wealth; in other words, a person may use property rights to exercise power over another even though the former has no financial interest in doing so. See 49–56 and 265–6 below.

[8] Which was clearly stated by Dixon J in *Victoria Park Racing and Recreation Grounds Ltd* v. *Taylor* (1937) 58 CLR 479, 509.

question which will be of importance in a tort action because the plaintiff will be seeking some form of protection for something in which he or she claims an interest, and the court will have to decide whether that form of protection is, or ought to be, available. To answer this question, a completely different form of argument is required, of which an example is summarized in the following proposition:

where the commercial value of an entity, whether tangible or intangible, has been brought about by the expenditure of time, effort, labour or money, the person who created that commercial value has a proprietary right to its commercial exploitation.[9]

This particular proposition is the conclusion of an argument designed to establish the right to use the fruits of one's effort, but the same form of argument could be, and would, indeed, have to be, used to establish any other of the rights which are incidents of the full concept of property. The important characteristic of such arguments is that they are designed to provide some good reason, grounded in morality[10] or in social or economic policy, why some or all of the incidents of the full concept of property ought to be attached to a particular thing.

It is, however, important to remember that the protection of property is only one of the functions of the law of tort and only one of the techniques available in it for the protection of economic interests. The fact that a person cannot convince a court that the thing in which he or she claims an interest ought to be recognized as having some or all of the incidents of property, does not mean that the law will not provide a remedy. To a limited extent the law of tort protects contractual interests in things (see Chapter 3). More importantly, the law of tort may also compensate for loss of monetary wealth, regardless of whether this is the result of interference with property rights (or, for that matter, contractual rights). Indeed, a distinction is sometimes drawn between protecting something by recognizing it as property and protecting it by creating a tort, as in the Law Commission Report on Breach of Confidence published in 1981.[11]

The reason the Commission drew this distinction was that it assumed that if confidential information was classified as property, certain undesirable

---

[9] D. Libling (1978) 94 *LQR* 103, 119. For a brief account of classic justifications for private property see A. Ryan, *Property* (Milton Keynes, 1987), chs. 4–7. Put crudely, the main competitor to 'moral' justifications for property such as Libling's (which are based on some nexus between the property and its 'owner') are 'economic' (see M. Crommelin in D. J. Galligan (ed), *Essays in Legal Theory* (Melbourne, 1984)) or 'utilitarian' justifications which see property rights as the best way to ensure the efficient or beneficial use of resources. K. Gray [1991] *CLJ* 252 suggests three questions relevant to the issue of whether any particular resource should be recognized as property: (a) can others be physically excluded from access to the benefits of the resource by reasonable means? (b) can the resource be adequately protected by some legal means other than attribution of the quality of being property? and (c) would it be anti-social to allow people to exclude others from the benefits of the resource?

[10] Witness, for instance, the debate about whether human body parts should be recognized as property: Nuffield Council of Bioethics, *Human Tissue, Ethical and Legal Issues* (London, 1995).

[11] Law Com. No. 110, esp. para. 2.10.

consequences would follow, because there are certain important respects in which confidential information is unlike other forms of property, notably tangible property. The Commission felt that the normal rules of property law about the transfer of property and about priorities between competing innocent acquirers of property could not be applied to confidential information. It does not follow from this, however, that confidential information should not be treated as property for the purposes of the law of tort. If the law were prepared to award monetary compensation for wrongful exploitation of confidential information in a way analogous to that in which it awards damages for wrongful exploitation of land or chattels, there would seem to be no strong reason why we should not treat this as an example of the law of tort being used to protect property or something analogous to it,[12] even if, for certain other purposes, confidential information was not treated in the same way as paradigmatic property interests. At the end of the day, such questions of classification are of no fundamental importance in their own right, but they are useful to the extent that they enable us to see connections between superficially different legal phenomena.

The fact that there are serious discussions about whether the law of breach of confidence, for example, should be treated as part of the law of property or as part of the law of obligations illustrates the complex relationship between these two areas, which is a legacy of the early shift from using proprietary actions[13] to using personal actions to protect title to property.

2. APPROPRIATION

Possession and the Right to Possess

In this book the term 'appropriation' or, more relevantly from the legal point of view, 'misappropriation', is used to mean taking property away from, or taking possession of property as against, a person who is in possession of it or from a person who has a right to immediate possession of it. As a result of this emphasis on possession, title to property is a relative concept in the law of tort. For example, a registered owner of land who has neither possession nor the right to immediate possession can be guilty of trespass; and the owner of chattels can be guilty of both trespass and conversion. This suggests that at bottom the law of tort is seeking to protect the right to use property, which is often a purely economic interest (although perhaps less often in the case of realty than of other forms of property). Appropriation removes the power to use; and this, rather than the abstract relationship of 'owner' to property, is tort law's main concern.

[12] See F. Gurry, *Breach of Confidence* (Oxford, 1984), 56.
[13] Including in this actions such as detinue which were seen as part of the law of (personal) property.

The law of tort protects both actual possession and the right to possess.[14] In relation to land, the tort of trespass protects possession as such, while the action of ejectment or, in modern terms, the action for possession of land, which is 'an offspring of trespass',[15] protects the right to immediate possession. The main reason tort law protects mere possession is in order to discourage indiscriminate seizure of property. One result of this is that a person may succeed in an action for trepass to land against a dispossessor even if that person's possession was wrongful as against another person who has the right to immediate possession of the land. Conversely, the fact that the law of tort protects only possession and the right to immediate possession means that a person, such as a landlord, who enjoys, for example, the right to manage the property and to alienate it but who, for the duration of the lease, has neither possession nor the right to immediate possession, cannot sue a misappropriator; furthermore (as already noted), the landlord may be liable in trespass at the suit, for example, of the tenant.[16]

In relation to chattels, the tort of trespass protects only possession, while an action in conversion can be brought by a person in actual possession, or a person with the right to immediate possession.[17]

The concept of possession is not limited to actual physical occupation or custody. A person can be in possession of real property which that person is not, at the time, physically occupying;[18] or of chattels which are not, at the time, in the person's physical custody.[19] Whether a person has sufficient control over land which he or she occupies or over chattels in his or her custody so that the person will be held to be in possession of the property is a question of fact, degree, and policy.[20] Possession is a root of title, whereas mere occupation or custody is not.

The notion of possession is limited to property which can be physically occupied or controlled; that is, land and chattels.[21] So misappropriation is a wrong which can only be committed in relation to land and chattels.[22] However, the tort of trespass to land can also be used to protect legal interests in land, such as easements or *profits à prendre* (for example, fishing and

---

[14] It should be noted that the law of tort does not protect title as such. Historically, it was the equity courts, not the common law courts, which protected title.

[15] Fleming, 49.   [16] e.g., *Inverugie Investments Ltd* v. *Hackett* [1995] 1 WLR 713.

[17] Concerning claims by parties with reversionary rights see A. Tettenborn [1994] *CLJ* 326.

[18] *Ocean Estates Ltd* v. *Pinder* [1969] 2 AC 19, 25–6 *per* Lord Diplock.

[19] Goode, 62–3.

[20] Cf. D. R. Harris in *Oxford Essays in Jurisprudence, Series I*, 72–80 (concerning chattels).

[21] The term 'chattel' includes documents which represent documentary intangibles, e.g., bills of lading and cheques: Goode, 66–7. A lease is, technically, personal property, not real property: a 'chattel real'. But for all practical purposes, the law treats leases as interests in land.

[22] A conversion action can be brought in respect of specified coins but not of a sum of money, for which the proper action is (a restitutionary) one for money had and received: *Orton* v. *Butler* (1822) 5 B & Ald. 652; *Foster* v. *Green* (1862) 7 H & N 881.

timber-cutting rights), which do not confer a right to possess the land but only a right to use or exploit it.[23]

A right merely to occupy land may be conferred by contract (called a 'licence'), but if the occupation is exclusive, in the sense that the occupant may exclude all other persons (including the owner) from the land, the licence (if for a term and in consideration of periodical payments) will usually[24] be interpreted as conferring a right of exclusive possession and, therefore, as a lease (that is, a proprietary interest in land), at least for the purposes of determining whether the conditions for the creation of a lease were satisfied; for determining the applicability of legislation protecting residential tenants;[25] and for determining the rights of successors in title of the grantor.[26]

Possession, as such, is often a valuable economic resource because if the possessor did not occupy or control *this* property, he or she would have to be expend resources to gain occupation or control of some other property. So the (wrongful) possessor who can use the tort of trespass or the tort of conversion to protect possession can, thereby, protect a valuable economic interest. At common law the usefulness of these remedies was enhanced by the rule that the defendant could not plead *ius tertii*; that is, D could not plead that some third party had a better title to the property than the plaintiff in possession. In relation to chattels, there were exceptions to this rule when D was defending on behalf of and by the authority of the true owner or had already made satisfaction to the true owner.[27] The effect of the rule against pleading *ius tertii* was that a wrongful possessor could get a remedy for dispossession even when D could prove that P had no right to possess the property. In respect of chattels, the scope of application of the rule has been very considerably[28] curtailed by section 8 of the Torts (Interference with Goods) Act 1977,[29] but it still applies to actions for trespass to land. It is thought better to protect even wrongful possession for the sake of discouraging disturbance of the dispossessor by others with no better claim to the land.[30]

As a general rule, a defendant is allowed to plead *ius tertii* in an action for possession of land (an ejectment action) brought by a person who claims only on the basis of a right to immediate possession. There are two exceptions to

---

[23] See Fleming, 43. Limited interests in chattels can only be based on possession: Goode, 54–6, 58–9, 65. In *Mason* v. *Clarke* [1955] AC 778 the House of Lords assumed that an equitable *profit à prendre* could be protected by the law of trespass. But historically, this must be wrong. See 283 below and *Moreland Timber Co.* v. *Reid* [1946] VLR 237.

[24] Gray, 706–32. The absence is not conclusive against the existence of a lease.

[25] See Housing Act 1988.   [26] See generally Megarry and Wade, 633–5.

[27] See Law Reform Committee Report No. 18 (Cmnd 4774, 1971), paras. 51–78.

[28] G. Battersby [1992] *Conv.* 100.

[29] The main justification for abolition was the risk that the defendant might be liable twice over to the wrongful possessor and to the owner: Law Reform Committee Report No. 18, para. 58. See also s. 7 of the Act.

[30] The scope of the protection given to actual possession is slightly narrowed by the doctrine of trespass by relation, which deems a person with a right to immediate possession to have been in actual possession from the date the right of entry accrued and not from the date of entry into possession.

this rule: first, a defendant who is a trespasser *vis-à-vis* P cannot plead *ius tertii*; and, secondly, a defendant who has acquired possession through another cannot plead, in an action brought by the latter or by anyone claiming through the latter, that the title is *defective*.[31] These rules make sense when it is remembered that the action for possession of land was originally developed to resolve disputes about title, although this is not its main modern use.

The right to immediate possession can also, obviously, be of great economic value. For example, a tenant has a right to immediate possession between the granting of the lease and entry into actual possession. If the tenant could not protect this interest against intruders, the lease would become worthless even while the liability to pay rent continued. The economic value of the right of the landlord to take possession of premises on expiry of the lease is equally obvious. Indeed, for many landlords the demised premises are purely an investment. The same is true, *mutatis mutandis* of the owner of hired chattels.

The economic aspect of the interest of landlords in the demised premises is well illustrated, in a slightly different context, by cases in which landlords have attempted to gain possession of rent-controlled premises by a variety of devious means.[32] Tenants are now protected by the Protection from Eviction Act 1977 which makes it an offence to evict or harass a tenant during the duration of the lease, and makes it unlawful to evict a tenant whose lease has expired otherwise than by proceedings in court for possession of the premises.[33] Of course, the Act does not guarantee that a tenant will not be dispossessed by an unscrupulous landlord; but in such a case, the tenant can claim damages under section 27 of the Housing Act 1988;[34] and at common law in a trespass action, the court can make an example of the landlord by an award of exemplary damages in addition to compensatory damages and an order for delivery up of possession to the tenant.[35]

The law recognizes that property is often seen primarily as an economic resource. In the tort of conversion, for example, not only are damages the prime remedy, but also an action in conversion can be brought even if D has disposed of the goods to someone else and so is no longer in possession of them.[36] In such a case, the only remedy available is damages. As an armchair generalization about human nature, it is probably true that real property more often has non-economic value in addition to its economic value than do

---

[31] Fleming, 50.

[32] *Perera* v. *Vandiyar* [1953] 1 WLR 672; *Mafo* v. *Adams* [1970] 1 QB 548. Cf. *Chapman* v. *Honig* [1963] 2 QB 502.

[33] See further 34 below.   [34] See 34 below.

[35] *Drane* v. *Evangelou* [1978] 2 All ER 437.

[36] In California, an unsuccessful attempt was made to sue in conversion in respect of the use of body tissue taken from a patient and used to develop a cell-line capable of producing a number of important and lucrative products: R. S. Magnusson (1992) 18 *Melb. ULR* 601, 621–2.

chattels (or, for that matter, intangible property).[37] But this statement ought not to be pressed too far. On the one hand, much land is owned and occupied for commercial rather than personal purposes, and the value of such real property to its owner is likely to be purely economic. On the other hand, chattels, particularly expensive or old chattels, often have non-economic value for their owner; and loss of intangible property can cause emotional upset.[38]

The Main Characteristics of Torts Protecting Possession

Strict Liability

Trespass to Land

Trespass to land, so far as it protects against misappropriation, is a tort of strict liability. This means that provided the acts which form the basis of the claim are voluntary[39] D will be liable even if D was completely ignorant of the facts which rendered the acts trespassory,[40] and even if D acted in perfect innocence and good faith. Thus, P does not have to prove that D acted carelessly or negligently;[41] nor, *a fortiori*, that D intended to trespass. The logic of these principles is that possession and the right to possess, being the core of the notion of property as it relates to land and chattels, deserve protection in their own right regardless of any fault on the part of the misappropriator. It is in this sense that the interest in possession is at the top of the hierarchy of legally protected interests: it is protected in itself and for its own sake.

In relation to mere possession, the lack of a defence of mistake encourages people to take special care to respect boundaries and helps to reduce the number of situations in which possessors may be encouraged to indulge in (possibly violent) self-help to protect the security of their landholding. Furthermore, when a person's claim is based on the right to immediate possession, and the issue at stake is the title to the land, the absence of a defence of mistake is essential to the aim of protecting security of tenure. Proprietary rights can be acquired by adverse possession;[42] the special sanctity accorded to property rights would be impaired if the 'owner' had to prove some fault on the part of the trespasser in order to stop time running.

---

[37] For a strong statement of this view see Goode, 51–2. An extreme example of real property which has more than financial value is the statutory property right in a burial plot: *Reed* v. *Madon* [1989] Ch. 408.

[38] Witness the effects of recent financial scandals such as that involving loss of pension benefits by people badly advised not to join or to transfer out of occupational schemes.

[39] See P. Cane (1982) 2 *OJLS* 30, 35.

[40] *Basely* v. *Clarkson* (1681) 3 Lev. 37; 83 ER 565.

[41] On the distinction between carelessness and negligence see P. Cane (1982) 2 *OJLS* 30, 36.

[42] e.g. *Buckinghamshire CC* v. *Moran* [1990] Ch. 623 (noted [1990] *CLJ* 23). The limitation period for actions for recovery of land is 12 years: Limitation Act 1980, s. 15.

It is sometimes suggested that liability for trespass to land does, or ought to, depend on proof of negligence.[43] The argument is based on the fact that liability for personal injuries caused by unintentional trespass requires proof of negligence,[44] and that 'inevitable accident'[45] is a defence to an action in trespass for damage to property.[46] But this argument fails to draw a distinction between misappropriation of property and physical damage to property. The proposition that a party in possession who has no better right to possess than the plaintiff should not be allowed to retain possession no matter how it was acquired is justifiable and, indeed, essential to the security of property rights; and the fact that liability for physical damage to property depends on proof that the damage came about in a particular way does not, in itself, throw doubt on this rule about liability for misappropriation.[47]

Appropriation of Chattels

The form of trespass to chattels constituted by carrying away (that is, by misappropriation) is also a tort of strict liability in the sense just described. So long as the misappropriator acted voluntarily, he or she is liable no matter how innocent or mistaken about the fact that the act violated someone else's possession, and regardless of the fact that the act was done without fault. As in the case of trespass to land, it is sometimes argued that liability for trespass to goods depends, or ought to depend, on proof of carelessness.[48] But once again, the argument is based on the fact that liability in trespass for physical damage to chattels is based on negligence. There seems nothing in this to suggest that liability in trespass for misappropriation should also be based on negligence.

Conversion involves interference with or exercising control over a chattel in a way inconsistent with someone else's possession of it or with someone else's right to immediate possession of it, and in circumstances where the defendant's dealing with the goods is inconsistent with the plaintiff's possession or right to possession. Sometimes the circumstances speak for themselves (as it were), as in the case of delivery of goods under a contract of sale, which normally amounts to conversion by both vendor and purchaser (whether or not the contract is effective to pass title).[49] In other cases, a demand for return might be necessary to render the dealing unequivocally inconsistent with the plaintiff's rights.[50] Where a person mistakenly thinks he or she is restoring

---

[43] Salmond, 45.

[44] *Fowler* v. *Lanning* [1959] 1 QB 426; *Letang* v. *Cooper* [1965] 1 QB 232.

[45] Inevitable accidents are events not caused by any carelessness on the part of the defendant: *The Marpesia* (1872) LR 4 PC 212, 220; *The Albano* [1892] P 419, 429.

[46] *National Coal Board* v. *J. E. Evans & Co. Ltd* [1951] 2 KB 861.

[47] Concerning cases falling short of misappropriation, see 49 and 84 below.

[48] Salmond, 99.

[49] Torts (Interference with Goods) Act 1977, s. 11(2) extends this rule to receipt of goods by way of pledge in cases where the delivery is itself a conversion.

[50] Denial of title is not, of itself, conversion: Torts (Interference with Goods) Act 1977, s. 11(3).

the goods to their true owner, or where a warehouser simply returns goods to the depositor, the dealings may be seen as equivocal.[51]

Since the prime remedy for conversion is damages equal to the value of the converted chattels, there is a view that an act will amount to a conversion only if it is serious enough to justify awarding the full value of the thing converted.[52] In effect, this would limit conversion to disposal, loss or destruction, alteration of identity, and appropriation.

It is often said that, in order to amount to conversion, the interference must be 'intentional', but this is defined in such a way as to be synonymous with 'voluntary'. Conversion is a tort of strict liability in the same way as trespass. A person can be liable in conversion even if unaware of P's right to possession, and even if that person had no intention, by dealing with the chattel, to deprive P of possession or to deny the plaintiff's right to possession.[53] Thus, for example, an auctioneer who honestly and reasonably, but wrongly, believes that the vendor has good title to the goods put up for sale, is liable to the true owner for conversion of the goods sold.[54] Conversely, an owner of goods does not forfeit the law's protection of property rights in the goods merely by being negligent in failing to protect the goods from being misappropriated.[55]

The Torts Require a Positive Act

Why, then, are the torts of trespass and conversion so often spoken of as being torts of intention? There may be an historical explanation for this.[56] It may also be explained by the fact that these torts are usually committed by the doing of deliberate acts; that is, a person who takes possession of land or chattels, or deals with them in some other way which amounts to a conversion, will not normally do so absent-mindedly but will have meant to take possession of the land or to deal with the chattel. It is also true that these torts cannot be committed purely by nonfeasance.[57] So, it is not conversion simply to fail to take care of goods in one's possession unless this amounts

---

[51] See generally Fleming, 58–62, 64.   [52] W. L. Prosser (1957) 42 *Cornell LQ* 168.

[53] Cf. S. Hedley (1984) 100 *LQR* 653, 670–1.

[54] *R. H. Willis and Son (a firm)* v. *British Car Auctions Ltd* [1978] 2 All ER 392. Banks have special protection from liability under Cheques Act 1957, s. 4. See generally A. M. Dugdale and K. M. Stanton, *Professional Negligence*, 2nd edn. (London, 1989), 174–9. The Unsolicited Goods and Services Act 1971 provides a recipient of unsolicited goods with a defence to an action for conversion if certain conditions are met.

[55] Contributory negligence is no defence to a claim in conversion (Torts (Interference with Goods) Act 1977, s. 11(1)) except in an action against a bank falling within Cheques Act 1957, s. 4: Banking Act 1979, s. 47. On liability of a goods owner in negligence see *Moorgate Mercantile Co. Ltd* v. *Twitchings* [1977] AC 890, esp. Lord Fraser of Tullybelton at 925G–H. See also *Debs* v. *Sibec Developments Ltd* [1990] RTR 91.

[56] P. Cane (1982) 2 *OJLS* 30, 35–39.

[57] Conversely, mere failure by a goods owner to look after goods does not affect the owner's rights against a converter: *Moorgate Mercantile Co. Ltd* v. *Twitchings* [1977] AC 890.

to a breach of the possessor's duty as a bailee.[58] It is not conversion merely to fail to return goods,[59] nor is it a trespass merely to remain on land; but in either case a deliberate refusal to return goods or to leave land when asked to do so may amount to tortious behaviour. Because nonfeasance is often the result of mere absent-mindedness, it is tempting to equate nonfeasance with carelessness and positive acts with intentional conduct. However, both 'negligence' and 'intention' as they are used in the law of tort refer to the consequences of one's actions, not to the actions themselves.[60] Intention involves intending consequences, and carelessness involves foreseeability of consequences. In these torts the relevant legal consequences, namely dispossession of another or the denial of another's right to possess, need not have been either intended or foreseeable.[61]

There is another possible explanation in relation to conversion. Conversion is constituted by action inconsistent with a person's rights. Actions by themselves may be equivocal in this regard;[62] and proof of an intention to deny a person's rights might render acts unequivocal which, in themselves, are equivocal.[63]

Why do these torts require positive acts? There is no obvious answer to this question, but it is probably related to the general reluctance of the law of tort to impose liability for mere nonfeasance. This is so even in situations where the adverse consequences of nonfeasance are intended or foreseeable. Where liability for consequences is strict, the arguments based on morality and causation which are usually cited in support of the law's reluctance to impose liability for nonfeasance seem even stronger. From another point of view, possession and the right to possession are well protected by the law against even innocent and mistaken positive interference; to protect them to this extent also against mere nonfeasance would be to accord to property interests a value which even the common law is unwilling to ascribe.

Actionability Per Se

Trespass to land and to chattels is said to be 'actionable *per se*', which means without proof of actual damage (such as physical damage to the property or economic loss) resulting from the tort. This proposition is not of importance in relation to misappropriation because deprivation of possession or interference with the right to possession can always be seen as damage in the

---

[58] Torts (Interference with Goods) Act 1977, s. 2(2); see also *Balsamo* v. *Medici* [1984] 1 WLR 951.

[59] *Howard E. Perry & Co. Ltd* v. *British Railways Board* [1980] 2 All ER 579. But see G. Samuel (1982) 31 *ICLQ* 357, 379–81. There is a view that not all cases of unjustified detention constitute conversion: N. E. Palmer (1981) 45 *Conv.* 62, 67–8; if this is correct, then the abolition of detinue may have left a gap in the law.

[60] Cane (1982) 2 *OJLS* 30, 36.

[61] But see *Moorgate Mercantile Co. Ltd* v. *Finch* [1962] 1 QB 701.

[62] See 30 above.   [63] See e.g. *Penfold's Wines Pty Ltd* v. *Elliott* (1946) 74 CLR 204.

relevant sense. However, the notion of actionability *per se* is important to the present discussion because it indicates that the tort of trespass protects interests other than economic interests. One of the most important of these interests is privacy. Trespass to land protects possessors of land from unwanted intruders (who have no legal justification for entry) even if such intruders in no way damage the land or reduce its economic value to the occupant. The right to exclude intruders is an important aspect of the right to manage. Actionability *per se* is particularly useful in protecting against deliberate intrusions; it plays an important part in protecting citizens from abuse of the powers of the police and other governmental bodies to enter land on official business and to seize property. The principle is, perhaps, less important in relation to chattels than realty because interference with chattels more often damages them.[64]

Remedies

As has already been noted, full protection of possession and the right to possession requires the availability of specific remedies, that is, orders that D return the misappropriated property to P. If protection against misappropriation were seen as part of the law of property, there could be no doubt that specific return would be the prime remedy. But the use of the law of obligations for this purpose meant that the personal remedy of damages also became available to protect possession. As a matter of principle, one would expect damages designed to protect possessory interests to be related to the value of the property misappropriated. However, because the law of obligations is chiefly concerned with compensating for damage or loss caused by breach of obligation, it might also be argued that damages ought to be related to the actual loss suffered as a result of the misappropriation. Suppose, for example, that the value of the property at the date of the court's decision that D misappropriated it is greater than its value at the date it was misappropriated because the misappropriator improved it. Who should reap the benefit of the increased value? Should P be entitled to recover more, in money terms, than was lost? We will examine the law's answer to this question in due course. This 'clash' of obligation-based and property-based principles runs throughout the law of damages as it relates to torts involving property, even when the tortious conduct consists in damaging or destroying property rather than misappropriating it. In this latter context, however, the usual question is whether damages should be limited to the reduction in the value of the property brought about by the tort rather than being measured by the cost of restoring the property to its former state by doing 'uneconomical' repairs or

---

[64] Fleming, 53, doubts that it applies to chattels. In *Thurston* v. *Charles* (1905) 21 TLR 659 substantial damages were held recoverable against a person who showed a private letter to someone to whom the owner of the letter did not wish it to be shown.

restoration. Here, the law's concern with loss predominates over its concern with property as such.

Real Property

Occupants   The rights of residential tenants are protected in a variety of ways. 'Statutorily protected tenancies'[65] can be terminated only on certain grounds. It is unlawful for a landlord to regain possession of residential premises on the expiry of a tenancy (other than a statutorily protected tenancy[66] or an 'excluded tenancy'[67]) except by process of law.[68] It is an offence to evict a residential tenant during the currency of the lease;[69] and it is an offence for a landlord or a landlord's agent to do acts (including persistent withdrawal or withholding of services) intended or likely to cause a sitting residential tenant to give up possession of the premises.[70]

If a landlord unlawfully deprives a tenant of occupation of the premises, or if the tenant gives up occupation as a result of unlawful harassment, the tenant is entitled to damages[71] in the nature of tort damages assessed according to the difference between the value of the premises to the landlord occupied and unoccupied;[72] that is, on the basis of the gain to the landlord resulting from the wrong rather than the loss to the tenant; or, in other words, according to the value of the landlord's reversionary interest in the premises.[73] This statutory right to damages is additional to any claim at common law for trespass or breach of contract.[74] But of course, the tenant may not recover twice over for loss of occupation.[75]

From the claimant's point of view, a common law action for trespass has a number of advantages over the statutory claim. First, a claim in trespass can be brought for losses other than loss of occupation (such as damage to person or chattels). Secondly, a claim for trespass can be brought even if the

---

[65] As defined in s. 8(1) of the Protection from Eviction Act 1977.

[66] Protected tenancies include those under the Rent Act 1977. On expiry, such a tenancy ceases to be a protected tenancy and becomes a 'statutory tenancy'. Statutory tenants enjoy the protection of the prohibition on self help: *Haniff* v. *Robinson* [1993] QB 419.

[67] One of the categories of excluded tenancy is one granted as a temporary expedient to a trespasser: Protection from Eviction Act, s.3A(6); cf. Housing Act 1985, s. 79(4). Note that self-help can be exercised against tenants under excluded tenancies only if the tenancy has been lawfully terminated.

[68] Protection from Eviction Act 1977, ss. 3, 3A, as amended and inserted by Housing Act 1988, ss. 30 and 31; Housing Act 1985, s. 82(1) (secure tenancies); Housing Act 1988, s. 5(1) (assured tenancies). The prohibition of self-help extends to enforcement of a possession order: *Haniff* v. *Robinson* [1993] QB 419.

[69] Protection from Eviction Act 1977, s. 1(2).

[70] *Ibid.*, s. 1(3),(3A) as amended by Housing Act 1988, s. 29. Harassment can constitute an offence under the Act even if it does not constitute a civil wrong: *R.* v. *Burke* [1991] 1 AC 135.

[71] Housing Act 1988, s. 27. In *McCall* v. *Abalesz* [1976] QB 585 it was held that statutory harassment offences did not give rise to a common law cause of action for damages.

[72] Housing Act 1988, s. 28; but ignoring certain prospective development gains: s. 28(3)(c),(6).

[73] N. Madge [1993] *New LJ* 844 and 880; [1995] *New LJ* 937 and 1060.

[74] *Kaur* v. *Gill, The Times,* 15 June 1995.

[75] S. 27(5); *Mason* v. *Nwokorie* (1994) 26 Housing LR 60.

tenant is still in occupation; under the Act a claim for damages will not lie if the tenant is in occupation, even in cases in which the tenant gave up possession but has since been restored to possession.[76] In other words, statutory damages cannot be recovered for temporary unlawful deprivation of possession. In a sense, this follows logically from the fact that the measure of damages is the financial gain to the landlord as a result of securing the reversion: a landlord who does not secure the reversion realizes no gain. Thirdly, exemplary damages are available in a trespass action,[77] but are probably not available under the statute.[78] Fourthly, the elements of a claim in trespass which the plaintiff must prove are much less complex than the elements of the statutory claim. Fifthly, the damages awarded in a statutory action can be reduced if the tenant or those living with the tenant misbehaved as tenants; or if the tenant unreasonably refused an offer of reinstatement by the landlord.[79] Sixthly, agents of the lessor cannot be liable for statutory damages,[80] whereas they may be liable in trespass. Finally, it is a defence to a statutory claim based on withdrawal or withholding of services for the landlord to prove that there was reasonable cause to believe that there were reasonable grounds for withdrawing or withholding the services.[81] Honest mistake of this sort would not be available as a defence to a trespass action; nor would 'contributory fault'.

On the other hand, the statutory action has a number of advantages over common law liability for trespass. First, a trespass action will not lie for unlawful eviction as such in the absence of trespass to land, property, or person.[82] So, not all forms of harassment which may constitute an offence will be actionable as trespasses. Secondly, not all of the categories of residential occupier protected from eviction by the Protection from Eviction Act could bring a trespass action for deprivation of possession (as opposed to trespass to goods or person). For example, tenants who hold over after the expiry of the lease are protected from eviction by section 3 of the Act, but could not sue in trespass because their proprietary interest in the premises has come to an end. Thirdly, although exemplary damages are available in a trespass action in addition to damages for financial and non-pecuniary losses and are probably not available in statutory actions, the total damages available in a trespass action might well be considerably less than the landlord's gain from the eviction, which is the measure of damages under the statute.

---

[76] S. 27(6), on which see *Tagro* v. *Cafane* [1991] 1 WLR 378.

[77] *Drane* v. *Evangelou* [1978] 2 All ER 437.

[78] Although there is no express provision for such damages, there are cases in which courts have awarded aggravated and/or exemplary damages under the Act (see Law Commission Consultation Paper No. 132 (1993), *Aggravated, Exemplary and Restitutionary Damages*, para. 3.46). But such awards are inconsistent with the decision of the Court of Appeal in *AB* v. *South West Water Services Ltd* [1993] QB 507 that exemplary damages are only available in respect of causes of action in which such damages had been awarded prior to 1964.

[79] Housing Act 1988, s. 27(7).
[81] S. 27(8)(b).

[80] *Sampson* v. *Wilson*, [1995] 3 WLR 455.
[82] *Perera* v. *Vandiyar* [1953] 1 WLR 672.

Besides statutory protection of the lessee's tenure, there is also statutory protection for another of the incidents of property—the right to dispose of or alienate the property. It is often a term of the lease that the tenant must obtain the landlord's consent before assigning the lease to a third party or before subletting or borrowing money against the security of the tenant's interest in the property. If the landlord unreasonably withholds consent, the tenant may seek a declaration to that effect.[83] Alternatively, the tenant may bring an action for breach of statutory duty under section 4 of the Landlord and Tenant Act 1988.[84] In such an action the tenant could claim either an injunction requiring the landlord to comply with the duties under the Act, or damages for breach of duty.

If a contract conferring a right to occupy for residential purposes is interpreted as a licence, the rights of the licensee are rather different from those just outlined. If the licence was entered into before 27 November 1980, the licensee might enjoy some statutory protection from termination of the licence by the licensor.[85] Furthermore, it is unlawful for a licensor to recover the premises after the expiry of the licence (unless it is an excluded licence) except by process of law;[86] and it is an offence unlawfully to evict a residential licensee or to do acts intended or likely to cause such a licensee to give up occupation.[87] Residential licensees are also entitled to tort damages for unlawful eviction under sections 27 and 28 of the Housing Act 1988. However, in the absence of statutory protection, the licensee's rights against the licensor are purely contractual, not 'proprietary', so that the licensee's remedy, if any, will be to claim an injunction to restrain the licensor from entering the premises contrary to the terms of the licence,[88] or specific performance of the agreement, or damages for breach of contract.[89] The licensee will not be able to bring an action for trespass for loss of occupation or any other loss.

Concerning the rights of licensees (whether residential occupiers or not) against successors in title of the licensor,[90] the law is in an unsettled state. The position appears to be that a contractual licence does not bind a successor in title (not even one with notice of the contractual rights of the licensee)

---

[83] *Mills* v. *Cannon Brewery Co.* [1920] 2 Ch. 38.

[84] For background to this Act see Law Com. No. 161 (1985); S. Shaw [1988] *New LJ* 918.

[85] See Megarry and Wade, 1118–22. Under the Housing Act 1988, s. 36, licences entered into on or after 15 Jan. 1989 enjoy none of the protections attaching to assured tenancies under that Act.

[86] Protection from Eviction Act 1977, ss. 3, 3A as amended and inserted by Housing Act 1988, ss. 30 and 31. On licences created by restricted contracts entered into between 28 Nov. 1980 and 14 Jan. 1989, see Housing Act 1980, s. 69(1).

[87] Protection from Eviction Act 1977, s. 1, as amended by Housing Act 1988, s. 29.

[88] The licensee could also successfully resist a claim for possession: see e.g. *Tanner* v. *Tanner* [1975] 1 WLR 1346.

[89] See generally Salmond, 80–84.

[90] The offences of unlawful eviction (Protection from Eviction Act 1977, s. 1(2)) and doing acts intended to cause a residential occupier to leave the premises (s. 1(3)) can be committed by 'any person'.

unless the successor in title took the land as a constructive trustee in favour of the licensee.[91] If the successor did take as a constructive trustee, it might be arguable that, in addition to equitable remedies as beneficiary, the licensee should be able to sue the successor in trespass. Although the interest of the licensee would, strictly, be 'equitable' rather than 'legal', it is anachronistic, since the fusion of law and equity in the nineteenth century, to draw a sharp distinction between the two bodies of law, at least in this context. In other cases, it would appear that the licensee would have no rights at law or in equity against a successor in title.

As against a third party other than a successor in title, it would seem to follow from the above that, since the contractual licensee would have no legal or equitable rights against the third party, the licensee could not sue the third party in trespass for disturbance of possession. However, it is possible to argue as a matter of policy that a licensee should be able to protect occupation against wrongful interference by strangers even if the licensee would have no rights against a successor in title of the licensor.[92] The case of the stranger who 'dispossesses' a contractual licensee is quite different from that of a successor in title to the licensor: the case of the latter raises land law questions which that the former does not.[93]

Some licensees of local authorities enjoy the protection accorded to 'secure tenants' under Part IV of the Housing Act 1985,[94] unless the licence was granted as a 'temporary expedient' to a trespasser.[95] Such licensees also enjoy the protection of section 1 of the Protection from Eviction Act 1977 (concerning unlawful eviction or harassment); and of section 3 of that Act (concerning recovery of occupation on the expiry of the licence),[96] and are entitled to damages under sections 27 and 28 of the Housing Act 1988.

There is also a statutory scheme of protection for business tenants. Under Part II of the Landlord and Tenant Act 1954 the tenant is entitled to a new tenancy on the expiry of the old one. If a new tenancy is refused and provided the ground of refusal is not some fault on the tenant's part, the tenant may be entitled to statutory 'compensation for disturbance', which is

---

[91] *Ashburn Anstalt* v. *Arnold* [1988] QB 1; J. Hill (1988) 51 *MLR* 226. Licences created by estoppel are usually assumed to bind both the parties to the estoppel and successors in title 'in equity': see Megarry and Wade, 804. The argument in the following text applies to such licences as well. The distinction between contractual and estoppel licences is unclear: Hill (1988) 51 *MLR* 226, 233.

[92] At common law a spouse *qua* spouse had certain rights to occupy the matrimonial home in cases where it was the sole property of the other spouse: *National Provincial Bank Ltd* v. *Ainsworth* [1965] AC 1175. According to Lord Upjohn (at 1232), the spouse would be entitled to sue a third party in trespass. The rights of a spouse in cases where the other spouse is the sole owner of the matrimonial home are now dealt with by statute: Matrimonial Homes Act 1983.

[93] See also 37 below.

[94] The scope of which was modified by Housing Act 1988, ss. 35 and 38.

[95] Housing Act 1985, s. 79(4).

[96] Unless they are occupants of a hostel: s. 3A(8); see also *Mohamed* v. *Manek, The Times*, 28 Apr. 1995.

calculated as a multiple of the rateable value of the premises.[97] The aim of the statutory scheme is to provide a stable base for business, and to protect the goodwill of the business, which may suffer if it is forced to relocate.

Landholders   We must now consider the remedies available to landholders against unlawful entrants or occupants. A person who successfully brings an action for ejectment (that is, for possession of land) is entitled to an order for possession. Actions for ejectment are most commonly brought against defaulting mortgagors and against tenants who remain in possession contrary to the terms of their lease (for example, after the period of the lease or a notice to quit has expired, or despite non-payment of rent).[98] Actions for possession against what are commonly called 'squatters'[99] are relatively rare. Neither homelessness nor squatting is a modern phenomenon, of course; but both gained a much increased position in people's consciousness in the late 1960s.[100] In the words of one writer, 'the occupations which particularly attracted the title of squatting were motivated by varying mixtures of self-help and protest'.[101]

The most common targets of such protest were local authorities whose ownership of vacant properties was seen as a dereliction of the duty of government to provide for the homeless. By way of defence, local authorities often claimed that premises were left vacant because they were unfit for human habitation and that the council lacked the funds to make them habitable or to demolish them and redevelop the site. The courts accepted the validity of such arguments by holding that, even if the council was in breach of its duty to house the defendant, the latter's only remedy was to apply to the Minister for an order against it.[102] Owners who kept properties vacant

---

[97] See generally S. Tromans, *Commercial Leases* (London, 1987), 162–93; T. M. Aldridge, *Leasehold Law* (looseleaf service, London), Pt. I, ch. 4; Pt. VI, ch. 4, s. 5.1; Law Com. No. 208 (1992).

[98] On such actions see National Consumer Council *Ordinary Justice* (London, 1989), 338–49. There is an offence of harassing a debtor: Administration of Justice Act 1970, s. 40.

[99] '[O]ne who, without any colour of right, enters upon an unoccupied house or land, intending to stay there as long as he can': *McPhail* v. *Persons, Names Unknown* [1973] Ch. 447, 456 *per* Lord Denning MR. See generally P. Walter and J. Harris, *Claims to the Possession of Land* (London, 1987), ch. 5.

[100] The first 'tactical' occupation of private property is believed to have taken place on 1 Dec. 1968 when about 40 protestors under the banner 'London Squatters Campaign' occupied a block of flats for about an hour. Some have proposed legislation which would allow community groups to take over empty property provided the owner has no plans to use it.

[101] A. M. Pritchard, *Squatting* (London, 1981), 1.

[102] *Southwark LBC* v. *Williams* [1971] Ch. 734. Similarly, the fact that a local authority is in breach of its statutory duty to provide camp sites for gypsies does not, by itself, provide a defence to possession proceedings or to a claim for an injunction to enforce compliance with a planning enforcement notice (on the latter see *Reigate and Banstead BC* v. *Brown*, The Times, 3 Mar. 1992. If the decision to bring possession proceedings was itself unreasonable and, therefore, *ultra vires*, the gypsies would have a defence: *West Glamorgan CC* v. *Rafferty* [1987] 1 WLR 457. However, that defence can only be raised by way of an application for judicial review, and not in answer to a claim for possession: *Avon CC* v. *Buscott* [1988] QB 656.

because they had been bought purely as investments were also sometimes targets.[103] In such cases the protest embodied the idea that real property is a social resource which people ought not to be allowed to deal with as if it had no worth beyond its economic value. In this respect, too, the law takes the side of the landowner: while necessity is a defence to an action in trespass, homelessness does not constitute necessity in the relevant sense.[104] One of the main incidents of property is the right to manage; and in this context, the law has been prepared to give considerable protection to that right even in cases where the owner chooses to leave the property derelict or unused.

A property owner whose property is occupied by unlawful entrants may be unable to ascertain the identity of some or all of them. The procedure made available by RSC Order 113 and CCR Order 24, Part I was designed chiefly to overcome this problem. It also provides a very short route to a final order for possession. The landowner may issue an originating summons claiming possession even if the names of the occupants cannot be discovered, and five clear days[105] after it has been served (or even less in case of emergency), the court may make an order for possession. An even more speedy procedure for use against squatters is contained in CCR Order 24, Part II.[106] The procedure only applies to buildings (not open land). An application for an 'interim possession order' (IPO) must be made within 28 days of the applicant becoming aware of the presence of the squatters. Hearing of the application for an IPO is to take place 'as soon as possible' after the application is made. If an IPO is made, all squatters must leave the premises within twenty-four hours of service of the IPO (which must take place within forty-eight hours of its being made). No claim for damages or loss of profits can be added to the application for an IPO. A final possession order can be made not less than seven days after the grant of an IPO.

Injunctions are available for trespass to land. Another tactic open to landowners faced with unwanted intruders is some form of self-help. Self-help can be used against squatters or other unlawful entrants but not against holding-over tenants or licensees.[107] The obvious first step is a request to leave.[108] As a matter of common law, reasonable force could be used to remove the intruders and their chattels if such a request fell on deaf ears.[109] The scope

[103] Pritchard, *Squatting*, n. 101 above, 12.

[104] *Southwark LBC* v. *Williams* [1971] Ch. 734.

[105] In the case of residential property; two days in the case of other land.

[106] See Consultation Paper, *New Procedures to Combat Squatting in Houses, Shops and Other Buildings*, Lord Chancellor's Department, July, 1994.

[107] Unless they fall into the category of 'excluded tenants or licensees': Protection from Eviction Act 1977, ss. 3 and 3A (see Housing Act 1988, ss. 30, 31). See also Consumer Credit Act 1974, s. 92(2),(3).

[108] However, the mere sending and receipt of a letter demanding delivery up of possession of the land does not amount to a re-entry into possession sufficient to stop time running against the owner: *Mount Carmel Investments Ltd* v. *Peter Thurlow Ltd* [1988] 1 WLR 1078.

[109] *McPhail* v. *Persons Unknown* [1973] Ch. 447, 456–7; *Hemmings* v. *Stoke Poges Golf Club Ltd* [1920] 1 KB 720.

for using force is somewhat reduced by section 6 of the Criminal Law Act 1977[110] which creates offences of using or threatening violence (whether against persons or property) for the purposes of securing entry to premises. These offences can be committed even when the premises are occupied by trespassers.[111] However, they can only be committed when there is someone on the premises opposing the entry. Furthermore, they cannot be committed by a person who is or who is acting on behalf of a 'displaced residential occupier' or a 'protected intending occupier';[112] and it is an offence for a trespasser to fail to leave premises when required to do so by such a person.[113] In the case of long-term occupation, the owner might attempt to flush the intruders out by cutting off essential services such as gas and electricity. It has also been held, in a case concerning a lawful tenant, that cutting off the electricity or gas supply to premises is not, in itself, a tort.[114]

One of the dangers of self-help is that in the wrong hands it can degenerate into harassment.[115] In one case concerning a lawful tenant, the owner tricked the tenant into vacating rent-controlled premises by a false statement to the effect that he would arrange alternative accommodation.[116] The decision of the Court of Appeal in favour of the tenant, who sued the owner in deceit, was that he had been deprived of something of value, namely the right to occupy rent-controlled premises. It is unlikely that a court would view a squatter who had been similarly tricked as entitled to relief.

In addition to, or instead of,[117] an order to the trespasser to leave, the landowner is entitled to a monetary remedy in the so-called action for mesne profits.[118] The basic measure of damages is the value of the use—normally[119] this means the market letting value.[120] Damages are recoverable regardless of whether the landowner can show that the property could or would have been

---

[110] As amended by Criminal Justice and Public Order Act 1994, s. 72.

[111] See A. Ashworth [1978–9] *JSWL* 76.

[112] These terms are defined in s. 12A of the Criminal Law 1977 Act which was inserted by s. 74 of the Criminal Justice and Public Order Act 1994.

[113] Criminal Law Act 1977, s. 7, as substituted by s. 73 of the Criminal Justice and Public Order Act 1994.

[114] *Perera* v. *Vandiyar* [1953] 1 WLR 672. But tenants, licensees, and, query, holding-over tenants are protected by the Protection from Eviction Act 1977 (as amended by Housing Act 1988, s. 29). It is an offence to evict a 'residential occupier' (s. 1(2)); or to do acts (including the persistent withdrawal or withholding of services) intended, or (in the case of a landlord or landlord's agent) likely, to cause a residential occupier to leave the premises (s. 1(3),(3A)).

[115] According to one estimate, nearly 1 in 10 private tenants is harassed each year: *Law and Order in Private Rented Housing* (Campaign for Bedsit Rights, 1994); see *Independent*, 14 Jan. 1994. Concerning harassment by mortgagees desirous of exercising a power of sale see D. G. Barnsley [1991] *JSWL* 220.

[116] *Mafo* v. *Adams* [1970] 1 QB 548.   [117] *Reed* v. *Madon* [1989] Ch. 408.

[118] *Swordheath Properties Ltd* v. *Tabet* [1979] 1 WLR 285. RSC Ord. 15, r. 1 (CCR Ord. 5, r. 1) allows a claim for mesne profits to be joined with an action for ejectment.

[119] For an exceptional case see *Ministry of Defence* v. *Ashman* [1993] 40 EGLR 144. See also *Ministry of Defence* v. *Thompson* [1993] 40 EGLR 148.

[120] The owner can also recover the costs of regaining possession, and damages for harm done to the property.

let to someone else if it had not been occupied by the defendant; or, in other words, regardless of whether the landowner has suffered any economic loss (in the sense of an opportunity cost) as a result of the wrongful occupation.[121] This rule (conveniently called by one judge, the 'user principle'[122]) is a reflection of the 'real' aspect of possession proceedings, and it may allow the landowner to recover recompense over and above his or her economic interest in the property. Such damages may be justified as compensation for the lost opportunity to bargain for the use of the property;[123] or as a means of preventing the defendant being unjustly enriched;[124] and, in the case of wilful trespassers, as a deterrent.[125]

Chattels

The Basic Scheme   The law about remedies for wrongful interference with goods amounting to misappropriation is contained in sections 3–7 of the Torts (Interference with Goods) Act 1977. The court can choose between three forms of order:[126]

(a) an order for delivery of the goods[127] and any consequential damages; or

(b) an order for delivery of the goods, but giving the defendant the alternative of paying damages by reference to the value of the goods, together, in either alternative, with payment of any consequential damages; or

(c) damages.

---

[121] *Inverugie Investments Ltd* v. *Hackett* [1995] 1 WLR 713. But if the value of the use to the defendant is less than the rent for which the owner could and would have let the premises if the defendant had not been in occupation, the owner can claim the higher amount by way of damages for loss suffered as a result of the trespass.

[122] *Stoke-on-Trent CC* v. *W. & J. Wass Ltd* [1988] 1 WLR 1406, 1416 *per* Nicholls LJ.

[123] See R. J. Sharpe and S. M. Waddams (1982) 2 *OJLS* 290.

[124] *Ministry of Defence* v. *Ashman* [1993] 40 EGLR 144 *per* Hoffman LJ at 146–7; E. Cooke (1994) 110 *LQR* 420.

[125] See D. Friedmann (1980) 80 *Col. LR* 504; S. Hedley (1984) 100 *LQR* 653, 678–9; 298–300 below.

[126] The owner of converted goods can also exercise self-help; but possession of goods subject to a regulated hire purchase or conditional sale agreement can be recovered only by a court order: see Harvey and Parry, 291–3, 295–6.

[127] Concerning goods subject to a regulated hire purchase or conditional sale agreement, see also Consumer Credit Act 1974, s. 133 (Harvey and Parry, 295–6). Under s. 4 of the 1977 Act an interlocutory order for delivery up may be made pending the determination of the dispute about the goods (see RSC Ord. 29, r. 2A and CCR Ord. 13, r. 7(1)(d)). The jurisdiction to make such an order is wide, and is not limited to cases where there is a risk that the goods will be lost, destroyed, or otherwise unaccounted for: *Howard E. Perry & Co. Ltd* v. *British Railways Board* [1980] 2 All ER 579. Such an order is akin to the relief available in proceedings in replevin, on which see Salmond, 122–3. There may also be some overlap between s. 4 and the rules about *Mareva* injunctions—for a straightforward account of these see P. S. Atiyah, *Pragmatism and Theory in English Law* (London, 1987), 55–61.

The plaintiff can choose between (b) and (c), but it is in the discretion of the court whether to make an order of type (a).[128] If the court makes a type (b) order, D can satisfy it by returning the goods. But if the damages to which P would have been entitled are less than the full value of the goods, the court can require P to pay the defendant the difference. Similarly under section 6, a person who improves goods in the honest but mistaken belief of having a good title to them, or a person who, in good faith, purchases improved goods from the improver (or from someone who purchased them from the latter), is entitled to an allowance in the calculation of damages to reflect the value of the improvements.

Section 7 is designed to prevent a person being held liable to pay more, in total, than the value of the goods. At common law this could come about in two ways: misappropriation of goods could be actionable not only at the suit of the true owner but also at the suit of a person with a right to possession as against the defendant (for example, a finder of the goods); secondly, the measure of damages for conversion at common law was the full value of the goods even if the plaintiff, the possessor of the goods, had only a limited interest in them because, for example, he or she was only a bailee.[129] Where all the claimants are before the court, the court must give relief in such a way as to avoid excessive liability. Where only one claimant is before the court, and is entitled to damages disproportionate to that person's interest in the goods, the claimant is liable to account to the other interested parties. If, as a result of such accounting, another party receives damages disproportionate to that other's interest, the other must account to the defendant.

This remedial regime represents an important conceptual shift in the law. The common law rules reflected a curious amalgam of proprietary ideas and principles of the law of obligations. Thus, the basic remedy was, and still is, damages; an order for delivery will normally be made only when the goods have some particular non-economic value[130] such that damages would not be an entirely appropriate remedy.[131] On the other hand, the basic measure of

---

[128] Concerning cases in which a wrongdoer mixes P's goods with his or her own in such a way that they are unidentifiable (though, in theory, separable) or affixes property to his or her own in such a way that it is inseparable, see P. Matthews [1981] *CLP* 159; P. Birks [1992] *CLP* (*Pt. 2*) 69 and in N. Palmer and E. McKendrick (eds.), *Interests in Goods* (London, 1993), ch. 16; G. McCormack (1990) 10 *LS* 293 See also *Coleman* v. *Harvey* [1989] 1 NZLR 723. Concerning changes in the form or nature of goods, see Matthews (1981) 10 *Anglo-American LR* 121: on common law tracing generally, see 290–1 below.

[129] *The Winkfield* [1902] P 42; *Chabbra Corporation Pte Ltd* v. *Jag Shakti (Owners)* [1986] AC 337. See also *O'Sullivan* v. *McCann* [1992] New LJ 717. However, where D had an interest in the goods, P could recover only to the extent of P's interest. Assuming that the law of bailment can be treated as part of the law of tort, the right of a bailee (or a bailor) with only a limited interest in chattels to recover damages representing the full value of the chattels constitutes an exception to the general rule that a person may not recover in tort damages for financial loss resulting from damage to the property of another: P. S. Atiyah (1967) 83 *LQR* 248, 253.

[130] Understood broadly; e.g., in *Howard E. Perry & Co. Ltd* v. *British Railways Board* [1980] 2 All ER 579 the goods (steel) were not of any special intrinsic value; but because of a steel strike, steel was in very short supply.

[131] *Cohen* v. *Roche* [1927] 1 KB 169, 180–1 *re* detinue.

damages was, and still is, the value of the goods rather than the loss to P (or the gain to D) as a result of the conversion. Viewing misappropriation as a breach of obligation for which damages was available as a remedy meant, amongst other things, that a plaintiff could bring an action in conversion against a wrongdoer who was no longer in possession of the goods. It also had the consequence that a wrongdoer could be held liable twice over. On the other hand, the 'value' measure of damages made it very difficult to deal in a fair and rational way with the case where the converter had improved the goods[132]—the result depended on the date at which value was assessed, and this differed in detinue (where it was the date of judgment)[133] and conversion (where it was the date of conversion).[134]

The Measure of Damages   As stated already, the basic measure of damages is the value of the goods, which means the market value.[135] This is straightforward in cases where P intended to sell the goods. If P had the goods for personal use, and if a reasonable substitute is available in the market, the damages will represent the cost of purchasing a substitute. If a near-substitute is available, it may be appropriate to award, as consequential damages, any difference in value between the appropriated goods and such substitute as is available, or the cost of adapting the substitute. If no near-substitute is available, it may be necessary to award the cost of making a replacement.[136] If P is a non-commercial user, there may be a case for awarding, in addition to the market value of the goods, damages representing any extra personal value which P put on the goods.[137] Such damages would, in the terms of this book, protect a non-economic interest.

If the appropriated chattel was used by P to earn profits, the market cost of a substitute may represent only an approximation to the true value of the chattel as a going concern because the latter, but not the former, will take account of the chattel's profit earning potential.[138] To this extent, the law does not properly protect the plaintiff's economic interest in the chattel. However, if the court also awards as consequential damages any loss of profits suffered or likely to be suffered as a result of the chattel being unavailable for use,[139] P will not be undercompensated at the end of the day.

---

[132] D. M. Gordon (1955) 71 *LQR* 346. Some of the anomalies in the law which Gordon discusses have been removed by the 1977 Act. However, it is still the case that a goods owner who can recover the goods without recourse to a court can take the advantage of any improvements done by the wrongdoer without making any allowance for their value.

[133] *Rosenthal* v. *Alderton* [1946] KB 374.

[134] *Mercer* v. *Jones* (1813) 3 Camp. 477; 170 ER 1452.

[135] Thus, in the case of negotiable instruments, the value of the instrument is its face value or its sale value, not the value of the paper on which it is written: *International Factors Ltd* v. *Rodriguez* [1979] QB 351.

[136] *J. E. Hall Ltd* v. *Barclay* [1937] 3 All ER 620.   [137] Harris, 44–6, 366.

[138] *Ibid.*, 359–63.

[139] This may include compensation for the loss of a chance of financial gain: *Howe* v. *Teefy* (1927) 27 SR(NSW) 301 (misappropriation of racehorse). See generally J. Knott (1993) *LMCLQ* 502.

In some cases, awarding the market value of converted goods might allow P to recover more than the financial loss flowing from the tort. Consider, for example, liability for the removal or mining of substances on or under land. The traditional approach was to award the owner the market value of the material removed, less the cost of severing it (if D had not acted wilfully) and of bringing it to the surface.[140] If the owner could not or would not have removed and marketed the substance, such an award would allow the owner to recover more than the financial loss flowing from the tort. A more appropriate measure of damages might be a royalty: such an award would compensate the owner for diminution in the value of the land as a result of the mining but at the same time allow the defendant to keep the fruits of its own efforts. The issue was discussed in a New South Wales case[141] in which it was held, by majority, that the proper measure of damages was the market value of gravel removed from P's land and not a royalty, despite the fact that P had not bought the land to exploit the gravel, it could probably not have obtained planning permission to operate a commercial gravel pit, and even though D could have removed the gravel lawfully in exercise of a statutory power and was in the habit of paying a royalty for gravel removed in exercise of the power. One of the judges[142] justified the decision on the ground that the award of a royalty would have allowed D to benefit from its own wrong, and that the award of market value prevented unjust enrichment. Another possible way of supporting the larger award would be to say that, whereas the award of a royalty would have compensated P for the financial loss flowing from exploitation of the land (given that P could not and would not have exploited it personally), it would not have compensated P for the non-financial loss consequent on being deprived of the freedom to decide that the land should remain unexploited.[143] Whether damages for such non-financial loss are recoverable in cases involving interference with property rights is a moot point, although there is some authority for the award of damages for distress caused by invasion of property rights.[144] At all events, freedom not to exploit implies freedom to exploit; and so an award of damages for non-financial loss would not be appropriate in a case (such, perhaps, as the one presently under discussion) where the owner was not legally free to exploit the property in the way the defendant did.

The willingness to award damages representing gains made by tortious conduct which do not correspond to financial loss suffered by the victim of the tort ('disgorgement damages'), in order to strip tortfeasors of benefits derived from their wrongdoing and for the sake of deterrence, is one of the ways in which the law of tort particularly protects property interests. Both disgorgement and deterrence can be achieved by awards of exemplary

---

[140] *McGregor on Damages*, 15th edn. (London, 1988), paras. 1320–31.

[141] *Bilambil-Terranora Pty Ltd* v. *Tweed Shire Council* [1980] 1 NSWLR 465.

[142] Mahoney J, at 494.   [143] This approach was suggested to me by Jane Stapleton.

[144] See 13 above.

damages under one of the heads recognized in *Rookes* v. *Barnard*,[145] but such awards are only made against persons who act in wilful disregard of another's rights. The law will also sometimes strip innocent wrongdoers of benefits in order to prevent unjust enrichment. So if a person converts goods by retaining them contrary to the terms of a hiring agreement, the owner is entitled to damages representing the market rate of hire.[146] As in the case of the claim for mesne profits in an ejectment action, the plaintiff can recover such damages even without proving that the property would or could have been hired out at the market rate to anyone else. Such cases differ from the mining case just considered in two ways: here the law does not strip the tortfeasor of any profits made by the tort but only awards damages representing expense saved (in the mining case the award of a royalty would have been equivalent). Secondly, it will often not be possible to interpret an award of 'use damages' or mesne profits (unlike a royalty in the mining case) as compensating for financial loss because in many cases mere use will not significantly reduce the value of the property used. On the other hand, such damages might, according to the particular facts, be seen as compensating P for (the non-financial) loss of the freedom to decide that the property should remain unexploited; and they could be viewed in this way even if the unauthorized use did not reduce the value of the property.

What happens if the value of the goods changes between the date of conversion and the date of judgment? This may come about in three different ways: inflation may increase the nominal but not the real value of the goods; fluctuations in supply and demand may affect the real value of the goods; and improvements to the goods made by the wrongdoer, or damage to the goods, may affect their real value. One way of dealing with all of these questions is to lay down a rule concerning the date at which damages are to be assessed. For a long time the rule was that the date of assessment in conversion was the date of conversion; but it has now been held that the proper date for assessment must depend on the facts of the case because the aim of awarding damages is to compensate for loss suffered.[147] Indeed, the three different causes of fluctuations in value really demand rather different treatment.

Let us deal first with fluctuations due to inflation. The main argument for assessing damages according to currency values at the date of judgment is that any increase in the nominal amount of the award between the date of the tort and the date of judgment is no loss to the defendant because D is theoretically in a position to invest funds equal to the amount of the liability in such a way as to mitigate or eliminate the effects of inflation. On the other hand, if P goes into the market to buy substitute goods before the date of judgment (as the duty to mitigate loss may well require), and is awarded only the nominal cost of the purchase, P suffers a real loss because of having had to use

---

[145] [1964] AC 1129.
[146] *Strand Electric and Engineering Co. Ltd* v. *Brisford Entertainments Ltd* [1952] 2 QB 246.
[147] *IBL Ltd* v. *Coussens* [1991] 2 All ER 133.

resources which cannot, therefore, be invested to counter the effects of inflation.[148]

There are several possible answers to this line of argument. First, if the substitute goods which P buys will themselves increase in value in line with inflation, then P does not suffer from inflation by spending money to buy them; so only their nominal cost should be recoverable. Secondly, even if the goods do not increase in value in line with inflation, P can, in theory, be compensated for the effects of inflation by an award of pre-judgment interest at a rate which incorporates the rate of inflation. The basic rule governing the choice of a rate of interest, at least in commercial cases, is that the rate should reflect the commercial cost of borrowing in the relevant period.[149] Commercial rates for borrowing will not necessarily compensate fully for inflation, and to the extent that they do not there is an argument for assessment in currency values as at the date of judgment. Another advantage for P of judgment date assessment, as opposed to assessment at some earlier date plus an award of interest, is that in some cases the lump sum award might be non-taxable but the award of interest on it taxable. In principle, P should not bear the risk of inflation, and this is so whether stress is laid on the property aspect or the obligation aspect of conversion. Assessing damages at the judgment date is one technique for avoiding this; but there are other techniques, and the courts should deal with each case individually.[150]

Secondly, we must consider fluctuations in the real value of the goods. If the value of the goods has fallen in real terms, commitment to the principle that P should normally only recover to the extent of financial loss would dictate recovery of only the reduced value. However, in *Solloway* v. *McLaughlin*[151] P deposited shares with a broker who sold them. When P wanted to close his account with the broker, the latter bought in an equal number of shares at a lower price than that at which the deposited shares had been sold. The Privy Council, applying the date of conversion rule, held that P could recover the difference between the value of the shares D had sold and the value of the shares which had been redelivered to P. In this case it does not seem that P suffered any loss as a result of the conversion; but the broker clearly made an improper gain which should have been disgorged on restitutionary principles. This may be a better explanation of the decision which, on any view, compensated P beyond his economic interest in the shares.

If goods have fallen in value because they have, for example, been

---

[148] D. Feldman and D. Libling (1979) 95 *LQR* 270; I. N. Duncan Wallace (1980) 96 *LQR* 101. For an economic argument in favour of the earlier date see s. Rea (1982) 14 *Ottawa LR* 465.

[149] *Metal Box Ltd* v. *Curry's Ltd* [1988] 1 WLR 175.

[150] In *Tate & Lyle Food and Distribution Ltd* v. *Greater London Council* [1982] 1 WLR 149 (affirmed on liability by House of Lords [1983] 2 AC 509), Forbes J held that the interest rate chosen should be appropriate to the general characteristics of P (such as size and prestige) but disregarding any special characteristic which might affect P's personal borrowing capabilities.

[151] [1938] AC 247; cf. *BBMB Finance (Hong Kong) Ltd* v. *EDA Holdings Ltd* [1990] 1 WLR 409.

damaged, P's rights should depend on whether there would be a cause of action in respect of the damage. If P would have such a cause of action against the converter, then the value of the undamaged goods should be awarded. If P would have a cause of action against some third person but not against the converter, the value of the damaged goods should be awarded in the conversion action, and P should be left to pursue the third party.[152] If P would have no cause of action in respect of the damage, only the value of the damaged goods should be awarded in the conversion action. The question of liability for the damage should be dealt with separately from the question of liability for the misappropriation because the two causes of complaint raise quite different legal issues.

If goods have risen in value in real terms as a result of changes in the balance of supply and demand in the market, commitment to the loss principle might seem to dictate that P should recover the increased value. This conclusion would suggest that the date for assessment of damages in such cases should be the date of judgment rather than the date of conversion. However, it is important, in defining the loss for which P is to be compensated, not to lose sight of principles of mitigation. If it is reasonable to expect P to have mitigated the loss by purchasing goods to replace those converted, the value of the goods for the purposes of assessing damages ought to be their value at the date on which the replacement ought to have been bought. There is authority[153] for the proposition that if D denies liability it is reasonable for P to await the outcome of the trial before deciding whether to take steps to mitigate or repair the effects of the tort. However, because denials of liability are a feature of most cases which go to trial, it seems wrong to argue that they ought to give P a justification for delaying in taking steps to mitigate loss; unless, perhaps, D was clearly waging a war of attrition. However, even in a case where D acts unreasonably, the correct approach may be to impose a penalty in costs or by an unfavourable award of interest.

As already noted, if the increase in value is a result of improvements to the goods done by the wrongdoer, section 6 of the Torts (Interference with Goods) Act 1977 requires allowance to be made for the improvements in assessing the damages payable by D provided D honestly believed that D had good title to the goods at the time the improvements were made.[154] But even

---

[152] It might be argued that it would be fairer to award the value of the undamaged goods and leave the converter to recover from the third party. But the converter would not have title to sue for damage to the goods because at the time they were damaged the converter was neither owner nor lawful possessor of them: *The Aliakmon* [1986] AC 785. So the final result of such an approach might seem fair only in cases in which the acts of the converter were, in some strong sense, the cause of the damage.

[153] *Dodd Properties Ltd.* v. *Canterbury City Council* [1980] 1 WLR 433.

[154] As the s. appears to apply only to the assessment of damages, a court would probably not make an order for the delivery of goods in a case in which it thought that an allowance should be made for improvements. Treating the innocent improver more generously than the guilty is consistent neither with the idea that remedies for conversion are designed to protect property interests (why should the property owner be forced to pay for improvements which were not

if D did not act honestly in this sense, an application of the date of conversion rule would often[155] allow D to reap the value of the improvements. There are two situations in which the goods owner will be able to take the benefit of the improvements, and thus gain disproportionately to his or her financial interest in the goods, namely where, by exercising lawful self-help, the owner is able to seize the goods back without recourse to court action; and where, under section 12 of the Torts (Interference with Goods) Act 1977, a bailee of goods, having made reasonable but unsuccessful attempts to communicate with the owner, sells the goods. The bailee is under an obligation to account to the owner for the proceeds of sale, less the expenses of the sale. In these cases, the only hope of the improver lies in an independent action against the owner, based on restitutionary principles, for recovery of the value of the improvements. Whether such an action would succeed in unclear.[156] This difference between recovery by court order and recovery by self-help seems difficult to justify. The goods owner should not be given a financial incentive to use self-help.

Finally, damages for consequential loss flowing from the conversion are recoverable. The basic rule appears to be that all losses flowing directly and naturally from the misappropriation are compensatable. For example, in *Howe* v. *Teefy*[157] the hirer of a racehorse was awarded, as damages for its having been taken away, the loss of the chance to make money out of training and racing it and out of betting on it and selling information about it to other punters. If, as a result of the conversion, P has been deprived of the use of the goods, the cost of hiring a substitute could be recovered, if this has been incurred; but even if not, the reasonable hire value of the goods could be awarded.[158] As in other contexts, P may be able to recover the hire value of the goods even if they would not have been hired out if they had not been converted. Such a rule prevents unjust enrichment and may deter wrongful dealing with goods.

---

requested and maybe not wanted? See P. Matthews [1981] *CLJ* 340, 355–7), nor with the idea that they are meant to compensate for financial loss, or with the idea that wrongdoers ought not to benefit from their own wrongs (conversion, even if innocent, is, after all, a legal wrong). The only possible justification is that it may deter the wilful wrongdoer from further wrongdoing. The common law similarly distinguished between the innocent and the guilty improver but, unlike the Act, it treated the negligent improver as guilty: *ibid* 345–6.

155 But not always: *ibid*. 341–2, 344–5, 346.
156 See Goff and Jones, 172–7; Matthews [1981] *CLJ* 340, 346–57.
157 (1927) 27 SR(NSW) 301.
158 *Strand Electric and Engineering Co. Ltd* v. *Brisford Entertainments Ltd* [1952] 2 QB 246.

3. EXPLOITATION SHORT OF APPROPRIATION

Real Property

Here we are concerned with interferences such as using land for access,[159] or for parking,[160] for storing goods[161] or tipping waste;[162] invasions of airspace, whether temporary[163] or permanent;[164] and placing scaffolding or other structures on adjoining land to facilitate work on buildings on the defendant's land.[165] The basic rule applicable to all these cases is that since proprietary rights have been interfered with, and provided the title to the land is not in issue, the owner is, *prima facie*, entitled to an injunction to restrain further interference and damages to compensate for past interference.[166] However, the court has a discretion to refuse an injunction and to award damages in lieu of an injunction.[167] Such interferences will usually amount to trespass, and so the trespasser will be liable even if ignorant of the owner's rights and even if the interference with those rights was done without intention or negligence.[168] Furthermore, because trespass is actionable *per se*, P will be entitled to relief even if the trespass has caused no damage in the past and will cause none in the future. In this context the law protects the landowner's right to use land and to regulate its use by others regardless of whether these rights are of any economic value.

Injunctions versus Damages

An important issue raised by these rules concerns the circumstances in which the court ought to exercise its discretion to refuse an injunction. My argument in this section will be that courts should be much more willing than they currently are to refuse an injunction and award damages in lieu.

First, we should distinguish between cases in which the landowner actually

---

[159] e.g. *Jaggard* v. *Sawyer* [1995] 1 WLR 269; *Bracewell* v. *Appleby* [1975] Ch. 408; *Behrens* v. *Richards* [1905] 2 Ch. 614; *Phillips* v. *Homfray* (1871) LR 6 Ch. App. 770.

[160] e.g. *Patel* v. *W. H. Smith (Eziot) Ltd* [1987] 1 WLR 853.

[161] e.g. *Penarth Dock Engineering Co. Ltd* v. *Pounds* [1963] 1 Lloyd's Rep. 359.

[162] e.g. *Whitwham* v. *Westminster Brymbo Coal and Coke Co.* [1896] 2 Ch. 538.

[163] e.g. *Woollerton and Wilson Ltd* v. *Richard Costain Ltd* [1970] 1 WLR 411.

[164] e.g. *Kelsen* v. *Imperial Tobacco Co. (of Great Britain and Ireland) Ltd* [1957] 2 QB 334.

[165] e.g. *John Trenberth Ltd* v. *National Westminster Bank Ltd* (1980) 39 P & CR 104.

[166] But note that we are not currently concerned with cases involving either physical damage to property or 'amenity damage' resulting from interference with use and enjoyment. Rather, we are concerned with financial loss to P or benefit to D resulting from exploitation of the land.

[167] Supreme Court Act 1981, s. 50.

[168] Contrast Fleming, 70. Fault is, no doubt, relevant to liability for physical damage to property (see 91 below) and to liability for amenity damage (see 85 below); but the rule of *prima facie* entitlement to an injunction to restrain exploitation suggests that liability for interference with the right to exploit is strict. However, in *League Against Cruel Sports* v. *Scott* [1985] 2 All ER 289 it was held that the liability of a master of hounds for trespass by hounds depended on proof of intention or negligence. This decision may be explained by the fact that the liability is really for failure to prevent trespass.

wishes the unlawful use of the land to stop and cases in which the owner does not wish to stop D using the land but wants to be paid for the use. In the former type of case an injunction seems, at first sight, to be an appropriate remedy to enforce the owner's right to decide that the land should not be used for the purpose in question. By contrast, in cases of the latter type it might seem, at first sight, that the appropriate remedy would be an award of damages equivalent to the value of a licence to use the land for the required purpose.

However, even when the owner apparently wants the trespass to stop, it is not always clear that an injunction is the more appropriate remedy. It is possible to imagine cases in which P wants to stop D using land but where it would seem undesirable and unjust to grant an injunction. For example, if (as in *Behrens* v. *Richards*[169]) D has been using the land in an unlawful way for a long time,[170] and if the unlawful use is financially important to D and inflicts no economic loss (including in this term, property damage) on P, then a court might feel justified in using its discretion to refuse an injunction, especially if there was evidence that P was acting out of spite.

On the other hand, consider the case of *John Trenberth Ltd* v. *National Westminster Bank Ltd*.[171] In order to comply with their statutory duty to keep their building safe, the defendants sought P's permission to erect scaffolding on the latter's land to facilitate repairs to the building on their land. P refused permission despite the offer of an indemnity against loss or damage. The defendants went ahead and erected the scaffolding despite the refusal of permission. No actual damage was caused to P's land. The trial judge held that P had not refused permission as a bargaining counter to extract payment from the defendants but out of a genuine desire that the scaffolding should not be erected on its land. On the other hand, in his Lordship's view, the defendants had acted in flagrant disregard of P's rights merely in order to save themselves the extra expense involved in demolishing the building and erecting a replacement. The judge not only awarded an injunction but also refused to suspend its operation until the work was complete on the ground that, no actual damage having been caused, there was no way of compensating P for the suspension because the reason it wanted to stop the use of its land was not primarily financial. The judge also held that in such circumstances, a *quia timet* injunction could be awarded to restrain erection of the scaffolding and that a mandatory injunction would go at the interlocutory stage to order removal of the scaffolding and debris.

---

[169] [1905] 2 Ch. 614; see also *Armstrong* v. *Sheppard* [1959] 2 QB 384, 396–7 *per* Lord Evershed MR.

[170] But not long enough to give rise to a prescriptive right of user. The law of prescription recognizes that in certain circumstances it is reasonable to protect long use by treating it as having been lawful, despite lack of evidence of a grant of a right to use: see generally Megarry and Wade, 869ff. A majority of the Law Reform Committee has recommended the total abolition of prescriptive rights: 14th Report, Cmnd 1300, 1966.

[171] (1980) 39 P & CR 104.

These two cases display a sharp divergence in judicial attitudes to property rights. On the one hand is the idea that property rights confer near-absolute freedom to use one's land in the way one chooses.[172] This idea can also be seen at work in a line of cases which decide that a landowner has a right to extract subterranean water flowing in undefined channels beneath the land even if this inflicts economic loss, property damage, or, incredibly, personal injury, on a neighbour under whose land the water also flows.[173] On the other hand is a view that land, even land in private ownership, is a social resource, and that landowning carries with it an obligation to exercise one's rights as owner in a responsible and reasonable way. Here, also, we see a clash of property ideas and obligation ideas: the law of obligations is basically concerned with compensating for losses inflicted by tortious conduct rather than with redressing interference with property rights as such. We have noted the influence of obligation ideas even in the law relating to remedies for misappropriation where, it might be thought, an attitude of absolute respect for property rights would be most justified. In the context of use and exploitation of property there would seem to be less threat to the institution of property involved in taking account of factors such as whether the owner suffered any actual loss or damage and the reasonableness or otherwise of the conduct of the parties to the dispute. Nevertheless, the basic correctness of the approach in the *Trenberth* case was affirmed by the Court of Appeal in *Patel v. W. H. Smith (Eziot) Ltd.*[174]

A strong justification for this strict approach in some cases is that since easements can be acquired by prescription[175] it is important that an owner whose land is being unlawfully used by another should have a readily available remedy to stop time running even if the owner has not yet suffered any economic loss as a result of the trespass and is unlikely to suffer such loss at least until the defendant has acquired rights over the property. Ironically, this justification applies to some cases in which injunctions have been refused, such as *Behrens* v. *Richards*; but does not to apply to other cases in which the strict rule has been most emphatically asserted, such as *Trenberth*.

The law's attempt to strike a balance between the interests of landowners and others who want to use land lies in the discretion to refuse an injunction and in the two conditions which must be satisfied before a court can exercise that discretion,[176] namely that damages would be an adequate remedy and that to award an injunction would be oppressive to the defendant. Damages will be adequate if the injury to P's rights is small, can be estimated in money, and can be compensated for by a small monetary payment. These two

---

[172] Cf. *Goodson* v. *Richardson* (1874) 9 Ch. App. 221, 223–4.

[173] *Bradford Corporation* v. *Pickles* [1895] AC 587; *Langbrook Properties Ltd* v. *Surrey County Council* [1970] 1 WLR 161; *Stephens* v. *Anglian Water Authority* [1987] 1 WLR 1381.

[174] [1987] 1 WLR 853. Both judges in this case declined to say that *Behrens* v. *Richards* had been wrongly decided.

[175] See Megarry and Wade, 869–92.

[176] *Shelfer* v. *City of London Electric Lighting Co.* [1895] 1 Ch. 287.

conditions are related in the sense that if the cost to D of complying with an injunction would be greater than any ensuing economic benefit to P then a court may consider that granting an injunction would be oppressive.[177]

The emphasis in these principles on the adequacy of a money payment as compensation for P's injury might seem to rule out refusal of an injunction in cases where P will suffer no loss as a result of the trespass, and where P's motive for bringing the action is non-economic. This was the view taken by the judge in the *Trenberth* case. On the other hand, since the law recognizes the category of nominal damages as a remedy for torts, such as trespass,[178] which are actionable *per se*; and since the purpose of such damages is to acknowledge that P's rights have been infringed even when no economic loss has been suffered as a result, it does not follow that the absence of economic loss rules out an award of damages. Indeed, in *Behrens* v. *Richards* nominal damages were awarded to mark the fact that P's property rights were being interfered with. The basic question is the extent to which the law of tort ought to protect the owner's desire to control use of the land.

On the other hand, an award of nominal damages might seem a poor recompense for the 'forced sale' of the owner's right to control the use of land, even if the owner has no desire to make money out of so doing; and *a fortiori* if the owner did want to exploit the property for financial gain. The latter was the position in *Woollerton and Wilson Ltd* v. *Richard Costain Ltd*[179] where the jib of a crane which D was using in its building operations was allowed to swing in the wind when not in use, leaving it free to intrude on P's airspace. The judge accepted that the fact that P had suffered and would suffer no financial loss made the award of an injunction more, not less, appropriate.[180] He also seems to have acknowledged that P's motive was financial: it wanted D to pay for the right to overfly the land. The judge decided that since D had offered P insurance cover plus a substantial sum for the right to allow the crane to swing over P's land, and since the trespass had been the result of inadvertence rather than flagrant disregard for P's rights, it was appropriate to suspend the operation of the injunction to allow the work to be finished.[181] A fairer solution would have been to refuse an injunction and to award P damages calculated as the reasonable value of a licence to intrude on the airspace.[182] Such a solution is now made possible by the Access to Neighbouring Land Act 1992 under which a court can make an order

---

[177] e.g. *Bracewell* v. *Appleby* [1975] Ch. 408; *Rileys* v. *Halifax Corporation* [1907] Law Times Rep. 278. Similarly, in calculating damages in lieu of an injunction, the court will not award an extortionate amount: *Jaggard* v. *Sawyer* [1995] 1 WLR 269.

[178] Salmond, 515–6.

[179] [1970] 1 WLR 411. See generally A. J. Wait [1989] *Construction LJ* 117.

[180] For criticism see J. A. Jolowicz [1975] *CLJ* 224, 246–7.

[181] The correctness of this decision has been doubted: *Charrington* v. *Simons & Co. Ltd* [1971] 1 WLR 598, 603. For a theoretical argument in favour of allowing the landowner to 'hold construction companies to ransom', see A. Brudner (1987) 7 *OJLS* 339, 365–8.

[182] See *LJP Investments Pty Ltd* v. *Howard Chia Investments Pty Ltd* (1989) 24 NSWLR 490 and 499.

granting access to land subject to conditions (*inter alia*) that the person granted access pay compensation for any loss inflicted on the neighbour as a result of the entry, and also pay a 'fair and reasonable sum by way of consideration for the privilege of entering' the land. But access may be granted only in order to facilitate works of 'preservation' (including alteration, adjustment, improvement, or demolition incidental thereto). So the Act would not apply to a case such as *Woollerton v. Costain*.

The unwillingness of courts to award damages in lieu of an injunction in cases where P will suffer no economic loss as a result of exploitation of land is apt to produce unfair and unsatisfactory results. The obstacle in the way of awarding such damages appears to be the assumption that substantial damages in lieu of an injunction can only be justified if P suffers economic loss. But it is clear that damages for trespass may be awarded in respect of the past in order to deprive defendants of an unjust enrichment gained by unlawful use of another's property.[183] The claim for mesne profits does exactly this. Furthermore, in *Penarth Dock Engineering Co. Ltd v. Pounds*,[184] where D bought a pontoon from P but failed to remove it from P's dock within a reasonable time, damages were awarded representing the cost of berthing the pontoon elsewhere for the appropriate period despite the fact that P had suffered no economic loss as a result of the delay. It is also clear that exemplary damages can be awarded in trespass,[185] and this enables a further deterrent element to be injected into the remedy in cases involving flagrant disregard of P's rights. There seems no reason of principle why such damages ought not also to be available in lieu of an injunction in respect of future trespass.[186]

I would argue that the courts should be more willing to consider the costs and benefits to the two parties of the award of an injunction and to award damages in lieu if the costs of complying with an injunction would significantly outweigh the benefits of that remedy. In this context, it is worth noting the distinction between trespass and nuisance. The successful plaintiff in a nuisance action is also *prima facie* entitled to an injunction. But to succeed in nuisance a plaintiff must show that actual damage has been or is likely to be suffered as a result of D's actions, and that what D did amounted to an *unreasonable* interference with the use and enjoyment of P's land. The issue of unreasonableness makes relevant to liability, *inter alia*, questions of the relative merits of the parties. Trespass, on the other hand, is actionable

---

[183] The unjust enrichment rationale is not needed where P will suffer economic loss (such as additional costs of maintenance) as a result of the trespass. In *Jaggard v. Sawyer* [1995] 1 WLR 269 the Court of Appeal seems to have gone further and treated loss of a chance to bargain for a licence as financial loss for which compensation in lieu of an injunction could be awarded.

[184] [1963] 1 Lloyd's Rep. 359.

[185] e.g. *Drane v. Evangelou* [1978] 2 All ER 437.

[186] An even better solution to the *Costain*-type case might be a statute allowing such use of airspace subject to satisfactory conditions and safeguards: G. Dworkin (1970) 33 *MLR* 552, 556–7.

per se, and the question of relative merits is relevant, if at all, only to the court's discretion to refuse an injunction.[187] Trespass involves some physical intrusion onto the property of another whereas nuisance may not. Nuisance normally involves interference with the use and enjoyment of P's land by some action done off the land (although it need not be done on D's land); but there is no reason, in principle, why acts done *on P's land* could not constitute a nuisance, and there is New Zealand authority directly supporting this view.[188]

If we assume that something done on P's land can constitute a nuisance as well as a trespass, it is difficult to see why, as a matter of policy, the balancing exercise relevant to liability for nuisance ought not also to be relevant to liability for trespass, at least when the crux of the complaint is exploitation or use of the land falling short of appropriation.[189] The answer to this might be that it would be undesirable (even if technically possible) to treat acts done on P's land as nuisance, and that such acts ought to be subject to a stricter regime of liability exactly because they involve the doing of acts on P's land. If this argument is convincing, perhaps the courts should not preserve a discretion to refuse an injunction in cases of trespass even in extreme cases.

The discussion so far has proceeded on the assumption that if an injunction is awarded, it will be enforced, and the trespassory use will come an end. But this assumption ignores the fact that the parties might bargain around the injunction so as to allow the wrongful conduct to continue in return for some payment or other consideration. In other words, the final outcome of the case might be the same regardless of whether the court awards an injunction or not. However, if the court awards an injunction, it gives P a powerful bargaining weapon which can be used to extract from D much more than P might have been able to obtain without it.[190] An injunction enables P to

---

[187] But not all intrusions onto the property of another constitute trespasses: some are justified by law and others by the consent of the owner. Furthermore, consent may be implied, but probably only where it would be obviously absurd not to and not simply because it would be unreasonable for the owner not to allow the visitor onto the land.

[188] *Paxhaven Holdings Ltd* v. *A-G* [1974] 2 NZLR 185; *Clearlite Holdings Ltd* v. *Auckland City Corporation* [1976] 2 NZLR 729. There are, of course, cases, such as *Kelsen* v. *Imperial Tobacco Co. (of Great Britain and Ireland) Ltd* [1957] 2 QB 334 and cases of overhanging trees which involve intrusions into airspace clearly amounting to nuisances, but since the intruding items are attached to something on the land of the defendant, these cases do not establish the point at issue.

[189] *Didow* v. *Alberta Power Ltd* [1988] 5 WWR 606.

[190] Some courts have explicitly recognized this: *Goodson* v. *Richardson* (1874) 9 Ch. App. 221, 224; *Eardley* v. *Granville* (1876) 3 Ch. D 826, 832; *Woollerton* v. *Costain* [1970] 1 WLR 411, 415; *Bracewell* v. *Appleby* [1975] Ch. 408, 416; *AB Consolidated Ltd* v. *Europe Strength Food Co. Pty Ltd* [1978] 2 NZLR 515, 525 (a breach of confidence case). The danger of unconscionable use of the bargaining power conferred by an injunction is greatest where the injunction requires the defendant to take positive action: *Isenberg* v. *East India House Estate Co.* (1863) 3 De GJ & S 263, 273; 46 ER 637, 641. In *Carr-Saunders* v. *Dick McNeil Associates Ltd* [1986] 1 WLR 922 Millett J, in assessing damages in lieu of a mandatory injunction which would have required the demolition of a building, took into account the fact that the award of such an injunction would have enabled P to extract from D far more than the financial loss suffered as a result of the nuisance.

decide the nature and set the level of compensation (within limits set by the value to D of continuing the wrongful conduct), whereas when the court awards damages it decides the level (and the nature) of the compensation. This bargaining advantage conferred by the award of an injunction is the economic value to P of the injunction as opposed to an award of damages. Of course, the value of the injunction to P will depend on the relative bargaining strengths of the two parties; but the injunction gives P a source of strength lacking in pre-trial bargaining aimed at settling a claim.

From one point of view, this reduces the importance of the distinction between protecting the right to control the use of property *per se*, and protecting the financial interest in controlling such use: it is true that it is only by the award of an injunction that the landowner is enabled to protect the right to control the use of land for its own sake—an award of damages amounts to a forced sale of that right or to the granting to the defendant of a licence to use the land in return for a money payment. However, it is not true that the award of an injunction will inevitably result in the cessation of the unlawful conduct. If the owner's real motive in seeking a remedy was to make an economic gain, the owner may well bargain with D for monetary or other compensation as the price of release from the injunction. But even if the owner's professed motive was non-economic (that the unlawful conduct should cease in circumstances where it was causing no economic loss; or despite an award of compensation equal to any economic loss suffered), the owner might still use the injunction as a bargaining counter to extract compensation from D in return for allowing the unlawful conduct to continue. Since the law does not require, as a condition of awarding an injunction, that P satisfy the court that he or she really wants the unlawful activity to stop, and since the law does not seek to control the way P uses any remedy awarded, there may be a case for the courts viewing the award of an injunction not so much as a way of protecting property rights as such, but as a means of giving to P a bargaining counter which will facilitate the use of property rights to economic advantage.[191]

If the courts took such an approach, some cases might take on a different complexion. Consider, for example, the *Trenberth* case.[192] Despite the protestations of P that it had a genuine desire that the scaffolding should not be constructed on its land, the fact that it was a company and not a private individual makes it implausible to think that it had any legitimate non-economic reason for preventing such a temporary use of its land, especially given that D had offered financial guarantees in return for the use. By awarding an injunction the court was giving to P an extremely strong bargaining weapon. Even if P intended to use its injunction to bring the trespass to an end, the law would at least be justified in drawing a distinction between commercial

[191] This use of ownership rights was recognized by Lord McNaghten in *Bradford Corporation v. Pickles* [1895] AC 587, 600–1.
[192] (1980) 39 P & CR 104.

and non-commercial landowners in appropriate cases and in weighing the relative financial interests of commercial disputants. The law's starting point—that property interests are intrinsically valuable and worthy of protection as such, should not be taken so far that the realities of life (namely that real property is often viewed as a economic resource, and often as nothing more than an economic resource), are ignored in favour of investing real property with a mystical quality which it may not have, even for private individuals, in a society as mobile and materialistic as ours. This is not to say that land is never more than a commodity to its owner; but it should mean that the law recognizes that in many cases the owner's main reason for wanting to control the use of land is to make a financial gain.

It might be argued that another justification for awarding an injunction is to deter the wrongdoer from future trespassing. Such an argument would be particularly pertinent where D acted deliberately. However, there are two weaknesses in this argument. First, if we accept that it is sometimes unreasonable for landowners to insist that trespassory use of their land stop and reasonable to force them to accept monetary compensation as the price of the user, it follows that in such cases the message we want to give to potential trespassers is that they should negotiate for use of the land with the landowner rather than that they should not contemplate use of the land. This message would effectively be given by an appropriate award of damages. Secondly, since the landowner can bargain with the trespasser for release from the injunction, the award of an injunction might itself only give the message that use ought to be paid for. It is, at all events, wrong to assume that only an injunction could perform a deterrent function: damages can also perform this function, especially if the quantum of damages equals or exceeds the financial benefit to the defendant in using the land. We have already seen that damages for trespass can be calculated so as to deprive D of any financial benefit obtained from the trespass, and that exemplary damages can be awarded to teach wilful trespassers that wrongdoing will not pay.

It is time to pause and summarize the argument. The prime remedy for the trespassory use of land is the injunction. However, there are cases where, considering the relative merits of the parties and the financial ramifications of the situation, the award of an injunction does not seem a reasonable way of resolving the dispute. This may be so whether or not the wrongful conduct has inflicted economic loss on the defendant. There is an argument for saying that unless the court is convinced that P has a genuine and reasonable non-financial reason for seeking the award of an injunction such that the injunction will be used to bring an end to the trespassory conduct, or unless it thinks it desirable to give P a weapon to use in negotiating a settlement with D, it should not award an injunction but should assess for itself P's legitimate economic interest in controlling the use of the property and award damages to reflect that interest.

Monetary Compensation

Damages for trespassory use of land can be awarded either in respect of the past or, in lieu of an injunction, in respect of the future. Exemplary damages can be awarded in appropriate cases, as can compensatory damages calculated according to the financial loss suffered or likely to be suffered in the future by the plaintiff. The rules about restitutionary compensation for the benefit gained by the defendant by using the property are somewhat confused. There is nineteenth-century authority for the proposition that the plaintiff cannot recover the reasonable value of the use of land,[193] and the cases already examined on the award of damages in lieu of an injunction seem to assume that damages for the future can normally be awarded only to compensate for actual loss likely to be suffered. But there is more recent authority to suggest that the value of the wrongful use can be recovered even if P suffers no financial loss as a result of the unauthorized use,[194] and this seems more consistent with other cases which allow damages for use of land and chattels which have been misappropriated,[195] and for unauthorized use of chattels.[196] On the other hand, in *Stoke-on-Trent CC v. W. & J. Wass Ltd*[197] it was held that the owner of a franchise to hold a market in a particular place could not recover damages representing the reasonable value of the use of the franchise by someone who held a market in that place without permission. This case may be technically distinguishable on the ground that it was not an action in trespass but it seems hard to explain on any more principled basis.

Non-Possessory Interests

We have been dealing so far with trespassory use which interferes with possessory interests in land. The law of tort also protects against unauthorized use other interests in land such as easements and *profits à prendre*. Furthermore, a right to enter and use land may be conferred by a contract (called a 'contractual licence') or by bare permission to enter (a 'bare licence') without creating any recognized proprietary interest in the land. The legal effect of mere permission to enter is to render the licensee's entry non-trespassory. But such a licence can be revoked at any time by the licensor, and after the lapse of a reasonable period in which the licensee can leave the land he or she becomes once again a trespasser. If a licence is coupled with a legally recognized proprietary interest in land such as a right to cut timber (a *profit à prendre*), then the licence is enforceable to the same extent and in

---

[193] *Phillips* v. *Homfray* (1871) LR 6 Ch. App. 770; but this rule strictly only applies to restitutionary claims and not to claims for damages in tort. On the latter, see *Whitwham* v. *Westminster Brymbo Coal and Coke Co.* [1896] 2 Ch. 538; Burrows, 296.

[194] *Penarth Dock Engineering Co. Ltd* v. *Pounds* [1963] 1 Lloyd's Rep. 359.

[195] See 40, 44–5 above.   [196] See 89 below.   [197] [1988] 1 WLR 1402.

the same way as the interest. The licensee's remedies for breach of a contractual licence will be contractual, not 'proprietary'; so the licensee will not be able to sue the re-entering owner in trespass, although in some cases the licensee may be entitled to an injunction (for breach of contract) or specific performance to restrain revocation and to enforce the right to enter.[198]

As against third parties who interfere with a contractual licensee's entry or use the licensee will, of course, have no contractual rights; and it is unclear whether or when the licensee will be entitled to recover damages in the tort of trespass for interference with the right to use the land. As noted earlier, it would appear that a contractual licence to enter and use land would not bind a successor in title of the licensor even if the successor had notice of the license.[199] As against other third parties, there is a case for allowing licensees in appropriate cases to sue people who interfere with rights of user in trespass. There is no good reason of policy why the mere fact that the licensee does not have a proprietary interest in the land should protect him or her against liability in the way it protects a purchaser of the land.[200]

Chattels

Wrongful detention of goods for a limited period is an actionable interference for which damages may be awarded representing the loss suffered by the owner as a result of the detention.[201] Merely using another's chattel without permission does not amount to conversion,[202] but it may amount to trespass. If the owner would have used the goods had D not been using them, the obvious measure of damages would be the cost of hiring a substitute because this is the measure of the owner's loss. But even if the owner did not need to hire a substitute, or did not suffer any financial loss by being deprived of the use of the goods, he or she could recover the reasonable hire value of the goods.[203] As in other contexts involving interference with property rights which cause no financial loss, the justification for recovery is that it prevents unjust enrichment and may deter wrongful use of goods.

Property rights to use goods which are protected by the tort of trespass attach not only to ownership of goods but also to bailment. Although bailment is a contract, the rights of the bailee are not limited to contract because bailment confers a right to possession. In addition, a person may have a purely contractual right to use goods, and we will consider in Chapter 3 the extent of legal protection of such contractual rights.

---

[198] *Verrall* v. *Great Yarmouth BC* [1981] QB 202. For detailed discussion see Salmond, 80–84.
[199] See 36–7 above.   [200] See further 37, above and 110 below.
[201] *Brandeis Goldschmidt & Co Ltd* v. *Western Transport Ltd* [1982] 1 All ER 28.
[202] Unless, perhaps, it is so serious that it involves obvious defiance of P's rights: Fleming, 57.
[203] *Strand Electric and Engineering Co. Ltd* v. *Brisford Entertainments Ltd* [1952] 2 QB 246.

Intangible Property

General Considerations

Once we move away from the paradigms of property—land and chattels—to deal with intangible property,[204] we enter the area of what we might call 'property in a metaphorical sense'. The metaphor resides, first, in the obvious fact that intangible property does not possess all the characteristics of the paradigms of property; it cannot, for example, be physically possessed or occupied.[205] But the metaphor extends further than this in two directions. First, in relation to any particular intangible asset, it is possible to ask whether the law does, or ought to, treat it as property; or, in other words, as capable of being the subject of proprietary rights and interests. Secondly, if the law does treat a particular intangible asset as property, it does not automatically follow that the asset will have all the legal characteristics of the paradigms of property: the law may accord to it some, but not other, protections which attach to the paradigms of property. Of course, the fact that a particular intangible asset does not enjoy the legal status of property or does not receive the full protection accorded to the paradigms of property does not mean that, *pro tanto*, it is without legal protection. Property is only one of the concepts which the law uses as a basis for legal protection of intangible (and tangible) assets; others are contract and wrongful infliction of economic loss. One of the merits of saying that intangible assets are property in only a metaphorical sense is that it emphasizes the choice involved in deciding to accord legal protection to an intangible asset by classifying it as property.

A clear example of this process at work is the case of *Ex parte Island Records*,[206] which involved what is known as 'bootlegging', that is, the unauthorized recording of live musical performances and the reproduction and sale of the recordings. Bootlegging is a criminal offence, but the question in this case was whether it was also a civil wrong against the perpetrators of which an injunction[207] could be awarded. The Court of Appeal decided that a right of action in tort could not be based on the statutory provision which created the criminal offence because it was not designed to protect individual

---

[204] Here we are concerned with 'pure intangibles' as opposed to 'documentary intangibles' (that is, intangible property transferable by physical transfer of the document which represents it). For present purposes the law relevant to documentary intangibles, such as rights embodied in bills of lading and negotiable instruments, is that relating to chattels which we have already discussed; see Goode, 66–8.

[205] Remember that we are not here dealing with documentary intangibles. Of course, pure intangible property often has physical form—the book in which the copyright material is contained, or the product on which a registered trade mark is printed or which infringes a patent. But here we are concerned primarily with the intangible property itself and not with its physical manifestations.

[206] [1978] Ch. 122.

[207] More precisely, an *ex parte Anton Piller* order; that is, an order requiring the defendant to disclose relevant material in his or her possession.

performers. Nevertheless, both Lord Denning MR and Waller LJ were prepared to find in favour of the plaintiffs (who were artists, songwriters, and
recording companies) on the basis that by virtue of exclusive recording contracts between the performers and the record companies the plaintiffs had
rights *in the nature of property rights* which could be protected from interference by an injunction. This reasoning, called by one judge 'the injury to property argument',[208] has since been held to be wrong,[209] but it does illustrate
well the creative process of reasoning by which intangible assets can be
accorded legal protection by being treated as property interests. Rights in performances are now defined by statute[210] and are protected by means of
actions for breach of statutory duty, which we will consider in more detail in
Chapter 4.

The intangible assets which have been longest recognized as property interests are patents, trade marks, copyright, and designs. These interests, which
are of great economic importance, have for a long time received considerable
statutory protection. For the purposes of exposition, this statutory law and
its judge-made accretions are usually treated as part of the law of 'intellectual property' rather than of the law of tort. However, the juridical techniques used in this area of the law are in many important ways similar to
those used in the common law property torts. Infringement of a statutory
intellectual property right is, in effect, a (statutory) tort. Since one of my chief
concerns in this book is to examine forms of and techniques for protecting
economic interests, the similarities between common law and statutory torts
must be exposed. For this purpose, there is no need to consider in detail the
precise scope and nature of these statutory property rights, but it is necessary
to consider in some detail the remedies provided for interference with the various rights.

Even more importantly, I will examine the extent to which the common
law of tort can provide protection, beyond that provided by the various statutory regimes, for intangible assets. We will, in due course, consider three main
techniques which the law of tort can use to accord such additional protection. The first technique (which will be discussed in this Chapter) was mentioned above: it is the injury to property argument. The second (which will
be discussed in Chapter 4) was also mentioned above: it is to allow an action
for breach of a statutory provision; and such an action may be allowed in
some cases even if the relevant statutory provision does not, in its terms, provide that a civil action can be brought by someone injured by breach of it.
The third technique (which will be discussed mainly in Chapters 3 and 4)
involves creating a tort based on the intentional infliction of economic loss;

---

[208] *Rickless* v. *United Artists Corporation* [1988] QB 40, 53 *per* Sir Nicolas Browne-Wilkinson
VC.

[209] In *Lonrho Ltd* v. *Shell Petroleum Co. Ltd (No. 2)* [1982] AC 173, 187; see *Rickless* v. *United
Artists Corporation* [1988] QB 40, 54 *per* Sir Nicolas Browne-Wilkinson VC.

[210] CDPA, ss. 194–7.

examples of such torts are conspiracy, interference with contract, deceit, malicious falsehood, causing loss by unlawful means, and unfair competition. Some of these torts are well-established, while others are in their formative stages.

The Main Statutory Property Rights

Trade Marks

The tort of passing off, which we will consider in more detail later, is designed to protect traders against competitors who seek to 'pass off' their goods or services as being those of another trader by misleadingly using some name, mark, sign, get-up, or description (etc.) used by that other trader, with the aim of reaping the benefits of the other trader's business reputation or, as it is usually put, 'goodwill' which, loosely, means the power to attract and retain customers.[211] The registration of a trade mark[212] is another way of protecting such things as trade and product names; product marks, designs, packaging, and descriptions; and devices, words, signatures, and so on, which identify a person as connected with the provision of a service. The tort of passing off and the law of registered trade marks protect essentially the same interest, namely trading goodwill. However, whereas the tort of passing off protects the actual goodwill which the name, mark, get-up, or description helps to create and sustain,[213] in the case of a registered trade mark, the property which the law protects is the mark itself. So, for instance, non-use of a registered trade mark may lead to its being expunged from the register;[214] whereas, provided the goodwill which the mark (etc.) has generated continues to exist, the non-use of the mark will not prevent an action for passing off being brought.[215]

The relationship between the law of registered trade marks and the tort of passing off (or of unregistered marks, as it is often referred to)[216] is complex.

---

[211] Reputation and goodwill are not strictly the same thing: reputation generates and sustains goodwill and reputation, as such, is not protected by the tort of passing off (see Phillips and Firth, 279–82). Passing off always involves exploitation of reputation in order to divert loyal customers.

[212] Cornish, chs. 15–17; Phillips and Firth, ch. 21. 'A registered trade mark is a property right': Trade Marks Act 1994 (TMA), s. 2(1); see also s. 22.

[213] But in some cases the protection offered by the tort of passing off is very similar to that offered by trade mark law; e.g., the protection of the use of the word 'champagne': *J. Bollinger* v. *Costa Brava Wine Co.* [1960] Ch. 262; *Taittinger* v. *Allbev Ltd* [1993] FSR 641; B. Lynch [1993] *New LJ* 1304. In this context the common law has come very close to recognizing a property right in the unregistered mark. Under TMA, s. 49 an association can register a collective trade mark which can be used by all members of the association.

[214] Trade marks are initially registered for 10 years, and the registration is renewable for periods of 10 years at a time (TMA, s. 42). Non-use for 5 years justifies expungement: s. 46(1)(a),(b). Thus, registration of a trade mark potentially confers a perpetual monopoly.

[215] *Ad-Lib Club* v. *Granville* [1972] RPC 673.

[216] But this is misleading because passing off can be, and often has been, used indirectly to protect registered marks by effectively extending the protection offered by the trade marks legislation.

Section 2(2) of the TMA expressly preserves the law of passing off; under section 5(4) of the Act a mark may not be registered if its use would amount to passing off; and under section 11(3) the use of a pre-existing unregistered mark in a locality, which use could be protected by a passing off action, does not constitute infringement of a relevant registered trade mark.

The statutory protection of trade marks has certain advantages as compared with the tort of passing off. First, once a trade mark is registered it is protected from the date of registration even if it has not been used;[217] whereas a mark (etc.) will be protected by the law of tort only if it has been used long enough to generate goodwill. Secondly, the fact that the existence of a mark has been publicized by its being placed on a register which can be searched no doubt makes it less likely that a competitor will employ a similar mark and less easy for the latter to argue that use of the similar mark did not infringe the plaintiff's rights. At common law P will have to prove, not just that D used the mark (etc.), but also that the use of the mark by P had generated goodwill which D's use was calculated to exploit. Thirdly, the protection given by a registered mark may be wider in geographical terms than that offered by the tort of passing off because registration provides protection throughout the UK whereas the goodwill attaching to an unregistered mark may only exist in a limited area.[218] Fourthly, under certain circumstances a registered trade mark can be 'assigned' (that is, sold) even though the goodwill of the business, which the mark fosters, is not assigned along with it.[219] Other traders can also be licensed to use trade marks. On the other hand, the common law protects marks (etc.) only as a means of protecting goodwill; and so, as a general rule, common law protection does not attach to use of the mark except in the course of the business the goodwill of which the mark fosters.[220] If the user of an unregistered mark ceases to trade, no other trader can claim protection for the use of that mark unless the latter has acquired the goodwill of the business. The mark again becomes 'public property'.

The two main practical functions of the tort of passing off are to provide protection for marks which are, for some reason, unregistrable; and to protect registered marks against conduct which does not amount to infringement under the trade marks legislation. In these respects, the balance between passing off and trade mark law has been considerably altered by the Trade Marks Act 1994. In the first place, it has been made easier to secure registration of a trade mark; and the definition of what may be a trade mark has been considerably extended to include, for instance, the shape of goods or their packaging (TMA, s. 1(1)). Under the old law, for example, the design of the standard Coca-Cola bottle, although distinctive in shape and strongly identified with the product it contains, was not registrable as a trade mark;[221]

---

[217] TMA, s. 9(3).   [218] Phillips and Firth, 288.   [219] TMA, s 24(1).
[220] *Star Industrial* v. *Yap* [1976] FSR 256.
[221] *In re Coca-Cola Co.* [1986] 1 WLR 695.

but the law of passing off provided a means of protecting such a design.[222] Secondly, prior to the 1994 Act, trade mark law only prevented the use of registered marks in relation to goods and services identical to those for which the mark was registered.[223] Passing off, by contrast, could be committed by the use of a mark in relation to similar goods or services; and the common law had begun to move in the direction of protecting unregistered marks against 'dilution'[224] by use in relation to dissimilar goods and services.[225] Now, use of a registered mark in relation to similar or even dissimilar goods or services may amount to infringement of the registered owner's rights.[226] Thirdly, the TMA now provides certain protection for owners of foreign marks well known in the UK without the need to use the law of passing off.[227] The overall result of these changes may be that the law of passing off will become rather less important than it has been in the past.

Because the basis of an action for infringement of a trade mark is interference with a property right, the proper person to bring the action is the registered proprietor;[228] and under certain circumstances, a licensee may sue.[229] There are four prohibited forms of infringement of trade marks:[230] the first involves using a sign identical to a registered trade mark in respect of identical goods or services. Liability for this form of infringement is strict (that is, it attaches simply to use of the mark). The second form involves using an identical sign in relation to similar goods and services or a similar sign in relation to identical or similar goods and services. This form of infringement only occurs if use of the sign generates a likelihood of confusion on the part of the public (including the likelihood of association with the trade mark); and in this respect it is similar to passing off. The third form of infringement covers 'dilution' of a mark by use of an identical or similar sign in relation to dissimilar goods or services. This form of infringement can be established even if the infringing use creates no risk of confusion. Like the first form, and unlike the second form, it is designed to protect trade marks as property.

The fourth form of infringement is directed at the use of trade marks in comparative advertising. It is permissible to use a trade mark to identify goods and services as those of the trade mark owner unless the use is not 'in accordance with honest practices in industrial or commercial matters' and 'without due cause takes unfair advantage of, or is detrimental to, the distinctive character or repute of the trade mark'. This is similar to the sort of conduct against which the tort of injurious falsehood is directed. The

---

[222] *Reckitt & Colman Products Ltd* v. *Borden Inc.* [1990] 1 WLR 491.

[223] Trade marks are registered in relation to specified goods or services.

[224] This is a complex concept. For a brief discussion see R. Annand and H. Norman, *Blackstone's Guide to the Trade Marks Act 1994* (London, 1994), 156–7.

[225] *Taittinger* v. *Allbev Ltd* [1993] FSR 641.

[226] TMA, ss. 10(2) and 10(3) respectively; see further below.

[227] For discusssion see Annand and Norman, *Blackstone's Guide to the Trade Marks Act 1994*, n. 224 above, 30–2.

[228] TMA, s. 14(1).   [229] TMA, ss. 30–31.   [230] TMA, s. 10.

usefulness of that tort (which will be considered in more detail later) in relation to comparative advertising is limited in at least three ways. To amount to injurious falsehood the comparison must involve an untrue statement; it must be malicious; and it must be about the plaintiff's goods, not the defendant's. In other words, the comparison must disparage P's product, not praise D's.[231] On the other hand, of course, the tort is not limited in its operation to the use of registered trade marks.

Because trade marks are property, the prime remedy[232] for infringement is an injunction, following the basic principle of English law that a person whose property rights are being infringed is, in the absence of special circumstances, entitled to have that infringement stopped.[233] Whereas in some contexts[234] it is a condition of specific relief that damages be an inadequate remedy, this is not the case in relation to the award of injunctions to restrain infringements of statutory intellectual property rights.[235] The case of *Ex parte Island Records*,[236] which was considered above, shows the importance of distinguishing between seeking an injunction to restrain infringement of a property right and seeking an injunction to restrain breach of a statutory duty or prohibition designed to protect intangible assets. Whereas the former type of injunction will be granted as a matter of course once an infringement of a property right is established, injunctions to restrain breaches of statutory duties[237] or prohibitions[238] will issue only if the statutory provision in question is interpreted by the court as intended to give individuals the right to bring a civil action, and only if actual damage has been or is likely to be suffered as a result of the breach.

In addition to and in order to ensure compliance with an injunction restraining infringement of a trade mark, the court may order that infringing articles (that is, articles impressed with the offending mark) be delivered up to the plaintiff or someone else and be forfeited or destroyed; or that the offending mark be erased from the goods.[239] The remedies of injunction and delivery up may be awarded even though the infringement was innocent (that is, even though D did not know and had no means of knowing of P's rights), and without proof of actual damage suffered or likely to be suffered by P as a result of the infringement. Declarations are also available to assist owners of trade marks to enforce their rights.

---

[231] *White* v. *Mellin* [1895] AC 154.

[232] See generally T. A. Blanco White and R. Jacob (eds.), *Kerly's Law of Trade Marks and Trade Names*, 12th edn. (London, 1986), 317–329.

[233] F. H. Lawson, *Remedies of English Law*, 2nd edn. (London, 1980), 185.

[234] e.g. appropriation of chattels (42 above); or where the gist of the tort in question is damage.

[235] Indeed, the converse is true: damages in lieu of an injunction will be awarded only if damages would be an adequate remedy: see 51 above.

[236] [1978] Ch. 122.   [237] Salmond, 251–6.

[238] *Lonrho Ltd* v. *Shell Petroleum Co. Ltd (No. 2)* [1982] AC 173.

[239] TMA, ss. 15–19.

Monetary remedies are available for infringement of a trade mark. Nominal damages can be awarded for the mere fact of infringement, even without proof of loss; this is a corollary of the proprietary nature of the rights of the trade mark owner. Exemplary damages could, perhaps, be awarded in appropriate circumstances if D flagrantly flouted P's rights.[240] Neither nominal nor exemplary damages protect the owner's financial interest in the mark. Compensatory damages can be awarded in respect of loss already suffered and, in lieu of an injunction, for loss likely to be suffered in the future as a natural and direct result of the infringement.[241] It appears that such damages (in contrast to an account of profits) can be awarded even if D neither knew nor had means of knowing of P's rights in the mark.[242] The normal measure of damages is profits lost as a result of the infringement, although in suitable cases P might be awarded a reasonable fee for granting a licence to use the mark even if no loss of profits was suffered as a result of D's wrongful actions (for example, because P did not produce or market goods of the type to which D affixed the mark). With the exception of damages in lieu of an injunction, the remedy of damages is available as of right; whereas the other monetary remedy—an account of profits—is an equitable remedy which lies in the discretion of the court. The nature of the remedies of damages and account and the relationship between the two are discussed in greater detail below.

Patents[243]

A patent is a statutory right which confers a monopoly (for twenty years)[244] in the marketing of particular goods or the use of a particular process. The basic purpose of the patent system is to encourage innovation by giving the innovator a protected opportunity to recoup development costs free from competition from other producers who might copy a product or process for commercial gain.[245] Whereas the tort of passing off complements and supplements the statutory protection of trade marks, there is no common law tort which performs this function in relation to the patent system.[246]

[240] See 71 below.

[241] *A. G. Spalding & Bros.* v. *A. W. Gamage Ltd (No. 2)* (1918) 35 RPC 101.

[242] *Gillette (UK) Ltd* v. *Edenwest Ltd, The Times*, 9 Mar. 1994. There is a suggestion in this case that an account of profits might not be available against an innocent infringer. In relation to infringement of a patent neither damages nor an account is available against an innocent infringer: 68 below. Damages for breach of copyright may not be awarded against an innocent infringer, but an account of profits may: see 00 below. It is hard to imagine a principled justification for this pattern of rules.

[243] Cornish, Pt. II; Phillips and Firth, Pt. II. Concerning the protection of plant varieties (etc.) see Phillips and Firth, ch. 25.

[244] Patents Act 1977, s. 25.

[245] Acts done privately and not for commercial gain cannot constitute infringment of a patent: Patents Act 1977, s. 60(5)(a). For a sceptical assessment of this 'economic' justification for patents see Phillips and Firth, ch. 9. The main competitor to economic justifications for intellectual property rights are 'moral' justifications based on the idea that a creator has a right to the creation by virtue of being its creator.

[246] Copying another's product and selling it is not passing off in the absence of some misrepresentation that the copied product is that of the original producer.

Like a registered trade mark, a patent is a property right.[247] Section 60 of the Patents Act 1977 defines infringement of a patent: put very crudely, infringing a patent involves using or dealing with a patented product or process for commercial ends without the consent of the proprietor of the patent.[248] Proceedings for infringement of a patent may be brought by the proprietor[249] or by an exclusive licensee.[250] The remedies available are an injunction; an order for delivery up or destruction of products which infringe the patent, or of articles in which that product is inextricably incorporated;[251] damages; an account of the profits derived by the wrongdoer from the infringement;[252] and a declaration that the patent is valid and has been infringed.[253] The principles relevant to the award of each of these remedies are those developed by the courts prior to the coming into effect of the Act.[254]

Because a patent is property, an injunction may issue (and, presumably, a declaration and orders for delivery up and destruction may be made) simply on proof of infringement and without proof either that the proprietor has suffered any loss as a result of the infringement or (except where the infringement consists in using or offering for use a patented process)[255] that D was in any way at fault in doing the infringing actions. However, an award of damages or an account of profits may not be given if D can prove that at the date of the infringement he or she did not know, and had no reasonable grounds for knowing, that the patent existed.[256] The basic measure of damages for infringement of a patent, as in the case of infringement of a trade mark, is either loss of profits resulting from the infringement or a royalty for use of the patent. If the subject of the patent is inextricably incorporated into some larger item, or if some patented process is used as part of the process of producing a product, P is entitled to recover the full amount of any loss of profits even though it is only partly the result of infringement of the patent.[257] In this respect, too, the patent owner may be compensated beyond its financial interest in the patent: the infringer is stripped of the fruits of lawful activity, presumably to obviate difficulties of proving causal link and as an additional deterrent.

[247] Patents Act 1977, s. 30(1) provides that a patent is personal property. It also provides that a patent is not a chose in action; in other words, a patent is to be treated as analogous to a chattel rather than to an intangible, such as a debt. It is not clear what the force of this provision is.

[248] Cornish, 162–9. Note that there are certain forms of 'secondary' or 'contributory' infringement.

[249] Patents Act 1977, s. 61(1).   [250] Patents Act 1977, s. 67(1).

[251] The defendant would receive no allowance for value added; cf. the position where a goods owner seizes converted goods without recourse to legal proceedings, 48 above.

[252] But a plaintiff may not be awarded both damages and an account of profits: Patents Act 1977, s. 61(2).

[253] The court may also make a declaration that an act does not, or that a proposed act would not, constitute an infringement of the patent: Patents Act 1977, s. 71.

[254] Patents Act 1977, s. 61(6).   [255] Patents Act 1977, s. 60(1)(b).

[256] Patents Act 1977, s. 62(1).

[257] *Meters Ltd* v. *Metropolitan Gas Meters Ltd* (1911) 28 RPC 157; *United Horse-Shoe and Nail Co. Ltd* v. *Stewart* (1888) 5 RPC 260.

Copyright[258]

Copyright is a property right which subsists in original literary, dramatic, musical, or artistic works; in sound recordings, films, broadcasts, or cable programmes; and in the typographical arrangement of published editions of copyright material.[259] The first owner of a copyright is, basically, the author of the copyright material.[260] In the most common case, copyright lasts until fifty years after the death of the author.[261] There is no common law tort which protects the same interest as the copyright legislation. The common law does protect confidential information (although the law of tort plays only a limited role here); and in relation to hitherto unpublished material, alternative claims for breach of copyright and breach of confidence are often made.[262] But the law of copyright is designed to protect much more than 'information' understood in any narrow sense. In relation to published material, copyright takes over exactly where the law of confidential information leaves off, namely when the work in question ceases to be confidential and is released into the public arena.

Copyright may be infringed by copying, by issuing copies to the public,[263] by performance or broadcast, and by adaptation (for example, translation).[264] Acts such as these, or the authorization of such acts,[265] amount to infringement if done without the licence of the copyright owner, regardless of whether the infringer knew or had means of knowing that the acts constituted an infringement of copyright. Certain other acts (called 'secondary infringements') can constitute infringement if the person doing them without the licence of the copyright owner knew or had reason to know that they infringed the owner's rights. These acts are: importing an infringing copy; possessing or dealing in it; providing means for making an infringing copy; permitting premises to be used for infringing performances; and providing apparatus for infringing performances.[266] However, the notion of infringement is subject to Chapter III of Part I of the Copyright, Designs and Patents Act 1988 which deals with acts permitted in relation to copyright works. These are acts which would otherwise amount to infringements, and the provisions of Chapter III protect, for example, copying for the purpose of

[258] Cornish, Pt. IV; Phillips and Firth, Pt. III; Dworkin and Taylor, *Blackstone's Guide to the Copyright, Designs and Patents Act 1988* (London, 1989). Concerning public lending right and resale royalty rights see Phillips and Firth, chs. 15 and 16 respectively.

[259] CDPA, s. 1.

[260] CDPA, s. 11. On assignment of copyright, see CDPA, s. 90.   [261] CDPA, ss. 12–15.

[262] See e.g. *Lion Laboratories Ltd* v. *Evans* [1985] QB 526.

[263] With the exception of the rental of sound recordings, films, and computer programs, the phrase covers only the first issuing of the copyright material and not subsequent dealings in it: the latter, including lending of books, are secondary infringements: Cornish, 298, 361–3.

[264] CDPA, ss. 16–21.

[265] Authorization is different from facilitation: *CBS Songs Ltd* v. *Amstrad Consumer Electronics PLC* [1988] AC 1013. There are certain other forms of 'secondary' or 'contributory' infringement: Cornish, 294–6.

[266] CDPA, ss. 22–26.

research and private study, or for the purposes of Parliamentary or judicial proceedings.

An infringement of copyright is actionable by the copyright owner or by an exclusive licensee.[267] Except as against the copyright owner, the rights of an exclusive licensee are the same as those of the owner;[268] this means, among other things, that an exclusive licensee is treated as having property rights in the copyright material and its typographical arrangement. The remedies for infringement of copyright are the same as those for infringement of 'any other property right';[269] these are injunctions, damages, and accounts of profits;[270] as well as declarations; and orders for delivery up,[271] or for destruction or forfeiture to the plaintiff[272] of infringing copies or other articles associated with the infringement. In addition, in cases where the owner would be entitled to an order for delivery up, he or she may be entitled to exercise self-help and seize and detain infringing copies found available for sale or hire.[273] The owner may not use force, and must inform the police before exercising the right. In considering whether to make an order for destruction or forfeiture of infringing copies or other articles associated with the infringement, the court must consider whether the other remedies available in an action for infringement are adequate to compensate P and protect P's interests;[274] in other words, an order for destruction is a remedy of last resort.

A copyright owner who claims damages (but not any other remedy, including an account of profits) is not entitled to the remedy where it is shown that at the time of the infringement the defendant did not know and had no reason to believe that copyright subsisted in the work to which the action relates.[275] In assessing damages, the court may have regard to the flagrancy of the infringement and to any benefit accruing to the defendant by reason of the infringement, and award such additional damages as the justice of the case may require.[276] This provision certainly allows the award of aggravated damages because these are treated as compensatory; but might also allow the award of exemplary damages (which could include an amount representing profits made by the defendant).[277]

The basic measure of damages for infringement of copyright is the depreciation in the value of the copyright caused by the infringement.[278] Damages

---

[267] CDPA, ss. 96(1) and 101(1).   [268] CDPA, s. 101(1).

[269] CDPA, s. 96(2).   [270] CDPA s. 96(2).   [271] CDPA, s. 99.

[272] CDPA, s. 114.

[273] CDPA, s. 100. An *Anton Piller* order is designed to secure for a potential plaintiff access to the premises of a potential defendant whom the former believes may have on the premises pirated audio or video cassettes, or other goods which infringe intellectual property rights, to enable P to search for the pirated goods and relevant accounts and business records. See Cornish, 47–50.

[274] CDPA, s. 114(2).   [275] CDPA, s. 97(1).

[276] CDPA, s. 97(2); cf. s. 229(3) *re* design rights.

[277] See Cornish, 307–8; Law Commission Consultation Paper No. 132, para. 3.54.

[278] *Sutherland Publishing Co. Ltd* v. *Caxton Publishing Co. Ltd* [1936] Ch. 323, 336 *per* Lord Wright MR.

are at large, so that the measure adopted in a particular case may represent loss of profits or a royalty, and may include consequential losses. For example, if D markets a cheap paperback edition of a more expensive hardback book being marketed by P, this may have damaged P's prospects of earning from a paperback edition.[279]

Design Rights

A design right[280] is a property right (lasting fifteen years)[281] in an original design as defined in section 213 of the Copyright, Designs and Patents Act 1988. The design right provisions apply basically to industrial designs, the vast majority of which are now excluded from the copyright regime.[282] The boundary between design rights and patents is regulated by section 213(3)(a) of the CDPA which provides that a design right does not subsist in a method or principle of construction. The first owner of a design right is the designer; or, if the design was made to a commission, the person who commissioned the design; or, if the design was created by an employee in the course of employment, the employer.[283] As in the case of copyright, the exclusive licensee of a design right has the same property rights as the owner against all except the owner.[284] Infringement of a design right consists (subject to the exceptions contained in Chapter II of Part III of the 1988 Act) either in making, or authorizing the making of, articles to that design or in making, or authorizing the making of, a design document recording the design for the purpose of enabling such articles to be made,[285] in either case without the licence of the design right owner. Secondary infringement consists (subject, again, to Chapter II) of dealing commercially with an article which the person knows, or has reason to know, infringes a design right.

An action for infringement of a design right can be brought by the owner or an exclusive licensee.[286] The remedies available are the same as those for infringement of copyright, except that there is no statutory right of self-help, and, further, that in the case of secondary infringement of a design right, where D shows that the infringing article was innocently acquired, the only remedy available in respect of the infringement is damages not exceeding a reasonable royalty in respect of the act complained of.[287]

[279] Cornish, 43–44.
[280] Cornish, 384–9; Phillips and Firth, ch. 24. Concerning registered designs, see 192–3 below.
[281] CDPA, s. 216.
[282] Concerning the relationship between (1) copyright and design right, see CDPA, s. 51; M. F. Flint, C. D. Thorne, and A. P. Williams, *Intellectual Property: The New Law* (London, 1989), 134; G. Dworkin and R. D. Taylor, *Blackstone's Guide to the Copyright, Designs and Patents Act 1988* (London, 1989), 147; Cornish, 389; (2) design right and registered designs, see Dworkin and Taylor *Blackstone's Guide to the CDPA*, 147, 151.
[283] CDPA, s. 215. On assignment of design rights see CDPA, s. 222.
[284] CDPA, s. 234.
[285] CDPA, s. 226.
[286] CDPA, ss. 229(1) and 234(2).
[287] CDPA, s. 233(2).

*General Points concerning Remedies for Infringement of Statutory Intellectual
Property Rights*

There are a number of general points which deserve to be made about the
remedies available for infringement of statutory intellectual property rights.
The first is that the non-monetary remedies—injunctions, declarations, orders
for delivery up, forfeiture, and destruction—are available without proof that
P has suffered or is likely to suffer any loss as a result of the infringement. In
other words, infringements of statutory intellectual property rights are actionable *per se*. Moreover, except in cases where an action does not amount to
infringement of a particular statutory intellectual property right unless D
knew or ought to have known of P's rights, the non-monetary remedies are
available even against innocent infringers, that is, infringers who did not
know and had no reason to know that the right in question existed. Nor
would it be a defence for the infringer to say that he or she took all reasonable care not to infringe a right which that person knew, or had reason to
believe, existed. The only question in cases where P seeks a non-monetary
remedy is whether D's acts actually amounted to an infringement of P's
rights. In this way, statutory intellectual property rights are like other common law property rights protected by the law of tort.

However (secondly), when it comes to claims for monetary compensation—damages and an account of profits—the property analogy has not
always been carried to its logical conclusion. A party who infringes a statutory intellectual property right may not be liable to pay monetary compensation in respect of loss suffered by P or gains made by that party if the latter
can prove that he or she neither knew nor had reason to believe that the right
in question existed. But it should be noted that it is no defence for D to say
that he or she took all reasonable care to avoid infringing a right known to
exist. In this way, the pattern of remedies for infringement of statutory intellectual property rights is the converse of that which some writers[288] maintain
applies to common law property rights in real property and chattels. It is
sometimes argued that it is a defence to a claim in respect of interference with
property rights in land or chattels that one took all reasonable care to prevent one's actions infringing another's acknowledged property right, but that
it is not a defence that one took all reasonable care to ascertain the existence
of the right which one's action has infringed. It was argued above that in relation to unlawful appropriation or exploitation of land or chattels, neither
plea constitutes a defence. But in relation to exploitation of statutory intellectual property rights, mistake as to the existence of the infringed rights
often constitutes a defence to a claim for monetary compensation, while mistake as to the infringing nature of one's acts does not.

Thirdly, it is necessary to say something about the assessment of monetary

[288] e.g. Fleming, 76–7.

remedies for infringement of statutory intellectual property rights. Account of profits is a discretionary remedy which was developed by the courts of equity. It is designed to strip D of net profits made as a result of the infringement of P's rights. An account of profits is different from (for instance) an award of mesne profits in an action for possession of land: the latter, which is usually calculated by reference to the market rent of the premises, is analogous to an award of damages measured by the reasonable value of a licence to exploit an intellectual property right.[289] There is no immediately obvious reason of principle why account should be available as a remedy for exploitation of a statutory intellectual property right but not for exploitation of a common law property right.

It is sometimes said that an account of profits, unlike awards of damages which are calculated in a fairly rough and ready way, requires the financial accounts of the defendant to be scrutinized to ascertain what profits have actually been made, and that this requirement of precision may preclude frequent use of the remedy because in many situations it will be by no means a straightforward matter to decide what proportion of D's profits is properly attributable to infringement of P's rights and what proportion to D's own exertions.[290] It is not clear whether this restrictive attitude represents the current approach of the courts.[291]

An account has two considerable advantages over (compensatory) damages, in theory at least. The first is that it enables a plaintiff to strip the defendant of profits which P could never have made because, for example, the demand for P's goods outstripped the latter's capacity to produce them and D's infringing activities had no adverse effect on profits derived from goods actually marketed. In other words, an account of profits may be granted even though P has suffered no financial loss as a result of the infringement of rights. In such cases, an account potentially protects more than P's economic interest in the property right by going beyond the amount which P could have demanded by way of a licence fee or royalty (which, in a free market, would always be less than the net profit the licensee expected to make by exploiting the right). A similar result could be achieved by an award of exemplary damages (at least in cases of flagrant infringement), but it is open to doubt whether exemplary damages are available in respect of infringement of intellectual property rights.[292] The second potential advantage of an account is that it may be used as a powerful bargaining counter to persuade D to settle: settling may be preferable for the defendant to the expense and inconvenience

---

[289] There is some authority for the view that the plaintiff must elect between damages and an account: A. S. Burrows, *Remedies for Torts and Breach of Contract*, 2nd edn. (London, 1994), 305; and in relation to infringement of a patent, s. 61(2) of the Patents Act 1977 expressly so provides.

[290] This apportionment question does not arise if the court makes an order for delivery up, forfeiture, or destruction.

[291] Burrows, 304–5.

[292] See 65 and 71 above.

of rendering an account.[293] In this respect the account operates in a similar way to an injunction to restrain interference with common law property rights.

So far as damages are concerned,[294] the basic statutory measure is the same as the ordinary tortious measure: damages are designed to put the plaintiff in a position as if the infringement of rights had not occurred. If P has incurred expenses as a result of the infringement (for example, the cost of advertising to warn consumers that D's goods are not P's despite the fact that they carry P's trade mark) then such expenses are recoverable. If P has suffered a loss of profits as a result of the infringement this, of course, is recoverable. As we have already seen, a plaintiff may not be able to prove any loss of profits if the infringing activities of the defendant have not deprived P of any sales, and if P could not or would not have met the demand which D satisfied. Such a plaintiff may, perhaps, recover damages by showing that he or she could and would have licensed the defendant to exploit the property rights.[295] In such a case the measure of damages is a reasonable royalty or licence fee.

In relation to land and chattels, we have seen that a plaintiff can recover (disgorgement) damages in tort measured in terms of a reasonable rent for the premises or hire charge for the goods even if P could not or would not have let or hired the property if D had not appropriated or used it. There is a dictum (in a case concerning infringement of a patent) supporting a similar approach in relation to intellectual property.[296] However, in another patent case Lord Wilberforce disapproved such an approach.[297] His Lordship was influenced by the fact that the plaintiffs in that case had not claimed an account of profits which would, of course, have enabled them to recover profits made by the defendant without proving that they themselves had suffered any financial loss. However, this point does not seem relevant in a case where P claims a royalty or licence fee. It is not obvious why a plaintiff should be allowed to strip a defendant of profits even though these were not made at the expense of P's profits, and at the same time should not be able to require a defendant to pay for the unlawful use of property simply because P has not suffered any financial loss as a result of the infringement of rights.

[293] Phillips and Firth, 167.

[294] Whether in respect of the past or, in lieu of an injunction, in respect of the future. In the case of misappropriated chattels, if D pays P their value, title to the chattels vests in the defendant (Torts (Interference with Goods) Act 1977, s. 5). Similarly, if the infringer of a statutory intellectual property right pays damages in respect of future infringements, the right to use the property vests in the infringer.

[295] In the case of patents, the Patents Act 1977, s. 48 makes provision in certain cases for compulsory licences (see Cornish, 205–10). In addition, the patent owner may apply to the Comptroller of Patents for an entry to be made in the register to the effect that licences under the patent are to be available as of right (s. 46). If such an entry is made then in an action for infringement of the patent, if the defendant undertakes to take such a licence no injunction may be issued and damages are limited to double the appropriate licence fee: s. 46(3)(c).

[296] Watson, Laidlaw & Co. v. Pott, Cassels & Williamson (1914) 31 RPC 104, 120 per Lord Shaw.

[297] General Tire Co. v. Firestone Tyre Co. Ltd [1975] 1 WLR 819, 833.

The technical point that a claim for such profits can be made by way of an equitable remedy (account of profits) while a claim for a licence fee is made by way of a claim for common law damages (the prime purpose of which is to compensate for loss), is exactly that—a mere technicality. It should also be remembered that an award of exemplary damages (if available) may, in effect, give P a royalty regardless of whether P could or would actually have charged D a licence fee. Furthermore, in cases where P is not a competitor of D (for example, in cases of non-competitive infringement of copyright), and so could not prove either loss of profits or loss of the chance to grant a licence, it is not obvious that an infringer should be free of liability to pay any form of monetary compensation.

This discussion makes it clear that there is an important distinction between the remedy of account, which strips the defendant of net profits made by exploitation of property, and disgorgement damages which require D only to pay P a sum representing expense saved by not paying rent or a licence fee or royalty for using the property. Account is available in respect of infringement of statutory intellectual rights but not, apparently, in respect of exploitation of property rights in tangibles. Conversely, it is doubtful whether disgorgement damages are available in respect of infringement of statutory intellectual property rights whereas they are available in respect of tortious exploitation of tangible property. It is hard to explain these facts in a principled way.

Confidential Information

The cause of action for breach of confidence[298] is particularly interesting for our purposes because there has been much debate about its proper juridical basis; or, in other words, by what juridical technique confidential information is or should be protected. In particular, it is not clear to what extent confidential information is treated by the law as property.[299] We have already noted that the Law Commission took the view that, at least for the purposes of rules about transfer and priorities between competing innocent acquirers, confidential information ought not to be treated as property.[300] Also, the fact that the obligation of confidence may be destroyed if the information loses its confidential character[301] and the fact that breaches of confidence may be

[298] Cornish, ch. 8; F. Gurry, *Breach of Confidence* (Oxford, 1984); Goff and Jones, ch. 35. Concerning criminal liability see J. T. Cross (1991) 11 *OJLS* 264.

[299] Gurry, *Breach of Confidence*, 46–56; N. E. Palmer and P. Kohler in N. Palmer and E. McKendrick (eds.), *Interests in Goods* (London, 1993), ch. 7.

[300] See 24 above.

[301] The Law Commission took the view that it is a positive requirement for success in an action for breach of confidence that the information should not have lost its secret character: Law Com. No. 110, paras. 4.15–31 and 6.67. While such a rule would prevent the award of an injunction in respect of non-secret information, it would not prevent an award of monetary compensation for loss suffered by P or for profits made by D in the past as a result of the original

justified in the public interest,[302] both suggest that the property analogy is by no means entirely apposite to confidential information.

The question we are concerned with here relates to remedies for breach of confidence: to what extent is confidential information treated as property for the purposes of deciding what remedies are available for breach? It should be said at this stage that the law of breach of confidence extends well beyond the territory covered by this book. I am concerned primarily with cases in which confidential information is used by a person in such a way as to inflict financial loss on another or to make a financial gain. I am not concerned with cases in which the law of confidential information is used simply to protect privacy or, more particularly, an interest in keeping certain information private.[303]

In commercial contexts, the law of confidential information provides a way of protecting trade 'secrets'[304] which might also be patentable. But the two methods of protecting information are quite different. The law of confidential information only enables information to be protected by keeping it secret, whereas the main point of a patent is to protect the information even though it is public knowledge. In many cases, the mere marketing of a product will enable others to discover the information necessary to reproduce it; and so the law of confidential information would not, by itself, provide adequate protection for the technical information needed for its production. In other cases, trade secrets are often protected by a combination of patents and agreements not to disclose secret information concerning the production of the patented items.[305] The law of confidential information also overlaps, to some extent, with the law of copyright.[306] Once again, however, the law of copyright is basically designed to protect published information; furthermore, the concept of infringement of copyright is concerned, more than is the notion of breach of confidence, with the form as opposed to the substance of the exploitation of the proprietor's creation: only certain types of 'publication' count as infringements of copyright, whereas, on the whole, any disclosure of

---

breach of confidence; nor would it prevent an award for loss likely to be suffered or profits likely to be made in the future as a result of the breach: see Law Com. No. 110, para. 6.70. See also *A-G* v. *Guardian Newspapers Ltd (No. 2)* [1990] 1 AC 109, esp. Lord Goff at 286–7.

[302] Y. Cripps, *The Legal Implications of Disclosure in the Public Interest*, 2nd edn. (London, 1995). See also 255–9 below.

[303] e.g., *Argyll* v. *Argyll* [1967] Ch. 302; *Stephens* v. *Avery* [1988] Ch. 449; *Hellewell* v. *Chief Constable of Derbyshire* [1995] 1 WLR 804, 807.

[304] This term has to be understood broadly: information may qualify for protection simply because it took time and effort to acquire. The acquirer is allowed to protect investment of time and energy against those who seek to 'reap without sowing': *Interfirm Comparison (Australia) Pty Ltd* v. *Law Society of New South Wales* (1975) 6 ALR 445.

[305] Cornish, 265. The law of confidence cannot be used effectively to extend the period of protection for an invention beyond that allowed under the patent system by restraining disclosure of secrets concerning the method of production of the patented product: *R.* v. *Licensing Authority Established under Medicines Act 1968, ex parte Smith Kline & French Laboratories Ltd* [1990] AC 64, 107 *per* Lord Templeman.

[306] Cornish, 217–8.

confidential information, in whatever form, can amount to a breach of confidence.[307]

Liability for breach of confidence rests on breach of an obligation of confidence. Such an obligation can arise from a contract (for example, between employer and employee); or 'in equity' out of circumstances which would make it unconscionable to disclose the information (for example, where a person imparts information to another on the understanding that it is confidential);[308] or as a matter of public policy (as in the case of disclosure of information in circumstances where such disclosure is detrimental to national security).[309] So far as tort liability is concerned, a contractual relationship of confidence could generate tort liability for interference with contractual relations if a third party were, for example, to induce a contracting party to breach a contractual obligation of confidence. This form of tortious liability will be discussed in Chapter 3. There is some authority for the proposition that inducing breach of an equitable obligation is actionable;[310] it is not clear whether such an action would be seen as an action in tort.[311] The way it is classified would affect the remedies available. Liability based on public policy is, perhaps, most appropriately treated as tortious liability.

Treating confidential information as property would involve imposing liability for breach of confidence not on the basis of an obligation of confidence, but rather on the basis of the nature of the asset which the plaintiff claims to 'own'. For this reason, a distinction has to be drawn between calling confidential information 'property' simply to convey the idea that a court will give a remedy for breach of contract or if some ground of equitable intervention is made out;[312] and, on the other hand, treating confidential information as analogous, so far as remedies are concerned, to tangible property (or, in other words, giving it the same status as a statutory intellectual

---

[307] On information communicated orally see *Fraser* v. *Thames Television Ltd* [1984] QB 44.

[308] Based on breach of the duty 'to be of good faith': *Fraser* v. *Evans* [1969] 1 QB 349, 361 *per* Lord Denning MR.

[309] *A-G* v. *Guardian Newspapers Ltd (No. 2)* [1990] 1 AC 109. Where the Crown seeks to restrain the publication of government information, at least where the publication is by a person other than the original recipient, it is not enough for it to show that the publisher, by reason of knowledge of the confidentiality of the information, is under an equitable duty not to disclose it. The Crown must also show a public interest in non-disclosure: Lord Keith of Kinkel, *ibid.*, 256; Lord Brightman, 267; Lord Griffiths, 270; Lord Goff of Chieveley, 282.

[310] *Prudential Assurance Co. Ltd* v. *Lorenz* (1971) 11 KIR 78; see also P. M. North (1971) *JSPTL* 149, 157–8. A person who induces a breach of trust is liable as a (constructive) trustee: C. Harpum (1986) 102 *LQR* 114, 141–2; and it has been said that this rules out tort liability for procuring a breach of trust: *Metall und Rohstoff AG* v. *Donaldson Lufkin & Jenrette Inc.* [1990] 1 QB 391, 481. This distinction between tortious and equitable liability makes no sense except in historical terms, and there is a real need for rationalization of principles of secondary liability. See P. Sales [1990] *CLJ* 491, 502–10.

[311] P. Elias and K. Ewing [1982] *CLJ* 321, 330, n. 36. *China and South Sea Bank* v. *Tan* [1990] 1 AC 536.

[312] Gurry, *Breach of Confidence*, 47; I. C. F. Spry *The Principles of Equitable Remedies*, 3rd edn. (London, 1984), 324–6.

property right).[313] For present purposes, this distinction is of some, but only limited, importance. It is not necessary to classify confidential information as property in the second sense in order to make available as remedies injunctions, or damages in lieu of an injunction, or orders for delivery up and destruction,[314] or damages, or an account of profits.[315] Injunctions and damages can be awarded for breach of contract; injunctions, damages in lieu of an injunction, and an account of profits can be awarded if a ground of equitable intervention is made out.

Classifying confidential information as property is a way in which the courts could make the common law remedy of damages[316] available (for tortious interference with a property right) in circumstances where there has been no breach of contract. The fact that damages are sometimes available, even in the absence of breach of contract, for infringement of statutory intellectual property rights justifies the conclusion that there is no intrinsic reason why the remedy should not also be available for breach of confidence, at least where the loss suffered as a result of the breach is financial.[317] Existing authority does not, however, unequivocally support the award of damages for past loss (as opposed to an award for the future in lieu of an injunction) in the absence of a breach of contract.[318] Use of the property analogy could justify such an award of damages for past loss.

As for the measure of damages, there seems little reason why this should depend on the juridical basis of liability for breach of confidence.[319] According to the circumstances,[320] it may be appropriate to measure damages by profits lost,[321] by the value of a licence to exploit the information,[322] by the cost of acquiring the information;[323] or, in cases involving 'public'[324] or

---

[313] Gurry, *Breach of Confidence*, n. 312 above, 46–56.

[314] Law Com. No. 110, paras. 4.102–4.

[315] *A-G* v. *Guardian Newspapers Ltd (No. 2)* [1990] AC 109.

[316] Including damages representing gain to D in the absence of corresponding loss to P.

[317] In relation to damages for mental distress see Law Com. No. 110, paras. 4.79–82 and 6.106.

[318] See Law Com. No. 110, paras. 4.75–77; contrast Gurry, *Breach of Confidence*, n. 312 above, 434. The position is different in New Zealand: *Aquaculture Corporation* v. *New Zealand Green Mussel Co. Ltd* [1990] 3 NZLR 299.

[319] Gurry, *Breach of Confidence*, n. 312 above, 448–51.

[320] *Talbot* v. *General Television Corporation Pty Ltd* [1980] VR 224.

[321] *Dowson & Mason Ltd* v. *Potter* [1986] 1 WLR 1419; or loss of a chance of financial gain: *Aquaculture Corporation* v. *New Zealand Green Mussel Co. Ltd* [1990] 3 NZLR 299; *Talbot* v. *General Television Corporation Pty Ltd* [1980] VR 224; *Saunders* v. *Parry* [1967] 1 WLR 753, 766. Losses consequent on a breach of confidence may be very difficult to assess: Gurry, *Breach of Confidence*, n. 312 above, 446–7.

[322] Gurry, *Breach of Confidence*, n. 312 above, 445.

[323] *Seager* v. *Copydex Ltd (No. 2)* [1969] RPC 250. The judgment of Lord Denning has been criticized on a number of grounds, including that it puts too much emphasis on reversing D's unjust enrichment as opposed to compensating P for losses. But there seems no reason of substance not to treat confidential information as property and to compensate P for misappropriation of its value if this seems appropriate on the facts of the case. The important thing is to mould the remedy to the facts of the case. See further Gurry, *Breach of Confidence*, n. 312 above, 442–7.

[324] *A-G* v. *Guardian Newspapers Ltd (No. 2)* [1990] AC 109. Concerning exemplary damages see G. Jones [1989] *CLP* 49, 62–3.

'domestic' secrets, as well as in appropriate commercial cases, by the profits made by D in exploiting the information.

Under the Law Commission's proposals for a statutory tort of breach of confidence, the court would also have the power to make an 'adjustment order' in cases in which it would be unfair to award either an injunction (thus giving P the exclusive right to the information) or damages in lieu of an injunction (thus giving D the exclusive right of exploitation).[325] Instead, the court would have the power to determine the extent (if at all) to which each of the parties will be free to exploit the information (for example, by granting licences to use it to third parties). It could also require the defendant, in addition to paying damages in lieu of an injunction, to make a fair and equitable contribution to expenses incurred by P preparatory to exploiting the information, which are likely to be wasted if D is allowed to use it. Conversely, if D is to be restrained by injunction from exploiting the information, P could be required to make such a contribution to the defendant's wasted expenditure.[326]

Treating confidential information as property could also justify imposing liability for innocent breach of confidence; that is, for a breach committed by a person who neither knew nor ought to have known that the information was confidential. By definition, a person who breaks a contractual obligation of confidence would not be innocent in this sense; and equitable principles of unconscionability would not justify awarding a remedy against an innocent discloser. At present the law appears normally to impose no liability on a person who neither knew nor ought to have known that the information was confidential.[327] Furthermore, the Law Commission thinks that the creation of an obligation of confidence should rest on express or implied agreement to treat the information as confidential.[328] The Commission also thinks that a person who receives information impressed with an obligation of confidence, however arising, should be subject to that obligation as soon as, but not before, the person acquires the information and knows or ought to know that the information is confidential. This basic rule would apply whether or not the person gave value for the information, and would be relevant to the award of any remedy.[329]

We have already seen that the rules regarding liability for innocent infringement of statutory intellectual property rights are not uniform. Sometimes innocent infringers are liable to pay monetary compensation, sometimes not; and some forms of infringement are defined in terms of knowledge or means of knowledge, others not. There is a good case for making liability for breach

---

[325] Law Com. No. 110, paras. 6.110–112.

[326] Cf. *Spur Industries Inc.* v. *Del E. Webb Development Co.* (1972) 494 P2d 700 in the context of nuisance.

[327] Regarding indirect or third party recipients see Law Com. No. 110, paras. 4.11–12. The original or direct recipient will normally know or have reason to believe that the information is confidential. But see P. M. North (1971) 12 *JSPTL* 149, 158–9.

[328] Law Com. No. 110, para. 6.11.   [329] Law Com. No. 110, paras. 6.52–55.

of confidence depend, at least, on knowledge or means of knowledge of the confidential nature of the information. After all, the essence of breach of confidence is betrayal of trust, and if a person did not know and had no reason to believe that trust was being reposed in him or her, then it is difficult to see how the person can be said to have breached a confidence. In commercial contexts, the desirability of fostering competition should make us suspicious of any rule which would allow a person to treat information as confidential without taking any steps sufficient to put the reasonable person on notice that it was secret.[330]

Goodwill

Goodwill is a product of the business reputation by means of which a trader or provider of services attracts and retains customers and clients. The claim of goodwill to be classified as property arises from the elements of, and the remedies for, the tort of passing off.[331] At least in its classic form,[332] passing off consists of 'passing off' one's goods or services as being those of another by creating the likelihood of confusion between one's own goods or services and those of that other. The tort can be committed in all innocence; in other words, all that is required is that the defendant's actions in fact create the likelihood of confusion, whether or not D intended this result or was negligent as to its possibility. Passing off is a tort of strict liability, and there is authority for the proposition that even monetary compensation can be awarded against an innocent defendant.[333]

On the other hand, there is one respect in which passing off is unlike the other property torts we have so far considered. In order to succeed in an action P must show actual financial damage (or at least the likelihood of such damage) beyond mere imitation, flowing from the tort.[334] Where P and D are direct competitors, likelihood of damage follows from the likelihood of confusion; but in other cases, more will be required to establish likelihood of damage.[335] This requirement of damage or its likelihood puts passing off in the same category as nuisance—the basis of both torts is interference with property rights, but the tortious nature of the cause of action is reflected in the requirement of damage. The fact that goodwill is viewed as property, even

---

[330] There should be no liability for breach of confidence where a person merely fails to make inquiries which would have revealed the confidential nature of the information. The burden should rest on the discloser to put the recipient on notice that the information is being conveyed in confidence. But the decision in *Smith, Kline & French Laboratories (Australia) Ltd* v. *Secretary of Community Services and Health* (1990) 95 ALR 87 perhaps goes further.

[331] Cornish, 403–26.

[332] For discussions of modern developments see Phillips and Firth, 274–82 and S. Naresh [1986] *CLJ* 97.

[333] *Gillette (UK) Ltd* v. *Edenwest Ltd*, The Times, 9 Mar. 1994; contrast *10th Cantanae Pty Ltd* v. *Shoshana Pty Ltd* (1987) 79 ALR 299, 319–323 *per* Gummow J.

[334] But see *Draper* v. *Trist* [1939] 3 All ER 513, 518.   [335] Cornish, 417–22.

though passing off is not actionable in the absence of damage or the likeli-hood of damage, provides a good illustration of the fact that the concept of 'property' can be used to justify a variety of legal consequences. Calling an asset 'property' does not necessarily mean that all of these legal consequences will be available to protect the asset. As a result, use of the concept without explanation is both dangerous and relatively uninformative.

The remedies available for passing off are the usual remedies available for interference with property rights: injunction,[336] account of profits, and dam-ages. Special damages may be awarded for loss of profits, and general dam-ages may be awarded for injury to goodwill (that is, for non-pecuniary loss).[337] An injunction and nominal damages are available merely on proof of likelihood of damage.[338]

There is another tort which protects goodwill: injurious falsehood. This tort covers damaging another's business reputation by disparaging the other's goods or services with statements which are false and fraudulent. It involves damage to but not exploitation of a property right. It will be considered later in this Chapter under the heading of damage to property.

Character or Personality[339]

The commercial exploitation of characters, whether real (for example, a well known show-business or sporting personality) or fictional (for example, Mickey Mouse or Postman Pat) is long established and can be highly lucra-tive.[340] Character merchandising presents the law with two challenges. The first is whether and how to protect legitimate exploiters from piracy; the sec-ond is whether and how to protect individuals against exploitation of their *persona* without their consent.

Concerning the first, franchising and sponsorship are two contractual tech-niques used for facilitating character merchandising;[341] preventing piracy is rather more difficult. Application of the name or signature or a likeness of a personality to goods may enable an application for a registered trade mark to be made,[342] or it may attract the protection of the law of passing off.[343] A drawn or photographic likeness of a personality will attract the protection of the law of copyright. But English law does not recognize character or

---

[336] A final perpetual injunction to restrain passing off effectively gives P a perpetual monop-oly. Note Lord Bridge's worries on this score in *Reckitt & Colman Products Ltd* v. *Borden Inc.* [1990] 1 WLR 491, 495.

[337] *Spalding* v. *Gamage* (1918) 35 RPC 101.

[338] *Draper* v. *Trist* [1939] 3 All ER 513, 525–7 *per* Lord Goddard CJ.

[339] T. Frazer (1983) 99 *LQR* 281; J. Holyoak [1993] *JBL* 444.

[340] Cornish, 420–2, 425–6; Phillips and Firth, ch. 22; G. Hobbs [1980] *EIPR* 47 and 79.

[341] Phillips and Firth, 310–14.

[342] For a discussion of the likely impact of provisions of the TMA on character merchandis-ing see Annand and Norman, *Blackstone's Guide to the Trade Marks Act 1994*, 213–7.

[343] *Ibid.*, 217–24; H. Carty (1993) 13 *LS* 289.

personality, as such, to be intellectual property. Because of the anti-competitive effect which the recognition of legally protected merchandizing rights would have, it may be thought that it is for Parliament to recognize new rights in the nature of property rights in intangible assets so that the exact nature and extent of such rights and their forms of legal protection can be carefully spelt out from the beginning.[344]

Nor has English law been very willing to protect individuals against exploitation of their personality without their consent partly, perhaps, because of understandable uneasiness about treating *personae* as property, at least in the case of real as opposed to fictional characters. If the name or likeness of a real person is used in such a way as to damage the person's reputation, that person may be able to bring an action for defamation regardless of whether he or she suffers any financial loss thereby.[345] But in general English law gives very little protection to a person's privacy and is even unwilling to strip a person of financial gains made by unauthorized exploitation of a *persona* or to compensate for distress caused thereby.

In *Kaye* v. *Robertson*[346] the Court of Appeal granted an injunction to restrain a malicious falsehood consisting of an implication that Kaye had consented to the publication in a newspaper of a story about him. The court's real concern was that the publication would have invaded Kaye's privacy. Since English law does not protect privacy as such, it found the threatened damage required to complete a cause of action in malicious falsehood in the fact that if the story had been published Kaye would have lost the ability to sell it to the highest bidder. It is surely an indictment of English law and society that judges feel the need to impute a desire to make a profit to someone in order to protect them from unwanted attention by the press. In future, the slowly developing tort of harassment[347] may help in cases such as this.

Fruits of Labour

How much further may the concept of property be pushed in the interests of providing protection for intangible assets?[348] One writer has argued that:

where the commercial value of an entity, whether tangible or intangible, has been brought about by the expenditure of time, effort, labour or money, the person who created that commercial value has a proprietary right to its commercial exploitation.[349]

The law does already protect the expenditure of time and effort as such in some contexts. For example, the labour of preparing a table or other

---

[344] See e.g. *RCA Corporation* v. *Pollard* [1983] Ch. 135, 154 *per* Oliver LJ.
[345] *Tolley* v. *J. S. Fry & Sons* [1931] AC 333.   [346] [1991] FSR 62.
[347] *Khorasandjian* v. *Bush* [1993] QB 727. But see Report of the Committee on Privacy and Related Matters, Cm 1102 (1990), paras. 6.23–4.
[348] See A. Terry (1988) 51 *ALJR* 296.   [349] D. Libling (1978) 94 *LQR* 103, 119.

compilation is protected by the law of copyright even if the compiler has no copyright in the individual items of the material compiled.[350] But as a statement of the present law the quoted passage surely goes too far. For instance, it has been held that the originator of encoded satellite television transmissions has no common law property right in the waves produced by the transmissions;[351] that the organizers of a dog show have no property right in the taking of photographs at the show which they can assign as 'sole photographic rights';[352] and that the compère of a television quiz show has no copyright in the 'format' of the show or of phrases used regularly in it.[353] Nor is it clear that this would be a desirable proposition for the law to adopt. The essence of commercial activity and competition is the expenditure of time, effort, labour, and money to generate income and commercial value. To protect the first person who entered a field of commercial endeavour simply because he or she was the first would spell the end of healthy competition.[354] On the other hand, the recognition of some property rights is a precondition of the existence and operation of a market and of relationships of exchange. The difficult job is to strike a balance between creating too many and creating too few property rights.

There is no doubt that certain forms of competition are unfair, but the definition of unfairness in this context is notoriously difficult, and the courts have always been unwilling to undertake the task. The advantage of the concept of property is that it can be used to protect assets from unauthorized use regardless of whether that use is unfair in any sense other than that it was done without the consent of the 'owner' of the asset. The corresponding disadvantage of the concept is that it enables business people to eliminate unwanted competition. The argument that it is for the legislature to strike the appropriate balance between competition and protection from it is not, of course, a conclusive one; otherwise the tort of passing off and other torts which can be used to protect traders against competition would be universally condemned as judicial usurpations of legislative power.[355] But the argument should at least warn us against the development of broad or general principles which would have the effect of casting a thick blanket of protection over all the fruits of human endeavour.

[350] CDPA, s. 3(1); see e.g. *Elanco Products Ltd* v. *Mandops (Agrichemical Specialists) Ltd* [1979] FSR 46.

[351] *BBC Enterprises Ltd* v. *Hi-Tech Xtravision Ltd* [1990] Ch. 609; affirmed on other grounds [1991] 2 AC 327 (HL).

[352] *Sports and General Press Agency Ltd* v. *'Our Dogs' Publishing Co. Ltd* [1916] 2 KB 880. There is also a large industry in producing copycat photographs by plagiarising famous images; e.g. photographs of Madonna in 'Marilyn Monroe poses'.

[353] *Green* v. *Broadcasting Corporation of New Zealand* [1989] 2 All ER 1056. For general discussion see A. Martino and C. Miskin [1991] *New LJ* 813; s. Lane and P. Smith [1993] *New LJ* 1265 and 1305.

[354] Consider the contemporary debate about the extent to which manufacturers of very well known products ought to be allowed to prevent supermarket chains selling their own 'look-a-like' brands.

[355] Cf. *Reckitt & Colman Products Ltd* v. *Borden Inc.* [1990] 1 WLR 491.

4. INTERFERENCE WITH USE AND ENJOYMENT

Real Property

In some cases, at least, to use another's land is also to interfere with its use by its 'owner'. In this section we are concerned with interferences with land which fall short of 'using' it in any but a stretched sense. The most important tort which protects the owner's right to use land is nuisance; but the tort of trespass also plays a part. For example, in an Australian case a television camera crew and a reporter entered the premises of the plaintiff, which had been for some time carrying on an investment business in such a way as to cause dissatisfaction amongst some of its customers.[356] The reporter continually harassed persons who were on the premises and the camera operators not only took video tape of the lobby of the office but also opened interior doors. This conduct was held to constitute a trespass because P had not expressly authorized the entry, and any implied invitation was limited to entry by persons *bona fide* wishing to do business with P. The plaintiff sought an interlocutory injunction to restrain the showing of the film taken; its main concern appears to have been that if the film were shown, its business might suffer. The problem for the judge was to find a ground on which the award of an injunction could be justified. There was no danger of repeated trespass; and the judge was prepared to accept that the film did not contain confidential information. However, he did hold that an injunction could be granted in circumstances such as this in order to restrain the publication of material which had been acquired by unconscionable means, provided P could show that otherwise irreparable damage, in the sense of damage not properly compensatable by an award of damages, would be suffered. But since, if trespass were proved, an award of exemplary damages could be made regardless of whether P had suffered or was likely to suffer economic loss, the judge thought that there was no reason to award an injunction. The decision that an injunction could be awarded for unconscionable conduct is open to some doubt in this country.[357] But the interest of the case, for our purposes, is that it illustrates that the tort of trespass can be used against persons who interfere with the quiet enjoyment of land; and also that a claim for damages for trespass would encompass financial loss resulting from the wrong.

Title to sue is essentially the same in both trespass and nuisance.[358] As a general rule,[359] the plaintiff must have a proprietary (or possessory) interest

---

[356] *Lincoln Hunt (Australia) Pty Ltd* v. *Willesee* [1986] 4 NSWLR 457. See also *League Against Cruel Sports Ltd* v. *Scott* [1985] 2 All ER 489 (incursions by hunting dogs). Apart from a tort action, another possibility is a complaint to the Broadcasting Complaints Commission: Broadcasting Act 1981, s. 54; *R.* v. *Broadcasting Complaints Commission, ex parte British Broadcasting Commission The Times,* 29 Oct. 1992.

[357] A. H. Hudson (1988) 104 *LQR* 18.   [358] *Re* nuisance see G. Kodilinye (1989) 9 *LS* 284.
[359] But see *Khorasandjian* v. *Bush* [1993] QB 727.

in the land. Mere occupation as a licensee is not enough unless, perhaps, the licence is one which confers a right of exclusive possession, but is not a lease because, for instance, it is not for a term of years.[360] While this rule is understandable in relation to misappropriation and even, perhaps, in relation to unauthorized use,[361] it seems much less sensible in relation to interference with use and enjoyment. After all, the consequences of such interference are suffered primarily by the occupier; and there is a case for saying that title to sue in these torts ought to be related to the nature of the damage suffered. The rule governing the right of a reversioner to sue in nuisance exemplifies this approach: a person whose only interest in property is to have it back when someone else's interest in it comes to an end can sue for nuisance committed before the interest matures if (but only if) the nuisance adversely affects the reversionary interest because it results in some permanent or long-term damage to the property.[362] Conversely, if there is a continuing nuisance then a party with an interest in the property can recover for loss caused by the nuisance even if the nuisance began before the interest was acquired.[363] It might also be argued that if a lawful occupier of premises suffers an interference with the use or enjoyment of it, the occupier should be entitled to recover damages in trespass or nuisance for the interference.

The main differences between trespass and nuisance are (as we have already seen[364]) first, that in nuisance only unreasonable interferences with use and enjoyment are actionable; whereas in trespass any unauthorized interference with possession is actionable except one justified on the basis that it would be absurd not to imply a licence to enter. Secondly, whereas trespass is only committed by physical encroachment onto land, nuisance usually, though not necessarily, consists of things done off the plaintiff's land. Thirdly, trespass is actionable without proof of damage whereas nuisance is actionable only if P can show that damage has already been suffered or is likely to be suffered in the future as a result of the nuisance.[365]

The first difference is neatly illustrated by the case of overflying aircraft. The classic view is that proprietary (and possessory) interests in land relate not only to the surface of the land but also to the subsoil and the airspace above it. Thus it is a trespass to encroach on airspace or to dig into the subsoil as much as it is to walk on the surface. However, section 76(1) of the Civil Aviation Act 1982 provides that:

---

[360] See 27 above.   [361] But see further 57–8 above.

[362] *Simpson* v. *Savage* (1856) 1 CB(NS) 347. The rarely invoked tortious liability for waste is liability for damage to the lessor's reversionary interest. For a modern example, see *Mancetter Developments Ltd* v. *Garmanson Ltd* [1986] QB 1212.

[363] *Masters* v. *Brent LBC* [1978] 2 All ER 664.   [364] See 53 above.

[365] There are a few exceptional cases, but most of these can be explained as cases in which P was seeking to prevent an easement or analogous right being lost by failure to complain about interference: R. A. Buckley, *The Law of Nuisance* (London, 1981), 105–6. In other words, P was seeking to protect *title*.

No action shall lie in respect of trespass or nuisance by reason only of the flight of an aircraft over any property at a height above the ground which . . . is reasonable, or the ordinary incidents of such flight, so long as the provisions of any Air Navigation Order . . . have been duly complied with and there has been no breach of section 81.

Furthermore, in *Baron Bernstein of Leigh* v. *Skyviews & General Ltd.*[366] it was held that it did not constitute trespass to fly over land at a height of many hundreds of feet taking aerial photographs of a house below. The policy underlying the statutory provision is clear: civil aviation would be rendered impossible if the ordinary overflight of aircraft were actionable as trespass. The *Bernstein* case goes somewhat further in that the plaintiff's complaint was, no doubt, not just that the aircraft had flown over the property but that photographs of the house had been taken by someone in it. This, it might be argued, is an undue invasion of privacy; but English law does not protect privacy as such.[367] It might also be thought that the owner of a stately home could have a financial interest in aerial photographs of the home: the owner might want to sell them to visitors or to license someone else, for a fee, to produce and sell such photographs. This would be a legitimate way of exploiting the owner's right to use the property.[368] However, *Bernstein* seems to rule out such arguments, at least in cases where the overflight as such could not be said to involve an unreasonable interference with the owner's right to enjoy the land. Even if the overflight could be called unreasonable, this would not get to the heart of the matter because there is authority for the proposition that sketching[369] or broadcasting[370] or photographing[371] what one sees on another's land is not actionable. In other words, there is no right not to be viewed in the use of one's premises. This rule has little to recommend it, at least where the landowner can establish that he or she has suffered economic loss or that someone has made a profit as a result of the viewing.

Neither the statute nor the *Bernstein* case rules out liability for nuisance in respect of overflight. The statute does say that no action for nuisance will lie, but only in respect of 'reasonable' overflight; this makes the provision strictly redundant as regards nuisance because a nuisance is, by definition, an 'unreasonable' interference with rights.

A fourth difference between trespass and nuisance may lie in the standard of liability. In relation to misappropriation[372] and exploitation,[373] it was argued above that liability for trespass is strict in the sense that it is not necessary either that the defendant knew or had means of knowing of the rights of the plaintiff; and in the sense that liability does not depend on proof that

[366] [1978] QB 479.   [367] See D. J. Seipp (1983) 3 *OJLS* 325, 334–7, 353–7.
[368] Cf. *LJP Investments Pty Ltd* v. *Howard Chia Investments Pty Ltd* (1989) 24 NSWLR 490, 495–6.
[369] *Hickman* v. *Maisey* [1900] 1 QB 752, 756.
[370] *Victoria Park Racing and Recreation Grounds Co. Ltd* v. *Taylor* (1937) 58 CLR 479.
[371] *Sports and General Press Agency Ltd* v. *'Our Dogs' Publishing Co. Ltd* [1916] 2 KB 880.
[372] See 30 above.   [373] See 49 above.

D intentionally or negligently interfered with those rights. On the other hand, it seems fairly clear that liability for physical damage to land depends on proof of fault no matter in which tort the action is framed.[374] What is the position in relation to interference with use and enjoyment? The justification for drawing a distinction between misappropriation and physical damage is that in relation to the former the law of tort provides an important means of securing title, and this function can only be fully performed if liability is strict. In relation to exploitation of land, strict liability can be justified as a means of protecting the right to decide how one's land will be used (which is one of the positive incidents of property). But in relation to damage, the choice between strict and fault liability depends on moral and economic arguments; liability for damage does not perform proprietary functions: the right that one's property should not be damaged or destroyed is a negative incident of property. Since the late nineteenth century, at least, the balance of such moral and economic arguments has been seen by the courts to be in favour of fault liability. There seems no reason of principle why the conditions of actionability in respect of amenity damage (that is, non-physical damage resulting from interference with use and enjoyment) should be any more strict than those applying to physical damage, especially where the landowner claims to have suffered economic loss in addition to non-pecuniary loss.

What do the cases say about the standard of liability in trespass for amenity damage? The question was not directly addressed in *Lincoln Hunt* v. *Willesee*,[375] but the tone of the judgment seems to support strict liability on the basis that the right of the owner of land to exclude unwanted intruders deserves the degree of protection which strict liability affords. If the only interest at stake were the right to use and enjoy one's land free from interference, then strict liability might not be appropriate. But since trespass involves intrusion onto property and not just interference with its use, a stricter standard of liability is appropriate because the interest being asserted is the right to control entry. If the essence of the complaint, even if made in a trespass action, is amenity damage, there is no reason why liability in trespass should be stricter in respect of this type of damage than it is in respect of physical damage.

As for nuisance, the question whether liability is strict or fault-based is one of the most difficult and obscure issues in the whole of the law of tort. One thing, at least, is clear: a nuisance is not just any interference with the use of land but only an unreasonable interference; furthermore, a variety of factors are relevant to the issue of unreasonableness, of which one is whether the defendant took all reasonable precautions to reduce the interference to a

---

[374] There is no direct authority for this proposition in the case of trespass to land, but there are many nuisance cases which support it: F. A. Trindade and P. Cane, *The Law of Torts in Australia*, 2nd edn. (Melbourne, 1993), 619–20. But see G. Cross (1995) 111 *LQR* 445.

[375] [1986] 4 NSWLR 457.

minimum.[376] On the other hand, the fact that D took all reasonable precautions to reduce the interference to a minimum will not necessarily prevent an activity constituting a nuisance if it nevertheless causes a substantial interference. In this way, liability in nuisance is stricter than that in negligence. But in practical terms, the issue of whether D acted reasonably is of crucial importance in nuisance as in negligence. Furthermore, as already argued, there is no good reason of policy why liability for interference with the use of land should be any stricter than that for physical damage to property except, perhaps, that interference with use is more likely than the infliction of physical damage to be a continuing problem.[377] Indeed, there is nineteen-thth-century authority for the proposition that liability for physical damage to property is stricter than liability for amenity damage.[378] It would be strange, indeed, if this rule had become reversed in the twentieth century.

The remedies available for trespass and nuisance are injunctions and damages in lieu of an injunction[379] (these are called 'equitable remedies'), and 'common law' damages for past loss.[380] Injunctions are available to restrain nuisances because, although damage is essential to a cause of action in nuisance, the definition of nuisance is in terms of interference with property rights. Damages may be awarded at common law for past non-pecuniary loss;[381] it is also clear that damages for economic loss (for example, loss of profits) resulting from an interference with amenities are recoverable.[382] If damages are awarded in lieu of an injunction, they will usually represent the diminution in the value of the premises as a result of the tort; but they may include an amount calculated with reference to any gains which the defendant has made or is likely to make from the nuisance.[383] Whether or not there has been any diminution in the value of the premises, damages for non-pecuniary loss may be awarded.

Damages in lieu of an injunction are theoretically important because they represent damages for loss which has not yet occurred. Indeed, a *quia timet* injunction and damages in lieu thereof may be awarded even if no damage has yet occurred, provided there is a strong probability that damage will occur in the future.[384] This point can be generalized: whenever an injunction

[376] Trindade and Cane, *The Law of Torts in Australia*, n. 374 above, 598–602.

[377] Although not necessarily: in *Miller* v. *Jackson* [1977] QB 966 there was a continuing risk of cricket balls landing on the roof or in the garden of the plaintiff's property.

[378] *St Helen's Smelting Co.* v. *Tipping* (1865) 11 HLC 642.

[379] On damages in lieu of an injunction see J. A. Jolowicz [1975] *CLJ* 224.

[380] Including the cost of abating a nuisance, if this was a reasonable way of mitigating damage: *Proprietors of Strata Plan No. 14198* v. *Cowell* (1989) 24 NSWLR 478.

[381] On the assessment of such damages see *Bone* v. *Seale* [1975] 1 WLR 797.

[382] *Campbell* v. *Paddington Corporation* [1911] 1 KB 869; *Andreae* v. *Selfridge & Co. Ltd* [1938] Ch. 1; *Page Motors* v. *Epsom & Ewell BC* (1982) 80 LGR 337; *Lincoln Hunt (Australia) Pty Ltd* v. *Willesee* [1986] 4 NSWLR 457; *Dunton* v. *Dover DC* (1977) 76 LGR 87, 93; *Carr-Saunders* v. *Dick McNeil Associates Ltd* [1986] 1 WLR 922.

[383] *Carr-Saunders* v. *Dick McNeil Associates Ltd* [1986] 1 WLR 922.

[384] *A-G* v. *Manchester Corporation* [1893] 2 Ch. 87. There are useful discussions in *Barbagallo* v. *J. & F. Catelan Pty Ltd* [1986] 1 QdR 45.

can be awarded in a tort action then, in theory at least, a *quia timet* injunction may be awarded in suitable circumstances; and damages may be given in lieu of such an injunction even though no injury has yet occurred; or in lieu of an ordinary injunction in respect of damage which has not yet occurred. In theory, of course, liability to pay such compensation arises in equity, not at common law; but this distinction is purely formal and is, anyway, anachronistic.

One remedy which English courts have not seen fit to contemplate is the award of an injunction to the plaintiff who has 'come to the nuisance' conditional on payment to the defendant of the cost of complying with the injunction.[385] The award of such a remedy would involve a recognition that in some cases at least, the plaintiff's interest in making a claim in respect of amenity damage is essentially financial; and that in such cases it is reasonable, given that D's activity was in place before P moved into the area, that P should pay for the financial benefit which will accrue by removal of the nuisance.[386] The mutual sharing of benefits and burdens involved in the award of such a remedy might be thought particularly appropriate in cases where, as in nuisance, the liability rules require a balancing of the interests of the two parties.

Today, the common law of nuisance has been largely eclipsed by planning legislation[387] and by statutory controls over noise, smells, and so on,[388] as a means of avoiding conflicting land use. Planning laws can only go a certain distance in regulating what is done or built on land,[389] and the law of nuisance (both statutory and judge-made) retains an area of operation within the interstices of planning law. Also, of course, planning authorities can make mistakes and permitted use or development may constitute a nuisance. The common law of nuisance or negligence may provide a remedy in such a case, although probably against the 'wrong' party (that is, the occupier rather than the planning authority).[390]

Would an action against the planning authority stand any chance of success? This question leads us into the complex area of public authority liability, which will be dealt with in more detail in Chapter 5. There is New Zealand authority to support such an action in circumstances in which the

---

[385] As in *Spur Industries Inc.* v. *Del E. Webb Development Co.* (1972) 494 P2d 700. If P is awarded an injunction, it is theoretically open to D to bargain with P to achieve this result; but in practice P may hold all the cards.

[386] Cf. the Law Commission's proposal for adjustment orders in actions for breach of confidence: 77 above.

[387] On enforcement of planning controls see D. Heap, *An Outline of Planning Law*, 10th edn. (London, 1991), ch. 12; J. Alder *Development Control*, 2nd edn. (London, 1989), ch. 9. A party who has an interest in or occupies land in relation to which a 'stop notice' is wrongfully issued may be able to claim compensation: Heap, *An Outline of Planning Law*, 278–9.

[388] Justices can make orders for the abatement of statutory nuisances and the High Court can issue injunctions: R. Buckley, *Law of Nuisance* (London, 1981), chs. 10 and 11.

[389] But some uses of land which do not constitute a nuisance may infringe planning law: B. Hough [1992] *JPL* 906.

[390] e.g., *Miller* v. *Jackson* [1977] QB 966.

authority failed to require a formal application to dispense with a condition stipulating a certain distance between adjoining properties before a building permit was issued. As a result, the plaintiff's view was obstructed by the new building, and she was awarded damages for the consequential diminution in the value of her premises.[391] However, in *Ryeford Homes Ltd* v. *Sevenoaks DC*[392] it was held that there was insufficient proximity between a planning authority and any individual adjoining landowner to create a duty of care; and that, as a matter of policy, an action should not be allowed because planning was a regulatory function involving the exercise of judgment on policy grounds in the interests of the community as a whole—inevitably some individual landowners would be adversely affected. Moreover, if the loss suffered was purely economic, it could not be recovered in the absence of reliance by the plaintiff on the decision of the planning authority. These three grounds of decision are consistent with recent leading decisions of the House of Lords. The only doubt about their correctness in general terms arises in relation to the second argument: it is surely not the case that all 'planning mistakes' are supportable by sound arguments of policy. Allowing houses to be built too close to a cricket pitch or failing to require formal application to be made for dispensation from planning regulations are examples of simple carelessness; and there seems no reason why they should never, as a matter of principle, be actionable.

Chattels

There is no tort which deals specifically with interference with the use of chattels. A number of torts might be used to deal with such cases. It is possible to imagine situations where a person might carry chattels away or misappropriate them, not for the purpose of using them or with the intention of permanently depriving the owner of the chattels, but simply with the aim of preventing the owner from using the chattels. Such actions would amount to trespass, if not to conversion. The clamping of car wheels might also in certain circumstances amount to trespass.[393] But interference with the use and enjoyment of chattels need not involve a trespass to the chattels. For instance, interference with the use of a radio or television by noise might amount to a private nuisance; or preventing a person using a car by obstructing the highway might amount to public nuisance actionable by the car owner on proof of special damage.

In a New Zealand case[394] P was deprived of the use of a vessel as a result

---

[391] *Craig* v. *East Coast Bays City Council* [1986] 1 NZLR 99.

[392] [1989] *New LJ* 255.

[393] The police are authorized to use clamps by Road Traffic Regulation Act 1984, s. 104.

[394] *Nauru Local Government Council* v. *New Zealand Seamen's Industrial Union of Workers* [1986] 1 NZLR 466.

of unlawful industrial action in respect of which the Union admitted liability
for inducing breaches of contract by seamen. The vessel was used to provide
a shipping service which was revenue-earning but not profitable. It was,
therefore, argued by the defendants that P had suffered no financial loss as a
result of the tortious behaviour. However, it was held that because P had
been deprived of the use of its property it was, *ipso facto*, entitled to compensation,[395] the quantum of which would depend on the facts of the particular case.[396] Possible measures in the case of a non-profit-earning chattel
would be the cost of hiring a substitute or interest on the value of the chattel. In *Nauru Local Government Council* v. *New Zealand Seamen's Industrial
Union of Workers*, a small amount was awarded under this head without any
clear indication being given of how it was arrived at. The measure of inter-
est-on-capital-value was rejected, however, because the vessel would not have
earned profits even if it had been in use. In addition, P was awarded the cost
(which it had actually incurred) of keeping the vessel in a state of readiness,[397]
this being held a reasonable thing to have done.

5. DAMAGE

Land and Chattels

For the purposes of the present discussion, 'damage' includes 'destruction';
and 'damage to property' includes 'loss of property'. Physical damage to
property and loss of property are not, of course, the same thing.[398] One writer
concludes that loss, unlike damage, is purely financial injury; and, therefore,
that recovery for it in a tort action is, and should be, more restricted than for
physical damage.[399] This conclusion is not justified. Certainly, it is often
difficult for a plaintiff to recover in tort (whether for conversion[400] or negligence[401]) for loss of goods. However, the basic reason for this lies not in the
nature of loss as opposed to damage, but in the circumstances in which loss
typically occurs. Cases of loss which find their way into the law reports typically involve theft by a third party. In such cases the plaintiff will often wish
to sue someone other than the thief (who may either have disappeared or not
be worth suing). The basis of such an action will be failure to prevent loss
rather than causing loss; and the difficulty of this ground of action resides in

---

[395] Protecting a non-economic interest. See esp. Somers J [1986] 1 NZLR 466, 481–2.

[396] Cf. *Birmingham Corporation* v. *Sowersby* [1970] RTR 84.

[397] It was also awarded an amount in respect of amortization, plus additional expenses
incurred in recommissioning the vessel after the strike.

[398] *Fothergill* v. *Monarch Airlines Ltd* [1981] AC 251, 273B (see also [1978] QB 108, 114).

[399] J. A. Weir [1965] CLJ 186, 187.   [400] See 32 above.

[401] e.g. *Morris* v. *C. W. Martin & Son Ltd* [1966] 1 QB 716; *Deyong* v. *Shenburn* [1946] KB
227; *Stansbie* v. *Troman* [1948] 2 KB 48. Contrast *Balsamo* v. *Medici* [1984] 1 WLR 951, 959
(concerning a bailee); *Lockspeiser Aircraft Ltd* v. *Brooklands Aircraft Co. Ltd*, *The Times*, 7 Mar.
1990; N. E. Palmer [1983] CLP 91, 99.

the relative unwillingness of the law of tort to impose liability for pure omission. But where some positive act of misfeasance facilitates the theft of property, the fact that the injury suffered is loss of rather than physical damage to property is and should be no bar to recovery.[402]

This conclusion is reinforced by cases which illustrate a similar unwillingness on the part of the courts to impose liability for failure to control third parties, even in cases of physical damage as opposed to loss.[403] In terms of the focus of this book, the plaintiff's interest in property (whether purely financial or not) will not differ according to whether the property is damaged or lost. What may differ is the extent to which the law will protect the interest.

Causing physical damage to land or chattels is, of course, a form of interference with property rights.[404] So the basic rule is that an action in tort can be brought in respect of physical damage to land or chattels only by the legal owner[405] or by someone with a possessory interest in the damaged asset at the time when the damage was inflicted:[406] a person who has only a contractual interest in the property cannot sue in tort in respect of physical damage to it.[407] There are two statutory exceptions to the temporal element of this basic rule. First, under Part I of the Consumer Protection Act 1987, which creates a regime of liability for defective products, loss of or damage to property is deemed to occur at the time it first becomes reasonably discoverable, and a person is entitled to sue in respect of such loss or damage only if he or she had an interest in the property at the date of discoverability of the loss

---

[402] e.g. *Dove* v. *Banham Locks Ltd* [1983] 1 WLR 1436. But in *Balsamo* v. *Medici* [1984] 1 WLR 951 D was held not liable in negligence for the loss of P's money even though D had been positively negligent in not ensuring that the person D handed it over to was the person P meant to receive it. S. Whittaker ((1985) 48 *MLR* 86) concludes that the decision is justifiable on insurance grounds, but not on conceptual grounds.

[403] *Smith* v. *Littlewoods Organization Ltd* [1987] AC 241. For a more expansive view of this case see Markesinis (1989) 105 *LQR* 104; and see generally J. Stapleton (1995) 111 *LQR* 301, 305–17.

[404] Causing damage to goods is a form of interference with goods: Torts (Interference with Goods) Act 1977, s. 1(b),(c), and (d). It may be possible to circumvent the Act in cases where D is a bailee: N. E. Palmer (1978) 41 *MLR* 629. Polluting a river so that the crops of a riparian owner are destroyed is a form of interference with common law proprietary rights: *Jones* v. *Llanrwst UDC* [1911] 1 Ch. 393, 402; it may also interfere with a statutory licence to extract water: *Scott-Whitehead* v. *National Coal Board* (1987) 53 P & CR 263.

[405] Equitable title is not enough: *Leigh & Sillavan Ltd* v. *Aliakmon Shipping Co. Ltd* [1986] AC 785, 812.

[406] The Torts (Interference with Goods) Act 1977 deals specifically with assessment of damages in cases in which more than one person has title to sue in respect, *inter alia*, of damage to goods: see 42 above. There may be cases in which the Act would not apply and in which the common law rule that a bailee can recover damages for the full extent of the damage to the goods despite the fact that his or her interest is limited, would apply (N. E. Palmer (1978) 41 *MLR* 629, 637, n. 38: this rule constitutes an exception to the basic rule stated in the text). The common law rule made some sense in relation to misappropriation, but its rationale is harder to discern in cases of unintentional damage: J. G. Fleming (1959) 32 *ALJ* 267, 267.

[407] *Leigh & Sillavan* v. *Aliakmon Shipping Co.* [1986] AC 785. In contract a person may, in certain cases, recover for damage to goods even if, at the time of the damage, that person did not own them or bear risk of their being damaged: e.g. *Linden Gardens Trust Ltd* v. *Lenesta Sludge Disposals Ltd* [1994] 1 AC 85.

or damage. Secondly, section 3 of the Latent Damage Act 1986, which deals with claims in negligence in respect of (latent) 'damage to property',[408] provides that where a person acquired an interest in property after the damage occurred but before it became discoverable, that person has a cause of action in respect of that damage. Both provisions seem apt to overcome the problem which arises where property suffering from latent damage changes hands: under the basic rule the purchaser would not have title to sue, and the vendor would have little incentive to sue (and could not be forced to do so by the purchaser).

Liability for physical damage to property, whether land or chattels, normally depends on fault in some form or other. This is true even when the action is framed in one of the so-called 'strict liability' torts. As we saw earlier, it is a defence to an action for trespass to goods in respect of physical damage to the goods that the damage was the result of 'inevitable accident' (that is, an event not caused by any carelessness on the part of the defendant).[409] There is no direct authority in relation to trespass to land but as a matter of principle, a similar rule should apply.[410] Liability for physical damage resulting from a public or private nuisance depends at least on proof of foreseeability of damage of the type that occurred;[411] and in some cases (for example, damage caused by trees overhanging the highway[412]), it depends on proof of negligence in the sense of failure to take reasonable precautions against foreseeable and significant risks of damage. So far as private nuisance is concerned, there will be no liability so long as the defendant's land use was reasonable; but if it was not, there can be liability even if D exercised reasonable care to avoid the nuisance.[413]

Liability for damage to property can also arise under the rule in *Rylands* v. *Fletcher*, which concerns liability for the escape of dangerous things from land. An occupier of land may be liable under the rule despite taking all reasonable care to prevent the escape, but there can be no liability unless damage of the type inflicted was foreseeable.[414] Under Part I of the Consumer

---

[408] Where the damage arises out of the acquisition of a defective building or chattel, property damage must be taken to mean damage to property other than the defective property itself or to some part of complex property other than the defective part: *D. & F. Estates Ltd* v. *Church Commissioners* [1989] AC 177.

[409] *National Coal Board* v. *J. E. Evans & Co. Ltd* [1951] 2 KB 861.

[410] *Esso Petroleum Co. Ltd* v. *Southport Corporation* [1956] AC 218, 242 *per* Lord Radcliffe; *Mayfair Ltd* v. *Pears* [1987] 1 NZLR 459. In *Home Brewery Co. Ltd* v. *William Davis & Co. (Leicester) Ltd* [1987] QB 339 the judge assumed that liability for trespass to land depended on the flooding being reasonably foreseeable: see esp. 354D–F.

[411] *Cambridge Water Co.* v. *Eastern Counties Leather PLC* [1994] 2 AC 264. But note *Wringe* v. *Cohen* [1940] 1 KB 229 concerning liability for 'buildings collapsing into the street' (J. Spencer [1989] *CLJ* 55, 82).

[412] *British Road Services Ltd* v. *Slater* [1964] 1 WLR 498; *Noble* v. *Harrison* [1926] 2 KB 332.

[413] *Cambridge Water Co.* v. *Eastern Counties Leather PLC* [1994] 2 AC 264.

[414] *Cambridge Water Co.* v. *Eastern Counties Leather PLC* [1994] 2 AC 264. See also P. Cane (1982) 2 *OJLS* 30, 53–4; *Mason* v. *Levy Auto Parts Ltd* [1967] 2 QB 530 (escape of fire); A. I. Ogus [1969] *CLJ* 104.

Protection Act 1987 compensation for damage caused by a defective product to real or personal property (other than the product itself) can be recovered if the property was of a description ordinarily intended for private use and was in fact intended mainly for private use by its owner. This Act supposedly introduces a form of strict liability; but, apart from the fact that in certain circumstances the Act imposes liability on suppliers and importers regardless of fault on their part, the basis of liability is far from being strict.[415] Strict liability in the form of vicarious liability can, of course, be imposed in certain circumstances in respect of damage to tangible property, but only if a recognized tort has been committed; and normally, as noted, liability in tort for physical damage to property depends on proof of fault in some sense.[416]

So far as concerns assessment of damages for physical damage to property,[417] the basic rule is that the measure of damages is the difference between the value of the property before it was damaged and its present value. However, in accordance with the principle that P must take reasonable steps to mitigate loss, the most common basis for the assessment of damages is the reasonable cost of repair.[418] If the cost of restoring the property to its former state exceeds the diminution in the value of the property resulting from the damage, the diminution in value may impose an upper limit on the award unless P can convince the court that there is some special reason why the cost of repairing the property should be awarded (for example, because it has some subjective value over and above its mere financial value).[419] This will be more easily done in the case of land or buildings than in the case of chattels because, in the case of real property, selling the damaged premises and buying a substitute is often not a realistic option. So in the case of buildings, the measure adopted will often depend on whether P acquired the property

---

[415] J. Stapleton (1986) 6 *OJLS* 392; C. Newdick (1987) 103 *LQR* 288.

[416] For examples of statutory liability of various degrees of strictness see Environmental Protection Act 1990, s. 73(6) (deposit of waste); Civil Aviation Act 1982, s. 76(2); Nuclear Installations Act 1965, ss. 12 and 13 (the Act applies only to actual personal injury or property damage; it does not cover the increased risk of either if it falls short of 51%, nor economic loss consisting, e.g., of the diminished value of property near an installation: *Merlin* v. *British Nuclear Fuels Ltd* [1990] 2 QB 557); Water Industry Act 1991, s. 209; Animals Act 1971, s. 2(1) (but note the various defences); and Merchant Shipping (Oil Pollution) Act 1971 (discussed in greater detail in Ch. 9). Concerning EC developments in respect of liability for damage caused by waste see P. Sands (1990) 53 *MLR* 685, 691–3; J. T. Smith (1993) 5 *J Environmental L* 91, 105–6; Commission Green Paper on Remedying Environmental Damage, COM(93)47 final, 14 May 1993. Concerning liability for services see J. Stapleton, *Product Liability* (London, 1994), 325, 335–6.

[417] Harris, 347–51, 353–64; Burrows, 156–167.

[418] *Darbishire* v. *Warren* [1963] 1 WLR 1067, 1071 *per* Harman LJ; *Hansen* v. *Gloucester Developments Pty Ltd* [1992] 1 Qd R 14.

[419] e.g. *Hollebone* v. *Midhurst and Fernhurst Builders Ltd* [1968] 1 Lloyd's Rep. 38; *Ward* v. *Cannock Chase DC* [1986] Ch. 546: rebuilding must be legally permissible (e.g. planning permission must be obtainable); but if not, an equivalent amount may be awarded to enable P to build a substitute somewhere else.

as an investment[420] or for personal occupation. If the latter, then the court might well[421] award the cost of repair even if this exceeds the reduction in the value of the property as a result of the tort.[422] In addition to the cost of repair, P may be able to recover financial losses consequential on the damage, such as the cost of hiring or renting a substitute while repairs are done, or damages for loss of the use of the property or loss of profits.[423]

If a building is destroyed as a result of a tort then, once again, P may well recover the cost of rebuilding, unless the property was acquired solely as an investment. In some cases the court might award the cost of purchasing new premises even if that cost exceeds the pre-tort value of the damaged premises, if purchasing alternative premises was a reasonable way of mitigating losses arising from the tort.[424] In the case of goods, market value (that is, the cost of replacement) would be the appropriate measure whether P had the goods as an investment or for personal use, even if P had acquired the goods for less than market cost.[425] In addition, P can recover for consequential losses such as the cost of hiring a substitute until a replacement is obtained, or loss of profits during that period.[426]

By and large, these rules properly protect a person's financial interest in property.[427] In some cases it has been held that damages for loss of the use of a damaged chattel may be recovered even though a substitute was not hired

[420] *C. R. Taylor Ltd* v. *Hepworths Ltd* [1977] 1 WLR 659.

[421] But not necessarily: *Bradburn* v. *Lindsay* [1983] 2 All ER 408.

[422] e.g., *Harbutt's Plasticine Ltd* v. *Wayne Tank & Pump Ltd* [1970] 1 QB 447.

[423] See also *Ironfield* v. *Eastern Gas Board* [1964] 1 WLR 1125; *Patel* v. *London Transport Executive* [1971] RTR 29.

[424] *Dominion Mosaics & Tile Co. Ltd* v. *Trafalgar Trucking Co. Ltd* [1990] 2 All ER 246.

[425] *Ibid.*

[426] *Ward* v. *Cannock Chase DC* [1986] Ch. 546. Damages for loss of use of the building may also be recovered if the pecuniary loss resulting from loss of use was foreseeable.

[427] But note that a person may recover for damage to goods even without having suffered any loss thereby by reason of the fact that the person has been paid the full value of the (undamaged) goods by the purchaser (*The Sanix Ace* [1987] 1 Lloyd's Rep. 465: the vendor is liable to account to the purchaser); or has been indemnified for the loss by an insurer (to whom the owner's right of action passes by subrogation (*The Charlotte* [1908] P 206); or because another has paid for the repairs (*Jones* v. *Stroud DC* [1986] 1 WLR 1141, 1150–1). Furthermore (1) a bailee can recover in full for damage to the bailed property even though the bailee's interest in it is limited (*The Winkfield* [1902] P 42: the bailee is liable to account to the bailor); (2) a person who takes out a policy of insurance upon goods may recover under the policy for the full amount of any damage to the goods even if the assured's interest in the goods is limited, provided the policy was intended to cover all those with an interest in the goods (*The Albazero* [1977] AC 774: the assured is liable to account to anyone with an interest in the goods); (3) Where A enters into a contract for the carriage of goods and it is contemplated at the time of contracting that proprietary interest in the goods will be transferred from the owner to another during the currency of the contract, then if the parties to the contract intended (expressly or impliedly) that the contract should be one for the benefit of all persons who had or might acquire an interest in the goods, the original contractor can recover damages for breach of contract representing the actual loss suffered by all of the persons having an interest in the goods (*The Albazero*; this principle does not apply where, under a bill of lading or toher document, the right of action for breach of contract passes with title to the goods). In all such cases, the plaintiff can recover for damage to goods beyond his or her financial interest in the goods.

and although the chattel was not normally used to earn a profit.[428] Such cases compensate beyond financial interest; and although such 'compensation' may be justifiable in cases of misappropriation or wrongful use of chattels (even if unintentional),[429] in order to protect the distinction between 'what is mine and what is yours', it seems less justified in the case of unintentional damage to chattels.

If the cost of repairing or replacing a building or a chattel increases between the date of the tort and the date of judgment, the question may arise whether the cost of repair or replacement ought to be assessed at the date of the tort or at the date of judgment. If the cost has risen solely as a consequence of inflation, then the plaintiff should not have to bear the cost of inflation.[430] If, at the date of the trial, the repairs have not been done or a replacement has not been procured, the burden of inflation since the date of the tort can be placed on the defendant by assessing damages as at the date of judgment, or assessing them at some earlier date and awarding pre-trial interest at rate which takes account of the rate of inflation in the relevant period. If the cost has risen in real terms as a result of a change in the balance of supply and demand then damages ought to be assessed, in accordance with normal principles, either at the date of the tort or at some later date at which it would have been reasonable for the plaintiff to mitigate the loss by doing the repairs or acquiring a substitute.[431]

Suppose that cost-of-repair damages are awarded but that even when the repairs are done the property will not be worth what it was worth before it was damaged. Can the plaintiff recover, in addition to the cost of repairs, damages representing residual diminution in value after the repairs are done? In answering this question it needs to be remembered that the plaintiff is entitled to recover only the *reasonable* cost of repairs; so if the residual diminution in value is simply the result of the fact that 'reasonable' damages are insufficient to allow a first-class job to be done, allowance could not be made for the diminution.[432] But suppose that it would be imposssible to restore the property to its former value no matter how much was spent on repairs. Sometimes in such cases, the property could be treated as having been destroyed, and then the cost of replacement or diminution in the (resale) value would be the appropriate measure. But a person might be awarded the cost of repairing a house (for example) or a rare or unique antique or heirloom, even though the property could not be restored to its former state in some respect: no matter how cunningly repaired, a vase which has been broken

---

[428] R. A. Buckley, *Modern Law of Negligence*, 2nd edn. (London, 1993), 197–8; *The Mediana* [1900] AC 113; *The Chekiang* [1926] AC 637; *Birmingham Corporation* v. *Sowersby* [1970] RTR 84.

[429] See 41 and 44 above. Regarding deprivation of use other than by damage, exploitation or misappropriation, see 88 above.

[430] See 45 above.   [431] See 47 above; P. Cane (1984) 10 *Mon. ULR* 17, 17–23.

[432] *Dodd Properties Ltd* v. *Canterbury City Council* [1979] 2 All ER 118, 124 *per* Cantley J at first instance.

may be worth less than a vase which had never been damaged; or a house which has suffered structural damage may be capable of being rendered safe and sound, but still bear marks of the damage which affect its value. Ought the person, in addition to the cost of repair, to be awarded damages representing residual diminution in the value of the damaged property? Since the residual diminution in value is the result of the physical damage, and since the basic measure of damages in tort is diminution in value (the cost of repairs being a subsidiary measure), there would seem no reason why such residual diminution should not be compensatable.

The prime remedy for physical damage to property is damages for past loss. But a plaintiff who frames a case in nuisance may be able to obtain an injunction, or damages for future anticipated loss in lieu of the injunction.[433] Indeed, a *quia timet* injunction or damages in lieu thereof may be awarded even before any physical damage has occurred, provided there is a strong probability that damage will occur in the future.[434] The technical reason for the availability of the injunction in nuisance actions is that the gist of the tort of nuisance, at least in its classical form, is interference with property rights.

The boundaries of nuisance and negligence have now broken down to such an extent that not only are damages for physical damage recoverable in actions for nuisance,[435] but also the standard of liability in such proceedings is fault. Furthermore, the courts now seem to take the view that, even in cases where the alleged cause of the damage is a continuing situation so that nuisance would seem the obviously appropriate cause of action, it makes no difference to the rules of liability whether the action is framed in nuisance or negligence. Add to this the fact that certain continuing sources of physical danger have always been seen as the province of the tort of negligence (for example, unsafe systems of work or defective buildings which endanger occupants), and the conclusion appears justified that if a situation for which one person is responsible presents a continuing source of physical danger to the person or property of another, the latter ought to be able to obtain an injunction to restrain continuance of the unsafe activity.[436] It would need to be

---

[433] e.g., *Miller* v. *Jackson* [1977] QB 966; contrast *Bolton* v. *Stone* [1951] AC 850 (negligence). See also *Pennington* v. *Brinsop Hall Coal Co.* [1877] 5 Ch. D 769. The damages may include the cost of measures to abate the nuisance: see e.g. *Barbagallo* v. *J. & F. Catelan Pty Ltd* [1986] 1 Qd R 245.

[434] See 86 above.

[435] Whereas originally the tort was only concerned with amenity damage: see F. H. Newark (1949) 65 *LQR* 480.

[436] J. R. Spencer ([1989] *CLJ* 55, 81) says, 'the plaintiff can *always* ask for an injunction to prevent a threatened harm where a claim for damage would succeed [on any basis] if the threat materialized' (emphasis and bracketed material added). As a generalization, this is incorrect: if personal injury or damage to property (other than the defective property itself) resulted from the negligent production of a dangerous building or chattel, this would be recoverable; but damages would not be awarded at common law for the cost of removing the danger before *any* physical damage had been caused by it. It is unlikely that a court would be prepared to award an injunction or damages in lieu thereof 'in equity' in such a situation. An injunction might, however, be available in cases where some physical damage had already been caused, in order to prevent repetition.

recognized, of course, that the award of an injunction would give the plaintiff considerable bargaining strength *vis-à-vis* the defendant; but as in other cases, the court should also be in a position to award damages in lieu of an injunction.

The fact that an injunction and damages in lieu thereof can be awarded in respect of injury which has not yet occurred contrasts with the unwillingness of English courts, especially in the context of liability for the supply of defective buildings[437] to award damages representing the cost of removing a substantial danger of future damage. The technical difference between equitable and common law remedies cannot satisfactorily explain this discrepancy. There is, no doubt, a desire to discourage speculative litigation, but the risk of such claims can be all but eliminated by requiring evidence that the risk is very high.[438]

Finally, we must consider the law governing remoteness of damage. In most contexts, the rule of remoteness relevant to actions in respect of physical damage to property is that foreseeable damage is recoverable. The question we need to consider here is whether only foreseeable damage is recoverable; and in particular, whether damage attributable to the plaintiff's lack of resources or impecuniosity is recoverable. To this issue the distinction between foreseeability and directness as tests of remoteness is apparently thought not to be important: the leading case on impecuniosity, *The Liesbosch*,[439] was decided on directness principles but is, nevertheless, treated as still relevant, despite the *Wagon Mound* decisions.[440] In *The Liesbosch* the plaintiff's dredge was sunk by the negligence of the defendants. Because all P's funds were tied up in the contract for dredging on which the vessel was engaged, it could not afford to buy a new dredge immediately but only to hire a replacement. The total costs associated with hiring were considerably greater than would have been the costs of buying a new dredge. The House of Lords held that P could not recover damages for the loss attributable to

---

[437] See 210–11 below.

[438] J. Stapleton (1988) 104 *LQR* 213, 232.

[439] *Owners of Dredger 'Liesbosch'* v. *Owners of Steamship 'Edison'* [1933] AC 449; cf. *Ramwade Ltd* v. *W. J. Emson & Co. Ltd* [1987] RTR 72.

[440] *Overseas Tankship (UK) Ltd* v. *Morts Dock & Engineering Co. Ltd* [1961] AC 388; *Same* v. *Miller Steamship Co. Pty Ltd* [1967] 1 AC 617. The decision in *The Liesbosch* can be explained in terms of foreseeability: *Perry* v. *Sidney Phillips & Son* [1982] 1 WLR 1297, 1307 *per* Kerr LJ. The issue of impecuniosity is relevant to the assessment of damages throughout the law of tort, and the discussion here should be borne in mind in other contexts where it is relevant. A particularly difficult issue concerns liability for interest as compensation for the late payment of a debt or damages (as opposed to interest payable under a contract and as opposed to statutory interest on the judgment debt). See generally F. A. Mann (1985) 101 *LQR* 30. The High Court of Australia has held that where a person pays money away, or where money is withheld from a person as a result of a breach of contract or of negligence, the person is entitled to damages representing the opportunity cost of the money or representing interest on money borrowed to replace it, provided that such loss is not too remote according to the ordinary rules of remoteness in contract and tort. The court expressly put aside the question of the impact of the rule in *The Liesbosch* in this context, but it clearly meant the general principles it enunciated to apply to actions in tort as well as to actions in contract: *Hungerfords* v. *Walker* (1989) 84 ALR 119.

its impecuniosity. The decision is open to two interpretations. One is that P's impecuniosity was an extrinsic factor which broke the chain of causation between D's negligence and P's loss; the other is that the principle that D must take its victim as found does not apply to business losses.

The validity of the *Liesbsoch* principle has been doubted;[441] but it was applied in *Compania Financiera 'Soleada' S.A.* v. *Harmoor Tanker Corporation Inc.*,[442] where it was held that P could not recover additional interest charges it had to pay because of its weak financial position. On the other hand, in *Martindale* v. *Duncan*[443] a taxi driver who could not afford to have his damaged taxi repaired until he received authorization for the repairs from his insurer was awarded damages for loss of profits during the delay. In *Perry* v. *Sidney Phillips & Son*[444] P was awarded damages for anxiety and inconvenience even though these were the result of delay in repairing his house caused by his lack of funds to do so.

All of these decisions might be reconcilable on foreseeability principles by saying that where P is a private individual or a 'one-person' business impecuniosity and its effects are foreseeable. So, for example, in *A.-G.* v. *Geothermal Produce N.Z. Ltd*[445] P was a family company which had just started a rose growing business. The defendant's contractor negligently destroyed the crop with spray; P lacked the funds to make good the damage, and eventually had to give up its plan for long-term development of a rose growing business. The *Liesbosch* principle was held not to apply; Cooke J stressed that it was foreseeable that a family company would lack the resources to meet an unexpected major financial crisis, especially one which interrupted a long term development plan.

The *Liesbosch* was distinguished in *Dodd Properties Ltd* v. *Canterbury CC*,[446] in which P delayed in repairing a building damaged by the negligence of D, partly because the cost of repair would have strained its resources and partly because it wanted to await the outcome of the trial. By the date of the trial the cost of doing the repairs had risen considerably because of inflation, and the question arose which party should bear the increase. The Court of Appeal distinguished *The Liesbosch* on two grounds. The first was that lack of resources was only one of the reasons why P had delayed the repairs; the second was that the case should be approached in terms of mitigation principles, not remoteness of damage principles, and that a plaintiff could not reasonably be expected to do what it could not afford to do in order to reduce its losses.

In essence, *Dodd Properties* decides that P acted reasonably in waiting until the outcome of the trial was known to do the repairs. This proposition is questionable because it confuses the issue of how to deal with inflationary

---

[441] e.g.*Taupo BC* v. *Birnie* [1978] 2 NZLR 397, 409 *per* Cooke J.
[442] [1981] 1 WLR 274.
[443] [1973] 2 All ER 355; cf. *Mattocks* v. *Mann* [1993] RTR 13.
[444] [1982] 1 WLR 1297.   [445] [1987] 2 NZLR 348.   [446] [1980] 1 WLR 433.

increases in the *quantum of damages*[447] with that of whether the plaintiff ought to have taken steps to mitigate the losses for which damages are to be awarded. The prospect of inflation by itself does not provide a sound reason for allowing a person to sit around and take no steps to ameliorate their position; and it is at least arguable that a party who is not unable to pay for repairs but simply unwilling to do so for commercial reasons ought not to be relieved of the duty to mitigate by doing the repairs. Moreover, the distinction between remoteness and mitigation[448] is highly suspect. Why should a defendant be allowed to plead the plaintiff's impecuniosity if P's case is framed in terms of remoteness of damage but not if it is framed in terms of mitigation of damage? Remoteness and mitigation are really two sides of one coin: any particular loss is not reasonably foreseeable and is, therefore, too remote if, *inter alia*, the sufferer ought reasonably to have taken steps which would have enabled it to avoid that loss. A person ought not to be expected to foresee loss which is the result of unreasonable failure on the part of another to act in their own best interest.[449]

The *Liesbosch* principle does not apply where impecuniosity did not exist before the tort was committed but was generated by it.[450] It is, finally, worth noting that to the extent that *The Liesbosch* is the source of a special rule concerning remoteness of damage, that rule probably applies to economic loss regardless of whether it is, in a factual sense, a consequence of physical damage to property.

Goodwill

The essence of passing off is competing unfairly by seeking to take advantage of another trader's or business's commercial reputation to attract business. The passing off of one's own goods or services as those of another will only bring advantage if the reputation of that other is a good one. The tort of injurious falsehood,[451] on the other hand, may provide a remedy in respect of unfair competition[452] consisting of making false statements with the aim of

---

[447] On which see 45 above.

[448] Which is well entrenched in the law: see *The Liesbosch* itself [1933] AC 449, 461.

[449] Such an approach seems to underlie the decision in *Perry* v. *Sidney Phillips & Son* [1982] 1 WLR 1297.

[450] *Archer* v. *Brown* [1985] QB 401 (deceit); *Taupo BC* v. *Birnie* [1978] 2 NZLR 397.

[451] See generally Salmond, 392–5; Fleming, 709–14; Cornish, 427–31.

[452] Although not all cases of damage to goodwill involve competition: e.g. *Lincoln Hunt* v. *Willesee* [1986] 4 NSWLR 457. This case also shows how a tort (here trespass to land) which is not designed to protect goodwill can be used to this end. Nor do all cases of injurious falsehood necessarily involve competition. Suppose, e.g., maliciously false statements about a person's product are published in a consumer advice magazine by someone wishing, for reasons other than competition, to injure the producer. See also *Kaye* v. *Robertson* [1991] FSR 62; noted 80 above.

damaging a person's commercial activities[453] in an attempt to deprive the person directly of financial gain or to make one's own product or services relatively more attractive than the other's. Whereas passing off only protects traders with an established commercial reputation, injurious falsehood can protect even newcomers to or on-off participants in the market.

Goodwill is recognized by the law as a form of property, and the gist of the tort of passing off, as we have seen, is interference with property rights. By contrast, the gist of the tort of injurious falsehood is the causing of damage. The elements of the tort are: (1) the making of a false statement concerning a person's goods, services, business, or occupation; (2) maliciously, that is, dishonestly, not believing its truth, or for some improper motive, that is, not for the protection of one's own legitimate interests;[454] and (3) pecuniary damage[455] caused by the false statement. Although the tort can be committed in non-competitive situations, the main justification for the requirement of malice is probably the preservation of competition.[456] In this light, it seems strange that exploiting another's goodwill, as opposed to damaging it, should ever be actionable without proof of fault.

Regarding the requirement of damage, injurious falsehood was originally not actionable *per se*; to succeed, the plaintiff had to prove actual pecuniary loss. This is still the law, except that section 3 of the Defamation Act 1952 provides that the plaintiff need not prove pecuniary loss if (a) the statement was 'calculated' (in the sense of 'likely') to cause pecuniary loss, and was published in writing or other permanent form;[457] or (b) the statement was calculated to cause a person pecuniary damage in respect of any office, profession, calling, trade, or business held or carried on by that person at the time of the publication.[458] Since the tort is most often used in commercial contexts, in practice the typical plaintiff will not have to prove pecuniary loss: it will be presumed from the making of the statement. This opens up the possibility that, although in theory the tort is designed primarily to protect a person's financial interest in his or her commercial reputation, in practice it may

---

[453] Understood in a wide sense: the injured person need not be a trader or business provided the damage relates to some commercial transaction or activity. E.g., one of the earliest uses of the tort was against persons who made false statements about title to property which another was attempting to sell. Furthermore, the statement need not be such as to lower a person in the estimation of others, but only such as to damage the person financially by causing people to hold some false view about his or her commercial activities; for example, a false assertion that a person had given up business to join a religious order might be actionable: Salmond 393.

[454] Presumably, the element of untruth would rule out mere strengthening of one's competitive position as a justification: see further 156 below.

[455] Damages for injury to reputation as such appear not to be recoverable in this tort; nor are damages for distress except by way of an award of aggravated damages in a case where pecuniary loss has or is deemed to have been suffered: *Joyce* v. *Sengupta* [1993] 1 WLR 337.

[456] So business people owe no duty of care actionable in negligence not to injure their competitors by 'negligent falsehoods': *Spring* v. *Guardian Assurance PLC* [1993] 2 All ER 273, 290a–b, 294h–j. In non-competitive contexts, see 100 below.

[457] Cf. the distinction between libel and slander in the law of defamation.

[458] Cf. s. 2 of the 1952 Act in respect of slanderous defamation.

be used to protect some other interest—for example, feelings, or a desire for vengeance.

Injunctions are available as a remedy for injurious falsehood.[459] Declarations are also available, and are particularly useful when the statement casts doubt on the plaintiff's title to property. Damages for past pecuniary loss, whether nominal, compensatory, or aggravated[460] are available.

Reputation[461]

Here we are concerned with 'personal' reputation rather than commercial reputation; with statements which are likely cause a person to lose esteem in the eyes of others as opposed to those which are likely to cause a person to lose some commercial or financial advantage.[462] Of course, the two may overlap, in that a statement which causes people to think less of a person may also damage that person's commercial prospects.[463] In such a case, the person may sue either in defamation or for injurious falsehood.[464] The distinction between 'personal' and commercial reputation all but disappears in cases where a commercial corporation sues for defamation.[465] But in theory, at least, a false statement which injures a person's financial prospects without lowering the person in the esteem of others will be actionable, if at all, as

---

[459] It is not clear why this is so. The obvious similarities between this tort and the tort of defamation suggest that, at some level, injurious falsehood involves interference with rights. Indeed, it is tempting to argue that the latter involves interference with property rights of some sort or another: denials of title to land, chattels, or intangible property (in the last case, in the form of malicious threats to sue for alleged infringement of statutory property rights: Cornish, 59–61); casting aspersions on the quality of land or goods; false statements which damage goodwill (note, particularly, cases of 'inverse passing off', where A claims not that A's goods or services are B's, but that B's goods or services are A's; this may amount to injurious falsehood—see J. D. Heydon, *Economic Torts*, 2nd edn. (London, 1978), 106–7). The tort was certainly originally concerned with property, but it is now, at least in theory, wider because it may cover any false statement about a person (other than one concerned solely with personal reputation) which causes a third party to act to the person's financial detriment. Furthermore, the requirement of malice and the original need to prove special damage weaken the property analogy. At all events, because damage is the gist of the tort, an injunction would, presumably, only be awarded if damages would be an inadequate remedy.

[460] See *Joyce* v. *Sengupta* [1993] 1 WLR 337. Query whether exemplary damages are available for this tort.

[461] Salmond, ch. 8; M. A. Jones, *Textbook on Torts*, 4th edn. (London, 1993), ch. 13.

[462] This distinction is explored in *Drummond-Jackson* v. *British Medical Association* [1970] 1 WLR 688; see also *Bell-Booth Group Ltd* v. *A-G* [1989] 3 NZLR 148. A distinction is drawn between the governmental and commercial reputations of governmental bodies: such bodies cannot sue in defamation in respect of the former: *Derbyshire CC* v. *Times Newspapers Ltd* [1993] AC 534.

[463] e.g. *Sim* v. *H. J. Heinz Co. Ltd* [1959] 1 WLR 313.

[464] *Joyce* v. *Sengupta* [1993] 1 WLR 337. An injurious falsehood action has the advantage for the plaintiff that it may qualify for legal aid, and the disadvantage for the defendant that it does not carry an absolute right to jury trial.

[465] Fleming, 529; Salmond, 423. See also R. Kidner [1992] *JBL* 570.

injurious falsehood which, because it requires proof of malice, is very much harder to establish.[466]

We do not normally think of reputation as property. But the way it is protected by the tort of defamation is, in some respects, analogous to the way property rights are protected. Liability for defamation is strict: the main defences to a defamation action (justification, privilege, and fair comment) are based on a public interest in the free flow of information which defeats the plaintiff's right to good repute in the circumstances of the case, rather than on any lack of fault on the part of the defendant. The only defence which directly mitigates the harshness of the liability rule is that contained in section 4 of the 1952 Act, which allows a person who defames another 'innocently' to make an offer of amends and to plead that offer in defence to the action if it is not accepted. Furthermore, injunctions are available as a remedy (although in order to discourage 'gagging writs', an interlocutory injunction will not normally be available in cases where D intends to plead justification). Finally, in many cases defamation is actionable *per se*, that is, without proof of special damage (which means, primarily, financial loss).

On the other hand, a person will be held to have published a defamatory statement only if its communication to a third party was foreseeable; and, therefore, only if the person ought to have taken reasonable precautions to prevent communication.[467] More importantly, the main defences operate in such a way that in practice few completely innocent defamers are likely to be held liable. A defence of justification or absolute privilege can succeed even if the defamer acted deliberately out of spite or ill-will (that is, maliciously). The defences of fair comment and qualified privilege can succeed provided only that the defamer did not act dishonestly, or out of spite or ill-will, or for an ulterior motive; it matters not how careless or careful the defamer might have been in publishing the defamatory words.

Although the standard accounts of the tort of defamation say that the tort protects reputation,[468] it should be noted that damage to reputation is presumed from the fact that a defamatory statement has been made; and a defamatory statement is one which bears a meaning capable of causing people to think less of the plaintiff (or to shun or avoid him or her). It matters not that no one actually believed the statement,[469] or that no one thought less of or shunned the plaintiff as a result of the making of the statement. So the tort of defamation can be used for purposes other than protecting a person's

---

[466] The tort of deceit deals with cases where a person acts to his or her own detriment as the result of a false statement aimed at him or her. The tort of deceit has been rendered largely redundant by the tort of negligent misstatement; similarly, there is an argument for saying that the tort of injurious falsehood has been rendered redundant: J. Mesher (1971) 34 *MLR* 317, 322. But it is necessary to distinguish injurious falsehood used as a weapon of commercial competition from its use in other contexts. In the former situation, the requirement of malice is justified for the preservation of competition.

[467] *Huth* v. *Huth* [1915] 3 KB 32.   [468] e.g. Salmond, 145.

[469] *Theaker* v. *Richardson* [1962] 1 WLR 151.

interest in a good reputation.[470] The statement may, in fact, have hurt feelings more than reputation; the plaintiff may bring an action out of a desire for revenge, or in order to exploit the situation to reap a financial gain at the expense of the defendant (thus risking accusations of 'gold-digging').[471]

As already noted, in many cases defamation is actionable *per se*. This is so if the defamatory statement takes the form of a libel as opposed to slander; or even if it is slander, provided one of a number of exceptions is satisfied. For our purposes, the most important of these is contained in section 2 of the 1952 Act: slander is actionable *per se* if the allegedly defamatory statement is,

calculated to disparage the plaintiff in any office, profession, calling, trade or business held or carried on by him at the time of the publication . . . whether or not the words are spoken of the plaintiff in the way of his office, profession, calling, trade or business.

Where defamatory statements meet this description, the overlap between injurious falsehood and defamation is at its greatest.[472]

In cases where defamation is actionable *per se*, the tort is obviously capable of protecting interests other than financial interests. But in all cases damages can be recovered for 'special damage', which primarily means financial loss resulting from the defamation. Under this head a person could recover not only out-of-pocket loss but also the loss of prospective advantages such as income or profits.

In recent years, courts have found difficulty with establishing the proper relationship between defamation and other torts. The basic rule of English law is that, if the facts of a case satisfy the elements of two different causes of action, the plaintiff may sue in either or in both concurrently. On the other hand, courts are sometimes reluctant to allow plaintiffs, by choosing one cause of action, to succeed in claims which would fail if the another available cause of action had been chosen. Thus in New Zealand it has been held that an action in negligence will not lie in respect of a defamatory statement which, being protected by qualified privilege, would not attract liability in defamation unless it was malicious.[473] The House of Lords has rejected this approach.[474] It has also been held that an action for 'lawful means' conspir-

---

[470] For an accusation see R. Shillito [1994] *New LJ* 194; and for a rebuttal see B. Taylor [1994] *New LJ* 312.

[471] Even more contrived mercenary motives have been suggested. When an action brought by Elton John against the *Sun* newspaper was settled out of court, the judge who was due to hear the case was reported to have said that his court had been turned into 'a supine adjunct to a publicity machine for pop stars and newspapers': *Independent*, 13 Dec. 1988.

[472] Fleming, 529, cites Australian authority for the proposition that a corporate plaintiff could not recover damages for 'reputation as such', but such a proposition could not stand with s. 2 of the Defamation Act 1952.

[473] *Bell-Booth Group Ltd* v. *A-G* [1989] 3 NZLR 148; *South Pacific Manufacturing Co. Ltd* v. *New Zealand Security Consultants and Investigations Ltd* [1992] 2 NZLR 282.

[474] *Spring* v. *Guardian Assurance PLC* [1994] 3 WLR 354.

acy[475] or injurious falsehood[476] may be brought in respect of defamatory statements, but that only damages for pecuniary loss and not for injury to reputation as such may be recovered in such actions. This qualification seems sound because it rests on a specification of the interests which the different torts are designed to protect. The elements of the tort of defamation are desinged to strike a balance between the individual's interest in good reputation and society's interest in freedom of speech, and people should not be allowed to upset this balance by suing for injury to reputation in any other cause of action than defamation.

Other Dignitary Interests

Reputation is sometimes called a 'dignitary interest'. The other most important dignitary interests are privacy and personal liberty. Privacy as such is not protected by the law of tort, although it does receive some indirect protection through the tort of trespass to land, for example. Personal liberty is protected by the tort of trespass to the person in its 'wrongful imprisonment' form.[477]

It seems even stranger to call personal liberty a property interest than it does to give this description to reputation.[478] Once again, however, the protection of personal liberty by the law of tort bears some of the hallmarks of its protection of property interests. First, wrongful imprisonment is actionable *per se*. Secondly, it is a strict liability tort in the sense that provided the act of imprisonment was deliberate the defendant is liable for all loss and damage suffered as a direct result of the imprisonment.[479] Thirdly, the most important defences to claims for wrongful imprisonment—defence of one's person or property, and lawful authority—depend on the recognition that the defendant was acting in defence of a right which is, under the circumstances, more important than the plaintiff's right to personal liberty.

Liberty is a dignitary interest, but it is also a financial interest: personal liberty is normally a precondition of generating substantial income and of disposing of one's labour and capital as one wills.

6. CONCLUSION

It is now necessary to gather together some of the threads which run through this Chapter. We have seen that the law of tort protects property interests in

---

[475] *Lonrho PLC* v. *Fayed (No. 5)* [1993] 1 WLR 1489.

[476] *Joyce* v. *Sengupta* [1993] 1 WLR 337.　　　　　　　　　　　　[477] Salmond, 128–131.

[478] Mesher (1971) 34 *MLR* 317, 319: 'wrongful detention is regarded more like physical injury than financial loss'.

[479] Note that the discussion under the heading 'Intention or negligence must be shown' in Salmond, 141–2, relates to liability in trespass for *personal injury*. Fleming, 79, recognizes that wrongful imprisonment does not fit the supposed requirement of intention or negligence.

a number of ways. It can be used to resolve disputes about title. In cases where title is not in dispute, it can be used (1) to protect the right to use and exploit property to financial advantage, or to strip a person of benefits gained by wrongful exploitation or use; (2) to compensate for loss suffered as a result of interference with use and enjoyment of property; and (3) to compensate for damage done to property. There are, then, at least four different types of disputes about property with which the law of tort deals: title disputes, user disputes, interference with use (or 'amenity damage') disputes, and physical damage disputes. These types of dispute correspond to different incidents of the right of property.

The two chief characteristics of tortious protection of property interests are actionability *per se* and strict liability. However, we have seen that these two characteristics are by no means universal in their application. Tortious remedies are sometimes only available if loss has been or is likely in the future to be suffered. Still, an injunction is normally available simply on proof of infringement of a property right;[480] and monetary compensation can sometimes be awarded even if the plaintiff has suffered no financial loss. As for the standard of liability, this varies from malice through negligence to complete innocence. In this respect, the torts which protect property in competitive contexts are the most bewildering because of the variety of standards of liability found in them.

The argument that tortious liability for competitive activities should depend on proof of a dishonest motive is easy to understand—even liability for negligence seems out of place in this context. Is it not extraordinary, then, that an injunction to restrain passing off can be awarded against an innocent defendant, while the Law Commission has proposed that liability, even for competitive exploitation of trade secrets, should rest on knowledge or means of knowledge of the secret nature of the information? The juristic logic of these different rules is apparent: the traditional categories of property, equity, and damage carry with them distinctive criteria of liability. But in less conceptual terms, the logic is less clear. We have also noticed in a couple of contexts differences between liability in trespass and nuisance which seem difficult to rationalize in terms of the interest being protected.

Three lessons emerge: first, tort law protects property interests, plural. Property is a complex bundle of legal rights, and the strands need to be separated in order to understand how each right is protected. Secondly, the traditional divisions between torts both distort and obscure the principles according to which the various interests are protected. Thirdly, the case of the 'competition torts' shows the importance of paying attention to the social function which the legal protection of the various property interests is meant to perform.

Finally, consideration of the way the law of tort protects property interests

---

[480] But note that specific return of chattels will only be ordered if damages are an inadequate remedy.

shows that the basic principle governing the assessment of tort compensation, namely that the plaintiff should be fully compensated for losses suffered but no more, applies more straightforwardly to damage disputes (whether damage to amenities or physical damage) than it does to user disputes. In user disputes the courts often award monetary compensation even though the plaintiff can prove no loss in order to achieve restitutionary, deterrence or punishment goals. And whereas in damage actions exemplary damages, which can help to achieve each of these goals, are exceptional, awards directed to these ends play a much more important role in user disputes.

3

Contractual Interests

INTRODUCTION

The considerable breadth and depth of the protection afforded to various property interests by the law of tort is matched by a powerful disinclination to provide significant protection for contractual interests. The explanation for this varies from area to area, and the relationship between principles of tort liability and principles of contractual liability is so complex that generalizations are very dangerous. However, the distinction between property and obligation, of which the distinction between property and contract is an aspect, pervades English law: owning something and being owed something are concepts located on opposite sides of a very deep divide.[1] Witness the law of bankruptcy and insolvency where the basic principle (subject to exceptions) is that the property available for distribution to unsecured creditors is property owned by the debtor. Property in the custody of or under the control of the debtor but owned by another or in which another has a proprietary interest is, *pro tanto* unavailable. In other words, 'it is a basic policy of insolvency law to adopt the non-bankruptcy ordering of rights and thus to respect proprietary rights held by another prior to the debtor's bankruptcy'.[2] It is of great importance to unsecured creditors of a bankrupt to know whether a third party owns (or has some proprietary interest in) property in the bankrupt's custody or control, or is merely owed some obligation by the bankrupt in respect of it.

The contractual interests we will consider in this Chapter can be divided into two broad categories: the first category contains contractual interests in property; the second contains contractual rights relating to property and services, including rights that the performance of contractual obligations should be of a particular standard, quality, or value. Contractual interests in property must be contrasted with property interests (which were dealt with in Chapter 2). They are discussed in section 1 of this Chapter. The second and larger section of the Chapter deals with rights under contracts which do not have property as their subject matter.

Two other distinctions should be drawn at this stage. The first is between interference with contractual interests by third parties and interference by the

[1] See e.g. *MacJordan Construction Ltd* v. *Brookmount Erostin Ltd* [1992] BCLC 350.
[2] R. M. Goode (1987) 103 *LQR* 433, 435. See also H. Anderson in E. McKendrick (ed.), *Commercial Aspects of Trusts and Fiduciary Obligations* (Oxford, 1992).

other contracting party. This distinction which, in traditional legal terms, is related to the doctrine of privity of contract,[3] is one source of the complexity of the relationship between tort and contract. The other distinction is that between existing contractual rights or interests and what are sometimes called 'mere contractual expectancies'.[4] Perhaps surprisingly, the law of tort is prepared to afford certain protection even against conduct which hinders the acquisition of contractual rights but does not interfere with existing contractual interests. This Chapter is concerned primarily with existing contractual interests; contractual and other expectancies will be considered in Chapter 4.

Issues to be examined in this Chapter include: when should the law of tort reinforce the stability of contractual relations by protecting them against attack by third parties? When, if ever, should a contracting party be allowed to sue another contracting party in tort in respect of breach of the contract? What is the rleevance of the distinction between intentional and negligent interference with contractual rights? As in other chapters, I will consider relevant statutory causes of action which are analogous to common law causes of action in tort.

1. CONTRACTUAL INTERESTS IN PROPERTY

Real Property

Appropriation and Exploitation

We have already discussed contractual licences to enter, use, or occupy land.[5] As we saw, although a contractual licensee may be able to claim contractual remedies against the licensor (including, in some cases, an injunction or specific performance) and, in certain circumstances, recover damages for unlawful eviction, the licensee cannot sue the licensor for trespass if the latter interferes with the former's entry, use, or occupation. As against third

---

[3] Third party tort liability for interference with contract can be justified in economic terms if one takes the view, as do economic analysts of law, that one of the functions of tort law is to resolve disputes in the way the parties would have if they had been in a position to make an agreement about the subject matter of their dispute; and if one assumes that a person is unlikely (because of high 'transaction costs') to be able to reach an appropriate agreement with a third party.

[4] The term 'contractual expectancy' is defined at 150 below. I have used the term despite a risk of confusion caused by the fact that contract lawyers often think of a contractual expectancy as an expectation of performance under an existing contract (which I call a 'contractual interest'), because I wish to emphasize that the relationship between tort and contract can be fully understood only by considering future as well as existing contracts; and because I wish to contrast contractual expectancies with non-contractual expectancies. But it must be noted that so-called 'damages for loss of expectation' in the contractual context and in the context of the discussion in this Ch. of concurrent actions are damages for failure to perform an existing contract.

[5] See 36–7 and 57–8 above.

parties, contractual licences as such do not, it seems, bind successors in title either at law[6] or in equity; nor, apparently, can a contractual licensee sue other third parties who interfere with entry, use, or occupation of the land. The distinction between proprietary (and possessory) interests in land and contractual interests in land is, therefore, of great significance, at least so far as common law tort liability is concerned. Why is this so? In attempting an explanation, it is probably necessary to deal separately with the licensee's rights against the licensor on the one hand, and the former's rights against third parties on the other.

First, however, we should observe that the distinction between contractual interests and proprietary interests is, from some points of view at least, quite arbitrary. It does not, for example, rest on the fact that contractual interests are the product of agreement between the parties whereas proprietary interests are not. It is true that proprietary interests (in particular, equitable proprietary interests) can arise without agreement, but in most cases they are the result of agreement between the 'vendor' and the 'purchaser'. Thus, there can exist side by side and arising out of one and the same transaction a contractual right of entry coupled with a proprietary right, for example, to cut wood. Also, we have seen that an agreement which gives a right of exclusive possession for a term will normally be treated as a lease (that is, a proprietary interest in land). The fact is that the law elevates some interests (which may be the product of agreement) into property interests, while others it relegates to the lesser category of contractual interests. In general terms, the most obvious criterion of categorization is the perceived social importance of the particular interest at the time the classification was made.[7]

Why, then, does the law of tort draw a sharp distinction between proprietary and contractual interests. The obvious answer, on the basis of what was said in the last paragraph, would be that the law of tort can provide protection for interests in property which is better than that which the law of contract can provide; and because property interests are, by definition, of more social importance than mere contractual interests, the law of tort recognizes this by drawing a distinction between them and by according its protection only to proprietary interests in property. The force of this explanation depends on the truth of the assertion that tort law can provide better protection to interests in land than contract law. As against the owner (in contractual terms, the licensor), this was undoubtedly once true: even if the licensor revoked the licence in breach of contract, the only contractual remedy available to the licensee was damages for breach of contract. Now, however, the rule appears to be that whether a contractual licence is revocable

---

[6] The rules of privity would bar a contractual action; and a contractual licence, not being an interest in land, could not run with the land.

[7] In the case of agreements for the occupation of residential premises which give exclusive possession, classification of the interest as a lease serves, *inter alia*, to afford to the licensee the protection of the Housing Act 1988.

depends on the terms of the contract; and if, as a matter of construction, it is irrevocable under the circumstances in which the licensor purported to revoke it, the licensee may be awarded an injunction to restrain revocation[8] or even specific performance of the terms of the licence.

If this is a correct statement of the present law, the advantage of tort would not lie in the available remedies,[9] but rather in the fact that the licensor under a contractual licence can exercise a degree of control,[10] by the terms of the licence, over the extent to which the licence will be irrevocable, whereas the rights of a person who enjoys a proprietary interest in land are more or less defined by law. In other words, as against the landowner the main advantage of tort law for the potential plaintiff is that the protection it provides is less subject to control and modification by the landowner than is the protection afforded by contract law. Looked at from the other side, the law refuses to recognize all interests in land as proprietary in order to reserve to landowners a certain degree of choice, via freedom of contract, as to how their land is used.

As against third parties, the situation is very different. Here, there is no real choice between tort and contract because the doctrine of privity of contract would, as a matter of principle, normally rule out contractual liability against strangers to the contract. In this context, the logic of denying tort liability would appear to be that to recognize it would amount to protecting interests which are neither proprietary nor (as against the defendant) contractual, as well as if they were proprietary and better than if they were contractual. In other words, there can be no liability for third party interference with contractual interests in land exactly because such interests in land are seen as inferior to proprietary interests in land, and to impose such liability would get too close to elevating contractual interests to the status of proprietary interests. Seen from the other side, third parties do not have the power which the landowner has to define their obligations towards the licensee by contract, and they should not be burdened with obligations which, because of their non-modifiable nature, are akin to 'proprietary obligations'. This argument perhaps receives indirect support from the fact that, when the law is prepared to enforce obligations arising from contracts in respect of land

[8] The licensee can also resist a claim for possession.

[9] Remember that this book is about financial interests. If a licensor attempted physically to remove a licensee in breach of an irrevocable licence, the licensor might be liable in tort for assault and battery, whereas liability in contract might be limited to financial loss; but this advantage of tort law is not relevant to our present discussion. So far as damages for financial loss are concerned, the rules of tort law are in some ways more advantageous to plaintiffs than the rules of contract law, and in other ways less advantageous. I will consider this point in greater detail in the discussion of concurrent actions in tort and contract in respect of the quality of services.

[10] But only a degree: the process of interpreting a contract gives the court a degree of power, too. Also in some circumstances, the law limits the power of the landowner to choose between creating a proprietary as opposed to a contractual interest: licences which give exclusive possession are normally treated as leases.

('restrictive covenants') against third parties, it does so by elevating them into proprietary interests which can, therefore, 'run with the land'.

On the other hand, perhaps a distinction should be drawn between successors in title and other third parties. It has just been argued that there is logic in not using tort law to protect contractual interests in land which are unenforceable in contract against the defendant. But this argument seems to apply more strongly to purchasers than to complete strangers. An important aspect of the legal protection given to proprietary interests is that the purchaser of such an interest takes free from encumbrances which do not themselves enjoy the status of proprietary interests. It is, therefore, logical that the law of tort should not assist the holder of a contractual interest against a successor in title. This argument would apply particularly in relation to registered title to land if the interest the plaintiff claimed was unregistered.[11] But there may be less reason why the law of tort should not protect the holder of a non-proprietary interest against a complete stranger who claims no competing proprietary interest, especially if tort liability for interference with a contractual interest in land required proof of knowledge of the plaintiff's interest and of an intention on the part of the third party to interfere with it; and if actual financial loss had to be proved to establish liability. Tort liability for intentional infliction of actual financial loss would bear neither of the two chief hallmarks of the tortious protection of property interests, namely strict liability and actionability *per se*. To allow the imposition of such liability on a stranger at the suit of a licensee would not, therefore, elevate the licensee's interest to the level of a proprietary interest.

Even if liability were strict, so that, for example, the interferer could in suitable cases be sued for trespass to land, such tort liability need not be viewed as an elevation of the licensee's interest to the status of a proprietary interest: although strict liability is a common feature of the tortious protection of proprietary interests, strict tortious liability is not limited to this context. There is nothing conceptually impermissible about strict liability for personal injuries, for example. On the other hand, if a stranger could be held liable in trespass for interference with a contractual interest in land without proof of actual damage, this would invest the interest of the plaintiff with one of the distinctive hallmarks of property. It might be argued that trespass ought not to be actionable *per se* in such circumstances. At all events, there is arguably no good reason of theory or policy why stranger third parties who interfere with contractual interests in land should not, under certain circumstances, be liable in tort.

In the light of this analysis (which supports the imposition of tort liability in certain circumstances on strangers but not on successors in title), it comes as a surprise that there is a certain amount of case law which supports the imposition of tort liability for interference with contractual interests in land

[11] R. J. Smith (1977) 41 *Conv. (NS)* 318.

on successors in title.[12] The most extreme case is *Esso Petroleum Co. Ltd* v. *Kingswood Motors (Addlestone) Ltd*.[13] This was an action for interference with contract; A, the registered proprietor of land, attempted to avoid a solus tie agreement between it and the plaintiff relating to the land by transferring the land to a third party. Bridge J awarded an injunction against A and the transferee to compel re-transfer of the land to A even though the transferee had been registered as proprietor. It has been suggested that the proper approach to such a case would be to allow A to plead a defence of justification based on its property rights over the land.[14] Such a defence would prevent the law of tort being used to outflank property law. Also relevant are dicta of Megaw LJ in *Binions* v. *Evans*[15] to the effect that a successor in title could be sued in tort for interference with contract for having attempted to evict a contractual licensee, provided the successor knew of the licence when he or she acquired the premises. It is by no means clear that the elements of liability for interference with contract could be established in such circumstances;[16] assuming that they could, the dictum runs counter to arguments from general principle.[17]

On the other hand, the policy considerations underlying the general principle are not entirely straightforward. We have seen that there is an argument for allowing successors in title to take free of encumbrances, especially if the successor's title is registered and the encumbrance is not. However, the licensee will have a strong moral claim if the successor knew of the licensee's interest when the successor contracted to buy the property, and an even stronger claim if the successor covenanted with the vendor to observe the terms of the licence.[18] So far as the law of tort is concerned, the proper approach to such cases may be to allow a defence of justification based on the exercise of property rights unless the successor in title has covenanted

---

[12] Cf. the rules about when successors in title are bound by equitable interests in the land: C. Harpum (1986) 102 *LQR* 267, 271–2.

[13] [1974] QB 142.

[14] Smith (1977) 41 *Conv. (NS)* 318, 321. Cf. *Edwin Hill and Partners* v. *First National Finance Corporation PLC* [1989] 1 WLR 225, 233; but note *Swiss Bank Corporation* v. *Lloyd's Bank Ltd* [1979] 2 All ER 853, 870 *per* Browne-Wilkinson J who wishes to keep separate cases (a) where P seeks to enforce a covenant concerning the use of property, contained in an agreement between P and another, against a successor in title, and (b) where P sues a third party for inducing a breach of contract between P and another. Only in the latter type of case could a defence of justification be raised. Furthermore, an action in tort would lie only if the terms of the covenant were such that the actions of the successor could put the original covenantor in breach: R. O'Dair (1991) 11 *OJLS* 227, 232.

[15] [1972] Ch. 359, 371. [16] Smith (1977) 41 *Conv. (NS)* 318, 322–6.

[17] Note that more is required to justify the imposition of a constructive trust on the purchaser: *Ashburn Anstalt* v. *Arnold* [1989] Ch. 1.

[18] The predominant motive of the vendor in securing a covenant from the purchaser that the latter will respect the contractual rights of the licensee may be to protect the vendor against the licensee rather than to protect the licensee against the purchaser. But this does not weaken the force of the licensee's moral claim against the purchaser. There is some authority for the proposition that the purchaser would, in such circumstances, be a constructive trustee of the covenantee's rights: *Swiss Bank Corporation* v. *Lloyd's Bank* [1979] 2 All ER 853, 871 *per* Browne-Wilkinson J.

with the vendor to observe the terms of the latter's contract with the second party. The argument for this compromise would be that it preserves the primacy of property rights but also gives proper weight to binding agreements entered in to by the property owner about the way those rights will be exercised. It does not seem unfair to hold a property owner to an agreement freely entered into concerning the way the property will be used. The plaintiff's moral claim is stronger still in a case such as *Esso* v. *Kingswood* where the defendants deliberately set out to destroy the solus tie. In such a case, too, the law of tort should protect P's contractual interest in the land.

Interference with Use and Enjoyment

The main tort which protects the interest in the use and enjoyment of land is nuisance, although we have seen that trespass may also play a part in this context.[19] The basic rule is that a contractual licensee has no title to sue in either trespass or nuisance. It has already been argued[20] that this rule makes little sense in relation to amenity damage, and that an occupier of land ought to be entitled to sue in respect of amenity damage regardless of whether the occupier has a proprietary interest in the land. Of course, the occupier should only be able to recover for damage to his or her interest as occupier and not for damage to the interest of the licensor.

Physical Damage

Two main questions arise here: first, can a contractual licensee recover the cost of repairing or rebuilding damaged premises? Secondly, can a licensee recover damages for financial loss consequent upon such damage? If D damages property in which P has a contractual interest with the intention of inflicting economic loss thereby, the latter may be able to sue for interference with contract.[21] Subject to this, however, the basic legal answer to both questions would appear to be negative: in order to sue for damage to real property, P must have a proprietary interest in the property at the time of the damage. The same basic rule applies to cases of physical damage to chattels, and we will discuss it further in that context. There are, as we have already seen,[22] two exceptions to the temporal element of the rule which are important in cases of latent damage; and one corollary of these exceptions is that a person may recover damages even though, at the time the property damage occurred, that person had only a contractual interest (or, indeed, no interest) in the property. But, in order to recover, the person must still have a proprietary or possessory interest in the property at the time when the cause of action on which the suit is founded arose.

---

[19] See 82 above.   [20] See 83 above.   [21] See 115 below.
[22] See 90 above.

It should be noted that the two questions posed above may raise different policy issues. If a licensee is under a contractual obligation to keep the premises in repair, there is good reason to allow recovery for the cost of repair or reinstatement from a person who tortiously damages the premises. The fact that the loss is purely financial does not seem crucial: the distinction between the cost of making good physical damage to property and the financial loss flowing from damage to property only matters in cases where awarding the cost of repair could not be justified on purely financial or economic grounds. In such cases an award of the cost of repair would have to be justified on non-financial grounds. But in other cases the cost of repair is purely financial loss, even if it is claimed by and awarded to the owner of the property.

The question of whether a contractual licensee should be entitled to recover damages for financial loss consequent upon damage to the property is one which has, *mutatis mutandis*, been much discussed by courts and commentators in relation to contractual interests in chattels, and it will be considered at greater length in that context.

Chattels

Appropriation, Exploitation, and Interference with Use[23]

As in the case of real property, the law of tort draws a sharp distinction between proprietary (and possessory) interests in chattels, and merely contractual interests in chattels. In order to sue for trespass to goods P must have possession of those goods (as opposed to mere custody); and to sue in conversion P must have a right to immediate possession of the goods.[24] As in the case of land, proprietary interests in chattels most commonly arise as a result of agreement;[25] here we are concerned with agreements about chattels which do not generate a right of possession.

Contractual interests in chattels[26] are not normally enforceable against a purchaser of the goods.[27] However, as in the case of land, there is authority for the proposition that if D, knowing of the contractual rights of P in the goods in question,[28] intentionally interferes with those rights in such a way

[23] In the last case, to the extent that the torts of trespass and conversion can be used to protect the right to quiet use and enjoyment.

[24] *Elliott Steam Tug Co. Ltd* v. *Shipping Controller* [1922] 1 KB 127, 139.

[25] The main source of possessory interests in chattels is bailment, and most forms of bailment are based on contract.

[26] Including documentary intangibles such as shares.

[27] *Port Line Ltd* v. *Ben Line Steamers Ltd* [1958] 2 QB 146; but see *Lord Strathcona SS Co.* v. *Dominion Coal Co.* [1926] AC 108; Treitel, 561–3.

[28] The requirement of knowledge is problematic. As we will see later (120 below), there appears to be a general rule that D can be liable for interfering with a contract between P and C even if D did not actually know of the existence of the contract or of its relevant terms,

as to cause damage to P, D may be liable in tort for interference with contractual rights.[29] In relation to real property, as we have seen, such liability
is difficult to reconcile with rules of property law designed to ensure certainty
and security of title and, in particular, with the principle of the finality of the
land register. Because chattels are generally considered to be less important
than land, and because any reasonably extensive system for the registration
of title to chattels (even very valuable chattels) would be extremely expensive
and difficult to operate in practice,[30] tort liability for interference with contractual interests in chattels does not seem as problematic in policy terms as
does the analogous liability in relation to land.[31] Furthermore, in relation to
chattels, because they are moveable, the greatest practical problems are not
caused by successors in title seeking to defeat the rights of persons contractually interested in the goods but by persons with contractual interests seeking to defeat the rights of the owner by disposing of the goods.[32] These
problems are dealt with by rules of sales law concerning priorities between
competing interests, and by the law of tort, which affords the true owner an
action in conversion in cases where the basic rule applies that the transferor
of goods can give no better title than the transferor has: *nemo dat quod non
habet.*

provided D was reckless as to its existence or, perhaps, provided D ought reasonably to have
known that it existed. But Treitel (at 563–4) and Browne-Wilkinson J in *Swiss Bank Corporation*
v. *Lloyd's Bank Ltd* [1979] Ch. 548, 572 take the view that D can be liable in tort for interfering
with a contract between P and C as to the use of C's chattel only if D actually knew of the relevant contractual terms. The policy argument in favour of this position is that, were the rule
otherwise, an undesirable element of uncertainty would enter into commercial transactions.
C. Harpum (1986) 102 *LQR* 267, 273 says that equitable interests in chattels are enforceable
against a successor in title who paid for the goods only if the latter had 'notice' of the interest;
notice here means actual knowledge or recklessness. If recklessness is enough to bind the successor in equity, the only reason for requiring actual knowledge in tort would be, to use the
words of Browne-Wilkinson J ([1979] Ch. 548, 572), to prevent the law of tort being bedevilled
with equitable refinements. But the idea that recklessness is an equitable refinement unknown to
the law of tort is wrong.

[29] *BMTA* v. *Salvadori* [1949] Ch. 556; *Rickless* v. *United Artists Corporation* [1988] QB 40;
Treitel, 563–5. If the contract interfered with by D is specifically enforceable, P will have an equitable charge over the property in question (entitling P to an injunction to restrain D from dealing with the property inconsistently with P's rights), unless D was a purchaser of the property
for value without notice of P's rights. Since 'notice' in this context embraces recklessness, then
unless D could be liable in tort even though only negligent as to P's interest (as to which see
n. 28 above), tort liability will, in practice, be superfluous in this situation: *Swiss Bank
Corporation* v. *Lloyd's Bank* [1982] AC 584, 598E–F *per* Buckley LJ. But see A. Tettenborn [1982]
CLJ 58, 83. In *MacJordan Construction* v. *Brookmount Erostin* [1992] BCLC 350 an unsuccessful attempt was made to extend the principle stated in the text to a contractual right to have a
retention fund established.

[30] Cf. R. M. Goode (1976) 92 *LQR* 528, 567.

[31] But note that a purchaser for value of land is more easily fixed with notice of equitable
interests than the purchaser of chattels: Harpum (1986) 102 *LQR* 114, 123–6; 102 *LQR* 267, 273.

[32] Goode, ch. 15.

Physical Damage

Here, too, the basic rule applies: a person with a merely contractual interest in goods at the time they are damaged cannot claim compensation for the damage.[33] Once again, liability for intentional interference with contractual rights seems to represent an exception to the general rule.[34] But it is now clearly established in English common law that there can be no liability in tort for negligently causing physical damage to property at the suit of a person whose only interest in the property at the time the damage was done was contractual.[35] We have already seen,[36] however, that there are two statutory exceptions to this rule which allow recovery to a person who has a proprietary or possessory interest in the goods at the time damage to them became discoverable. In the case of 'patent' damage, the date the damage occurs and the date it becomes discoverable will coincide; in the case of latent damage, the statutory exceptions overcome the problem which arises when the property changes hands between the date of occurrence of the damage and the date of discoverability. In such a case, without the exceptions, the purchaser could not recover damages in respect of the damage; and the vendor would have little incentive to sue (and could not be forced to do so by the purchaser).

Of course, these statutory exceptions deal not only with the case where P had a contractual interest in the goods at the time they were damaged, but also where P had no interest in them at all at that time. Problems of latent damage most commonly arise in relation to real property, and typically in cases involving acquisition of a building which has been badly constructed. This case and that of the acquisition of chattels which have been badly made are dealt with below.[37]

Despite a decision of the US Supreme Court to the same effect as the English rule,[38] various American courts have found three ways round the rule, all in shipping cases involving claims by time charterers in respect of physical damage to the chartered vessel. One is based on the admiralty law notion of 'community of venture';[39] a second rests on the fact that in the leading Supreme Court case the charterer's only claim was for profits lost as a result

---

[33] On the distinction between cost of repairs and consequential loss see 112 above.

[34] See 126–8 below.

[35] *Leigh & Sillavan Ltd* v. *Aliakmon Shipping Co. Ltd* [1986] AC 785; *Candlewood Navigation Corporation Ltd* v. *Mitsui OSK Lines Ltd* [1986] AC 1; see further 000 below. The position is different in Australia: *Caltex Oil (Australia) Pty Ltd* v. *Dredge 'Willemstad'* (1976) 136 CLR 529; and in Canada: *Norsk Pacific Steamship Co* v. *Canadian National Railway Co.* (1992) 91 DLR(4th) 289 (J. G. Fleming [1993] *Tort LR* 68). On the question whether a right to immediate possession will amount to sufficient title to sue see *Transcontainer Express Ltd* v. *Custodian Security Ltd* [1988] 1 Lloyd's Rep. 128. It would, perhaps, be strange if a right to immediate possession were sufficient in conversion but not for an action in negligence.

[36] See 90 and 112 above.   [37] See 207–18.

[38] *Robins Dry Dock & Repair Co.* v. *Flint* (1927) 275 US 303.

[39] *Amoco Transport Co.* v. *S/S Mason Lykes* (1985) 768 F2d 659.

of the vessel being laid up and not also for hire charges payable during the period of inactivity;[40] and the third depends on holding that a time charterer can have a possessory interest in a vessel by virtue, for example, of having spent a large amount modifying it so that it can be used with the damaged vessel 'as an integrated unit'.[41] The third exception seems unarguable as a matter of English law; and the second exception is clearly not recognized in England.[42]

The first exception is more problematic. In the case in point, a ship carrying P's cargo was damaged by D and alternative transport for the goods had to be arranged; P, however, remained liable under the bill of lading for the original freight charges. P was allowed to recover them and the cost of alternative transport. These facts are analogous to those of the famous hypothetical case involving road transport posed by Lord Roche in *Morrison Steamship Co. Ltd* v. *Greystoke Castle (Cargo Owners)*;[43] his Lordship said that the goods owner would be allowed to recover the cost of alternative transport. But the value of this dictum is usually discounted on the basis that the case (although not the example) concerned the admiralty rules of 'general average contribution'.[44] Under these rules, a cargo owner may be liable to contribute to the cost of repairing a damaged vessel on which goods are being carried; and *Morrison* decides that a cargo owner so liable may recover financial loss from the person who caused the damage.

Intangible Property

Although the law draws a clear distinction between the owner of a statutory intellectual property right and a person licensed by contract to exploit the right, such contractual licensees are given special statutory protection. The exclusive licensee of a patent[45] and, subject to the terms of the licence, the exclusive licensee of a trade mark,[46] have the same rights to sue for infringement as the proprietor; in other words, the licensee, too, is treated as having property rights. Similarly, the exclusive licensee of copyright or of a design right is treated as having the same rights as the owner against all except the owner.[47] As against the owner, the licensee is restricted to contractual rights under the licence; so the licensee can be sued for infringement by the owner for exceeding the terms of the licence and can sue the owner for breaches of the terms of the licence.

---

[40] *Venore Transportation Co.* v. *MV Struma* (1978) 583 F2d 708.

[41] *Domar Ocean Transportation Ltd* v. *M.V. Andrew Martin* (1985) 754 F2d 616.

[42] *Chargeurs Réunis Compagnie Française* v. *English & American Shipping* Co. (1921) 9 Lloyd's Rep. 464; *Candlewood* v. *Mitsui OSK* [1986] AC 1; see further P. S. Atiyah (1967) 83 LQR 248, 266–7.

[43] [1947] AC 265, 280.

[44] *Murphy* v. *Brentwood DC* [1991] 1 AC 398, 468 *per* Lord Keith of Kinkel.

[45] See 66 above.   [46] See 63 above.

[47] See 68 and 69 above.

The policy underlying these provisions is clear enough: the whole point of according statutory protection to intellectual property is to enable its original owner to control its commercial exploitation. The protection of intellectual property against unauthorized exploitation would be very difficult and cumbersome if authorized users were not able to protect the property rights against third-party infringement. It is less clear why a person with a contractual right to exploit land or chattels should not be able to sue strangers in tort for infringement of their contractual rights. It is, of course, true that land and chattels are often not acquired solely, or at all, for commercial exploitation; but if land or some chattel is acquired for this reason, and the owner licenses another to exploit it, it is arguable that the licensee should be entitled to sue in tort[48] a stranger (as opposed to a successor in title)[49] who interferes with the licensee's rights over the land, even if the interference is not intentional.[50]

The licensee of a statutory intellectual property right may be awarded a remedy (such as an injunction or an account of profits) even if no financial loss resulted from the infringement, and there seems no intrinsic reason why the same rule should not apply to interference with contractual rights to exploit land[51] or chattels. Tort liability for intentional interference with contractual rights would only lie if actual damage had resulted from the interference or if a likelihood of actual damage could be established.

In relation to contractual interests in other intangibles, such as confidential information[52] or a statutorily protected performance,[53] there may be liability in tort for interference with contracts relating to the use of such intangibles. But otherwise, in the absence of statutory provision making a tort action available, a person with a mere contractual interest in the exploitation of an intangible could not sue in tort in respect of unauthorized exploitation even if the law recognized the intangible as property.

---

[48] In trespass or nuisance, for instance.

[49] Although, as we have seen, the arguments for treating a successor in title differently are stronger in relation to land than in relation to chattels.

[50] In which case there might be liability for intentional interference with contract.

[51] If the right of exploitation constitutes an easement or *profit à prendre*, it will be enforceable by a tort action. Here we are concerned with purely contractual rights of exploitation.

[52] F. Gurry, *Breach of Confidence* (Oxford, 1984), 290–308; P. M. North (1971) 12 *JSPTL* 149, 150–153.

[53] *Rickless* v. *United Artists Corporation* [1988] QB 40. In such a case the relevant right is correlative to a statutory duty which is held to give rise to a right of action in an individual. Thus *Rickless* established that the relevant legislation gave an individual right of action to the performer, but *RCA Corporation* v. *Pollard* [1983] Ch. 135 established that a recording company which had an exclusive recording contract with the performer had no such right of action under the legislation. Rights in performances and recordings are now created by CDPA, Pt. II, and infringement is actionable as a breach of statutory duty. This does not rule out actions for interference with contract, but an action for breach of statutory duty would be preferable because an injunction to restrain breach could be obtained without proof of any fault on the part of the defendant, and damages could be awarded unless D could negative negligence: CDPA, s. 182. These provisions will be considered at greater length in Ch. 4.

2. CONTRACTUAL RIGHTS RELATING TO PROPERTY AND SERVICES

Tort Liability of Non-contracting Parties

Here we are dealing with contractual rights *simpliciter*, without any compli-
cating proprietary aspects.[54] To the extent that property is involved, we are
concerned with contractual provisions about the supply and receipt of property rather than with P's interest in the property. In this context, 'interference
with contractual interests' refers broadly to acts which render contractual
rights financially less valuable, profitable, or advantageous, or contractual
obligations financially more onerous. Such interference may come about in a
number of ways, which we will consider separately.

Deliberate Interference

Interference with the Performance of the Plaintiff's Contracting Partner[55]

Two torts are relevant in this context: interference with contract and intimidation. We are concerned with tortious liability for the infliction of economic
loss (damage or the likelihood of damage must be proved in both of these
torts) in a number of different factual situations:

(a) D induces C not to comply with some term or terms of a contract
between C and P (interference with contract by direct persuasion);[56]

(b) D personally disables C from complying with the terms of a contract
between C and P (interference with contract by direct disablement);

(c) D, acting through a third party (for example, by inducing the third
party not to comply with the terms of a contract between C and the
third party, or not to comply with a statutory duty[57]) disables C
from complying with the terms of a contract between C and P (interference with contract by indirect disablement);[58]

---

[54] So equitable principles will not normally play any part in this context because contracts not
involving property are rarely specifically enforceable.

[55] Cf. American Law Institute, *Restatement (Second) of Torts*, s. 776; and see C. E. Carpenter
(1928) 41 *Harvard LR* 728; P. Burns (1980) 58 *Can. BR* 103; D. B. Dobbs (1980) 34 *Ark. LR* 335;
J. Danforth (1981) 81 *Col. LR* 1491; H. S. Perlman (1982) 49 *U of Chicago LR* 61; D. C. Dowling
(1987) *U of Miami LR* 487.

[56] An argument against this form of liability is that the induced party is a free agent, and that
this severs the moral link (and, perhaps, also the causal link in a legal sense) between D's action
and the failure to comply with the contract: Dobbs (1980) 34 *Ark. LR* 335. A distinction is sometimes drawn between inducing or persuading a person not to perform a contract and merely
informing the person of reasons not to perform. But even if this distinction is accepted (see J. D.
Heydon, *Economic Torts*, 2nd edn. (London, 1978), 30–1) it does not meet the point because persuasion could not, at least in many cases, be said to render the contract 'breaker' an unfree agent.
Thus, it is important to find justifications for this form of liability which focus on the nature of
D's conduct as such rather than on the mere fact that it resulted (in a factual sense) in a failure
of contract compliance.

[57] *Associated British Ports* v. *Transport and General Workers' Union* [1989] 1 WLR 939 (CA).

[58] On (a)–(c), see *Merkur Island Shipping Corporation* v. *Laughton* [1983] 2 AC 570, 606–9.

(d) D causes loss to P by making a threat against C (to which C yields) that if C does not fail to comply with some term or terms of a contract between C and P, D will act in a particular way which will cause economic loss to C (for example, D will not comply with the terms of a contract between D and C) (three-party intimidation).[59]

In each case, D may be acting alone or in concert with others: in this context, it is irrelevant whether or not D is part of a conspiracy. The phrase 'failure to comply with some term or terms of a contract' has been used throughout in order to indicate that the action involved need not amount to a breach of contract actionable at the suit of the plaintiff.[60] But it must, for present purposes, amount to a failure to comply with some obligation imposed by a term of an *existing*[61] contract:[62] we are not concerned here with cases which involve no failure to comply with some term or terms of an existing contract to which P is a party.[63]

In all of the situations outlined above, P is given an action in tort in respect of a failure to comply with the terms of a contract against a person who is not a party to the contract. Such actions unsettle contractual principles in a number of ways. First, the tort action may lie even where a contract action would not because the failure to comply with the contract did not amount to an actionable breach. Secondly, the action in tort lies against a party who could not be sued in contract because of lack of privity.[64] Thirdly, the measure of recovery in tort may be more generous than that in contract (because, for example, of more generous remoteness rules) even though the source of P's loss is failure to comply with the contract.

Because of this unsettling effect on contractual principles, and because

---

[59] Concerning two-party intimidation see 000 below.

[60] *Torquay Hotel Ltd* v. *Cousins* [1969] 2 Ch. 106 (contract contained a clause excluding liability for the relevant breach); contrast the apparent position *re* the tort of inducing breach of statutory duty (or breach of an equitable obligation): *Associated British Ports* v. *TGWU* [1989] 1 WLR 939, 952 *per* Neill LJ; 959 *per* Butler-Sloss LJ; 964–5 *per* Stuart-Smith LJ. A common objection to tort liability for interference with contract which is not based on the doing of some unlawful act is that P may still sue the contract 'breaker', so that P's contractual rights have not, in one sense, been interfered with because, adopting the Holmesian view of the nature of contractual rights (M. Howe (ed.), *The Common Law* (Boston, 1963), 233–8), P can still sue for damages. But there may be tort liability even if the contract 'breaker' could not be sued successfully for damages. This shows that the tort is protecting P's financial interest in performance rather than P's financial interest as such. English tort law, at least, does not accept the Holmesian view of the nature of contractual rights.

[61] The contract must, of course, be valid: it would not be actionable to induce e.g. non-performance of an illegal contract.

[62] It is not tortious intentionally to deprive a contracting party of the opportunity to claim a remedy for interference with contract: *Law Debenture Trust Corporation PLC* v. *Ural Caspian Oil Corporation Ltd* [1994] 3 WLR 1221; P. Cane (1995) 111 LQR 400.

[63] So we are not concerned with facts such as those in *Rookes* v. *Barnard* [1964] AC 1129 in which the action taken by C against P was in accordance with the terms of the contract. The case is an example of causing loss by unlawful means (that is, threatening a breach of contract), not of interference with contract.

[64] But the mere possbility of liability for intimidation does not 'outflank' the doctrine of privity: see Treitel, 566.

interference with contracts, even existing contracts, is an almost inevitable concomitant of competition and is a central feature of much industrial action by workers, several conceptual devices are used to restrict the scope of the torts. First, D must have intended to injure P or at least have been reckless as to the possibility of injury. It is not enough that D failed to take reasonable care to prevent injury to P.[65] D must also have known of the existence of the contract and of its relevant terms. But knowledge is judged objectively so that if, for example, it was common knowledge that business of a particular type was conducted on a contractual basis or on particular contractual terms, D would be treated as knowing this.[66] In other words, it may be enough that D was negligent as to the existence of the contract,[67] but not that D was merely negligent in bringing about the failure of compliance with its terms. By contrast, liability for breach of contract is often strict.

The requirement of intention to injure serves another purpose: without it, a defendant might be faced with a very large number of actions brought by unsuccessful competitors or by 'incidental victims' of D's activities such as customers of the employers of striking workers.[68] This fact by itself would not justify the requirement: without it the law could provide more powerful deterrents to the sort of conduct in question.[69] But it reinforces the reasons based on the desirability of preserving competition and not unsettling contractual principles too much.

The second conceptual restriction is that P must prove that financial loss has already been suffered as a result of the interference with contract or that

[65] But see *Millar* v. *Bassey*, *Independent*, 26 Aug. 1993. It must follow that wrongs which can be committed negligently or entirely without fault could not constitute unlawful means for the purposes of these torts. But contrast *Nicholls* v. *Richmond Corporation* [1983] 4 WWR 169.

[66] Salmond, 360; Heydon, *Economic Torts*, n. 56 above, 33–4; but see n. 28 above.

[67] But this statement may be too strong: the main English authorities perhaps only support the proposition that D must have been reckless as to the existence of the relevant contract terms. It is, at all events, clear that an honest and conscious doubt about whether a contract exists will exonerate D: *Smith* v. *Morrison* [1974] 1 WLR 659. The argument against any more stringent requirement than actual knowledge is that if the rule were otherwise ordinary commercial activities and ordinary competition would be unduly restricted. This argument is weakened if the objective standard of knowledge is applied to common business practice. In the context of industrial relations, views on the proper width of liability for interference with contract are a function of views about the proper power balance between capital and labour.

[68] But see *Falconer* v. *ASLEF* [1986] IRLR 331. In 1994 the Prison Officers Association (without admission of liability) paid compensation (totalling £230,000) for wrongful imprisonment to 200 mental patients locked into their rooms for several days as part of an industrial action by prison officers against their employers: *Independent*, 15 Dec. 1994. For the view that intention to injure is not an ingredient of interference with contract see *Associated British Ports* v. *TGWU* [1989] 1 WLR 939, 963F–G, 966F–G *per* Stuart-Smith LJ. The basis of this view is that liability for interference with legally recognized rights is strict. So the rule would also apply to inducing breach of an equitable right (*Prudential Assurance Co. Ltd* v. *Lorenz* (1971) 11 KIR 78), inducing breach of a statutory right (*Associated British Ports* at 963–5 *per* Stuart-Smith LJ), and interference with a private right (Elias and Ewing [1982] *CLJ* 321, 347–51).

[69] As is recognized by s. 235A of the Trade Union and Labour Relations Consolidation Act 1992 (as inserted by s. 22 of the Trade Union Reform and Employment Rights Act 1993) which does not create liability to pay damages but does allow individuals who are incidental victims of unlawful industrial action to obtain an order restraining such action: G. S. Morris [1993] *PL* 595.

it is likely to be suffered in the future. By contrast, in strict theory damage is not the gist of an action for breach of contract: an injunction or nominal damages may be awarded even without proof of financial loss or its likelihood. Thirdly, in situations (c) and (d) above[70] liability will arise only if D's action was independently unlawful: it is only if D directly interferes with the performance of a contract[71] that liability attaches to D's conduct even though the means by which the interference was effected were intrinsically lawful. The meaning of 'unlawful' in this context is a matter of some difficulty and, hence, a source of uncertainty as to the exact scope of the torts. There is authority for the view that an act can constitute unlawful means only if, in addition to being independently unlawful, it is also independently actionable.[72] But there is also authority to the contrary;[73] and any such rule would render tort liability for causing loss by unlawful means largely superfluous.

Conduct otherwise actionable may be justified if D was acting in defence or furtherance of some legitimate interest. Where, as in all the cases we are currently considering, P's interest is in the performance of a contract, a defence of justification would probably fail if D's only interest was the furtherance of D's own commercial well-being.[74] D would probably have to establish that what had been done[75] was done under statutory authority; or to protect some other legal interest of D which was equal or superior to that of P[76] or to protect some public interest; or, possibly, to protect some moral or ethical principle.[77] In other words, intentionally interfering with contracts,

---

[70] J. D. Heydon, *Economic Torts*, 31; *Middlebrook Mushrooms Ltd* v. *Transport and General Workers' Union* [1993] ICR 612; or, on another view, in all situations but the first: W. V. H. Rogers, *Winfield & Jolowicz on Tort*, 14th edn. (London, 1994), 523; *Clerk & Lindsell on Torts*, 16th edn. (London, 1989), 818–9. For a very useful discussion see R. O'Dair (1991) 11 *OJLS* 227, 231–4.

[71] Or directly induces a breach of statutory duty or of an equitable obligation: *Associated British Ports* v. *TGWU* [1989] 1 WLR 939, 959 *per* Butler-Sloss LJ; 963 *per* Stuart-Smith LJ.

[72] *Lonrho Ltd* v. *Shell Petroleum (No. 2)* [1982] AC 173.

[73] *Associated British Ports* v. *TGWU* [1989] 1 WLR 939; *Lonrho PLC* v. *Fayed* [1990] 2 QB 479 (interference with trade); *Daily Mirror Newspapers Ltd* v. *Gardner* [1968] 2 QB 762; *Acrow (Automation) Ltd* v. *Rex Chain Belt Inc.* [1971] 1 WLR 1676; *Brekkes* v. *Cattel* [1972] 1 Ch. 105.

[74] See generally Heydon, *Economic Torts*, 38–47; J. F. Lever 'Means, Motives and Interests in the Law of Torts', in A. G. Guest (ed.), *Oxford Essays in Jurisprudence, Series I* (Oxford, 1961), 64–5.

[75] Should there be a rule that D's action must have been reasonable? See R. O'Dair (1991) 11 *OJLS* 227, 243–5.

[76] In *Edwin Hill & Partners* v. *First National Finance Corporation* [1989] 1 WLR 225 the Court of Appeal held that a mortgagee was justified in entering an arrangement with the mortgagor under which, instead of exercising its power of sale, the mortgagee agreed to redevelopment of the property and, as a condition of redevelopment, required the mortgagor to terminate a contract with the plaintiff architect. Although it was not found as a fact that P's contract post-dated the mortgage, the court seems to have assumed that it did, and so the case appears to establish that D can be justified in interfering with a contract between P and C in order to protect contractual rights which were created before the contract between P and C came into existence. But let us assume that P's contract predated the mortgage and that D knew of it when it entered the arrangement with the mortgagor. It could be argued that a defence of justification should still succeed because D was acting to protect a proprietary interest by interfering with a contractual (and hence legally inferior) interest. To hold otherwise, it might be said, would effectively

even if done by intrinsically lawful means, is a form of unfair competition: if it is done purely to improve one's own competitive or financial position[78] it is actionable. *A fortiori*, it would not be possible to justify interference with contract by unlawful means.[79] This shows that while contractual rights are not as well protected by the law of tort as are property rights, they do receive greater protection than the interest which every person has in accumulating wealth. Contractual rights are legally protected in a way that the 'right to trade and compete' is not.

Because interference with contract is the most common means by which unions and workers can bring pressure to bear on employers against whom they have a grievance, there is a complex set of statutory immunities from actions in tort[80] for interference with contract.[81] The basic aim of the statutory provisions is to preserve what is seen as the right of workers to engage in conduct 'in contemplation or furtherance of a trade dispute'[82] which would otherwise be tortious, in order to preserve and further their legitimate interests as employees. When such legislation was first enacted, the 'trade dispute' formula provided total immunity against tort liability to individuals engaged in industrial action directed towards an economic goal. In recent years, however, this immunity has been considerably reduced.[83] Furthermore, since 1982[84] it has been possible to sue unions to which officials and strikers belong if the officials commit torts outside the scope of the statutory immunities, on the basis that unions are vicariously liable in certain circumstances for the

elevate P's interest to proprietary status. On the other hand, it could be argued that D should have negotiated a release of P's rights. For further discussion see R. O'Dair (1991) 11 *OJLS* 227, 234–243. On the question whether justification could be claimed if D interfered with a contract between P and C in order to protect rights against P created after the contract between P and C but without knowledge of that contract, see S. Gardner (1982) 98 *LQR* 279, 289–92; Treitel, 564–5.

[77] *Brimelow* v. *Casson* [1924] 1 Ch. 302.

[78] Or, *a fortiori*, solely or predominantly to injure another.

[79] On the justification of unlawful means see further 000 below.

[80] However, it appears that courts may be prepared effectively to 'extend' the statutory immunities to other causes of action: *Universe Tankships Inc. of Monrovia* v. *International Transport Workers Federation* [1983] 1 AC 366; see Wedderburn, 650–4. But note that workers involved in industrial action are not (and never have been) immune from liability for breach of their employment contracts: see K. D. Ewing, *The Right to Strike* (Oxford, 1991), esp. ch. 2.

[81] Trade Union and Labour Relations (Consolidation) Act 1992 (TULRCA), s. 219; P. Elias and K. Ewing [1982] *CLJ* 321. Note that the statute distinguishes between breach of and interference with contract. I am using the latter term to include the former.

[82] On the definition of 'trade dispute', see Wedderburn, 553–71.

[83] *Ibid.*, ch. 8; B. Simpson (1991) 54 *MLR* 418. The immunity does not attach to action to enforce trade union membership (TULRCA, s. 222), action taken because of dismissal for taking unofficial action (s. 223), 'secondary action' (s. 224), action designed to exert pressure to recognize a union (s. 225), or action taken without compliance with the statutory provisions concerning strike ballots (s. 226). For the purposes of liability in tort, Crown servants are deemed to be employed under contracts of service: s. 245. The Secretary of State has the power to make codes of practice (s. 203). While non-compliance with a code does not, of itself, render a person 'liable to any proceedings', an Industrial Tribunal must take Code provisions into account when relevant: s. 207.

[84] Employment Act 1982, ss. 14–16. See now TULRCA, ss. 20–23; also Wedderburn, 530–40.

acts of their officials. Both injunctions and damages are available in actions against unions, but awards of damages are limited in some cases. The normal situation in which the statutory immunities become relevant is when an employer seeks to restrain union officials from instructing the members of their union to take industrial action.[85] But the immunities could also provide protection against actions by other workers.[86]

Damage is the gist of the tort of interference with contract. Damages for loss already inflicted are calculated according to tortious, not contractual, principles.[87] The basic aim of damages is to put P in the position he or she would have been in if the contract had not been interfered with. Expenses incurred as a result of the interference are recoverable,[88] as are damages for consequential non-pecuniary loss.[89] It is unclear whether exemplary damages would ever be available.[90] The main head of damages will usually be loss of profit.[91] The rules of remoteness in tort may be different from those in contract. In particular, while the basic rule in contract is that losses are recoverable if they were in the reasonable contemplation of the parties at the time the contract was made, it is unclear what the rule of remoteness is in torts involving the intentional infliction of economic loss. The possibilities are that only intended damage is recoverable, or that damage foreseeable at the date of the tort is recoverable, or that damage directly attributable to the tort is recoverable even if unforeseeable. On the analogy of deceit,[92] the last may be the correct rule. Thus, the quantum of damages in tort may be greater than that in contract. This illustrates a more general point, namely that the term 'financial interest' has a legal definition (or, perhaps more accurately, a number of legal definitions) in addition to the less formal definition given in

[85] Despite curtailment of the statutory immunities, employers remain quite unwilling to use the law to deal with industrial disputes. During the miners' strike of 1984–5 neither the National Coal Board nor its major customers made much use of the courts: such litigation as there was emanated from small firms and working miners. This suggests that even if unions and union officials did not enjoy statutory immunities, tort law might still not be an important factor in industrial relations. See generally R. Benedictus [1985] *ILJ* 176; S. Evans (1983) 12 *ILJ* 129 and 'Picketing under the Employment Acts' in P. Fosh and C. R. Littler (eds), *Industrial Relations and the Law in the 1980's* (London, 1985); S. Auerbach (1988) 17 *ILJ* 227.

[86] *Thomas* v. *National Union of Mineworkers* [1986] Ch. 60.

[87] Heydon, *Economic Torts*, 36.

[88] *BMTA* v. *Salvadori* [1949] Ch. 556. Concerning expenses incurred in anticipation of the interference, see 156, n. 36 below.

[89] *Pratt* v. *British Medical Association* [1919] 1 KB 244, 281–2; *GWK Ltd* v. *Dunlop Rubber Co. Ltd* (1946) 42 TLR 376. In *Thomas* v. *National Union of Mineworkers (South Wales Area* [1986] Ch. 20 Scott J invented a new tort of harassment to justify restraining pickets from harassing workers (that is, causing them non-pecuniary loss) on their way to work. Although the existence of this tort was doubted by Stuart-Smith J in *News Group Newspapers Ltd* v. *SOGAT '82* [1987] ICR 181, 205–6, harassment as a form of compensatable damage has received recent support: *Khorasandjian* v. *Bush* [1993] QB 727.

[90] See 302 below.

[91] In the United States, restitutionary damages for profits made by D by interfering with the contract are recoverable: *Federal Sugar Refining Co.* v. *US Sugar Equalization Board Inc.* (1920) 268 F 575.

[92] *Doyle* v. *Olby (Ironmongers) Ltd* [1969] 2 QB 158.

Chapter 1. The legal nature of a person's financial interest in a particular situation depends on the legal causes of action available to protect the person's financial interest (in the non-legal sense).[93]

Injunctions may be awarded to restrain interference with contracts[94] and, presumably, to restrain intimidation. The basis of the award of injunctions is, no doubt, that the legal rights[95] of the plaintiff are threatened, albeit indirectly, by the actions of the defendant.

It might be thought suprising that in an economy based on competition there should ever be legal liability for inflicting economic loss by intrinsically lawful means in the course of commercial competitive activity. The explanation perhaps lies in the distinction between existing contractual rights and mere contractual expectancies: it could be argued that, while it is contrary to the whole notion of competition to impose liability for depriving someone of a mere hope of entering into advantageous financial arrangements, it is not inimical to fair competition to require traders to respect the existing rights to financial benefit which their competitors have secured by their own efforts, because the whole basis of the modern competitive economy is the possibility of stable contractual arrangements.[96] Put another way, in terms of fair competition, contractual rights rank more highly than the 'right' to trade and compete. The law of tort is, to this extent, prepared to protect contractual rights.

There is also a puzzle why, in competitive contexts, the law of tort is ever prepared to give A a tort action (other than one based on an independent tort which constitutes 'unlawful means') against B in respect of a failure by C to perform a contract in a case where A could, in theory at least, sue C for breach of contract.[97] Furthermore, it is not necessarily morally objectionable to persuade someone to withdraw from a contract: the contract may itself be morally objectionable.[98] The mystery deepens when it is recalled that the damages awarded in a tort action against the interferer may be greater than

[93] See 8 above.

[94] But a final injunction would, presumably, only issue if damages would not be an adequate remedy, since damage is the gist of the tort. An injunction would usually not be awarded when it would compel the performance by the induced party of a contract of a sort which would not normally be specifically enforced against the contracting party in a contract action: *Warren v. Mendy* [1989] 1 WLR 853. Actions arising out of labour disputes rarely proceed beyond the stage of an interlocutory injunction; actions for damages are extremely rare: R. Lewis and B. Simpson, *Striking a Balance* (London, 1981), 212ff; Wedderburn, 684–705.

[95] Some writers say that the tort of interference with contract treats contractual rights as a form of property: C. E. Carpenter (1924) 41 *Harvard LR* 718, 742; D. C. Dowling (1987) 40 *U of Miami LR* 487, 505; D. B. Dobbs (1980) 34 *Ark. LR* 335, 351–4; D. Friedmann (1980) 80 *Col. LR* 540, 515, n. 54. This is clearly incorrect in a legal sense: actionability *per se* and strict liability, which are central features of tortious protection of property rights, are not a feature of the torts which protect contracts from interference.

[96] J. Danforth (1981) 81 *Col. LR* 1491.

[97] Dowling argues that it should be easier to establish tort liability for interference with contractual expectancies than with contractual rights because in relation to the latter there will, in theory, always be the possibility of contractual liability: (1987) 40 *U of Miami LR* 487, 513.

[98] Dobbs (1980) 43 *Ark. LR* 335, 343.

could be awarded in contract against the contracting party. The answer, in competitive contexts, must be that there is a public interest not just that contracts be kept but also that competition be preserved by providing remedies against unfair (or 'anti') competitive practices. A trader is entitled to have views about the morality of the conduct of competitors; but provided competitors do not act unlawfully, the trader should not give effect to those views about their behaviour by interfering with their contracts. Freedom to contract embraces the freedom to contract 'immorally'. Competition, like all forms of liberty, paradoxically requires restraint on the part of all those exercising it in order to flourish. Of course, the law of tort plays only a very minor role in the preservation of competition: legislation concerning monopolies, mergers, and restrictive trade practices is, in practice, much more important. Some aspects of such legislation will be examined in Chapter 4.

The rationale for third party liability in the industrial relations context is quite different. Employers and workers are not in (direct) competition,[99] and the interests which workers seek to further by inflicting economic loss on their employers and by damaging the competitive position of their employers *vis-à-vis* other traders often go beyond their own immediate financial interests. So the statutory immunities from tortious liability for interference with contract (which is the only ground of liability to which they apply) operate whether the means used were unlawful or not. The narrowing of the statutory immunities in the 1980s was the product of a fundamental change of view about the relative strengths of workers and employers, and about the importance of affording workers some coercive tools with which to counteract the power which attaches to the ownership of capital and of industrial property, both tangible and intangible.

Interference with the Plaintiff's Performance

In this section we are concerned with actions of the defendant which interfere with the plaintiff's performance of some obligation or obligations under a contract between P and a third party, or which make it more expensive for P to perform obligations under such a contract. An example of the latter is *Dimbleby & Sons Ltd* v. *National Union of Journalists*[100] in which, as a result of a strike by journalists, it cost P more than it otherwise would have to provide copy to meet contracts with its printers.

In the former type of case, P may suffer economic loss in two ways: P may be liable to the third party for breach of contract, and P may lose the benefit of the consideration given for contractual undertakings. An example of this type of case is 'two-party intimidation', in which D makes a threat against P (to which P yields) that if P does not fail to comply with the terms of a

---

[99] But unionized and non-unionized workers are in competition in the job market, and the unlawfulness of industrial action taken to enforce a closed shop can be seen as designed to foster maximum competition in the labour market.

[100] [1984] 1 WLR 67 (CA; affirmed [1984] 1 WLR 427).

contract between himself and C, D will act in a way detrimental to P.[101] The damage to P may be the direct result of D's own actions, or it may be brought about by D indirectly through a third party.

Again, the basic rule applicable to such cases is that there can be no tort liability without proof of intention to injure; and, at least in cases where the interference was indirect, P would have to establish that unlawful means had been used. But tort actions in such cases do not unsettle contractual principles: P is not suing D in respect of a failure by another to comply with a contract, but rather in respect of P's own contractual performance or lack of it. Therefore, the main justifications for the requirement of intention in this context must be the desire not to inhibit competition or workers' industrial action unduly,[102] and the desire not to precipitate a multiplicity of actions.

Incidental Interference

Here we are concerned with conduct which is not designed to interfere with contractual rights but which incidentally (and unintentionally) does so. Suppose, for example, that an insurer, in breach of contract, refuses to pay a claim made under a fire policy because an investigator employed by the insurer wrongly certifies that the fire was caused in a way which entitles the insurer to refuse to meet the claim.[103] The basic rule is that there can be no liability for unintentional interference with contract, so that if the investigator's mistake was the result of negligence alone, the insured would have no right of action against the investigator.

Damage to Property of a Third Party

The basic rule of no liability for incidental interference with contractual rights has been most often invoked in cases where P's contractual rights are rendered less valuable or P's contractual obligations more onerous as a result of damage to the property of a third party caused by D's negligence. In *Cattle* v. *Stockton Waterworks Co.*[104] it was held that D could not be liable for tortiously damaging the land of a third party for whom P had contracted to do some work with the result that it became more expensive for P to perform the contract. In the course of delivering the judgment of the Court, Blackburn J gave the famous example of a mine flooded by a tortious act: to allow an action in the present case would be to establish a principle which would entitle not only the owner of the mine to sue but also the workers, and not just for damage to their tools and clothes but also for loss of wages.[105] In *Spartan*

---

[101] Of course, C might also be able to sue D for inducing breach of contract, but here we are assuming that the loss resulting from P's failure of compliance is suffered by P.

[102] Wedderburn, 614–7.   [103] S. Todd (1992) 108 *LQR* 360.

[104] (1875) LR 10 QB 453. See also *Simpson & Co.* v. *Thomson* (1877) 3 App. Cas. 279, 289–90 *per* Lord Penzance; cf. *Société Anonyme de Remorquage à Hélice* v. *Bennetts* [1911] 1 KB 243.

[105] Cf. *Adams* v. *Southern Pacific Transport Co.* (1975) 50 Cal. App.(3d) 37; *Stevenson* v. *East Ohio Gas Co.* (1946) 73 NE2d 200, 203–4 *per* Morgan J.

Steel & Alloys Ltd v. *Martin & Co. (Contractors) Ltd*[106] a majority of the Court of Appeal held that where a person negligently damages property of a third party, and as a result causes damage to the plaintiff, P may recover only to the extent that the loss consists of physical damage or economic loss causally consequential upon such damage; there can be no recovery for economic loss consisting of the increased cost of complying with existing contracts, or for loss of profits on existing contracts, or for of loss of income on anticipated contracts.

Despite a dissent on the part of Edmund Davies LJ and an expression of doubt as to the correctness of the majority decision in *Spartan Steel* on the part of Lord Roskill in *Junior Books Ltd* v. *Veitchi Co. Ltd*,[107] the rule that there can be no liability in tort for purely economic loss (that is, loss not consequential upon physical damage to the person or property of the plaintiff) resulting from negligently caused physical damage to the property of a third party is firmly entrenched in the law.[108] In *Candlewood Navigation Corporation Ltd* v. *Mitsui OSK Lines Ltd*[109] the Privy Council held that the time charterer of a ship (who has only a contractual and not a possessory interest in it) could not recover for loss of profits suffered as a result of the ship having been damaged by the defendant's negligence and, thus, being unable to trade while it was undergoing repair.

Many of the cases involving physical damage to property owned by third parties concern the cutting-off of essential services such as gas or electricity, or damage to strategic facilities such as bridges. In such cases the courts are afraid that to allow an action in one case would lead to a flood of claims, many of which might be for small amounts of damages but which, in aggregate, would impose a heavy burden of liability on the defendant. There is Australian[110] and Canadian[111] authority for allowing recovery for economic loss[112] consequent upon damage to the property of a third party if the

---

[106] [1973] QB 27; applied in *Muirhead* v. *Industrial Tank Specialities Ltd* [1986] QB 507. See also *Shell & BP South African Petroleum Refineries (Pty) Ltd* v. *Osborne Panama SA* (1980) 3 SALR 653, aff'd (1982) 4 SALR 890.

[107] [1983] 1 AC 520, 547; see P. Cane, 'Economic Loss and Products Liability' in C. J. Miller (ed.), *Comparative Product Liability* (London, 1986), 48–52.

[108] It is sometimes suggested that there is an exception to this rule in cases where P and the third party are engaged in a 'joint venture', that is, a contractual arrangement involving profit sharing; R. Hayes (1979) 12 *Melb. ULR* 79, 108–13; but see P. Cane (1980) 12 *Melb. ULR* 408, 412–3, and *Wimpey Construction (UK) Ltd* v. *Martin Black & Co. (Wire Ropes) Ltd* [1982] SLT 239. A further extension of the joint venture idea is to cases in which a ship or lorry owner and an owner of cargo or goods being carried on it have a community of interest in the state of the vessel or lorry; on which see 116 above.

[109] [1986] AC 1.

[110] *Caltex Oil (Australia) Pty Ltd* v. *The Dredge 'Willemstad'* (1976) 136 CLR 529; cf. *New Zealand Forest Products Ltd* v. *A-G.* [1986] 1 NZLR 14. In fact, in *Spartan Steel* itself the damaged cable supplied only P's factory, and D knew this.

[111] *Norsk Pacific SS Co. Ltd* v. *Canadian National Railway Co.* (1992) 91 DLR (4th) 289.

[112] In the *Willemstad* case the loss consisted of the increased cost of performing existing contracts. There are dicta in two of the judgments which suggest that loss of expected profits on existing contracts would not be recoverable; but the distinction between additional cost actually

number of persons directly affected is small; but this authority has not found favour in England, perhaps on the basis that people ought to protect their financial interests in the property of others by making suitable contractual arrangements with the property owner.

Nuisance

A head of liability under which there can, contrary to the basic principle, be recovery for unintentional interference with contractual interests is nuisance.[113] In private nuisance, the requirement that the plaintiff have a proprietary interest in the affected land, and the necessarily localized nature of private nuisance, obviate the danger of a large number of claims. Furthermore, the requirement that the plaintiff have an interest in the land enables it to be said that what is being protected is a property interest, even in cases where the nub of P's complaint is interference with contractual rights.

More problematic is public nuisance: unintentional obstruction of a highway or a public waterway may amount to a public nuisance,[114] and it is quite clear that economic loss consequent on a public nuisance can be recovered by a person who has suffered special damage.[115] The fact that a nuisance made it more expensive for P to perform existing contracts, or disabled P from doing so, could amount to special damage. There is no limitation device built into the tort of public nuisance which would necessarily prevent a large number of claims being brought as a result of something directly analogous to the cutting-off of an essential service or the damaging of a bridge,[116] and yet this has not, so far, been seen as a reason to deny liability in this sort of case. The right interfered with by a public nuisance is a public right; the claim for damages is a derivative one, based on the injury suffered. Public nuisance constitutes a straightforward exception to the principle of no liability for unintentional interference with contractual rights. It is not clear how, if at all, this exception can be justified.

---

incurred and profits not made seems fortuitous: see Hayes (1979) 12 *Melb. ULR* 79 and Cane (1980) 12 *MULR* 408. The judges did not discuss the loss of future contracts.

[113] e.g. *Campbell* v. *Paddington Corporation* [1911] 1 KB 869. It should be noted that this case (which is an example of direct disablement of the plaintiff) allows recovery for interference with contractual expectancies as well as with existing contractual rights.

[114] Liability in this form of public nuisance depends on proof of fault, at least in the sense of foreseeability of damage: *Overseas Tankship (UK) Ltd* v. *Miller Steamship Co. Pty Ltd* [1967] 1 AC 617, 639 *per* Lord Reid. Liability for oil pollution is considered in greater detail in Ch. 9.

[115] *Tate & Lyle Food Distribution Ltd* v. *Greater London Council* [1983] 2 AC 509: the House of Lords held both that D was not liable in negligence because the loss was purely economic, and that D was liable in public nuisance. The anomaly was disguised because there was only one plaintiff who was obviously affected much more than anyone else. See also G. H. L. Fridman (1951) 2 *WA Ann. LR* 490; G. Kodilinye (1986) 6 *LS* 182.

[116] 'Special damage' means damage over and above that which constitutes the nuisance. Thus, the notion of special damage might limit recovery to those who suffer 'significant amounts' (however defined) of economic loss. But such persons might, nevertheless, constitute a large group. For a statement of the view that nuisance liability would be much more restricted than I suggest, see (1974) 88 *Harvard LR* 444.

The use of the law of nuisance in industrial relations contexts deserves special attention. There is a statutory immunity from action arising out of picketing at a worker's own place of work for the purpose of peaceful persuasion or communication of information.[117] Picketing which does not fall within this immunity may be actionable as a public or a private nuisance. In *Thomas* v. *National Union of Mineworkers*[118] Scott J also invented a new tort of harassment of workers by picketers. These torts can be used to protect interests in the due performance of contracts. The test of liability is not whether D intended to injure P but whether D's conduct was unreasonable (in the light of the interests of the parties) and resulted in economic loss to P. Because the two nuisance torts protect property rights (whether in private or public property), the balance of this calculation is, from the start, adjusted in favour of P. It is noteworthy that under these heads individuals engaged in industrial action may be liable in tort even in the absence of proof that they intended to inflict economic loss on the plaintiff.

Tort Liability of Contracting Parties

The Principle of Concurrency of Causes of Action

In the last section we were concerned with tort liability in respect of conduct which interferes with the performance of a contract to which P is a party but which does not consist of a failure by D to comply with the terms of *that* contract, and which may not consist in failure to comply with the terms of *any* contract. In this section we are concerned with tort liability arising out of failure by D to perform, either properly (misfeasance) or at all (nonfeasance), some term of a contract between D and P. In other words, we are considering situations in which the P may be entitled to sue D in tort instead of suing D in contract.

A person who could claim against D in contract will want to claim against D in tort instead only if thereby some benefit can be secured or some restriction on liability in contract can be avoided. It is often seen as a danger of permitting concurrent actions that, by allowing breaches of contract to be treated as torts, the law will license the evasion and subversion of rules of contract law.[119] This way of approaching concurrent liability assumes a particular relationship between tort and contract liability in which contract is primary and tort is secondary. This approach will be examined further in Chapter 6.

---

[117] TULRCA, s. 220; Wedderburn, 540–53. There is also a government Code on Picketing (SI 476/1992) which advises that normally no more than six workers at a time should mount a picket.

[118] [1986] Ch. 20; see 123 above.

[119] e.g. *Société Commerciale de Réassurance* v. *ERAS (International) Ltd* [1992] 2 All ER 82, 85.

The basic rule of English law is that if, on the facts of the case, the plaintiff can establish that a tort has been committed, P may sue in tort even though, on those facts, P could also establish a breach of contract.[120] The plaintiff is said to have concurrent rights of action in tort and contract. The most important application of this principle of concurrency of causes of action is in relation to breaches of contractual duties of care which also constitute tortious negligence. There is, in theory at least, another type of case in which a breach of contract might also be actionable as a tort: if breach of contract can constitute unlawful means for the purposes of the tort of causing loss by unlawful means, an intentional breach of contract might be actionable in tort.[121] A threat by D not to comply with a contract with P unless P acts to his or her own detriment is certainly actionable as intimidation, which is a form of causing loss by unlawful means. There seems no logical reason why actually breaching a contract should not constitute unlawful means.[122] If this is so, then at least some[123] intentional breaches of contract might be actionable as torts.

In general terms, a person is unlikely to be able to sue in tort in respect of 'contractual nonfeasance', such as failure to perform a contractual obligation at all; or failure to perform it on time;[124] or failure to deliver the correct quantity of goods or goods of the correct description; and this would be so even if it could be proved that the breach of contract was the result of negligence. In such cases, the unwillingness of the law of tort to compensate for nonfeasance is likely to be called in aid to justify refusing an action. Of course, the distinction between nonfeasance and misfeasance is a notoriously fuzzy one, and there is no intrinsic reason why failure to supply the correct quantity of goods, for example, should not be treated as misfeasance. The law of tort is often prepared to allow actions in respect of nonfeasance if it can be said that the defendant was under a positive duty to take action; and a contractual duty to deliver a particular quantity of goods could be treated as the source of such a positive duty.[125] But the fear of turning every breach of contract into a tort is likely to lead courts to take the position that breaches of contract such as those mentioned above are not actionable in tort.

---

[120] *Henderson* v. *Merrett Syndicates Ltd* [1994] 3 WLR 761; C. French (1982) 5 *Otago LR* 236; W. D. C. Poulton (1966) 82 *LQR* 346; J. A. Weir, *International Encyclopedia of Comparative Law* (The Hague, 1976), xi, ch. 12; G. H. L. Fridman (1977) 93 *LQR* 422; P. Cane, 'Contract, Tort and Economic Loss', in M. Furmston (ed.), *The Law of Tort* (London, 1986).

[121] See further 132 below.   [122] But see 124–5 above.

[123] But not all intentional breaches of contract are torts: see *Perera* v. *Vandiyar* [1953] 1 WLR 672, discussed below; but note that this case predates *Rookes* v. *Barnard* [1964] AC 1129 which established that breaches of contract can constitute unlawful means for the purposes of tort liability.

[124] *The Albazero* [1977] AC 774, 846–7 *per* Lord Diplock.

[125] e.g. *Stansbie* v. *Troman* [1948] 2 KB 48; but contrast *Quinn* v. *Burch Bros* [1966] 2 QB 370.

Furthermore, even cases of contractual 'misfeasance' are not necessarily actionable in tort.[126]

However, having said that not all breaches of contract will be actionable in tort, and having given examples of breaches of contract which would probably not be actionable in tort, it is much more difficult to lay down any general principle which would enable us to predict whether particular breaches of contract would be held actionable in tort or not. One suggestion is that obligations to achieve a contractually specified result, which there was no duty to achieve apart from the contract, would only be actionable in contract;[127] but if the breach of contract consists in the bad performance of skilled services (that is, misfeasance), then it would normally be actionable in tort.[128] What this seems to mean is that, if the contractual obligation is one to take reasonable care to achieve a particular result, a concurrent action in tort for negligence could lie. But if the contractual standard of liability is strict because, as a matter of interpretation, the defendant warranted that the particular result would be achieved, no concurrent action in tort for negligence would lie.[129]

While such a distinction between duties to achieve results and duties to take care to achieve results would be relatively straightforward to apply, its logic is by no means clear. First, in one respect it is question-begging: the law of tort does not normally impose strict liability (at least in name)[130] in respect of the supply of goods[131] or services, so that any duty to achieve a particular result will, as such, only normally be actionable in contract.[132] But this does not tell us why negligence in failing to achieve that result should not be actionable independently in tort. Secondly, it is not clear why some contractual duties (for example, those of a seller of goods under the implied warranties of quality in the Sale of Goods Act 1978) are strict, while others (for example, the implied terms as to the quality of services under the Supply of Goods and Services Act 1982) are duties of reasonable care. There is no obvious reason why suppliers of goods should not be liable only for negligence, or why the suppliers of services should not be required to take the risk that their 'product' will fall short of the required standard.

Thirdly, it is clear that, in some cases at least,[133] non-contracting parties

---

[126] e.g. *Perera* v. *Vandiyar* [1953] 1 WLR 672.

[127] For a historical justification of this approach, see V. Palmer (1983) 27 *Am. JLH* 85.

[128] B. Morgan (1980) 58 *Can. BR* 299, 307–8.

[129] What if liability was, in a particular case, strict as a matter of tort law, but liability under the contract was only for negligence? Here there would clearly be an argument, on traditional assumptions about the relationship between tort and contract, for not allowing a concurrent tort action, as is the rule in German law, on the basis of a general principle that concurrent tort liability should be no more onerous than that imposed by the contract.

[130] The doctrine of *res ipsa loquitur* can be used effectively to impose strict liability.

[131] But note Consumer Protection Act 1987, Pt. I to the extent that it imposes strict liability for defective products.

[132] Concerning the standard of liability in contract see Treitel 737–40, esp. 739–40 *re* services.

[133] But not others; e.g. late delivery: *Bart* v. *British West Indian Airlines Ltd* [1967] Lloyd's Rep. 239; *BDC Ltd* v. *Hofstrand Farms Ltd* (1986) 26 DLR(4th) 1.

can sue in tort for negligence in the performance of strict contractual duties: the essence of *Donoghue* v. *Stevenson*[134] is that it enables a third party to sue a manufacturer in tort for negligence in respect of the supply of defective goods for which, if sued in contract, the manufacturer could be held liable to a purchaser without proof of fault. In one respect, of course, having to sue in tort rather than contract is disadvantageous: the plaintiff in a tort action will usually have to prove fault.[135] But in other respects, as we shall see, tort is sometimes more advantageous to the plaintiff than contract, and it is not clear why a third party should be able to take these advantages while a contracting party cannot. It would surely be extraordinary if a third party could sue in tort in respect of negligent supply of defective goods but a contracting party could not do so in similar circumstances. If the third party deserves the protection of tort law, then so does a contracting party if that protection is greater than contract law gives. Once it is conceded that concurrent actions are sometimes properly available, it simply restates the issue to answer that the contracting party should not be allowed to sue in tort by virtue of also having a right of action in contract.

Nor is the relevance of the distinction between the two types of duty obvious in the case of tort liability for deliberate breach of contract. If, for example, breaching a contract is used as a form of pressure to coerce the other party into acting to his or her detriment, there is an argument for saying that P ought to be entitled to recover in contract the loss flowing from the breach, and in tort[136] the loss flowing from the detrimental action which P was pressured into taking, regardless of the nature of the contractual term breached.[137] The defendant in such a case has committed two wrongs: breach of contract and intentionally using unlawful pressure to cause a person to act to his or her detriment. In such a case, P ought to be entitled to remedies in respect of both wrongs. In such a case, too, an action in tort in respect of loss intentionally caused by non-compliance with a contract is different from an action in the tort of negligence in respect of breach of a contractual duty of care. In the latter case, although the defendant has technically committed two wrongs they are, in effect, only one; and the choice between tort and contract actions is a choice between the more and the less advantageous way of seeking a remedy for that wrong. But in the former case, there are two distinct wrongs which may have inflicted two distinct lots of damage. We may conclude that if the loss caused to the plaintiff by a deliberate breach of contract would have been suffered even if the breach had not been deliberate, then the distinction between breaches of contract which are actionable in tort and

[134] [1932] AC 562.

[135] Although by virtue of the operation of the doctrine of *res ipsa loquitur*, less often in actions in respect of defective goods than in many other cases. The current discussion must, of course, be read subject to Pt. I of the Consumer Protection Act 1987.

[136] But the tort analysis may be unnecessary: *both* losses might satisfy the contractual rules of remoteness.

[137] On this see further 154–5 below.

breaches which are not will be as relevant here as in the case of negligent breaches.

Finally, we should note that rights of action in tort concurrent with a right of action in contract may be created by statute. It is a breach of statutory duty for a local authority to interfere with the selection of subcontractors under a contract or to terminate a contract on 'non-commercial grounds'.[138] Such breach is actionable at the suit of any person who suffers loss or damage as a result. It is also a breach of statutory duty for a person to terminate a contract for the supply of goods or services on 'union membership grounds'. The duty is owed to the other contracting party and to any other person 'adversely affected'.[139] If 'termination' in these provisions includes breach of contract, to that extent they create a form of concurrent liability in contract and tort so far as the other contracting party is concerned.

Dismissal of an employee on grounds related to union membership or activities is deemed to be unfair for the purposes of the employment protection legislation;[140] and compensation can be awarded not only against the employer but also against third parties who put pressure on the employer to dismiss the employee.[141] An employee who is dismissed in breach of the Sex Discrimination Act 1975 or the Race Relations Act 1976 has a cause of action under the legislation independently of any claim for breach of contract or unfair dismissal.[142] The legislation also makes it unlawful, *inter alia*, for an employer to dismiss an employee for making a claim against the employer under it; and it has been suggested that there may be a principle of public policy which would support tort liability in other contexts for dismissal on the ground that the employee sued the employer.[143] Breach of contracts other than employment contracts might also constitute a breach of various provisions of the anti-discrimination legislation, and so might be independently actionable.

Practical Ramifications of the Concurrency Principle

The practical importance of whether an tort action for negligence is available concurrently with a contract action lies in the differences between tort liability and contract liability.[144] The most important of these differences are as follows:

[138] Local Government Act 1988, ss. 17 and 19.

[139] Trade Union and Labour Relations (Consolidation) Act 1992, s. 145. Apparently as a result of a drafting error, termination is not mentioned in s. 187 concerning refusal to deal on union recognition grounds. Under s. 146, action short of dismissal taken against an employee on grounds related to union membership or activities can also give grounds for complaint (and a right to compensation: s. 149) not only against the employer but also against third parties who put pressure on the employer to take the action (s. 150).

[140] Trade Union and Labour Relations (Consolidation) Act 1992, s. 152.

[141] *Ibid.*, s. 160.   [142] On discrimination law generally see further 000–000 below.

[143] G. Pitt (1989) 52 *MLR* 22, 32–4; on tort liabiity for contempt of court see further 000 below.

[144] In respect of contribution between wrongdoers, it now makes no difference whether D is sued in tort or contract: Civil Liability (Contribution) Act 1978, s. 6(1).

Limitation of Actions

The limitation period for an action in contract begins to run from the date of breach whereas in tort actions the basic rule is that the period begins to run from the date the damage (which forms the gist of the action)[145] occurs.[146] There are some statutory departures from the basic rules. In product liability actions under Part I of the Consumer Protection Act 1987 in respect of property damage, the period begins to run from the date the damage first becomes reasonably discoverable.[147] In actions under the Defective Premises Act 1972 the limitation period begins to run from the date of completion of the relevant work. In 'actions for damages for negligence' other than actions in respect of personal injuries, the period begins to run either from the date the damage occurs or from the date the damage becomes discoverable, whichever is the later.[148] It has been held that the phrase 'actions for damages for negligence' does not include actions for breach of a contractual duty of care.[149]

The basis for the difference between the starting date of the basic period of limitation in contract (which relates to the breach) and that in tort (which relates to the damage) is said to be that damage is the gist of an action in negligence but not of an action for breach of contract. This is a relatively weak justification because, in general, if no loss has been suffered as a result of a breach of contract, substantial damages will not be recoverable;[150] it does, however, serve to emphasize the point that liability for breach of contract is liability for interference with rights rather than simply liability for the infliction of damage.

In practical terms, this difference in the starting date of the limitation period is of great importance and has generated a considerable amount of litigation, much of it concerned with the question of when damage occurs in cases where the damage remains undiscoverable for some time after it occurs. This particular issue is now dealt with in the Latent Damage Act 1986 which provides that in cases of damage (other than personal injury) which was undiscoverable at the date it occurred, the limitation period runs either for six years from the date the damage occurred or for three years from the date when the damage became reasonably discoverable, whichever is the later; and in the Consumer Protection Act 1987, which deems property damage caused

---

[145] J. Stapleton (1988) 104 *LQR* 213 and 389.

[146] The period is 6 years, except in actions under Pt. I of the Consumer Protection Act 1987, where it is 3 years for all claims.

[147] Consumer Protection Act 1987, s. 5(5).

[148] Latent Damage Act 1986, s. 1 (inserting new ss. 14A and 14B into the Limitation Act 1980).

[149] *Société Commerciale de Réassurance* v. *ERAS (International) Ltd* [1992] 2 All ER 82. This result can be supported in two ways: first, the problem which the Act was designed to overcome was generated by the tort rule that time does not begin to run until damage occurs, not by the contract rule; secondly, current judicial ideology favours keeping contract and tort quite distinct: see further 482 below.

[150] Cf. conversely *Moore* v. *Ferrier* [1988] 1 WLR 267, 280E–F *per* Bingham LJ.

by defective products to occur when it becomes discoverable. As already noted, the provisions in the Latent Damage Act do not apply to actions for breach of contract, and this represents a very important practical difference between actions in tort and actions in contract: it makes tort even more attractive in cases of latent damage than it often is in cases of damage which is obvious as soon as it occurs.

Of particular relevance for our purposes are cases concerning purely economic loss. Suppose, for example, that a solicitor drafts a document which is defective in the sense that it will not achieve its desired legal effect; does the client suffer economic loss at the date the defective document comes into force or only at some later date when the client tries to rely on it or enforce it? In *Moore & Co. Ltd* v. *Ferrier*[151] the Court of Appeal held that it was a question of fact in every case when damage occurred; and that, on the facts of the case, the plaintiff had suffered economic loss when it received an ineffective covenant in restraint of trade drafted by the defendant solicitor and before it actually tried to enforce the covenant against the other contracting party. Similarly, it has been held that an insured suffers loss upon entering a voidable (re)insurance policy even though the insurer does not discover the grounds of voidability until some time later.[152] However, negligent professional advice or services will not always produce immediate financial damage; for example, the negligent drafting of a will causes immediate financial damage neither to the testator nor to beneficiaries.[153] If a valuer negligently overvalues property, a mortgagee suffers no loss at the date of the advance but only when, and if, it fails to recoup its investment.[154] More problematically, it has been held that where, as a result of a solicitor's negligence, a cause of action is struck out, the plaintiff suffers no loss until the date of the striking out even if the cause of action has been materially reduced in value prior to that date by reason of there being a real risk of its being struck out.[155]

A distinction needs to be drawn between purely economic loss consisting of the difference between the value of something acquired or received and what was paid for it on the one hand, and economic loss consequential upon such loss on the other. Loss of the former type will often be suffered at the date of acquisition or receipt,[156] while consequential loss may only be suffered some time later.[157] Of course, it may not always be easy to quantify the

---

[151] [1988] 1 WLR 267; cf. *Forster* v. *Outred* [1982] 1 WLR 86; *Bell* v. *Peter Browne & Co.* [1990] 2 QB 495. But see *UBAF Ltd* v. *European American Banking Corporation* [1984] QB 713.

[152] *Iron Trade Mutual Insurance Co. Ltd* v. *J. K. Buckenham Ltd* [1990] 1 All ER 808; *Islander Trucking Ltd (in liq.)* v. *Hogg Robinson & Gardner Mountain (Marine) Ltd* [1990] 1 All ER 826.

[153] J. M. T. (1982) 98 *LQR* 514, 515.

[154] *First National Commercial Bank PLC* v. *Humberts* [1995] *New LJ* 345.

[155] *Hopkins* v. *MacKenzie, The Times*, 3 Nov. 1994. The Court of Appeal held that until the date of striking out the plaintiff's loss was only potential, not actual. But the same could be said in relation to *Moore* v. *Ferrier*, for instance.

[156] For the implications of this in the building context see R. O'Dair (1992) 55 *MLR* 405.

[157] This distinction was crucial in *First National Commercial Bank* v. *Humberts* [1995] *New LJ* 345.

loss suffered by receiving a worthless asset: in the case of an ineffective covenant in restraint of trade the loss, if calculated at the time the covenant was received, would consist of the value of the chance that the covenantor would not comply with the covenant in the future; and this would, in turn depend on a number of imponderable factors.[158] In practical terms, however, the importance of the fact that damage occurs at the date of acquisition is often not so much that it enables the plaintiff to bring an action at that date, but that it starts the basic limitation period running.

In many cases involving defective documents the damage will be latent; and having employed an apparently competent lawyer to draft the document, the defect would not normally be reasonably discoverable until reliance on it was actually challenged.[159] So the practical importance of the *Moore* v. *Ferrier* approach may not be great given the provisions of the Latent Damage Act.

Contributory Negligence

If a negligent breach of contract also amounts to a tort, the defendant may have the damages reduced on account of contributory negligence by the plaintiff.[160] This means that in any case where P has a choice between an action for breach of a contractual duty of care and an action in negligence, contributory negligence will be an available defence regardless of the cause of action chosen.[161]

Assessment of Damages

Heads of Damage   There are differences between tort and contract in terms of heads of recoverable damage. First, the basic rule in contract is that damages for mental distress,[162] hassle, and inconvenience can be recovered only if the aim of the contract was to secure freedom from such non-pecuniary damage[163] or to provide positive non-pecuniary benefits such as enjoyment;[164] or if they are 'directly related to physical inconvenience and discomfort resulting from the breach of contract'.[165] In tort, on the other hand, it is at least arguable that damages for non-pecuniary loss (other than nervous shock in the technical sense) can always be recovered if the loss are consequent upon some other actionable damage. Secondly, exemplary damages may be avail-

---

[158] [1988] 1 WLR 267, 277 *per* Neill LJ.

[159] But see A. McGee (1988) 104 *LQR* 376, 378–9.

[160] *Barclays Bank PLC* v. *Fairclough Building Ltd* [1994] 3 WLR 1057. See also Law Com. No. 219.

[161] For criticism of this rule see M. J. Smith (1988) 4 *Construction LJ* 75.

[162] Which may include distress caused by injury to reputation: *McLeish* v. *Amoo-Gottfried & Co.*, *The Times*, 13 Oct. 1993.

[163] *Heywood* v. *Wellers* [1976] QB 446; *Hayes* v. *Dodd* [1990] 2 All ER 815.

[164] *Jarvis* v. *Swan Tours Ltd* [1973] 1 QB 233; *Bliss* v. *SE Thames RHA* [1985] IRLR 308. See M. G. Bridge (1984) 62 *Can. BR* 323; P. H. Clarke (1978) 52 *ALJ* 626; B. S. Jackson (1977) 26 *ICLQ* 502.

[165] *Watts* v. *Morrow* [1991] 1 WLR 1421.

able in tort (but not in negligence actions[166]), but such damages are not, *per se*, available in contract.[167]

There may be some difference between contract and tort concerning liability for 'pure loss of a chance'[168] to secure a financial gain or avoid a financial loss. It is clear that if, as a result of a breach of contract, a plaintiff loses a chance of gaining some benefit, P can recover damages proportional to that chance even if this is the only loss P suffers as a result of the breach.[169] There is also ample authority for allowing recovery for loss of a chance in negligence actions against professionals who could be sued either in contract or in tort. A solicitor may be liable in contract or tort for failure to issue a writ within the limitation period with the result that a client loses the chance to launch successful litigation.[170] The measure of damages is the value of the primary claim discounted according to the risk of failure of the action. It does not follow from this that a professional adviser will always be liable (either in contract or tort) to a client for loss of a chance of acquiring some benefit. For example, it is unlikely that a stock or commodity broker could successfully be sued for giving negligent advice to a client who failed as a result to realize an anticipated profit[171] because stock and commodity dealing is such a speculative activity that advice regarding good and bad investments can easily be wrong without being negligent; so, too, can advice about the chances of success in litigation. But merely failing to issue a writ in time is a different matter; here, there is no room for argument that the failure was the result

---

[166] The technical reason is that exemplary damages were not awarded in negligence actions before 1964 (see 302 below). A more principled explanation is that negligence does not entail deliberation. But suppose that an employer cynically fails to comply with reasonable safety standards in a factory in order to save money, and that an employee is injured as a result. Such conduct might fall under the second head of exemplary damages in *Rookes* v. *Barnard* [1964] AC 1129. It has been held that aggravated (compensatory) damages cannot be awarded in personal injury actions, whether in tort or contract, because the aim of such actions is to compensate P and not to discriminate between degrees of fault on the part of D: *Kralj* v. *McGrath* [1986] 1 All ER 54.

[167] Treitel, 861–2; but see *McCall* v. *Abalesz* [1976] QB 585, 594.

[168] It is clear that if the loss of a chance is a consequence of the suffering of some other compensatable damage (e.g. personal injuries: *Mulvaine* v. *Joseph* (1968) 112 Sol. J 927) damages may be recovered for that loss. The whole process of assessing damages for post-judgment loss of income in personal injury actions is one of assessing the value of lost chances.

[169] Treitel, 845; *Obagi* v. *Stanborough (Developments) Ltd*, *The Times*, 15 Dec. 1993; *Sellars* v. *Adelaide Petroleum NL* (1994) 120 ALR 16, 25–6.

[170] *Kitchen* v. *Royal Air Force Association* [1958] 1 WLR 563. In 1958 solicitors were liable to their clients in contract only. But the case was cited without disapproval by Lord Bridge of Harwich in *Hotson* v. *East Berks HA* [1987] AC 750, 782, which supports the sensible view that it applies to actions in tort and contract. See also *Dickinson* v. *Jones, Alexander & Co.* [1989] *New LJ* 1525 (negligent handling of a claim for relief ancillary to divorce); *Thompson* v. *Howley* [1977] 1 NZLR 16 (negligent settlement of a claim for less than true value); *Murray* v. *Lloyd* [1989] 1 WLR 1060 (loss of chance to become a statutory tenant); *Allied Maples Group Ltd.* v. *Simmons & Simmons* [1995] 1 WLR 1602.

[171] Cf. *Stafford* v. *Conti Commodity Services Ltd* [1981] 1 All ER 691; *Merrill Lynch Futures Inc.* v. *York House Trading Ltd* [1984] LS Gaz. R 2455.

such argument if a broker simply failed to place an order for a stock or commodity which, as it turned out, rose in value.

In *Midland Bank Trust Co. Ltd* v. *Hett, Stubbs & Kemp*[172] it was held that a client could sue a solicitor in contract or tort for loss of the chance of exercising an option to buy land. In *Moore* v. *Ferrier*[173] it was held that, for the purposes of deciding when a cause of action for negligence accrued as a result of the negligent drafting of an ineffective covenant in restraint of trade, economic loss was suffered when the ineffective covenant was entered into. It followed from this that if an action for negligence against the solicitor had been brought at that date, substantial damages could have been awarded representing the chance that the covenantor would default at some time in the future. These two cases are particularly important because it is possible to rationalize recovery for a lost chance in the cases mentioned in the last paragraph by saying that what D undertook to secure for P was a chance of gain:[174] the project on which the parties were engaged was, by its nature, speculative. In *Midland Bank* v. *Hett, Stubbs & Kemp*, by contrast, the element of chance was not inherent in the task undertaken by D (namely, to register an option to purchase) but in the fact that P could choose to exercise it or not. Similarly, in *Moore* v. *Ferrier* the element of chance was not inherent in the project of drafting an effective covenant in restraint of trade but rather arose from an extrinsic factor, namely the possible future conduct of the covenantor. Nevertheless, the loss of a chance of making a financial gain and of avoiding financial loss (respectively) was allowed to form the gist of an action in tort.

There is even some authority for the proposition that in suitable cases there may be recovery for loss of a chance by a plaintiff whose only cause of action lies in tort. In one case a company which ran a 'holiday stamp' scheme received compensation for loss of a batch of stamps calculated according to the face-value of the stolen stamps discounted for the chance that only a proportion of the stamps would be presented for payment.[175] In another, underwriters were compensated in tort for loss of the chance to avoid potential liability under a policy issued without authority.[176] In a New Zealand case[177] P was awarded tort damages for loss of the use of a vessel partly on the basis, as one judge put it,[178] that the compensation could be seen as recompense for the loss of a chance of earning future profits. The High Court of Australia has gone so far as to hold that there can be liability in tort[179] for causing the

---

[172] [1979] Ch. 384.   [173] [1988] 1 WLR 267.

[174] Cf *Sellars* v. *Adelaide Petroluem* (1994) 120 ALR 16 33 *per* Brennan J.

[175] *Building and Civil Engineering Holidays Scheme Management Ltd* v. *Post Office* [1965] 1 All ER 163.

[176] *Pryke* v. *Gibbs Hartley Cooper Ltd.* [1991] 1 Lloyd's Rep. 603.

[177] *Nauru Local Government Council* v. *New Zealand Seamen's Industrial Union of Workers* [1986] 1 NZLR 466.

[178] Richardson J, *ibid.*, 476.

[179] As well as in contract and under s. 52(1) of the Trade Practices Act 1974 (Cth) (misleading or deceptive conduct).

loss of a business opportunity even if there was less than an even chance that the opportunity would have materialized, provided the chance of its materializing was not negligible. Damages would be assessed according to the chance that the opportunity would have materialized.[180]

In *Ross* v. *Caunters*[181] Megarry V-C held that a disappointed beneficiary under a will drafted by the defendant solicitor could recover damages in a negligence action for the loss of a legacy resulting from the fact that the beneficiary's spouse witnessed the will. This decision was not followed in the Victorian case of *Seale* v. *Perry*;[182] one of the grounds for refusing recovery was that the legatee's interest was a mere *spes successionis* in the sense that until his death the testator could have altered his will to exclude the plaintiff from benefiting under it. However, on proper analysis, while a holding in favour of the legatee involves compensating for failure to secure a benefit, it does not involve compensating her for the loss of a chance. If the legatee brought an action before the death of the testator, the claim certainly would be one for the loss of a chance. But once the testator has died, the chance that the legatee may be disinherited has disappeared and the legatee's interest ceases to be a mere *spes* in the above sense.[183] At all events, in *White* v. *Jones*,[184] in which it was held that a solicitor owed a duty of care to intended legatees in drafting the will, none of their Lordships seems to have felt that the nature of the legatee's loss presented any barrier to the imposition of tort liability.

Would an action during the testator's lifetime succeed? This, it seems, would depend on the precise facts of the case. Suppose a solicitor gives bad advice to a testator about the management of the testator's property with the result that the testator's estate is so diminished that a beneficiary's legacy cannot be paid (in full). An action by the beneficiary against the solicitor (even if brought after the testator's death) would fail, apparently on the ground that until the testator dies a beneficiary has no interest in property mentioned in the will which would support an action in respect of dealings with the property.[185] If the action were in respect of a defect in the will, it could only succeed if the defect was practically irreparable;[186] otherwise, the plaintiff ought to persuade the testator to repair it.

On the basis of this case law it might be supposed that there is no bar on recovery in tort for lost chances. However, when, in *Hotson* v. *East Berks HA*,[187] a plaintiff attempted to recover damages for the loss of a 25 per cent chance of avoiding a particular medical condition, the House of Lords held

---

[180] *Sellars* v. *Adelaide Petroleum* (1994) 179 CLR 332.   [181] [1980] Ch. 297.
[182] [1982] VR 193.
[183] How should one analyse the loss in the following case? A punter lays a bet on a four-horse accumulator. The fourth horse romps home, but a subsequent stewards' inquiry declares the result void because the race was started early. The punter sues the race organizer: *The Times*, 21 Sept. 1994.
[184] [1995] 2 WLR 187.   [185] *Clarke* v. *Bruce Lance & Co.* [1988] 1 WLR 881.
[186] *Hemmens* v. *Wilson Browne* [1994] 2 WLR 323.   [187] [1987] AC 750.

that since he could not prove on the balance of probabilities that he would not, but for the negligence of the defendant, have developed the condition he could not succeed in tort. The flaw in the reasoning of the House of Lords is that it does not squarely address P's argument, which was that if D had not been negligent P would have had a one in four chance of not contracting the condition; and there was medical evidence to establish this proposition on the balance of probabilities.[188] There are dicta in the judgments which suggest that damages for loss of a chance may be recoverable in some personal injuries cases;[189] but one writer, assessing them in the context of the reasoning as a whole, concludes that the House of Lords would be unlikely to award such damages if it considered the issue of recovery for loss of a chance squarely in a personal injuries action.[190] Another suggests that there is a relevant difference between loss of the chance of making a financial gain and loss of the chance of physical health which would justify excluding personal injury cases from any rules allowing recovery for loss of a chance;[191] but such discrimination against personal injury victims seems difficult to justify.

In *D. & F. Estates Ltd* v. *Church Commissioners for England*[192] it seems to have been held that in an action at common law in tort for negligence against a builder or other party responsible for defects in premises or chattels, the cost of repairing the property in order to forestall damage to the property itself or to persons or other property could not be recovered.[193] Since such damages would represent the cost of avoiding the chance of (liability for) future loss or damage, the case stands as authority for the proposition that in the context of the acquisition of defective buildings or chattels[194] damages may not be recovered for the loss of a chance of avoiding financial loss or physical damage in the future. Of course, the case goes much further than this in that it denies liability for the cost of averting future damage even when it is certain to occur.

There seem to be two main grounds for unwillingness to allow recovery for loss of a chance. In cases where, as in *Hotson*, the loss of which there was a chance has actually materialized, the courts do not seem prepared to depart from the all-or-nothing balance of probabilities test of causation by awarding damages proportional to the risk, judged before the loss materialized, that

---

[188] J. Stapleton (1988) 104 *LQR* 389.

[189] [1987] AC 750, 782–3 *per* Lord Bridge and 768 *per* Lord Mackay.

[190] Stapleton (1988) 104 *LQR* 389, 394.

[191] T. Weir in Olivier Guillod (ed.), *Développements récents du droit de la responsabilité civile* (Zurich, 1991), 122.

[192] [1989] AC 177.

[193] Of course, if the defective property caused damage to 'other property' belonging to the plaintiff, the cost of repairing this could be recovered. Lord Oliver said that if, in order to remedy such damage, it was necessary also to remedy the defect in the property, damages for that could also be recovered. See further 208–14 below.

[194] But if the plaintiff can frame the case in nuisance, a *quia timet* injunction may be awarded even though no loss has yet occurred provided the court is satisfied that there is a sufficiently high chance of loss occurring in the future.

it would occur. Unless P can prove on the balance of probabilities that D's tort caused the loss of which there was a chance, no damages will be awarded. On the other hand, in cases where the loss of which there is a chance has not, at the time of the trial, yet materialized, the courts seem unwilling to entertain speculative actions in which an award of damages proportional to the risk might be claimed; or even, in the absence of personal injury or property damage, to award damages for loss which P can prove, on the balance of probabilities, will occur.[195] In other words, the courts are unwilling to depart from the all-or-nothing balance of probabilities test of causation and to award damages, whether proportional to risk or not, in cases where the defendant's contribution to the risk was 50 per cent or less; and they are unwilling to entertain actions for damages for the cost of forestalling future loss even if the balance of probabilities test is satisfied in relation to that loss.

The cases we have considered concerning the loss of a chance of making a gain fall into the first category of cases in which, at the time of the trial, the chance of making the gain has passed. In all of these cases it seems to have been a condition of liability that P prove on the balance of probabilities that but for the negligence of D a gain would have been made by utilizing the capital in some other profitable way. The case of *Moore* v. *Ferrier*, on the other hand, falls into the second category of cases in the sense that the Court of Appeal was prepared to contemplate an action for damages for the risk of future loss before that loss had materialized.[196] None of the cases involve a departure from the balance-of-probabilities test of causation: P must prove on the balance of probabilities that but for D's negligence there would have been a chance of making a gain or avoiding a loss.[197] But they all run counter to the unwillingness underlying *Hotson* and *D. & F. Estates* to award damages in tort proportional to the chance of making a gain or avoiding a loss; and *Moore* v. *Ferrier* runs counter to the unwillingness which underlies *D. & F. Estates* to award damages for economic loss which has not yet occurred.

Can this difference of approach be explained? One possibility might be to say that if, but only if, the purpose for which the defendant was employed was to secure for P a chance of avoiding a loss or making a gain, damages for loss of that chance will be recoverable in tort and contract (provided the loss is not too remote).[198] This principle would explain most of the cases, and it would overcome another source of anxiety about claims for loss of a chance, namely the risk of a very large number of claims.[199] This risk does not, of course, present itself in contractual claims for loss of a chance, nor in

---

[195] *D. & F. Estates* v. *Church Commissioners* [1989] AC 177.

[196] But if the purchaser of a voidable insurance policy sued a negligent broker before an insured event had occurred, recovery would be limited to the premium paid.

[197] The same principle applies in contract: *Sykes* v. *Midland Bank Executor and Trustee Co. Ltd* [1971] 1 QB 113.

[198] Cf. *Waribay Pty Ltd* v. *Minter Ellison* [1991] 2 VR 399.

[199] J. Stapleton, *Product Liability* (London, 1994), 284–5.

concurrent claims against professionals; nor even in pure tort claims (such as *Ross* v. *Caunters*) which arise out of contractual misfeasance. Moreover, few of the cases we have considered in this section present any really serious problem of quantifying the lost chance, which is a further worry about some lost chance claims. Nevertheless, it must be admitted that neither *Hotson* nor *D. & F. Estates* created a risk of a multiplicity of claims or any serious difficulty of quantification. So at the end of the day, the law seems simply inconsistent in its treatment of lost chance claims.

Quantum of Damages The basic difference between contract and tort, so far as concerns the quantum of damages, is often said to be that it is only in contract that damages for expectations or benefits not realized (as opposed to losses actually suffered or expenses actually incurred) can be recovered. Put another way, the aim of damages in contract is to put the plaintiff in the position he or she would have been in if the contract had been performed; while the aim of an award of tort damages is to put the plaintiff in the position he or she would have been in if the tort had not been committed. However, the application of this basic distinction to concurrent actions in contract and tort is by no means straightforward. In the first place, we should note that, at least in cases where the alleged breach of contract consists in the performance of some service in such a way as to constitute a breach of a contractual duty of care,[200] and the alleged tort consists of negligent performance of the service, the two measures will produce the same formula: in this context, performing the contract and not committing the wrong add up to the same thing.[201]

Secondly, we must note an ambiguity in the terms 'expectation' and 'gain'. There are two different complaints which might be made by a person who makes a bad investment which fails to generate a hoped-for gain. One is that if the investment had been a good one a gain would have been realized which will not now materialize. The other is that if the bad investment had not been made, another investment could have been made which would have generated a gain greater than that actually realized. The first complaint is (we might say) about the actual cost of the investment, the second is about the opportunity cost of the investment.[202]

It seems clear that a complaint of the first sort will only sound in contract. But a contract will only support such a complaint if D warranted that the investment would realize a specified gain for P.[203] Breach of a contractual duty to take care in giving investment advice or performing investment-related services will not support a complaint of the first type. So, for exam-

---

[200] As opposed to breach of a warranty on the part of the service provider to secure a particular result.

[201] *Banque Bruxelles Lambert SA* v. *Eagle Star Insurance Co. Ltd* [1995] 2 WLR 607, 616–7.

[202] *Gates* v. *City Mutual Life Assurance Society Ltd* (1986) 63 ALR 600, 608.

[203] *Watts* v. *Morrow* [1991] 1 WLR 1421. In other words, liability for breach of contract in such a case will be strict.

ple, a surveyor only undertakes to exercise reasonable care to alert a purchaser or mortgagee to defects which might make the property worth less
than the purchase price or the proposed mortgage; in the absence of express
words (or 'necessary implication'), the surveyor does not warrant that it has
a particular value (even if he or she expresses an opinion about its condition
which implies such a value). Therefore, even if the action is framed in contract, a purchaser normally[204] cannot recover the cost of putting right the
defects but only the difference between contract price and market value;[205]
and a mortgagee will recover the difference between the amount actually lent
and the amount which would have been lent if the truth had been known.[206]
Similarly, in *Esso Petroleum Ltd* v. *Mardon*,[207] in which P suffered loss as a
result of a negligent misstatement by D as to the likely throughput of a petrol
station, Lord Denning MR expressed the opinion that regardless of whether
the basis of liability was tortious (for misrepresentation) or contractual (for
breach of a term concerning throughput) P ought to be awarded not only
damages for loss of the capital put into the business and for interest paid on
an overdraft, but also for loss of profits for the period P owned the lease and
for a reasonable period thereafter during which P could find another business
to invest in. But the oil company did not warrant that the petrol station
would have a specified throughput and so P was not to be put into the position he would have been in if the statement had been true.

In other words, the contract defines what the defendant has undertaken to
do; and this, not the cause of action, determines the quantum of damages. So,
for example, a lawyer undertakes to exercise reasonable care to procure for
a litigant a particular benefit as a result of litigation, and so the litigant is not
restricted to recovering amounts spent on the unsuccessful litigation or on
fruitless consultations with the lawyer, but may recover the amount of the
expected recovery suitably discounted to take account of the chance that
the court would have found in whole or in part for the defendant.[208] By

---

[204] But see P. A. Chandler (1990) 106 *LQR* 196.

[205] *Phillips* v. *Ward* [1956] 1 WLR 471; *Perry* v. *Sidney Phillips & Son* [1982] 1 WLR 1297,
1302; *Watts* v. *Morrow* [1991] 1 WLR 1421 (E. Macdonald [1992] *New LJ* 632 criticizes the case
on the ground that damages ought to have been calculated on the opportunity cost basis). By
contrast, designers of structures may be held, in contract, to have warranted the quality of their
design: Treitel, 754.

[206] *Baxter* v. *F. W. Gapp & Co. Ltd* [1939] 2 KB 271. Concerning the effect of subsequent
fluctuations in the general level of property values on the rights of mortgagees and purchasers
against valuers see *Banque Bruxelles Lambert* v. *Eagle Star Insurance Co.* [1995] 2 WLR 607.

[207] [1976] QB 801.

[208] *Kitchen* v. *Royal Air Force Association* [1958] 1 WLR 563. But the result could be explained
in terms of opportunity cost: it can be assumed that if the plaintiff had known that the solicitor
would act negligently, P could and would have found another solicitor who would have brought
the litigation to a successful conclusion. The High Court of Australia has held that in a case
where a lawyer negligently fails to commence proceedings within the limitation period, the damages are assessed at the date when the claim became statute-barred (*Nikalaou* v. *Papasavas* (1988)
82 ALR 617); or, in a case where an action is struck out for want of prosecution, at the date
when the action was dismissed (*Johnson* v. *Perez* (1988) 82 ALR 587). An insurance broker who
negligently fails to procure a policy as requested by a client is liable for amounts which would

extension, even if the plaintiff's only cause of action is in tort, it is the nature of the job being performed by the defendant which defines the loss. So in *Ross v. Caunters*,[209] in which a third-party beneficiary under a will successfully sued the defendant solicitor for negligence in having the will executed with the result that the plaintiff's legacy was defeated, the testator's aim in consulting the solicitor was, *inter alia*, to procure a benefit for P; and so P could recover damages for the value of that benefit. By the contract between the solicitor and the testator, the former had undertaken to secure a benefit for the plaintiff, not just to exercise care so to do.

A claim for loss of expectation on the opportunity cost basis can be made either in contract or in tort and even if the defendant's only obligation was to take reasonable care in advising about the value of the investment. But such a claim will succeed only if the expected gain was not too remote in law and was the result of the negligent conduct. In *County Personnel (Employment Agency) Ltd* v. *Alan R. Pulver & Co.*[210] the plaintiff, acting on the advice of its solicitor, the defendant, entered into an extremely disadvantageous sub-lease. P intended to use the sub-demised premises to conduct an employment agency business, and one of the heads of damages claimed was loss of prospective profit on resale of the lease and the associated goodwill of the business conducted on the premises. Bingham LJ, delivering the main judgment in the Court of Appeal, held that if D had been told that P intended, once the business was established, to sell the sub-lease and the associated goodwill, then the loss would be sufficiently proximate as a matter of law. Causation would be established if P could show that if D had not been negligent it would not have entered the sub-lease but would instead have invested in and made a profit on the resale of another lease and associated business. Because the evidence only showed that P would not have entered the sub-lease if it had known the truth and not that it would have made an alternative investment, the proper measure of damages was the cost to P of extricating itself from the disadvantageous transaction by surrendering the sub-lease (or, in other words, the actual financial cost of entering the sub-lease).[211] The causation requirement means that whether or not an opportunity cost claim will succeed depends, in every case, on how P would have reacted if the truth had been known; whereas this issue is irrelevant if D warranted a particular outcome.[212]

The reason why it is only in contract that damages can be recovered for the fact that an investment does not yield an expected gain is said to be that

have been payable to the client under the policy (but not for losses consequential upon the fact that P did not receive the insurance monies at the expected time): *Ramwade Ltd* v. *W. J. Emson & Co. Ltd* [1987] RTR 72.

[209] [1980] Ch. 297.

[210] [1987] 1 All ER 289. See also *G. & K. Ladenbau (UK) Ltd* v. *Crawley & de Reya* [1978] 1 All ER 682.

[211] Cf. *Hayes* v. *Dodd* [1990] 2 All ER 815.

[212] *Swingcastle Ltd* v. *Alastair Gibson (A Firm)* [1991] 2 AC 223.

a person should, as a general rule, only be liable for failure to secure a gain for another if that person undertook, in a legally binding way, to secure that gain. If no such undertaking was given, liability should only arise for doing something which prevented another realizing a similar gain in another way. It has been argued, however, that allowing recovery on the opportunity cost basis is effectively equivalent to allowing recovery on the contractual basis because in a perfectly competitive market an equally profitable alternative investment will always be available.[213] But markets are never perfectly competitive, and unless a court is prepared to assume in the plaintiff's favour that such an alternative investment would have been available, it may not be possible for P to prove that such an investment could and would have been made.

Remoteness of Damage   The rules of remoteness of damage in contract are, in general terms, less generous to the plaintiff than those in tort.[214] In contract, unless the occurrence of the loss can be called a serious possibility the defendant will be liable only if D knew of the particular circumstances which gave rise to the loss. In tort, on the other hand, a person can often be held liable for very unlikely losses arising out of circumstances of which that person had no knowledge. The contract rule may have the effect of encouraging disclosure of information relevant to settling the terms of the contract and to buying insurance.[215]

One suggested justification for the difference between the contract and tort rules is that contract law is primarily concerned with protecting purely economic interests; and that these are less important and so less worthy of protection than interests in personal safety.[216] This argument receives indirect support from the fact that when damages for physical injury or loss are claimed in a contract action the contractual rule of remoteness seems to operate similarly in practice to the tort rule.[217] Another common argument is that, because the parties to a contract can regulate their legal relations in advance, a party who wishes to increase the burden of the other's potential liability should stipulate to that end. This explanation is not entirely satisfactory. In cases where tort liability is based on the fact that the parties were in a 'business' relationship before the tort occurred, the argument that the plaintiff ought to have stipulated the extent of the defendant's potential liability for remote losses may apply with equal force, especially in cases where the reason why P is suing in tort is that no consideration was given for D's advice or service.[218]

At all events, as far as concurrent liability in tort and contract is concerned,

---

[213] H. Collins, *The Law of Contract*, 2nd edn. (London, 1993), 184–5, 372–6, 381–4.
[214] But the rules governing intervening causation are similar in tort and contract: *Beoco Ltd v. Alfa Laval Co Ltd* [1994] 3 WLR 1179.
[215] W. Bishop (1983) 12 *JLS* 241.
[216] J. A. Weir, *International Encyclopedia of Comparative Law*, xi, ch. 12, s. 17.
[217] *Vacwell Engineering Co. Ltd* v. *BDH Chemicals Ltd* [1971] 1 QB 88.
[218] As in *Hedley Byrne* v. *Heller* [1964] AC 465.

Parsons v. *Uttley Ingham & Co.*[219] casts some doubt on the position as stated above. In this case, Lord Denning proposed that the distinction between tort and contract be replaced with a distinction between physical injury or damage and economic loss consequent upon it on the one hand, and economic loss (such as loss of profits or opportunities of gain) on the other, on the basis that the former should be more generously compensated for than the latter. This distinction may rest on the idea that economic loss is not as worthy of compensation as physical damage, or on the notion that plaintiffs should take steps to protect themselves against economic loss.[220]

Scarman LJ (with whom Orr LJ agreed) rejected Lord Denning's suggested distinction and attempted to assimilate the contract and the tort rules in respect of losses of all types by saying that the difference between the 'serious possibility' test of contract and the 'foreseeability' test of tort was semantic, not substantial; and by holding that the serious possibility test applied only to the type of loss and not to its exact extent.[221] If anything, this rule is more generous than the tort rule: as we have seen,[222] there is authority for the rule that the extent as well as the type of economic loss suffered has to be foreseeable if it is to be recoverable in tort, at least if D is a large commercial entity.[223] The main effect of Scarman LJ's approach (that is, a uniform test of remoteness for all *types* of loss) would be felt in cases where the loss was caused by unusual circumstances unknown to either party. His Lordship does not seem to have intended to relieve contracting parties of the obligation to reveal unusual circumstances of which they knew. This appears from his comments about cases of concurrent liability in tort and contract: here there could be no justification for applying different remoteness rules according to the cause of action chosen unless either the contract made express provision different from the tort rules, or the plaintiff had knowledge relevant to the likely extent of the loss which the defendant did not have.

It seems, therefore, that in cases of concurrent liability in tort and contract the rules of remoteness of damage will be the same unless the contract makes express special provision or unless P knew of relevant facts of which D was ignorant. In the latter case, an action in tort could be more beneficial to P than an action in contract. In the former case it may be that despite Scarman LJ's view a court might now hold not that the remoteness rule in a contract

---

[219] [1978] QB 791.

[220] Cf. Lord Denning's approach in *Lamb* v. *Camden LBC* [1981] QB 625; but note that this was a case of property damage.

[221] Cf. *Banque Bruxelles Lambert* v. *Eagle Star Insurance Co.* [1995] 2 WLR 607, 620 (economic loss); *Vacwell Engineering* v. *BDH Chemicals* [1971] QB 88 (property damage). For criticism of Scarman LJ's approach see Treitel, 878.

[222] See 96–8 above.

[223] The rule was laid down in the context of liability for additional loss attributable to impecuniosity. The contract rule concerning lack of means appears to be that extra loss resulting from lack of funds is recoverable provided D knew of P's impecuniosity and the additional loss was a likely consequence of the lack of means: *Monarch SS Co.* v. *Karlshamns Oljefabriker (A/B)* [1949] AC 196, 224; Treitel, 877.

action would be different from that in a tort action, but that the contractual limitation on recovery governed the tort action as well as any contract action. It is clear that in cases of concurrent liability any contractual exclusion clause would apply to the tort action in the same way as it would apply to a contract action.[224] By parity of reasoning, a contractual clause imposing a remoteness rule more limited than that in tort should also operate to limit tort liability in cases of concurrent liability.

This position could be justified on the basis that:

a party who has, by his choice, exposed himself to contractual liability of a certain extent, should not have his choice outflanked by the subsequent unilateral decision of the other to sue in tort or be deprived of the beneficial incidents of contractual liability.[225]

On the other hand, the weakness in this argument is that it fails to take account of the fact that by allowing concurrent liability at all the law potentially allows the plaintiff to deprive the defendant of beneficial incidents of contractual liability; but there is no apparent reason, on this view, why D should have to stipulate expressly in the contract to preserve those incidents, and lose the benefit of them if this is not done. If liability based on *choice* is to be preferred to liability imposed by law, why should the rules of contract law not always prevail over tort law? The difficulty arises from treating liability based on expressions of will as contained in contracts as primary, and treating liability imposed by law as secondary. If it were accepted that liability imposed by law (whether statute law or common law) is primary, then concurrent liability would follow logically; and it could, consistently, be made subject to modification by agreement in cases where this was acceptable in policy terms.[226]

Exclusion Clauses

We must consider further the application of contractual exclusion clauses in concurrent tort actions. As already stated, effective contractual exclusion clauses apply in such a tort action. In other words, a concurrent tort action cannot be used to escape the operation of an effective contractual exclusion clause.[227] In this context it is worth noting the provisions of the Unfair Contract Terms Act 1977. This Act lays down tests for the effectiveness of

---

[224] *Coupland* v. *Arabian Gulf Petroleum Co.* [1983] 3 All ER 226; *Elder Dempster & Co. Ltd* v. *Paterson Zochonis & Co. Ltd* [1924] AC 522, 548 *per* Viscount Finlay; *Hall* v. *Brooklands Auto Racing Club* [1933] 1 KB 205, 213 *per* Scrutton LJ.

[225] Weir, *International Encyclopedia of Comparative Law*, xi, ch. 12, 27–8.

[226] See Cane in Furmston, *The Law of Tort*, 130. Indeed, so many of the rules of contract law are rules 'imposed by law' that contract could itself be legitimately viewed as a set of institutionally imposed rules selectively subject to exclusion, qualification and modification by agreement of the parties.

[227] *Central Trust Co.* v. *Rafuse* (1986) 31 DLR(4th) 481, 522.

exclusion provisions which are essentially the same whether the provision is contained in a contract or not and whether the action is brought in tort or in contract. It also draws a distinction between personal injury (and losses consequential upon it) on the one hand, and other losses on the other, and (in the case of business liability) entirely prohibits exclusion of negligence liability in respect of the former, but only subjects exclusions of liability for the latter to a test of reasonableness.[228] It thus silently supports the exclusion from this book of personal injuries and the bracketing of property damage with economic loss.

3. BASIC ISSUES

It is useful at this stage to summarize some of the basic issues which emerge from the discussion in this Chapter.[229] The first concerns the relationship between contractual rights and property rights. The question for the law of tort is when, if ever, contractual rights in property ought to be enforceable against a third party to the contract who has a proprietary or possessory interest in the property. In one direction pulls the idea that property rights are in some sense superior to contractual rights. Another factor which pulls in this direction is the impact of tort liability on the land registration system. In the other direction pulls the idea that a property owner ought not to be allowed to ride roughshod over another's contractual rights in the property, at least if the owner undertook not to do so and, perhaps, even if the owner just knew of the other's contractual rights.

Secondly, in cases where the contractual rights interfered with are not rights in property, the basic issue is when, if ever, the law of tort ought to be available to reinforce the stability of contractual relations against attack by third parties. The argument for some tort liability in this context rests on the importance of contracting in a market economy. The most vociferous opponents of such liability tend to be those who wish to champion the interests of workers, for whom interference with contracts between their employers and the latter's customers is a prime means of furthering their industrial interests.

Thirdly, quite different issues are raised by actions in tort by one contracting party against the other in respect of breaches of contract. One question concerns whether, in the absence of a statutory right of action, concurrent rights of action in tort should ever be recognized? The argument against allowing them rests ultimately on the idea that contractual liabilities, being self-imposed, are legally prior and superior to tort liabilities, which are externally imposed. The idea is challengeable in two respects: legal restrictions on freedom of contract suggest that self-imposed liabilities are not

---

[228] Under s. 7 of the Consumer Protection Act 1987 exclusion of liability is prohibited whether the damage suffered is personal injury, or loss of or damage to property.

[229] Each of these issues will be considered further in later chs.

always seen as being superior; and, anyway, it is not true that all contractual liabilities are self-imposed, nor that all externally imposed liabilities can be modified by agreement. It might be argued that only the legislature ought to be able to impose liabilities on contracting parties and that the courts should leave them free of external control. But since much of the law of contract consists of common law rules which externally regulate the rights and oblig-ations of the parties, this argument, too, is weak. Another issue arises if con-current liability is accepted: in the absence of relevant statutory provisions, which breaches of contract should be actionable in tort? A final issue con-cerns the extent to which the rights of the plaintiff in the tort action should be shaped by reference to the contract between the plaintiff and the defen-dant: to what extent should a party, by suing in tort, be able to succeed in the claim when that party would not succeed in a contract action? The law's general answer to this question seems to be that the effect of express or implied terms (such as exclusion clauses) in the contract cannot be evaded, but that extra-contractual rules of contract law (concerning limitation of actions, for instance) can be.

Fourthly, we have the cases in which a person's contractual obligations are rendered more onerous or their contractual rights are rendered less valuable by conduct not aimed at that person. Here, two main issues seem to under-lie the law's unwillingness to allow tort actions: the fear of unleashing a flood of claims, and the desire to encourage people to protect their contractual interests in ways other than by bringing tort actions.

4

Other Assets

INTRODUCTION

This Chapter is concerned with financial assets, other than property and contractual rights, which receive protection from the law of tort. These assets fall into three groups. First there are expectancies. Expectancies are of two types: contractual and non-contractual. A contractual expectancy[1] consists of the chance (viewed objectively) or expectation (viewed subjectively) of entering into a financially advantageous contractual arrangement in the future; a non-contractual expectancy consists of the chance or expectation of making a gain in the future by some means other than a contractual arrangement. The second group of assets consists of what are sometimes called 'trade values' or, in other words, intangible assets (other than property or contractual rights), the product of someone's effort and skill, which can be exploited to make financial gains. The third group of assets consists of monetary wealth in all its forms; the interest being protected here is an interest in the preservation of the financial status quo. This last category is, in some sense, residual, because into it can be put all cases of actionable financial loss which do not fall into any of the other more specific categories.

Section 1 of this Chapter deals with expectancies (first contractual, then non-contractual); section 2 deals with trade values, and section 3 with monetary wealth. In the discussion of contractual expectancies we will examine again some of the issues about competition and labour relations which were discussed in Chapter 3. As in previous chapters, we will see that statutory causes of action play an important (and increasing) role in supplementing and extending the protection which the common law of tort provides to various economic interests. In the discussion of trade values we will return to a theme which was prominent in Chapter 2, namely that the law of tort has at its disposal a variety of alternative juridical techniques for redressing interferences with economic interests which have different characteristics and which can provide different patterns of protection. In this Chapter, too, we will examine further aspects of the complex relationship between tort and contract.

---

[1] On the use of this term see 107 above.

1. EXPECTANCIES

Contractual Expectancies

In the light of the relative unwillingness of the law of tort to protect contractual interests under existing contracts, it might seem surprising that contractual expectancies receive any protection at all.[2] In fact, there are several ways in which the law of tort protects the interest in making advantageous contracts in the future. The main functions of the law of tort in this context are to prevent the abuse of economic power in the market-place (as, for example, by unions in industrial disputes; or by employers who adopt discriminatory employment practices); to restrain excess concentration of economic power (this is the province of competition law); and to ensure that participants in the market are not given inaccurate information which might hinder the making of informed economic choices (this is the purpose of rules about pre-contractual misrepresentation). In economic terms, the role of tort law can be seen as achieving results which the parties could have achieved for themselves by contractual arrangements but for the existence of barriers to free and equal contracting caused, for example, by maldistribution of information or excessive monopolization (which economists call 'transaction costs').

Interference with the Making of Contracts

Common Law: Liability for Actions Done to Further Financial or Commercial Interests[3]

This category of case is sometimes referred to by the name 'interference with trade' or 'interference with business', even though it embraces cases falling within the 'nominate' torts of conspiracy and intimidation. In competitive contexts, 'trade' and 'business' consist most importantly of the making of advantageous contracts.[4] For convenience I will normally use the phrase

---

[2] Cf. P. S. Atiyah (1985) 5 *OJLS* 485, 487.

[3] Cf. American Law Institute, *Restatement (Second) of Torts*, s. 766B.

[4] It is clear that 'interference with trade/business' extends beyond interference with subsisting contracts: *J. T. Stratford & Son Ltd* v. *Lindley* [1965] AC 269, 324 *per* Lord Reid; *Merkur Island Shipping Corporation* v. *Laughton* [1983] 2 AC 570, 609 *per* Lord Diplock; *Clerk and Lindsell on Torts*, 16th edn. (London, 1989), 850–1. But it is unclear whether all cases of interference with advantageous business opportunities are covered: *Lonrho PLC* v. *Fayed* [1990] 2 QB 479, 493 *per* Woolf LJ. See further H. Carty (1988) 104 *LQR* 250, 273–4; (1983) 3 *LS* 193; W. V. H. Rogers (ed.), *Winfield and Jolowicz on Torts*, 14th edn. (London, 1994), 547. In *Department of Transport* v. *Williams, The Times*, 7 Dec. 1993 the Court of Appeal held that interference with the building of a motorway by 'wilful obstruction of the exercise of statutory functions' constituted the tort of unlawful interference with business. Concerning conduct which deprives a person of the ability to claim a legal remedy see *Law Debenture Trust Corporation* v. *Ural Caspian Oil Corporation* [1995] Ch. 152; Cane (1995) 111 *LQR* 400.

'interference with trade'[5] to mean 'interference with the making of a future contract or contracts'. There are a number of fact situations in which the law of tort may give a remedy in respect of conduct which 'interferes' with contractual expectancies in the sense that the conduct prevents or inhibits the making of contracts:

1. Two or more persons act in concert to injure another by interfering with that other's trading activities (conspiracy to injure or, as it is sometimes called, 'simple conspiracy'.[6]

2. Two or more persons act in concert in an unlawful way and thereby interfere with another's trading activities (conspiracy to use unlawful means or 'unlawful means conspiracy').

3. A, by inducing or procuring another to use unlawful means,[7] interferes with B's trading activities.

4. A, by using unlawful means, interferes with B's trading activities (causing loss by unlawful means,[8] or 'unlawful interference with trade').[9]

5. A, by making a threat (to which B yields) to take unlawful action against B if B does not act in a particular way (which will be to B's detriment), causes B to act in a way detrimental to B's trading activities (two-party intimidation).

6. A, by making a threat (to which C yields) that he will take unlawful action against C if C does not act in a particular way (which will cause detriment to B), causes C to interfere with B's trading activities (three-party intimidation).

In the last four situations it is irrelevant whether A was acting in concert or alone. In the first four situations, the mechanism of causing loss might involve either interference with B's making of a contract or contracts with others, or interference with the making of a contract or contracts with B by

---

[5] Recognized as a tort in *Hadmor Productions Ltd* v. *Hamilton* [1983] 1 AC 191 and *Merkur Island Shipping Corporation* v. *Laughton* [1983] 2 AC 570.

[6] This head of liability is historically associated with anti-competitive restrictive practices such as cartels and boycotts, but it may be relevant in other contexts. See e.g. *Gulf Oil (Great Britain) Ltd* v. *Page* [1987] Ch. 327 (spiteful publication of a true statement).

[7] On inducement of breach of statutory duty (or of an equitable obligation) as unlawful means see *Associated British Ports* v. *Transport and General Workers' Union* [1989] 1 WLR 939 (CA).

[8] This phrase is wider than 'interference with trade' because it extends beyond interference with contractual expectancies.

[9] This head of liability is so broad that it includes all the others except the first. It is, therefore, sometimes argued that there is a 'genus' or 'umbrella' tort of causing loss by unlawful means (or 'unlawful interference with trade'). It also covers the torts of deceit and injurious falsehood; but, of course, these torts are actionable in their own right, whereas not all 'unlawful means' are. Deceit which induces a person to enter a contract is considered below, as is deceit which causes other financial loss. If the unlawful means are independently actionable P may be able to escape the limitations on this tort, such as the need to prove intention to injure. For an interesting example of independent actionability involving trespass to land, see *XL Petroleum (NSW) Pty Ltd* v. *Caltex Oil (Australia) Pty Ltd* (1985) 155 CLR 448. Concerning causing loss by unlawful means as it might relate to covenants about the use of land, see R. J. Smith (1977) 41 *Conv.* 318, 326–7.

third parties. It will be noted that none of these fact situations has been described as involving 'interference with contract'. The reason for this is that the tort of interference with contract only applies to interference with rights under existing contracts. This limitation on the scope of this tort is important only in respect of those forms of the tort which can be committed without the use of unlawful means—namely, direct persuasion and, perhaps, direct disablement. In all cases involving the use of unlawful means, it appears that the distinction between existing contractual rights and contractual expectancies is not crucial to establishing a *prima facie* case, although it may be important in connection with the defence of justification, which I will discuss in a moment. When unlawful means are used with the intention of inflicting economic loss on the plaintiff,[10] P's chance of recovering damages is not dependent on the interest invaded being a right under an existing contract rather than a contractual expectancy.[11]

There are two actionable forms of interference with trade which do not require proof that the defendant used independently unlawful means: the first form of conspiracy (situation 1 above), and inducement of breach of a statutory duty (or of an equitable obligation) (situation 3 above).[12] Whereas one-person interference with contract (in the form of direct persuasion and, perhaps, in the form of direct disablement) may be actionable even if unlawful means have not been used, interference with trade cannot, except in situation 3 above, be committed by one person acting alone, unless unlawful means were used.[13] In this important respect, contractual expectancies are less well protected from interference by the law of tort than are existing contractual interests. The reason inducement of breach of a statutory duty or of an equitable obligation can be tortious even if not intrinsically unlawful is, apparently, that the rights correlative to statutory duties and equitable obligations are seen as being analogous to contractual rights. On this basis, one would presume that the rules which make certain forms of interference with contract actionable only if intrinsically unlawful would also apply, *mutatis mutandis* to interference with statutory or equitable duties.

From one point of view the first form of conspiracy is anomalous:[14] why

---

[10] Or, perhaps, in the case of conspiracy to use unlawful means, even without such an intention; see 156 below.

[11] *Merkur Island Shipping Corporation* v. *Laughton* [1983] 2 AC 570, 609 *per* Lord Diplock, on which see R. Simpson (1987) 50 *MLR* 506, 509, n. 11.

[12] *Associated British Ports* v. *Transport and General Workers' Union* [1989] 1 WLR 939, 959 *per* Butler-Sloss LJ; 963 *per* Stuart-Smith LJ. But on inducing breach of trust see *Metall und Rohstoff AG* v. *Donaldson Lufkin & Jenrette* [1990] 1 QB 391, 481.

[13] *Allen* v. *Flood* [1898] AC 1. For arguments in favour of the recognition of liability for intentional infliction of economic loss without use of unlawful means see P. Burns (1980) 58 *Can. BR* 103; R. F. V. Heuston (1986) 20 *UBCLR* 33. If such a principle were adopted, great weight would fall on the defence of justification as a means of keeping the liability within bounds; and this would require consideration of the relative interests of the parties. See also G. H. L. Fridman 'The Protection of Business Relations by the Law of Torts', in G. H. L. Fridman (ed.), *Studies in Canadian Business Law* (Toronto, 1981).

[14] See e.g. Carty (1988) 104 *LQR* 250, 253; see also Simpson (1987) 50 *MLR* 506, 509.

should an act, which would not be actionable if done by one person alone, even if that person is a large corporation, be actionable just because it is done by two acting in concert, even if their combined power is much less than that of some large corporations?[15] However, it should be noted that the elimination of this anomaly would not produce a simple equation in which contractual interests (or other analogous rights) were protected even against intrinsically lawful interference, whereas contractual expectancies were only protected against intrinsically unlawful interference. We have seen that certain forms of liability for interference with contractual interests are only actionable if intrinsically unlawful; and I have just argued that the same must be true, *mutatis mutandis* of interference with rights analogous to contractual rights. Viewed in this light, the anomaly is that interference with either contractual (and analogous) interests or contractual expectancies is ever actionable in cases where no intrinsically unlawful means were used.

It is not clear whether the term 'unlawful means' bears the same meaning here as it does in the context of the tort of interference with contract; or even whether it bears the same meaning in the context of the three 'torts' (conspiracy, intimidation, and interference with trade[16]) relevant in this context. The phrase definitely includes interference with contract (that is, as unlawful means rather than as a tort in its own right) unless, in the circumstances, it is protected by section 219 of the Trade Union and Labour Relations (Consolidation) Act 1992 (TULRCA); and inducing breach of statutory duty (or of an equitable obligation).[17] It is unclear whether the unlawful means have to be independently actionable;[18] except that where a conspiracy to use unlawful means is committed in contemplation or furtherance of a trade dispute then, by virtue of section 219(2) of TULRCA, the conspirators will usually[19] only be liable where the means used would, if employed by an individual acting alone, be actionable in tort.

A particularly contentious issue, which arises most starkly in the context of fact situation 4 above, is whether breach of contract can or should constitute unlawful means. The doctrinal argument for an affirmative answer is that *Rookes* v. *Barnard*[20] establishes that threatening a breach of contract can constitute unlawful means; and it would be inconsistent to classsify a threat

[15] *Lonrho* v. *Shell Petroleum (No. 2)* [1982] AC 173, 188–9 *per* Lord Wilberforce.

[16] In the sense in which it describes fact situation 3 above, rather than in its umbrella sense, in which it covers all five fact situations.

[17] On infringing statutory prohibitions or breaching statutory duties as species of unlawful means, see *Associated British Ports* v. *TGWU* [1989] 1 WLR 939 (CA); P. Elias and K. Ewing [1982] *CLJ* 321, 351–6; Simpson (1987) 50 *MLR* 506, 509–11.

[18] See 000 above. *Lonrho PLC* v. *Fayed* [1990] 2 QB 479 (reversed in part [1992] 1 AC 448) appears to establish that where they are directed against a third party and not against the plaintiff, they do not have to be actionable by P: see J. M. Eekelaar (1990) 106 *LQR* 223, 225–7. And in *Associated British Ports* v. *TGWU* [1989] 1 WLR 939 Butler-Sloss LJ (at 961) and Stuart-Smith LJ (at 965) seem to have taken the view that when inducing breach of statutory duty is relied upon as unlawful means, there need be no independent cause of action against either the inducer or the induced. See further 197 below.

[19] Wedderburn, 581–2.   [20] [1964] AC 1129.

as unlawful means, but not the act itself. The doctrinal argument for a negative answer is that classifying an intentional breach of contract as unlawful
means would subvert the doctrine of privity in cases where the plaintiff was
not a party to the contract breached; and if P was a party, it would allow
evasion of the rules of contract law which would govern P's claim if brought
in contract. The latter situation has already been discussed.[21] As regards the
former, suppose that D and C make a contract under which D is to confer
some benefit on P. Unless P can bring his or her case within one of the exceptions to the doctrine of privity,[22] P will not be able to sue D in contract for
failing to confer the benefit unless (on the assumption that breach of contract
can constitute unlawful means for the purposes of the law of tort) D breaches
the contract with the intention of harming P. Why, it might be asked, should
D's state of mind affect liability when it is normally irrelevant to the existence of liability in contract?

How does one choose between the affirmative and the negative answer to
the question whether breach of contract should be capable of constituting
unlawful means? Perhaps it could be argued that there is a moral difference
between breaching a contract unintentionally and doing so with the aim of
harming the other party; and that this moral difference justifies imposing the
more stringent 'penalties' of the law of tort. On the other hand, and more
specifically, it has been argued that to recognize breach of contract as unlawful means for the purposes of the law of tort would 'outflank' the statutory
immunities for acts done in contemplation or furtherance of a trade dispute,
since these immunities do not protect workers from tort liability for breach
of their employment contracts.[23]

The requirement of unlawful means is best understood in terms of the two
main areas of practical operation of the various torts currently under consideration. Intentional infliction of economic loss on one's competitors by
lawful conduct is of the very essence of the free market. In the industrial relations context, the requirement acknowledges the economic advantage conferred by ownership of the means of production. Outside these contexts, it is
less easy to justify, and insistence upon it may produce undesirable results.[24]

It seems clear that all of these torts require proof that D intended to injure P.

[21] See 132 above. Carty (1988) 104 *LQR* 250, 260–2 argues that intentional breach of contract
or threats of breach of contract should, in two-party cases (that is, where P and D are the contracting parties), be treated as a form of economic duress for which the only remedies would be
contractual or restitutionary (see Treitel, 374–7). It is difficult to assess this proposal in the
abstract—it is necessary to decide, in the light of the differences between the various remedies
available for breach of contract, for tort, and for economic duress, whether any of these remedies ought not to be available as a matter of policy in particular cases (cf. J. Beatson, *The Use
and Abuse of Unjust Enrichment* (Oxford, 1991), 17). Wedderburn ((1982) 45 *MLR* 556) argues
that the notion of economic duress should have no place in industrial relations law, because 'the
essence of collective bargaining is power and 'coercion' of one side by the other' (560).

[22] Treitel, 576–88.

[23] Wedderburn, 637–8. See also S. Fredman (1987) 104 *LQR* 176, 180.

[24] As in *Law Debenture Trust Corporation* v. *Ural Caspian Oil Corporation* [1995] Ch. 152.

There are dicta to this effect in relation to 'interference with trade'.[25] Intention to injure is, *ex hypothesi*, an element of simple conspiracy, and was assumed by the House of Lords to be an element of unlawful means conspiracy in *Lonrho PLC* v. *Fayed*.[26]

So far as the defence of justification is concerned, simple conspiracy can be justified if its sole or predominant purpose was the furtherance of the conspirator's own financial or commercial self-interest[27] but unlawful means conspiracy cannot be so justified.[28] There is also authority for the view that unlawful 'interference with trade' cannot be justified by self-interest where the unlawful act relied upon is interference with a contract between P and C, or where D has committed a fraud against C or has intimidated C.[29] Furthermore, we have seen that interference with existing contracts can probably never be justified by self-interest even if unlawful means are not used.[30] Even so, as a matter of principle and given the wide range of unlawfulness which might form the basis of an action, it is perhaps unlikely that there is a general rule that the use of unlawful means could never be justified. But it is surely the case that unlawful means would be harder to justify than lawful ones. Unlawful conduct is not always unjustifiable, but it often (perhaps usually) is.[31]

Two points need to be made about the statutory immunities enjoyed by those engaged in trade disputes. First, by virtue of section 219(2) of TULRCA, simple conspiracy is usually[32] not actionable when committed in contemplation or furtherance of a trade dispute. Secondly, the statutory immunity for action in contemplation or furtherance of a trade dispute only applies to acts and conspiracies which involve interference with contract. This means that unlawful interference with trade is protected by TULRCA only if the 'unlawful means' used involve interference with a contract.[33] Interference with the performance of equitable obligations (such as an obligation of confidence),[34] or of a statutory duty; or interference with private rights[35] (assuming that these are capable of giving rise to liability in tort) are not protected.

Damage is the gist of all of the torts currently being considered; so the main remedy is damages,[36] but an injunction[37] may also be available to restrain

---

[25] *Lonrho PLC* v. *Fayed* [1990] 2 QB 479, 489 *per* Dillon LJ; 492 *per* Ralph Gibson LJ.

[26] [1992] 1 AC 448.   [27] *Crofter Hand Woven Harris Tweed Co.* v. *Veitch* [1942] AC 435.

[28] *Lonrho PLC* v. *Fayed* [1992] 1 AC 448.

[29] *Lonrho PLC* v. *Fayed* [1990] 2 QB 479 (CA).   [30] See 121 above.

[31] J. D. Heydon (1970) 20 *U of Tor. LJ* 131, 171–82; Wedderburn, 622–3.

[32] Wedderburn, 581–2.

[33] *Hadmor Productions Ltd* v. *Hamilton* [1983] 1 AC 191, 231: protected acts cannot constitute unlawful means for the purposes of tort liability.

[34] See Wedderburn, 648–50.   [35] Elias and Ewing [1982] *CLJ* 321, 347–51.

[36] *Messenger Newspapers Group Ltd* v. *National Graphical Association* (1982) [1984] IRLR 397: damages for unlawful interference with business can be recovered for expenses incurred in anticipation of the tort in order to protect property or business. Aggravated (but perhaps not exemplary) damages are also available. Damages for injury to reputation and feelings are not available in an action for conspiracy: see 102–3 above.

[37] Or an order under s. 235A of TULRCA (inserted by s. 22 of the Trade Union Reform and Employment Rights Act 1993).

unlawful action.[38] In some cases, such an injunction may not be available at the suit of an affected individual but only at the suit of the Attorney-General either *ex officio* or *ex relatione*.[39] It is unclear what the rule of remoteness of damage is in these torts. This depends to some extent on whether P must prove that D intended to injure. If so, then it may be that damages could only be recovered for intended consequences, although such a rule would be narrower than that which applies either to the tort of deceit or even to the tort of negligence. It is more likely that liability can arise for all foreseeable consequences and even, perhaps, for all direct consequences, as in deceit.

Statutory Liability

There are a number of statutes (etc.) which, in effect, impose liability, *inter alia* for interfering with the making of contracts. Such interference may take the form of hindering the making of contracts by two or more third parties, or even of refusal or failure by the defendant to make a contract with the plaintiff. Liability for this latter form of interference involves a departure from one of the tenets of the principle of freedom of contract, namely that individuals may contract or refuse to contract with whomever they will. Where liability is envisaged it may, indeed, be tortious to refuse or fail to make a contract.

The 'statutory' causes of action (some of which, at least, are viewed as statutory torts[40]) differ in at least one important respect from their common law counterparts: liability does not always depend on proof of intention or even of negligence. The two main areas to consider are discrimination law and competition law.

Discrimination Law   Under the Sex Discrimination Act 1975 (SDA)[41] and the Race Relations Act 1976 (RRA),[42] victims of discrimination in matters of employment can be awarded compensation by an industrial tribunal.[43] Compensation is also payable if the respondent to a discrimination claim has, without reasonable justification, failed to comply with a recommendation made by an industrial tribunal (under SDA, s. 65(1)(c) or RRA, s. 56(1)(c)) that action be taken to reduce or obviate the effect on the complainant of the

---

[38] In *News Group Newspapers Ltd* v. *SOGAT '82* [1987] ICR 181 an injunction was granted to restrain intimidatory threats. See also *Femis-Bank (Anguilla) Ltd* v. *Lazar* [1991] Ch. 391.

[39] *Gouriet* v. *Union of Post Office Workers* [1978] AC 435. This statement assumes that unlawful means need not be independently actionable.

[40] e.g. *Duke* v. *GEC Reliance Ltd* [1988] AC 618, 642: 'the statutory tort of operating differential retirement ages'; *Alexander* v. *Home Office* [1988] 1 WLR 968, 975: 'tort of unlawful racial discrimination'.

[41] S. 65(1)(b). See now also Disability Discrimination Act 1995.

[42] S. 56(1)(b). In Britain, discrimination on religious grounds is not unlawful; nor is discrimination on political grounds, on which see House of Commons Employment Committee: 1990–1 Second Report: Recruitment Practices (HMSO).

[43] See generally Wedderburn, 458–82.

discriminatory acts complained of.[44] There used to be a low ceiling on compensation in employment cases (never more than £11,000), but in a sex discrimination case in 1993 the European Court of Justice held that the ceiling was inconsistent with EC law, and damages must now compensate for all the loss and injury actually suffered as a result of the discriminatory treatment.[45] Victims of discrimination in other contexts can claim damages in a county court in proceedings which are described in the statutes as 'like . . . any other claim in tort'.[46]

A distinction has to be drawn between direct and indirect discrimination. The former involves discriminatory action against a member of the protected group by virtue of membership of that group; whereas the latter involves discriminatory action which consists of setting an unjustifiable condition or requirement which does not single out individual members of the protected group but does, in fact, discriminate against them. For example, a ban on the wearing of hats in a pub does not single out Sikhs but it does indirectly discriminate against them. No compensation is payable for unintentional indirect discrimination;[47] but compensation is payable in cases of direct or intentional indirect discrimination.[48] The basic aim of compensation under these provisions is 'restitution'.[49] Compensation can be awarded for injury to feelings;[50] and, more importantly for our purposes, for loss of future earnings (if, for example, the complainant was refused a job or a promotion[51]) or of any other valuable benefit, and for any other quantifiable loss arising out of the unlawful act.

In practice, the context in which claims for financial loss are most likely to be made is employment; but discrimination in other areas, such as housing,[52] may well cause financial loss, and the scope for claims is large. Given this potential, civil litigation in the anti-discrimination field is a relatively rare phenomenon. Several reasons have been suggested for this:[53] superior courts,

---

[44] SDA, s. 65(3); RRA, s. 56(3). Such recommendations are not specifically enforceable.

[45] *Marshall* v. *Southampton and South West Hampshire AHA (Teaching) (No 2)* (Case C-271/91) [1994] AC 530 given effect by Sex Discrimination and Equal Pay (Remedies) Regulations, SI 2798/1993 and by the Race Relations (Remedies) Act 1994.

[46] SDA, s. 66; RRA, s. 57.

[47] But this provision may be inconsistent with EC law; as may be the rule that exemplary damages are not available in statutory discrimination actions. See B. Fitzpatrick in B. Hepple and E. M. Szyszczak (eds.), *Discrimination: The Limits of Law* (London, 1992), 79–80.

[48] SDA, s. 66(3); RRA, s. 57(3); but see *James* v. *Eastleigh BC* [1989] IRLR 318 and B. Napier [1989] *New LJ* 1494.

[49] *Alexander* v. *Home Office* [1988] 1 WLR 968, 975 *per* May LJ.

[50] SDA, s. 66(4); RRA, s. 57(4). See *Alexander* v. *Home Office* [1988] 1 WLR 968. But exemplary damages are not available: *Deane* v. *Ealing LBC* [1993] ICR 329.

[51] Or, of course, if the complainant was dismissed; but this does not fall within the area of present concern because it involves breach of contract: see 133 above.

[52] See e.g. Commission for Racial Equality, *Annual Report, 1993*, 14–15. The RRA and the SDA also cover discrimination e.g., in the provision of professional, banking, and insurance services, and of transport and educational facilities; and in the operation of hotels, restaurants, and places of entertainment.

[53] B. A. Hepple [1983] *CLP* 71; Sir Nicolas Browne-Wilkinson [1988] *CLP* 237.

which have tended to take a legalistic and literal attitude towards interpretation of the legislation, have also used the rules of evidence in this area in such a way as to make proof of indirect discrimination very difficult;[54] legal aid is not available for claims brought before industrial tribunals, where most discrimination litigation takes place;[55] class actions, which have been a significant feature of discrimination litigation in the United States, are unknown in Britain, as is organized and concerted use of the civil law as a tool for dealing with systemic discrimination; and damages awards have traditionally been very low.[56] There are signs of change in recent decisions on the interpretation of the legislation and on the rules of evidence.[57] So far as damages awards are concerned, the recent removal of the statutory cap on damages for discrimination was followed by some very large damages awards and settlements.[58] But the civil law still plays only a minor role in redressing discrimination. It may come to play a much bigger role: large damages awards may make employers and others think twice before engaging in discriminatory action; and the amount of publicity which tends to surround major discrimination cases gives them an impact well beyond their immediate context.[59]

Women are also protected by the Equal Pay Act 1970.[60] The legal technique

---

[54] This is important because although it seems that the legislation has not done much to improve the lot of women or racial minorities, it has eliminated a great deal of overt and direct discrimination.

[55] The EOC and the CRE have power to assist individuals who wish to pursue complaints of discrimination before an industrial tribunal or a county court. In 1993 the CRE received 1,630 requests for assistance. The Commission supplied representation in 250 cases and some other form of assistance in a further 1,174 cases: CRE, *Annual Report 1993*. In 1994 the EOC received 1,629 requests for assistance; it supplied representation in 108 cases and other asssitance in a further 7: *Annual Report 1994*.

[56] Cf. K. O'Donovan and E. Szyszczak, *Equality and Sex Discrimination Law* (Oxford, 1988), 221–3.

[57] Statistical evidence about treatment of the protected group as a whole used to be thought relevant to claims of indirect discrimination but not to claims of direct discrimination. But it is now relevant to both types of claim: *West Midlands Passenger Transport Executive* v. *Singh* [1988] ICR 614. It has been argued that this development makes it clear that discrimination is not like traditional torts between individuals, but rather concerns systemic wrongs: J. Gardner (1989) 105 *LQR* 183.

[58] The very largest awards/settlements were in the region £300,000–£500,000, but most have been in the range £20,000–£40,000. According to the Equal Opportunities Commission, since removal of the cap the average award has risen sevenfold: *Taking the Cap off Discrimination Awards* (1994). It has been estimated that the total cost of claims against the armed forces for unlawful dismissal of pregnant women between 1978 and 1990 may amount to more than £100 million. The EAT has laid down principles for the assessment of awards in such cases: *Ministry of Defence* v.*Cannock* [1994] IRLR 509. The effect should be to bring awards in discrimination cases more or less into line with awards in cases of unfair dismissal not involving unlawful discrimination.

[59] Such publicity can be avoided by settling out of court and by inserting a confidentiality clause in the settlement contract. It is impossible to know how many cases are settled out of court.

[60] Which is backed up by Art. 119 EC. See generally Wedderburn, 487–503. Concerning maternity rights, see Wedderburn, 483–6.

used in the Act is contract,[61] not tort: a term is implied into every employment contract with a woman employee requiring equal treatment with men in respect of a range of conditions of service (not just basic pay). The history of the Act's operation once again shows the importance and value of external pressure (from EU institutions) in forcing the pace of social and legal change in Britain: EC rules required the addition of the concept of 'equal pay for work of equal value' to the concepts of equal pay for 'like work' and 'work rated as equivalent', which were enshrined in the original legislation.[62]

Competition Law[63]

Competition Between Traders
Article 85 of the Treaty of Rome prohibits the prevention, restriction, or distortion of competition within the Common Market, and Article 86 prohibits abuse of a dominant market position. There is authority for the proposition that a breach of Article 86 is actionable in English law as a breach of statutory duty;[64] and it is generally assumed that the same would apply to breaches of Article 85.[65] It had been argued, on the basis of principles of European law, that the only remedy available in domestic courts for breach of these Articles was an injunction because orders to desist (and fines) are the only remedies available in European law: damages cannot be awarded under European law for breach of one of these Articles. However, it now seems accepted that damages are available in English law for such breaches, apparently on the basis that if an action for breach of statutory duty is available then both injunctions and damages must be available as remedies. On the other hand, it was held in *Bourgoin SA* v. *Ministry of Agriculture, Fisheries and Food*[66] that breach of Article 30 of the Treaty of Rome, which prohibits the imposition by Member States of quantitative restrictions on imports within the Community, is not actionable in English law as a breach of statutory duty. The basis of the decision was that the usual remedy in English law for invalid government action is judicial review and that damages are not available. This reasoning was apparently approved by Lord Goff in *Factortame (No 2)*,[67] but it is not clear that it is consistent with the approach of the European Court in *Francovich* v. *Italy*[68] that in certain circumstances Member States can be

---

[61] Other examples of the use of contractual techniques to achieve goals related to those which tort law pursues in the broad area of controlling market power are tenancy protection and fair rent legislation, and unfair dismissal provisions.

[62] By contrast, EC law says very little about race discrimination: G. Bindman [1994] *New LJ* 352.

[63] See generally Whish.

[64] *Garden Cottage Foods Ltd* v. *Milk Marketing Board* [1984] AC 130.

[65] In *Application des Gaz SA* v. *Falks Veritas Ltd* [1974] Ch. 381 Lord Denning MR said, obiter (at 396), that Arts. 85 and 86 created 'new commercial torts'.

[66] [1986] QB 716.

[67] *R.* v. *Secretary of State for Transport, ex parte Factortame Ltd (No 2)* [1991] 1 AC 603, 671.

[68] [1992] IRLR 84.

liable to pay damages for breaches of EC law. At all events, *Bourgoin* is of no direct relevance to actions against private defendants for breaches of Articles 85 and 86.

The availability of actions for damages for breach of these Articles is potentially of very great importance: they could constitute an important aid to enforcement by the European Commission, whose resources are over-stretched.[69] On the other hand, a number of arguments have been used against allowing such actions for damages:[70] the Commission has much greater expertise in these matters than any national court is likely to have; proving a breach and consequent damage would require complex economic investigation and argument which court procedures are not designed to facilitate and which judges are not competent to undertake; effective civil actions in this context require facilities for class actions which do not exist in English law; availability of damages could lead to a flood of claims, and to forum-shopping if damages were available in some Member States but not in others; and it is, anyway, doubtful whether damages awards actually do much to promote competition.

There are also a number of relevant provisions in domestic statutes. Under section 25(3) of the Resale Prices Act 1976 breaches of sections 1 (resale price maintenance agreements between suppliers unlawful), 2 (such agreements between dealers unlawful), 9 (such agreements between individual suppliers and dealers unlawful), and 11 (withholding supplies from dealer unlawful) are actionable as breaches of statutory duty. The Director General of Fair Trading may also apply for an injunction or any other appropriate relief (s. 25(2)).

Under section 35(2) of the Restrictive Trade Practices Act 1976 a failure to register a restrictive agreement is similarly actionable.[71] Furthermore, there is an argument that damages may be recoverable for contempt of court in the form of giving effect to a restrictive agreement held contrary to the public interest by the Restrictive Practices Court.[72] Under section 93(2) of the Act, the Director General of Fair Trading may seek an injunction to enforce compliance with any order made by the Secretary of State pursuant to a report of the Monopolies and Mergers Commission to the effect that a monopoly reference raises public interest issues. Breach of such an order is not a criminal offence, but section 93(2) provides that this does not limit 'any right of any person to bring civil proceedings in respect of any contravention or apprehended contravention of such an order'. It is not clear whether any such proceedings could be brought—it depends on whether a court would be prepared to treat contravention as a breach of statutory duty actionable at the

[69] D. G. Goyder, *E.C. Competition Law*, 2nd edn. (Oxford, 1993), chs. 25, 26.

[70] F. Jacobs [1983] *European LR* 353; J.-M. Claydon [1983] *ECLR* 245; M. Friend and J. Shaw (1984) 100 *LQR* 188.

[71] Whish, 173.

[72] Whish, 169; Sir Gordon Borrie and N. Lowe, *The Law of Contempt*, 2nd edn. (London, 1983), 281–4.

suit of individuals.[73] This provision also applies to orders made pursuant to an adverse report made under the Competition Act 1980 in respect of anti-competitive practices in connection with the production, supply, or acquisition of goods, or the supply or securing of services, within the United Kingdom.

By contrast, section 26(a) of the Fair Trading Act 1973 expressly provides that contravention of an order made under section 22 of the Act (pursuant to a report by the Director General of Fair Trading that a consumer trade practice has an adverse effect on consumers)[74] does not give rise to civil liability. But even where they are available, private actions for damages, although ideologically important, play an insignificant practical part in UK competition law.[75]

A rather specialized form of anti-competitive practice is the making of threats to sue for infringement of a trade mark,[76] patent,[77] a design right,[78] or a registered design.[79] Because intellectual property rights can, in the last resort, only be protected by litigation, such threats to sue are of very great commercial signficance. Even if the threat is believed to be groundless, the uncertainty and the expensive and time-consuming nature of litigation may lead a competitor to think that it would be economically more sensible to capitulate than to fight. The common law offers relatively little protection here: both the tort of malicious institution of legal proceedings[80] and that of injurious falsehood[81] require the plaintiff to prove that the defendant did not hold a genuine and honest belief, based on reasonable grounds, that the proceedings were justified.[82] Hence the statutory protection. The protection is limited in various ways. For instance, merely informing a person of the existence of the right in question does not constitute a threat of proceedings. The person making the threats can escape liability by proving that the acts in

[73] The attitude of English courts to Arts. 85 and 86 EC suggests that a contravention might be held actionable.

[74] See Harvey and Parry, 310–11. On the relationship between the Competition Act and the Fair Trading Act see Whish, 119–20.

[75] The White Paper, *Opening Markets—New Policy on Restrictive Trade Practices*, Cm 727 (1989) proposed sweeping changes to competition law to bring it more in line with EC law; and a 1992 Green Paper, *Abuse of Market Power*, Cm 2100, proposed reform of certain aspects of the Fair Trading Act and the Competition Act: see Whish, 730–7. In the former, the Government expressed the hope that private actions would play an increasingly significant part in any new regime, and proposed certain measures to encourage such actions: paras. 5.15–19. Current government policy is against radical reform of competition law and policy despite continuing pressure from bodies such as the National Consumer Council, which favours civil actions: National Consumer Council, *Competition and Consumers* (May, 1995). Concerning the role of private actions in Australian restrictive trade practices law see M. Brunt (1990) 17 *Melb. ULR* 582.

[76] Trade Marks Act 1994, s. 21.   [77] Patents Act 1977, s. 70.

[78] CDPA, s. 253.   [79] Registered Designs Act 1949, s. 26.

[80] Salmond, 404–14.   [81] Cornish, 429–30; J. D. Heydon, *Economic Torts*, 82.

[82] Cf. *Granby Marketing Services Ltd* v. *Interlego AG* [1984] RPC 209 in which P attempted to get around the lack of a statutory prohibition on threatening proceedings for copyright infringement by bringing an action for wrongful interference with contract. The action failed because the threat of proceedings had been made *bona fide*.

respect of which proceedings were threatened constitute or, if done, would constitute, an infringement of the relevant right. Any 'person aggrieved' by an actionable threat may sue, whether or not he or she was the person to whom they were made. The remedies available are a declaration that the threats were unjustifiable, an injunction to restrain continuance of the threats, and damages for loss suffered.

Competition in the Market for Labour and for Goods and Services

Under section 145 of TULRCA a person must not 'refuse to deal with' a supplier or prospective supplier of goods or services on the ground that work to be done for the purposes of the contract would be, or would be likely to be, done by persons who are or are not union members. Under section 187 a person must not refuse to deal on the ground that a supplier or prospective supplier does not or is not likely to recognize, or negotiate or consult with, a union. Such refusal is actionable as a breach of statutory duty at the suit of the disappointed supplier or any other person adversely affected by the refusal. But it might be very difficult to prove a case under these provisions. Moreover, large damages awards are perhaps unlikely to be made: damages for being deprived of the chance of tendering would be heavily discounted because of their speculative nature. Where a person actually refuses to contract with another on a prohibited ground, the latter would be under a duty to mitigate the loss by finding alternative work; and in many cases this requirement would operate to keep the award low.

These provisions are part of a wider plan to restrict the adoption and operation of union closed shops. Also part of this plan is section 137 of TULRCA which prohibits refusal of employment on the ground that a person is or is not a member of a union or is unwilling to become or to cease to be a union member; and section 138 which prohibits refusal of the services of an employment agency on such grounds. Breach of either provision gives rise to a right of complaint to an industrial tribunal, and the available remedies include compensation 'assessed on the same basis as damages for breach of statutory duty' which 'may include compensation for injury to feelings' (TULRCA, s. 140). Compensation can also be awarded against a person who exerts pressure to induce such action by calling or threatening to call industrial action (TULRCA, s. 142). In the light of these provisions, section 174 of TULRCA, which confers upon workers a right not to be unreasonably excluded or expelled from a trade union in cases where membership of a particular trade union is a condition of obtaining or retaining employment, seems largely redundant.[83]

---

[83] This section protects both existing contractual rights and contractual expectancies. But note that dismissal of an employee in order to enforce trade union membership is automatically unfair (TULRCA, s. 152). See also TULRCA ss. 64 and 66(4).

Anti-Competitive Practices by Public Authorities

Under section 17 of the Local Government Act 1988, local authorities[84] must not, *inter alia*, exclude persons from tendering for public supply or works contracts, or refuse to enter into such a contract on the basis of 'non-commercial' considerations (as defined in s. 17(5)).[85] The effect of section 19(10) is to prevent the use of contractual terms to achieve non-commercial ends.[86] Non-compliance with the statute is actionable as a breach of statutory duty (s. 19(7)) at the suit of any person who suffers loss or damage as a consequence. Under this Act, therefore, failure to enter a contract (and termination of a contract) may amount to a tort.[87] Where an action is brought by an unsuccessful tenderer, damages are limited to the reasonable costs of making the tender.[88] An application for judicial review is available as an alternative to a civil action for damages;[89] but such an application would be a relatively unattractive option because the most a disappointed tenderer could expect would be that the local authority would be forced to find some commercial reason not to award any particular contract to the plaintiff. This might not be too difficult, given that the definition of 'non-commercial matters' does not cover all fields of social policy; and given the flexibility inherent in notions such as 'value for money'.

Damages, interim orders in the nature of an injunction, and other remedies are also available for breach of the provisions of various sets of regulations[90] which implement EC Directives dealing with the award of works and supply contracts by governmental and certain non-governmental bodies. As a result, both making a contract and failure to make a contract may, in effect, be a tort; and actions may be brought by successful or unsuccessful tenderers.

Competition in the Supply of Essential Services

Under the Telecommunications Act 1984 the Secretary of State has power to grant licences for the running of telecommunications systems (as defined in the Act). The Minister may attach conditions to such licences in order to further the aims of the legislation, which include the protection of consumers and the maintenance and promotion of effective competition between persons engaged in commercial activities connected with telecommunications in the United Kingdom.[91] If a licence-holder contravenes or appears likely to

---

[84] And other authorities listed in Sch. 2 to the Act. There are many ways in which the exercise by governmental bodies of their statutory powers can have an effect on competition; concerning government financial support for industry see T. Sharpe (1979) 95 *LQR* 205; on central governnment contracting policy see T. Daintith [1979] *CLP* 41, 50–3.

[85] See also ss. 18 and 19(1)–(4).

[86] Contracts may not be terminated for non-commercial reasons: s. 17(4)(c)(ii).

[87] At common law, failure of a member of a common calling to provide services without reasonable ground for refusal is actionable. N. E. Palmer, *Bailment* (2nd edn., London, 1991), 973 says that the failure of a common carrier to accept goods for carriage is actionable in *tort*.

[88] Local Government Act 1988, s. 19(8).   [89] S. 19(7)(a).

[90] Such as the Public Works Contracts Regulations 1991, the Public Supply Contracts Regulations 1991 and the Utilities Supply and Works Contracts Regulations 1992.

[91] Telecommunications Act 1984, s. 3(2)(b).

contravene any condition attached to the licence, the Director General of Communications may issue an order to secure compliance with the condition(s). The obligation to comply with such an order is a duty owed to any person who may be affected by a contravention of it.[92] If a person suffers loss or damage as a result of a breach of such a duty, or of any act which induces such a breach or interferes with the performance of such a duty,[93] that person can bring an action for breach of statutory duty.[94] If the person sued is the person who owes the duty, that person can plead that all reasonable steps were taken and all due diligence exercised to avoid contravening the order.[95] If the defendant is a person who induced the breach or interfered with the performance of the duty (for example, an employee of the licence-holder), that person will be liable only if he or she acted 'wholly or partly for the purpose of achieving that result'. The Director General may also bring an action for an injunction or other appropriate relief to enforce an order made by him or her. The Gas Act 1986 (s. 30), the Water Act 1989 (s. 22), and the Electricity Act 1989 (s. 27) establish similar regimes of liability except that they do not impose liability for inducing breach of, or for interference with the performance of, the duty to comply with an enforcement order.

Interference with the Making of Contracts by Physical Damage to Property of a Third Party

We have already considered the issues relevant here in two other contexts, namely that concerned with recovery for physical damage to property in which the plaintiff has a contractual interest, and that concerned with damage to contractual interests by physical damage to third-party property. When considering the latter, we saw that there is normally no liability for unintentional interference with contracts. Here we are concerned with cases in which the defendant, by causing physical damage to the property of a third party, interferes with the plaintiff's trade. The classic fact situations involve the cutting off of essential services,[96] or damage to strategic infrastructure such as bridges,[97] as a result of which the plaintiff loses profits on expected

---

[92] S. 18(5).

[93] This provision for compensation for inducing breach is designed to allow civil actions in respect of loss caused by industrial action by workers. It puts telecommunications workers at a disadvantage because the statutory immunities for trade disputes will not apply to actions which fall under the provision unless the aim of the strike justifies classifying it as a trade dispute and it was no part of the purpose of the strikers to bring about a breach of the licence-holder's duty (which is very unlikely to be the case). See H. Carty (1984) 13 *ILJ* 165; Wedderburn, 658–9.

[94] Telecommunications Act 1984, s. 18(6).

[95] S. 18(7).

[96] e.g. *Elliott* v. *Sir Robert McAlpine & Sons Ltd* [1966] 2 Lloyd's Rep. 482 (telephone; concerning the liability of British Telecom see British Telecommunications Act 1981, s. 23; and of the Post Office, Post Office Act 1969, s. 29); *Spartan Steel & Alloys Ltd* v. *Martin & Co. (Contractors) Ltd* [1973] QB 27 (electricity). But contrast *New Zealand Forest Products Ltd* v. *Attorney General* [1986] 1 NZLR 14.

[97] *Norsk Pacific Steamship Co.* v. *Canadian Pacific Railway Co.* (1992) 91 DLR(4th) 289.

contracts.[98] Once again, a person who suffers purely economic loss as a result of unintentional physical damage to the property of another cannot normally recover damages for that loss in a negligence action.[99] If the damage was deliberately inflicted with the intention of causing financial loss to the plaintiff, P might be able to sue D for intentionally causing loss by unlawful means. But a person cannot be liable for negligent interference with contractual expectancies merely on the basis of having caused physical damage to property belonging to a third party.[100]

Apart from the question of how this rule is to be justified, which we will consider in Chapter 10, the main issue arising is how to reconcile the rule with the rules about nuisance, which we will now consider.

Interference by Nuisance with the Making of Contracts

We saw in the last chapter that economic loss is recoverable both in private and in public nuisance.[101] Such loss might result from interference with existing contractual rights or with contractual expectancies. For example, the unintentional blocking of a road or canal might make it more expensive for persons to perform existing contracts, and might deprive them of future business.[102] Such liability for purely economic loss consequent upon a nuisance is problematic. As we have seen, there is a general ban on recovery for purely economic loss consequent on unintentional physical damage to the property of a third party even if the property damage affects the conduct of business by P on P's land and so might fall within the definition a of private nuisance. Is there any good reason why a landowner should be entitled to recover for purely economic loss consequent on, for example, a noise nuisance or the blocking of a view, but not for economic loss consequent on the cutting of an electricity cable which supplies the land? A possible reason may be that physical damage to the property of a third party is more likely to affect a large number of landowners and generate a flood of claims than is a noise nuisance or the blocking of a view, for instance. As we will see in Chapter 10, fear of a flood of claims is one of the chief justifications for the refusal of liability for economic loss resulting from third-party property damage.

[98] See also *Weller* v. *Foot and Mouth Disease Research Institute* [1966] 1 QB 569; *Domar Ocean Transportation Ltd* v. *MV Martin Andrew* (1985) 754 F2d 616, discussed 116 above.

[99] Cf. *Petition of Kinsman Transport Co.(II)* (1968) 388 F2d 821; *State of Louisiana* v. *MV Testbank* (1985) 752 F2d 1019. The rule has not been adopted in Australia: *Caltex Oil (Australia) Pty Ltd* v. *Dredge 'Willemstad'* (1976) 136 CLR 529; or in Canada: *Norsk* n. 97 above.

[100] Would the same rule apply if, for example, a contractor working for a building owner negligently disconnected the electricity supply to the building without causing any damage to the owner's property but thereby causing the shutdown of computers which a tenant in the building used to trade on the stock market? To the extent that the justifications for the basic rule (on which see 454 below) apply to this case there is no reason why the result should not be the same.

[101] See 128–9 above.

[102] e.g. *Union Oil Co.* v. *Oppen* (1974) 501 F2d 558 (successful action by commercial fisherman whose business activities were affected by an oil spill); Comment (1974) 88 *Harv. LR* 444; W. Bishop and J. Sutton (1986) 15 *JLS* 347, 359; B. Feldthusen, *Economic Negligence*, 3rd edn. (Toronto, 1994), 259–64.

In the light of this reason, liability for economic loss in pub.
seems particularly problematic because public nuisances often af
number of people. There appears to be no good reason why a litig
be able to recover for economic loss by pleading it as consequent
unintentionally caused public nuisance when such recovery would be denied
if the claim were framed in negligence.[103]

Finally, note that the discussion above[104] of the use of the torts of private
and public nuisance in the industrial relations context is relevant here too.

Conduct Affecting the Value of Contractual Expectancies

The cases to be considered in this section fall into two fact patterns: the first
is where a person is induced to enter a contract as a result of some statement
or action of another which led the person to think that the contract would
be more valuable than it turned out to be; the second is where the negligent
performance of some service deprives a person of some contractual
expectancy or renders it less valuable.

Common Law

Misstatements which Induce Contracts[105]   Here we are concerned with misstatements and actions which imply statements which are false. The most
common way in which misstatements cause financial loss is by inducing the
representee to enter a contract.[106] The law's concern here is not so much to
ensure that contracting parties have sufficient information on which to base
their economic choices: the basic rule is that mere failure to disclose relevant
information is not tortious. Rather, the main aim is to make good the effects
of the giving of inaccurate information which influences economic choices.
Liability can exist in cases whether the representor is a third party or the other
contracting party. Where the representor is the other contracting party, the
representee may also be able to bring an action in contract. In such cases, the
representee may be able to sue both in contract and tort,[107] provided the two
actions are not theoretically incompatible; if they are, P must choose between
them, but this choice is free. It is not usual to think of liability for misstatements which induce contracts as involving the protection of contractual

---

[103] But note *State of Louisiana* v. *MV Testbank* (1985) 752 F2d 1019, noted P. S. Atiyah (1985)
5 *OJLS* 485: ship collision causes chemical spill and closes shipping lane; 41 claims were brought
representing shipping interests, marina and boat rental operators, seafood enterprises, and fishermen. Court of Appeals held (see 1030), *inter alia*, that recovery would be denied in the absence
of damage to the property of the plaintiffs whether the action was framed in public nuisance or
negligence.

[104] See 129.   [105] See generally Treitel, ch. 9.

[106] Misstatements which induce contracts are usually called 'misrepresentations', but I will use
the terms 'misstatement' and 'misrepresentation' interchangeably in this context. The plaintiff
will often be the buyer under the contract, but may be the seller: consider e.g. an action against
an estate agent for undervaluing a house which the agent is employed to sell.

[107] See 130 above.

expectancies, but it is important to treat them in this way in order to understand properly the relationship between tort and contract. The crucial point is that at the time of the alleged tort, the interest which the plaintiff was trying to protect by relying on the defendant's statement was the interest in entering a contractual arrangement which measured up to P's hopes of making a gain or, at least, not suffering a loss.[108]

The protection given to the representee's expectations varies according to whether the misstatement was fraudulent, negligent, or 'purely innocent'. The law of tort does not give any remedy for purely innocent misstatement: outside defamation, there is no strict tortious liability for statements. This means that a person induced to enter a contract as a result of a purely innocent misrepresentation will have an action only if the misrepresentor was the other party to the contract. It also means that the only remedies for innocent misrepresentation are contractual: rescission and/or damages for breach of contract,[109] if the statement is held to be a term of the contract; or rescission for misrepresentation or damages in lieu of rescission.[110] The principles governing whether a misstatement which induces a contract will be held to be a term of the contract are complex and vague; and they have been rendered much less important than they once were because there are now non-contractual remedies for negligent misrepresentation,[111] and because damages (in lieu of rescission) can now be awarded for any non-fraudulent[112] misrepresentation. Before these remedies existed, the only way a court could award damages for a non-fraudulent misrepresentation which induced a contract was to hold the statement to be a term of the contract; and if it did this then, prior to the passing of the Misrepresentation Act 1967, the only remedies available were remedies for breach of contract: the right to rescind for misrepresentation was lost.[113]

Rescission for breach of contract only operates from the date of rescission, and so damages for breach of contract can be recovered in addition to rescission for breach (which is more accurately called, and will hereafter be called, 'termination'). Rescission for misrepresentation (which will, hereafter, be called simply 'rescission') operates retrospectively, so that the contract is treated as never having existed. A contract will be rescinded only if the parties can be substantially restored to their pre-contractual financial positions: *restitutio in integrum* must be possible. This means that property and other

---

[108] Cf. J. A. Weir [1963] *CLJ* 216, 220: *Hedley Byrne* v. *Heller* introduced tort liability for 'negligent promotion of contractual relations'.

[109] Depending on whether the statement is held to be a condition, a warranty, or an innominate term.

[110] Misrepresentation Act 1967, s. 2(2).

[111] Before the passing of the Misrepresentation Act 1967 there were only two categories of actionable misrepresentation, namely fraudulent and innocent (it was not clear until 1972 that *Hedley Byrne* applied to pre-contractual misstatements); the latter category encompassed both negligent and purely innocent misrepresentations.

[112] That is, negligent or purely innocent.

[113] See now Misrepresentation Act 1967, s. 1(a).

benefits transferred under the contract must be capable of being returned either *in specie* or in the form of some reasonable equivalent. The representee may also be able to recover from the representor an 'indemnity' for amounts paid under the terms of the contract to third parties.[114] Rescission or termination will, of course, only be available as remedies in cases in which the defendant is the other party to the contract. Damages in lieu of rescission are in the discretion of the court; this may apply to the quantum of damages as well as to the basic question of whether they will be awarded at all.

If the misstatement was fraudulent in the sense that the defendant knew it was false and made it with the intention that the plaintiff should detrimentally rely on it,[115] then the remedies available are termination of the contract and/or damages for breach of contract, if the misstatement is held to be a term of the contract; or rescission for misrepresentation, plus restitution and indemnity (but not damages in lieu of rescission);[116] and (in either case) damages in tort for deceit.

If the misstatement was negligent, the available remedies are termination of the contract and/or damages for breach of contract, if the misstatement is held to be a term of the contract; or rescission for misrepresentation or damages in lieu of rescission; and (in either case) damages in tort for negligence. Such tort damages are available under two heads: at common law under the principles first stated in *Hedley Byrne* v. *Heller*[117] and *Esso* v. *Mardon*,[118] and under section 2(1) of the Misrepresentation Act 1967.

The main differences between these two sources of damages for negligent misstatement are these: first, under the Act an action will lie only if the misrepresentor was the other party to the contract,[119] whereas at common law damages may be recoverable in respect of a misrepresentation which induces the representee to enter into a contract with a third party. Such common law liability may arise if the representor explicitly undertook responsibility to the representee for the accuracy of the representation[120] (or, perhaps, to an

---

[114] J. Cartwright, *Unequal Bargaining* (Oxford, 1991), 139–40.

[115] Or, in other words, if the false statement was 'aimed at the plaintiff'. Deceit falls within the definition of the 'innominate tort' of causing loss by unlawful means considered above. Here we are dealing in particular with deceit which induces a person to enter a contract.

[116] Of course, these remedies are only available where the misrepresentor is the other party to the contract.

[117] [1964] AC 465. In 1964, R. Stevens (27 *MLR* 121, 122) said this: 'The development of a complex commercial system, and in this century a more general participation in that system by the population a large, has made the absence for a general remedy for statements leading to financial loss appear increasingly anachronistic'.

[118] [1976] QB 801.

[119] So an agent cannot be sued under the Act, only the principal: *Resolute Maritime Inc.* v. *Nippon Kaiji Kyokai* [1983] 1 WLR 857.

[120] *Hedley Byrne & Co. Ltd* v. *Heller & Partners Ltd* [1964] AC 465. It is unlikely in reality that a person will explicitly and positively undertake responsibility; positive undertakings are more likely to be 'implied' or imposed. The notion of 'undertaking' is more important in cases, such as *Hedley Byrne*, where the defendant disclaims such an undertaking; cf. *Pacific Associates Inc.* v. *Baxter* [1990] 1 QB 993. *Smith* v. *Bush* [1990] 1 AC 831 establishes that non-contractual disclaimers are subject to the Unfair Contract Terms Act 1977. But liability for fraudulent

ascertainable class of persons of whom the representee was one)[121], or where it is reasonable to impose responsibility.[122] Secondly, at common law silence (that is, failure to speak) may (albeit rarely) give rise to liability for negligent 'misstatement', whereas under the Act the defendant must actually have made a statement.[123] Thirdly, at common law the burden of proof on the issue of negligence rests on the plaintiff, whereas under the Act it rests on the defendant.

Fourthly, at common law the plaintiff has to prove that the defendant was negligent at the time the statement was made, whereas under the Act the defendant has to prove that he or she had reasonable cause to believe the truth of the statement up until the contract was made. In other words, the Act imposes a duty to disclose information (of which the representor knows or ought to know) which affects the truth of the original statement, which may not exist at common law.[124] Fifthly, the Act says that the statement is to be treated as if it had been made fraudulently. This 'fiction of fraud' has a number of actual or potential ramifications:[125] first, there can be no liability under section 2(1) unless, as required in the tort of deceit, the defendant made the statement with the intention that the plaintiff should rely on it.[126] Secondly, the measure of damages in claims under section 2(1) is that applicable to the tort of deceit. This means that the rule of remoteness of damage applicable to claims under the Act is that laid down in *Doyle* v. *Olby (Ironmongers) Ltd*,[127] namely that the plaintiff can recover for all losses which are a direct consequence of the tort;[128] whereas in a negligence action, only foreseeable loss is compensatable. Thirdly, a misrepresentation as to credit or creditworthiness is not actionable in deceit or under section 2(1) unless it is in writing signed by the defendant.[129] Fourthly, whereas an action will lie for negligent misrepresentation at common law only if P's reliance on it was reasonable, it seems that a party who has relied on a fraudulent misrepresentation can sue even if a reasonable person would not have so

misstatement cannot be excluded or disclaimed: *S. Pearson & Sons Ltd* v. *Dublin Corporation* [1907] AC 351; *Commercial Banking Co. of Sydney Ltd* v. *R. H. Brown & Co.* (1971) 126 CLR 337.

[121] *Caparo Industries PLC* v. *Dickman* [1990] 2 AC 831.   [122] See further 176 below.

[123] *Banque Keyser Ullman SA* v. *Skandia (UK) Insurance Co. Ltd* [1990] 1 QB 665, 790.

[124] See Cane (1981) 55 *ALJ* 862, 867, n.42, 868, n.48 and accompanying text.

[125] There may be others. E.g. (1) a person who personally tests the accuracy of an innocent or negligent misrepresentation cannot be said to have relied on it; but this rule does not apply to fraudulent misrepresentations: Treitel, 303; (2) there is a special limitation rule for actions 'based upon' fraud: Treitel, 314; (3) there may be a special rule concerning notice of rescission in cases of fraud: Treitel, 332–3. Concerning advantages of a fraud action over an action under s. 2(1) see R. Hooley [1992] *New LJ* 60.

[126] *Banque Keyser Ullman* v. *Skandia Insurance* [1990] 2 QB 665, 790.

[127] [1969] 2 QB 158.

[128] *Royscot Trust Ltd* v. *Rogerson* [1991] 2 QB 297. For detailed criticism see I. Brown and A. Chandler [1992] *LMCLQ* 40.

[129] By virtue of the Statute of Frauds Amendment Act 1828, s. 6: *UBAF Ltd* v. *European American Banking Corporation* [1984] QB 713. The section does not apply to actions at common law: *W. B. Anderson & Sons* v. *Rhodes (Liverpool) Ltd* [1967] 2 All ER 850.

relied;[130] but there is no authority that this rule applies to claims under section 2(1). Fifthly, contributory negligence is no defence to a claim in deceit;[131] but in *Gran Gelato Ltd* v. *Richcliff (Group) Ltd*[132] Nicholls V-C held that contributory negligence is available as a defence to a claim under section 2(1) on the ground that the action under the section is akin to an action in negligence. Most commentators agree with this view of the nature of the liability under section 2(1) and deplore the introduction into it of elements of the tort of deceit on the basis that they are inappropriate in the absence of proof of fraudulent conduct.

In cases where the defendant is the other party to the contract, the main constraint governing the availability of these various remedies arises from the effect of rescission which, as we have seen, is to bring the contract to an end as from the date it was made. It is, therefore, not possible to claim both rescission and remedies for breach of the contract. But subject to this, any of the remedies can be claimed cumulatively or in the alternative subject, of course, to the proviso that the plaintiff may not recover more than his or her total economic loss. In cases where the defendant is a third party, the only remedy available is tort damages.

The next question to consider is the measure of damages available under the different heads. There is authority for the proposition that the measure of damages in lieu of rescission under section 2(2) if the 1967 Act is the difference between the value of the contractual performance received by the representee and the value it would have had if the representation had been true.[133] Damages for consequential loss[134] are not available. Damages for negligence at common law and under section 2(1) of the 1967 Act[135] entitle P to be put back into the position P would have been in if the misstatement had not been made. Thus, P can recover the difference between the price and the actual value of what was received.[136] If the representee rescinds the contract, he or she can also recover amounts spent in reliance on the contract and other consequential losses. If the representee affirms the contract, he or she may also be able to recover reliance and consequential losses provided, had the representee known the truth, he or she would not have entered the contract.[137] But if the contract would have been made even if the truth had been known, but the representee would have paid less, the representee may be limited to recovering on the shortfall of value measure on the ground that

---

[130] Treitel, 312–14; *Lonrho PLC* v. *Fayed (No 2)* [1992] 1 WLR 1, 5–6.

[131] *Alliance & Leicester Building Society Ltd* v. *Edgstop Ltd* [1993] 1 WLR 1462.

[132] [1992] Ch. 560.

[133] *William Sindall PLC* v. *Cambridgeshire CC* [1994] 1 WLR 1016.

[134] That is, amounts spent in reliance on the contract and other losses consequential upon having been induced to enter the contract: Treitel, 337–8.

[135] On the relationship between damages under s. 2(2) and s. 2(1) of the 1967 Act see s. 2(3).

[136] This is normally assessed as at the date of acquisition, but this is not an inflexible rule: *Naughton* v. *O'Callaghan* [1990] 3 All ER 191. See also *Smith New Court Securities Ltd* v. *Scrimgeour Vickers (Asset Management) Ltd* [1994] 1 WLR 1271.

[137] *Davies & Co. (Wines) Ltd* v. *AFA Minerva (EMI) Ltd* [1974] 2 Lloyd's Rep. 27.

the other losses would have been suffered even if the truth had been known.[138]

As we saw in the last chapter,[139] such tort damages may include damages for failure to realize expected gains measured according to the likely value of the next best investment available to the plaintiff, subject to proof, on the balance of probabilities, that P would have made that investment and realized a gain. The possibility of recovering such damages might be particularly important in cases, to which I have not adverted so far, in which P, rather than being induced to enter a disadvantageous contract, is induced not to enter a potentially advantageous contract.[140] Suppose, for example, that a doctor negligently advises a patient that he or she is not in sufficiently good health to take a particular job in which the patient would have earned more than he or she is currently earning; or suppose that a bank negligently advises a client that a company with which it wishes to make a lucrative contract is not creditworthy, with the result that it does not enter the contract. In such cases, provided P can prove that if he or she had known the truth they would have entered the advantageous contract, there seems no reason of principle why P should not recover in tort (subject, of course, to the duty to mitigate losses) the value of lost expectations under the contract which did not materialize. In an analogous New Zealand case the Court of Appeal held that damages could be recovered for the loss of the chance of making substantial profits from a land development which had been prevented by the negligent refusal of a government Minister to grant consent for the sale of shares in the development company to a Japanese corporation.[141]

Damages at common law for deceit (and possibly under s. 2(1) of the 1967 Act[142]) go one step further and entitle the plaintiff to damages for all consequential losses which are the intended or direct result of the misstatement[143] (including loss of profits on the opportunity cost basis[144]). Furthermore, additional losses suffered by the representee by reason of impecuniosity are probably recoverable, at least if the impecuniosity is a result of the deceit.[145] It

---

[138] Cf. *JEB Fasteners Ltd* v. *Marks, Bloom & Co.* [1981] 3 All ER 289, 306e (result affirmed [1983] 1 All ER 583).

[139] See 136–145 above; D. W. McLauchlan (1987) 6 *Otago LR* 370; *Gates* v. *City Mutual Life Assurance Ltd* (1986) 63 ALR 600, 607–8. Note particularly *McNally* v. *Welltrade International Ltd* [1978] IRLR 497. Also note *V. K. Mason Construction Ltd* v. *Bank of Nova Scotia* [1985] 1 SCR 271 (Canada).

[140] The plaintiff may, nevertheless, enter *a* contract: suppose that as a result of a misrepresentation that valuable goods are worth very little, P contracts to sell them at a gross undervalue.

[141] *Takaro Properties Ltd* v. *Rowling* [1986] 1 NZLR 22; reversed on the issue of negligence by Privy Council [1988] AC 473.

[142] See 170 above.

[143] *Doyle* v. *Olby (Ironmongers) Ltd* [1969] 2 QB 158. It is unclear whether exemplary damages can be recovered in deceit: *Mafo* v. *Adams* [1970] 1 QB 548; *Archer* v. *Brown* [1985] QB 401. For Australia see *Musca* v. *Astle Corporation Pty Ltd* (1988) 80 ALR 251: exemplary damages available, but award may be reduced or no award may be made where the loss suffered by P is greater than the benefit derived by D from the tort.

[144] *East* v. *Maurer* [1991] 1 WLR 461.   [145] *Archer* v. *Brown* [1985] QB 401.

was held in *Smith, Kline & French Laboratories Ltd* v. *Long*[146] that where, as a result of the deceit, a manufacturer is induced to sell goods at an under-value, the *prima facie* measure of damages is the difference between the price and the market value of the goods sold, rather than the difference between the price and the cost of producing the goods. This rule was supported by drawing an analogy with damages for conversion;[147] the justification given for the rule in cases of conversion was that 'it does not lie in the mouth of the defendant to suggest that the owner might not have found a purchaser or hirer'.[148] But this explanation seems of little relevance to *Smith, Kline & French* in which the basis of P's claim was that if it had not sold the goods to the third party it would have sold them to someone else at a higher price. In fact, the rule provides another instance of recovery in tort for gains not realized, calculated on the opportunity cost basis.

In one respect, damages for breach of contract go one step further than damages in tort for deceit: if,[149] as a matter of interpretation of the contract, D warranted that P would make a particular gain which does not material-ize, then P can recover damages calculated, not on an opportunity cost basis, but on the basis of the gain the representee would have reaped from the investment if D's statement about it had been true. Suppose, for example, that as a result of a misstatement to the effect that particular property is worth £500,000, P is induced to enter a contract to purchase that property for £450,000; and that the property turns out to be worth only £400,000. Suppose, further, that if P had not bought this property, he or she could and would have spent £450,000 in buying another property worth at least £475,000. In tort P could recover no more than the difference between the value of the property and the gain which would have been realized by mak-ing the next best investment, that is £75,000. But in a contract action P might recover the difference between the actual value of the property and what it would have been worth if it had been as D represented it to be, namely £100,000. It does not follow from this, of course, that the plaintiff in a con-tract action will always recover such 'loss of expected gain' damages; for example, where the property acquired would only have been worth what P paid for it even if it had been as D represented it, no damages will be recov-erable.

On the other hand, damages greater than the plaintiff's financial loss (that is, damages in the nature of a penalty) cannot be recovered in contract;[150] and the rules of remoteness governing damages for consequential loss recoverable in a contract action are, as we saw in the last chapter,[151] in some respects less generous to the plaintiff than those in the tort of negligence.

---

[146] [1989] 1 WLR 1. *Restatement (Second) of Torts*, s. 549(2) goes even further and allows damages in deceit on a contractual basis where the representor is the other contracting party.

[147] See 43 above.

[148] [1989] 1 WLR 1, 10 *per* Slade LJ.

[149] But only if: *Watts* v. *Morrow* [1991] 1 WLR 1421.

[150] Treitel, 845–6.   [151] See 145–7 above.

There is one other respect in which the rules governing damages for breach of contract may be less advantageous to the plaintiff than those in tort. In contract, the plaintiff can recover, *inter alia*, damages for losses incurred in reliance on the contract as well as damages for gains not realized. But suppose that P made a bad bargain in the sense that the amount P had to spend in the attempt to realize the gains which, according to D's representation, the contract offered was greater than any gain P could ever have made out of the contract even if D's statement had been true.[152] In such a case, if D can prove that P made a bad bargain (which may be difficult to do), P's damages are limited to the gain reasonably expected and do not cover wasted expenditure which could never have been recouped from the contract.[153] On the other hand, by suing in tort P could recover all amounts spent in reliance on the contract. However, if P made a bad bargain, a court might hold that part of the reliance loss was the result of P's own negligence[154] and reduce the damages accordingly.[155] Even so, the tort measure might yield a different (and, perhaps, higher) figure than the contract rule.

The upshot of the fact that there are a number of different heads under which damages for misrepresentation may be recoverable is that we cannot fully define what we mean by a person's 'financial interest' in a transaction (or, in other words, we cannot accurately state the value of the person's contractual expectancy) without reference to the quantum of recovery available under the various heads of legal liability open on the facts of the case. It is a striking feature of the law in this area that the victim of misrepresentation is given a wide choice of causes of action unhindered by qualms about whether any particular cause of action is contractual or tortious, or about the 'proper relationship' between contract and tort.[156]

---

[152] Of course, the essence of a claim for misrepresentation is that P was induced to make a bad bargain in the sense that the price paid to the other contracting party was too high. But here we are concerned with amounts subsequently spent in reliance on the contract rather than the price paid.

[153] *CCC Films (London) Ltd* v. *Impact Quadrant Films Ltd* [1985] QB 16.

[154] e.g. if a commercial party dealing at arm's length did not take independent advice: *James McNaughton Paper Group Ltd* v. *Hicks Anderson & Co.* [1991] 2 QB 113, 127 *per* Neill LJ.

[155] A misrepresentation is normally actionable as a breach of contract only if a reasonable person would have relied on the statement in the way P did. In tort, too, P has to show that reliance on D's statement was 'reasonable'. In tort cases, reasonableness of reliance is usually said to be relevant to duty of care; but there is some authority for the view that it may be taken into account in reduction of damages rather than as automatically defeating the claim. See R. A. Buckley, *Modern Law of Negligence*, 2nd edn. (London, 1993), 114–5; F. A. Trindade and P. Cane, *The Law of Torts in Australia*, 2nd edn. (Melbourne, 1993), 372; P. Cane (1992) 108 LQR 539, 544. Cf. *McLellan* v. *Fletcher* (1987) 3 PN 202. In cases in which contributory negligence can be pleaded as a defence to a claim for breach of contract (see 136 above) there seems no reason why this preferable approach should not be followed there, too.

[156] The recent history of the law on misrepresentation is a chapter of historical 'accidents'. Consider the chronology: *Hedley Byrne* in 1964, the Misrepresentation Act in 1967, and *Esso* v. *Mardon* in 1976. Actions in tort in respect of misrepresentations made by contracting parties have been abolished in New Zealand by s. 6 of the Contractual Remedies Act 1979, on which see F. Dawson and D. W. McLachlan, *The Contractual Remedies Act 1979* (Auckland, 1981), ch. 2; S. M. D. Todd *et al.*, *The Law of Torts in New Zealand* (Sydney, 1991), 159–61.

Perhaps the most vexed issue in this area of the law is whether, and if so when, a third party can recover damages in tort for loss suffered as a result of relying on a misstatement made to another. Some professions are more at risk in this respect than others: advice given by solicitors to their clients, for example, rarely affects third parties at all directly, whereas the work of professionals involved in the construction industry and of members of 'reporting professions' such as auditors and accountants, often affects large numbers of third parties quite directly.

In technical terms, the question to be answered is what constitutes a 'special relationship' for the purposes of common law liability in tort for negligent misstatement: it has been the law since 1964 [157] that such liability depends on there being a special relationship between the plaintiff and the defendant. A special relationship will exist if the statement was made by D to P in the course of performing a contract between D and P (for example, by a professional to a client), or if P was induced by D's misstatement to enter a contract with D (in other words, if the statement was made in the course of precontractual negotiations between the parties).[158] It may also exist if the statement was made by D to P in circumstances where D undertook or assumed (or where a court is prepared to treat D as having undertaken or assumed[159]) (legal[160]) responsibility for its accuracy, or where D ought to have realized that P would treat the statement seriously and rely on it— crudely put, in business or commercial situations.[161]

But where the statement was not made to the plaintiff but to some third party, the courts have reacted to a fear that to allow liability would be potentially to subject defendants to liability to persons who they could never reasonably have been expected to foresee would rely on their statements. Because words can 'travel far and fast', the class of such 'third party plaintiffs' could be large, and this might impose a burden of liability on defendants which was both 'unfair' in some sense and also difficult to insure against; the full membership of the class might also be unidentifiable at the time D was making the statement, thus making it difficult for D to do the cost-benefit analysis relevant to deciding whether to make the statement at all, and if so, how much to charge for it.

But this fear has not led the courts to deny liability entirely to third-party plaintiffs. Rather, liability has been allowed in some situations in which there was no real danger of unleashing a flood of claims. As far back as 1952,

---

[157] *Hedley Byrne* v. *Heller* [1964] AC 465.
[158] *Esso Petroleum Ltd* v. *Mardon* [1976] QB 801.
[159] *Caparo* v. *Dickman* [1990] 2 AC 605, 628 *per* Lord Roskill; 637 *per* Lord Oliver; 655 *per* Lord Jauncey.
[160] But see *White* v. *Jones* [1995] 2 WLR 187, 212 *per* Lord Browne-Wilkinson.
[161] But see *Caparo* v. *Dickman* [1990] 2 AC 605, 636–7 *per* Lord Oliver. It is normally assumed that there would be no liability for statements made in social situations; but see *Chaudhry* v. *Prabhakar* [1989] 1 WLR 29 which may, however, rest on an unjustified concession: see May LJ at 38–9.

Denning LJ had said that liability to third parties would depend on proof that the defendant knew that the statement would be conveyed to a particular third party for the purposes of a particular transaction.[162] In *Hedley Byrne* v. *Heller*[163] itself P was a third party, but the House of Lords was prepared to treat the case as if it were a two-party case, apparently on the basis that D knew that the information was to be passed on to a third party (it may not be necessary that P's identity be known by D[164]) for a particular[165] purpose.

Denning LJ's 1952 approach was endorsed by the House of Lords in *Caparo PLC* v. *Dickman*.[166] The ratio of the case is that an auditor performing statutory functions for a company[167] owes no duty of care to prospective purchasers of shares whether or not they already own shares. The auditor's only duty is to the company and to its members in respect of their current shareholdings.[168] So a company auditor owes no duty of care to existing creditors of the company who make further advances in reliance on the published accounts of the company; nor, *a fortiori*, to potential creditors.[169] It is unclear what broader propositions the judgments in *Caparo* justify. However, I would suggest that the following statements can be said to have enjoyed majority support. First, whether a duty of care in the making of statements is owed in any particular circumstances depends not on any undertaking or assumption of (legal) responsibility by the defendant, but on whether the court thinks that, all things considered, a duty ought to be imposed.

This proposition deserves some elaboration. The notion of an assumption or undertaking of responsibility is derived from *Hedley Byrne* v. *Heller*. In that case, it was recognized that an adviser faced with a request for information can take one of three courses of action: refuse to give the requested information, give it but expressly disclaim (legal) responsibility for its accuracy, or simply give it. There is, in fact, another possibility: the adviser might give the information and expressly accept (legal) responsibility for its accuracy; although in reality it is unlikely that an adviser would do this, even if the advice was given in performance of a contract to advise. In *Hedley Byrne* itself the bank adopted the second course; so it made sense, in that case, to say that it had not accepted (legal) responsibility for the accuracy of its state-

---

[162] *Candler* v. *Crane Christmas & Co.* [1951] 2 KB 164.   [163] [1964] AC 465.

[164] A. M. Honore (1967) 8 *JSPTL* 284, 288–9; *Caparo* v. *Dickman* [1990] 2 AC 605, 638 *per* Lord Oliver. But to the extent that *Junior Books* v. *Veitchi* [1983] 1 AC 520 establishes any general proposition, it would seem to require knowledge by D of P's identity and the precise nature of P's commercial requirements. See further 208 below.

[165] *Caparo* v. *Dickman* [1990] 2 AC 605, 638A *per* Lord Oliver.

[166] [1990] 2 AC 605. Cf *Anthony* v. *Wright, Independent*, 27 Sept. 1994.

[167] It would be different if an accountant was employed directly by a would-be investor or creditor: *Caparo* [1990] 2 AC 605, 629 *per* Lord Roskill; see also *Huxford* v. *Stoy, Hayward & Co.* (1989) 5 BCC 421.

[168] But on the question of causation see [1990] 2 AC 605, 626–7 *per* Lord Bridge.

[169] *Al Saudi Banque* v. *Clarke Pixley* [1990] Ch. 313. See also *Mariola Marine Corporation* v. *Lloyd's Register of Shipping*, [1990] 1 Lloyd's Rep. 547 (Lloyd's owes no duty of care to the purchaser of a ship in respect of a survey made for the previous owner).

ment, but that if it had it could have been held liable. It was, therefore, often argued that tortious liability for negligent misstatements is assumed, not imposed. But this conclusion does not follow. As I have said, if an adviser 'speaks' without disclaimer, the adviser may either expressly accept (legal) responsibility for what is said or simply speak. If the latter course is adopted, then any undertaking of (legal) responsibility will be, at best, implied; and an implied undertaking is, to all intents and purposes, an imposed undertaking.

The idea that *Hedley Byrne* liability is assumed was given what many thought was its final quietus by *Smith* v. *Eric S. Bush*[170] in which the House of Lords held that non-contractual disclaimers of (legal) responsibility are subject to the Unfair Contract Terms Act 1977. This means that even if an adviser expresses an unwillingness to accept legal responsibility for advice given, that expression may be of no legal effect; in other words, an adviser may be held liable in tort even if it is clear that he or she did not intend or wish to accept legal liability. So disclaimers operate as attempts to exclude legal liability; such legal liability will normally arise independently of any expression by the defendant of an intention or willingness to accept it, and expressions of unwillingness to accept legal liability are of limited effect. However, in the light of the decisions of the House in *Henderson* v. *Merrett Syndicates Ltd*[171] and *White* v. *Jones*[172] it may unfortunately be that the imposition of liability in cases of negligent misstatement must be rationalized in terms of assumption of responsibility.

The second general proposition which enjoyed majority support in *Caparo* is that before a duty will be imposed the court must be satisfied that D knew or ought to have known that P, whether individually or as a member of an 'ascertainable class',[173] was likely or, perhaps, very likely, to rely on the statement for the purposes of a particular, or a particular type of, transaction.[174] Thirdly, however, the defendant will owe a duty of care only if the statement was made for the purposes of that,[175] or that type of, transaction;[176] whether it was so made depends ultimately not on the defendant's intentions but on the court's judgment, given all the circumstances of the case, including any statutory provisions relevant to the making of the statement,[177] of whether

[170] [1990] 1 AC 831.

[171] [1994] 3 WLR 761. See also Lord Goff's judgment in *Spring* v. *Guardian Assurance PLC* [1994] 3 WLR 354. [172] [1995] 2 WLR 187.

[173] [1990] 2 WLR 358, 384 *per* Lord Oliver. See also *Aiken* v. *Stewart Wrightson Members Agency Ltd* [1995] 1 WLR 1281.

[174] *Galoo Ltd* v. *Bright Grahame Murray (a firm)* [1994] 1 WLR 1360; *Deloitte Haskins and Sells* v. *National Mutual Life Nominees Ltd* [1993] AC 774.

[175] e.g. *McCullagh* v. *Lane Fox and Partners*, *The Times*, 25 Jan. 1994.

[176] Cf. *Al-Nakib Investments (Jersey) Ltd* v. *Longcroft* [1990] 1 WLR 1390 with *Morgan Crucible Co. PLC* v. *Hill Samuel & Co. Ltd* [1991] Ch. 215. See also *Pisano* v. *Fairfield City Council* [1991] Aust. Torts Rep. 81–126.

[177] In *Caparo*, the Companies Act provisions about the functions of auditors. Doubt has been cast on the interpretation accepted by the House of Lords of the purpose of these provisions: D. Howarth [1991] *CLJ* 58, 86. See also *Deloitte Haskins and Sells* v. *National Mutual Life Nominees Ltd* [1993] AC 774.

the defendant should be treated as having made the statement for the particular purpose, or type of purpose, for which the plaintiff relied on it.

It is obvious that these statements are very abstract, and they leave much to be decided on the facts of individual cases. In *Smith* v. *Eric S. Bush/Harris* v. *Wyre DC*[178] the House of Lords held that where a property valuer values a property for a mortgagee in circumstances where the valuer knows, or ought to know, that the mortgagor is very likely to rely on the valuation in purchasing the property, the valuer owes a duty of care to the mortgagor.[179] These two cases have a number of noteworthy features. First, as already noted, the duty was held to arise even though the defendant expressly disclaimed responsibility for the accuracy of the valuation. Secondly, in only one of the cases before the House was the valuation report made available to the plaintiff. Thirdly, however, the plaintiff in both cases had paid for the report; and it was well known among valuers that a very high proportion of house purchasers, especially purchasers of modest properties such as were involved in these cases, rely on building society valuations and do not buy independent surveys.

The courts are clearly concerned to limit the scope of liability for negligent misstatement, but the above general principles of liability are by no means as narrow as they might be. For example, they would appear to leave open the possibility of liability to a large, though 'ascertainable', class of persons. It may well be that the key concept is 'purpose': for what purposes should the law allow particular statements to be relied upon?[180] The use of this concept will often impose a limit on liability; but does it have any logical foundation? On the one hand, it may be seen as giving effect to the speaker's expectations: the person might not have spoken at all if he or she had realized that P would rely on what was said in the way P did; or the speaker might have said something different, or might have charged (more) for the advice. Recipients of advice ought, perhaps, to be encouraged to enquire about the purposes which the speaker had in mind. On the other hand, if the use to which the recipient put the advice is a reasonable one, and if it was not clear from what the advisor said that he or she did not intend the advice to be relied upon for that purpose, it might be argued that P should be allowed to recover. At the end

---

[178] [1990] 1 AC 831; T. Kaye (1989) 52 *MLR* 841. Cf. *Rutherford* v. *Attorney-General* [1976] 1 NZLR 403.

[179] The Law Commission once suggested a completely different approach to the type of situation in this case involving the abolition of the principle of *caveat emptor* in relation to contracts for the sale of land, and the imposition on the seller of a duty to disclose to prospective buyers all relevant facts about the property: Consultation Paper on *Caveat Emptor in Sales of Land* (1988); criticised by S. M. Waddams (1989) 105 *LQR* 377. The Royal Institute of Chartered Surveyors made similar proposals: [1989] *New LJ* 903. But the Law Commission resiled from its proposals: *Let the Buyer be Well Informed* (1989).

[180] It should be noted that the idea of purpose also plays an important part in other areas of tort law: liability for breach of statutory duty or negligent performance of statutory powers: see 220 and 239 below; and in product liability: Consumer Protection Act 1987, ss. 3(2)(a) and (b) for example.

of the day, courts have to choose to favour one party or the other: to be 'pro-plaintiff' or 'pro-defendant'; and the concept of 'purpose' does not relieve them of this choice.

Negligent Services A good example of this category of case concerned a defendant which provided a service to farmers of collecting cattle semen for artificial insemination and storing it. D negligently supplied P with the wrong semen,[181] as a result of which fewer calves were conceived than was expected, and the calves that were born were much less valuable than those which would have been produced if the correct semen had been used. D was held liable in tort for damages representing the difference between the price the farmer received for the calves which were born and the price he would have received if the anticipated number of pedigree claves had been born.[182] The principles governing liability in such cases are, no doubt, analogous to those governing liability for negligent statements which induce contracts.

A crucial feature of this case was that P and D were not in competition with one another. We should not deduce from it any general principle of liability for negligently depriving a person of some contractual expectancy for such a principle would be unduly subversive of free markets. This is why there are various restrictions, such as the requirements of intention and unlawfulness, on liability for interference with contracts and contractual expectancies.

Statutory Liability

There are a number of important statutory provisions which create liability for misstatement.[183] The Financial Services Act 1986 imposes liability[184] on any person responsible for securities listing particulars (s. 150) and prospectuses (s. 166) to any person who acquires securities and suffers loss in respect of them as a result of any untrue or misleading statement in the particulars or the prospectus or of the omission of any matter required by the Act to be included in the relevant document. These provisions go further than the common law in that they impose liability for statements which are misleading, even if they are not false; in this way, they could impose liability for mere omission of relevant details even if those details are not required by the Act to be included, where the effect of the omission is to render what is stated misleading. Liability is essentially for failure to take reasonable care in

[181] Note that the semen was not defective. If it had been, there could have been no liability in tort under English law: see 208 below.

[182] *Port* v. *New Zealand Dairy Board* [1982] 2 NZLR 282.

[183] Concerning civil remedies for insider dealing see Criminal Justice Act 1993, s. 63(2); and more generally E. Lomnicka in R. Plender (ed.), *Legal History and Comparative Law: Essays in Honour of Albert Kiralfy* (London, 1990); L. C. B. Gower, D. D. Prentice, and B. G. Pettet, *Gower's Principles of Modern Company Law* 5th edn. (London, 1992), 640–2.

[184] Additional to any liability which may arise from any other source: Financial Services Act 1986, ss. 150(4) and 166(4).

making the false or misleading statements or in not issuing a correction; and liability does not arise where the purchaser of the securities knew that the statement was false or misleading.[185] Whether the defendant reasonably believed that the statement was neither false nor misleading is judged at the time the securities were acquired, not at the time the particulars were published or the prospectus was delivered for registration.

In the light of these provisions, it comes as a surprise that the Trade Descriptions Act 1968 does not impose civil liability for applying false descriptions to goods, or for making false statements in relation to services in the course of a business; and the better view appears to be that the courts would not impose liability for breach of statutory duty in respect of breaches of the Act.[186] Furthermore, section 1(4) of the Property Misdescriptions Act 1991, which makes it an offence to make a false of misleading statement about a prescribed matter in the course of an estate agency or property development business, provides that 'no right of action in civil proceedings in respect of any loss shall arise, by reason only of the commission of' the offence. On the other hand, the Director General of Fair Trading has power to seek an injunction to restrain the publication of misleading advertisements.[187]

Section 5(1) of the Financial Services Act 1986 provides that a person who enters an agreement with a person who is carrying on investment business without being authorized to do so under the Act may recover money or property paid or transferred to the other party under the agreement and compensation for any loss suffered as a result of entering the agreement. The restitutionary remedy is available against 'the other party to the transaction in question or the party to whom, under the transaction in question, the investor's money or property had been paid or transferred'.[188] The compensation payable is such as the parties agree between themselves or as is determined by the court on application by either of them. Section 62 of the Act[189] allows actions for breach of statutory duty for contravention of a wide range of rules, regulations, requirements, and conditions contained in the Act or made (or which could be made) under it, and for contravention of rules of self-regulating organizations and recognized professional bodies. Such actions

---

[185] Financial Services Act 1986, ss. 151, 167.

[186] R. Lowe and G. Woodroffe, *Consumer Law and Practice*, 3rd edn. (London, 1991), 227–8; W. R. Cornish (1972) 12 *JSPTL* 126, 138.

[187] Control of Misleading Advertisements Regulations 1988, reg. 5; these regulations are designed to protect competitors of the advertiser as well as consumers. See further *Director General of Fair Trading* v. *Tobyward Ltd* [1989] 1 WLR 517 and 398 below.

[188] *Securities and Investments Board* v. *Pantell (No 2)* [1993] Ch. 256, 270 *per* Scott LJ.

[189] See also ss. 71(1), 91(4), 104(4), 131(7), 171(6), 184(8), 185(6), Sch. 11, para. 22(4). Ss. 56(2), (3) and 57(5), (6), and (7) entitle a party to compensation for loss suffered as a result of transferring money or property (which is later recovered) under an agreement entered into as a result of the unsolicited marketing or unauthorized advertising of investment products. These provisions would allow recovery, for example, of interest on money or dividends on shares.

may be brought by any 'private investor'[190] who suffers loss as a result of the contravention, subject to defences and other incidents applying to actions for breach of statutory duty. There need be no particular relationship between the plaintiff investor and the defendant; all that need to be proved is a causal relationship between the breach and the loss. Neither section 5 nor section 62 gives a right of rescission of the contract entered into by the investor.

Sections 6 and 61 of the Act provide for representative actions brought by the Securities and Investment Board at the Board's expense on behalf of investors. Under these sections the court can issue injunctions to restrain contravention of the authorization provisions of the Act and of a variety of rules, regulations, requirements, and provisions contained in or made under the Act. The court can also order a party in contravention or 'any other person who appears to the court to have been knowingly concerned in the contravention' to take steps to restore the parties to the position they were in before the transaction was entered into. This is a statutory remedy of rescission and restitution. Any order made must be designed to restore all the parties to their former positions.[191] A restitutionary order can be made against a party, even a party knowingly concerned, despite the fact that the person has received nothing under the transaction.[192] Finally, the court can order a party in contravention to pay into court amounts representing profits made or losses inflicted by such contravention;[193] the court then distributes such amounts among the persons who entered the transactions which generated the profits or occasioned the losses. This provision is noteworthy in two respects: first, it allows the bringing of what is, in effect, a class action for compensation, contrary to the usual idea that class actions for damages are not possible because the issues relevant to assessment of damages vary from individual case to individual case and are not common to the claims of all of the members of the class. By contrast, rescission and restitution orders must relate to specific transactions.[194] Secondly, the provision allows the defendant to be stripped of profits. This can be viewed either as a punitive measure or as restitutionary, in that the profits were made at the investors' expense and by using their money: on the latter view, the action would resemble a claim for an account of profits made by exploiting a person's property.

In the United States, the civil law has played an important role in enforcing securities laws, but it is not clear that it will play a similar role in this country. This matter will be discussed in a little more detail in Chapter 8.

Mention might also be made here of the City Panel on Takeovers and

---

[190] S. 62A, added by Companies Act 1989, s. 193(1); see also the Financial Services Act 1986 (Restriction of Right of Action) Regulations 1991 (SI 489/1991).

[191] *Securities and Investments Board* v. *Pantell (No 2)* [1993] Ch. 256.

[192] *Ibid*. This is a very strong deterrent provision.

[193] The SIB can apply for a *Mareva* injunction: *Securities and Investments Board* v. *Pantell* [1990] Ch. 426. See also *Securities and Investments Board* v. *Lloyd-Wright* [1993] 4 All ER 210 (SIB not required to give undertaking as to damages); D. Crighton [1994] *JBL* 8.

[194] *Securities and Investments Board* v. *Pantell (No 2)* [1993] Ch. 256.

Mergers, a non-statutory body which makes and polices the City Code on Takeovers and Mergers.[195] The Panel exercises great remedial flexibility. In one incident the Panel required Guinness to pay compensation to certain former shareholders in Distillers, which it had taken over. These shareholders had been induced to sell their shares in Distillers to Guinness at a lower price than had been paid for certain other shares in Distillers by a purchaser acting in concert with Guinness; this concerted action constituted a breach of the Takeover Code. There are several noteworthy features of this sequence of events: first, the Panel has no coercive powers but operates purely by consent; secondly, the shareholders who were to be compensated did not have to take any steps on their own behalf: the procedures of the Panel were activated by a rival takeover bidder. Thirdly, the shareholders entitled to compensation were not identified at the time of the Panel's decision: Guinness used the media to inform shareholders of their rights, and to invite them to apply for compensation.[196] In short, the incident involved, in effect, a class action brought by a non-member of the class.

Section 67 of the Companies Act 1985 imposes liability for loss or damage suffered by persons who subscribe for shares or debentures in a company on the faith of untrue statements included in a prospectus.[197] The liability rests on directors and promoters of the company and on persons who authorize the issue of the prospectus. Under section 68 there is a defence that the person sued reasonably believed the statement to be true (or to be a fair representation of a statement by an expert which the defendant reasonably believed to be competent) up until the time the shares or debentures were allotted (or, in the case of a fair representation, until the prospectus was issued).

Non-contractual Expectancies

Here we are chiefly concerned with prospects of making financial gains by means other than the making of an advantageous contract. The most important example is the interest of a beneficiary under a will. In *Ross* v. *Caunters*[198] it was held that P, a disappointed beneficiary, could recover from D, a solicitor who had negligently allowed P's spouse to witness the will, the value of the legacy P would have received under the will but for D's negli-

---

[195] Cane [1987] *CJQ* 324.

[196] But success in alerting small investors to their entitlement was, predictably perhaps, limited: [1990] *NLJ* 239.

[197] See also Companies Act 1985, s. 78.

[198] [1980] Ch. 297; see Cane (1980) 96 *LQR* 182; A. Briggs (1981) 131 *NLJ* 343. The decision was applied in *Watts* v. *Public Trustee* [1980] WAR 97 (cf. *Gartside* v. *Sheffield, Young & Ellis* [1983] NZLR 37) but vigorously rejected in Victoria: *Seale* v. *Perry* [1982] VR 193; Cane (1983) 99 *LQR* 346; H. Luntz (1983) 3 *OJLS* 284.

gence. Similarly, in *White* v. *Jones*[199] the House of Lords held that P, a disappointed beneficiary, was owed a duty of care by a solicitor who negligently delayed in preparing a will giving effect to the testator's declared intention to benefit P, with the result that the testator died before a will was executed. The High Court of Australia has imposed liability in favour of a beneficiary on a solicitor who delayed in telling the executor that the testator had died; during the period of delay the value of the estate fell so that the beneficiary received less than he would have if the estate's assets had been realized earlier.[200]

The chief argument of policy in favour of the results in these cases seems to be that unless the disappointed beneficiary can sue there would be no effective remedy against the solicitor because the estate, which could, of course, claim in contract against the solicitor, has suffered no loss. To refuse a remedy would be unfair to disappointed beneficiaries; and, in the absence of an effective remedy, the law would provide solicitors with no real incentive to take care. On the other hand, the imposition of liability in tort on the solicitor in favour of the disappointed beneficiary has been criticized on a number of grounds. First, it is said that it would be more desirable to amend the law of wills to allow unintended legatees to be stripped of their windfall and the true intentions of the testator to be given effect to.[201] This solution would not deal with a case such as *Hawkins* v. *Clayton*; nor with situations where, for example, a solicitor advises that a will is not necessary, or fails to advise that a will would be revoked on marriage.[202] Nor would it give lawyers any incentive to take care in the preparation and execution of wills.

Secondly, it is said that the beneficiary's interest in such cases is a pure expectation which does not properly fall within the province of tort law. The beneficiary is being compensated simply for not having secured a benefit. In *Seale* v. *Perry*[203] this was an important ground of decision against the plaintiff: it was said that P's interest was a mere *spes successionis*. Two things should be borne in mind in this regard: first, we saw in the last chapter that the law of tort is by no means unwilling to allow recovery for gains not realized especially in circumstances such as those in the will cases where one of the very purposes for which the testator consulted the solicitor was to obtain a will which would benefit the plaintiff. Secondly, we should distinguish between cases in which the loss to the plaintiff is still capable of being remedied by the donor (in which case, the solicitor should escape liability)[204] and cases where it is too late to do anything. For example, while still alive a testator can, of course, alter the will so as to deprive unintended beneficiaries of prospective gains; but once the testator has died, this option is unavailable,

---

[199] [1995] 2 WLR 187.
[200] *Hawkins* v. *Clayton* (1988) 78 ALR 69; J. G. Fleming (1989) 105 *LQR* 15.
[201] H. Luntz (1983) 3 *OJLS* 284; Tony Weir (1995) 111 *LQR* 357.
[202] Nor where, e.g., a solicitor fails to register a mortgage in favour of a third party.
[203] [1982] VR 193.   [204] See n. 212 below.

and the fact that the beneficiary's interest is in securing a benefit arguably provides no good reason why the solicitor should not be held liable in tort to the beneficiary.

A third problem is that in the will cases the beneficiary recovers for economic loss even though he or she did not rely, in the sense of act to his or her detriment upon, anything said or done by the solicitor. Given the emphasis on reliance in *Hedley Byrne* v. *Heller*, which is seen as providing the modern basis for the tort liability of professional advisers, some have thought the absence of reliance to be fatal to liability in the will cases. In *Ross* v. *Caunters* the absence of reliance was dealt with by saying that the case was properly seen as in a line of succession from *Donoghue* v. *Stevenson* (in which liability was not based on reliance) rather than from *Hedley Byrne* v. *Heller*, and by pointing out that the plaintiff had suffered loss even though he had not relied on the solicitor.[205] In *White* v. *Jones* the House of Lords rejected the analogy with *Donoghue* v. *Stevenson*, but implicitly accepted that reliance goes to causation rather than to duty of care, so that if P suffers actionable loss as a result of D's negligence even though P has not relied on anything said or done by D, then the absence of reliance by P on D is not, in itself, a bar to the imposition of tort liability on D in favour of P.

Fourthly, the decision in *Ross* v. *Caunters* was criticized on the ground that, since the remedy given to the beneficiary is effectively one for breach of the solicitor's duty to the testator, it ought to be conceptualized as contractual, not tortious. A contractual analysis of the solicitor's liability to the disappointed beneficiary is far from straightforward;[206] and it was rejected by both the majority and Lord Mustill in dissent in *White* v. *Jones*.

What is the juristic basis of the liability of the solicitor in these cases? In *Ross* v. *Caunters* Megarry V-C based his decision in favour of the beneficiary on *Donoghue* v. *Stevenson*: the solicitor had acted negligently with the result that the beneficiary had failed to receive a legacy. P was, by virtue of being named in the will, in the direct contemplation of the solicitor; and it was part of the very purpose of the transaction between the testator and the defendant to benefit P. Such reasoning did not find favour with the majority of their Lordships in *White* v. *Jones*, who preferred to explain the liability of the solicitor in terms of the concept of assumption (or 'undertaking') of responsibility. The obvious difficulty of applying this concept to the facts of the will cases is that in many circumstances there will have been no dealings between the defendant solicitor and the disappointed beneficiary. Indeed the latter may not even know of the existence of the testator, the will, or the solicitor.[207]

---

[205] Cf. *San Sebastian Pty Ltd* v. *Minister Administering the Environmental Assessment and Planning Act 1979* (1986) 68 ALR 161, 168–9. See also Cane in P. Cane and J. Stapleton (eds.), *Essays for Patrick Atiyah* (Oxford, 1991), 360–2.

[206] K. Barker (1994) 14 *OJLS* 137.

[207] In fact, in *White* v. *Jones* itself, there had been relevant contact between the beneficiaries and the solicitor, but the plaintiffs' case was not based on this. Lord Nolan ([1995] 2 WLR 187, 231) clearly found it easier, because of this contact, to justify a decision in the plaintiffs' favour,

This led Lord Mustill to dissent on the ground of lack of what he called 'mutuality' between the parties. In *Hedley Byrne* there had been such mutuality because the plaintiff had requested for a declared purpose information which the defendant had then supplied. Lord Goff overcame this problem in an unsatisfying way by saying simply that the solicitor's assumption of responsibility to the testator (arising out of the solicitor's contractual agreement to draft the will) 'should be held in law to extend to the intended beneficiary'.

Lord Browne-Wilkinson thought that a duty of care could be owed by a professional adviser even in the absence of mutuality, as shown by the fact that a duty of care is owed by fiduciaries to their beneficiaries. Mutuality, his Lordship said, was only one basis on which a duty of care to avoid economic loss could be imposed. The crucial thing was that the defendant had taken on the job of drafting the will knowing that the beneficiary was 'wholly dependent' on the solicitor to do the job carefully.[208] The grave defect in the approaches of both Lords Goff and Browne-Wilkinson is that they give almost no guidance on when doing a job will carry with it a potential liability to persons who will foreseeably be injured if care is not taken. Lord Nolan seems to have gone so far as to say that embarking on any 'potentially harmful activity' (such as driving a car) could generate liability under the 'assumption of responsibility' principle.[209] In fact, the concept of 'assumption of resonsibility' is too vague and open-textured to provide a useful criterion of liability in this or any other context.[210] In my view, the better approach is that of Megarry V-C in *Ross* v. *Caunters*: his Lordship stressed the unique features of the will cases—the fact that if the beneficiary was not given a remedy there would be no effective remedy; the fact that the identity of the intended beneficiary was known to the solicitor and that the very purpose for which the testator engaged the solicitor was to secure a benefit for the intended beneficiary. The approach of the majority of the House of Lords, by contrast, clearly demonstrates a major flaw in any attempt to fit all instances of liability under a single overarching criterion, namely that any such criterion is almost bound to be so broad and open-textured as to give, by itself, very little guidance for the resolution of cases which have not yet been before a court.

Although this was not made explicit in *White* v. *Jones*, the 'Ross v. Caunters principle' only applies in cases where, by the time of the beneficiary's complaint, it is beyond the power of the testator (or donor in the case of an *inter vivos* gift) to remedy the loss to the beneficiary. So a

although he expressly denied that liability could not be imposed in the absence of such contact. It seems that Lord Mustill (in dissent, at 228) might have been prepared to contemplate a decision in favour of the plaintiffs if their case had been based on the dealings between themselves and the solicitor. But neither Lord Goff nor Lord Browne-Wilkinson put any weight on the contact between the parties.

[208] See esp. [1995] 2 WLR 187, 213–4. [209] *Ibid.*, 230.
[210] Cf. Lord Mustill, *ibid.* 228.

solicitor cannot be held liable to disappointed beneficiaries for failing to press a testator to make provision in the will for particular persons whom the testator refuses to include;[211] or for drafting an ineffective will or deed of *inter vivos* gift in circumstances where the donor refuses to put matters right by executing a fresh will or deed.[212] Nor does a solicitor owe a duty to beneficiaries under a will to take care in advising a testator about dealings with property which is left to them in the will.[213] It should also be said that the principle in *Ross* v. *Caunters* could only apply in cases where the true intentions of the testator were known and could be proved.

2. TRADE VALUES

The term 'trade value' describes the interest of a person who has, by effort and exertion and often by skill, created a situation which can lawfully be exploited for financial gain; the person's interest is in preventing others from exploiting the situation which that person has created. Some trade values—patents, trade marks, copyright, and registered designs—have been accorded the status of property rights by statute; others, such as goodwill, have been accorded similar status by the common law. These property rights were examined in Chapter 2. The question to be considered here is the extent to which the law of tort can be used to protect trade values which have not been accorded such status. Looked at from the other side, the question in issue here is sometimes put in terms of whether the law recognizes a general tort of 'unfair competition' or 'misappropriation of trade values' in addition to other more specific torts which regulate competition. The recognition and protection of property rights is a juristic technique for restricting competition and encouraging innovation and investment; but it is not the only one. And just as the creation of property rights can have undesirable anti-competitive effects, so could the use of other techniques with similar aims. A balance needs to be struck between encouraging competition on the one hand, and innovation and investment on the other.

The Relationship between Common Law and Statute

An important preliminary issue concerns the relationship between common law liability and statutory regimes which protect trade values. To the extent that such statutory regimes are treated by the courts as exhaustive, there will

---

[211] *Sutherland* v. *Public Trustee* [1980] 2 NZLR 536.

[212] *Hemmens* v. *Wilson-Browne* [1994] 2 WLR 323. A solicitor might be liable in respect of an *inter vivos* gift if the gift attracted a tax liability which could have been avoided by careful advice: A. Haydon [1995] *CLJ* 238, 240.

[213] *Clarke* v. *Bruce Lance & Co.* [1988] 1 WLR 881.

be no room for the development of common law rules protecting trade values other than those recognized by statute, or for the development of rules protecting statutorily recognized interests in situations in which the statute provides no protection.

As a matter of principle, one would expect that courts would be less willing to allow the common law to be used to protect trade values which are recognized by statute in situations where the statute affords no protection than they would be to afford protection to trade values which are not recognized at all by statute. This expectation seems to be borne out by the law. Thus, in Chapter 2 we saw that the common law tort of passing off[214] and the statutory regime for the registration of trade marks exist side by side, and the protection each offers overlaps to some extent with that offered by the other.[215] But this is not seen as problematic, apparently because the tort and the statute protect different property interests: the tort essentially protects the trader's interest in goodwill, which may be partly generated and sustained by use of a mark, whereas the statute protects the trader's interest in the mark itself. So the tort and the statute are seen as being complementary rather than in conflict. Similarly, the common law of confidence can be seen, in commercial terms, as complementary to the statutory protection afforded to patents; but in legal terms, the two regimes operate in quite different realms, the former protecting secrets, the latter protecting information which is, by virtue of the marketing of the invention, in the public domain. So while, in legal terms, these cases involve separate bodies of law running in adjacent streams, in terms of commercial and functional reality they form part of a single picture; and in commercial terms, the common law may, in effect, extend the protection afforded by the statutory regimes.

On the other hand, there are cases in which courts have refused to allow the law of tort to be used to protect a commercial interest which is, in practical terms, identical to that protected by a statutory regime. For example, in *CBS Songs Ltd* v. *Amstrad Consumer Electronics PLC*[216] the plaintiffs argued that the defendants were in breach of their copyright by selling in large numbers to the public tape recorders which could be used to copy commercially recorded audio tapes onto blanks: the claim was that by so doing the defendants were 'authorizing' breaches of copyright by the machine owners. The House of Lords held that the acts of the defendants amounted only to 'facilitation' of breaches of copyright, and that this was not a form of infringement recognized by the legislation.[217] In the alternative, the plaintiffs argued that the defendants owed them a duty of care not to cause or permit or facilitate infringements of copyright, and thus cause them foreseeable financial loss. Lord Templeman answered this argument in the following terms:[218]

---

[214] Supplemented by the tort of injurious falsehood.   [215] See 61–3 above.
[216] [1988] AC 1013.
[217] The position is different in Australia: Phillips and Firth, 362–6.
[218] *Ibid.*, 1059–60.

The pleading assumes that we are all neighbours now, Pharisees and Samaritans alike, that foreseeability is a reflection of hindsight and that for every mischance in an accident-prone world someone solvent must be liable in damages . . . The rights of [the copyright owner] are to be found in the [Copyright] Act of 1956[219] and nowhere else. Under and by virtue of that Act Amstrad owed a duty not to infringe copyright and not to authorize an infringement of copyright. They did not owe a duty to prevent or discourage or warn against infringement.

It is the second sentence of this quotation which does the work; the first seems curiously at odds with the facts, which did not involve a mischance or an accident but at the least a reckless disregard of the commercial interests of the plaintiff. The underlying rationale for the decision seems to be that it is for Parliament, and not the courts, to decide the extent to which competition should be restrained and the interests of one enterprise accorded priority over those of its competitors by the recognition of property rights. This argument, by itself, does not go nearly far enough: the protection accorded to goodwill, for example, is not a creature of statute but an invention of the judges.

A possible technical explanation of these two different approaches is that in the former instances (at least in the case of liability for passing off), the common law tort protects a property right whereas in the latter case, the tort of negligence only protects P's interest in making financial gain; or, in other words, the lack of a property right cannot be made good by suing for mere financial loss: property trumps obligation. In terms of substance, however, this explanation only presses the inquiry one step further back: why are some interests better protected by the common law than others by being classified as property interests? The answer to this question, in relation to *CBS* v. *Amstrad*, may be that in the court's opinion, at least, P was asking it effectively to extend the protection afforded to a statutory property right rather than to protect some identifiably separate interest.[220] But viewed in the wider context of unfair competition, this distinction loses some of its appeal: in the former instances the common law is prepared to castigate certain competitive practices as unfair in the absence of legislative condemnation, while in the latter cases it is not.

The issues raised by *Paterson Zochonis Ltd* v. *Merfarken Packaging Ltd*[221] were somewhat different: this was an action by a copyright owner against a printer[222] who printed copyright labels to the order of competitors of P whose plan was to use them to pass off their own goods as P's. The defendant had committed a breach of copyright, and P claimed that damages for such breach should include compensation for all losses which were a foreseeable result of

---

[219] Now the Copyright, Designs and Patents Act 1988.

[220] Cf. R. v. *Licensing Authority Established under the Medicines Act 1968, ex parte Smith Kline & French Laboratories Ltd* [1990] AC 64 in which the House of Lords refused to allow the applicant effectively to extend its patent monopoly by invoking the law of confidentiality.

[221] [1983] FSR 273.

[222] The court was concerned with a motion by the defendant for the striking out of certain parts of the statement of claim.

the infringement, including the losses inflicted by the passing off. The court rejected this contention because, in the words of Oliver LJ, 'the plaintiff's case ultimately depends on the existence, alongside the statutory duty not to infringe copyright, of a parallel common law duty owed to the copyright owner to take reasonable care not to infringe copyright'.[223] The court felt that to impose such a common law duty would involve an unacceptable extension of the statutory protection afforded to copyright. The plaintiff also argued that independently of the copyright infringement D owed it a common law duty of care and that it ought to have taken steps to ascertain whether the material it was printing was the subject of copyright owned by its customers and whether the use to which they intended to put the material was lawful. It was held that the claim in negligence must also fail.[224]

This decision is clearly more justifiable than that in *CBS* v. *Amstrad*: to require printers to take steps to ascertain that the material they are reproducing is not copyright would be to impose a very onerous duty. Furthermore, to hold the printer liable for the torts of the competitors would be to impose liability for the acts of third parties in circumstances where, on general principles, the law of tort would normally not impose liability. On the other hand, printers of defamatory material are strictly liable; but this discrepancy is, perhaps, to be explained on the ground that spreading the effective protection of the copyright legislation would inhibit economic activity more than the legislature intended, whereas the law of defamation does not inhibit legitimate economic activity because we value personal reputation more highly than financial profit. At all events, the Court of Appeal in *Paterson Zochonis* rejected the defamation analogy as irrelevant.

Statutorily Protected Trade Values

Moral Rights

The term 'moral rights'[225] is used to refer to interests of a copyright owner other than the interest in commercial exploitation of the copyright material. They are created by the Copyright, Designs and Patents Act 1988 (CDPA). The rights (stated very crudely and without the numerous statutory qualifications and exceptions[226]) are the right to be identified as the author of a copyright literary, dramatic, musical, or artistic work on occasions when that work is issued or displayed in public ('the right of paternity');[227] the right

---

[223] [1983] FSR 273, 285; cf. Robert Goff LJ at 295.

[224] Robert Goff LJ expressly rejected the argument that the fact that the loss suffered was purely economic ruled out the imposition of a duty of care: [1983] FSR 273, 299–300.

[225] Cornish, 309–16; Phillips and Firth, 8–9 and ch. 18.

[226] The qualifications and exceptions are designed to ensure that moral rights do not impose an undue restriction on business activity which involves the use of copyright material.

[227] CDPA, ss. 77–79. This right has to be asserted by the author, and delay in so doing must be taken into account in assessing damages.

not to have one's copyright work subjected to derogatory treatment by addition, deletion, alteration, or adaptation ('the right of integrity');[228] the right not to have a literary, dramatic, musical, or artistic work falsely attributed to one as author or director;[229] and the right not to have certain private or domestic photographs or films issued to the public or shown or broadcast to the public.[230] Infringement of moral rights is actionable as a breach of statutory duty owed to the person entitled to the right.[231] At common law, the right of paternity and the right not to be falsely identified as author can, to a certain extent, be protected indirectly through the tort of passing off; and the latter right, as well as the right of integrity, receive indirect protection from the tort of defamation.

These rights are called 'moral rights' because they are seen as protecting the copyright owner's[232] non-pecuniary interest in the work or the owner's 'artistic integrity'. They can be readily derived from a view which sees intellectual property primarily as a recognition of the value of self-expression rather than as a legal technique for promoting the efficient use of resources. Because these rights are seen as personal in nature they cannot be assigned, although they can be transferred on death.[233] Furthermore, in the case of the right of integrity the court may, if it thinks it an adequate remedy in the circumstances, grant an injunction restraining the doing of any act unless a disclaimer is made dissociating the author or director from the treatment of the work. This reflects the idea that this right is primarily designed to protect the author's reputation.

However, it should not be thought that none of these rights is of financial significance. Failure of attribution or false attribution of authorship or derogatory treatment might cause financial loss to the author; although the author might have difficulty proving the causal link between loss of income and the infringement of the right—in which case an injunction might mitigate the adverse financial consequences. Furthermore, the rights can be waived, and acts done with the consent of the person entitled to the right do not constitute infringement of the right;[234] consent and waiver are analogous to licensing exploitation of intellectual property rights, and the power to do so reflects the commercial value of the rights. It may be to a person's financial advantage, for example, to have a work 'mutilated' for popular consumption, and the right to sue the mutilator who acts without consent would, in such cases, be of obvious financial value because, as a corollary of the granting of an injunction to restrain future infringements, an account of

---

[228] CDPA, ss. 80–83. The rights of paternity and integrity last as long as the copyright in the relevant work.

[229] CDPA, s. 84. This right subsists for 20 years after a person's death.

[230] CDPA, s. 85.   [231] CDPA, s. 103(a).

[232] But note that the right to object to false attribution can be asserted by any person; and the right of privacy can be asserted by the person who commissions the taking of the photograph or the making of the film even though that person is not the first owner of the copyright.

[233] 226 CDPA, ss. 94, 95.   [234] CDPA, s. 87.

profits could be ordered.[235] Indeed, the waiver provisions may be among the most important in practice: large users of copyright material may regularly be able to require authors to waive their statutory rights in return for more carefully defined and circumscribed contractual rights; and specific groups of copyright owners may band together to bargain with copyright users in the way the Performing Rights Society already does.[236]

The CDPA does not say anything specific about the remedies available for breach of a moral right. Both injunctions and damages are available in actions for breach of statutory duty. Since moral rights basically protect non-pecuniary interests, it is to be presumed that damages for non-pecuniary loss will be available. In a copyright action, the court has power to award 'additional damages' assessed in the light of the flagrancy of the breach of copyright and of any profits made by the infringer.[237] It is not clear whether such additional damages will be available in an action concerning breach of a moral right; although, as already noted, an account of profits could be awarded as a concomitant of the award of an injunction.

Rights in Performances

The CDPA also confers rights in respect of dramatic, musical, literary, or artistic performances[238] on performers and persons having exclusive recording rights in relation to performances. The relevant provisions[239] are designed to deal with the problem of bootlegging, that is, unauthorized commercial recording and broadcasting of performances and commercial sale and broadcasting of such recordings. Because copyright attaches to the permanent form to which the created material is reduced rather than to the material itself, there can be no copyright in performances as such. Prior to the Act, bootlegging was a statutory criminal offence, and it had been held that the statutory provisions in question (which did not expressly mention civil actions for damages) gave rise to a right of civil action in performers but not in recording companies.[240]

Under the Act, infringement consists of doing any of the prohibited acts without the consent of the person entitled to the relevant right. The rights last for 50 years from the end of the calendar year in which the performance took place;[241] the rights are not assignable, but the performer's rights are transmissable on death.[242] As in the case of moral rights, infringement of rights in performances is actionable as breach of statutory duty.[243] Orders for delivery up of illicit recordings can be made,[244] and there is a right in the

---

[235] R. P. Meagher, W. M. C. Gummow, and J. R. Lehane, *Equity, Doctrines and Remedies*, 3rd edn. (Sydney, 1992), 662.

[236] Cornish, 261–3. [237] CDPA, s. 97(2). [238] Cornish, 358–61.

[239] CDPA, Pt. II. [240] *Rickless v. United Artists Corporation* [1988] QB 40.

[241] CDPA, s. 191. [242] CDPA, s. 192. [243] CDPA, s. 194.

[244] CDPA, ss. 195, 203, 204.

person entitled to apply for such an order personally to seize illicit recordings.[245]

Rights in Cable and Satellite Transmissions

Whereas moral rights are protected by actions for breach of statutory duty,
the economic interest of a broadcaster in charging for the reception of television programmes transmitted by cable or satellite is protected by affording
to the broadcaster the same rights as a copyright owner,[246] even though the
broadcaster has no proprietary right in the waves generated by such transmissions.[247] So if a broadcaster makes an exclusive agreement with a manufacturer of receiving equipment for the production and marketing of such
equipment in return for a share of the proceeds of sale, it has a statutory
cause of action against any other manufacturer who, without the broadcaster's permission, markets such equipment.[248] The CDPA also gives a cause
of action against anyone who, without the broadcaster's permission, pub-
lishes information which is 'calculated' to enable or assist persons to receive
cable or satellite transmissions.

Registered Designs[249]

Under the Registered Designs Act 1949 (as amended by CDPA)[250] it is possible to register the design of features of shape, configuration, pattern, or orna-
ment applied to an article by any industrial process,[251] provided it is an
aesthetic feature, that is, a feature which appeals to and is judged by the eye,
and provided the article to which it is applied is of a type which is usually
judged by aesthetic criteria by those who acquire or use it.[252] The original
proprietor of a registered design is its author or, if the author was comis-
sioned or employed by another to create it, that other person. The right given
by registration (which is not stated to be a property right) is a monopoly right
to deal commercially in articles to which the design has been applied. The
right lasts initally for five years, but can be extended for four further periods
of five years each. Infringement of the right consists of doing any act which
the registered proprietor has the exclusive right to do, without the propri-

---

[245] CDPA, ss. 196, 204.   [246] CDPA, s. 298.

[247] *BBC Enterprises Ltd* v. *Hi-Tech Xtravision Ltd* [1990] Ch. 609; affirmed on other grounds
[1991] 2 AC 327.

[248] *Ibid.*

[249] Cornish, 374–81; Phillips and Firth, ch. 24. On design rights, see 69 above.

[250] The text of the 1949 Act is contained in Sch. 4 to the CDPA.

[251] A design is applied by an industrial process if it is applied to more than 50 single articles.

[252] On the relationship between registered designs and copyright, see Phillips and Firth, paras.
24.2–4; and CDPA, s. 53 discussed in M. F. Flint, C. D Thorne and A. P. Williams, *Intellectual
Property: The New Law* (London, 1989), 135. On the relationship between registered designs and
design rights, see CDPA, s. 213(3)(c). See generally Dworkin and Taylor, *Blackstone's Guide to
the Copyright, Designs and Patents Act 1988* (London, 1989), ch. 12.

etor's consent, either in relation to an article or a kit of components intended to be assembled into an article; or of making anything enabling such an article to be made.

Injunctions may be granted to restrain infringement, and an account of profits could be ordered as a concomitant; damages may not be awarded against an innocent infringer.[253] In certain circumstances, licences to exploit registered designs are available as of right;[254] in such cases, if a defendant in infringement proceedings undertakes to take such a licence, no injunction can be awarded and the measure of damages or the amount payable by way of an account of profits is limited to twice the licence fee which would have been payable if such a licence had been granted before the earliest infringement.

Unfair Competition

In Chapter 2 we considered whether the common law was likely to extend the mantle of protection afforded to property rights any further than it presently extends by recognizing new property rights in trade values. We saw that English law has been very unwilling to recognize a property right in one's personality and in other products of effort and exertion.[255] Here we will consider the same question from a slightly different angle: could protection be given to currently unprotected trade values by developing a tort of unfair competition?[256] This approach deals with the issues in terms of the law of obligations rather than the law of property; the interest which would be protected by such a tort is not a property interest in the thing exploited but the contractual expectations attached to the product of the plaintiff's effort and exertion. Such a tort, if it existed, would differ from the tort of interference with trade (or causing loss by unlawful means) in that it could be committed without the use of unlawful means. It would be a version of the tort which in the United States is identified by the phrase 'the *prima facie* tort doctrine',[257] that is, intentionally causing loss without lawful justification.[258]

There are at least four objections to the recognition of such a tort. The first is precedent: the English case law concerned with the intentional infliction of economic loss (in the absence of interference with any recognized property

---

[253] Registered Designs Act 1949, s. 9.   [254] S. 11A.   [255] See 79–81 above.

[256] See A. Terry (1988) 51 *MLR* 296; T. Sharpe (1979) 95 *LQR* 205, 211–13.

[257] Heydon, *Economic Torts*, 128–32.

[258] R. F. V. Heuston (1986) 20 *UBCLR* 33. S. 52 of the Australian Trade Practices Act 1974 (and parallel legislation in several of the States) provides civil actions for 'conduct which is misleading or deceptive or is likely to mislead or deceive.' This provision was originally intended as a consumer protection device, but it has been much used by commercial litigants. A large number of such actions have concerned exploitation of trade values, and many of the principles of the tort of passing off have been applied to them: M. Blakeney (1984) 58 *ALJ* 316. It is unclear how far beyond traditional passing off the provision is capable of being extended; but on its face the section is very broad: W. Pengilley [1987] *Aust. Bus. LR* 241; R. S. French (1989) 63 *ALJ* 250. It should be noted that there is no requirement of intent to mislead or deceive; nor, of course, of intent to injure.

right) seems to allow recovery in only four situations: where there has been a conspiracy to inflict economic loss;[259] where there has been interference with an existing contract[260] or inducement of breach of a statutory duty or of an equitable obligation;[261] where unlawful means have been used;[262] and where a false statement has knowingly been made.[263] Under the law as it stands, there can be no liability for intentional interference with contractual expectancies in the absence of concerted action and without the use of unlawful means or the making of a statement known to be false.

The second objection to the recognition of such a tort is that it would require the court explicitly to weigh the commercial interest of the plaintiff and the interest of the defendant pleaded as justification for what was done; or, put another way, it would require the courts to decide which competitive practices are unfair. Under the present law, on the other hand, judicial discretion is restrained by the requirement to show conspiracy, deceit, interference with existing contractual rights, or unlawful action. Some of the force of this argument is removed when it is observed that the courts have considerable discretion to decide what constitutes unlawful means; and the proposed formulation would have the advantage of forcing the courts to justify their decisions in policy terms rather than hide behind the cloak of 'unlawfulness'.

The third objection to recognition of a tort of unfair competition is that it would give too much legal protection to the purely economic 'right to trade'. It is true that English common law imposes liability for intentional infliction of personal injury or physical damage to property without lawful justification; but, it is said, economic loss is different and less worthy of the law's attention, at least when it is the result of commercial competition. This is an argument of some substance, provided it is rephrased so that the relevant distinction is between economic interests and non-economic interests: there is no good reason why tangible property should receive better protection than other economic interests in cases where the owner's interest in it is purely economic.[264]

The fourth objection is related to the third: a common law tort of unfair competition would unduly inhibit competition and commercial activity. Of course, the restriction of liability to cases of 'unfair' competition is meant to restrict the restraint on competition to cases where it is 'justified' in order to preserve 'full competition'; in other words, unfair competitive activity is really anti-competitive activity. But the nub of this objection is, I think, that it is for Parliament, and not the courts, to decide where the limits of fair competition lie; and this it has done in intellectual property legislation. The obvious weakness of this objection is that taken to its logical conclusion there would be no common law tort liability for passing off, breach of confidence, and so on, to the extent that these heads of liability can be used effectively

---

[259] See 152 above. [260] See 118 above. [261] See 153 above.
[262] See 153 above. [263] See 168 above. [264] See 12 above.

to protect intellectual property rights in ways in which the relevant legislation does not protect them. This objection is the sort of blanket argument which can conveniently be used by courts to justify denying liability in particular cases without having to give concrete arguments in favour of the refusal. The fact that there is much legislation on the topic of unfair competition should, of course, make the courts wary about developing the common law in such a way as effectively to broaden the statutory protection of economic activity. But unless we are prepared to say that the sole function of the courts is to interpret and apply legislation, the existence of statutory provisions in a particular area does not provide a conclusive argument against parallel common law developments.[265]

A possible source of development of a general tort of unfair exploitation of trade values is the judgment of Lord Diplock in *Erven Warninck BV* v. *Townend & Sons (Hull) Ltd*[266] which contemplates the extension of the tort of passing off into new realms;[267] but it is by no means clear how far beyond the classic passing off fact pattern (a misrepresentation leading consumers to confuse the defendant's goods with the plaintiff's) the development might go. One writer thinks that switch selling would now be actionable even though it does not involve confusion.[268] It might be thought, too, that adaptation of the tort of passing off to restrict use of the word 'champagne'[269] is a move in the direction of extending the tort to cover practices which do not involve deception and misrepresentation but 'only' unfair exploitation of the fruits of another's efforts and investment (for example, merchandising of some character or personality without permission[270]).

At the end of the day, however, the basic issue is not whether we adopt one juridical technique (property) or another (interference with contractual expectancies),[271] but rather where the proper balance lies between freedom of competition and encouragement of effort and innovation; and, perhaps more importantly, who should decide where this line lies.[272] There is an argument for saying that the courts should not get too heavily involved in regulating competition;[273] but much depends here on what one means by 'too heavily'. The common law is already actively involved in the area of exploitation of trade values, and the only question appears to be whether the courts feel that

---

[265] See *Erven Warnink BV* v. *Townend & Sons (Hull) Ltd* [1979] AC 31, 743 *per* Lord Diplock; *Reckitt & Colman Products Ltd* v. *Borden Inc.* [1990] 1 WLR 491.

[266] [1979] AC 731, 742–3.

[267] Cornish, 404, 422–6; G. Dworkin [1979] *EIPR* 241; J. Holyoak (1990) 106 *LQR* 564.

[268] Dworkin [1979] *EIPR* 241, 245; switch selling involves a trader leading passers-by to think that it sells product A, but when they enter the shop only offering them product B. It involves no representation that the two products are in any way related.

[269] See 61, n. 213 above.   [270] See also Cornish, 425–6; H. Carty (1993) 13 *LS* 289.

[271] There are other possible theoretical bases for protection; for example, some equitable notion of unconscionable conduct: Terry (1988) 51 *MLR* 296, 312.

[272] Cf. Heydon, 'Restrictive Trade Practices and Unfair Competition', in E. Kamenka and A. Tay (eds.), *Law and Social Control* (London, 1980), 143.

[273] Terry (1988) 51 *MLR* 296, 313–5.

they have gone as far as they should go, or as far as they can go without entering areas which are so controversial that involvement in them carries a considerable risk of damaging respect for the role of the courts in the competition area. All these matters are, of course, the stuff of finely balanced judgment. In 1988 Hoffman J said that he thought 'quite plainly unarguable' the proposition that:

the plaintiffs were entitled to an injunction to restrain any deliberate acts calculated to cause damage to their business and goodwill . . . [or] that any intentional act which is calculated to cause damage to the plaintiff's business or goodwill is actionable per se.[274]

3. MONETARY WEALTH

Typical forms of monetary wealth are debts owed by banks or other financial institutions to depositors and securities such as shares. But my concern here is not only with tortious conduct which reduces monetary credit balances or the value of securities, but also with tortious action which increases a person's financial indebtedness to others. So I am concerned with tortious conduct which has an adverse affect on a person's monetary position.

Intentional Infliction of Damage

The intentional torts which we considered earlier in this Chapter have a role to play here. The most obvious illustration is intimidation in *Rookes* v. *Barnard*[275] where the loss suffered by P as a result of the threats used by D was his job, and hence his income. But other torts—conspiracy,[276] deceit, causing loss by unlawful means,[277] and the incipient tort of harassment[278]—

---

[274] *Associated Newspapers Group PLC* v. *Insert Media Ltd* [1988] 1 WLR 509, 511. The defendants made an arrangement with newsagents allowing them to insert advertising leaflets into newspapers published by the plaintiffs. This was held to amount to passing off and was restrained by injunction ([1990] 1 WLR 900; [1991] 1 WLR 571). In the proceedings before Hoffman J the plaintiffs unsuccessfully moved to amend the pleadings to add as grounds for the award of an injunction that 'the defendants' deliberate acts were calculated to cause damage to the plaintiffs' business and goodwill' and that 'they constituted unfair trading by debasing and devaluing the plaintiff's goods'.

[275] [1964] AC 1129.

[276] *Allied Arab Bank* v. *Hajjar (No. 2)* [1988] QB 944; *Metall und Rohstoff AG* v. *Donaldson Lufkin & Jenrette Inc.* [1990] 1 QB 391.

[277] The Computer Misuse Act 1990 creates offences of unauthorized access to a computer and unauthorized modification of computer material which could form the basis of actions for causing loss by unlawful means. At present, conspiracy and negligence would appear to be the only possibly available causes of action. However, it has been suggested that 'more than three quarters of reported computer security incidents are caused by natural hazards, such as fire or flood, or by human mistakes or basic system failures': 'Computer Bill will do little to help security', *Independent*, 5 May 1990, 3.

[278] For the potential role of this tort in employment contexts see I. Mackay and J. Earnshaw [1995] *New LJ* 338.

may also apply in situations where the plaintiff's loss is purely monetary. For example, a person might, by relying on a false fraudulent misstatement, be led to give money to the rogue or to some third party; or a person might, by fraud, incur debts in the plaintiff's name. Of course, the defrauder will usually not be worth suing; but if he or she is an employee of a third party, the latter may be vicariously liable;[279] and if the rogue acts in concert with others, the co-conspirators may be worth suing.

There can also be tort liability for inducing breach of, or interfering with the performance of, a statutory duty or an equitable obligation.[280] Further, inducing breach of statutory duty or interfering with the performance of a statutory duty[281] can constitute unlawful means for the purposes of other torts. In *Associated British Ports* v. *TGWU*[282] Butler-Sloss and Stuart-Smith LJJ took the view that if the plaintiff rested an action directly on inducement of breach of statutory duty, it would succeed only if the breach involved was itself actionable (although the means used to effect the inducement need not be independently actionable); but that a plaintiff could rely on inducement of breach of a statutory duty as unlawful means even if the actions of neither the inducer nor the induced were independently unlawful. If this is correct, it renders the tort of inducement of breach of statutory duty superfluous.

Another relevant head of liability is malicious[283] institution of legal proceedings and malicious abuse of legal process.[284] Provided P has suffered some actual damage, damages may be recovered for non-pecuniary loss, such as loss of reputation and mental distress, as well for pecuniary loss such as the cost of defending oneself against the wrongful action, and loss of income. It used to be tortious in certain circumstances for a third party with no direct interest in the proceedings to promote or support legal proceedings, but the torts of maintenance and champerty (the latter of which involved supporting litigation in return for a share of the proceeds, if any) were abolished in 1967.[285] Given that these torts could be committed even if D honestly believed

---

[279] *Lloyd* v. *Grace, Smith & Co.* [1912] AC 716; *Uxbridge Permanent Benefit Building Society* v. *Pickard* [1932] 2 KB 248; *United Bank of Kuwait* v. *Hammoud* [1988] 1 WLR 1051. There can also be vicarious liability for misfeasance in a public office: *Racz* v. *Home Office* [1994] 2 AC 45.

[280] *Associated British Ports* v. *TGWU* [1989] 1 WLR 939; Elias and Ewing [1982] *CLJ* 321, 351–6; Simpson (1987) 50 *MLR* 506, 509–10. But on inducing breach of trust see *Metall und Rohstoff AG* v. *Donaldson Lufkin & Jenrette Inc.* [1990] 1 QB 391, 481. See also *Barretts & Baird (Wholesalers) Ltd* v. *IPCS* [1987] IRLR 3.

[281] *Department of Transport* v. *Williams, The Times*, 7 Dec. 1993.

[282] [1989] 1 WLR 939.

[283] 'Malice' means personal spite or ill will, or other improper motive.

[284] Salmond, 404–14; Fleming, ch. 27. It is not tortious to defend a civil action even with a dishonest defence or untruthful evidence: *Metall und Rohstoff* v. *Donaldson Lufkin & Jenrette* [1990] 1 QB 391. Litigation may be used as a form of commercial pressure in order to interfere with D's trade; and if this, rather than vindication of P's rights, is the predominant purpose of the institution of litigation, P may be liable in tort: *Ibid.* 469; *Speed Seal Products Ltd* v. *Paddington* [1985] 1 WLR 1327. See further 266–8 below.

[285] Criminal Law Act 1967, s. 14(1). For an account of the common law see Fleming, 624–8. Although maintenance and champerty are no longer either criminal or tortious, 'trafficking in

on reasonable grounds that the proceedings were justified and even if they were successful, it is not surprising that they were abolished. Very many law suits are quite legitimately financed by 'interested parties', and a rule which would outlaw all forms of contingency fee arrangements with lawyers now seems unnecessary and undesirable given the limited availability of civil legal aid.

Supporting proceedings on improper grounds may amount to contempt of court,[286] but contempt of court does not, by itself, constitute a tort.[287] It has been held, however, that to induce or assist another to act in contempt with the intention of injuring a third party can constitute the tort of unlawful interference with trade,[288] and there seems no reason, in theory, why it should not be tortious for D intentionally to injure P by supporting legal proceedings against P in contempt of court. It has recently been said that although maintenance is no longer tortious it is still 'unlawful', so that an order for costs can be made against a third party who financially supports litigation; and that to this end, an order may be made requiring the supporter's identity to be revealed 'in order that justice should be done as to the costs of litigation'.[289] This decision might be seen as supporting the classification of contempt of court as unlawful means for the purposes of the law of tort.

There can be statutory liability for abuse of legal proceedings. We saw earlier[290] that groundless threats of proceedings for infringement of trade marks, patents, design rights, and registered designs are actionable. A related statutory cause of action is given by section 12 of the Housing Act 1988[291] which provides for the award of compensation for loss or damage suffered as a result of a landlord obtaining an order for possession of protected premises by concealment or fraud.

Indirectly related to, although quite distinct from, malicious prosecution is false (or 'wrongful') imprisonment.[292] Being a form of trespass, wrongful imprisonment is actionable *per se*; but, of course, damages can be awarded for financial loss resulting from the confinement. False imprisonment involves deliberate action which restrains the plaintiff, but there might also be liabil-

---

litigation' is contrary to public policy: *Trendtex Trading Corporation* v. *Crédit Suisse* [1982] AC 679; *Singh* v. *Observer Ltd* [1989] 2 All ER 751, 756j. Thus, a contract to assign a cause of action may be invalid. Whether it is or not depends on whether the assignee has 'a genuine and substantial interest in the success of the litigation': see Treitel 598–601. See also *Giles* v. *Thompson* [1994] 1 AC 142; *Grovewood Holdings PLC* v. *James Capel & Co. Ltd* [1995] 2 WLR 70; *Ward* v. *Aitken, The Times*, 19 June 1995.

[286] *A-G* v. *News Group Newspapers PLC* [1989] QB 110.

[287] *Chapman* v. *Honig* [1963] 2 QB 502. But it may constitute a breach of contract: *Midland Marts Ltd* v. *Hobday* [1989] 1 WLR 1143. See also *Pickering* v. *Liverpool Daily Post and Echo Newspapers PLC* [1991] 2 AC 370. Perjury is not a civil wrong for which damages can be recovered: *Hargreaves* v. *Bretherton* [1959] 1 QB 45.

[288] *Acrow (Automation) Ltd* v. *Rex Chainbelt Inc.* [1971] 1 WLR 1676.

[289] *Singh* v. *The Observer Ltd* [1989] 2 All ER 751.   [290] See 162 above.

[291] Cf. Rent Act 1977, s. 102.

[292] Salmond, 128–31; Fleming, 27–30; see 103 above.

ity in negligence for loss resulting from carelessness leading to confinement.[293] Where a person is imprisoned as a result of legal process, the only possible tort liability would be for malicious prosecution,[294] even if the conviction is later quashed. But there is now a statutory scheme for compensation for 'miscarriages of justice'. Under the scheme, the Secretary of State decides whether there is a right to compensation, but the quantum is decided by an independent assessor appointed by the Secretary of State.[295] The entitlement decision could, no doubt, be challenged by an application for judicial review, but probably not otherwise.

Finally, mention should be made of the 'public law' tort of misfeasance in a public office.[296] If a public authority causes financial loss to a citizen by taking action which it knows it does not have power to take, or[297] by exercising a power out of personal spite or ill will, or for some other improper motive (that is, maliciously), then it can be liable in damages.[298] Despite several attempts on the part of litigants to persuade courts otherwise, the tort is not committed merely when a public authority acts *ultra vires*. The plaintiff must also establish that the defendant knew that what it was doing was *ultra vires*; or that it acted maliciously. In theory, an authority might act out of malice even if it does not know that what it is doing is illegal (although, query, not vice-versa); but, in practice, knowledge and improper motive will usually go together.

Unintentional Infliction of Damage

Damage to Property of a Third Party

We have seen that there can be no liability in tort for unintentional interference with contractual interests or contractual expectancies as a result of

[293] e.g., by failure to maintain a door lock in proper working order, or by negligently locking a reader into a library at closing time: P. Heffey (1983) 14 *Melb. ULR* 53. In 1989 a woman committed to a psychiatric hospital as a result of a negligent medical report was awarded £27,500 damages for wrongful detention: *Independent*, 8 May 1989.

[294] Salmond, 131–2; Fleming, 30–31.

[295] Criminal Justice Act 1988, s. 133. Concerning the government's international obligations to compensate for detention, see European Convention on Human Rights, Art. 5(5); *R. v. Home Secretary, ex parte Weeks, The Times*, 15 Mar. 1988. See also European Convention, Arts. 13 and 50. The UK would appear, on the basis of *Weeks*, to be in breach of Art. 13 in relation to the breach of the Convention found to have occurred in that case.

[296] Sir William Wade and C. F. Forsyth, *Administrative Law*, 7th edn. (Oxford, 1994), 789–96; P. P. Craig, *Administrative Law*, 3rd edn. (London, 1994), 636–8. On the meaning of 'public office' see B. Gould (1972) 5 *NZULR* 105, 117–9; R. C. Evans (1982) 31 *ICLQ* 640, 644–6.

[297] The requirements are alternative, not cumulative: *Bourgoin SA v. Ministry of Agriculture, Fisheries and Food* [1986] QB 716.

[298] If the power is statutory (or 'prerogative' and, query justiciable), then liability will arise only if it has been exercised *ultra vires*. If the power is derived from contract, and is not subject to any relevant statutory limitations, then malice by itself will render exercise of the power unlawful: *Jones v. Swansea CC* [1990] 1 WLR 54 (reversed on other grounds [1990] 1 WLR 1453). Malicious exercise of contractual powers by a private person is not, as such, actionable: *Chapman v. Honig* [1963] 2 QB 502; see 267 below.

causing damage to property of a third party. *A fortiori*, of course, there can be no liability for unintentional infliction of economic loss (that is, reduction of monetary wealth) as a result of causing damage to property of a third party.

Substandard Services

Financial Services[299]

Common Law My concern in this section is not with tort claims in respect of substandard services made by a client who has a contract with the service provider for the provision of the services: these were dealt with in Chapter 3.[300] Here I am concerned with claims by third parties, and with claims by 'second parties' in circumstances where there is no contract (for example, a claim against an NHS doctor or hospital or against a government body[301]).

There is no doubt that in some circumstances at least damages may be recovered in tort for purely economic loss caused by substandard financial services, whether these take the form of statements or acts.[302] *Hedley Byrne* v. *Heller*[303] established such liability in the case of statements, and the decision in *Henderson* v. *Merrett Syndicates Ltd*[304] makes it clear that the *Hedley Byrne* principle can apply to acts and omissions as well as words. The currently accepted basis for the imposition of liability for negligence in the performance of financial services is assumption of responsibility. Thus, in *Henderson* v. *Merrett* it was held that underwriting agents at Lloyd's had assumed responsibility for the performance of underwriting services (accepting and reinsuring risks) to 'indirect names'; and in *Aiken* v. *Stewart Wrightson Members Agency Ltd*[305] it was held that an underwriting agent owed a duty to present and future members of syndicates to take care in buying reinsurance on the basis that in the circumstances of the case the agent had 'clearly intended' to buy insurance on behalf of future as well as present syndicate members. Unfortunately, the concept of assumption of responsibility is so vague that it gives little or no guidance on the sorts of case in which a duty of care will be imposed.[306]

---

[299] In the Financial Services Act 1986 the term 'financial services' means, basically, the giving of investment advice and dealing in investments. Here it is used in a wider sense to mean commercial services other than services associated with the manufacture of chattels or the construction of buildings (these are dealt with below under the headings of 'Defective Chattels' and 'Defective Premises'). Services, such as valuing and surveying, associated with the acquisition of goods and buildings (as opposed to their production or construction), fall within the category of financial services: e.g. *Smith* v. *Bush* [1990] 1 AC 831.

[300] See 106–149 above.

[301] Claims against governmental bodies in respect of purely economic loss present great problems in relation to duty of care, which will be discussed in Ch. 5.

[302] On 179 above the word 'services' was used in contrast to 'statements' and as a synonym for 'acts'. In this context the word 'services' covers both statements and acts.

[303] [1964] AC 465.   [304] [1994] 3 WLR 761.

[305] *The Times*, 8 Mar. 1995.   [306] See further 185 above.

It is clear that providers of financial services will not automatically be liable in tort to anyone who suffers foreseeable economic loss as a result of negligence in the performance of the services. For instance, the New Zealand Court of Appeal has held that insurance investigators employed by insurers to investigate claims owe no duty of care to insured persons or to creditors or shareholders of insured parties;[307] and the House of Lords has held that a classification society employed by a shipowner to certify that repairs have been properly carried out owes no duty of care to cargo owners.[308] These decisions are perhaps best explained on the basis that in the court's view the insured and the cargo owner each had an adequate remedy in contract against the insurer and the shipowner respectively.[309]

It has been held that mortgagees, receivers, and the like owe a duty to unsecured creditors, guarantors, and so on, as well as to the debtor. However, this duty is only to act in good faith in the exercise of powers given ' "for the special purpose of enabling the assets comprised in the . . . security to be preserved and realised" for the benefit of the [secured creditor]'.[310] The duty is said to arise in equity and to be inconsistent with the existence of any duty of care in tort. A mortgagee owes no general duty to take care in exercising the powers of a mortgagee because the interests of the mortgagee may be in conflict with those of the mortgagor and of other interested parties. On the other hand, once the mortgagee decides to sell, reasonable care must be taken to obtain a 'proper price'.[311] There seems little point in insisting that the secured creditor's duty arises in equity rather than in tort (except, perhaps, as a shorthand way of specifying what the duty is), so long as the content of the duty and the remedies for its breach are tailored to the circumstances so as to recognize the potential conflicts of interest between the various

---

[307] *South Pacific Manufacturing Co. Ltd* v. *New Zealand Security Consultants and Investigations Ltd* [1992] 2 NZLR 283.

[308] *Marc Rich & Co. AG* v. *Bishop Rock Marine Co. Ltd (The Nicholas H)* [1995] 3 WLR 227; Cane [1994] *LMCLQ* 363; [1995] *LMCLQ* 433. For Lord Lloyd of Berwick (dissenting) the fact that the damage in this case involved the destruction of physical property provided a powerful argument in favour of liability. Lord Steyn gave the fact much less weight. In my view, since the property was a commercial asset, its physical nature was largely irrelevant.

[309] See generally J. Stapleton (1995) 111 *LQR* 301. The House of Lords has also said that third parties who act for or deal with trustees normally owe no duty of care to beneficiaries to check that the trustee is not misbehaving: *Royal Brunei Airlines Sdn Bhd* v. *Tan* [1995] 3 WLR 64.

[310] *Downsview Nominees Ltd* v. *First City Corporation Ltd* [1993] AC 295, 314. But the position may be different if the company is being managed under an administration order made under the Insolvency Act 1986: *ibid.*, 316. See also *China and South Sea Bank* v. *Tan* [1990] 1 AC 536: a secured creditor owes no duty to a guarantor to realize the security at the best possible price, but only to ensure that it is not imperfect, surrendered, lost, or altered in condition.

[311] *Cuckmere Brick Co. Ltd* v. *Mutual Finance Ltd* [1971] Ch. 949 as interpreted in *Downsview Nominees* [1993] AC 295, 315. Cf *Standard Chartered Bank Ltd* v. *Walker* [1982] 1 WLR 1410; *American Express International Banking Corporation* v. *Hurley* [1985] 1 All ER 564. See also *Palk* v. *Mortgage Services Funding PLC* [1993] Ch. 330.

interested parties.[312] Whatever its source, the duty is non-contractual and it protects an interest in financial wealth.

The duties of company directors in respect of the day-to-day running of the company have also traditionally been seen as arising in equity out of the fiduciary relationship between the directors and the company. On this basis, directors owe no duty to individual shareholders of the company. Several policy justifications for this rule have been suggested: to avoid multiplicity of suits; to prevent double recovery (that is, by both shareholders and the company); to protect the interests of creditors of the company; and that recovery by the company will restore the shares to their former value without the need for action by the shareholders.[313] For what they are worth, these justifications also count against imposing a duty of care in tort on directors in favour of shareholders. Furthermore, it has been said that to impose such a duty would unduly hamper commercially advantageous management of the affairs of the company by the directors.[314] It has been suggested, however, that there are good reasons to allow individual shareholders (and, *a fortiori*, ex-shareholders) to sue in tort in respect of intentional wrongdoing by directors.[315] It has also been argued that directors should be under a common law tort duty to take reasonable care to keep shareholders informed about the affairs of the company so as to facilitate participation in the affairs of the company by individual shareholders and protection of their financial interests.[316]

Courts have been extremely unwilling to impose tort liability for negligent failure to protect a person from suffering financial loss[317] or to warn person of impending loss.[318] So an employer owes no duty to employees to protect their property from being stolen;[319] an occupier of premises probably owes no duty to lawful visitors to protect their property from being stolen;[320] a bank normally owes no duty of care to advise a person signing security documents either about the nature of their obligations under the security or to take independent advice.[321] School authorities are not required to take out first party accident insurance to cover pupils involved in dangerous sports nor

---

[312] But the classification of the duty may have an important impact on issues such as the effect of a clause in the mortgage purporting to exclude the duty, on the rights of purchasers from the mortgagee and on conflicts of laws: A. Berg [1993] *JBL* 213, 233, 238–9, 239–41 respectively. Whether it should make a difference is debatable.

[313] M. J. Sterling (1987) 50 *MLR* 468, 475.

[314] V. Finch (1992) 55 *MLR* 179, 205. For a quite different view see M. J. Trebilcock (1969) 32 *MLR* 499.

[315] Sterling (1987) 50 *MLR* 468.   [316] Finch (1992) 55 *MLR* 179.

[317] e.g. *Balsamo* v. *Medici* [1984] 1 WLR 951 (noted S. Whittaker (1985) 48 *MLR* 86; see further N. E. Palmer [1983] *CLP* 91).

[318] A lender who fails to take reasonable steps to ensure that a surety is properly advised about the financial risks of the transaction may be fixed with notice of the surety's rights against the borrower with the result that the surety will be entitled to avoide the contract of guarantee: e.g. *Barclay's Bank PLC* v. *O'Brien* [1994] 1 AC 180; H. W. Wilkinson [1995] *New LJ* 792. This principle generates no entitlement to damages.

[319] *Deyong* v. *Shenburn* [1946] KB 227.

[320] *Tinsley* v. *Dudley* [1951] 2 KB 18; *Ashby* v. *Tolhurst* [1937] 2 KB 242.

[321] *Barclays Bank PLC* v. *Khaira* [1992] 1 WLR 623.

are they required to advise parents of the children of the wisdom of taking out such insurance.[322] Similarly, an employer is under no duty to provide personal accident insurance for employees,[323] or to warn employees of special risks attendant on their work and advise them to take out insurance to protect themselves against such risks.[324] Furthermore, breach of the employer's statutory duty to insure against liability for personal injuries suffered by employees as a result and in the course of their employment is not actionable in tort.[325]

In *Banque Keyser Ullmann SA* v. *Skandia (UK) Insurance Co. Ltd*[326] an insurance underwriter knew that an insurance broker was fraudulently representing to creditors that insurance policies had been taken out as security for their debts when in fact they had not been. The Court of Appeal held that the insurer was under no common law duty in tort to tell the creditors of the fraud despite the fact that there was no way that the creditors could find out for themselves about the fraud. The insurer had not explicitly undertaken to tell them;[327] and a duty to tell, the court said, would conflict with the rule that parties in contractual negotiations are under no positive 'obligation to speak' (silence cannot, normally, amount to an actionable misrepresentation). Anyway, the plaintiffs could sue the brokers for damages (and had, in fact, settled their claim against them).

The underlying legal problem in the cases mentioned in the last two paragraphs resides in the general principle that the law of tort does not impose liability for negligent failure to act as opposed to negligent positive action; or, in other words, that it does not impose liability for failing to prevent harm occurring as opposed to causing harm. As a general rule, the unwillingness of the law to impose liability for failure to act is even greater in cases of economic loss (including loss of property) than in cases of physical damage, whether to persons or property.[328] But this general principle is riddled with

---

[322] *Van Oppen* v. *Trustees of Bedford School* [1990] 1 WLR 235.

[323] The employer is under a statutory duty to take out insurance to cover employees against injuries caused by the negligence of the employer or those for whom it is responsible: Employers' Liability (Compulsory Insurance) Act 1969.

[324] *Reid* v. *Rush & Tompkins Group PLC* [1990] 1 WLR 212. In essence, the court held that there could be no such duty in tort given that the employment contract contained no relevant term and that no such term could, on ordinary principles, be implied into it.

[325] *Richardson* v. *Pitt-Stanley* [1995] 1 All ER 460.

[326] [1990] 1 QB 665 (affirmed on different grounds [1991] 2 AC 249); J. G. Logie [1989] *CLJ* 115, 126–7; F. A. Trindade (1989) 105 *LQR* 191.

[327] For an example of liability based on an express undertaking to act to protect from financial loss see *Marac Finance Ltd* v. *Colmore-Williams* [1988] 1 NZLR 625. For examples of undertakings implied from a course of conduct see *L. Shaddock & Associates Pty Ltd* v. *Parramatta City Council* (1981) 36 ALR 385 (purely financial loss); *Brown* v. *Heathcote CC* [1987] 1 NZLR 720 (PC) (property damage). But the existence of a limited contractual undertaking to speak may make it harder, not easier, to impose a tortious duty: *Bank of Nova Scotia* v. *Hellenic Mutual War Risks Association (Bermuda) Ltd (The Good Luck)* [1990] 1 QB 818 (reversed on irrelevant grounds [1992] 1 AC 233); see 315 below.

[328] This distinction runs through the judgments in *Van Oppen* [1990] 1 WLR 235.

exceptions.[329] Most relevantly in this context, liability for failure to protect is, in some situations at least, imposed on those who have control over children, on employers *vis-à-vis* their employees, and on professional advisers *vis-à-vis* their clients.[330] So the issue in this context is not whether, in general terms, persons *in loco parentis*, or employers or professional advisers, can be held liable for failure to take reasonable care to protect their charges, employees, or clients against loss, but whether such liability can extend to purely financial loss and whether it can extend to a duty to insure or advise that insurance be taken out.

Statutory Liability   There is a heterogeneous collection of relevant statutory provisions. For instance, section 10 of the Local Land Charges Act 1975 creates a liability to compensate for loss caused by the issue of inaccurate certificates by registering authorities.[331] Under sections 22 and 23 of the Data Protection Act 1984 an individual who suffers damage as a result of inaccuracy in personal data about him or her held on computer by a data holder (called in the Act a 'data user'), or as a result of loss or unauthorized destruction or disclosure of personal data, can recover damages. The data user is given a defence of reasonable care.[332] Of particular importance in this context are credit reference agencies: inaccurate data held and divulged by such agencies may lead to a consumer being unreasonably refused credit for the acquisition of goods or services.[333] In other words, these provisions are also relevant to the protection of contractual expectancies.

There are statutory provisions concerning disclosure by auditors of banks and other companies in the financial services sector of information about the affairs of the bank or company.[334] The information in question might well be relevant to protecting investors from financial loss. The provisions relieve auditors of any obligation of confidence of which disclosure might constitute a breach; and they empower the Secretary of State to make rules or regulations imposing obligations of disclosure if the relevant professional bodies do not make appropriate internal rules setting out when, and what sort of, infor-

---

[329] Cane, *Atiyah's Accidents Compensation and the Law*, 5th edn. (London, 1993), 63–72; Logie [1989] *CLJ* 115.

[330] See particularly *Penn* v. *Bristol & West Building Society*, *The Times*, 19 June 1995: solicitor acting for co-owner in connection with the sale of a house owes a duty of care to the other co-owner (even if not a client of the solicitor) to ascertain that it has the latter's authority to act.

[331] For the position at common law see *Ministry of Housing and Local Government* v. *Sharp* [1970] 2 QB 223.

[332] R. Sizer and P. Newman, *The Data Protection Act* (Aldershot, 1984), 114–8; K. Gulleford, *Data Protection in Practice* (London, 1986), 75–9.

[333] See further Harvey and Parry, 299–301. See also B. Napier [1991] *New LJ* 497.

[334] Financial Services Act 1986, s. 109; Building Societies Act 1986, s. 82(8)-(11); Banking Act 1987, s. 47. Under s. 179 of the Financial Services Act various regulatory bodies are under an obligation not to disclose without consent certain information received in the course of performing their functions under the Act. This section has been held not to be civilly actionable: *Melton Medes Ltd* v. *Securities and Investments Board* [1995] 2 WLR 247.

mation ought to be disclosed.[335] The provisions do not expressly impose civil liability for failure to disclose. Failure to observe a code of practice issued by a professional body would not, as such, be actionable, but it might provide good evidence of negligence, and might encourage a court to impose a common law duty of disclosure. Breach of an obligation imposed by a statutory rule or regulation might give rise to an action for breach of statutory duty, but it is very difficult to be confident about this.

A provision of enormous potential[336] significance is section 214 of the Insolvency Act 1986.[337] Under section 213 of the Act (which has a long history), the liquidator of a company can apply to the court for an order that any person who was a knowing party to fraudulent trading by a company in the course of being wound up (whether insolvent or not), should contribute to the assets of the company. Because it is often difficult to prove intent to defraud, section 214 (which was introduced in the Insolvency Act 1985) imposes liability to contribute to the assets of an insolvent company on any director[338] who knew or ought to have concluded, before the commencement of the winding up, that 'there was no reasonable prospect that the company would avoid going into insolvent liquidation'. There is a defence that the director took every step which ought to have been taken with a view to minimizing the potential loss to the company's creditors.[339] The facts which the director ought to have known or ascertained, the conclusions which the director ought to have drawn from them, and the steps the director ought to have taken in the light of them, are judged objectively; but if the particular director was exceptionally knowledgeable, skilled, or experienced, this will raise the standard of care required (s. 214(4)(b)).[340] The amount of the contribution is such as the court thinks proper; but the contribution is to compensate the creditors, not to punish the director.[341]

In effect, this section creates civil liability for negligent trading by an insolvent company. It prevents directors hiding behind the corporate veil.[342] The

---

[335] The Auditing Practices Board has made a number of such rules.

[336] But research suggests that the section is widely seen as posing an empty threat: C. Williams and A. McGee, 'Rules fit to curb "unfit" directors', *The Times*, 15 Oct. 1992.

[337] H. Rajak [1989] *New LJ* 1374 and 1458; D. D. Prentice (1990) 10 *OJLS* 265; L. S. Sealy, *Disqualification and Personal Liability of Directors*, 3rd edn. (Bicester, 1989), chs. 5 and 6.

[338] This term includes a 'shadow director' (s. 214(7)), that is, 'a person in accordance with whose directions or instructions the directors of the company are accustomed to act' (Companies Act 1985, s. 741(2)). A major creditor might fall within this definition: *Re A Company* (1988) 4 BCC 424.

[339] Note that the provision does not say 'every reasonable step' or 'reducing loss'. The point of, and the difficulty in applying, this test arises from the fact that the best way of protecting the interests of creditors may be to continue trading with a view to improving the fortunes of the company.

[340] T. E. Cooke and A. Hicks [1993] *JBL* 338.

[341] *Re Produce Marketing Consortium Ltd (No. 2)* [1989] BCLC 520.

[342] The court cannot relieve a director of liability under s. 214 of the 1986 Act by recourse to Companies Act 1985, s. 727: *Re Produce Marketing Consortium Ltd* [1989] 1 WLR 745. S. 310(3) of the Companies Act 1985 (as substituted by s. 137 of the Companies Act 1989) allows the company to take out insurance to indemnify directors against liability under, *inter alia*, s. 214

cause of action, however, belongs to the liquidator of the company;[343] and any contribution ordered will not accrue to the benefit of any particular creditor, but rather will probably swell the assets available for distribution to creditors generally (rather than only the victims of the wrongful trading),[344] in accordance with the rules of insolvency law. Furthermore, it is common for creditors to require directors to give personal guarantees of the company's debts, and the Act does not say how priorities between such guarantees and the statutory cause of action are to be worked out; the existence of the statutory liability may well make such guarantees more common.[345] On the other hand, the section provides protection for persons who provide goods and services to insolvent companies thinking the company is solvent, without the need for the creditors to take any action on their own behalf.

Medical Services

Negligent performance of medical services typically causes personal injury. Economic loss resulting from such negligence is normally consequential upon personal injury, and so outside the scope of this book. However, there are at least two types of case in which negligent performance of medical services can cause economic loss in circumstances where, even if it also causes personal injury, some, at least, of the economic loss will not be consequent upon the personal injury. The first type of case in question involves unsuccessful sterilization operations leading to the conception and birth of an 'unwanted' child (so-called 'wrongful life' cases). English courts have been very resistant to allowing the child to sue the doctor, but parents have been allowed to recover for losses including the cost of rearing the child. In *Emeh* v. *Kensington AHA*[346] the mother was awarded damages for loss of future earnings and the cost of maintaining the child. In a later case, a father was awarded the cost of private education for the child.[347] The other type of case involves negligence leading to the death of a foetus or newly born child. In *Kralj* v. *McGrath*[348] the plaintiff's child died soon after birth as a result of negligence on the part of the doctor who delivered it. The judge held that the plaintiff could recover damages, *inter alia* for the financial cost of going through another pregnancy in order to replace the dead child.

---

of the 1986 Act. On Directors' and Officers' (D & O) liability insurance generally see D. Jess, *The Insurance of Commercial Risks*, 2nd edn. (London, 1993), ch. 7; V. Finch (1994) 57 *MLR* 880.

[343] For a discussion of duties owed directly to creditors see R. Grantham [1991] *JBL* 1.
[344] D. D. Prentice (1990) 10 *OJLS* 265, 272.
[345] On the relationship between a charge and directors' contribution see *ibid.* 271–2.
[346] [1985] QB 1012; criticised P. R. Glazebrook [1992] *CLJ* 226.
[347] *Benarr* v. *Kettering Health Authority* [1988] *New LJ* 179.
[348] [1986] 1 All ER 54.

Services Associated with the Production of Goods and the Construction of Buildings

The common law seems to draw a distinction between services associated with the manufacture of goods and the construction of buildings (such as design or surveying or engineering or building services) on the one hand, and 'financial services' on the other hand. The basis of the distinction is by no means clear; the distinction is not a surrogate for one between personal injury and physical damage to property on the one hand and purely financial loss on the other, because substandard services associated with the production of goods and buildings can cause loss of both types. It may simply be that in the case of chattels and buildings there is a tangible product of the service which causes the loss, and we naturally concentrate on that product in thinking about liability in such situations.[349] The distinction does, however, create serious anomalies. For example, the law is much more willing to impose strict liability for products, especially chattels, than for services; and for manufacturing defects than for design defects.[350] Adherence to the distinction has also created a situation in which, for instance, a surveyor who negligently over-values a building may be liable in tort to the purchaser for economic loss suffered by purchasing the building in reliance on the valuation;[351] but a surveyor involved in the construction of a defective building may not be sued in tort by the purchaser for economic loss suffered by acquiring a defective building (see below).

Common Law

Defective Chattels

If a chattel causes personal injury, or if it damages property, the victim can recover damages in tort from any person associated with its manufacture or supply whose negligence in the course of manufacture or supply caused or contributed to the plaintiff's personal injury or property damage.[352] The victim can (subject, of course, to the rules about contributory negligence, intervening cause, and remoteness of damage) recover such damages, whether he or she was the purchaser of the chattel or just a user of it or, even more remotely, a mere bystander. But can the purchaser (that is, the owner) of such a chattel recover from persons in the chain of manufacture and supply *in tort* for negligence:

    (a) damages representing the difference between the price of the chattel and what it was worth;[353] or

---

[349] J. Stapleton, *Product Liability* (London, 1994), 323–8.   [350] *Ibid.*
[351] *Smith* v. *Bush* [1990] 1 AC 831.   [352] *Donoghue* v. *Stevenson* [1932] AC 562.
[353] The principles discussed at 92–3 above concerning the choice between diminution in value and cost of repair are also relevant here.

(b) the cost of repairing the defect in the chattel in order to render it reasonably safe; or

(c) the cost of repairing the chattel to bring it up to a reasonable standard of quality; or

(d) damages for any damage to the chattel itself caused by the defect; or

(e) economic loss consequential on the chattel's defectiveness, such as loss of profits or the cost of hiring a substitute?[354]

In other words, can the purchaser recover damages for financial loss consisting of or consequent upon the defectiveness of the chattel? The short answer to this question is: only in rare circumstances, if at all.[355]

If the chattel has caused damage to property belonging to the purchaser, other than the defective chattel itself, the purchaser can recover damages not only for that property damage but also for economic loss consequential upon that damage. If D knew exactly why P wanted to buy the particular chattel, and especially (or perhaps only) if it was custom-built to meet P's requirements (which the defendant was aware of); and if D assured P personally that the chattel would meet P's requirements, and P acquired the chattel in reliance on that assurance, the purchaser might be able to recover damages under the heads stated above even if the chattel neither had caused, nor was likely in the future to cause, damage to any person or to any property other than the chattel itself.[356] The correct analysis of this head of liability appears to be that it is allied to liability for misstatement inducing the entering of a contract.[357] The difference between it and liability under *Hedley Byrne* v. *Heller* in situations not related to the provision of chattels is that the degree of proximity required in this context appears to be greater—there can be no liability to classes of plaintiffs in respect of types of transactions,[358] but only to an individual plaintiff whose precise requirements are known to the defendant. Thus, ironically, 'purely financial interests' are better protected than financial interests in tangible property.

Defective Premises

There are at least five types of situation in which tort actions in respect of property damage and economic loss resulting from the construction and supply of defective premises are important. First, there are cases in which a pur-

---

[354] With the substitution of the word 'building' for 'chattel', these heads of loss are also relevant to the discussion in the next section of defective premises.

[355] The leading cases are *D. & F. Estates Ltd* v. *Church Commissioners* [1989] AC 177; *Murphy* v. *Brentwood DC* [1991] 1 AC 398.

[356] This proposition in based on *Junior Books* v. *Veitchi* [1983] 1 AC 520; cf. *The Diamantas Pateris* [1966] 1 Lloyd's Rep. 179. An action in respect of defective chattels failed in *Muirhead* v. *Industrial Tank Specialities Ltd* [1986] QB 507 because D and P were not in a sufficiently close degree of proximity in this sense.

[357] For the purposes of limitation of actions, the damage in such a case is probably suffered (and so the cause of action probably accrues) at the date of acquisition of the defective chattel. The regime under the Latent Damage Act, discussed on 211 below, could apply here.

[358] See *Caparo Industries* v. *Dickman* [1990] 2 AC 605; see 176 above.

chaser or lessee wishes to sue the vendor or lessor in respect of the state of the premises at the date of acquisition. The basic rule of contract law in relation to the acquisition of premises is *caveat emptor*: the purchaser or lessee must take steps to satisfy himself or herself that the premises are in good condition and suitable for the use to which they are to be put; and in the absence of misrepresentation by the vendor or lessor, the latter is not normally liable (unless the contract contains express provisions imposing such liability) for the state of the premises as acquired by the purchaser or lessee. The law of tort follows this rule: the vendor or lessor as such owes the purchaser or lessee no duty of care in respect of the state of the premises.[359] This rule does not apply, however, in cases in which the vendor[360] or the lessor[361] has personally done positive acts (such as designing or building the premises) which have contributed to or caused the defective state of the premises. In such cases, the vendor or lessor is dealt with in the capacity of builder, designer or whatever.

The second type of case in which the law of tort is important is that in which a subsequent purchaser from or a lessee of the original purchaser wishes to sue a person (whom I shall call 'the builder') responsible for the defective state of the premises. In this type of case, P will be at one remove from, and will have no contractual relationship with, the builder; if P is to sue the builder, it will have to be in tort.[362]

The third type of case we must consider is that in which a building owner, or one of the parties involved in the construction of the building, wishes to sue someone in the chain of construction or supply with whom P has no contract: usually a subcontractor. This factual situation is of very great importance in relation to buildings because the construction industry is organized in such a way that subcontracting is the most common form in which the construction of substantial structures is arranged. A variant of this type of case arises where the person wishing to sue the subcontractor is a purchaser or lessee from the building owner; this variant raises, in addition, issues associated with the second type of case.

The fourth type of case is that in which a building owner or a subsequent

---

[359] *Cavalier* v. *Pope* [1906] AC 428; *Bottomley* v. *Bannister* [1932] 1 KB 458; *McNerny* v. *Lambeth LBC* (1989) 21 Housing LR 188. There is an exception in the case of the letting of furnished premises if personal injury is suffered: *Collins* v. *Hopkins* [1923] 2 KB 617.

[360] *Anns* v. *Merton LBC* [1978] AC 728.

[361] *Targett* v. *Torfaen BC* [1992] 3 All ER 27.

[362] *D. & F. Estates* [1989] AC 177 was this type of case. But suppose that A contracts with B for the construction of a building on its land which, in the contemplation of the contracting parties, will be occupied or possibly bought by a third party. Suppose further that A transfers its interest in the property (including the building, but not including the benefit of the building contract) for full value to C before building starts (or, at least, before its is completed) and that after transfer, due to a breach of contract by B, some defect is introduced into the building. A can recover full damages for breach of contract even though the loss falls on C: *St Martin's Property Corporation Ltd* v. *Sir Robert McAlpine Ltd* (*sub nom. Linden Gardens Trust Ltd* v. *Lenesta Sludge Disposals Ltd* [1994] 1 AC 85. In such a case A would have to account to C. But in the absence of a fiduciary relationship between A and C, C could not force A to sue. In the *St Martin's* case itself, A and C were wholly-owned subsidiaries of the same parent.

purchaser or lessee wishes to sue a local authority in respect of the exercise of statutory powers or duties to supervise the design or construction process. The fifth type is that in which a person who is in a contractual relationship with the builder wishes to sue the latter in tort in order to gain the benefit of some rule of tort law, most usually a more generous limitation rule. We discussed in Chapter 3 some of the issues raised by this type of case. One would expect that there could be no liability in tort concurrent to liability in contract in a case where, if the parties were not in a contractual relationship, there could be no tort liability. But doubt is cast on this assumption by the view of Lord Keith in *Murphy* v. *Brentwood DC*[363] that the architect of a defective chimney could be liable to its owner (who had employed the architect) not only in contract but also concurrently in tort for the cost of repairing the chimney.

The basic rule governing liability for economic loss in cases such as these is analogous to that we have already considered in relation to chattels.[364] If, but only if, the defect in the premises causes personal injury or damage to property other than the defective premises then damages for such injury or damage may be recovered in a tort action.[365] But this statement must be qualified in relation to local authorities exercising regulatory functions: their liability depends ultimately on the proper interpretation of the statutory provisions under which they operate, and the question whether they would be liable for personal injury or damage to 'other property' was not decided in *Murphy* v. *Brentwood DC*.[366]

By way of exception to the basic rule, damages may be recoverable for the cost of repairing or replacing defective premises, even in the absence of personal injury or damage to other property, if the plaintiff was in a relationship of proximity with the defendant as close as that which existed between the parties in *Junior Books* v. *Veitchi*.[367] A subsequent purchaser or lessee

---

[363] [1991] 1 AC 398, 466 explaining the result in *Pirelli General Cable Works Ltd* v. *Oscar Faber & Partners* [1983] 2 AC 1. See also *Nitrigin Eireann Teoranta* v. *Inco Alloys Ltd* [1992] 1 WLR 498, 503–4.

[364] The leading cases are *D. & F. Estates* v. *Church Commissioners* [1989] AC 177 and *Murphy* v. *Brentwood DC* [1991] 1 AC 398. For detailed discussion of the latter case see the 1st ed. of this book at 511–18.

[365] Contrast the position in Canada: *City of Kamloops* v. *Neilsen* (1984) 10 DLR (4th) 641; *Rothfield* v. *Manolakos* (1989) 63 DLR(4th) 449; *Winnipeg Condominium Corporation No. 36* v. *Bird Construction Co. Ltd* (1995) 121 DLR(4th) 193 (subsequent purchaser v. builder, architect, and subcontractor); Australia: *Bryan* v. *Maloney* (1995) 128 ALR 163 (subsequent purchaser v. builder) and New Zealand: *Invercargill CC* v. *Hamlin* [1994] 3 NZLR 513 (purchaser v. local authority). The DoE has proposed that subsequent purchasers should have a right of recovery in respect of costs of repair and reinstatement but not in respect of consequential economic losses: 'Latent Defects Liability and BUILD Insurance' (Consultation Paper, Apr., 1995), paras. 36–8.

[366] [1991] 1 AC 398, 457 *per* Lord Mackay; 463 *per* Lord Keith; 479 *per* Lord Bridge; 492 *per* Lord Jauncey. The liability of local authorities is much wider in New Zealand: *Stieller* v. *Porirua CC* [1986] 2 NZLR 84; *Craig* v. *East Coast Bays CC* [1986] 1 NZLR 99 (contrast *Ryeford Homes Ltd* v. *Sevenoaks DC* [1989] *New LJ* 255).

[367] [1983] 1 AC 520. The parties, the main contractor, and a supplier of a subcontractor were held not to be in a sufficient relationship of proximity in *Simaan General Contracting Co.* v.

would be even less likely to be able to establish the existence of such a relationship than the original owner.[368] As stated above, this head of liability is correctly viewed as derived from the principles first laid down in *Hedley Byrne* v. *Heller*.[369] Another technique which has been used in an action by a building owner against a nominated supplier of materials to a contractor to achieve a similar result is to hold that the plaintiff and the defendant were parties to an implied collateral contract, the consideration for which was the entering into of the contract with the contractor by the plaintiff, and the main term of which was a warranty of quality based on a verbal assurance of quality given by the supplier.[370]

For exceptional cases where the cost of repairing the defective premises themselves may be recoverable, there is a generous regime of limitation rules in section 1 of the Latent Damage Act 1986 which may help building owners (amongst others) whose cause of action relates to latent damage. An action may be brought within a period of six years from the date the relevant 'damage' occurs; or three years from the date when the damage becomes reasonably discoverable, subject to a longstop of fifteen years from the date of the alleged breach of duty.[371] However, the Act was drafted against the background of rules of tort law which were thought to allow recovery for the cost of repairing defective premises in a significant number of cases. The decisions in *D & F Estates* and *Murphy* v. *Brentwood DC*[372] have deprived the Act of much of its area of operation in relation to buildings.[373]

It is worth noting at this stage that the cases fall into two quite distinct

Pilkington Glass Ltd (No. 2) [1988] QB 758. The main contractor was, in effect, seeking an indemnity from the supplier directly rather than by suing the subcontractor. On indemnity actions see also 439 below.

[368] See Cane in C. J. Miller (ed.), *Comparative Product Liability* (London, 1986), 64.

[369] *Murphy* v. *Brentwood DC* [1991] 1 AC 398, 466 *per* Lord Keith; 481 *per* Lord Bridge; cf. *D. & F. Estates* v. *Church Commissioners* [1989] AC 177, 215 *per* Lord Oliver. For the purposes of limitation of actions, the damage in such a case probably occurs (and so the cause of action probably accrues) at the time of acquisition of the premises. A couple of other exceptions to the basic rule (of doubtful validity) can be gleaned from *Murphy*: (1) repair costs may be recoverable to forestall (liability for) personal injury to or damage to the property of a neighbouring property owner or member of the public using the highway: Lord Bridge at 475; *Morse* v. *Barratt (Leeds) Ltd* (1993) 9 Construction LJ 158; but note Lord Oliver's reservation at 489; (2) the cost of repairing a building may be recoverable if the damage to the building was caused (a) by some component of it which was supplied and erected entirely by someone other than the person responsible for building the damaged part: 470 *per* Lord Keith; 497 *per* Lord Jauncey; or (b) by 'ancillary equipment' such as a boiler or electrical wiring: 478 *per* Lord Bridge; 497 *per* Lord Jauncey. A further query might be raised in relation to a situation where defective work to part of a building owned by A damages another part owned by B: *Lindenberg* v. *Canning* (1992) 62 BLR 147, 161.

[370] *Shanklin Pier* v. *Detel Products Ltd* [1951] 2 KB 854.

[371] The DoE has proposed that the longstop be reduced to 10 years in line with provision of the Consumer Protection Act 1987 concerning defective products: 'Latent Defects Liability and BUILD Insurance' (Consultation Paper, Apr. 1995), para. 27.

[372] See n. 364 above.

[373] The decisions in these cases have also profoundly affected the operation of s. 3 of the Act, the wording of which seems to assume that 'damage' to the defective property itself qualifies as 'damage to property' for the purposes of tort law.

groups. First, there are those in which the plaintiff and the defendant are 'on the same contractual chain'. Such chains are very common in the building industry, especially in the case of major building contracts: the building owner hires a contractor who, in turn, hires subcontractors, and both enter into contracts with suppliers for the supply of materials. The owner may also hire an architect or engineer to supervise the project for him. All of the parties may be involved in the planning of the project and be aware of the identity of the others and, in general terms anyway, of the provisions of the contracts to which they are not party. In some cases, the contracts between the various parties may, to some extent, be integrated. In cases where one party on such a contractual chain brings an action against another party on the chain with whom the former is not in a direct contractual relationship, the main policy issue is whether P ought to be required to pursue a contract action against an immediate contracting party (leaving the latter to sue the subcontractor for an indemnity), rather than being allowed to sue the subcontractor directly.

But it is also not uncommon for there to be an additional 'collateral contract' between the building owner and a subcontractor. For example, in *Greater Nottingham Co-operative Society Ltd* v. *Cementation Piling and Foundations Ltd*[374] P had entered a separate contract with the subcontractor concerning piling work, but the terms of the contract were only concerned with the quality of the piling and said nothing about liability for negligent operation of the piling machinery, which was the cause of the plaintiff's economic loss. It was held, in effect, that where the plaintiff and the subcontractor are in a contractual relationship but the contract is silent on the subject matter of their dispute, the court cannot make good the omission of the contract by imposing liability in tort.

At first sight, this case appears to rest on the principle that no wider liability can be imposed in a tort action than could be imposed in a contract action arising out of the same facts and between the same parties. But this interpretation might seem difficult in the light of the fact that under section 13 of the Supply of Goods and Services Act 1982 there is implied into contracts for services rendered in the course of a business a term that the supplier of the service will use reasonable care and skill. Although the contract in this case was made before the Act came into operation, an equivalent term was normally implied at common law. The court in *Cementation* recognized that in terms of *Junior Books* v. *Veitchi*, the existence of the contract put the plaintiff and the defendant in the closest possible degree of proximity to one another. So if it is correct to view the decision in *Junior Books* as based on reliance on an assurance of quality, the decision in *Cementation* must rest on the fact that there was no actual representation by D that its employees would exercise care in operating the piling machinery.

[374] [1989] QB 71.

It is hard to see why such a representation should have been necessary. One can understand the idea that when A makes something for B, A gives no warranty as to its quality outside the ambit of any contract between them (including any terms implied into it by law); but it is much harder to understand the proposition that A cannot be held liable outside contract for loss caused by negligence in the making of something which does not cause that thing to be defective but rather increases the cost to B of acquiring it. The result is all the more extraordinary when it is realized that the head contractor might well not be liable for such negligence, so that if B cannot recover from A, B might not be able to recover at all; in other words, B might not be able to recoup its loss by suing the head contractor in contract or by suing the subcontractor in tort.

The second group into which the 'building cases' fall do not involve contract chains in the sense described above. In such cases, P may have been in no way involved in the building project; P may, for example, be a purchaser or a lessee of a building built for P's vendor or lessor, who was a party to a contractual chain. The courts seem not to discriminate between this type of case and the true contractual chain. But in terms of 'commercial reality' the two types of case are quite different. A party to an integrated contractual chain may be in a better position to protect its interests as against remote links in the chain than is a person who contracts with a member of the chain after the building work is complete.

The discussion so far of liability in the tort of negligence to an acquirer of defective chattels or premises may be summarized by saying that the acquirer may not recover damages for purely economic loss attributable to the defect. The status of this general rule, which is well supported in the cases, has been thrown into considerable doubt by the renewed emphasis on the concept of assumption of responsibility in cases such as *Henderson* v. *Merritt Syndicates*[375] and *White* v. *Jones*.[376] In the former case the defendant underwriting agents and the plaintiff Names were remote parties in a chain of contracts, but Lord Goff nevertheless held that the defendants had assumed responsibility towards the plaintiffs. On the other hand, his Lordship thought that the case was exceptional on its facts because of the close relationship between Names and underwriting agents on the Lloyd's market; and that in analogous cases in the building context, such as *Simaan* v. *Pilkington Glass* there would normally not be a sufficiently close relationship between remote parties on a contractual chain to support a finding of assumption of responsibility between them. His Lordship acknowledged the difficulty created by *Junior Books* v. *Veitchi*, but did not seek to resolve it.

It could be argued that the concept of assumption of responsibility explains and justifies the result in *Junior Books* because in that case there was a close relationship between the defendant subcontractor and the plaintiff factory

[375] [1994] 3 WLR 761.   [376] [1995] 2 WLR 187.

owner; but also that on its different facts, the decision in *Simaan* is also explicable in terms of that concept. But the wider point to be made is that if assumption of responsibility is, as the recent cases suggest, the proper basis of liability for purely economic loss, the blanket ban on recovery in tort for purely economic loss flowing from acquisition of a defective building or chattel may not be sustainable in cases where there is a close relationship between the plaintiff and the defendant. In turn, doubt may be thrown on the distinction between financial services on the one hand, and building and manufacturing services on the other, even though Lord Goff might be thought to have tried indirectly to preserve it by his comments about *Simaan* in *Henderson*.

An entirely different explanation of the economic loss cases (including the defective building and chattel cases) is that liability in tort will not arise if the plaintiff could reasonably have been expected to take steps to secure protection from economic loss (typically by contract) in such a way as that the loss would ultimately fall on the defendant.[377] Some such principle could explain the result in *Simaan*, for instance, where the plaintiff had a right of action in contract against an intermediate party who, in turn, had a contractual right of action against the defendant. But it does not explain the results in *Hedley Byrne* v. *Heller*, *Junior Books* or *Henderson*, nor is it obviously consistent with the blanket rule in *D & F Estates*. An attraction of the principle is that it denies the protection of the law of tort to those who could reasonably be expected to buy protection in the market-place while extending it to those who could not. But despite decisions such as *Smith* v. *Bush* in which the courts have been sensitive to the realities of the market-place, the current law seems quite a long way from endorsing this vision of distributive justice as a general principle underlying tort liability for negligently inflicted economic loss.

Statute

Defective Chattels
Part I of the Consumer Protection Act 1987 introduced a scheme of 'strict liability' for defective products. The definition of 'product' contained in section 1 of the Act includes in that term component parts of products. This means, amongst other things, that a plaintiff may choose to sue either in respect of the final composite product or in respect of some component comprised in it (or in respect of both). A producer (for example) of a composite product may be held liable for damage caused by the product even though it is attributable to a component supplied by a third party; on the other hand, a component manufacturer is not liable for damage solely attributable to some defect in the composite product in which the component was comprised.[378]

---

[377] J. Stapleton (1995) 111 *LQR* 301.   [378] Consumer Protection Act 1987, s. 4(1)(f).

Recoverable damage is defined in section 5(1) to mean 'death or personal injury or any loss of or damage to any property (including land)'. However, there is no liability for

the loss of or any damage to the [defective] product itself or for the loss of or any damage to the whole or any part of any product which has been supplied with the product in question comprised in it.[379]

Suppose, for example, that faulty brakes supplied to a car manufacturer by a component manufacturer cause damage to the car; such damage would not be compensatable under the Act.[380] Conversely, it is apparently not possible to sue the producer (etc.) of a composite product for damage to a component part of it because such an action in respect of damage caused by the composite product would depend on treating the composite product as 'the product itself' for the purposes of section 5.

Under the 1987 Act, property damage is recoverable only in respect of property 'ordinarily intended for private use, occupation or consumption' and which was 'intended by the person suffering the loss or damage mainly for his own private use, occupation or consumption'.[381] Furthermore, the Act does not apply to defendants who were not acting in the course of a business or with a view to profit.[382] In other words, the Act is basically a consumer protection measure. Damages for loss of or damage to property are not recoverable in cases where the claim (plus interest) does not exceed £275.[383]

An action in respect of property loss or damage can be brought under the Act by a person with an interest in the property at the earliest time at which the loss or damage became discoverable.[384] This is different from the common law rule, which gives the action to the person who owned the property at the time the loss or damage occurred. Thus, in cases where the loss or damage was latent in the sense that it became discoverable only some time after it had first occurred, the person who can sue under the 1987 Act is a person who had an interest in the goods at that later date, and not a person interested in them when they were damaged. The effect of this provision is similar to that of section 3 of the Latent Damage Act 1986, which gives a cause of action to a person who acquires property after damage to it has occurred but before the damage became discoverable. However, this latter provision creates an additional cause of action whereas under the 1987 Act, the only person who can sue is a person interested at the date the damage became

---

[379] S. 5(2). This may be in conflict with the EC Dir. on which the Act is based: R. Merkin, *A Guide to the Consumer Protection Act 1987* (London, 1987), 12–13. If damage is caused by a component not supplied with the product, liability may arise: A. M. Clark, *Product Liability* (London, 1989), 128.

[380] In this regard, the Act may be inconsistent with the Dir. See Stapleton, *Product Liability*, 278–9.

[381] S. 5(3).   [382] S. 4(1)(c).

[383] S. 5(4). This may be thought a strange limitation in a consumer protection measure: Clark, *Product Liability*, 129.

[384] S. 5(5).

discoverable. In relation to the Latent Damage Act, it has been questioned whether this somewhat dramatic change in the law was intended.[385] The wording of the 1987 Act does not admit of such doubts. On the other hand, the limitation regime under the Consumer Protection Act is less generous than that under the Latent Damage Act (see below).

There is another noteworthy feature of the 1987 Act which is advantageous as compared with the common law. Under the Act it is possible to sue not only the manufacturer but also any 'own brand' supplier, and any importer of the product; and under certain circumstances, any supplier of the product. We have also noted that the producer (etc.) of a composite product can be sued in respect of defects in component parts. In other words, actions can be brought against a variety of defendants who may not have been responsible for the defect in a causal sense.

The limitation period for actions under the Act (including those in respect of property damage) is three years from the later of the date on which the cause of action accrued and the date on which the damage first became discoverable, subject to a longstop of ten years from the date when the product was first put into circulation.[386] In the case of damage to property, these two dates will coincide by virtue of the rule contained in section 5(5) of the 1987 Act to the effect that damage to property is deemed to occur when it first becomes discoverable. This regime is less advantageous in the simple case of damage to other property, because the basic statutory limitation period is three years rather than six. Latent damage problems in relation to property are relatively unlikely to arise under the Act because of the prohibition on recovery for damage to the defective product itself.

Defective Premises

The main statute here is the Defective Premises Act 1982.[387] Under section 1 of that Act the cost of repairing buildings which are unfit for human habitation as a result of the use of unsuitable materials or of bad workmanship[388] can be recovered; presumably, damages for personal injury can also be recovered, as well as damages for consequential economic loss such as the cost of alternative accommodation while repairs are done. The requirement that the building be unfit for human habitation presumably means that the Act only applies where there is actual or threatened[389] danger to the health or safety of occupants; and it might also mean that damages could not be recovered under the Act for damage to 'other property' or for economic loss not consequential upon unfitness for human habitation.

---

[385] Treitel, 543, n. 76.

[386] On the meaning of this phrase, see Consumer Protection Act 1987, s. 4(2).

[387] S. 38 of the Building Act 1984 creates civil liability for breach of building regulations, but the section has not been brought into force.

[388] Whether misfeasance or nonfeasance: *Andrews* v. *Schooling* [1991] 1 WLR 783.

[389] *Ibid.*

The regime of liability under the Act has several advantages over the common law. First, it allows damages to be recovered before anyone suffers illness or injury; secondly, an action under the Act can be brought against anyone who 'takes on work for or in connection with the provision of a dwelling' (including a vendor or lessor who is involved in building on his or her own land), at the suit of the person to whose order the work is done or of any person who subsequently acquires a legal or equitable interest in the dwelling; so such persons have no problems in establishing the required degree of proximity with the defendant. But bystanders or members of the 'owner's' family cannot sue under the Act. Thirdly, not only can the person who does the work be sued, but also anyone who employed that person to do the work either under contract (a head contractor or a developer), or in exercise of statutory powers (a local housing authority).[390] At common law, on the other hand, an employer is not vicariously liable for the negligence of an independent contractor,[391] and only in rare cases will it be possible to sue the employer of an independent contractor for negligence in selecting or supervising the work of the contractor. Fourthly, the duty owed under section 1 of the Act cannot be excluded by contract.[392]

On the other hand, the Act has a number of features which explain why it has been very little used. First, it only applies to dwellings and not to other buildings; secondly, by virtue of the existence National House Building Council Scheme,[393] its practical area of operation is limited to alterations or extensions to existing dwellings,[394] and not to new houses. Thirdly, the limitation period under the Act is only six years and runs from the date the work is completed.

Under section 4 of the Act, a lessor[395] who has an obligation under the lease to maintain or repair the premises,[396] is subject to a duty (which cannot be excluded by contract) owed to all persons who may reasonably be expected to suffer personal injury or damage to their property, to take reasonable care to see that injury or damage is not caused by a defect in the

---

[390] It is not clear whether a local authority could be sued in respect of its own employee's inspection of premises under statutory powers; if it contracted the work out into the private sector it might be held liable.

[391] *D. & F. Estates* v. *Church Commissioners* [1989] AC 177.

[392] Defective Premises Act 1972, s. 6(3).

[393] A 10-year insurance scheme for new houses funded by a levy on registered builders; for details see A. M. Dugdale and K. M. Stanton, *Professional Negligence*, 2nd edn. (London, 1989), 187–90. Even though the scheme is not approved for the purposes of s. 2 of the Act (see 420below), it probably has the effect of discouraging claims under the Act in respect of new dwellings. So far as commercial buildings are concerned, it is very difficult for builders to buy latent damage insurance. The National Economic Development Office (NEDO) once recommended the establishment of an insurance scheme for commercial property: see Report of NEDO Insurance Feasability Steering Committee, *Building Users Insurance against Latent Defects* (1988) and 420 below.

[394] But the NHBC also runs a voluntary 6-year scheme to protect purchasers of newly converted and renovated houses.

[395] The provision does not apply to licences.

[396] Such an obligation need not be express but can be implied in a variety of situations.

premises of which he knew or ought to have known. It does not matter whether the defect arose before or after the commencement of the tenancy, but it must be attributable to a failure on the landlord's part to maintain or repair the premises.[397]

Under Part I of the Consumer Protection Act 1987 a person injured by a defective product which has been incorporated into a building may sue in respect of that product as a component of the building, but cannot sue in respect of the building as a 'finished product' because the act does not apply to realty. Nor can a mere vendor or lessor be sued under the Act for supplying the defective component by selling or letting the building.[398] An action can be brought under the Act in respect, *inter alia*, of property damage attributable to defective goods, but not for damage to the goods themselves or to the building in which they are incorporated.[399] Furthermore, the Act only applies to property of a type ordinarily intended for private use and in fact intended by the plaintiff for such use.

4. BASIC ISSUES

First, it is useful to tie together the material in this Chapter on intentional interference with the making of contracts, and that in the last chapter on intentional interference with existing contracts. The chief areas of operation of these bodies of law are commercial competition and employer–employee (that is, industrial) relations. There is an important contrast between legislative techniques for dealing with these areas of activity and the common law technique. Legislation usually defines a state of affairs which is thought undesirable as a matter of policy (for example, anti-competitive practices, or discriminatory employment practices, or union closed shops, or 'politically motivated' local authority contracting) and attempts to prevent such states of affairs materializing; and it sometimes provides a mechanism to compensate persons injured by acts which bring the states of affairs into existence (most commonly by giving an action for breach of statutory duty). The courts, on the other hand, have traditionally been loath to define what are considered to be unfair anti-competitive practices, unfair union tactics, and so on. Instead, the common law concentrates on the nature of the plaintiff's interest (was it contractual or not?), or on the quality of the defendant's conduct (was it intentional? was it independently unlawful? was it done in concert with others?), and on the nature of any interest asserted by the defendant in

---

[397] Defective Premises Act 1972, s. 4(3); *Rimmer* v. *Liverpool City Council* [1985] QB 1, 7D–E; *McNerny* v. *Lambeth LBC* (1989) 21 Housing LR 188.

[398] Consumer Protection Act 1987, ss. 46(3) and (4); Stapleton, *Product Liability*, 305–6.

[399] Consumer Protection Act 1987, s. 5(2).

justification of the conduct,[400] rather than on the state of affairs which provoked or which results from the clash of interests.

This unwillingness to confront issues of social morality (as opposed to the morality of individual action) caused the tort law of industrial relations to be structured in the way it is, as a set of common law rules about individual conduct subject to a set of statutory immunities against liability for individual conduct designed to protect concerted (social) action by unions. The unwillingness is also manifest in the rules of tort law which are concerned with excessive competition (or, as we might say, ultra-competitive activity). Here the law is based on the making of false statements (injurious falsehood); and on the appropriation of property interests. The concept of property is the analogy, in this context, of the notion of independent unlawfulness in the anti-competitive context: it provides an 'external' yardstick of liability. The courts have traditionally been, and still are, unwilling to embark on the project of defining, in any comprehensive way, what amounts to unfair ultra-competitive activity; or even to recognize explicitly that, for example, the interests of consumers and competitors do not always coincide in this context.

Secondly, an important feature of the common law's concentration on interests and conduct rather than on outcomes is that rules which are superficially similar in legal terms often deal with states of affairs and outcomes which are quite unrelated. The most obvious example is the general rule (to which the tort of nuisance represents the only exception), that there can be no tort liability for unintentional interference with contractual rights or contractual expectancies in the absence of negligent misstatement or the negligent rendering of services to the plaintiff. The policies which underlie and justify this general rule in the context of commercial competition are different from those which operate in the area of industrial relations; and both sets of policies are different from those which apply to interference by causing damage to property. In this respect, we have to dig beneath legal classifications, whether in terms of the plaintiff's interests or the defendant's conduct, and examine the states of affairs with which the legal rules are dealing. We must distinguish clearly the fact situations with which the law deals from the legal formulae into which the raw factual data is cast.

Thirdly, we have seen, in this Chapter particularly, how potentially important the tort of breach of statutory duty is in protecting financial interests in various fields of commercial activity. This is not because the courts have developed the tort in this area—the common law maintains its traditional unwillingness to allow actions for breach of statutory duty in respect of

---

[400] Judgments about desirable and undesirable states of affairs do creep in at the level of justification: the rule that conspiracy to injure can be justified by furthering one's own legitimate financial interests (*Crofter Hand Woven Harris Tweed Co.* v. *Veitch* [1942] AC 435) clearly endorses strike action by workers to improve pay and conditions; and the decision in *Scala Ballroom (Wolverhampton) Ltd* v. *Ratcliffe* [1958] 1 WLR 1057 involves a clear assertion of the undesirability of racial discrimination.

purely financial loss when the statute itself does not expressly provide for such an action. Rather, the legislature has increasingly adopted the technique of making breaches of statutory prohibitions and infringements of statutory rights actionable as breaches of statutory duty.[401] So we should examine the tort a little more. In the contexts with which we are concerned in this book, there seems little doubt that in the absence of express statutory words to the contrary,[402] liability will depend simply on proof first, that the defendant, by voluntary conduct, did the prohibited act or created the prohibited state of affairs, regardless of whether D intended to injure P thereby or of whether D was negligent in injuring P;[403] and, secondly, that D's conduct caused damage to P. In many of the instances we have discussed, proof of causation will be very difficult; and this, plus the cost and hassle of litigation, will probably ensure that the civil law is relatively little used in many of the contexts we have examined. An action for breach of statutory duty will lie only in respect of damage of the type which the statute was intended to provide protection against. Statutes rarely make explicit provision on this point, but in the contexts with which we are concerned, the only loss normally in issue will be purely economic loss; and so such loss will have to be held recoverable if the relevant provisions are to have any practical operation. Issues of remoteness of damage are also subsumed under this rubric.[404] It can be imagined that such questions could raise extremely complex issues in some of the areas we have examined, such as competition law.

The defences of contributory negligence and voluntary assumption of risk (*volenti non fit injuria*) are, in theory, available (unless excluded by statute) in actions for breach of statutory duty. It is not clear, however, that these defences would have much part to play in the sort of actions in respect of economic loss which we have considered. It is hard to see how it could be argued that a plaintiff had accepted the 'risk' of being the subject of unlawful anti-competitive or discriminatory action; and it would certainly be contrary to the whole purpose of anti-discrimination legislation, for example, to allow a defendant to argue that the plaintiff was partly at fault.

The last basic issue which needs to be introduced at this stage, and which underlies much of the law discussed in the last two chapters, is the relationship between contract and tort as bodies of law. Certain aspects of this issue were mentioned at the end of Chapter 3. Two other aspects are raised by the material in this Chapter: the first is the impact of arguments about the desirability (or otherwise) of allowing concurrent actions in contract and tort on the rules concerning liability for misrepresentations which induce contracts.

---

[401] But there are cases in which actions for breach of statutory provisions are expressly excluded: e.g. Radioactive Substances Act 1993, s. 46; Water Resources Act 1991, s. 100.

[402] As in the case, e.g., of indirect sex or race discrimination: see 158 above.

[403] This is ironical, given the well-documented unwillingness of the courts to interpret safety regulations as imposing strict duties: K. M. Stanton, *Breach of Statutory Duty in Tort* (London, 1986), 92–113.

[404] *Ibid.* 133.

The second concerns cases in which manufacturers, builders, or service providers are sued in tort by persons other than their clients: the fundamental question of legal policy in such cases is whether P ought to be denied an action in tort on the ground of being in a position to sue a third party in contract; or on the ground that P could and should have secured protection by making appropriate contractual arrangements with a third party. As we have seen, the law appears less willing to allow third-party tort actions in respect of services associated with the manufacture, production, and supply of goods and buildings than in respect of other services: in the latter case, the requirement of damage to other property imposes a limit on tort actions; but this requirement bears no obvious relationship to the question whether P ought to be relegated to whatever contractual rights he or she may have. The relationship between tortious and contractual liability is discussed in detail in Chapter 6.

5

Interests Competing with the Plaintiff's

1. THE IDEA OF COMPETING INTERESTS

The fact that the plaintiff has a legally recognized interest does not necessarily mean that interference with it will be actionable in tort: by no means all such interests are so protected. In some cases this is just because the protection of the interest in question is seen as the job of some other area of the law (such as criminal law). But in other cases, with which we are concerned in this Chapter, the reason is not that the particular interest falls outside the province of the law of tort but rather that the defendant is able to point to some competing interest which outweighs that of the plaintiff and justifies the law of tort in refusing to come to P's aid.

Such competing interests fall into two broad categories: individual and public. For example, in an action for inducing breach of contract the defendant may plead that he or she acted to protect some superior legal interest of D; or in an action for breach of confidence D may plead that some public interest justified the disclosure of the information. Such interests may figure in the reasoning justifying a refusal to impose tort liability in one of two ways: as in the examples just given, a competing interest may provide a defence to an action in respect of conduct which is *prima facie* tortious. On the other hand, it may lead the court to say that the conduct complained of was not tortious at all because, for example, it would be against the public interest to impose a duty of care in the particular circumstances of the case— the (limited) immunity from liability in tort enjoyed by advocates provides an instance of such reasoning. The practical importance of this distinction lies in allocation of the burden of proof or persuasion: the plaintiff will normally be responsible for establishing that there are no factors which prevent tort liability arising, whereas the onus of establishing defensive factors will normally rest on the defendant.

Statute plays a very important part in establishing competing interests. Sometimes a statute provides a defendant with a precise answer to the plaintiff's claim; examples are the immunity for certain otherwise tortious acts done in furtherance of a trade dispute, and the grounds of lawful arrest and lawful entry of premises contained in the Police and Criminal Evidence Act 1984. In other cases, however, statutory provisions figure in the reasoning in a more indirect way; for example, if a statutory authority is sued in tort for breach of statutory duty or negligent exercise of a statutory power, then in the absence of any express provision in the statute on civil actions for damages, the court will examine the scheme of the Act and decide whether an action for damages is consistent with its terms. This process is usually described as one of discerning the intention of the legislature or of the statute, but in reality it is an exercise in establishing the demands of public policy. In addition to statute-based competing interests, there are also, of course, competing interests recognized purely by the common law. For instance, the advocates' immunity prevents tort liability arising in certain cases, and the public policy defence to an action for breach of confidence may provide an answer to a claim in respect of *prima facie* actionable conduct.

Competing interests most commonly provide answers to claims in respect of *prima facie* tortious conduct in cases where the tort on which the cause of action is based is one which has the protection of a property interest (or some kindred type of interest) or of a contractual interest, as its juristic focus: trespass, for example, or defamation, or interference with contract. Where the interest which the plaintiff seeks to protect is simply one in protecting monetary wealth, and where the essence of the claim is that D's wrongful conduct inflicted economic loss on P, competing interests more commonly prevent tort liablity arising. Thus, we speak of justifying trespass or interference with contract,[1] and of raising a defence to a *prima facie* case of defamation. By contrast, in relation to the tort of negligence, which figures most prominently in the protection of monetary wealth as such, the position is quite different. In this tort, competing interests figure most prominently in the formal structure of the law of negligence at the level of duty of care where they appear as a sub-class of 'policy' arguments against the imposition of liability.

This difference between the place of competing interests in reasoning in these two different contexts may be a reflection of the law's judgment about the relative importance of the various interests at stake. When the interest which P seeks to protect is proprietary or contractual, the juridical and social importance of the interest is signalled by requiring D to provide a reason (in the form of some competing interest) why the interference with the interest in question should not attract tort liability. In such cases, P is not required to convince the court that there is no competing interest standing in the way of the imposition of tort liability.

It should be noted that not all 'policy' arguments or considerations relevant to the imposition and scope of tort liability are based on the existence of competing interests. In Chapter 10 we will discuss aims of tort law and justifications for tort liability; aims such as compensation and deterrence clearly influence the imposition and extent of tort liability, but they do not

---

[1] Cf. Race Relations Act 1976, s. 1(1)(b)(ii); Sex Discrimination Act 1975, s. 1(1)(b)(ii).

normally[2] figure in the formal reasoning which justifies decisions in particular cases. Rather they operate as high-level explanations of or justifications for the pattern of tort liability which has developed, as conceptual tools for the evaluation and criticism of existing patterns of liability and as starting-points for reform proposals.

This Chapter deals first with competing public interests and then with competing private interests. The interests surveyed are diverse, and no clear pattern emerges which would justify broad general statements about the role or function of tort law.

2. PUBLIC INTERESTS

Protection of Life and Property

There is a public interest in the protection of persons from death and bodily injury or illness, and in the protection of property from destruction, damage, or misuse. If the person or property in danger is the defendant's own, then a public interest and a private interest coincide, but the element of self-interest may weaken D's claim to special consideration in respect of any wrong committed in the course of taking protective action. The law looks more indulgently on acts done to preserve the person or property of another, especially if that other is the plaintiff. The most common situation is where tangible property is damaged or property rights are invaded in order to save a person from death or injury or some property (other than the damaged property) from destruction or damage.

As a factor which prevents tort liability arising, this public interest appears in the tort of negligence at the level of standard of care: risks may be justified in an emergency, for the sake of preserving life and property, which would not otherwise be justified. For example, drivers of emergency vehicles, such as fire engines, may be justified in taking risks which ordinary drivers should not take; although, of course, the greater the risk, the greater the care required to avoid damage. In this context, the law clearly does not bracket physical damage to property with personal injury: the risks justified to preserve property would be less than those justified to preserve persons from death or personal injury.[3] It is a question of balancing the value of that which was preserved against the value of that sacrificed in order to do so.

As an answer to *prima facie* liability, this public interest usually takes the form of the defence of necessity to actions for trespass.[4] What acts the defence

---

[2] The major exception is that the aim of compensation provides the starting-point of the rules about assessment of damages.

[3] *Esso Petroleum Co. Ltd* v. *Southport Corporation* [1956] AC 218, 228 *per* Lord Devlin.

[4] Salmond, 481–3; Fleming, 94–8.

will justify depends, once again, on the nature and source[5] of the evil avoided, the identity of the beneficiaries of D's action, and the seriousness of the interference with P's rights.[6] Such balancing of factors may involve difficult and controversial moral and social judgments. For example, homelessness has been held not to justify squatting.[7] When should a person effectively be required by law to allow his or her interests to be sacrificed to those of others? The law's general answer is: only in extreme cases in order to prevent death or personal injury, or to prevent destruction of or serious damage to property.[8]

This public interest may justify relieving D of liability for the interference as such with P's rights. But does it justify leaving P without compensation for loss or damage suffered as a result of D's actions? As a general rule, English common law recognizes no right to compensation in such circumstances. As a matter of morality or fairness, it might be said that the beneficiaries of the plaintiff's unintended benevolence (whether D or third parties) should pay compensation.[9] Such a principle is recognized where the actor is the government: statutory compensation is payable when land is compulsorily acquired for public purposes; or in certain cases where property rights are devalued by public works.[10] The common law also recognizes this principle.[11] The doctrine of 'general average contribution' in maritime law allows a shipowner who incurs expense to preserve cargo on the ship to recover a contribution to the cost from the cargo owners proportional to the value of their cargo saved; and it allows a cargo owner whose cargo is jettisoned to save the ship and other cargo on it to recover a contribution to making good the loss from those whose property was saved.[12] Maritime law also recognizes a doctrine of 'maritime salvage', which entitles a person who takes action at sea to save a ship from peril to recompense for so doing from those whose property is saved.[13]

---

[5] The defence will not be available if the need to act was the result of D's negligence: *Rigby* v. *Chief Constable of Northamptonshire* [1985] 1 WLR 1242.

[6] e.g., did D merely use P's property or was it damaged?

[7] *Southwark LBC* v. *Williams* [1971] Ch. 734. Nor does hunger justify theft. But if the continuance of life rather than its quality was at stake, the result would surely be different. Lord Denning's view was that the law should take a firm line, and 'trust that . . . distress will be relieved by the charitable and the good'. But can the State (whether in the form of the government or the courts) abdicate moral responsibility in this way?

[8] e.g. Police and Criminal Evidence Act 1984, s. 17(e).

[9] But what if the rescue attempt is unsuccessful? See D. Friedmann (1980) 80 *Col. LR* 504, 542–3. At least partial success is a requirement in the maritime law of salvage: F. D. Rose (1989) 9 *OJLS* 167, 198.

[10] Land Compensation Act 1973.

[11] *Burmah Oil Ltd* v. *Lord Advocate* [1965] AC 75. But its application in this case was reversed by statute: War Damage Act 1965.

[12] See generally Goff and Jones, 333–42. Such contributions may be recovered from a person whose negligence created the need to incur the expense or sacrifice the property: *Morrison Steamship Co. Ltd* v. *Greystoke Castle (Cargo Owners)* [1947] AC 265.

[13] By statute, the principles relevant to salvage at sea now also apply to aircraft and hovercraft (as well as lives). The measure of compensation is not limited to reimbursement for costs

The claim to compensation seems strongest in principle and easiest to satisfy in practice in cases, first, where D acts to save self or own property;[14] and, secondly, where the state acts in the public interest. Where a private individual acts to help a third party, the third party might be able to resist a claim for compensation on moral grounds if the help was uninvited (or, *a fortiori*, declined); and in practice, it might not always be easy to identify (all) the beneficiaries or to apportion the compensation fairly between them.[15]

Conversely, in cases where D acted to assist P, there is a moral argument for requiring P to compensate D for any expense or loss incurred, in addition to relieving D of liability for interference with P's rights and not requiring D to compensate P for loss or damage suffered in the attempt to help P, provided D acted reasonably and without negligence.[16] Indeed, the law of tort does allow a rescuer to recover damages (for loss suffered as a result of going to the rescue) from a person who negligently puts their person[17] or property[18] in a position of danger. The defendant's claim would be weakened if the assistance was uninvited, and weakened even more if the offer of assistance was specifically declined.[19]

The moral problem involved in allowing the defence of necessity to be pleaded against the person suffering injury, damage, or loss is that it forces that person to sacrifice his or her interests to those of another (or, in the case where D assists P, to some other interest of P which D deems more important than P does). And the moral problem involved in requiring the beneficiaries to pay the injured person compensation[20] is that this may force them, in effect, to pay for something they did not ask for and which, perhaps, they did not want. In other words, allowing the defence of necessity and awarding compensation in cases where the acquiescence of the person injured or benefited has not been obtained in advance forces that person to accept a val-

---

incurred, but includes recompense for services rendered and even an element of reward designed to encourage salvage. Those whose property is saved are liable to contribute to the compensation according to the value of their property which is saved. See generally Goff and Jones, ch. 16. See also F. D. Rose (1989) 9 *OJLS* 167.

[14] As in *Vincent* v. *Lake Erie Transportation Co.* (1910) 124 NW 221. Of course, P would, under current law, have a claim if D's own tort created the need to rescue.

[15] These problems do not arise, or, at least, not in acute form, in the maritime context. Where the sacrificed property is insured, the insurance *de facto* apportions the loss; and this perhaps provides a good reason for tort law not to intervene: Fleming, 94–5. But see Goff and Jones, 375, n. 97.

[16] If a third party (not D) gratuitously renders services to the victim of personal injuries caused by the defendant's negligence, P, as trustee for the third party, can recover the reasonable value of those services from D: *Hunt* v. *Severs* [1994] 2 AC 350.

[17] *Harrison* v. *British Railways Board* [1981] 3 All ER 679; the rescuer can, of course, recover from a third party who negligently created the danger. It is not clear whether this right extends to purely economic loss in the form of expenses incurred or income foregone.

[18] *Ogwo* v. *Taylor* [1988] AC 431.

[19] It is in cases of emergency medical treatment that the law is least receptive to such arguments on the part of a plaintiff. On this cf. Road Traffic Act 1988, ss. 157–8.

[20] Or in refusing the injured person compensation where he or she is the beneficiary.

uation of his or her interests[21] different from that which he or she assigns to them.

The crucial question is this: when is the law justified in giving effect to 'social' valuations of interests and ignoring the valuation assigned by the interest-holder? On the whole, English law is prepared to do this only in extreme circumstances. This explains, for example, the results in the nuisance and trespass cases considered in Chapter 2 in which a landowner has been held entitled to use the law of tort to protect his or her legal rights even when, judged from a social point of view, the landowner's interest in doing so is slight compared with D's interest in interfering with those rights. It also explains why, as we shall see later in this Chapter, English law has been traditionally unwilling to accept any general proposition that legal rights and powers must not be exercised for unacceptable ends. When the law refuses to force people to accept invasions of their rights or to pay for unrequested benefits, it is expressing a preference for requiring those who wish to invade rights or confer benefits to bargain in advance with the other party. Only where bargaining is impossible or impractical, or where one of the parties is in an unassailable bargaining position, is the law likely to intervene.[22] The obverse is that the law of tort is unwilling to require positive action unless a person has agreed or undertaken to act, or in extreme circumstances.

Law Enforcement

The Police and Criminal Evidence Act 1984 and a number of other statutes provide defences to actions for trespass to the person and to land and goods with a view to assisting the prevention and detection of crime and other unlawful conduct.

Discouragement of Illegal Conduct

As a matter of public policy, courts are reluctant to give legal remedies to a party who founds a cause of action on his or her own illegal act.[23] The judges do not wish to be seen as giving aid or encouragement to law breakers. At the same time, the courts are reluctant to deprive an injured person of compensation simply because he or she has done something wrong, unless the illegal act was a cause of or was closely associated with the loss. So, for instance, a person may be awarded damages for fraudulent misrepresentation even if the contract into which he or she was induced to enter was in some respect

---

[21] Namely, that they were worth saving at the expense of loss or damage to the rescuer.
[22] Cf. A. Brudner (1987) 7 *OJLS* 339, 365–8.
[23] *Holman* v. *Johnson* (1775) 1 Cowp. 341, 343; [1775–1802] All ER 98, 99.

unlawful, and even if the claimant was implicated in that unlawfulness.[24] It is thought wrong to allow D to keep ill-gotten gains when they were obtained by a fraud which was unrelated to P's illegal conduct. Conversely, in *Thackwell* v. *Barclays Bank PLC*[25] P sued the bank for negligence and conversion of a cheque which it had paid into the account of a person who had forged P's signature. Because the cheque represented the proceeds of a crime, it was held that P could not recover on the ground that the illegality was highly 'proximate' to P's loss.

These decisions have been said to rest on a general principle that damages in tort will not be awarded if to do so would cause 'affront to the public conscience'.[26] But the House of Lords has disapproved of such a free-wheeling approach,[27] and the correct approach seems to be to ask whether P's illegal conduct was the real or effective cause of the loss for which compensation is sought.

Control of Land Use

The 'public interest' in the use of private land is normally not, as such, a relevant factor in deciding whether a landowner has used land unreasonably and hence inflicted a nuisance on owners of neighbouring land;[28] or in deciding whether to award damages in lieu of an injunction.[29]

The Administration of Justice

Liability for Statements Made in Court

The law goes to considerable lengths to protect participants in the judicial process from tort actions in respect of things said for the purposes of such proceedings. Thus, statements made in preparation for or in the course of judicial proceedings by judges,[30] counsel, witnesses, jurors, and parties are protected by absolute privilege in the law of defamation.[31] Nor can state-

---

[24] *Shelley* v. *Paddock* [1980] QB 348; *Saunders* v. *Edwards* [1987] 1 WLR 1116.

[25] [1986] 1 All ER 676.

[26] *Thackwell* v. *Barclays Bank PLC* [1986] 1 All ER 676, 687.

[27] *Tinsley* v. *Milligan* [1994] 1 AC 340.

[28] Harris, 324, 327, n.1 and text, 328–9, 341–2. Concerning the impact of a grant of planning permission on liability for nuisance see *Gillingham BC* v. *Medway (Chatham) Dock Co. Ltd* [1993] QB 343.

[29] *Kennaway* v. *Thompson* [1981] QB 88.

[30] *Scott* v. *Stansfield* [1868] LR 3 Ex. 220. See generally A. Olowofoyeku, *Suing Judges: A Study of Judicial Immunity* (Oxford, 1993), esp. ch. 4.

[31] Salmond, 165–7; Fleming, 559–61. Accurate reports of judicial proceedings are also protected: Law of Libel Amendment Act 1888, s. 3; Defamation Act, 1952, ss. 8, 9. Similarly, a police informer cannot be sued for malicious prosecution: *Martin* v. *Watson* [1994] QB 425.

ments made in court form the basis of actions for deceit or conspiracy,[32] or for negligence.[33] This means that the maker of the statement cannot successfully be sued even if the statement was made out of malice with a view to injuring the plaintiff.

The justification for this privilege and immunity is obvious—it is of the utmost importance in an adversary system that no unnecessary constraints be put on freedom of speech before a court; and it may be[34] that in this context (as opposed to the Parliamentary context), even the protection which the law gives to malicious speech is justified. The possibility of being sued, even if unsuccessfully, might not only inhibit witnesses and others from appearing in court but might also undermine the credibility of what they say if it is thought that the fear of being sued might cause them to 'hold back'. On the other hand, the uncertainty about which tribunals are encompassed within the operation of these rules makes the law somewhat unsatisfactory in its practical operation. Both these points emerge clearly from statements of Lord Diplock in *Trapp* v. *Mackie*:[35]

In deciding whether a particular tribunal is of such a kind as to attract absolute privilege for witnesses when they give evidence before it, your Lordships are engaged in the task of balancing against one another public interests which conflict . . . that the law should provide a remedy to the citizen whose good name and reputation is traduced by malicious falsehood uttered by another . . . [and] that witnesses before tribunals recognized by law should . . . give their testimony free from any fear of being harassed by an action of [sic] an allegation, *whether true or false*, that they acted from malice.

It has been argued that an exception to the immunity should be created in the case of paid expert witnesses so that they could be sued in negligence (but not defamation, etc.) in respect of evidence they give and their preparatory work.[36] Whether this is a sound proposal depends partly on the likely effect of abolition of the immunity on the availability of experts willing to act as witnesses and on the credibility of their evidence; and partly on an assessment of the role of the expert witness. The first issue is largely a matter of speculation on which opinions will differ. The second issue turns on how best to characterize the role of expert witnesses. Are they properly seen as impartial sources of technical information for the court; or, by contrast, as part of the adversary process and hence entitled to be partisan while, nevertheless, owing duties to the court to act, if necessary, adversely to the interests of the

---

[32] *Hargreaves* v. *Bretherton* [1958] 3 All ER 122 (alleged perjury); *Marrinan* v. *Vibart* [1963] 1 QB 234 (applied in *Roy* v. *Prior* [1970] 1 QB 283); *Cabassi* v. *Vila* (1940) 64 CLR 130.

[33] *Evans* v. *London Hospital Medical College* [1981] 3 All ER 715. This decision, which was approved by the House of Lords in *X* v. *Bedforshire CC* [1995] 3 WLR 152, 187–8, establishes that the immunity of witnesses (including expert witnesses), at least in respect of liability in negligence, extends to statements made in the knowledge that they may give rise ot court proceedings in which the statement may be used as evidence.

[34] But see 231 below.   [35] [1979] 1 All ER 489, 494–5 and 492a–b.

[36] T. Hervey [1985] PN 102.

parties employing them in order to ensure the due administration of justice. The latter view seems more realistic[37] and suggests treating expert witnesses analogously to advocates.[38]

Liability for Court Orders[39]

The law also accords to judges considerable immunity from actions in tort arising out of things done in the course of judicial proceedings.[40] The common law apparently drew a distinction between inferior courts of limited jurisdiction and superior courts.[41] Judges of inferior courts were immune from liability provided they were acting within their powers,[42] and provided they did not act 'maliciously';[43] whereas judges of superior courts, acting as such, were immune from liability even for acts done maliciously, provided they did not exceed their powers. Any judge could be sued for acting maliciously[44] beyond power. Thus section 44 of the Justices of the Peace Act 1979 provided that *if* a justice could be sued for acts done within jurisdiction, the plaintiff had to plead and prove malice and 'lack of reasonable and probable[45] cause'. However, in *Re McC.*[46] a majority of the House of Lords held, obiter, that the rule that justices could be sued for acts done within their powers was not justified in modern conditions and, therefore, that the rule in section 44 had no field of operation. To this effect, section 108 of the Courts and Legal Services Act 1990 amended section 44 of the 1979 Act to give justices (and justices' clerk exercising the functions of a justice) complete immunity from action in respect of acts done within jurisdiction.

Section 45 of the 1979 Act, by contrast, provided positively that a justice could be sued for acts done without jurisdiction or in excess of power, even without proof of malice or lack of 'reasonable or probable cause'. But in *Sirros* v. *Moore*[47] Lord Denning MR was of the opinion that judges of inferior courts (not just magistrates) should be treated similarly to judges of superior courts, and that they should not be liable for acts done without jurisdiction in the absence of malice. This view has been given effect to (in respect of magistrates) by an amendment to section 45 contained in section

---

[37] I. R. Freckleton, *The Trial of the Expert* (Melbourne, 1987), ch. 8; J. Basten (1977) 40 *MLR* 174.

[38] Cf. *Palmer* v. *Durnford Ford* [1992] QB 483. Concerning advocates see 233–7 below.

[39] M. Brazier [1976] *PL* 397; B. Feldthusen (1980) 29 *UNBLJ* 73.

[40] Salmond, 402–4. The immunity extends to things done in execution of court orders in respect of which immunity exists.

[41] See R. Walker and R. Ward, *Walker & Walker: The English Legal System* 7th ed. (London, 1985), 183.

[42] Or unless any excess of jurisdiction was the result of a mistake of fact: *Sirros* v. *Moore* [1975] QB 118, 148 *per* Ormrod LJ.

[43] Which appears, in this context, to mean 'for an improper purpose or motive'.

[44] Which appears, in this context, to mean 'with knowledge of lack of jurisdiction'.

[45] That is, 'justifiable'.   [46] [1985] AC 528.

[47] [1975] QB 118, 136–7; cf. Ormrod LJ at 149.

108 of the Courts and Legal Services Act 1990, which gives justices (and justices' clerks exercising any of the powers of a justice) immunity from action in respect of acts done without jurisdiction[48] unless it is proved that the justice or clerk acted 'in bad faith'.[49]

The main argument for judicial immunity[50] goes as follows: the proper course for a party aggrieved by a court decision is to challenge the *decision* by ordinary means, such as appeal or an application for judicial review,[51] rather than to sue the judge, even if the judge acted out of malice, envy or hatred. It is not that judges should be entitled to engage in unseemly behaviour, but that the threat of such attacks on judges personally might open them to corrupt outside influences which could threaten their impartiality and independence.[52] Actions for damages would also by-pass the established means of correcting judicial errors, such as appeals and applications for habeas corpus. Furthermore, actions for, say, negligence or false imprisonment against a judge would, in effect, involve a rehearing of the original action by another court, often at the same level in the judicial hierarchy, and this would run counter to the law's proper concern with securing finality of litigation and might generate an unhealthy lack of confidence in the competence of the judiciary.[53] It is also sometimes argued that judicial liability could (and, in the case of magistrates, may even now) lead to 'defensive judging',[54] which seems to include undue caution in convicting those prosecuted for alleged offences. Whatever the merits of this argument in other contexts, it might be thought that in the administration of the criminal law by lay persons, caution in convicting alleged offenders was exactly the desirable approach.[55] Furthermore, any argument that there is a real danger of (a significant number of) unfounded or vexatious claims seems, at best, doubtful.

At all events, the moral claim of a person who, for example, is wrongfully

---

[48] This phrase is to be understood in a narrow sense and not in accordance with the extended sense given to the notion of jurisdiction in *Anisminic Ltd* v. *Foreign Compensation Commission* [1969] 2 AC 147: see *Re McC* [1985] AC 528, 536–47. This means that not every error which would justify quashing of a decision on an application for judicial review will found an action for damages. See also *R.* v. *Manchester City Magistrates Court, ex parte Davies* [1989] QB 631, 641 *per* Neill LJ.

[49] Under s. 53 of the 1979 Act the financial burden of civil liability may, in cases where it is thought reasonable, be borne by the public purse. But the Crown is not liable vicariously for the torts of judicial officers: Crown Proceedings Act 1947, s. 2(5).

[50] For detailed consideration of the rationale of judicial immunity see Olowofoyeku, *Suing Judges*, ch. 6.

[51] 51 Of course, if a judge of an inferior court acted out of malice or other improper motive, the decision would be *ultra vires* and could be quashed.

[52] *Sirros* v. *Moore* [1975] QB 118, 132 *per* Lord Denning MR; cf. *Scott* v. *Stansfield* [1868] LR 3 Ex. 220, 223 *per* Kelly CB.

[53] For a contrary view, see Brazier [1976] *PL* 397, 408–9.

[54] Editorial [1988] *New LJ* 837.

[55] In practice, lay magistrates are advised on the law relevant to the cases they try by their clerks, who are legally qualified; or, if no legally qualified clerk is available, by unqualified court officers (at least, so it was alleged in a leading article in the *Guardian*, 6 July 1989, 18). Such court officers presumably enjoy common law immunity from action.

imprisoned under a defective court order is strong, as is the case for providing some formalized mechanism for compensation.[56] If a judge has acted corruptly, he or she may be removed from office. But the likelihood of this happening is in inverse relation to the rank of the judge;[57] and, anyway, removal does not help the aggrieved person directly. In practice, however, negligence and incompetence are more important causes of wrong decisions than corrption, and it is against liability for negligence that the judicial immunity offers greatest protection. The Criminal Justice Act 1988 establishes a statutory compensation scheme to deal with 'miscarriages of justice'; and in some cases it might be possible to claim compensation under the European Convention on Human Rights.[58]

Immunity from liability for negligence also extends to other bodies and persons exercising judicial functions, such as administrative tribunals and officials,[59] and arbitrators.[60] The difficulty in applying this immunity is in distinguishing between judicial and other functions. For example, it has been held that an architect employed by a building owner to value and certify work done by a builder, or an auditor employed by a vendor of shares to value them for the purposes of sale, is not fulfilling a judicial function even though he or she has to make a decision on an issue (that is, the value of goods or services) in relation to which the two parties involved have conflicting interests. The most widely accepted reason for this is that the architect or auditor does not, while the arbitrator does, settle a *dispute* between the parties. But, as Lord Kilbrandon said in *Arenson* v. *Casson*,[61] the distinction between an actual dispute and a situation of potential dispute between parties with conflicting interests is not very satisfying.

A viable distinction might be based on the fact that judges and arbitrators are empowered to apply the law of the land and to decide disputed questions of law. In this sense, they form part of the machinery of government whereas architects and auditors perform no such governmental function.[62] It is to ensure the impartial administration *of the law* that judicial independence is maintained; it is not only the parties to a dispute who have an interest in the due administration of the law. The independence of arbitrators is not as well protected as that of judges in that they are appointed by the parties in dispute and have no security of tenure. However, this fact provides no reason not to attempt to make their position in relation to particular decisions as impregnable as possible by immunizing them from actions in respect of them.

[56] See Lord Templeman in *Re McC* [1985] AC 528, 559.
[57] Brazier [1976] PL 397, 400–3.   [58] See 199 above.
[59] *Partridge* v. *The General Council of Medical Education and Registration of the United Kingdom* (1890) 25 QBD 90; *Everett* v. *Griffiths* [1921] 1 AC 631.
[60] *Sutcliffe* v. *Thackrah* [1974] AC 727; *Arensons* v. *Casson, Beckman, Rutley & Co.* [1977] AC 405; *Palacath Ltd* v. *Flanagan* [1985] 2 All ER 161; F. Miller [1991] *New LJ* 633. Court-appointed sequestrators do not qualify for immunity: *IRC* v. *Hoogstraten* [1985] QB 1077.
[61] [1977] AC 405, 430.
[62] Cf. *O'Reilly* v. *Mackman* [1983] 2 AC 237 (CA).

This explanation has the advantage both that it explains why the line is drawn where it currently is, and also that it rests on the idea of impartiality and independence from control by private citizens. Furthermore, it is compatible with cases concerning administrative bodies cited above which associate the term 'judicial' with discretionary power to affect the legal rights of citizens.[63]

If a public body or official exercised a judicial function deliberately for an improper purpose, or knowingly exceeded its powers, the body or official might be liable in the tort of misfeasance in a public office.[64] If a private person (such as a private arbitrator) exercised judicial powers in such a way, he or she might incur liability for intentional infliction of economic loss, especially if the person exceeded his or her powers: in that case, the requisite element of unlawfulness would clearly be present.

As we will see later, English courts have become very unwilling to impose liability for negligence on public authorities exercising 'public functions'.[65] This unwillingness is not predicated on the function in question being judicial, but rests on a number of policy considerations, some of which are similar to those which support judicial immunity. It may be that the law is moving to a position where the negligent exercise of 'public functions' will rarely be actionable in tort. If so, judicial functions will simply represent a sub-class of public functions. At one extreme, High Court judges exercising judicial functions would be protected from tort liability except for malicious excess of power; at the other extreme, a public official might enjoy no immunity for malicious conduct and only limited immunity from liability for negligent exercise of public functions. The precise scope of the immunity of any particular official or body would depend on the nature of the function exercised and the manner of its exercise.

Liability of Lawyers for Negligent Conduct of Litigation

In *Rondel* v. *Worsley*[66] the House of Lords held that 'a barrister, like a judge, juryman and witness, is immune from being sued in respect of anything he says or does or omits to say or do in the course of performing his role in court'.[67] This immunity now extends to advocates who are not barristers;[68] and conduct covered by the immunity is beyond the remit of the Legal Services Ombudsman[69] The immunity now covers what can loosely be

[63] Cf. S. A. de Smith, *Judicial Review of Administrative Action* 4th edn. (J. M. Evans, (ed.)) (London, 1980), 337–9.
[64] See 262 below.   [65] See 238–46 below.   [66] [1969] 1 AC 191.
[67] *Saif Ali* v. *Sydney Mitchell & Co.* [1980] AC 198, 227 *per* Lord Salmon. For the position in Ontario, see *Demarco* v. *Ungaro* (1979) 95 DLR(3d) 385.
[68] Courts and Legal Services Act 1990, s. 62(1). See also Supply of Services (Exclusion of Implied Terms) Order 1982, reg. 2(1). There used to be a rule that barristers could not contract with their lay clients; but see now Courts and Legal Services Act 1990, s. 61. The immunity extends to liability under such a contract: see *ibid.*, s. 62(2).
[69] *Ibid.*, s. 22(7)(b).

described as the conduct of the case in court and out-of-court work which is 'so intimately connected with the conduct of the cause in court that it can fairly be said to be a preliminary decision concerning the way the cause is to be conducted when it comes to a hearing'.[70] On the basis of this principle, immunity has been held to attach (for instance) to advice about the plea to be entered by the defendant to a criminal prosecution;[71] to advice that there is no evidence to support a claim, on the part of a husband in maintenance proceedings, of misconduct by a wife;[72] to a refusal by counsel to ask all the questions or lead all the evidence suggested by the client;[73] to settlement of an action by compromise in court after oral evidence;[74] to failure to advise a client that he or she has a good defence to a prosecution and failure to object to inadmissible evidence.[75] Immunity has been held not to apply (for instance) to a failure at an early stage to advise the joining of certain parties to an action;[76] or to the compromising of appeal proceedings before the hearing of the appeal had begun.[77]

The immunity is potentially very wide. As defined it could cover anything done in court in the conduct of a case, and any advice about what ought or ought not to be done in court, or on the way the case ought to be conducted in court. It could also, presumably, cover advice on the conduct of a trial which never takes place. So what is left outside the immunity? In *Saif Ali* v. *Mitchell*[78] it was held that decisions whether or not to institute proceedings at all or against particular parties are not immune. But are these not direct counterparts of decisions made in court not to pursue an action further, or not to do so against a particular party? In fact, it might be thought that the only activities of advocates which are not caught by the immunity as defined are things not done in contemplation of litigation. This is not to say that the immunity will not be limited more narrowly than the terms in which it is stated could justify, but only that the present formulation of the immunity seems very wide.

---

[70] *Rees* v. *Sinclair* [1974] 1 NZLR 180, 187 *per* McCarthy P. The immunity of witnesses (other than paid experts) from actions in negligence appears to be wider: *Evans* v. *London Hospital Medical College* [1981] 1 All ER 715. The emphasis on the trial of actions in court may seem odd in the light of the fact that only a very small proportion of claims ever goes to trial and of the current vogue for 'alternative dispute resolution'. Some would say that the decreasing importance of trials in the professional lives of advocates supports the abolition of the immunity: J. Powell, *Counsel*, April 1995, 11.

[71] *Somasundaram* v. *M. Julius Melchior & Co.* [1988] 1 WLR 1394.

[72] *Rees* v. *Sinclair* [1974] 1 NZLR 180.

[73] *Rondel* v. *Worsley* [1969] 1 AC 191.

[74] *Biggar* v. *McLeod* [1978] 2 NZLR 9. Would the immunity extend to settlement at the door of the court, or earlier? A solicitor can be sued for settling contrary to the client's wishes: e.g. *Thompson* v. *Howley* [1977] 1 NZLR 16.

[75] *Giannarelli* v. *Wraith* (1988) 81 ALR 417.

[76] *Saif Ali* v. *Mitchell* [1980] AC 198. Nor should it attach to carelessly (by inertia) allowing an action to become statute-barred or to fail for want of prosecution (cf. *Gouzenko* v. *Harris* (1976) 72 DLR(3d) 293) or to end in judgment by default.

[77] *Donellan* v. *Watson* (1990) 21 NSWLR 335.

[78] [1980] AC 198.

None of the arguments in favour of the immunity is entirely convincing.[79] One argument is that an advocate has a duty not only to the client but also to the court,[80] and that these duties may conflict. Since the duty to the court is higher, the advocate might be required by it to do something which could adversely affect the client's case. But the mere doing of one's duty to the court to the detriment of one's client could never be called negligent—liability could only be justified where the advocate wrongly and negligently reached the conclusion that the duty to the court required action to the detriment of the client. So the basis of the argument must be that the fear of actions, even unfounded ones,[81] might have a negative effect on the conduct of advocates, and might lead them to prefer the interests of their clients to their duty to the court.

A similar argument is sometimes used in other contexts, notably in actions against governmental bodies[82] and against doctors; the courts seem to fear that the prospect of being sued may lead to undue caution in the performance of a person's or body's tasks or functions, or to the taking of unnecessary ('defensive') precautions. In the case of advocates, this may lead to prolixity of presentation and a consequent increase in the length and cost of trials.[83] But since it is acknowledged that such caution would be 'undue' and such precautions 'unnecessary', in the sense that failure to take them could not be categorized as negligent, the argument seems to involve an assumption and a condonation of ignorance of the law. In the case of advocates in particular, this is a flimsy foundation for the edifice of protection or immunity which is constructed upon it. Moreover, the assertion that the fear of liability would lead to defensive behaviour is, to say the least, unsupported by empirical evidence: there is no evidence for it, and some against it.[84] Furthermore, people who are not accorded the status of professionals are not, explicitly at least, given the benefit of the 'defensive practice argument', even though it may arguably be relevant to their activities.

The argument from conflict of duties is sometimes bolstered by saying that counsel would be hindered in doing their duty to the court when forced to make a quick decision in court in the heat of the moment and without the benefit of calm reflection if they operated under the fear of being sued (even if unsuccessfully) by their clients. Supported in this way, the argument would not seem to justify immunity in any case where there was time for reflection, even in relation to a matter to which immunity would attach if a decision on it was made in court. Furthermore, other professional groups, especially doctors, often have to operate under pressure, but they are not protected on this basis from the possibility of being sued; and, of course, the notion of

[79] See especially the judgment of Lord Diplock in *Saif Ali* v. *Mitchell* [1980] AC 198.
[80] Or, more portentously, 'to justice': D. L. Carey Miller (1981) 97 *LQR* 127.
[81] Cf. *Giannarelli* v. *Wraith* (1988) 81 ALR 417, 434 *per* Wilson J.
[82] See 241 below.   [83] *Rondel* v. *Worsley* [1969] 1 AC 191, 229 *per* Lord Reid.
[84] *Ibid.*, 714–5.

'reasonable care' which forms the basis of the legal concept of negligence takes account of the fact, if it be so, that the allegedly negligent conduct took place in an emergency, under pressure of time or circumstances.

A second argument in favour of immunity is that since a barrister is not free to refuse a brief in the area of his or her competency, immunity protects the barrister from the fear of action at the suit of a disgruntled client with a bad case which, given the choice, the barrister may not have taken on. However, barristers are not uniquely placed in this respect: a hospital doctor or a general practitioner employed by the National Health Service is not free to turn away a patient who has a condition which is difficult to treat—not only would this be considered ethically improper, but it might also result in the imposition of legal liability for failure to offer treatment.[85] Nor does the NHS doctor have the freedom to discourage unwanted patients by charging a higher fee; but the barrister does.[86] It is not clear why the barrister deserves an immunity which the doctor is denied; such immunity seems a very high price to pay for protection from what must, in practice, be the very small risk of being subjected to vexatious litigation (which is, anyway, unlikely to get very far). Another problem with this argument is that it would not seem to apply to advocates who are not barristers.

A third argument is similar to one used in support of the immunity accorded to judges: an action in negligence against an advocate would only succeed if it could be proved that, but for the advocate's negligence, the client would have won. Such proof would require a retrial of the issues which would undermine the finality of judicial decisions[87] and create an unhealthy and, in our society, unjustified disrespect for the competence of judges. This 'collateral challenge' argument, besides being used to support the immunity of judges and advocates, has an independent life of its own: as a general principle,[88] it is an abuse of the process of the court for a defendant to seek to relitigate in civil proceedings issues already decided against him or her in criminal proceedings.[89] It has been held that the collateral challenge argument can prevent an advocate being sued even in relation to actions which would not be protected by the advocate's immunity from actions in tort.[90] However, the collateral challenge argument can only provide protection where there has been a decision of a court, whereas the advocate's immunity may arise even in cases where a court has not pronounced upon it. This position has been acknowledged to be anomalous and creative of hardship.[91]

---

[85] *Barnett v. Chelsea and Kensington Hospital Management Committee* [1969] 1 QB 428.
[86] J. Hill (1986) 6 *OJLS* 183, 184.   [87] R. Jackson, *Counsel*, June 1995, 16.
[88] For exceptions see *Walpole v. Partridge & Wilson* [1994] QB 106.
[89] *Hunter v. Chief Constable of the West Midlands Police* [1982] AC 529. This principle is to be distinguished from estoppel, which prevents the relitigation of issues decided in a civil action by parties to the action or their 'privies'.
[90] *Somasundaram v. M. Julius Melchior & Co.* [1988] 1 WLR 1394; criticized by J. A. Jolowicz [1989] *CLJ* 196.
[91] *Somasundaram v. Melchior* [1988] 1 WLR 1394, 1400.

As just noted, the collateral challenge argument would not apply in cases where there was no court decision: for example, where an advocate negligently advises submission to a default judgment. Nor would it apply to advice not to institute proceedings or not to join parties. Furthermore, it might be thought that the exposure of incompetence amongst barristers would strengthen the judicial system rather than weaken it: judges in our system rely very heavily on counsel to present their cases fully and in the best possible way, and a finding that a decision of a court might, on the balance of probabilities, have been different if an advocate (not the judge) had acted differently would not seem likely to undermine (legitimate) public confidence in the system as a whole. It can also be argued that, since it may, in some cases, be very difficult to prove the causal connection between the advocate's negligence and the failure of the plaintiff's case, allowing negligence actions against advocates is a very costly way of regulating the quality of legal services. Ethical rules, taxation of costs, and the fact that barristers are hired (and fired) by other lawyers and not by lay persons, might provide cheaper methods of quality control.[92] On the other hand, quality control is only one function of tort law; the redress of individual grievances is another, and this may require the payment of compensation.

We may conclude that, even taken together, the justifications adduced for the immunity do not support it strongly. On the other hand, the immunity of the advocate is usually seen as just one aspect of the immunity from action of all those involved in the judicial process, including witnesses, parties, and judges. How, it might be asked, could we justify allowing advocates to be sued for negligence[93] when other participants in the litigation enjoy immunity from such actions? This objection could be met in the following way: first, the collateral challenge argument is much stronger in relation to judges than in respect of advocates; secondly, advocates, as opposed to non-expert witnesses and parties, are professional participants in the judicial process and ought to be answerable to their clients for the way they perform their professional duties; and thirdly, if advocates were liable to be sued for negligence, this might strengthen the case for removing the immunity from (query, paid) expert witnesses.

Liability of Parties for the Conduct of Litigation

In *Business Computers International Ltd.* v. *Registrar of Companies*[94] it was held that no duty of care is owed by one litigant to another as regards the

---

[92] Veljanovski and Whelan (1983) 46 *MLR* 700, 716–7; *Giannarelli* v. *Wraith* (1988) 81 ALR 417, 439 *per* Brennan J.

[93] No-one suggests that they should not enjoy immunity from liability for defamation, etc.: cf. M. Zander *Legal Services for the Community* (London, 1978), 135; P. C. Heery (1968) 42 *ALJ* 3, 6–7.

[94] [1988] Ch. 229; cf. *Bennett* v. *Commissioner of Police of the Metropolis* [1995] 1 WLR 488.

manner in which the litigation is conducted.[95] So in that case, a writ alleging negligence in the service of a winding-up petition at the wrong address was struck out as disclosing no reasonable cause of action. The main basis of the decision was a form of the collateral challenge argument: the proper way of controlling the conduct of litigation is by utilizing the rules and procedures of the court, and not by bringing civil actions for damages; if process has not properly been served, it can be set aside by the court. And, of course, the court can award costs against a party who causes an opponent to incur unnecessary expense by conducting the case inefficiently. The rule could also be supported by a wider argument that in the adversary system neither party to litigation owes a duty of care to the other; in a similar way, where two parties are each represented by a solicitor, the solicitor of one party does not normally owe a duty of care to the other party.[96]

The Conduct of Governmental Business

Discretionary Powers

General Principle of Liability

As a general principle, statutory governmental bodies are subject to common law tort liability in the same way as ordinary citizens and non-governmental bodies.[97] In relation to negligence, this principle was established in a number of nineteenth century cases concerning private statutory undertakings operating under private Acts of Parliament,[98] but it is taken as applying also to statutory governmental bodies. So far as central government ('the Crown') is concerned, section 2 of the Crown Proceedings Act 1947 provides that the Crown shall be liable in tort to the same extent 'as if it were a private person of full age and capacity' in respect of vicarious liability, employers' liability and occupiers' liability. There are a number of qualifications and exceptions to this general provision, the most important of which are: (a) statutory immunities or limitations of liability accruing to any government department or Minister also accrue for the benefit of the Crown; (b) the

[95] But a prosecutor may owe a duty of care to an accused in respect of conduct not covered by the advocate's immunity provided the prosecutor assumed some relevant responsibility to the accused: *Welsh* v. *Chief Constable of Merseyside* [1993] 1 All ER 692; *Elguzouli-Daf* v. *Commissioner of Police of the Metropolis* [1995] 2 WLR 173.

[96] *Allied Finance and Investments Ltd* v. *Haddow & Co.* [1983] NZLR 22.

[97] There is one head of common law tort liability which only applies to public bodies: misfeasance in a public office. See generally H. W. R. Wade and C. R. Forsyth, *Administrative Law*, 7th edn. (Oxford, 1994), 789–96; P. P. Craig, *Administrative Law*, 3rd edn. (London, 1994), 636–8. On the meaning of 'public office, see B. Gould (1972) 5 *NZULR* 105, 117–9; R. C. Evans (1982) 31 *ICLQ* 640, 644–6. See also 233 above. There may, of course, be statutory liability for loss caused by the exercise of a statutory power: e.g. Consumer Protection Act 1987, s. 14(7).

[98] *Mersey Docks Trustees* v. *Gibbs* (1866) LR 1 HL 93; *Geddis* v. *Proprietors of Bann Reservoir* (1878) 3 App. Cas. 430.

Crown is not liable for breaches of statutory duties resting only on its officers and not on other persons; (c) no statutory obligation binds the Crown unless the statute in question specifically so provides; (d) the Crown cannot be sued in respect of the judicial activities of its officials.

In practice, the most important head of tort liability so far as the exercise of discretionary powers is concerned is negligence, and it is on this tort that this section on discretions will focus.

Qualifications to the General Principle

The general principle of governmental liability stated above is subject to important qualifications. The most recent exposition of the law in this area is provided by Lord Browne-Wilkinson (with whom the other Law Lords agreed completely or substantially) in *X* v. *Bedfordshire CC*.[99] The cases dealt with in this decision came to the House on an application to strike out, and so some caution has to be exercised in determining what propositions of law it establishes. However, it now appears to be the law that a negligence action against a public authority in respect of the exercise of a statutory discretionary power will not succeed if (a) the imposition of a duty of care would be incompatible with the scheme of the statute conferring the discretionary power; or (b) the public authority's allegedly negligent conduct was not unreasonable in the public law sense of 'so unreasonable that no public authority properly understanding the limits of its power would have engaged in it'; or (c) the question whether the authority acted unreasonably in this sense raises 'non-justiciable issues'.

Compatibility   The test of compatibility in this context is essentially similar to the (set of) tests used in the tort of breach of statutory duty to decide whether a cause of action for damages in tort can arise out of breach of a statutory duty. It is a test of the 'intention of the statute'. Another way of stating the idea of compatibility is to say that the existence and scope of any common law rights or obligations arising out of the exercise of statutory functions must depend, in part at least, on the terms of the relevant statute.[100]

One specific factor relevant to compatibility is whether and to what extent the relevant statute allows people in the position of the plaintiff to participate in the decision-making process leading to the exercise of the statutory function, and the nature of any mechanisms ('alternative remedies') it establishes for dealing with grievances about that process. Common law liability is less likely to be imposed in respect of the performance of a function conferred by a statute which allows affected parties to participate and provides

---

[99] [1995] 2 WLR 152; Cane (1996) 112 *LQR* 000.

[100] *Governors of Peabody Donation Fund* v. *Sir Lindsay Parkinson & Co. Ltd* [1985] AC 210. See also *Philcox* v. *Civil Aviation Authority*, *The Times*, 8 June, 1995. The same idea has sometimes been expressed in terms of the conclusory concept of 'proximity': e.g. *Yuen Kun Yeu* v. *A-G of Hong Kong* [1988] AC 175. Cf. *Minories Finance Ltd* v. *Arthur Young (a firm)* [1989] 2 All ER 105; *Wood* v. *Law Society* [1993] *New LJ* 1475.

them with a grievance mechanism than in respect of the performance of a function conferred by a statute which gives few or no rights of participation and establishes no effective grievance mechanism. In *Jones v. Department of Employment*,[101] P made an unsuccessful application for unemployment benefit; he appealed successfully against the refusal of benefit, but then sought to recover the costs of the appeal[102] and damages for non-pecuniary loss by bringing an action in tort for negligence in the making of the decision not to award benefit. This action failed on the ground that the statute provided a detailed and adequate system of appeals against refusal of unemployment benefit (which the plaintiff had successfully utilized), and so there was no good reason to allow an action in tort in respect of the refusal of benefit.[103]

In the way I have stated it, the compatibility principle only applies to the exercise of statutory functions. However, an anlogous idea applies to the exercise of non-statutory governmental discretionary powers. For example, in *Hill v. Chief Constable of West Yorkshire*[104] it was held, in effect, that a common law duty of care could not arise in respect of the performance by the police of the function of investigating crime and apprehending criminals, because the purpose of this function was to protect the public at large and not specific individuals who might become victims of crime. Nor is the alternative remedies principle restricted in its application to statutory governmental functions or to alternative remedies provided by statute. In *Hill*[105] the mother of a victim of a mass rapist and murderer sued the police for alleged negligence in conducting the hunt for the criminal. One of the grounds on which the action was dismissed was that P could have sought monetary compensation under the Criminal Injuries Compensation Scheme (which is not embodied in a statute).

Indeed, the alternative remedies principle may be seen merely as an application of a wider principle to the effect that as against public authorities an action for damages in tort is a last resort, only to be allowed if there is no suitable alternative avenue of redress.[106] Thus in *Rowling* v. *Takaro Properties Ltd*[107] Lord Keith made the point that, if a governmental decision

---

[101] [1989] QB 1. See also *Mills v. Winchester Diocesan Board* [1989] Ch. 428.

[102] Legal aid is not available for appeals to social security tribunals, nor can costs be awarded to a successful applicant.

[103] But the application of this reasoning to the facts of the case is less straightforward. The plaintiff's aim in suing in tort was not to recover the equivalent of the unemployment benefit he had originally been refused: he had already obtained the benefit as a result of his successful statutory appeal. Rather, his aim was to recover costs and damages which he could not recover under the statute; the decision, therefore, turns not on the availability of an alternative remedy to achieve the result which the plaintiff sought to achieve by his tort action, but on the undesirability of allowing tort actions to be used to circumvent legal aid and costs rules and to obtain damages for non-pecuniary loss resulting from the refusal of unemployment benefit and the making of an appeal.

[104] [1989] AC 53.

[105] [1989] AC 53; cf. *Bennett v. Commissioner of Police of the Metropolis* [1995] 1 WLR 488.

[106] e.g., *Wood v. Law Society* [1993] *New LJ* 1475.

[107] [1988] AC 473.

can be successfully challenged by way of judicial review, its only adverse effect may be to delay the implementation of any project hindered by it. The implication of this is that delay by itself would not justify allowing an action for damages in tort in addition to the possibility of an application for judicial review. However, if, as in *Takaro* itself, the effect of delay is to cause economic loss then judicial review of the *ultra vires* decision could not be said to be a suitable alternative remedy because damages are not available for *ultra vires* as such.

Related to the test of compatibility is the so-called 'overkill' argument. The idea here is that the fear of being sued (even if unsuccessfully) may lead potential defendants to be unduly cautious in the performance of their statutory (and other) functions and to take 'defensive measures' designed to minimize the risk of being sued which, because of their cost in time and money, are not to the financial benefit either of the public or of potential plaintiffs.[108] This argument is not peculiar to cases against public authorities; it originated in actions against professionals (especially doctors) and has been extended to actions against governmental bodies. In its application to public authorities, the overkill argument is related to the test of compatibility by the idea that it cannot have been the intention of Parliament that public authorities should waste time and resources in defending themselves against common law claims for damages or the risk of such claims at the expense of the 'proper' performance of their statutory functions.

The overkill argument suffers from two grave defects. First, in most cases where it is used it is based on no (or, at least, no reliable) empirical evidence; and secondly, it depends on attributing to potential defendants an ignorance of the requirements of the law (which does not expect the taking of 'unnecessary precautions') and, more seriously, uses this ignorance as the basis for a legal rule. On the other hand, it may be that the overkill argument is properly viewed as a function of the fact that public authority defendants are often what have been called 'peripheral parties'.[109] Many tort actions against public authorities in recent years have concerned the exercise of regulatory functions. In such actions the claim against the authority is typically not that the authority caused the loss which P has suffered but rather that if the authority had exercised its regulatory powers (carefully) it could have prevented the loss which P suffered. *Anns* v. *Merton LBC*[110] established, among other things, that a public authority exercising statutory powers could, in an appropriate case, be held liable for failure to exercise those powers. This holding was important for two reasons: first, it opened the way for actions in tort in respect of failure to exercise statutory powers as opposed to failure to

---

[108] *Calveley* v. *Chief Constable of Merseyside* [1989] AC 1228; cf. *X* v. *Bedfordshire CC* [1995] 3 WLR 152, 183–4, 194; *Hill* v. *Chief Constable of West Yorkshire* [1989] AC 96; *Alexandrou* v. *Oxford* [1993] 4 All ER 328; *Osman* v. *Ferguson* [1993] 4 All ER 344; *Ancell* v. *McDermott* [1993] 4 All ER 355.

[109] J. Stapleton (1995) 111 *LQR* 301.　　　　　　　　　　　　[110] [1978] AC 728.

perform statutory duties; and it made possible the imposition of liability for failure to prevent loss or damage occurring as opposed to causing loss or damage. In respect of actions concerning the performance (or non-performance) of regulatory functions, it was potentially of great importance that the existence of statutory functions could be treated as establishing a special relationship between the regulatory authority and those for whose protection statutory functions were conferred on it,[111] so that failure to perform those functions and prevent loss being caused by the actions of some person whose conduct ought to have been regulated might be actionable.[112]

Because, in actions for negligence in the exercise of (or in not exercising) regulatory functions, it is not claimed that the authority caused P's loss but only failed to prevent its resulting from someone else's conduct, the responsibility of the authority for the loss may be seen as being signficantly less than that of person who caused the loss. It is in this sense that regulatory authorities may be seen as peripheral parties. At the same time public authorities are attractive targets for litigation because they have 'deep pockets' and because, by reason of the rules of joint and several liability, they can be held liable in full for a loss for which their responsibility was much less than that of someone else. The overkill argument (leading to a denial of liability) may, in this context, be seen as a way of giving effect to the idea that to hold fully liable for a loss a regulatory authority whose responsibility for that loss was much less than that of some other party would be to impose on the authority an unduly heavy burden of liability which might adversely affect the way it and other authorities perform their statutory functions. On the other hand, it might be thought that rather than relieving regulatory authorities of all liability, a better way of giving effect to the overkill argument in such cases would be the introduction of some sort of proportional liability. But the courts are not in a position to invent such proportional liability, even if they wanted to; and so the only way to deal with the problem is to immunize regulatory authorities from any liability.

If the 'peripheral parties' interpretation of the overkill argument is correct, it does not overcome the two grave objections to the argument stated earlier. But it does help to explain why the approach in *Anns* described above came under considerable attack,[113] and why cases since *Anns*[114] suggest that courts will be unwilling to read into statutes under which regulatory authorities[115]

---

[111] See e.g. *City of Kamloops* v. *Neilsen* (1984) 10 DLR(4th) 641.

[112] For arguments in favour of liability, see A. Rubinstein (1987) 13 *Mon. LR* 115–18.

[113] See esp. J. C. Smith and P. Burns (1983) 46 *MLR* 147.

[114] Especially *Yuen Kun Yeu* v. *A-G of Hong Kong* [1988] AC 175. See also *Curran* v. *Northern Ireland Co-ownership Housing Association Ltd* [1987] AC 718; *Sutherland SC* v. *Heyman* (1984–5) 157 CLR 424; *Davis* v. *Radcliffe* [1990] 1 WLR 821.

[115] Including professional and trade regulatory bodies which are established or recognized by statute or which operate with *de facto* government backing. See further *Wood* v. *Law Society* [1993] *New LJ* 1475; D. Feldman [1987] *PN* 23. Where the actions of such a body form the basis of a civil action against the body by a member of the relevant regulated group, there will often be a contract between the regulator and the plaintiff. If the contract establishes an appeal

operate, an intention that particular individuals should be entitled to sue in respect of allegedly negligent non-performance (or even performance) of regulatory functions.

On the other hand, although the mere existence of statutory powers which could be used to prevent loss occurring[116] will usually not lead to the imposition of a duty to take care to prevent such loss, if a public body expressly or impliedly undertakes to exercise its powers in such a way as would have prevented loss, then failure to act in that way, if negligent, may justify the imposition of liability.[117] This accords with the general principle that an undertaking to act in a particular way may generate liability for failure to act in that way, even though mere failure to act would not, of itself, be actionable. So, if a local authority voluntarily adopts a practice of providing prospective real estate buyers with information about road-widening proposals,[118] or if a drainage authority voluntarily adopts a practice of informing local councils, who are considering applications for building permits, of risks of flooding,[119] then failure to provide relevant information to an inquirer may be actionable. In some cases it is said that liability cannot arise under this principle unless the plaintiff relied on the defendant's undertaking.[120] An important weakness of this approach, in cases where reliance is not a necessary link in the causal chain, is that it discriminates against those most in need of protection, namely the ill-educated and ignorant. So the Privy Council has held that the plaintiff can recover in such a case even without having personally relied on anything said or done by the defendant.[121] These cases also make it clear that an undertaking can be implied from a course of conduct. If liability can be imposed on the basis of a course of conduct of which the plaintiff may not even have been aware, the language of undertaking seems inappropriate. We should recognize that the basis of liability in such cases is simply what seems fair and just.

Unreasonableness In *X* v. *Bedfordshire CC*[122] the House of Lords held that an action in negligence in respect of the exercise of a statutory discretionary power can succeed only if the allegedly negligent conduct was unreasonable

mechanism, this may exclude liability in tort. But tort law will be the most likely source of relevant legal principles where P suffers loss as a result of actions of a 'regulated person' which P seeks to recover from the regulator. Concerning the position of regulatory bodies under the Financial Services Act 1986 see 251 below.

[116] If use of the powers could not have prevented the loss then, *a fortiori*, a duty will not arise: *Curran* v. *Northern Ireland Co-ownership Housing Association Ltd* [1987] AC 718.

[117] e.g. *T* v. *Surrey CC* [1994] 4 All ER 577.

[118] *L. Shaddock & Associates Pty Ltd* v. *Parramatta CC* (1981) 36 ALR 385.

[119] *Brown* v. *Heathcote CC* [1987] 1 NZLR 720.

[120] *Sutherland SC* v. *Heyman* (1984–5) 157 CLR 424; it is not easy to discern the ratio of this case, but the proposition here attributed to it seems at least consistent with the majority of the judgments. See also *Parramatta CC* v. *Lutz* (1988) 12 NSWLR 293.

[121] *Brown* v. *Heathcote CC* [1987] 1 NZLR 720; see also Rubinstein (1987) 13 *Mon. LR* 75, 112; S. Todd (1986) 102 *LQR* 370.

[122] [1995] 3 WLR 152.QN

in the sense in which that term was defined in *Associated Provincial Picture Houses Ltd* v. *Wednesbury Corporation*.[123] The *Wednesbury* criterion of unreasonableness is not a test of liability in tort but of public law unlawfulness. In other words, *Wednesbury* unreasonable conduct is *ultra vires* and can attract public law remedies. The fact that conduct is *Wednesbury* unreasonable does not, as such, make it negligent and capable of forming the basis of a successful action for damages in tort. However, since the concept of *Wednesbury* unreasonableness relates to the substance of the decision (as opposed to the procedure by which it was reached), any act or decision which is *Wednesbury* unreasonable will almost certainly also be negligent. In fact, the *Wednesbury* definition of 'unreasonableness' is equivalent in essence to the test of negligence laid down in the medical negligence case of *Bolam* v. *Friern Hospital Management Committee*.[124] Under this latter test, a defendant will not be held negligent if it can be shown that a body of responsible professional opinion approved the allegedly negligent conduct, even if most professionals would have acted differently.

The adoption of *Wednesbury* unreasonableness as a pre-condition of liability in tort for negligence in respect of the exercise of statutory discretionary powers has two ramifications. The first is that negligence actions will only lie in respect of the substance of decisions and actions made and done in performance of statutory discretionary powers, and not in relation to the procedure by which decisions whether and how to act in performance of a statutory discretion were reached.[125] The second is that the effective criterion of negligent conduct in an action concerned with the exercise of a statutory discretion will be *Bolam* unreasonableness rather than the more commonly adopted test which would ask whether what D did was reasonable rather than whether what D did was so unreasonable that no reasonable person similarly placed would have done it. In these respects it seems that X v. *Bedfordshire* CC has significantly changed the law as it was widely understood before this decision. First, prior to the *Bedfordshire* case there was good reason to think that procedural impropriety by a public authority could form the basis of an action in negligence. For instance, in *Rowling Properties Ltd* v. *Takaro*[126] the issue before the Privy Council was whether failure to take legal advice before making a decision was negligent. The Board held, on the facts, that it was not, but nowhere suggested that if it had been liability could not have arisen. Secondly, prior to *Bedfordshire* there was no reason to think that as a general rule the criterion of negligence in respect of the exercise of statutory discretions was *Bolam* unreasonableness.

Non-justiciability   In *Bedfordshire* it was also held that a negligence action in respect of the exercise of a statutory discretion could not succeed if, in order to decide whether or not D had acted unreasonably, the court would

---

[123] [1948] 1 KB 223.   [124] [1957] 1 WLR 582.   [125] See [1995] 3 WLR 152, 171.
[126] [1988] AC 473.

have to adjudicate upon non-justiciable matters. Lord Browne-Wilkinson defined non-justiciability in terms of a variety of different phrases. Notably he said that decisions about the allocation of scarce resources[127] or involving the conscious taking of risks would be non-justiciable. However, at the end of the day it seems that non-justiciable matters are simply matters which, in the court's view, raise questions about the balancing of policy factors which the court feels it should not consider. This caution is apparently based on constitutional principles: basic separation of powers considerations require that courts should not interfere with the administrative process by granting judicial remedies where this would require them to 'second-guess' judgments by public authorities about the demands of public policy and the proper balance between public and private interests.

Conclusion

For a variety of reasons, the courts have shown reluctance to impose liability in negligence on public authorities in respect of the exercise of statutory (and other) discretionary powers. Most of the juridical techniques used to give effect to this reluctance are not peculiar to actions against public authorities. The idea of compatibility, for instance, applies to actions for breach of statutory duties by private citizens; and the concept of *Wednesbury* unreasonableness has a close analogy in the *Bolam* test of negligence. The overkill argument is well known in the general law of tort;[128] and the alternative remedies argument has counterparts in the law concerning the rights and obligations of citizens *inter se*: the general principle that contract remedies ought to be pursued in preference to tort remedies provides an analogy. The only technique which is recognizably peculiar to actions against public authorities is that which utilizes the concept of non-justiciability. This technique rests on a certain view of the proper constitutional relationship between the courts and the executive branch of government. The fact that so many arguments are available to ground a refusal to impose liability on public authorities leads one to the conclusion that, as a matter of general policy, the courts wish to protect public authorities from liability in negligence in respect of the exercise of discretions.

---

[127] This is controversial: resources are always limited, and private defendants cannot plead lack of resources; so why (it is asked) should public authorities be allowed to do so? In the context of judicial review, the position appears to be that a public authority is entitled to take resources into account in deciding how to exercise its powers, but that it may not be proper to allow lack of resources to be determinative. In the end, the extent to which lack of resources provides an answer in any particular case will probably depend on the relative value the court puts on the interests of the applicant on the one hand and competing calls on resources on the other. See, for instance, *R. v. Cambridge HA, ex parte B* [1995] 1 WLR 898; *R. v. Criminal Injuries Compensation Board, ex parte P* [1995] 1 WLR 845; *R. v. Gloucestershire CC, ex parte Mahfood, The Times*, 21 June 1995.

[128] A pertinent recent example is *Marc Rich & Co. AG v. Bishop Rock Marine Co. Ltd* [1995] 3 WLR 227, 251: the defendant was a non-statutory body performing essentially regulatory functions which Lord Steyn thought were of a public character.

Duties

When we turn to the performance of statutory duties, the position does not look all that different. A basic principle of general tort law is that an action for damages or an injunction in tort for breach of a statutory duty (whether in the form of misfeasance or non-feasance) will only succeed if the statute, either expressly or as interpreted by the court, provides for such an action. This general principle applies to actions against public authorities in the same way as it applies to actions against private defendants.[129] It is an application of the wider principle (discussed above) that common law actions based on statutory provisions take their characteristics, at least in part, from the statute. As noted above, a statute will only be interpreted as (impliedly) creating a right of action for damages if such an action is compatible with the scheme of the statute; and the criteria of compatibility are similar in this context as in the context of actions relating to the exercise of statutory discretions.

Although a statutory function may be called a 'duty' by the statute, the content of that duty may not be expressed in a sufficiently detailed way such that in every situation in which the duty falls to be performed the authority under the duty will know, just by reading the statute, what it must do. If this is so, the authority will have to make some decision or choice about what to do in exercise of its duty.[130] For example, local education authorities are under a statutory duty to provide sufficient school facilities for children in their areas; but the relevant statute contains no detailed definition or specification of what amounts to 'sufficient' facilities, and so each authority has a certain amount of choice in deciding what facilities to provide. In other words, local education authorities have a duty coupled with a discretion. The principles of law considered above in relation to liability for the exercise of statutory discretions are also relevant to the control of the exercise of such 'ancillary discretions'. So, for instance, if the exercise of an ancillary discretion raises issues which the court thinks are non-justiciable,[131] or if it was not *Wednesbury* unreasonable, a tort action for breach of statutory duty will not lie in respect of it.

---

[129] This rule creates what may be seen as an anomaly in that if mandamus or an injunction is sought to enforce a statutory duty in an application for judicial review, the applicant need only have a 'sufficient interest in the matter to which the application relates': RSC Ord. 53, r. 3(7). Even if this phrase is taken, in the context of attempts to enforce statutory duties for the individual benefit of the applicant, to require a personal interest (see R. v. *Felixstowe JJ, ex parte Leigh* [1987] QB 582), it is still easier to force a public body to perform a statutory duty than to obtain damages for its non-performance. See P. Finn (1983) 51 *ALJ* 493 and 571.

[130] P. Cane [1981] *PL* 11.

[131] e.g. *Danns* v. *Department of Health*, QBD, 9 June 1995.

Statutory Authorization

General Principle

Conduct will not be actionable in tort if it is authorized by statute. The effect of a plea of statutory authorization is to prevent a *prima facie* liability in tort arising. For this reason, it is misleading to call statutory authorization a 'defence'. Pleas of statutory authorization are not only available to public authorities. Indeed, the leading modern case on statutory authorization in the tort of nuisance concerned the activities of a private company.[132] But because a very large proportion of governmental activity is carried on under the provisions of particular statutes, public bodies are much more likely to be in a position to plead a statutory provision in this way than is a private defendant.

A plea of statutory authorization is not available in the case of every tort. Obviously, a statute will not authorize the breach of a duty which it imposes. It is usually said that a plea of statutory authorization could not succeed in an action for negligence. Two reasons are given for this assertion, but neither is entirely convincing. First, it is said that Parliament is unlikely ever to intend that the repository of a statutory function should be free to exercise it negligently; and secondly, that negligence, by its very nature, cannot be authorized in advance since it would be impossible to specify in words what it was that was being authorized because the concept of negligence is closely tied to the facts of particular cases. Both of these reasons ignore the fact that the concept of negligence (failure to take reasonable precautions to avoid foreseeable risks of damage) is wide enough to cover deliberate, and even intentional, as well as inadvertent, conduct. Even if inadvertent carelessness cannot, in any meaningful sense, be authorized in advance, deliberate or intentional conduct can be; liability in negligence is often the result of the conscious taking of risks, which can obviously be authorized in advance. Furthermore, Parliament often authorizes deliberate conduct which might otherwise be tortious: statutory powers to enter and search premises provide a classic example. It *is* unlikely that Parliament would authorize inadvertent carelessness; but it certainly does sometimes authorize the conscious taking of risks.

Trespass

The torts in relation to which pleas of statutory authorization are most important are trespass and nuisance.[133] Both involve interference with property rights, and such a plea amounts to the assertion of a statutorily endorsed public interest to trump the property rights of the plaintiff.[134] The nineteenth-

---

[132] *Allen v. Gulf Oil Refining Co. Ltd* [1981] AC 1001.

[133] A plea of *bona fide* execution of a valid law provided a successful defence to an action for interference with contract in *James v. The Commonwealth* (1939) 62 CLR 339.

[134] *Allen v. Gulf Oil* [1981] AC 1001, 1023 *per* Lord Roskill.

century case of *Cooper* v. *Wandsworth Board of Works*[135] provides a classic illustration of the operation of the defence: the plaintiff succeeded in an action in trespass against the Board following the demolition by it of part of a house in execution of an invalid demolition order. If the demolition order had been valid the demolition would have been lawful despite the fact that it would have been tortious if done without the support of such an order. Since, in fact, the order was invalid, it provided no authorization for the otherwise tortious action. This case also provides an illustration of the relationship between the public law concept of *ultra vires* and the private law concept of tortiousness: the action in trespass succeeded only because the demolition order was *ultra vires*. The Board had been given a discretionary power to demolish buildings in certain circumstances, and the decision whether to demolish was for it to make, subject only to the rules of *ultra vires* and of the private law of tort. But there may be cases where a public authority may be liable in tort merely because it commits a trespass regardless of whether, in so doing, it also acted *ultra vires* in any meaningful sense: for example, if, without the permission of the owner, peripatetic workers set up their camp on private land. In such a case, it seems simply superfluous to ask whether, in addition to being trespassory, the encroachment was also *ultra vires*.

Nuisance[136]

Authorization of a nuisance (in the sense of an unreasonable interference with the use and enjoyment of land rather than in the sense of a *prima facie* actionable nuisance) may be implied into a statute as well as expressly stated. In this respect, it is said that statutes have to be interpreted in a common sense way; so that, for example, a statute which expressly authorizes the construction of an oil refinery must be take as impliedly authorizing the operation of that refinery if the obvious intent of the legislature is not to be defeated.[137] But a statute will not be read as authorizing unnecessary acts.

Statutory authorization also extends to nuisances which are the inevitable result of or necessarily incidental to the doing of that which the legislature has authorized. It is for the defendant to establish that the nuisance was inevitable.[138] Where, as will usually be the case,[139] D has a certain degree of choice about where, when, or how the statutorily authorized activity will be

---

[135] (1863) 14 CBNS 180.

[136] Concerning the relationship between the grant of planning permission and liability in nuisance see *Gillingham BC* v. *Medway (Chatham) Dock Co. Ltd* [1993] QB 343; *Wheeler* v. *J. J. Saunders Ltd* [1995] 2 All ER 697.

[137] *Allen* v. *Gulf Oil* [1981] AC 1001. The countervailing argument, at least in relation to private developers, is that they should be required to specify precisely the activities for which authorization is sought: *ibid.* at 1020 *per* Lord Keith of Kinkel dissenting.

[138] *Manchester Corporation* v. *Farnworth* [1930] AC 171, 182 *per* Viscount Dunedin.

[139] But 'in the absence of negligence, a body is not liable for a nuisance which is attributable to the exercise by it of a duty imposed upon it by statute . . . even if by statute it is expressly made liable, or [expressly] not exempted from liability, for nuisance ': *Department of Transport* v. *North West Water Authority* [1984] AC 336, 344, 359–60.

conducted, the basic presumption is that the legislature intended it to be conducted without creating a nuisance.[140] This presumption is particularly strong in cases where the statute contains no provision for the payment of monetary compensation to victims of a nuisance created by the activity.[141] If, in a case where the presumption applies, the activity could have been carried on without creating a nuisance, any nuisance created will not be inevitable. It is not entirely clear what the phrase 'could have been carried on without creating a nuisance' means; but in *Allen* v. *Gulf Oil*[142] Lord Edmund Davies said that in order to prove inevitability D would have to show that the injury could not have been avoided no matter how much had been spent on precautions. This interpretation of inevitability seems to render superfluous the basic rule, enunciated by Lord Blackburn in *Geddis* v. *Proprietors of Bann Reservoir*,[143] that an action will lie in respect of the negligent exercise of statutory powers: conducting an activity without negligence normally means that reasonable precautions have been taken to avoid injury or damage to others[144] whereas, according the Lord Edmund Davies' test, the cloak of statutory authorization will only cover the activity if the injury or damage could not have been avoided no matter what precautions were taken. In relation to public authorities at least, Lord Edmund Davies's approach is even more questionable in the light of the decision in *X* v. *Bedfordshire CC*[145] to the effect that tort liability for the exercise of statutory discretions will only arise if the discretion was exercised in a way no reasonable authority in D's position would have done.

In *Page Motors Ltd* v. *Epsom & Ewell BC*,[146] a group of gypsies had camped on a field owned by the council beside which ran a road which gave access to the plaintiff's automotive garage. P's business suffered because the behaviour of the gypsies discouraged customers from using the access road. The council obtained an eviction order against the gypsies but delayed for five years in enforcing it because of political pressure from the county council and from Whitehall to await the formulation of a wider-ranging solution to the gipsy 'problem'. The Court of Appeal held that the liability of the council as occupier had to be judged according to the ordinary principles of the law of nuisance: had its actions interfered unreasonably with the use and enjoyment of P's land? However, the court then proceeded to hold that because the council was a public body it was reasonable for it to go through the 'democratic process of consultation' before deciding when and how to abate the nuisance; so it was justified in delaying longer before acting than a private landowner would have been (although not five years). Although this case did not involve

---

[140] *Managers of Metropolitan Asylum District* v. *Hill* (1881) 6 App. Cas. 193.

[141] *Allen* v. *Gulf Oil* [1981] AC 1001, 1016 *per* Lord Edmund Davies.

[142] [1981] AC 1001, 1015.   [143] (1878) 3 App. Cas. 430, 455.

[144] Or, as it is put in the context of nuisance, conducting it 'with all reasonable regard and care for the interests of other persons': *Allen* v. *Gulf Oil* [1981] A.C. 1001, 1011 *per* Lord Wilberforce.

[145] [1995] 3 WLR 152.   [146] (1982) 80 LGR 337.

the exercise of a statutory discretion, merely the exercise of the council's common law powers as landowner, nevertheless it does illustrate well that public authorities may have responsibilities to the public as a whole which should be taken into account in deciding whether to hold them liable in tort. The way the Court of Appeal did this in *Page Motors* was to interpret the term 'unreasonable' in the law of nuisance as bieng similar in meaning to *Wednesbury* unreasonableness. In this respect, the decision seem precisely in line with the approach in the *Bedfordshire* case.

Nuisance Clauses

Sometimes a statute contains a provision which expressly imposes or expressly preserves liability for nuisance. Such clauses are, as it were, the converse of authorizing provisions. They do not allow the imposition of liability for nuisances attributable to the exercise, according to its terms, of a statutory duty, provided the duty was performed without negligence; but if the nuisance is attributable to the exercise of a statutory discretionary power, then such a clause will make the authority liable even if it exercises its power without negligence.[147] In other words, the only effect of such clauses on the common law is to reverse the rule which allows an authority to escape liability if it exercises a statutory power without negligence. In other cases, application of common law rules would probably achieve the same result whether the clause existed or not.

Sometimes a statute contains a provision requiring a body to pay compensation to persons who suffer loss or damage as a result of the exercise of statutory functions; but the absence of such a clause is of equivocal significance: it will usually be interpreted to mean that the legislature intended the ordinary law of nuisance to apply, but it may sometimes be taken to signify that the legislature intended victims of nuisances to go uncompensated.[148] The proper interpretation of the absence of such a clause is decided on the facts of particular cases. As a matter of principle, it will often be right for individuals who suffer as a result of the performance of public works to be compensated at public expense; but this will not necessarily always be so. It is by no means clear that this question of principle should be left to be decided by courts on a case-by-case basis.

Rylands v. Fletcher

Another application of the basic idea of statutory authorization is to be found in the context of the rule in *Rylands* v. *Fletcher*. In *Dunne* v. *North West Gas Board*[149] it was held that the Board, in exercising its statutory functions in connection with the provision of gas, did not store gas in its pipes for its own purposes but for the general benefit of the whole public; so the rule in

---

[147] *Department of Transport* v. *North West Water Authority* [1984] AC 336, 344, 359–60.
[148] *Allen* v. *Gulf Oil* [1981] AC 1001, 1016 *per* Lord Edmund Davies.
[149] [1964] 2 QB 806.

Rylands v. *Fletcher* did not apply to its activities. The effect of this decision is to require proof of negligence by the plaintiff rather than to immunize the defendant from liability for loss or damage inflicted; but it does put 'public bodies'[150] in an advantageous position as compared with private individuals. This approach is hard to justify: the whole point of strict liability, as embodied in the rule in *Rylands* v. *Fletcher*, is to allocate the costs of risky activities to those who carry on the activity, no matter how carefully it is conducted. The argument for doing this in the case of public undertakings, especially the provision of essential services, seems very strong.

Exclusion Clauses

Finally, it should be noted that statutory provisions may, of course, exclude liability in tort for the protection of public or regulatory bodies. An example is section 187 of the Financial Services Act 1986 which exempts the Securities and Investments Board and Self Regulating Organisations (SROs) from liability in damages in respect of the performance of their functions under the Act, provided that what was done was not done in bad faith. The chief justifications put forward for this immunity were, first, that it would make it easier to attract high quality persons to serve on the boards of such bodies (although it is not clear why this aim requires immunity for the body as well as for its officers); and secondly, to minimise the risk that SROs would be less willing to take enforcement action against their members for fear of being sued. Recognised Professional Bodies (RPBs) are not as well protected: such a body may make it a condition of certification that no action for damages will be brought against the body or its officers in respect of the exercise of its statutory functions, but RPOs are not protected against actions by investors.

Statutes sometimes explicitly provide that duties imposed by the statute are not to give rise to civil actions. An example is section 67(10) of the Police and Criminal Evidence Act 1984 which provides that failure to comply with Codes of Practice made under the Act (which are embodied in statutory instruments and which require affirmative approval by both Houses of Parliament) does not 'of itself' render the police officer in breach liable to civil proceedings.[151]

---

[150] Would the reasoning in *Dunne* apply to the privatized gas industry? Private gas undertakers deliver gas 'for their own purposes', but they do so for the common benefit of themselves and the public.

[151] For other examples see K. M. Stanton, *Breach of Statutory Duty* (London, 1986), 10.

Freedom of Speech and Information

Defamation

Most of the defences available in a defamation action involve an assertion, in some form or other, of a public interest in freedom of speech.[152] The defence of justification, or truth, obviously rests on the idea that people ought to be free to publish the truth no matter how much damage that does to the reputation of another: undeserved reputations have no claim to be protected. Freedom to publish the truth is considered so important that the motive with which it is done is irrelevant: the defence can succeed even if D, out of nothing more than spite or ill-will or for some other improper reason, aimed to damage P's reputation.[153]

In some situations the law is even prepared to protect (by the defence of absolute privilege)[154] the publication of statements which are not (or, at least, cannot be proved to be) true, even if D was motivated by malice or spite; or did not believe the statements to be true, or did not honestly do so; or if the statement was irrelevant in the context in which it was made. The main situations in respect of which the defence of absolute privilege is available are proceedings in a court of law and proceedings in Parliament. The justification for absolute privilege is the public interest in the free and fearless performance of their duties by those involved in court proceedings and by Members of Parliament.

The protection which absolute privilege affords to Parliamentary proceedings has often been attacked on the basis that it is an invitation to Members of Parliament to reap political advantage by making unsubstantiated allegations in Parliament which they would not dare make outside. On the other hand, Parliament has an important role to play in ensuring upright conduct in the transaction of government business; and perhaps the strongest justification for absolute privilege is that it is often the airing of suspicions for which there is little or no evidence which leads, in the end, to the uncovering of actual wrongdoing. It can be argued that in Parliament and the courts and in other official investigatory forums, people should not be discouraged from voicing their suspicions and submitting them to proper public scrutiny simply because their motives in doing so are not entirely pure. The public

---

[152] The value of free speech also explains the extreme unwillingness of courts to award exemplary damages for defamation or for conspiracy to injure by making defamatory statements: *Femis-Bank (Anguilla) Ltd* v. *Lazar* [1991] Ch. 391.

[153] There are two exceptions: (1) if D bases a defence on a spent conviction, malice will defeat the defence; (2) in a prosecution for criminal libel a plea of justification will succeed only if the publication of the true statement(s) was 'for the public benefit'. Furthermore, the crime can be committed by publication to the person defamed alone. See generally J. R. Spencer [1977] *Crim. LR* 383 and 465.

[154] Salmond, 165–9; Fleming, 557–64.

interest in the bringing to light of wrongdoing should be seen as the chief justification of absolute privilege.

The difference between absolute privilege and qualified privilege[155] is that the latter can be defeated by proof of 'express' or 'actual' malice. Malice in this context means personal spite or ill will or other improper motive; or a lack of 'honest' belief[156] in the truth of the statement; or abuse of the occasion of privilege (that is, in other words, making the statement for a purpose other than that for which the privilege is conferred).

Section 7 of the Defamation Act 1952 gives qualified privilege to a wide variety of statements made in newspapers, mostly consisting of fair and accurate reports of proceedings, decisions, or findings of public bodies or associations whose activities are of public importance. The basic purpose of the provision is made clear by section 7(3), which removes the protection of qualified privilege from 'the publication . . . of any matter which is not of public concern and the publication of which is not for the public benefit'. Three important ideas are implicit in this subsection. The first is that a line has to be drawn between matters which are of public interest and matters which are of purely private interest. It is not always easy to draw this line, but it is a fundamental tenet of modern Western political philosophy of almost every ideological hue that there are some areas of life which are of legitimate concern only to persons actually involved. The second implicit idea is that a line has to be drawn between matters in which the public has a legitimate interest and matters which it may be 'interested in' but which it has no 'right to know'. The third implicit idea is that there may be matters in which the public has a legitimate interest but which it would be better if it did not know: here there may be a clash of two public interests, namely that in freedom of information and that in the maintenance of some value such as security or safety which may, in certain circumstances, be better protected by non-disclosure of sensitive information. Giving effect in particular circumstances to these three ideas might theoretically involve the making of difficult and contentious value judgements; but the dearth of litigation on these provisions would suggest that in practice they give rise to few problems.

Apart from statutory provisions which confer qualified privilege, there is a general common law principle that a statement may be privileged if the person making it was under a legal, social, or moral duty to make it, and the person(s) to whom it was made had a reciprocal and corresponding legal, moral, or social duty to receive it or interest in receiving it. Privilege may also arise where the maker of the statement had a legitimate interest in making it, such as the protection of the speaker's own reputation, provided the person(s)

---

[155] Salmond, 169–183; Fleming, 564–85.

[156] The word 'honest' in the phrase 'honest belief in . . .' is redundant; if a qualifier is used, a better word might be 'positive' because indifference to truth entails liability.

to whom it is made had a reciprocal duty to receive the information or an interest in receiving it.[157]

It is important to note that although, in a broad sense, the interest being protected by qualified privilege is the public interest in the free flow of information and freedom of speech, the privilege will attach to publication to the public generally only if the public generally does actually have a legitimate interest in receiving the information and the receipt of it is in the public interest. This rule is stated explicitly in section 7 of the Defamation Act 1952, considered above, but it also applies at common law.[158] So in Britain, media revelations about the private lives of public figures are not privileged simply because the person in question has chosen a public career,[159] or because all aspects of the person's life are interesting to members of the public: people may find interesting matters in which they have no legitimate interest. Indeed, in this country it is public figures who most often bring defamation actions in respect of publications concerning their private lives,[160] and who recover the largest awards of damages.

Nor will the defence be available to a person who thought they had a duty to make the statement or an interest in making it when, in fact, they did not; or to a person who mistakenly thinks that the person(s) to whom the statement was made had a duty to receive it or an interest in receiving it. It would, therefore, be more accurate to say that the defence of qualified privilege protects the public interest that the right people are told the right things by the right people rather than that it protects some vague 'public right to know'.

Unlike the defence of justification, which can protect statements of opinion as well as statements of fact, the defence of fair comment[161] protects only opinions (that is, 'comments'). The line between fact and opinion is not clear-cut either in reality or in law. In reality, what one person puts forward as a statement of opinion another may assert as a fact. As a matter of law, a defence of fair comment will only succeed if statements which the defendant alleges to be comments are sufficiently supported by a substratum of fact which is either stated or referred to in the publication complained of. Otherwise, the alleged comments will be treated as if they were statements of fact and the defendant will have to prove them to be true (or that they are protected by some other defence). In relation to statements of opinion, the essential difference between a plea of justification and one of fair comment is that the former can succeed only if the comment was a reasonable inference from true facts; whereas a defence of fair comment can succeed provided the

---

[157] Salmond, 171–2.   [158] *Blackshaw* v. *Lord* [1984] QB 1.

[159] The distinction between the public and the private activities of local authorities which underpinned the decision in *Derbyshire CC* v. *The Times* [1993] AC 534 that a local authority may not sue in defamation to protect its 'governmental reputation' may herald a change in this respect. Concerning the position in Australia see F. A. Trindade (1995) 111 *LQR* 199.

[160] Not least because legal aid is not available for defamation actions, and many ordinary people lack the resources to litigate.

[161] Salmond, 183–91; Fleming, 585–93.

opinion was a 'fair' inference from true facts. A comment can be fair even if it is unreasonable, provided it could be held by an honest person who was not actuated by 'malice' (in the sense of 'personal spite or ill will') towards the plaintiff.

Furthermore, although a plea of fair comment will succeed only if the statement of opinion complained of was on a matter of public interest, the requirement of public interest is interpreted less strictly than in the context of qualified privilege. Whereas a national newspaper, for example, would succeed in qualified privilege only if it could show that the public generally had a legitimate interest in the statements made, a newspaper could succeed in fair comment simply by showing that the subject matter was 'in the public domain',[162] even if it was of real concern to only a limited section of the public. The reason for this may be that a defence of qualified privilege can protect even false and defamatory statements of fact, whereas a plea of fair comment will succeed only if the comment was fair on the basis of facts which can be proved to be true.[163] It is important, therefore, that the defence of qualified privilege be limited to cases where the recipient of the statements complained of had a duty to receive or a personal interest in receiving the information.

The law thus gives special protection to statements of opinion. There are, perhaps, two (related) reasons for this: the first is that unhindered expression and exchange of opinions is of the essence of freedom of speech as a political and constitutional ideal; the second is that opinions, as it were, 'invite' debate and disagreement whereas statements of fact invite acceptance and belief. In this respect, in a liberal democracy statements of opinion need less to be controlled than statements of fact. On the other hand, if a statement of fact is true then the value of truth renders the motive with which it was stated irrelevant, whereas it is an abuse of freedom of speech to use the freedom to express opinions maliciously to injure another. For although statements of opinion invite dissent, they do not always receive it; or at least not from a sufficiently influential source or in such circumstances that a proper balance between competing opinions is achieved. Freedom of expressing opinions is required so that every opinion can be tested against competitors and so that only the best opinions will survive. It is not justified if it is used as a vehicle for injuring others.

Breach of Confidence

Public interest may operate so as to negative the existence of an obligation of confidence. For example, in *R.* v. *Licensing Authority Established under*

---

[162] Thus, the public conduct of public figures (but not their private lives) is a legitimate subject for comment.

[163] This was the rule at common law and it has survived the enactment of s. 6 of the Defamation Act 1952: *London Artists Ltd* v. *Littler* [1969] 2 QB 375, 391 *per* Lord Denning MR.

Medicines Act 1968, ex parte Smith Kline & French Laboratories[164] it was held that there was 'no principle of confidentiality in English law which would prevent the authority from making use of the [confidential] information supplied [to it] by the appellants for any of the purposes for which the licensing authority was established'.[165] In that case the applicant had sought to prevent the authority using confidential details of research done by the applicant in developing a particular drug in order to assess applications from other drug companies for product licences for 'generic' versions of the drug.

Public interest can also operate as a factor nullifying liability for breach of confidence by justifying the disclosure of information impressed with an obligation of confidence.[166] An initial distinction has to be drawn between confidential information 'belonging' to a private individual or body and confidential information 'belonging' to the state (that is, government information). As regards information in the first category, take the example of *Lion Laboratories Ltd* v. *Evans*[167] in which it was held, in an appeal from the grant of an interlocutory injunction, that public interest in the accuracy of breathalyser machines manufactured by P could justify former employees of P who, as employees, had received information in confidence about the operation of the machines, in making it available to a newspaper for publication. In this case the Court of Appeal treated the interest in keeping confidences as a public interest which, in certain circumstances, might come into competition with a public interest in disclosure. In other words, the interest in privacy which the law protects is a public interest and not a purely private interest. This characterization serves to strengthen the interest in privacy in any competition with the public interest in the free flow of information.

Although the interest in privacy is a public interest, in cases where the original imparter of the information was a private person the right of non-disclosure is established simply by showing that one of the grounds of an obligation of confidence (for example, contract) existed in this case.[168] On the other hand, in relation to government secrets, an obligation of confidence will arise only if the government can show that the public interest would be damaged if the information were published.[169] If it can do this, then although it is still open to the discloser to argue that nevertheless publication was in the

[164] [1990] AC 64.

[165] [1990] AC 64, 105. Cf. *In re a Company's Application* [1989] Ch. 477.

[166] See further Y. Cripps, *The Legal Implications of Disclosure in the Public Interest*, 2nd edn. (London, 1994), ch. 2.

[167] [1985] QB 526; see also *A-G* v. *Guardian Newspapers Ltd (No. 2)* [1990] 1 AC 109, 269 *per* Lord Griffiths.

[168] Or, more accurately, the mere disclosure of information contrary to the wishes of the confider is itself sufficient detriment: *A-G* v. *Guardian Newspapers (No. 2)* [1990] 1 AC 109, 255–6 *per* Lord Keith; but contrast Lord Griffiths at 270D–F; Lord Goff at 281–2.

[169] *A-G* v. *Guardian Newspapers (No. 2)* [1990] AC 109. The law of confidence has become very important in this area because by using it the government can have the issues involved tried by a judge alone, and it has the chance of recovering profits made by the discloser; in these ways the civil law is more attractive than the criminal law.

public interest it would, in practice, probably be difficult for him or her to convince a court that the public interest in disclosure outweighed the public interest in secrecy. The interest being protected in these cases is not an interest in privacy but rather an interest that sensitive government information should not be leaked.[170]

As in the case of defamation, there is a difference 'between what is interesting to the public and what it is in the public interest to make known'.[171] But this perhaps means no more than that it is for the court to decide whether the public interest requires publication. The defence of public interest in this context operates similarly to the defence of qualified privilege in defamation in that the mere fact that disclosure is in the public interest does not necessarily justify disclosure to the public: it may be more appropriate for the information to be disclosed to some individual or an official body. Conversely, as in the case of qualified privilege, the discloser must show that he or she had a personal duty to disclose the information: different recipients of confidential information may have different duties such that one may be justified in the public interest in disclosing it while another may not.[172]

Finally, it should be noted that professional advisers in financial services industries enjoy various statutory immunities from liability for breach of contract or confidence which might arise out of disclosure by them to regulatory authorities of information relevant to the discharge by those authorities of their statutory functions in respect, for instance, of breaches of the Financial Services Act or of money-laundering offences.[173]

Breach of Copyright[174]

Although the law of copyright is primarily designed to prevent unauthorized publication of information which is already public,[175] publication of

---

[170] The public interest in secrecy is well recognized in the law of discovery where a public interest immunity from disclosure is recognized: see Cane, *An Introduction to Administrative Law* (2nd edn., Oxford, 1992), ch. 15. On the other hand, 'leakers' are given a measure of protection by s. 10 of the Contempt of Court Act 1981. See generally Cripps, *The Legal Implications of Disclosure in the Public Interest*, n. 166 above, ch. 8.

[171] *British Steel Corporation* v. *Granada Television Ltd* [1981] AC 1096, 1168 *per* Lord Wilberforce.

[172] *A-G* v. *Guardian Newspapers (No. 2)* [1990] 1 AC 109, 182–3 *per* Donaldson MR; *W* v. *Edgell* [1990] Ch. 359, 388 (affirmed *ibid.*).

[173] See 000 above; *re* money laundering see e.g. Drug Trafficking Act 1994, ss. 50(3)(a), 51(5)(a), 52(3); Money Laundering Regulations 1993 (SI 1933/1993), reg. 16(4).

[174] Cripps, *The Legal Implications of Disclosure in the Public Interest*, 2nd edn., 178–93. Note that grant of a patent (Cornish, 150) or registration of a trade mark (Cornish, 456) or design (Registered Designs Act 1949, s. 43(1)) may be refused on grounds of public policy (see *In re Masterman's Application* [1991] RPC 89). It is on this ground that the European Patent Office has refused to grant a patent for the so-called 'oncomouse' and for a technique of correcting genetic defects in sperm.

[175] So the defence recognized in *A-G* v. *Guardian Newspapers (No. 2)* [1990] 1 AC 109 (at least in relation to third party recipients as opposed to the original confidant) to an action for breach of confidence that the material was now in the public domain does not apply to an action for

confidential information may also constitute a breach of copyright: copyright is the result of the act of creation, and material does not have to be made public in order to be protected by copyright law.[176] If public interest were not available as a defence to an action for breach of copyright, its utility as a defence to an action for breach of confidence would be much reduced. So public interest is also available as a defence to an action for breach of copyright.[177] The defence is a common law, not a statutory, one; but it is recognized by section 171(3) of the CDPA.

It has been said that copyright law 'is designed to effect a reasonable balance between the public interest in giving authors rights in order to promote cultural, social and economic progress and the public interest in free access, or access on reasonable terms, to copyright material'.[178] So the legislation which establishes copyright also permits a wide range of acts which would otherwise constitute infringements of the copyright owner's rights. In our terms, these provisions illustrate the role of public interest in negativing liability.

Public interest may also come into play at the level of remedies: in *Attorney-General* v. *Guardian*[179] Lord Jauncey said that a court might refuse to enforce the rights of a copyright owner whose own actions 'reeked of turpitude', or where the copyright work contained false statements designed to deceive the public or was grossly immoral. His Lordship also suggested that the same rule might apply in an action for passing off if, for example, P had deliberately set out to deceive the public by making false statements about its products. This approach is essentially an equitable one: equity will not assist an undeserving plaintiff by, for example, awarding an injunction or an account of profits to protect P's legal rights. It may be argued that such an approach would not be appropriate where the remedy sought was damages rather than an equitable remedy.[180] However, given that the principle seems well established and perfectly justifiable, this objection seems rather pointless. In theoretical terms this may be a case where, contrary to the normal principle,[181] English law recognizes a doctrine of abuse of (legal) rights.

The CDPA gives effect to a similar principle in section 81(6) which creates an exception to the (moral) right to object to derogatory treatment of copyright work.[182] Under this provision the right of integrity is not infringed by anything done for the purpose of avoiding the commission of an offence; or

infringement of copyright. Thus, the question of who owned the copyright in Wright's book was a matter of great potential importance: Y. Cripps [1989] *PL* 13, 14–15.

[176] There is a *de facto* exception to this: the moral right of paternity has to be 'asserted' by the author to be effective (CDPA, s. 78). Thus the right will only be effective against people generally once the work has been published and the right asserted in relation to it.

[177] *Lion Laboratories Ltd* v. *Evans* [1985] QB 526.

[178] G. Dworkin and R. D. Taylor, *Blackstone's Guide to the Copyright, Designs and Patents Act 1988* (London, 1989), 104.

[179] [1990] 1 AC 109, 294; cf. Lord Keith of Kinkel at 262; Cripps [1989] *PL* 13.

[180] Dworkin and Taylor, *Blackstone's Guide*, 121.

[181] See further 261–9 below.   [182] G. McFarlane [1989] *New LJ* 844.

complying with a statutory duty; or (in the case of the BBC) avoiding the inclusion in a programme of 'anything which offends against good taste or decency or which is likely to encourage or incite to crime or to lead to disorder or to be offensive to public feeling', provided that, if the author or director of the programme is identified, a sufficient disclaimer is given. This provision effectively prevents an author or director from obtaining a remedy for breach of statutory duty when the public interest justified the breach.

Public Interest and the Justification of Intentionally Inflicted Loss

Interference with contract can, as a general rule, only be justified[183] by the assertion of some superior right of the defendant, such as a property right or a prior contractual right.[184] But there is some authority for saying that interference with contract may be justified by asserting the public interest. In *Brimelow* v. *Casson*[185] the defendants, who were members of an actors' protection society, were held to be justified in inducing theatre proprietors to break their contracts with a theatrical manager who paid female chorus members employed by him at such a low rate that they were 'forced' into prostitution to survive. Whatever the scope of this defence, there are certain areas where it is clearly irrelevant. For example, it might be thought that *Brimelow* v. *Casson* could support the proposition that improving the pay of workers was justified in the public interest; but trade union legislation deals in detail and exhaustively with action which seeks to improve the lot of workers by inducing breaches of contract. In practice, most industrial disputes which get to court never go past the stage of the grant or refusal of an interlocutory injunction. The public interest plays an important role in the decision whether such an injunction to restrain industrial action by workers should be granted.[186]

'Simple' conspiracy, that is conspiracy to injure not involving the use of unlawful means, can be justified not only by assertion of some legal right but also by the assertion of legitimate self-interest.[187] For self-interest to be legitimate it is arguably necessary for the furtherance of self-interest to be, in some sense, in the public interest.[188] For example, freedom of competition is in the general public interest, and so the furtherance of one's own competitive position by means which are not unlawful is treated as being consistent with the furtherance of that public interest. The courts have adopted the approach that the best general policy for them to adopt in the face of conflicts

---

[183] Justification is a defence which nullifies *prima facie* liability.

[184] J. D. Heydon, *Economic Torts*, 2nd edn. (London, 1978), 38–47; see also 121–2 above.

[185] [1924] 1 Ch. 302; Heydon, *Economic Torts*, 42–4; Salmond, 365.

[186] *Associated British Ports* v. *Transport and General Workers' Union* [1989] 1 WLR 939 (CA).

[187] See generally Heydon, *Economic Torts*, 16–28.

[188] Cf. *ibid.* 24: 'It seems that if conspirers eliminate the plaintiff's competition without providing equivalent benefits to the public, they will not be justified'.

between competitors is neutrality. In economic terms, this approach is simplistic because lawful competition can itself lessen competition by facilitating the creation of monopolies. But the control of monopolies has been left largely to the legislature.

The protection of the legitimate interests of workers has also been treated by the courts as providing justification for simple conspiracy.[189] Once again, furtherance of the self-interest of workers can be seen as in the public interest because it provides a counterweight to the ability of employers, by virtue of their economic strength, to protect their own interests within the law.

The decision in *Scala Ballroom (Wolverhampton) Ltd* v. *Ratcliffe*[190] arguably goes further by allowing altruistic action designed to protect the interests of third parties to be pleaded in justification of simple conspiracy.[191] Such a defence would, in essence, be a defence of public interest because the courts would be unlikely to allow it to succeed unless they considered that what had been done did further some interest of the public generally. The *Scala* case concerned the public interest in eliminating racial discrimination. That interest is now, of course, embodied in statute; but even in 1958 it was possible to say that eliminating racial discrimination was a matter of public interest and not just a matter of interest to groups who were discriminated against. The courts are unlikely to relish the prospect of being expressly asked to decide which political or social causes justify conspiracies to injure.

On the other hand, if it be accepted that the true basis of self-interest, to the extent that it provides a legal justification, is that it also furthers some wider public interest, then perhaps the line between self-interest and altruism is logically indefensible. Furthermore, there is no apparent reason why the courts should be any more wary of admitting a defence of public interest in this context than they are in the context of breach of confidence. There are many areas of the law of tort in which the courts give effect, explicitly or implicitly, to 'public policy' arguments. The results may sometimes be controversial, but the courts are not always in a position to shirk the responsibility of deciding such matters; nor do they always wish to do so.

When it comes to justifying the use of unlawful means in torts such as intimidation or unlawful means conspiracy or several forms of interference with contract, the general question is whether the use of unlawful means can ever be (legally) justified. An analogous question arises when D argues that P should not recover in tort because he or she was acting illegally at the time the injury or damage was suffered. In the latter context, the general principle appears to be that the mere fact that P was engaged in an unlawful activity when injured does not provide D with a defence. Only if P's loss was a result

---

[189]   *Crofter Hand Woven Harris Tweed Co. Ltd* v. *Veitch* [1942] AC 435.
[190]   [1958] 1 WLR 1057; but there is considerable emphasis in the case on the fact that the union had many black members, and so this interpretation of it may be doubted.
[191]   Heydon, *Economic Torts*, 20–21.

of the unlawful action in a quite direct sense will recovery be denied.[192] Similarly, in the law of contract, the fact that the plaintiff was guilty of some illegal conduct in making or performing the contract will very often not affect recovery of damages for breach of contract.[193] In both contexts it is recognized that being in breach of a statute often involves no immorality because many modern statutes are purely 'regulatory'; but even if the plaintiff is to some degree morally at fault, this should not affect the recovery of damages if the illegal conduct is only incidentally related to the civil claim for damages. It is highly doubtful whether the civil law ought to be used to bolster the incentives given by the criminal law, at least if doing so defeats the prime function of the law of tort, namely compensation for loss suffered.

In this light, there seems a good argument for saying that there is no reason why illegal acts should *never* be justifiable in a civil action for intentionally inflicted loss. If the illegality is no more than incidental to the purpose which the defendant was pursuing, and if the interest D was seeking to protect was sufficiently important to outweigh the negative impact of the illegal conduct involved (because, for example, the illegality consisted of the breach of a merely regulatory provision), then it may be that a defence of justification should succeed.[194]

3. PRIVATE INTERESTS

The Relevance of Motive

We have already seen that private interests, such as property and contractual interests, may be pleaded in justification of actions which are intended to, and do, inflict economic damage on another. In this way, private interests can nullify *prima facie* liability in tort. But it is sometimes said[195] that the English law of tort also recognizes a very important liability-negating general principle, namely that no cause of action in tort can be founded on the exercise of a person's legal rights (or more accurately, powers) even if those rights are exercised maliciously[196] (that is, out of spite or ill will, or for an 'improper purpose' such as blackmail); or with the sole (or predominant) intention of causing damage to the plaintiff; or selfishly, for self-aggrandizement.[197] This

---

[192] See 227–8 above; Trindade and Cane, *The Law of Torts in Australia*, 2nd edn., 546–50; Fleming, 305–7.

[193] See generally Treitel, ch. 11. [194] Cf. Heydon (1970) 20 *UTLJ* 131.

[195] A classic, though dated, exposition is H. C. Gutteridge (1933–5) 5 *CLJ* 22. See also D. J. Devine [1964] *Acta Juridica* 148, 164–72; W. Friedmann, *Law in a Changing Society*, 2nd edn. (London, 1972), 103–5.

[196] Or 'morally reprehensibly': G. H. L. Fridman (1958) 21 *MLR* 484, 487.

[197] Although these three motives are distinct in theory, they may not be easily disentangled in practice: motives are often mixed. In particular, intention to injure is very often coupled with some other motive; so Fridman distinguishes between 'intention', which he calls the 'immediate end or purpose', and 'motive' which refers to some more remote purpose: (1958) 21 *MLR* 484,

is the converse of the principle, which we discussed at some length in the context of trespass[198] and nuisance,[199] that a person is entitled to use the law of tort to enforce legal rights (and, in particular, property rights) even though that person has no financial interest in doing so, and even if the only aim in doing so is to make things difficult for the defendant or to extract a financial payment from the defendant. Put another way, English law recognizes no doctrine of 'abuse of rights': it is normally open to a person to assert legal rights or to exercise legal powers to the full no matter what his or her motive in doing so, no matter how much damage this may inflict on others, and regardless of the fact that the right-holder will derive no tangible benefit from asserting the rights.

Although this statement of the principle captures its essence, it is too unqualified to be accurate.[200] In the first place, it is not true that the law imposes no limitations on the exploitation of legal rights. For example, in Chapter 4 we examined a wide variety of limitations on the freedom to further one's own interests by trade competition and the making of contracts for the sake, for example, of preserving competition and preventing race and sex discrimination. There are a great many limitations, deriving both from statute (for example, planning laws) and the common law (for example, the law of nuisance) on the exercise of real property rights. In the case of some of these limitations, failure to observe the restriction(s) imposed can give rise to liability in tort.

Secondly, sometimes the malicious exercise of a legal right can entail liability in tort. For example, a public body which exercises a legal power either for an improper purpose or knowing the act to be unlawful (or both), may be liable in tort for misfeasance in a public office.[201] Proof of actual malice[202] can defeat a plea of qualified privilege or fair comment in an action for defamation.[203] Thirdly, it is sometimes tortious to act with the sole or predominant intention of injuring another; for example, simple conspiracy consists of acting in concert with another with the intention of injuring a third party even though what is done is, in itself, a lawful exercise of legal powers.

---

488. Things are made even more difficult, at least from a moral point of view, by the fact that people's motives are often a mixture of the good and the bad. It is sometimes said that this fact, coupled with the difficulty of proving what a person's motives were, justifies extreme caution in making motive relevant to legal liability. But motives are important morally; and if the law is to command respect it must, to some extent at least, reflect morality.

[198] Recall the rule that necessity in the sense of homelessness is no defence to a claim for possession of land: *Southwark LBC* v. *Williams* [1971] Ch. 734.

[199] See 49–57 above.

[200] See J. F. Lever, 'Means, Motives and Interests in the Law of Torts', in *Oxford Essays in Jurisprudence, Series I* (Oxford, 1961), 55–65.

[201] See 233 above.

[202] Where malice is an element of a tort involving the making of statements it has another meaning in addition to spite or improper motive namely, lack of honest belief in the truth of the statement.

[203] These defences 'are assertions of a legal power to act': Fridman (1958) 21 *MLR* 484, 492.

On the other hand, the defendant may succeed in a plea of justification if he or she was acting out of self- interest.

So the above statement of the general principle should be amended by adding the qualification 'sometimes': sometimes the law of tort allows a person to exercise legal rights in the way described above. In other words, the mere fact that a person has asserted rights maliciously or selfishly or with the intention of injuring another will not entail tort liability or deprive the person of the protection of the law of tort. It is, therefore, necessary to discover which rights are protected in this extensive way.

Furthermore, from a moral or normative point of view, we should perhaps distinguish a little more carefully between the motives with which legal rights may be used. In particular, there may be a difference between a case where a person stands on legal rights in order to further their own financial interests, and one where the person does so even though no financial advantage will accrue as a result but where, perhaps, another will suffer financial detriment as a consequence. In the first case, provided the financial benefit likely to accrue to the defendant justifies any accompanying damage to the plaintiff, we might be prepared to say that D was entitled to act out of self-interest even though one motive of the action was to injure another. Thus, the tort of simple conspiracy is based on intention to injure; but furtherance of one's self interest can provide justification.

But where D stands to make no financial gain from asserting rights, then we may be more wary: in such a case, D's dominant motive may be simply to make things more difficult for P—this is 'malice' in the sense of the word adopted earlier. On the other hand, the fact that a person stands to make no financial gain from asserting rights does not mean that he or she may not gain some emotional satisfaction from asserting them or may not suffer some emotional injury, such as anxiety, if the rights are not respected. Should we give more or less (or equal) value to potential financial gains or losses than to potential emotional gains or losses? Is a person more or less or equally justified in seeking to protect financial interests and emotional interests? Are we justified in concluding from the fact that a person stood to gain nothing financially from asserting rights, that the person's sole or predominant motive was spite or ill-will against another?

The law has given no consistent answer to these questions. Many of the cases mentioned below involve selfish action to protect one's financial interests regardless of the injury this may cause to another; in general, the law allows this type of behaviour. But we saw in Chapter 2[204] that the law of tort also sometimes allows people to assert their property rights and to recover damages for unauthorized use of their property even though they were not using the property themselves and had no intention of using it. Allowing

---

[204] See 49–57 above.

recovery in such cases comes very close to what one writer once graphically called 'the consecration of the spirit of unrestricted egoism'.[205]

Discrimination Law

Indirect discrimination on grounds of sex[206] or race[207] can be justified if it serves some legitimate (often financial) interest of the discriminator.[208]

Competition Law

Allen v. *Flood*[209] decides that it is not tortious for one trader intentionally to inflict economic loss on another trader in the course of conducting business provided only that the acts which cause the loss are not themselves unlawful. As noted above, in relation to competition the basic approach of the common law is neutrality between competitors. There are, perhaps, two main grounds for this approach: the first is an unwillingness on the part of the courts to get involved in regulation of markets; and the second is the desire to have relatively objective criteria of actionability ('unlawfulness') as opposed to criteria which depend on determining whether a person acted from a good or a bad motive.[210] Neither ground is entirely satisfactory. As regards the first, we saw in Chapter 4 that the common law does regulate competition to some extent; it is not always neutral—it does sometimes protect against unfair competition. As regards the second ground, although the criterion of unlawfulness may not normally require examination of the state of a person's mind it is, nevertheless, a very unclear and uncertain concept; nor is it true that issues of liability never turn on motive, as was noted above.

At all events, both grounds are ignored in cases where a trader acts in concert with another to inflict injury on a competitor, for then the trader may be liable for simple conspiracy even if nothing was done which, if done by the trader alone, would have been unlawful. Anachronistic though it be in terms of the internal organization of trading corporations; and illogical though it be, in that there is no inherent relationship between numbers of actors and likely extent of damage inflicted, the common law makes the assumption that the element of combination upsets the equality of competition which justifies the law's basic approach of neutrality. However, D may justify his or her actions by establishing that they were done with the predominant motive of self-interest rather than with malice in the sense of a desire (as opposed to an intention) to injure another.

---

[205] Gutteridge (1933–5) 5 *CLJ* 22, 22.   [206] Sex Discrimination Act 1975, s. 1(1)(b)(ii).
[207] Race Relations Act 1976, s. 1(1)(b)(ii).
[208] For a discussion see R. Townshend-Smith, *Sex Discrimination in Employment* (London, 1989), 79–93.
[209] [1898] AC 1.   [210] *Allen* v. *Flood* [1898] AC 1, 118–9, 153.

Property Rights

A landowner commits no tort to a neighbouring landowner by abstracting subterranean water flowing in undefined channels beneath his or her land, no matter how much physical or pecuniary loss this causes to the neighbour and no matter how carelessly it is done.[211] This is so even if the landowner's only motive in extracting the water is to coerce the neighbour to buy the land at the landowner's price.[212] Nor is it a tort for an occupier of land to use it in order to observe activities being conducted on neighbouring land and to make a financial gain from doing so.[213] In both of these instances the law allows a person to exercise property rights for financial gain even though a neighbour is injured as a result.

But in this context, there is authority for the proposition that, if a landowner exercises property rights simply out of a desire to hurt another, the landowner may be liable in nuisance. The plaintiff in *Hollywood Silver Fox Farm Ltd* v. *Emmett*[214] bred silver foxes, which are very sensitive during the breeding season: if disturbed they are liable to refuse to breed or to miscarry or eat their young. After a disagreement between P and D (an adjoining landowner), the latter caused his son to discharge guns on D's own land as near as possible to P's breeding pens on the pretext of shooting rabbits but in fact, as the court found, in order to disturb P's animals. It was held that since P had acted maliciously, he could be held liable. Clearly D was entitled to shoot on his own land, and the hypersensitivity of P's activity might have prevented the amount of noise made from constituting a nuisance.[215] On the other hand, it is possible to argue that in this case the amount of noise was such that it would have been a nuisance even if innocently done. Not so, however, in *Christie* v. *Davey*[216] where it was specifically held that making noise

---

[211] *Stephens* v. *Anglian Water Authority* [1987] 1 WLR 1381. The principle does not apply to subsidence resulting from the extraction of minerals: *Lotus Ltd* v. *British Soda Co. Ltd* [1972] Ch. 123; nor to action of a lower landowner designed to stem the natural flow of water onto his or her land from higher land (the higher landowner is (understandably) not liable in tort for permitting the flow): *Home Brewery Co. Ltd* v. *William Davis & Co. (Leicester) Ltd* [1987] QB 339.

[212] *Bradford Corporation* v. *Pickles* [1895] AC 587. Of course, it does not follow from the fact that a landowner is entitled to extract water flowing beneath land even though this causes a neighbour financial loss by depriving the latter of the water, that the landowner should be free of liability for doing so carelessly in such a way as to cause the neighbour's land to subside. But such a line of reasoning was adopted in *Langbrook Properties Ltd* v. *Surrey CC* [1970] 1 WLR 161 and *Stephens* v. *Anglian Water Authority* [1987] 1 WLR 1381. On the other hand, if the subsidence itself only causes financial loss and can be repaired, there seems no strong reason to distinguish between the two cases. Under s. 24 of the Water Resources Act 1991 a licence is needed to abstract water from any 'source of supply'. Under s. 39(1) the water authority is under a duty (breach of which is actionable in damages: s. 60(2)) not to grant to a person a licence to extract water which derogates from another person's rights to abstract.

[213] *Victoria Park Racing and Recreation Grounds Co. Ltd* v. *Taylor* (1937) 58 CLR 479; nor is it tortious to block a view: *Aldred's Case* (1610) 9 Co. Rep. 57b: hence the aptly-named 'spite fence'.

[214] [1936] 2 KB 468.   [215] On this point see Salmond, 64–5.

[216] [1893] 1 Ch. 316.

in order to vex and harass one's neighbour could constitute a nuisance even if no action would have lain if the noise had been made innocently.[217] Unlike the cases in the previous paragraph, the facts of neither of these cases support the interpretation that the defendant was acting primarily out of self-interest, whether financial or otherwise.[218] In this context, as in that of competitive trade, the law distinguishes between self-interest and spite.

Abuse of Litigation

The tort of malicious institution of legal proceedings[219] is committed if, but only if, D acted out of malice (that is, spite or other improper motive), and if D did not honestly and reasonably believe that the proceedings were justified.[220] On the other hand, perjury is not a tort;[221] nor is it tortious to defend a civil action with a dishonest defence.[222] These latter rules are applications of the general immunity (discussed earlier) from civil actions based on things said or done (even maliciously) in court or in preparation for court proceedings.

How are we to explain these apparently inconsistent propositions? This may be possible by observing the limits of the immunity from action given to participants in the legal process. On the whole, it only extends to things said or done in court and to preparation for trials. It does not extend to the decision whether or not to institute proceedings. It should be noted, however, that

[217] It is not clear whether the principle in these cases, namely that malice can turn otherwise lawful activities into a nuisance, applies where D's acts are done in response to a nuisance committed against D by P: cf. *Fraser* v. *Booth* (1950) 50 SR(NSW) 113 (not liable) with *Stoakes* v. *Bridges* [1958] QWN 5 (liable).

[218] A technical way of reconciling *Bradford* v. *Pickles* and *Hollywood Fox Farm* v. *Emmett* is to say that a landowner has no legal right to the water percolating in undefined channels under the land, whereas a landowner does have a legal right to enjoy land without undue noise pollution: W. V. H. Rogers (ed.), *Winfield & Jolowicz on Tort*, 14th edn. (London, 1994), 413–4; cf. Fleming, 423. But since both involve conflicts of interest in the use of adjoining land, this does not explain why one interest is legally protected while the other is not.

[219] On what it means to 'institute' criminal proceedings, see *Martin* v. *Watson* [1995] 3 WLR 318. With a few exceptions, namely bankruptcy and insolvency proceedings, and the sanctions of imprisonment and siezure of property, in practice, only criminal proceedings are covered (but see *Little* v. *Law Institute of Victoria* [1990] VR 257, 267). The main reason given for excluding most civil proceedings is that the institution of civil proceedings does not, in itself, injure a person's reputation. In some cases, at least, this reason is weak. Also, it is not clear why the tort should be so closely tied to the protection of reputation since it also protects a person against deprivation of liberty and property. Why should it not also protect against economic loss? See *Winfield and Jolowicz on Tort*, 581–2.

[220] The word 'justified' has to be understood in a rather special sense: P need not prove that he or she was innocent, nor can D escape liability by proving that P was guilty; the only question is, did the proceedings end in P's favour, for whatever reason? This rule is supported by the undesirability of allowing collateral attacks to be mounted against court decisions. On the other hand, the ground on which the case was dismissed would often be relevant to deciding whether D *reasonably* believed that the proceedings were justified.

[221] See 198, n. 287 above.

[222] *Metall und Rohstoff AG* v. *Donaldson Lufkin & Jenrette Inc.* [1990] 1 QB 391.

it is not tortious simply to institute unjustified legal proceedings for an improper purpose. The public interest in the due administration of justice is taken to demand that liability only be imposed if D did not honestly believe that the proceedings were justified or, if D did believe they were justified, this belief was unreasonable.[223] It is not clear that this distinction between the institution and the conduct of proceedings is justified. If it is not necessary to protect parties from tort liability for maliciously and knowingly (or unreasonably) instituting unjustified proceedings, neither is it necessary to protect them from tort liability for maliciously and knowingly (or unreasonably) giving false evidence. And if it is not necessary to protect parties from tort liability in the latter situation, it does not seem necessary to protect other participants in the legal process from similar liability.

Even if the proceedings were validly commenced in the sense that the person instituting them honestly and reasonably believed that they were justified, there is some authority for the proposition that it may be tortious to use a validly instituted action (even a civil action) for an improper purpose.[224] On the other hand, it has also been held that it is not a tort vindictively to serve a valid notice to quit on a tenant;[225] and the same conclusion might well be reached if valid proceedings for possession were commenced out of a desire to 'punish' the tenant. But if the use of validly instituted proceedings for an improper purpose is actionable, the resulting situation is irrational. Why should it be actionable to use proceedings which were honestly and reasonably believed to be justified for an improper purpose but not actionable to institute such proceedings for such a purpose? And why should it be actionable to use validly instituted civil proceedings for an improper purpose when, in the case of most civil proceedings, it is not actionable to institute them for such a purpose even if the person instituting them does not honestly (or reasonably) believe them to be justified? What is the relevant difference between institution and use of proceedings? Both involve misuse of the judicial system to bring pressure on another.

It is undoubtedly true that legal proceedings are often used for purposes additional to or other than the vindication of legal rights. The difficult thing is to decide when this is acceptable and when it is not. For example, the institution of justified proceedings is often used as a means of extracting by way of settlement of the claim some benefit to which P has no legal entitlement

---

[223] Furthermore, the burden of proof on the issue of reasonable belief is on P: Fleming, 618.

[224] *Goldsmith* v. *Sperrings Ltd* [1977] 1 WLR 478; *Metall und Rohstoff* v. *Donaldson* [1990] 1 QB 391, 469–70. The 'tort of collateral abuse of process' is authoritatively established in Australia: *Williams* v. *Spautz* [1992] 107 ALR 635; Trindade and Cane, *The Law of Torts in Australia*, 2nd edn., 94–9.

[225] *Chapman* v. *Honig* [1963] 2 QB 502. So this case illustrates the proposition that 'abuse' of contractual powers is not *per se* tortious. (But see 000 above concerning malicious exercise of contractual powers by a public body). *A fortiori* the assertion in good faith of a legal right and threatening proceedings for infringement of the right cannot found an action in tort: *Granby Marketing Services Ltd* v. *Interlego AG* [1984] RPC 209.

(for example, an apology in a defamation action). This is accepted as quite legitimate. On the other hand, using litigation as part of a campaign to bring financial ruin on the defendant may be undesirable, and perhaps the courts should not allow themselves to be the means to such ends. It may be, however, that the public interest in the administration of justice dictates that the bringing of justified proceedings should be protected whatever the plaintiff's motive. Both positions are arguable, but the distinction between the institution and the use of proceedings seems irrelevant to the argument.

Analysis

Can anything general be said about this case law? Perhaps the only general observation to emerge is that the common law of tort has not taken a consistent attitude towards the use of legally protected rights for unacceptable motives. It is true that English law has no doctrine of abuse of rights: there is no general rule that legally protected rights must only be used for morally or socially acceptable purposes. But neither is it true that the law always allows such rights to be asserted for any purpose whatever. This is the sort of piecemeal result one would expect of the common law. On the other hand, a distinction which seems to explain many of the cases is that between self-interest, whether financial or not, and spite or vindictiveness. On the whole, it is not tortious to assert one's rights to the injury of another out of self-interest; but it may be actionable to do so out of spite. Of course, motives are often mixed, and it will usually be necessary to pick one motive as being predominant. The artificiality of this exercise is often seen as a conclusive objection to taking motive into account, but it does not seem to have worried English courts too much.

The general willingness of the law to allow people to protect and further their own interests at the expense of others may be seen as a product of liberal assumptions about the value of freedom of action for the individual. On the other hand, it runs counter to equally strong liberal arguments to the effect that the proper function of the law (and indeed, its only proper function) is to prevent harm to others. This 'harm principle' must extend to the exercise of legal powers if it is to be logically applied. At an abstract level, these cases on the harmful exercise of rights may be seen as the law's attempt to strike a balance between the value of individual freedom and that of providing protection from harm.

CONCLUSION

We have seen in this Chapter that the law of tort recognizes a diverse set of public and private interests which may be appealed to by defendants to limit the protection which the law is prepared to give to the plaintiff's economic interests. This ends the discussion of the relevant principles of tort law. In the next part I will examine the way in which tort law interacts with other sets of legal rules which also play a part in protecting economic interests.

PART III

The Wider Context of Tort Law

6

Tort Law and Other Legal Categories

INTRODUCTION

So far, we have considered that portion of the law of tort which is concerned with the protection of economic interests in the sense in which that expression was defined in Chapter 1. However, a proper understanding of the rules and principles of tort law and of their impact on social life requires an analysis not only of tort law itself but also of the wider legal and social environment in which it operates. The law of tort provides, *inter alia* a set of legal techniques for protecting economic interests; but other bodies of legal rules provide different techniques, and beyond the law there are yet more strategies available for the protection of such interests. So this Part of the book deals with a number of forms and sources of protection for economic interests which provide alternatives to the law of tort. The aim will be to give an account of such alternatives and to examine their relationship with and their impact on tort law.

This Chapter is concerned with other bodies of legal rules, apart from tort law, which play an important part in providing legal protection for economic interests. Unless we pay close attention to the interaction between tort law and these other bodies of law, we risk having an inadequate understanding of both. My aim is to break down some of the barriers between legal subjects which are erected for pedagogical and analytical reasons in order to expose more clearly the similarities and differences between related areas of the law.

1. SELF-HELP

In a broad sense, 'self-help' refers to any action which a person can lawfully take to protect interests which does not involve recourse to legal proceedings.[1] In the narrower sense relevant here, it refers to actions which the law permits a person to take because of that person's interest which would, for another individual without that interest, be unlawful. In the law of tort,

---

[1] The potential importance of self-help in this sense should not be underestimated. For a specific set of self-help proposals to deal with noise nuisance see D. Oliver and A. Waite (1989) 1 *J Env. L* 173.

self-help in this sense is available in aid of rights in tangible property. Thus under certain circumstances, a person entitled to possession of land or chattels may retake possession even though this action is an interference with the possession of the other, and so a trespass;[2] and the victim of a nuisance[3] may enter the land of another to abate the nuisance even though the victim commits a trespass in so doing. An occupier of land may, in certain cases, seize chattels of another on the land and retain them as security for the payment of compensation for damage done by the chattel.[4]

It should also be noted that a copyright owner may, under certain circumstances, seize and detain infringing copies found available for sale or hire; and the beneficiary of a performance right may sometimes seize illicit recordings.[5]

2. PUBLIC LAW

In the last chapter, we saw that one of the arguments used in actions against public authorities to justify limiting the tort liability of such bodies is that no duty of care should arise where there is an alternative remedy such as a statutory appeal (or a ministerial default power), or a non-tort compensation scheme,[6] or an application for judicial review.[7] The availability of an alternative remedy may lead a court to deny that the authority owed the plaintiff any duty of care in exercising its powers. The alternative remedy to which the plaintiff is restricted may not provide exactly what P wants. This was true in *Jones* v. *Department of Employment*[8] where the plaintiff was not able to recover through the appeal mechanism compensation for the financial loss (in the form of the costs of the appeal) and the non-pecuniary loss for which he sought damages in the tort action.[9] So far as judicial review is concerned, it is certainly true that if the aggrieved party is in a position to make an

---

[2] Concerning releasing a wheel-clamped car by damaging the clamp see *Lloyd* v. *DPP* [1992] 1 All ER 982, 991–2; G. Virgo [1992] *CLJ* 411.

[3] Or trespass by encroachment: *Burton* v. *Winters* [1993] 1 WLR 1077.

[4] On this last see *Jamieson's Towing and Salvage Ltd* v. *Murray* [1984] 2 NZLR 144. On self-help generally, see F. H. Lawson, *Remedies of English Law*, 2nd edn. (London, 1980), ch. 1; and on self-help in the law of tort in particular, see Salmond, ch. 25.

[5] See 68 and 192 above respectively.

[6] Such as the Criminal Injuries Compensation Scheme in *Hill* v. *Chief Constable of West Yorkshire* [1989] AC 53.

[7] See 239–41 above. An analogy to an application for judicial review is a motion to have pleadings or a cause of action struck out: *Business Computers International Ltd* v. *Registrar of Companies* [1988] Ch. 229.

[8] [1989] QB 1.

[9] In *Hill* v. *Chief Constable of West Yorkshire* [1989] AC 53, Mrs Hill might well have felt that a tort action had desirable features which making a claim to the Criminal Injuries Compensation Board would not have had: it publicised her grievance much more effectively than a claim to the Board would probably have done; it enabled her to make a public complaint against the police which she could not have made by an application to the Board; and if her claim had been successful, she might well have felt vindicated and comforted in a way that she may not have following a successful claim to the Board.

application before the decision in issue is acted upon or comes into effect, then having the decision quashed may be adequate in all respects except that of affording compensation for any financial loss suffered between the date the decision was made and the date it was quashed as a result of the making of the illegal decision. Given that the judicial review procedure can be relatively speedy in its operation, this may be no great hardship; although if P could prove that the authority had acted tortiously and that loss had been caused as a result, there seems no reason of principle why recovery for that loss should be denied. On the other hand, if the decision has been executed and P has suffered loss as a result, judicial review will be of no assistance; it is in this situation that a tort remedy is most needed.

We might conclude that the law of tort is seen as a technique of last resort for redressing grievances against public authorities. It seems a necessary (but not a sufficient) condition for the success of a tort action against a public authority (except, perhaps, one for misfeasance in a public office) that no statutory or public law remedy is available to the plaintiff which the court considers to be a suitable and adequate alternative.

3. LAW OF PROPERTY

In Chapter 3 we saw that in certain (unusual) circumstances the law of tort may provide a means of protecting a contractual interest in land or chattels against a person claiming a proprietary interest in the property. We concluded that in policy terms the cases concerning real property were the more problematic: so far as property law is concerned, contractual interests in land are not binding on successors in title. In other words, the law of property recognizes certain techniques for creating binding interests in land and refuses to enforce interests not created in an authorized manner. The conceptual dynamics of this situation are complex. Traditionally in English law, proprietary interests trump contractual interests, and contractual interests trump 'tort interests'. When the law of tort protects contractual interests in property it gives such interests priority over proprietary interests. The law of tort is implicated because the contractual interests in question are being enforced against a non-contracting party.

The reaction of one writer (Smith) to this situation is as follows:

The law of real property has been dealing with this issue for centuries. Thus contracts to create legal estates bind purchasers with notice, as do restrictive covenants, whereas contractual licences (on orthodox principles) do not bind purchasers . . . Even if one thinks that a purchaser with actual notice of an earlier contract should be unable to take advantage of a failure to protect it by registration, the correct approach is to reform the land charges and land registration legislation. Extension of tort principles is bound to cause undesirable uncertainty. It is submitted, therefore, that . . . where real property principles accord priority to a contract or conveyance over an earlier contract, it should not be open to the earlier contracting party to rely on tort.[10]

This quotation contains three very important ideas. The first is that the law of tort should not be used as a means of making good what are seen as deficiencies in other branches of the law. As we will see later in this Chapter, this argument has also been used in the context of the relationship between contract and tort. An assumption underlying this argument (and made explicit in the quotation) is that the 'deficient' branch of the law could not be reformed easily (or at all) by the courts. So the law of tort, which is usually seen as being more fluid than many other branches of private law, provides a possible means of by-passing more inflexible and less easily modified rules. When the alternative to using tort law is legislative reform, an argument in favour of reform (which the courts themselves find attractive in some contexts) is that the legislature is unlikely to do what is necessary, or that it will take a very long time to act; and that this justifies the courts in stepping in. Since in our system it is not open to the courts to amend statutes,[11] they are limited to solutions which can be achieved by means of techniques of statutory interpretation; or to a collateral approach which might involve using some area of the common law to modify the operation of the statutory rule 'in effect' and indirectly. It is the latter approach which is manifest in the cases which require the re-transfer of land the title to which has been registered. But often the force of a statute is so strong that the courts are unwilling to allow it to be undermined by changes in related rules of law.[12]

Even where the alternative to tort law is some other area of the common law, the courts not infrequently take the line that they will not allow one area of the law to be altered 'by a side wind' by applying principles from some other area of the law, or that the rule under attack is so firmly entrenched that it could only be altered by legislation. Attempts to use the law of tort effectively to create exceptions to the doctrine of privity of contract provide an example. None of this conceptual manoeuvring makes much sense except in terms of the interests which the courts see as most worthy of protection in particular situations. In other words, the attitudes which the courts take to the interrelationship between statute law and common law on the one hand, and between different areas of the common law on the other, depend a great deal on their perceptions of the merits of the particular cases in which the issue arises.

There is another related point: courts are unwilling to hold that a duty of care exists whenever there is some legal principle or rule dealing with the situation in issue. For example, in *Banque Keyser Ullman SA* v. *Skandia (UK)*

[10] R. J. Smith (1977) 41 *Conv.* 318, 328–9.

[11] On this option see G. Calabresi, *A Common Law for the Age of Statutes* (Cambridge, Mass., 1982).

[12] See the discussion of statutory intellectual property rights, above 186–9.

Insurance Co. Ltd[13] the Court of Appeal held that an action for damages in the tort of negligence could not be based on a breach of the duty of utmost good faith owed by the parties to an insurance contract because, as a matter of contract and statute law,[14] the only remedy available for breach of the duty was rescission of the insurance contract. This is another respect in which, so far as economic interests are concerned, the law of tort is seen as being a last resort, only available for use when no other suitable avenue for protection of the economic interest in question is available.

The second idea in the above quotation is that reforming property law rather than having recourse to tort law is the 'correct' approach; underlying this argument is a reassertion of the traditional hierarchy of legal values in which property trumps contract and tort. The word 'correct', which carries with it a connotation of technical purity, should be seen as an expression of a value judgement.

Thirdly, Smith argues that recourse to the law of tort would introduce 'undesirable uncertainty' into property law. This argument, too, is used in the contractual context. It can take two forms: the first, as in the quotation, says that the interaction of the two bodies of law would generate uncertainty. The case for this is clear in the context of registered land: if unregistered interests can too easily override registered interests, the basic rationale and practical operation of the register is undermined. On the other hand, the social desirability of recognizing some informal interests in land is reflected in section 70 of the Land Registration Act 1925 which allows certain types of unregistered interests in land to override registered interests in the land notwithstanding the fact that the registered owner may have no actual knowledge of them. Thus, there is no absolute principle in land law that only registered interests should be recognized.

The second form of the argument depends on the fact that many of the concepts of tort law (notably, unreasonableness and foreseeability) are inherently flexible and vague whereas property law, in particular, tends to utilize harder-edged concepts. This form of the argument is not particularly appropriate to the intentional economic torts with which Smith deals; it is most appropriate to the tort of negligence. It raises one of the fundamental dichotomies of the law: certainty versus flexibility. No-one denies that each plays an important part in all branches of the law; the issue, in any particular context, is the balance between them. The argument against tort law usually involves saying that in the context in question certainty is more important than flexibility. Whether this is so or not is ultimately a question for individual judgment. It is clear, however, that certainty and security are the highest values underlying the system of land title registration.

---

[13] [1990] 1 QB 665; affirmed on different grounds [1991] 2 AC 249.
[14] But the statute was not directly in point and so did not settle the issue.

4. MARITIME LAW[15]

Under this heading we will first consider some substantive rules special to claims arising out of maritime activities; and then certain procedural rules unique to claims brought in the Admiralty jurisdiction.

Substantive Rules

Historically, English maritime law, as applied by the Admiralty Court, was grafted on to the common law and was not an integral part of it. So there are, to this day, rules and doctrines applicable to maritime disputes which are not part of the general common law. We have come across two of these: the law of salvage and the doctrine of general average contribution.[16] Both of these sets of rules are a response to the peculiar perils involved in maritime activities. The law of salvage allows a person who saves a ship from peril to recover from the owners of the ship or of cargo being carried on it compensation representing expenses incurred by that person in saving the ship, reasonable remuneration for the services provided, and even a reward for the action taken. Under the doctrine of general average contribution, if the owner of a ship or of cargo being carried on it suffers loss or expense as a result of action taken to protect the ship or its cargo from peril, the owner may recover from those who benefit from that action a rateable contribution towards the loss or expense. Furthermore, those who make contributions can recover them from any person whose wrongful act made the action necessary. This latter rule, of course, allows recovery for economic loss consequential upon damage to the property of a third party; such loss is normally not recoverable in the law of tort.

Procedural Rules

The Admiralty jurisdiction is exercised by the Admiralty Court which is part of the Queen's Bench Division of the High Court. From our point of view, the important thing to realize is that tort actions may be brought in the Admiralty jurisdiction if they fall within one of the heads of such jurisdiction as enumerated in section 20 of the Supreme Court Act 1981. The most relevant heads are those contained in paragraphs (d),(e),(g),(j), and (q) of section

---

[15] See generally C. Hill, *Maritime Law*, 2nd edn. (London, 1985), ch. 4; D. C. Jackson, *The Enforcement of Maritime Claims* (London, 1985); *Halsbury's Laws of England*, 4th edn. (London, 1973), i; D. R. Thomas, *Maritime Liens* (London, 1980), chs. 1 and 2. The relevant law is obscure and complex, and the reader is referred to these works for full details.

[16] See 225 above.

20(2), namely claims for damage received by a ship,[17] for damage done by a ship (including oil pollution damage),[18] and for loss of or damage to goods carried in a ship, salvage claims,[19] and claims arising out of general average acts (that is, acts to which the doctrine of general average contribution applies). If a tort action is brought 'in Admiralty', the claim is governed by the rules of procedural and substantive law applicable to actions in that jurisdiction, including the rules about salvage and general average contribution already examined.

The most important feature of admiralty claims from our point of view which, of course, applies to tort claims brought in Admiralty, is that Admiralty claims are either *'in personam'* or *'in rem'*.[20] With one exception,[21] all claims actionable *in rem* are also actionable *in personam*;[22] but the converse is not true: some claims are only actionable *in personam*. The practical importance of the possibility of making an *in rem* claim is that it gives the court jurisdiction over a ship which is within the jurisdiction even if the personal defendant is not. Secondly, it gives the plaintiff security[23] either in the form of the ship itself or the proceeds of its sale or, most commonly, in some other form which the court permits the personal defendant to provide when D appears in person—which the arrest or (more often) the threatened arrest of the ship will usually force D to do.[24] But in theory, the crucial difference between an *in rem* claim and an *in personam* claim is that the latter can only give rise to a personal obligation in the defendant, whereas the former can give P proprietary rights in D's property (in particular, the ship). This means, first, that a successful plaintiff in an *in personam* action will rank only as an unsecured (judgment) creditor of the defendant if the latter goes bankrupt or insolvent; whereas the plaintiff in a successful *in rem* action will rank as a secured creditor.[25] Secondly, *in rem* claims are, in certain cases,[26] enforceable against a purchaser of the affected ship even if the purchaser had no

[17] 'Ship' includes 'any description of vessel used in navigation and . . . a hovercraft' (Supreme Court Act 1981, s. 24(1)).

[18] Supreme Court Act 1981, s. 20(5); on oil pollution damage, see Merchant Shipping Act 1971, s. 13 (as amended by Merchant Shipping Act 1988). Note also Supreme Court Act 1981, s. 20(3)(b): actions arising out of collisions between ships and similar cases are specifically mentioned as falling within the admiralty jurisdiction; but many such cases will fall under one of the other paragraphs as well.

[19] Including salvage claims in relation to aircraft while the aircraft is waterborne: Supreme Court Act 1981, s. 24(1).

[20] For a brief account of *in rem* actions see T. C. Hartley (1989) 105 *LQR* 640, 640–4.

[21] Supreme Court Act 1981, s. 22.

[22] An *in rem* claim and an *in personam* claim can be made concurrently; indeed, when a defendant enters an appearance to an *in rem* writ, an *in personam* claim automatically arises.

[23] The right to seize chattels as security exists in certain other situations as well: see 274 above.

[24] Thomas, *Maritime Liens*, 42–3.

[25] *Re Aro Co. Ltd* [1980] Ch. 196; Thomas, *Maritime Liens*, 65–73. On priorities between different maritime claims to the proceeds of a ship see *ibid.*, ch. 9.

[26] That is (1) where the ship is sold after the issue of the writ *in rem*; or (2) where the claim gives rise to a maritime (as opposed to a statutory) lien: Hill, *Maritime Law*, 109–10; but for a wider view see Jackson, *The Enforcement of Maritime Claims*, 253.

knowledge of the claim. Thirdly, whereas an (interlocutory) *Mareva* injunction[27] only imposes a personal obligation on D,[28] the interlocutory remedy of arrest available in *in rem* actions in Admiralty gives P a proprietary interest in the arrested property, and the court a power of sale.[29] So whereas the plaintiff in a non-Admiralty tort action can only obtain personal remedies (unless P can establish grounds for the award of the equitable proprietary remedy),[30] the plaintiff in a tort action brought in Admiralty may be able to obtain remedies with proprietary effects.

The important question is, which claims in Admiralty are *in rem* claims? Section 21(4) of the Supreme Court Act 1981 is the basic provision: in the case of claims under paragraphs (e),(g),(j), and (q) of section 20(2), an action *in rem* will lie where the claim arises in connection with a ship, and where the person who would be liable in an action *in personam* (the 'relevant person') was, at the time the cause of action arose, the owner or charterer of the ship or in possession or control of it. Such a claim[31] lies against the ship involved (provided that, at the time the action is brought, the relevant person is the sole beneficial owner or the demise charterer of the ship), or against any other ship of which, at the time the action is brought, the relevant person is the sole beneficial owner. It should be noted that this provision does not cover claims under section 20(2)(d) that is, claims for damage received by a ship; nor claims under section 20(3)(b) that is, claims arising out of collisions and other similar claims. For our purposes, the second omission is not important, but the first is so far as it relates to damage not caused by another ship (which is covered by s. 20(2)(e)). However, Jackson argues that *in rem* claims could be brought in relation to damage received by a ship before the 1981 Act and that, by virtue of section 20(1)(c) of that Act (which preserves pre-1981 jurisdiction), they can still be brought. It should be noted that an action *in rem* will lie not only against the ship involved but also against what are colloquially called 'sister ships'.

In rem claims can also, by virtue of section 21(3) of the 1981 Act, be brought in cases where there is a 'maritime lien or other charge on any ship, aircraft or other property . . . against that ship, aircraft or other property'. Maritime liens arise in various types of case including salvage claims,[32] and cases of damage done by a ship through fault of the person in charge of the ship;[33] but there is probably no lien in respect of oil pollution claims.[34] Cases

---

[27] A *Mareva* injunction restrains D from disposing of (or removing from the jurisdiction of the court) assets out of which any judgment against D in a pending action might be satisfied. For brief accounts, see Thomas, *Maritime Liens*, 73–7; P. S. Atiyah, *Pragmatism and Theory in English Law* (London, 1987), 55–61; R. Walker and R. Ward, *Walker and Walker's English Legal System*, 7th edn. (London, 1994), 289–92.

[28] But see J. M. Dine and J. J. McEvoy [1989] *CJQ* 236.

[29] On sale, P's proprietary rights attach to the proceeds. See also Supreme Court Act 1981, s. 22(6).

[30] See 287–90 below.   [31] Which is also described as a 'statutory lien'.

[32] Jackson, *The Enforcement of Maritime Claims*, 17–20.

[33] *Ibid.*, 20–2, 32–3.   [34] *Ibid.*, 23–4; cf. Thomas, *Maritime Liens*, 106–7.

which fall under section 21(3) also fall under section 21(4). But a claim under section 21(3) can be brought despite a change of ownership of the ship after the cause of action arose; and a maritime lien may exist in relation to an aircraft or other property, such as cargo. On the other hand, a claim under section 21(3) does not lie against 'sister' ships (or aircraft).

The Policy Basis of the Rules

The peculiarities of maritime law and the Admiralty jurisdiction can be explained historically. But is there any policy justification for the existence of substantive rules of law and of remedies and procedures which are confined, by and large, to maritime cases? The traditional justification for the law of salvage and general average contribution is that seafaring is regularly subject to perils of a type and intensity which do not affect other commercial endeavours. Furthermore, whereas in the case of accidents on land a stranger who came to the rescue rather than enlisting the aid of an organized rescue service might be characterized as an intermeddler who ought not to be allowed to demand payment for (unnecessary) services rendered, rescue services are not normally readily available beyond coastal waters to deal with maritime accidents. On the other hand, it has been argued that although such reasoning should make us wary about allowing salvage and similar claims arising out of accidents on land, there is no reason to impose an absolute ban on such claims.[35]

The theory underlying actions *in rem* is disputed.[36] On one view, they are a procedural device to encourage the personal appearance of the defendant (in order to prevent the ship being sold). This is the way *in rem* claims are most often used in practice, but the obvious theoretical defect of this view is that the plaintiff in an action *in rem* acquires proprietary rights enforceable against purchasers and in bankruptcy. The other main view is that the action *in rem* is a proprietary action against the thing in connection with which the plaintiff's substantive claim arises. This view is undermined by the availability of an action *in rem* against a sister ship, and also by the fact that it is ultimately the defendant who pays even in an action *in rem*.

But these views suggest policy reasons which could be used to support the availability of actions *in rem*. The first is that, in a world in which many individuals and institutions own assets situated in jurisdictions in which they are not present, the possibility of attaching and selling those assets gives the owner a very strong incentive to submit to the jurisdiction of the court and give security, even if personal service out of the jurisdiction would not be available or would be difficult to effect. Secondly, ships are very mobile and can be easily and quickly removed from the jurisdiction of the court, and thus

---

[35] F. Rose (1989) 9 *OJLS* 167.

made unavailable for satisfying any judgment given against the defendant. Arrest, which is an integral adjunct of actions *in rem*, helps to overcome the problem to which the mobility of ships gives rise. On the other hand, ships are not the only very mobile assets which a plaintiff may wish to realize to satisfy a claim: aircraft are also easily and quickly removed from one juris- diction to another. Actions *in rem* are, in some cases, available against air- craft, but not nearly so often as against ships. Also, air travel has made small chattels, such as diamonds and other valuable commodities, easily transfer- able from one country to another. More importantly, modern technology has made many intangible assets extremely and rapidly mobile; and many intan- gible assets can be disposed of very quickly, and even dissipated.

The response of English (non-maritime) law to these facts is the *Mareva* injunction,[37] an interlocutory order which restrains D from dissipating or removing from the jurisdiction assets from which P hopes to satisfy a claim. The *Mareva* injunction, unlike arrest, only imposes a personal obligation on the defendant; and, of course, the fact that a plaintiff is awarded a *Mareva* injunction does not affect the chance that any final relief awarded to P will have proprietary effects.[38]

The whole question of interlocutory and final proprietary relief in respect of property other than real property deserves attention in a way not tied to specific areas of the law or specific jurisdictional arrangements.

5. EQUITABLE PRINCIPLES AND THE LAW OF TRUSTS

The Law of Tort and Equitable Proprietary Interests

As we saw in Chapter 2, the law of tort plays a central role in English law in protecting legal, as opposed to equitable, property interests. Although, as a result of the Judicature Act reforms of the nineteenth century, the distinc- tion between law and equity is now much less important than it used to be, it still plays a central role in the law of property (of which, for present pur- poses, I treat the law of trusts as being a part).[39] One legacy of the distinc- tion is that the law of tort (which is, of course, part of 'law', not 'equity') does not protect equitable property interests. So, for example, even though a contractual licence may be binding in equity on a successor in title who took

---

[36] For detailed discussion, see Jackson, *The Enforcement of Maritime Claims*, chs. 3 and 11; also Thomas, *Maritime Liens*, 41–2.

[37] A. A. S. Zuckerman (1993) 109 *LQR* 432.

[38] See L. Collins (1989) 105 *LQR* 262, 263–5. It is also worth noting that a plaintiff who is awarded a *Mareva* injunction has to give an undertaking as to damages, whereas a plaintiff in an action *in rem* is only liable in damages if a ship is arrested in bad faith.

[39] But see B. Rudden (1994) 14 *OJLS* 81, 88. For our purposes, a trust can be defined as a legal relationship in which the title to property is split: legal title is held by the trustee(s), while the beneficial or equitable title to the property resides in the beneficiary or beneficiaries for whose benefit the trustee is obliged to hold and use the property.

the land as a constructive trustee in favour of the licensee, the licensee would not be able to sue the successor (or anyone else) in trespass.[40] The same general principle applies to chattels: a person with a purely equitable interest in goods cannot sue in negligence for physical damage to the goods,[41] nor for conversion of them.[42] In the context of a trust, it is the trustee, as the holder of the legal title, who may be able to use the law of tort to protect his or her (and indirectly, any beneficiary's) interest.

The distinction between torts and equitable wrongs is partly a function of the historical development of our court system. It can also be argued that common law property rights and equitable property rights perform different functions, the former being designed to mark and enforce the distinction between 'what is yours and what is mine', and the latter being designed as a means for enforcing standards of honesty and good faith in the management of (common law) property. Nevertheless, the fusion of the courts of law and equity has had a profound effect on our perception of the relationship between the substantive rules of law and equity, and the time has come to begin the process of creating a integrated law of obligations based not on the distinction between law and equity as such but on principles about which interests the law should protect and how it should protect them.

To this end I would suggest that, just as various features of the law of tort can be illuminated by observing that tort law has two quite distinct orientations (one towards the compensating for breaches of duty and the other towards the protection of rights),[43] it may be that our understanding of the law of trusts can be deepened by observing that while equity courts have traditionally been concerned with enforcing standards of probity and fair dealing this has been done chiefly by inventing (equitable) property rights. In other words, the law of trusts is oriented both towards sanctioning unconscionable conduct and towards protecting property rights.

Types of Trust

Trusts can be classified in a number of ways. One important classification distinguishes between trusts which come into existence as a result of a deliberate act of creation (express trusts) on the one hand, and those which are

---

[40] See 107 above.

[41] *Leigh and Sillavan Ltd* v. *Aliakmon Shipping Co. Ltd* [1986] 1 AC 785, 812.

[42] In *International Factors Ltd* v. *Rodriguez* [1979] QB 351 P was equitable owner of a company's book debts and had a contractual right to immediate possession of any cheques in favour of the company. It was held that P could sue for conversion of certain cheques on the basis (according to the majority) of the contractual right coupled with P's equitable title. This holding was justified by appeal to the fusion of law and equity. The majority also held that a contractual right to possession cannot ground a claim in conversion. As a general proposition, this must be wrong. It is correct to say that tort law does not protect contractual interests in chattels, but it is incorrect to say that a possessory interest in property cannot be created by contract; witness leases and contracts for the hire of chattels.

[43] See 22 above.

imposed by law (resulting and constructive trusts), on the other. For our purposes, resulting trusts can be bracketed with express trusts. The typical express trust is an ongoing arrangement under which the trustee manages and exploits property for the benefit of the beneficiaries, and distributes the fruits of that management in accordance with the terms of the trust. Express trusts perform a variety of social functions,[44] all concerned with the protection of economic interests.

The constructive trust is essentially a remedial device, although it is not technically a remedy. A holding that D is a constructive trustee for P of certain property usually[45] provides the legal foundation for an order requiring D to transfer (an interest in) the trust property to P or to the trustee of an express trust under which P is the beneficiary. Constructive trusts of land are most important in the context of marriage and informal domestic relationships.[46] Constructive trusts of chattels and intangibles can arise in a number of ways.[47] The only one of importance for our purposes is that D will be constructive trustee for P of an asset in D's hands if that asset represents the proceeds of unauthorized disposition by D of P's property, or the profits of unauthorized use by D of P's property.

Liability for Breach of Trust

Here we are concerned with the liability of trustees for breach of express trusts and of third parties for involvement in breaches of trust. Liability can usefully be divided into three categories: liability for losses suffered by the trust, liability for gains made at the expense of the trust, and liability for receipt of trust property.

Liability for Losses

Trustees[48] are, of course, liable to compensate the trust for losses suffered as a result of breaches of trust by them. In this respect, liability for breach of trust is essentially indistinguishable from tort liability.[49] The trustee's liability may be strict, as where the trustee makes an unauthorized investment of trust assets. A trustee is liable for loss suffered by the trust as a result of unauthorized investment no matter how reasonably or even innocently the trustee acted. By contrast, in handling the (legitimate) business affairs of the trust the

---

[44] G. Moffat, *Trusts Law: Text and Materials*, 2nd edn. (London, 1994), ch. 2.

[45] Confusingly, however, the language of constructive trust is also used in the context of personal equitable liability to compensate for losses or to account for gains.

[46] N. 44 above, ch. 13. The law of tort plays no significant role in this context.

[47] R. M. Goode (1976) 92 *LQR* 528, 534–5.

[48] If a person who is not a trustee acts as if he or she were a trustee, that person will be treated by the law as a trustee and will be subject to the same liabilities as a real trustee: C. Harpum (1986) 102 *LQR* 114, 127–30.

[49] The liability of the trustee was said to be an instance of liability for breach of a duty of care by Lord Browne-Wilkinson in *Henderson* v. *Merrett Syndicates Ltd* [1994] 3 WLR 761; this view is vigorously opposed by J. D. Heydon (1995) 111 *LQR* 1.

trustee is (only) required to exercise the skill of an ordinary prudent person of business (or, in the case of a professional adviser acting as trustee, the skill of a reasonable member of the profession in question). In exercising a discretion to dispose of the income of the trust the trustee's only duty is not to act unreasonably, that is, in such a way that no reasonable trustee would act.

These three standards of liability have obvious analogies in the law of tort: some tort liabilities (such as liability for interference with property interests) are strict, while others are based on lack of reasonable care; and in some cases (for example, actions in respect of alleged negligence by a doctor) the test of reasonable care comes rather close to imposing no more than a requirement that the defendant acted 'not unreasonably', because a doctor will not be held liable if he or she can prove that a responsible body of doctors would have acted as the allegedly negligent doctor did, even if others (who may be the majority) would have done otherwise. Strict liability in the law of tort performs two main functions: to protect property rights and to allocate risks to the activity which generates them. The strict liability of a trustee is usually explained as a strong deterrent; but it is not easy to see how the threat of liability can deter purely innocent conduct, and it is probably better explained as an outworking of the property rights of the beneficiary. In this light, the fact that liability for losses caused by management of trust property is not strict may be seen as a concession to the difficulty of the trustee's task. The fact that a trustee can be liable in respect of the distribution of trust property only for acting in a way that no reasonable trustee would have acted is a corollary of the discretionary nature of the trustee's function rather than, as in the case of doctors, a product of deference to their expertise and professional status.

A third party who was involved or who assisted or participated in a breach of trust may be held liable for losses suffered by the trust as a result. The third party will be liable according to equitable principles only if he or she acted 'dishonestly', that is with 'conscious impropriety', either knowing of the beneficiary's interest, or recklessly as to its existence.[50] As a general rule, third parties owe no duty of care to beneficiaries, although they may owe a contractual or a non-contractual duty of care to the trustee who may, in turn, be liable to the beneficiary for any loss suffered as a result of the third party's negligence. Third-party liability for losses caused by involvement in a breach of trust is analogous to tort liability for interference with contract, and the existence of the former head of liability has prevented the recognition of a tort of 'interference with a trust'.[51]

Whereas entitlement to damages in tort is limited by rules of remoteness, in equity the beneficiary can recover for all losses suffered as a result of the

[50] *Royal Brunei Airlines Sdn Bhd* v. *Tan* [1995] 3 WLR 64.
[51] *Metall und Rohstoff AG* v. *Donaldson Lufkin & Jenrette* [1990] 1 QB 391, 481–2.

breach of trust, however indirect or unforeseeable:[52] the claimant bears the burden of proving only that the losses for which compensation is claimed were, as a matter of fact, caused by the breach.[53] Furthermore, contrary to the position in tort, the claimant's tax liability is irrelevant to the assessment of equitable compensation.[54] These rules reflect the fact that, whereas the basic aim of the law of tort is compensation for losses suffered as a result of tortious conduct, equity is more concerned with vindicating the beneficiary's equitable property rights and sanctioning the defendant.

Liability for Gains

By virtue of being fiduciaries,[55] trustees are subject to very strict liability to account for gains made at the expense of the trust. A fiduciary must not exploit his or her position by competing with the principal (i.e. in this context, the beneficiary), for example, or by exploiting information acquired as fiduciary, or by exploiting the principal's property. If the interests of the trustee conflict with those of the beneficiary, the trustee must not promote his or her interests over those of the beneficiary. The trustee is liable to disgorge all gains which, as a matter of fact, resulted from the breach of fiduciary duty however remotely.

A fiduciary can be held liable for gains made even if he or she acted in all innocence and good faith,[56] even if the principal could not have acquired the benefit which the fiduciary acquired,[57] and even if the principal suffered no loss but actually benefited financially from the fiduciary's conduct.[58] Nor does it assist a fiduciary that the profit could not have been made but for his or her own skill and effort; however, the fiduciary may be awarded remuneration and even a share of the profits, especially if he or she acted in good faith.[59] This principle of strict liability, which dates from the eighteenth century, is usually justified by deterrence arguments. It has come under criticism

---

[52] Harpum (1986) 102 *LQR* 114, 119–20. Damages may be recovered for loss of a chance of financial gain caused by breach of trust: *Nestlé* v. *National Westminster Bank PLC* [1993] 1 WLR 1260.

[53] *Target Holdings Ltd* v. *Redferns* [1995] 3 WLR 352.

[54] *Bartlett* v. *Barclays Bank Trust Co. Ltd (No 2)* [1980] Ch. 515.

[55] See further 294 below.

[56] Cf. liability for unauthorized exploitation of another's real property or chattels; but contrast statutory liability for infringement of intellectual property rights: 70 above.

[57] In these two respects, cf. tort liability for unauthorized exploitation in conversion and trespass.

[58] *Boardman* v. *Phipps* [1967] 2 AC 46.

[59] *Boardman* v. *Phipps* [1967] 2 AC 46 (remuneration could be 'generous'); *O'Sullivan* v. *Management Agency & Music Ltd* [1985] Ch. 428 (award to D not to be as great as the benefit which could have been obtained if it had acted properly). For economic arguments in favour of such limited profit sharing see W. Bishop and D. Prentice (1986) 49 *MLR* 118. Profit-sharing is appropriate only where the profit is 'incidental', that is, not the product of the performance of the very task which forms the subject matter of the fiduciary relationship. This is essentially a question of causation: did the fiduciary's special position provide merely the opportunity for making a profit? Accounting in non-fiduciary contexts requires apportionment of gains between lawful and unlawful activity: see 71 above.

in recent years, especially in its application to commercial dealings: to what extent is it realistic or appropriate to hold people, such as company directors[60] and bankers,[61] who handle other people's money and intangible assets, liable according to principles which were developed in the context of family trusts of real property?[62]

Third parties who are dishonestly[63] involved in a breach of trust are also liable to account for gains made as a result. The requirement of fault contrasts with the fact that liability in tort for gains made by exploiting another's property is strict. This difference is a reflection of the different functions of legal and equitable property rights and the concern of equity with unconscionability.

Excursus on Proprietary Remedies The liability of trustees and of third parties to account for gains made by breach of trust which has just been discussed is called 'personal liability' and it is enforced by the 'personal remedy' of account of profits. To be contrasted with personal remedies are equitable 'proprietary remedies'.[64] Proprietary remedies are best described by reference to their two main characteristics: the first is that the beneficiary of a proprietary remedy can rank as a secured rather than an unsecured creditor in the bankruptcy or liquidation of the defendant.[65] As a matter of bankruptcy and insolvency law (special statutory provisions apart), having the priority of a secured creditor depends on having title to property in the hands of the debtor. The way proprietary remedies accord priority in bankruptcy is by recognizing that the beneficiary of the remedy has an equitable interest in the property in question. The second main characteristic of proprietary remedies is that such a remedy always relates to (and is a response to a claim to) some asset in the hands of the defendant at the time the remedy is awarded. Suppose that D receives an asset worth £X, but that by the time P claims it, the value of the asset has dropped to £X–Y; if P is awarded a proprietary remedy in respect of the asset, the most P can recover is £X–Y. On the other hand, if at the date of the claim the value of the asset has risen to £X+Z,

---

[60] But see Bishop and Prentice (1983) 46 *MLR* 289, 303. The legal title to the property which company directors manage is in the company.

[61] *Baden, Delvaux and Lecuit* v. *Société Générale pour Favouriser le Développement du Commerce et de l'Industrie en France SA* [1983] BCLC 325.

[62] Harpum (1986) 102 *LQR* 114, 125–6; for a different view see A. Tettenborn (1979) 95 *LQR* 68, 75–6, and [1980] *JBL* 10 (banks, solicitors, and other professionals should be held to higher standards for assistance in breach of trust than private persons). See also Moffatt, *Trusts Law: Text and Materials*, n. 44 above, ch. 15.

[63] I am assuming that the basis of liability for losses accepted by the Privy Council in *Royal Brunei Airlines* v. *Tan* [1995] 3 WLR 64 will also be applied to liability for gains.

[64] Proprietary remedies take a number of forms such as an order for the transfer of specific assets, an order entitling P to a proportionate share of an investment paid for partly with P's assets, or a lien or charge over property (if, for example, P had a security interest in the property in question). 'Proportionate share liability' enables P to recover profits made by use of the trust property.

[65] A. J. Oakley [1995] *CLJ* 377.

then a proprietary remedy may entitle P to recover some or all of £Z in addition to £X. By contrast, the quantum of a personal remedy is not tied to the present value of the asset received.

Proprietary remedies were creatures of equity, not the common law, and were not available in the common law courts. So, for instance, a plaintiff in a conversion action could (and can) only claim personal remedies. Even an order that D return some specific piece of property to P, such as may be made in a conversion action, is a personal remedy. It is true that by means of an order for specific return[66] P may succeed in capturing an increase in the value of the property since the date of its receipt by D, but this is an incidental side-effect of the remedy. An order for specific return would not, as such, entitle P to rank as a secured creditor of D.[67] Furthermore, proprietary remedies can only be had in aid of equitable rights in situations in which legal and equitable title reside in different persons.[68] There is also authority for the proposition that an equitable proprietary remedy is available only if there was a 'fiduciary relationship' between the plaintiff and someone through whose hands the property passed (not necessarily the defendant).[69]

In theory, at least, proprietary remedies may be awarded in respect of two quite different types of claims. In claims of the first type (which I shall call 'property claims'), P asserts that at the time of receipt of the claimed asset by D equitable property in the asset received resided in P (and remained in P thereafter). In claims of the second type (which I shall call 'non-property claims') P asserts that although at the time of receipt of the claimed asset by D equitable property in the asset did not reside in P, D should be treated as holding the asset on (constructive) trust for P. Claims in respect of gains made by trustees and third parties by breach of trust are typically non-property claims. Claims in respect of trust property received by a trustee or third party (which are discussed below) are property claims.

Because of their impact on the rights of creditors in bankruptcy, the use of equitable proprietary remedies is controversial, at least when used to vindicate non-property claims. For instance, some people doubt that proprietary remedies should ever be available on the basis that property in D's hands,

---

[66] And also by means of self-help, when it is allowed.

[67] If P had possession of the goods immediately before they were converted or has a right to immediate possession of the goods, and the trustee in bankruptcy or the liquidator refuses to surrender the goods, the latter will be liable in conversion: e.g. *Clough Mill Ltd* v. *Martin* [1985] 1 WLR 111 (goods sold subject to a so-called 'retention (or 'reservation') of title' clause). See generally G. McCormack, *Reservation of Title* (London, 1990), ch. 12.

[68] For criticism see Hanbury and Maudsley, 648–9. Technically, no separate equitable interest exists where the whole interest in the property, both legal and beneficial, is in the same person: *Commissioner of Stamp Duties* v. *Livingston* [1965] AC 694, 712. By a retention of title clause a seller may retain title to goods until they are paid for. If the buyer disposes of the goods and the third-party purchaser obtains legal title to them, equitable title to the proceeds may vest in the original seller, thus giving him or her the right to claim a proprietary remedy in respect of the proceeds. See Hanbury and Maudsley, 657–62; Goode (1976) 92 LQR 528, 547–52.

[69] Hanbury and Maudsley, 647–8; Goff and Jones, 83–6; but cf. Birks, 362. See below on fiduciary relationships.

which was acquired from a third party for him- or herself, should have been acquired by D (if at all) for P.[70] This is because the effect of a proprietary remedy in such a case is to create rather than simply to recognize the existence of a property right.[71] It is widely felt that because property rights are so well protected by the law they should be created by general rules with purely prospective application and not by decisions in individual cases which have retrospective force. By contrast, others argue that proprietary remedies should be more freely available than they are now;[72] as, indeed, is the case in the United States, for instance.[73]

Any judgment about the desirability or otherwise of extending the availability of equitable proprietary remedies must take account of the competing claims of unsecured (and secured[74]) creditors in bankruptcies and insolvencies because the usual reason for imposing such a remedy is to raise the plaintiff to the status of a secured creditor. Some judgment needs to be made, in particular categories of case, about the relative merits of the claims of the person seeking to establish a proprietary claim over assets in the hands of the bankrupt person or insolvent company and that person or company's other creditors. It can be argued that, in the absence of a wide-ranging system for the registration of interests in personal (as opposed to real) property, proprietary remedies in aid of rights which are often 'invisible' in commercial terms are an undue impediment to the profitable pursuit of commerce[75] especially if liability for interference with equitable interests can arise out of merely negligent failure to make inquiries.[76] On the other hand, a supplier of goods (for example) may be more willing to deal with a financially insecure business if it can protect itself in case of bankruptcy; and, in the long run, this may benefit all the creditors, both secured and unsecured, by enabling the company to trade itself into prosperity.[77]

Proprietary remedies are normally used to vindicate equitable property rights in gains made or property received by the defendant. They are not usually available in tort actions because a money judgment in a tort action gives rise to a relationship of debtor and unsecured creditor and no more, even if the claim relates to a gain made by the defendant.[78] As we have seen, however, there is one context in which proprietary remedies may be available in aid of tort claims as such, namely in Admiralty where a plaintiff may be given proprietary rights over a ship (etc).[79] In this context, a proprietary remedy may relate to loss suffered by the plaintiff as opposed to gain made by the

---

[70] See esp. R. M. Goode in E. McKendrick (ed.), *Commercial Aspects of Trusts and Fiduciary Obligations* (Oxford, 1992), ch. 7.
[71] R. M. Goode in A. Burrows (ed.), *Essays on the Law of Restitution* (Oxford, 1991), ch. 9.
[72] e.g. Goff and Jones, 93–102.   [73] See Goode (1976) 92 *LQR* 528, 560–3.
[74] e.g. *In re Goldcorp Exchange Ltd* [1994] 3 WLR 199, 221–2.
[75] Goode (1976) 92 *LQR* 528, 566–7; M. Lawson [1989] *JBL* 287.
[76] R. P. Austin (1986) 6 *OJLS* 444, 452–3.   [77] *Ibid.* 455.
[78] Cf. *Halifax Building Society* v. *Thomas*, unreported, 29 June 1995.
[79] See 279 above.

defendant. The function of such a proprietary remedy is to give P security for the payment of the judgment debt; it does not involve any claim by P to ownership of the asset(s) to which the remedy applies. The use of proprietary remedies in order to provide security for the payment of judgment debts may be thought even more objectionable than their use in support of non-property claims in respect of gains made. There is room for debate about whether the considerations which support their use in the admiralty context adequately justify it; and also whether those considerations are only applicable to actions in Admiralty.

Excursus on Tracing   Because an equitable proprietary remedy vindicates a claim of equitable title to property in the defendant's hands, such a remedy will be available (whether against a trustee or a third party) only if the property to which P claims to be entitled in equity can be 'traced' into property in D's hands.[80] Tracing is most important and most difficult where claimed property has passed through several hands before getting to D. Burrows defines tracing as 'the technique by which a person follows his property' either *in specie* or into other property for which it is substituted.[81] Birks, on the other hand, defines tracing as 'the exercise of identification by which the law decides whether and where value is located at any one moment'.[82] Birks' definition is wider than Burrows': Birks says that 'if money or some other valuable thing is exchanged for another thing or contributes to the purchase of another thing, it is plainly only by means of a fiction that we speak of tracing the first asset into the second'.[83] What we are actually doing, says Birks, is pinpointing the present location of the value of the original asset. Nevertheless, the imagery of tracing, on either definition, is of searching for and identifying something, or the product or value of something belonging to the plaintiff.

Although proprietary remedies are not available to vindicate common law property rights, the ability to trace property or its product or proceeds has some relevance at common law. In relation to chattels, tracing presents difficulties only when they are mixed with other chattels or their physical form is altered; and the common law developed (not entirely satisfactory) rules to deal with these situations.[84] Concerning money, suppose that X converts P's property (for example, by stealing it) and then sells it Y. Instead of suing Y in conversion for return of the property or for damages representing its value, P may (subject to any available defences) sue X to recover the pro-

---

[80] See generally Birks [1993] *LMCLQ* 218, 229–36. The equitable tracing rules differ according to whether the recipient was innocent or not: Harpum in P. Birks (ed.), *Frontiers of Liability, Volume 1* (Oxford, 1994), 18–19. A form of tracing is also relevant to personal liability for (the value of) property received in breach of trust in that the beneficiary must prove that the property received by D was trust property.

[81] A. Burrows, *The Law of Restitution* (London, 1993), 57.

[82] P. Birks, *Restitution—The Future* (Sydney, 1992), 111.

[83] *Ibid*. 112.   [84] See 42, n. 128 above.

ceeds of the sale in a common law personal action for 'money had and received'.[85] Suppose, further, that X transfers the proceeds of the sale to Z. P may sue Z at common law to recover the proceeds (once again, subject to defences, notably change of position and purchase for value without notice). It is a precondition of the success of such claims that P's property can be traced into the amount received by D.[86] The standard view is that the common law rules (unlike the equitable rules) do not allow money to be traced into a mixed fund.[87] Given the fusion of law and equity in the nineteenth century, it seems anachronistic that there should be two sets of tracing rules. The rules of tracing lay down the circumstances in which what P claims from D can be identified as, or as the proceeds of, property to which P has a good claim either in law or equity. There seems no good reason why these rules of identification should differ according to whether P's interest in the property is an equitable or a common law one.[88]

Liability for Receipt of Trust Property

A trustee who misappropriates trust property is, of course, strictly liable to account for its value whether or not the property is still in the trustee's hands. Such personal liability is analogous to common law liability to pay damages representing the value of converted property. As an alternative to such liability to account, a trustee who still has the property may, in appropriate circumstances, be ordered to restore it to the trust.[89] This remedy (which is also personal) is analogous to an order for the return of converted property. In cases where the misappropriated trust property or its proceeds are still in the trustee's hands, some form of proprietary remedy may be available.

A third party who 'knowingly' receives trust property in breach of trust may be liable to account for its value, or may be ordered to restore it. It is

[85] Goode, 70–1, 420–1; (1976) 92 *LQR* 360, 368–70, 375; Burrows (1983) 99 *LQR* 217, 236–7. If equitable title to the proceeds resides in P and tracing is possible, P may be able to claim an equitable proprietary remedy—for intance, if a thief steals goods and then sells them, the legal title in the proceeds will normally be in the thief but the equitable title will be in the true owner: Goode (1976) 92 *LQR* 528, 532 n. 21.

[86] The leading case is *Lipkin Gorman* v. *Karpnale Ltd* [1991] 2 AC 548. For cogent criticism of this requirement see S. Fennell (1994) 57 *MLR* 38, 42–6. There is a distinction between the claim, 'You have (received) (the proceeds of) my property' and the claim, 'You are richer because I am poorer'. Tracing is relevant to the first type of claim but not the second, which presupposes only a causal connection between your enrichment and my impoverishment. The claims under discussion here are of the second type because the proceeds of the sale of converted property belong at law to the seller, not the owner of the converted property.

[87] *Agip (Africa) Ltd* v. *Jackson* [1991] Ch. 547. This rule is particularly important in relation to money deposited in a bank account. Indeed, there is a view that merely depositing money in a bank account makes common law tracing impossible. However, both these propositions have been challenged; but because common law tracing is rarely used, the law is in an uncertain state. See generally F. O. B. Babafemi (1971) 34 *MLR* 12; Goode (1976) 92 *LQR* 359, 376–396; S. Khurshid and P. Matthews (1979) 95 *LQR* 79; Hanbury and Maudsley, 643–6; Goff and Jones, 68–93; Birks, 359–60.

[88] But they may differ according to the nature of the property in question, e.g. chattels or money.

[89] Or the court may declare that it is trust property.

unclear whether 'knowingly' means 'intentionally or recklessly' or 'negligently'.[90] What seems to be accepted is that in general personal liability for receipt of trust property depends on fault of some sort.[91] By contrast, common law liability (in conversion) for receipt of chattels is basically strict, and common law (restitutionary) liability for receipt of money is often strict (most commonly in cases where the money was paid by mistake or in ignorance). The strictness of common law restitutionary liability is softened by the defences of *bona fide* purchase for value without notice[92] and change of position.[93] The first of these defences is not generally available in answer to a claim for conversion, although there are a few exceptions to the rule *nemo dat quod non habet* in favour of *bona fide* purchasers without notice.[94] The general unavailability of the defence is explicable in terms of the function of legal property rights: full maintenance of the distinction between what is yours and what is mine requires that the general rule be strict liability for appropriation. It is for this reason, too, that contributory negligence is not available as a defence to a claim in conversion[95] and that the owner of chattels has no legal obligation to protect them by registration, for example.[96] Change of position cannot be pleaded by a 'wrongdoer',[97] and this term probably includes a converter of another's property. Anyway, change of position is said to be a defence to a claim in restitution, which (technically, at least)[98] a claim in conversion is not. Nor is the defence available to a person who changes position 'in bad faith'. A person knowingly involved in a breach of trust clearly could not rely on the defence.

How are we to explain the fact that third-party equitable liability for receipt of property is essentially fault-based whereas common law liability for receipt is basically strict? Three reasons may be suggested: first, the common law rule of strict liability was developed in non-commercial contexts and in circumstances where the facts about ownership of the most important forms of personal property were usually quite easily ascertainable. Secondly, the equitable remedy of account is more onerous than tortious damages, and this is compensated for by the less strict standard of liability in equity. Thirdly,

---

[90] It is unclear what the impact will be in this context of the decision in *Royal Brunei Airlines* v. *Tan*, [1995] 3 WLR 64.

[91] There are a couple of exceptional instances of liability for innocent receipt of trust property. These are of uncertain scope, but on the basis of them Birks argues (controversially) that personal liability for receipt should be (and is) strict: [1989] *LMCLQ* 296 and in *Frontiers of Liability, Volume 1*; cf. A. Burrows (1990) 106 *LQR* 20 and Harpum in *Frontiers of Liability, Volume 1*, 21–4. If Birks is right, then the defences of *bona fide* purchase for value without notice and change of position will assume great importance in this context.

[92] The meaning of this term at common law is shrouded in obscurity. See Goode, 406, n. 85; Goff and Jones, 761–2; A. Bell, *Modern Law of Personal Property in England and Ireland* (London, 1989), 461–2.

[93] The latter was recognized in *Lipkin Gorman* v. *Karpnale Ltd* [1991] 2 AC 548. See generally A. Burrows, *The Law of Restitution* (London, 1993), 421–31.

[94] See generally Goode, 393ff.   [95] See 31, n. 55 above.   [96] See 31 above.

[97] *Lipkin Gorman* v. *Karpnale Ltd* [1991] 2 AC 548, 580 *per* Lord Goff.

[98] But see further 296 below.

strict liability is necessary to preserve the integrity of legal property rights; by contrast, because equitable property rights are primarily designed to enforce standards of honesty and probity in the management of property, fault seems the appropriate basic standard of liability.

A third party who receives trust property in breach of trust may also be subject to a proprietary remedy provided the property or its proceeds are still in the third party's hands, and provided the third party was not a *bona fide* purchaser for value without notice. An 'innocent volunteer' (that is, a person who receives property *bona fide* and without notice of P's interest but who does not give value for it) may be able to plead change of position. By virtue of the fact that in equity a person can have notice of P's interest even without deliberately or recklessly ignoring it,[99] the standard of liability in this context is stricter than in relation to liability to account for property received. This is best explained as an outworking of the property rights of the beneficiary: if D has P's property D should, as a general rule, give it up. By contrast, if the issue is whether D should account, considerations of fault are more compelling.

Equity and the Protection of Economic Interests

Although the law of tort does not protect equitable property interests, the converse is not true: equity does give important protection to legal property interests and to other economic interests with which the law of tort is concerned. There are two forms of such equitable protection which deserve mention.

Equitable Remedies

First, equitable remedies are often available in aid of legal rights and interests. We have seen that injunctions and accounts of profits are available in intellectual property cases; injunctions are available in trespass and nuisance actions and in actions for breach of statutory duty, interference with contract, defamation, and so on. However, since the fusion of the courts of law and equity in the nineteenth century, the equitable nature of these remedies has been of little practical significance apart from the fact that they are discretionary.

---

[99] Harpum in *Frontiers of Liability, Volume 1*, 18–19; M. Bryan (1993) 109 *LQR* 368. On this basis, a person could have notice but yet act *bona fide*; but a person who acts recklessly or intentionally ignoring P's interest cannot be *bona fide*. S. Fennell (1994) 57 *MLR* 38, 55 suggests that '*bona fide*' should be understood to mean 'not in accordance with accepted standards of conduct'.

Fiduciary Relationships

Secondly, where parties are in what is called a 'fiduciary relationship', equity is prepared to provide remedies for abuse of the relationship.[100] The relationship between trustee and beneficiary is a fiduciary one, but it is special in that the fiduciary (the trustee) holds the legal title in property which, in equity, belongs to the beneficiary. Other fiduciary relationships do not involve split ownership of property. The list of fiduciary relationships, like the list of relationships which can give rise to a duty of care in tort, is not closed. Furthermore, the same relationship may give rise both to a fiduciary duty in equity and to a duty of care in tort or a contractual duty; the relationships of solicitor and client, and banker and customer[101] are examples. The main advantage to a plaintiff in a defendant being under a fiduciary duty is that a fiduciary is liable to account for profits made by exploiting his or her position as fiduciary; whereas liability for profits made by breach of duty is rarely imposed in contract or tort. More importantly, a fiduciary who makes a gain[102] as a result of a breach of fiduciary duty will usually be held to be a constructive trustee of that gain and subject to a proprietary remedy. Indeed, it is sometimes suggested that the fiduciary duty concept is merely a tool used by courts to justify awarding a proprietary remedy. So, for example, whereas a person who makes a profit from unauthorized disclosure of confidential information will normally be liable only to account personally for that gain, if the person is held also to have been in a fiduciary relationship with the plaintiff the latter will be able to claim a proprietary remedy. The nature of the fiduciary's liability for gains was examined earlier.[103]

Courts in Commonwealth countries have recently revived (or developed) the remedy of 'equitable compensation' for loss inflicted by breach of fiduciary duty. This remedy is seen as analogous to the liability of trustees (etc.) to make good losses suffered by the trust.[104] The precise contours of the remedy are unclear,[105] but it is perceived in various ways to be more extensive than common law damages. This makes it all the more important that courts develop a coherent and acceptable theory about when a fiduciary duty can be superimposed on a duty in contract or tort.[106] One view is that a fiduciary as such can owe no common law duty of care to the protected party;[107] but there are recent dicta of Lord Browne-Wilkinson to contrary

---

[100] J. C. Shepherd (1981) 97 *LQR* 51; R. Flannigan (1989) 9 *OJLS* 285; Goff and Jones, ch. 4.

[101] e.g. *Barclays Bank PLC* v. *Quincecare Ltd* [1992] 4 All ER 363.

[102] Including a bribe or secret commission: *A-G of Hong Kong* v. *Reid* [1994] 1 AC 324.

[103] See 286–7 above.   [104] See 284–6 above.   [105] J. D. Heydon (1995) 111 *LQR* 1.

[106] See generally L. Aitken (1993) 67 *ALJ* 596; J. Martin [1994] *Conv.* 13; W. M. C. Gummow in T. Youdan (ed.), *Equity, Fiduciaries and Trusts* (Toronto, 1989); *Clark Boyce* v. *Mouat* [1993] 3 NZLR 641.

[107] e.g. *Wickstead* v. *Browne* (1992) 30 NSWLR 1, 16–19 *per* Handley and Cripps JJA.

effect.[108] The competing views are underpinned by different approaches to the 'fusion' of law and equity.

Finally, it should be noted that there is authority for the existence of tort liability for inducing breach of a fiduciary duty.[109] Such liability would only arise if the defendant acted intentionally or recklessly. The status of this authority is not thrown into doubt by dicta denying the existence of tort liability for involvement in breach of trust[110] because there are no relevant equitable principles of liability dealing with secondary liability for breach of fiduciary duty.

6. LAW OF RESTITUTION

What is Restitution?

A restitutionary claim is, crudely put, a claim to some gain or benefit made or received by the defendant. Thus, claims for profits made by trustees and fiduciaries in breach of their duties (considered above) are restitutionary claims. In *Lipkin Gorman* v. *Karpnale Ltd*[111] the House of Lords accepted that restitutionary obligations are based on a general principle of unjust enrichment at the expense of another.[112] A gain made 'at the expense of' another may or may not correspond to a financial loss suffered by that other. If A pays B a sum of money, mistakenly believing that the money is owing to B, B's gain is A's loss and is, for that reason, at the expense of A. But if B makes productive use of A's property in circumstances where A would not or could not have made such use of the property, B's gain may be no loss to A, and in that case it will be at A's expense only if B acted unlawfully in using A's property because, for instance, B did not have A's consent to the use. In some circumstances, a restitutionary obligation will arise in respect of a gain only if that gain corresponds to a loss suffered by P. I shall call these 'obligations of restoration'. By contrast, sometimes a restitutionary obligation may arise in respect of gains regardless of whether they correspond to any loss suffered by the plaintiff; I shall call these 'obligations of disgorgement'. Obligations of disgorgement can only arise in relation to gains made by unlawful conduct of the recipient, whereas obligations of restoration may arise even in relation to gains which were not the result of unlawful conduct by the recipient or, indeed, of any conduct by the recipient, whether unlawful or not (as in a case of receipt of a payment made as the result of a

---

[108] *Henderson* v. *Merrett Syndicates Ltd* [1993] 3 WLR 761, 799.
[109] See 75 above.   [110] See 285 above.   [111] [1991] 2 AC 548.
[112] In addition to judge-made restitutionary obligations, there are various statutory restitutionary obligations such as to refund overpaid taxes. See also Torts (Interference with Goods) Act 1977, s. 7(4).

mistaken belief on the part of the payor, not induced by any conduct of the recipient, that it was owing to the recipient).

Scholars disagree about the relationship between claims for restoration and property rights. At one extreme is the view that, if P's claim is based on the assertion that at the time of the receipt by D, property in the benefit received resided in P (and remained in P thereafter), then P's claim (which I referred to earlier as a 'property claim') cannot be restitutionary because the continued existence of P's property right prevents unjust enrichment.[113] At the other extreme is the view that many obligations of restoration are based on the principle that the enrichment gained by D in fact belongs to P.[114] In the middle is the view that some claims for restoration rest on an assertion that D's enrichment belongs to P but that other claims for restoration rest on an assertion that although D's enrichment belongs to D, P has a good claim to it or, more commonly, its value.[115]

This difference of opinion is implicitly underpinned by different definitions of the terms 'benefit' and 'enrichment'. Receipt of something which belongs to another may not, in terms of the law of property, be an enrichment; but in a factual sense it may be. A person who steals another's property does not thereby acquire legal title to it and may be sued in the tort of conversion for return of the property or its value; but the thief may benefit in a factual sense by having stolen the property. On one view, therefore, causes of action in conversion cannot be restitutionary, whereas on another they may be. Receipt of property to which another has title may also be a benefit when the other's title is equitable rather than legal. If one follows the logic of the view that restitutionary claims and property claims are mutually exclusive, no claim based on an assertion by P of equitable title at the time of acquisition by D (that is, no property claim) would be properly analysed as restitutionary. By contrast, a claim that property to which D acquired title at the time of receipt ought to be impressed with an equitable interest in favour of P (that is, a non-property claim) would count as restitutionary.

Is there any good reason to resist the classification of property claims as restitutionary? Two reasons may be considered. First, if property claims are treated as part of the law of restitution, some parts of the law of tort (aspects of conversion, for instance) would strictly belong to the law of restitution, not to the law of tort. This would be messy if the law of restitution is to be treated as a separate department of the law of obligations alongside the law of contract, tort, and trusts. So there is a good practical reason not to classify as restitutionary any property claim which has traditionally been subsumed under one of these other heads. Secondly, if property claims are treated

---

[113] e.g. P. Birks in *Frontiers of Liability, Volume 1*, 31–2; [1983] *CLP* 141, 143; and in Birks, 13–16.

[114] S. J. Stoljar, *The Law of Quasi-Contract*, 2nd edn. (Sydney, 1989), discussed by Burrows, *The Law of Restitution*, 3–4.

[115] Burrows (1983) 99 *LQR* 217, 233, n. 60; *The Law of Restitution*, ch. 13.

as part of the law of restitution, then the defence of change of position (which appears to be a specialty of the law of restitution as currently defined) would, in theory, be available in answer to them. It might not be thought desirable that this defence should be available in answer to a claim that D ought to restore P's property as contrasted with a claim that D ought to make recompense for a loss suffered by P which corresponds to a gain made by D. In fact this is not a great problem because it is clear that the defence of change of position is a flexible one which will not necessarily be available in answer to all restitutionary claims. So the strongest argument for excluding property claims from the law of restitution is one of classificatory neatness.

Our main concern in this book is with cases in which the recipient's gain is the result of unlawful and, in particular, tortious conduct on the recipient's part. If and to the extent that a gain made by tortious conduct at another's expense corresponds to a loss suffered by that person, it may be recoverable according to ordinary tort principles by way of an award of compensatory damages. Because losses caused by tortious conduct are remediable regardless of whether or not they correspond to a gain made by D, the existence of an obligation to compensate renders superfluous any obligation to restore. Gains made by tortious conduct which correspond to losses may also be recoverable without reference to the tortiousness of the recipient's conduct. For example, if B fraudulently induces A to pay B a sum of money in the mistaken belief that B is C, A may be able to claim the money back either by way of a claim in the tort of deceit or simply on the ground that A mistakenly made the payment to B.[116] Claims in respect of gains which correspond to losses but which are not based on the tortiousness of the defendant's conduct are sometimes called 'autonomous' restitutionary claims. If and to the extent that a gain made by tortious conduct does not correspond to a loss suffered by the plaintiff, P's claim in respect of the gain will have to be based on the recipient's tort because it is only by so basing it that P can establish that the gain was at his or her expense. Moreover, P will succeed only if the tort in question is one which can give rise to claims for disgorgement.

Two questions must be considered. First, in cases where D's gain by a tort corresponds to a loss suffered by P and P could also make an autonomous restitutionary claim for restoration of the gain, what principles govern P's choice between a tort claim for compensation and autonomous restitutionary claim for restoration?[117] Secondly, in cases where D's gain by a tort represents no loss to P, what principles determine whether P will be able to recover an amount representing D's gain?

[116] In the restitutionary claim, B's wrongdoing will be relevant to defences such as change of position.

[117] It should be noted that a choice between a tort claim and an autonomous restitutionary claim can only arise where D's gain corresponds to a loss suffered by P. Moreover, the fact that a gain which corresponds to a loss is recoverable in a particular sort of tort claim for compensation tells us nothing about whether gains which do not correspond to losses would be recoverable by way of disgorgement in that sort of tort claim.

Concurrent Claims in Tort and Restitution[118]

Concerning the first of these questions, Goff and Jones discuss three possible bars to a tort claim which may not avail against a restitutionary claim: first, the limitation period for a restitutionary claim may be longer than that for a tort claim; secondly, the conflict of laws rules determining when a tort committed abroad is actionable in England may not be the same as the rules determining when a restitutionary claim arising out of the same facts would be actionable in England; and thirdly, the ban on assignment of a cause of action in tort may not apply to a restitutionary claim.[119] If, by choosing to claim in restitution rather than in tort, the plaintiff can take advantage of some favourable rule about limitation of actions, for example, it is necessary to ask whether, in the circumstances of the case at hand, P should be allowed to do so.[120] Would the policy of the tort rule be defeated by allowing P to frame the claim as one in restitution? And is there any good reason to have two different rules? In general, I would suggest that when two different causes of action protect the same interest, there is unlikely to be any good reason why a plaintiff should be able to gain an advantage over the defendant by choosing one cause of action rather than the other.[121] On the other hand, the recent acceptance by the House of Lords in *Henderson* v. *Merrett*[122] of the principle of concurrency in relation to actions in contract and tort suggests that a plaintiff would have a free choice between a tort claim and a restitutionary claim arising on the same facts.

Restitutionary Tort Damages and Account of Profits[123]

Suppose that D, by committing a tort against P, makes a gain at P's expense which does not correspond to any loss suffered by P. Two questions arise: first, should D be required to disgorge that gain? If so, secondly, should P's

---

[118] Some restitution lawyers talk about 'alternative analysis' of claims: Burrows, *The Law of Restitution*, 377; see also J. Beatson, *The Use and Abuse of Unjust Enrichment* (Oxford, 1991), 25–8. Note that the theory underlying alternative analysis is quite different from that said to underlie waiver of tort. The idea behind waiver of tort is that if P sues for the value of a gain (which does not correspond to a loss suffered by P) made by D as a result of tortious conduct, P must sue 'in restitution', not in tort because the only proper remedial response to torts is compensation. Alternative analysis, on the contrary, is concerned with the different substantive bases on which claims can be made in respect of gains made by D which correspond to losses suffered by P. The alternatives are to claim on the basis of the wrong or of an 'autonomous' ground of restitution which does not depend on proving a wrong. The two phenomena are similar in one respect: they both concern a choice between an action based on a wrong (such as a tort) and an action 'in restitution'.

[119] Goff and Jones, 728–31.   [120] Birks, 347–51.

[121] Cf. *Universe Tankships Inc of Monrovia* v. *International Transport Workers' Federation* [1983] 1 AC 366.

[122] [1994] 3 WLR 761.

[123] J. Glover (1992) 18 *Mon. ULR* 169.

successful claim be seen as lying in restitution or in tort? The latter question seems easy to answer: since D's obligation to disgorge the gain will (and must) be based on the tort which D has committed against P, that obligation is best seen as part of the law of tort.

The former question raises more complex issues. First, it should be noted that gains may be negative (expenses saved) or positive (profits made). In some circumstances it may be appropriate to require D to disgorge net profits, taking account of expenses saved, while in others it may be appropriate to limit P's recovery to expenses saved by D even if D has also made positive gains from the tort.[124] Secondly, there are three different remedies by means of which obligations of disgorgement can be imposed: tort damages (which I shall call 'disgorgement damages'), an account of profits and exemplary damages. There are various circumstances in which disgorgement damages can be awarded in tort actions. A person who seeks an order for the possession of land may also make a claim for 'mesne profits'; that is, for an award equal to the rental value of the premises;[125] a plaintiff in a conversion or trespass action arising out of the unauthorized exploitation of P's property is entitled to an award representing the reasonable hire value of the property;[126] a person who mines and removes material from another's land is required to pay the landowner damages representing the value of the mined material or a royalty on it.[127] There is also authority for the proposition that where a landowner develops land in such a way that the development causes a nuisance to a neighbour, the amount of any gain made by the landowner from the development can be taken into account in the assessment of P's general damages.[128] On the other hand, it has been held that damages are not recoverable representing gains from wrongful interference with the right to hold a market.[129] It has also been held that a secured creditor who was induced to make the loan by fraud was not entitled to recover any surplus on the sale of the security over and above the loss suffered as a result of the tort.[130]

Gains made by the defendant, whether or not they represent losses to the plaintiff, may also be recovered in actions for infringement of statutory intellectual property rights, for passing off, and for breach of confidence. In such actions, recovery is effected by means of the remedy of account of profits.[131] This remedy, being equitable in origin and unlike common law (disgorgement) damages, is technically discretionary, thus allowing the court in individual cases to make allowance for the relative merits of the parties in ordering an account. It has often been said that the remedy requires detailed

---

[124] See further 306–7 below.   [125] See 40–1 above.   [126] See 48, 57 above.

[127] See 44–5 above. It appears that restitutionary damages are available regardless of whether the tort in question is actionable *per se*, and regardless of whether the plaintiff suffered any loss. For the significance of this see D. Friedmann (1980) 80 *Col. LR* 504, 546–9.

[128] See 86 above.

[129] *Stoke-on-Trent City Council* v. *W. & J. Wass Ltd* [1988] 1 WLR 1406.

[130] *Halifax Building Society* v. *Thomas*, n. 78 above (CA).

[131] Query whether 'profits' includes expenses saved or is limited to positive gains made.

investigation of accounts to ascertain the profits made by the defendant, whereas common law damages for financial loss can be assessed on a relatively broad brush basis.[132] But there is no sound theoretical or practical justification for this distinction between the two remedies.

The remedy of account is not available against an innocent infringer of a trade mark or a patent;[133] nor, apparently, in respect of innocent breach of confidence.[134] On the other hand, account is available against an innocent infringer of copyright.[135] There is also authority for the proposition that a plaintiff cannot be awarded both damages for loss suffered and an account of profits made by the defendant.[136] Except to the extent that D's gain corresponds to P's loss, it is hard to see the reason for this since the two remedies protect different interests. For the same reason, there could be no objection to a plaintiff recovering both compensatory and disgorgement damages.

Exemplary Damages

The third mechanism by which a defendant may be required to disgorge gains is an award of exemplary damages.[137] Such damages are, by definition, additional to damages to compensate for loss suffered as a result of a tort. An award of exemplary damages may contain an element representing gains made by tortious conduct (regardless of whether they correspond to loss suffered by P), but it may also contain an additional element designed purely to punish the defendant (that is, an element which relates neither to loss suffered nor gain made). Purely punitive damages are, in effect, a fine payable to the plaintiff rather than the State.

In the law of tort there are three grounds on which exemplary damages may be awarded; two deserve mention in the present context.[138] Such damages may be awarded, first, in relation to 'oppressive, arbitrary or unconstitutional action' by persons exercising governmental (or 'public'[139]) powers.

---

[132] Burrows, *Remedies for Torts and Breach of Contract*, 304–5.   [133] See 65, 66 above.

[134] Cf. *Peter Pan Manufacturing Corporation* v. *Corsets Silhouette Ltd* [1964] 1 WLR 96 with *Seager* v. *Copydex* [1967] 1 WLR 923.

[135] See 68 above.   [136] Burrows, 305.

[137] Cane (1993) 5 *J Env. L* 149; Salmond, 518–21; Fleming, 241–3; Harris, ch. 18; Burrows, 270–85. Exemplary damages are distinguished from aggravated damages which, in theory, compensate the plaintiff for mental suffering (non-pecuniary loss) caused by the way in which or the motive with which the tort was committed, but which in practice are very difficult to distinguish from purely punitive damages (if they are compensatory, what does it mean to say that they are 'aggravated'?).

[138] *Rookes* v. *Barnard* [1964] AC 1129; the third ground is where exemplary damages are provided for by statute.

[139] *Bradford City MC* v. *Arora* [1991] 2 QB 507. It is clear from this case and from *Jones* v. *Swansea CC* [1990] 1 WLR 54 that exercises of contractual power can be public so as to attract liability to pay exemplary damages under this head and liability for misfeasance in a public office. Why is the category limited to governmental or public functions? If abuse of power is the basis of the category, then the rationale extends beyond the exercise of such power.

For example, exemplary damages are sometimes awarded against police officers in actions for wrongful imprisonment. In this type of case exemplary damages may, but need not, represent some gain made by the tort; their chief function is to signal the court's special disapproval of the abuse of power. They will only be awarded in cases where the official acted intentionally or maliciously, knowing that the action was *ultra vires* or with a reckless disregard for its legality.

More importantly, exemplary damages may be awarded in cases where,

the defendant's conduct has been calculated to make a profit for himself which may well exceed the compensation payable to the plaintiff . . . Where a defendant with a cynical disregard for a plaintiff's rights has calculated that the money to be made out of his wrongdoing will probably exceed the damages at risk, it is necessary for the law to show that it cannot be broken with impunity. This category is not confined to moneymaking in the strict sense. It extends to cases in which the defendant is seeking to gain at the expense of the plaintiff some object—perhaps some property which he covets—which either he could not obtain at all or not obtain except at a price greater than he wants to put down. Exemplary damages can properly be awarded whenever it is necessary to teach a wrongdoer that tort does not pay.[140]

Exemplary damages in this category clearly provide a means by which a person who has made gains at the expense of another may be required to surrender those gains.[141] But the prime aim of damages under this head is punitive, not restitutionary. Such damages are only available in cases where D has been guilty of calculated conduct designed to acquire some benefit at another's expense. Furthermore, damages awarded under this head are not limited to the amount of any gain made but may be awarded even if D made no gain by the tort.[142] The award of such damages is 'at large' (that is, a matter of discretion), although the classic opinion is that such awards should be 'moderate'.[143] Because the quantum of such damages is at large, exemplary damages are a very blunt restitutionary instrument. The plaintiff need not prove the extent of any benefit derived from the tort or the extent to which it was attributable to the wrong as opposed to D's own legitimate exertions. It would be much better if a clear distinction were drawn between disgorgement damages and purely punitive damages, the former being subject to requirements of proof of quantum of gain, causal link between the tort and the gain, and that the gain was not too remote a consequence of the tort.

[140] *Rookes v. Barnard* [1964] AC 1129, 1226 *per* Lord Devlin; cf. *Cassell & Co. Ltd v. Broome* [1972] AC 1027.

[141] In Australia it has been held that where the compensatory award exceeds the gain made by the defendant from the tort, exemplary damages will not normally be awarded: *Musca v. Astle* (1988) 80 ALR 251.

[142] *Cassell v. Broome* [1972] AC 1027, 1130 *per* Lord Diplock.

[143] *Rookes v. Barnard* [1964] AC 1129, 1227–8 *per* Lord Devlin. Presumably, this principle, and also the principle that the means of the defendant and the conduct of the plaintiff are relevant to assessing the damages, do not apply to any element in the damages referable to the profit made by the defendant, but only to the purely punitive element.

Exemplary damages under the second head are most commonly awarded in libel and trespass[144] actions. Such damages may be awarded only in relation to torts for which, prior to the decision in *Rookes* v. *Barnard*,[145] it had been held that exemplary damages could be awarded.[146] This rule has no rational basis but is a crude attempt to limit the availability of exemplary damages, which are thought by many judges to be undesirable. It is difficult to consider the justifications for exemplary damages without distinguishing between their punitive and disgorgement functions. The two most commonly used arguments against punitive tort damages are, first, that the civil law does not, as compared with the criminal law, give defendants sufficient protection against the imposition of what amounts to a criminal fine; and secondly, that there is no reason why the plaintiff should benefit from an award of punitive damages.[147] The first argument could be met by imposing more stringent requirements for the award of punitive damages than for the award of compensatory damages. The second could be met by providing that punitive damages were payable to the State, not to the plaintiff. It might be argued that such a provision would give undesirable encouragement to purely vindictive plaintiffs with no financial interest in the action. However, cases in which a tort could be established in the absence of either loss to P or gain to D would be very rare; and to deal with them it could be provided in addition that punitive damages could only be awarded as an adjunct to an award of either compensatory or disgorgement damages.

When should Disgorgement Damages be Available?

Awards of tort damages may be designed for compensation, disgorgement, or punishment. Compensation has for long been seen as the prime function of tort damages, and against this background disgorgement remedies and punitive damages are seen by many as requiring special justification. But this view is not universal. Professor Jones argues that if a tortfeasor makes a gain as a result of a tort, the tortfeasor should be required to disgorge that gain because compensation of losses and disgorgement of gains are equally justifiable responses to a tort.[148] Professor Birks, on the other hand, distinguishes between torts the main purpose of which is the prevention of enrichment, for

---

[144] *Drane* v. *Evangelou* [1978] 1 WLR 455; cf. *Guppys (Bridport) Ltd* v. *Brookling and James* [1983] 269 EG 846 (nuisance). There is also some authority for awarding such damages in relation to unlawful interference with trade: *Messenger Newspaper Group Ltd* v. *National Graphical Association* [1984] IRLR 397; and inducing breach of contract: *Warner* v. *Islip* [1984] *New LJ* 763.

[145] [1964] AC 1129.

[146] *AB* v. *South West Water Services Ltd* [1993] QB 507; Cane (1993) 5 *J Env. L* 149.

[147] For answers to both arguments see P. Birks, 'Civil Wrongs: A New World', *Butterworth Lectures 1990–1* (London, 1992), 80, 87–8.

[148] G. Jones, *Restitution in Public and Private Law* (London and Bombay, 1991), 73–82.

which disgorgement remedies would be available, and other torts.[149] In his view, negligence and defamation are examples of 'anti-harm' torts, and trespass and conversion are examples of 'anti-enrichment' torts. On the other hand, Birks recognizes the disgorgement element in exemplary damages, and accepts that deterrence (which he calls 'prophylaxis') provides a rationale for a restitutionary approach to wrongful conduct. This throws doubt on his distinction because neither exemplary damages nor the potential deterrent value of the disgorgement damages are, in theory, limited to the category of anti-enrichment torts as Birks defines it.

The current law of tort allows the imposition of an obligation of disgorgement as a response either (in many cases) to the exploitation of property without consent or (in a limited number of cases) to deliberate gain-seeking. This suggests two alternative justifications for obligations of disgorgement, namely to protect highly valued interests and to deter and express disapproval of especially objectionable conduct. The difficulty with giving effect to the first of these justifications is that it requires a relative ranking of interests which may be very difficult to achieve. Are we really prepared to accept the law's ranking in which real and personal property attracts fairly precise obligations of disgorgement while reputation is protected only by the much blunter tool of exemplary damages and bodily health and safety is primarily vindicated by a tort (negligence) which attracts no obligations of disgorgement at all? How are we to determine which interests deserve the protection of obligations of disgorgement and which deserve only the protection of obligations to compensate? Approaching the matter from an interest-related perspective, is there any reason not to adopt Jones' wide principle?

Turning to the deterrence justification, we should note that English law refuses to impose liability to disgorge gains made by deliberate contract-breaking.[150] It has been argued that the possibility of an award of damages for loss of contractual expectation, together with the remedies of injunction and specific performance, provides sufficient deterrent signals to would-be contract breakers.[151] A similar argument might be made in relation to torts which can be restrained by injunction, and (query or) for which damages for gains not realized can be awarded on an opportunity cost basis. On the other hand, cases may occur of deliberate wrongdoing which produces a gain for D but inflicts no loss on P in which an injunction or order for specific

---

[149] Birks, 329; cf. G. E. Palmer, *The Law of Restitution* (Boston, 1978), i, 138: disgorgement is called for when the wrong involves interference with property the right to use which is normally acquired by purchase.

[150] *Surrey CC* v. *Bredero Homes Ltd* [1993] 1 WLR 1361; Birks (1993) 109 *LQR* 518.

[151] I. M. Jackman [1989] *CLJ* 302, 318–21. I have paraphrased Jackman's argument: he does not speak of incentives and deterrence signals, but of 'institutional harm'. Relevant harm is done to a legal institution, such as contract or property, if persons are free to take the benefits of the institution without accepting the burdens. So a party should not be allowed to take the benefits of a secure contract without accepting the burdens attendant on performing it. This notion of institutional harm is vague: how do we know how heavy a burden of liability is needed to 'redress' (Jackman's word) the harm to the institution of contract done by breach of a contract?

performance would not be appropriate because, for example, the conduct in question is complete and irreversible.[152] In such a case an award of disgorgement damages might be the only way in which the law can express disapproval of D's conduct.

There is an economic argument against remedies for disgorgement of gains resulting from breach of contract: performance of a contract is economically efficient only when the net social benefits which would accrue from performance outweigh the net social costs. If society would benefit more from breach than from performance, then provided P is compensated for losses, if any,[153] resulting from the breach,[154] D should not be discouraged from acting in an economically efficient way; and it would discourage D from so acting if D also had to disgorge the profit expected as a result of breaching the contract, for this is the very net social benefit which, in economic terms, justifies the breach. The strength of this argument depends on how much weight is put on economic efficiency as a goal of the law of contract and how much on the moral idea that promises ought to be kept no matter what the financial cost.[155] Also, it would not rule out the award of disgorgement damages in cases where the contract breaker acted from some other motive than economic efficiency, at least if the breach could not also be justified in terms of efficiency.[156]

An analogous argument may be made in relation to some torts. Perhaps the most obvious is inducing breach of contract: in economic terms, D should not be discouraged from persuading C to break a contract with P and to contract with D instead unless the net social costs of D's action outweigh its net social benefits; if they do not, then provided D compensates P for P's financial losses, if any, D should not also be stripped of the very profits which make the tort economically efficient.[157] In the United States, inducing breach of contract has been held to give rise to a right to disgorgement of the inducer's profits;[158] but in England, there is only authority for requiring a person who induces a breach of contract to disgorge a payment made by the

---

[152] e.g. *Surrey CC* v. *Bredero Homes* [1993] 1 WLR 1361.

[153] P should not be allowed to make a bad bargain good by seeking to recover D's gains, any more than P should be allowed to do so by claiming compensatory damages on the reliance rather than the loss of expectation basis: Burrows, *Remedies for Torts and Breach of Contract*, 250–4.

[154] The requirement of compensation cannot be derived from the notion of efficiency alone; some notion of fair distribution of social wealth has to be added to it. In this context, I simply adopt the distributive principles inherent in the law as it is.

[155] G. Jones (1983) 99 *LQR* 443; Friedmann (1980) 80 *Col. LR* 504, 516–26. If a contract breaker is in a fiduciary relationship with the other contracting party, then under current rules the former will usually be a constructive trustee of gains made by the breach of contract.

[156] Birks [1987] *LMCLQ* 421.

[157] Cf. Friedmann (1980) 80 *Col. LR* 504, 553–4; see also H. S. Perlman (1982) 49 *U Chi. LR* 61.

[158] *Federal Sugar Refining Co.* v. *US Sugar Equalization Board* (1920) 286 F 575; Birks points out that P sought restitution against the inducer rather than damages against the contract breaker because P had made a bad bargain: Birks, 336–7.

other contracting party to the inducer as the price for putting an end to the inducement.[159] This latter liability is unlikely to be open to the economic objection;[160] furthermore, disgorgement is justified as a deterrent to commercial blackmail. Similar reasoning would apply to the recovery of sums paid in response to intimidation.[161]

Other torts require a slightly different analysis: the 'economic interpretation' of negligence sees it as the infliction of harm in circumstances where the net social cost of the harm outweighs the 'cost' of avoiding it. In reality, conduct held to be negligent often involves a conscious choice to cut corners, to take risks in the hope that no harm will result. If harm results which could have been avoided for a sum less than the cost of the harm inflicted then the defendant will, in theory, be liable. But the damages payable will represent the cost to the plaintiff of the harm inflicted on P; this will, *ex hypothesi*, be more than the cost of avoiding the harm, but it may be less than the benefit which D received by cutting corners. In other words, by cutting corners a person might save enough to compensate people who are harmed by the cost cutting and still have more left over. Should a victim of the cost-cutting be allowed to strip the cost-cutter of any such additional gains? Cases of continuing nuisance prompt the same question: should victims of pollution be allowed to recover damages representing the polluter's gain from the wrong as well as compensation for harm inflicted on them?[162]

The relevance of this type of analysis is particularly clear in relation to defamation: the gains made from defamation by the popular press, for example, are, no doubt, very large; while the cost of avoiding liability (especially given that defamatory material is often published after conscious deliberation) would probably be quite modest. Should a defamed person be entitled to strip the defamer of profits made by the tort? The law's direct answer to this question is in the negative;[163] but indirectly it gives a qualifiedly positive

---

[159] *Universe Tankships Inc. of Monrovia* v. *International Transport Workers Federation* [1983] 1 AC 366; in this case, the gain to D was also a loss to P.

[160] Cf. R. A. Posner, *Economic Analysis of Law*, 2nd edn. (Boston, 1977), 473.

[161] Threats and commencement of litigation are sometimes used as a commercial weapon. Such action may be tortious, or it may not. If it is tortious, should a claim for restitution of profits be allowed? Perhaps not, at least between commercial competitors: such liability might represent an undue barrier to competition. *A fortiori*, if the defendant's actions were not tortious. But see Friedmann (1980) 80 *Col. LR* 504, 537–8.

[162] See *Kirk* v. *Todd* (1882) 21 Ch.D 484 in which it was held that a person who had suffered loss as a result of the discharge of waste into a stream could not bring an action in respect of gains made from the tortious conduct (the technical issue concerned survival of actions). The case is of little value because Jessel MR asserted, unconvincingly, that D appeared to have got no benefit by fouling P's stream. Cf. *Stoke-on-Trent CC* v. *W. & J. Wass Ltd* [1988] 1 WLR 1406, 1415C–E *per* Nourse LJ. See also Friedmann (1980) 80 *Col. LR* 504, 531–2, but note that his discussion is somewhat hamstrung by his (self-imposed) requirement that the plaintiff seeking restitution show interference with a property right; see also *ibid*. 554–5 (but the discussion here fails to distinguish between deterrence in the sense of loss prevention and deterrence in the sense of cost-internalization (price deterrence: see further 475 below)); see, finally *ibid*. 557.

[163] Cf.*Stoke-on-Trent CC* v. *W. & J. Wass Ltd* [1988] 1 WLR 1406, 1415E *per* Nourse LJ.

answer by allowing the award of aggravated and exemplary damages in cases of deliberate defamation.

One technical issue raised by this discussion is causation: to justify an award of disgorgement damages it would have to be shown that D's gain was causally consequential on the tort (however causation is defined). This could present great practical difficulties in many cases: how does one determine how much of the newspaper's profits derived from its defamatory contents;[164] or how much an employer saved by skimping on precautions for employees' safety? And once one gets beyond the stage of simple 'but-for' causation, value judgements also need to be made: for example, should the court limit its enquiry to the edition of the newspaper in which the offending article appeared, or should it look for longer term increases in circulation?[165] Another technical difficulty arises in cases (nuisance cases provide the obvious, but not the only, example) where D's gain is made at the expense of a large number of people: how is D's gain to be apportioned between the claimants?

A deeper underlying question of principle concerns the circumstances in which it is proper or desirable to require a defendant to disgorge gains made by wrongful conduct. For instance, would it be inconsistent with the assumptions underlying the notion of fair competition to require a person who has injured a competitor by tortious conduct not only to compensate the competitor but also to give up all the profits attributable to the wrong? Should it matter if the injured party is not a competitor of the tortfeasor (as in the case of most defamation actions against newspapers)? When should the tortfeasor's motives and state of mind be relevant?[166] For instance, is there any justification for the current state of the law under which an innocent converter may be required to pay disgorgement damages, but a defamer may be required to do so only if the defamer acted in blatant disregard of the rights of the defamed and in order to make a profit? How do we decide whether the additional incentive of liability to disgorge over liability to compensate is necessary or justified?

Assuming an award of disgorgement damages is appropriate in the case at hand, another issue concerns the proper measure of such damages. The important distinction is between expenses saved and profits made. Awarding damages representing expenses saved by using another's property, for example, seems unproblematic: the market value of the use of the property should

[164] Cf. G. Jones [1989] *CLP* 49, 60.

[165] On the general issue of 'remoteness of gain' in restitutionary claims based on tortious conduct see Birks, 351–5.

[166] Birks' first criterion for 'restitution for wrongs' is did the tortfeasor deliberately set out to enrich himself or herself? There is a further question: should it make any difference whether the tort in question is one in which deliberately setting out to inflict harm is, or is not, sufficient for liability? Birks believes (Birks, 337) that the 'intentionality required for the tort [of interference with contract] would not automatically satisfy' the test of deliberate exploitation of wrongdoing. It could be argued that such a rule would be necessary to prevent undue legal control and inhibition of competition and industrial action.

be the *prima facie* measure of damages. But where the plaintiff seeks to recover actual profits made by the defendant, difficult apportionment problems may arise: how much of the profits are attributable to D's tortious conduct and how much to D's own legitimate efforts? As a general principle, tortfeasors should only be required to disgorge profits which are properly attributable to the tort. To require them to pay more could be said to go beyond disgorgement to punishment. If we are to punish tortfeasors we should do so expressly, and not under cover of disgorgement remedies.

Moreover, there may be cases where it would be undesirable to award any more than damages for expenses saved. We might feel, for instance, that innocent wrongdoers should normally not be required to disgorge profits but only to account for expenses saved. Or consider, for example, the case of trespass into airspace by the jib of a crane being used on a construction site: to award the neighbour any more than the market value of the right to overfly would be to give unjustified weight to the neighbour's property interest; and, in economic terms, it would produce an inefficient outcome. We noted above the argument, based on economic efficiency, for not awarding disgorgement damages at all for breach of contract. The law gives greater weight to property interests than to contractual interests; but even the former must, at some point, give way to wider considerations of social good.

7. LAW OF CONTRACT

General Issues

As we have seen, particularly in Chapters 3 and 4, the relationship between tort and contract is of crucial importance in a number of contexts to the protection of economic interests by the law of tort. It is now necessary to attempt to sort out the various aspects of that relationship. At the crudest and most general level, economic interests are sometimes divided up so that compensating for physical damage to tangible property is seen as a proper function for tort law while the protection of other economic interests (including nonproprietary interests in tangible property) is seen as properly belonging to other areas of the law, particularly contract. This approach is clearest in cases involving claims arising out of physical damage to property not belonging to the claimant, and in cases involving claims based on the state of tangible property acquired by the claimant.

But this approach is deficient in a number of ways. First, it ignores the role which tort law plays in protecting interests in intangible property. Secondly, it ignores the role of tort law in protecting tangible property from interference not consisting of physical damage: we have seen that misappropriation and unauthorized exploitation of tangible property are often tortious. Thirdly, it ignores the fact that tort law provides significant protection to contractual interests, contractual expectancies and, to a considerably lesser extent, to monetary wealth. It is sometimes said that liability under principles developed from those first enunciated in *Hedley Byrne* v. *Heller*[167] constitutes an exception to a general principle of no tort liability for 'purely economic loss'. This statement must, at least, be qualified so as to apply only to liability for negligent infliction of purely economic loss: tort law is by no means averse to protecting economic interests from intentional interference. But even so qualified, the statement relegates a very important head of tort liability to undue subordination. It is true that in some contexts the courts have shown very great reluctance to award damages for negligent interference with non-proprietary economic interests, but it is inaccurate to elevate this reluctance to a general principle.

If it is accepted that the law of tort does play an important role in protecting economic interests of various sorts, we must then consider the relationship between the protection provided by tort law on the one hand and contract law on the other. In doing this, it is important to draw a distinction between cases in which the plaintiff and the defendant in a tort action were in a 'relevant contractual relationship', and cases in which they were in no such relationship (including those in which they were in no contractual relationship at all). The notion of relevance is a difficult one, but its force can be illustrated by an extreme example:[168] suppose P employs D to build an extension to P's house; one Sunday afternoon, both P and D and their families are, quite independently, out visiting relatives when D's car collides with P's car as a result of negligent driving by D. The building contract between P and D is irrelevant to D's liability in negligence for the damage to P's car. Relevance is a matter of degree: a contract may be relevant to a particular transaction or incident between two parties even though it does not deal expressly with every aspect of that transaction or incident. Contracts are often silent about many of the potential causes of dispute between the contracting parties. If so, then a court in dealing with that dispute will be confronted with the possibility (and the normative choice) of rendering the contract relevant to the dispute by implying into it a term dealing with the cause of the dispute. Where a contract between P and D makes express or implied provision about the circumstances giving rise to the tort dispute between them, the impact of the contract on the tort claim turns on the content and effectiveness of those provisions.

---

[167] [1964] AC 465.

[168] A less extreme example was given by Lloyd LJ in *National Bank of Greece SA* v. *Pinios Shipping Co. (No 1)* [1990] 1 AC 637, 651. His Lordship spoke of the tort and the contract 'lying in different fields'. See also *The Good Luck* [1990] 1 QB 818, 901F–G: if it is correct to say that the example would support concurrent actions in contract and tort, it is not extreme enough to illustrate my point; but it does suggest limits to the application of the very narrow rules for the implication of terms into contracts adopted in *The Good Luck*. For other examples see *J. Lauritzen AS* v. *Wijsmuller BV (The Super Servant Two)* [1989] 1 Lloyd's Rep. 148, 156–7 (the question of tort liability was not discussed by the CA: [1990] 1 Lloyd's Rep. 1); and *Barclays Bank PLC* v. *Khaira* [1992] 1 WLR 623, 636.

Where a contract is silent about the circumstances which have given rise to a tort claim and the court declines to imply a relevant term into the contract, or where P and D were not in any contractual relationship at all, the issue is whether the law of tort can be used to make good the lack of contractual provision. This issue will often turn on whether P could and should have protected him or her self by negotiating an appropriate contractual arrangement with D or with someone else who was in a contractual relationship with D and who could pass liability on to D. In a situation where P could not have made an appropriate contractual arrangement with D or with an appropriate third party because, for example, there was no pre-tort relationship between them, then arguments about the proper provinces of tort and contract seem out of place. But difficult questions about the proper relationship between the two bodies of law arise in cases where P was in a pre-tort relationship with D or some appropriate third party and so could, in theory at least, have secured protection by contract but did not: should P have done so?

Whether or not P and D were in a relevant contractual relationship, another matter often arises which is of great importance but which we have not so far properly addressed. In Chapter 5 we examined interests which a defendant might assert in order to gain protection from tort liability. Although it was not presented thus in that context, the interest of a defendant in gaining protection from tort liability is itself an economic interest: it is usually an interest in the preservation of monetary wealth because tort liability usually takes the form of an obligation to pay money. One of the typical ways in which a contract is relevant to a tort claim is that D seeks to use some provision of it to limit tort liability or to exclude it entirely. Where P and D were in a pre-tort contractual relationship, any exclusion or limitation of liability clause in the contract which, as a matter of interpretation, covers the tortious conduct and is legally effective can be pleaded by D against P. Much more difficult are cases in which P and D are not in a (relevant) contractual relationship. Two situations need to be distinguished: first, D might wish to plead in answer to P's claim a limitation or exclusion of liability clause contained in a contract between P and C; secondly, D might wish to plead such a clause contained in a contract between D and C. Both situations raise questions of privity of contract.

With all these issues in mind, let us now look in more detail at particular areas of the law where the relationship between tort and contract is of importance.

Parties in a Relevant Contractual Relationship

Protection of Interests under Existing Contracts

Relevant Contract Covers the Tort

Where D's conduct amounts to a breach of a term (whether express or implied) of a contract with P, the fundamental juristic question is whether 'contract' ought to be treated as the only relevant juristic category.[169] This sort of question arises not only as between contract and tort but also, for example, as between contract and equity: when, if ever, should the parties to a contract be held to be in a fiduciary relationship? A similar issue may arise, as we have seen, as between 'restitution' on the one hand and tort on the other.[170] Questions may also arise within tort about the relationship between negligence and defamation, for instance.[171] Such overlaps of different causes of action are a function of the fact that divisions in the law between contract, tort, restitution, and so on are attempts to impose a degree of order on unruly reality; inevitably, reality is only partly amenable to such discipline, and many situations bear the characteristics of more than one legal category.

Categorization questions of this sort take two different forms. In some cases, conduct uncontroversially constitutes two different legal wrongs (tortious negligence, and breach of a contractual duty of care, for example); here, the only question is whether P ought to be allowed to choose freely between one categorization or the other or whether, on the contrary, the law should formulate a priority rule. In other cases, while it may be clear that conduct falls into one juristic category it may be a matter of dispute whether it falls into another as well; and if so, which one. For example, in *Hospital Products Ltd* v. *United States Surgical Corporation*[172] the question was whether the parties to a contract were also in a fiduciary relationship; while in *Banque Keyser Ullmann SA* v. *Skandia (UK) Insurance Co. Ltd*[173] one of the many issues was whether failure to warn a corporation that a fraud was being perpetrated on it by a third party constituted a tort as well as a breach of contract. In such cases, arguments about the desirability (or otherwise) of allowing a party to choose between two possible legal categorizations of conduct can be taken into account in deciding whether the conduct in question actually falls into more than one category. Thus, in *Banque Keyser Ullmann* the Court of Appeal refused to impose tort liability for breach of the duty of utmost good faith owed by parties to an insurance contract to each other because (among other reasons) the remedy of rescission of the insurance contract and restitution of benefits transferred under it, already existed.

---

[169] Concerning the preference given to contract, see 311 below.
[170] See 298 above.   [171] *Spring* v. *Guardian Assurance PLC* [1994] 3 WLR 354.
[172] (1984) 55 ALR 417.
[173] [1990] 1 QB 665 (affirmed on other grounds: [1991] 2 AC 249).

Whichever form the categorization question takes in a particular case, the underlying issue is the same, and concerns the proper approach to concurrent liability. As a general rule, English law allows concurrent liability in contract and tort.[174] This means that if D's conduct constitutes both a tort against P and breach of a contract between P and D P may choose to sue D either in tort or in contract (or in both) in respect of that conduct. In French law, by contrast, the basic rule is *non cumul*—P may only sue in contract. In practical terms, allowing concurrent liability enables a person to choose whichever of the available causes of action will produce the more favourable result.

The argument in favour of giving this choice is simple: if the law recognizes that a particular act constitutes two legal wrongs, why should a person not be entitled to complain of either? Just as the forms of action must not be allowed to rule us from the grave, nor must causes of action or 'the forms of legal thought'.[175] The traditional argument against concurrent liability in contract and tort (which I shall refer to as the 'preference for contract argument') is that if parties are in a contractual relationship, their rights and obligations *inter se* should be determined solely by reference to that contract. This preference for contract over tort may be based on a respect for the autonomy and freedom of choice of individuals and on a view that economic relations ought to be regulated by the market operating within the framework provided by contract law rather than by government regulation or court intervention in the name of justice or fairness through the medium of tort law or other branches of the law of obligations (such as trusts or restitution). In other words, contractual obligations, much more than tortious (or other legal) obligations, are seen as being the product of the free choice of the parties. The accuracy of this view of contract law is open to question.[176]

The most important differences between tort law and contract law so far as concerns the plaintiff's choice of cause of action in cases of concurrency relate to limitation periods, and remoteness and assessment of damages. But the rules of contract law dealing with these matters are no more the product of the choice of the parties than are the corresponding rules of tort law. The fact that the parties to a contract can modify the operation of such rules does not justify a general conclusion that the unmodified application of such rules is a function of the parties' choice.

In certain respects, being able to sue in tort instead of contract offers no advantage. In the first place, it is quite clear that even if P sues in tort any tort duty owed by D to P in the circumstances of the case can be no wider or more onerous than any corresponding obligation owed to P under the contract in those circumstances.[177] Secondly, if the contract contains any term

---

[174] *Henderson v. Merrett Syndicates Ltd* [1994] 3 WLR 761.

[175] T. Hadden (1971) 87 *LQR* 240.

[176] P. S. Atiyah, *Essays on Contract* (Oxford, 1986), ch. 2; H. Collins, *The Law of Contract*, 2nd edn. (London, 1993), ch. 5.

[177] *Tai Hing Cotton Mill Ltd* v. *Liu Chong Hing Bank Ltd* [1986] AC 80, 107 *per* Lord Scarman; *Henderson v. Merrett Syndicates* [1994] 3 WLR 761, 781. Given that obligations not

which, as a matter of interpretation, is apt to restrict or exclude liability for breach of the relevant contractual obligation, it will also exclude or restrict liability in tort.[178] If any such clause is caught by the Unfair Contract Terms Act 1977, then it may not be effective to exclude liability either in contract or in tort. Thirdly, in cases of concurrent liability in contract and the tort of negligence, contributory negligence can be pleaded as a defence to both causes of action.[179]

So which features of tort liability are more favourable to plaintiffs than the corresponding features of contract liability such that a plaintiff would be encouraged to frame an action in tort rather than contract? In most cases where concurrent actions will lie the standard of liability will be the same in tort and contract; and if it is different, it is likely to be less favourable in tort than in contract.[180] The most common reason for choosing tort rather than contract is that the limitation period in tort may be more favourable than that in contract.[181] In general, so far as actions for damages are concerned (and most 'concurrent' tort actions are actions for damages),[182] the justification for different limitation rules in tort and contract is extremely slight: it is said that the limitation period in tort begins to run when damage occurs because damage is the gist of most actions in tort, but that it begins to run from the date of breach in contract because the gist of an action in contract is the breach itself. But whether in contract or tort, if there is no damage then there can be no successful action for damages. Limitation rules represent a practical compromise between conflicting interests,[183] and there seems little reason why these rules ought to be tied to theoretical differences between the source of the obligation rather than to practical considerations relating to the circumstances in which the damage was inflicted and to the type of damage. For example, if the regime established by the Latent Damage Act 1986 is a good

expressly contained in the contract can be implied into it by the court, this rule at bottom seems to mean that any alleged non-express obligations must satisfy the rules for the implication of terms into contracts, which are quite stringent. The law of tort cannot he used to fill perceived gaps in the law governing the implication of terms into contracts. This means that if a party wishes to impose an obligation which could not be justified under the rules governing the implication of terms, that party must bargain for its express inclusion in the contract.

[178] Unless the contract expressly provides otherwise—which is extremely unlikely.

[179] *Barclays Bank PLC* v. *Fairclough Building Ltd* [1994] 3 WLR 1057.

[180] For the view that the standard of care may sometimes be higher in contract than in tort see *Duchess of Argyll* v. *Beuselinck* [1972] 2 Lloyd's Rep. 172.

[181] But this is more likely to be the case in actions concerning physical damage than in actions concerning economic loss: see 134–6 above.

[182] Entirely different issues arise in respect of claims for injunctions or specific performance, whether in contract or tort; both are discretionary remedies, and the element of discretion largely overrides rigid limitation rules. Questions about the acquisition of prescriptive rights over property ought to be dealt with quite separately from questions about liability to damages because they raise issues of title which claims for damages normally do not (conversion is an exception because if D is ordered to pay or is given the option of paying damages, title in the goods passes to D on payment of the sum awarded).

[183] From D's point of view, the sooner the period expires the better; and from P's point of view, the later the better.

one, there is no sound reason why it should not apply to contract actions for negligence as well as to tort actions. The problems of latent damage are the same whichever way the action is framed.

Rules about remoteness and assessment of damages vary as between tort and contract (and within tort), but it is not possible to say that one set of rules will always and in every case be more favourable to plaintiffs rather than defendants, or vice versa. There is authority for the rule that, where the same act is both a tort and a breach of contract, the applicable rule of remoteness should be the same regardless of the cause of action pursued, and that the rule applied should be the tort rule unless the contract provides otherwise or P failed to disclose to D information relevant to assessing in advance the likely scope of D's liability.[184] As regards the principle of assessment of damages, it was argued in Chapter 3 that there is much support for the view that in cases of concurrency the measure of damages should be related to the nature of the task 'undertaken' in the contract (it may, of course, be implied by law); and since, in such cases, the contractual duty will normally be at least as onerous as that imposed by the law of tort, there is no need or justification for different principles of assessment according to the cause of action pursued.

In summary, therefore, it can be argued that the law either should, or already does, adopt a single rule to deal with each of the issues which arise in concurrent actions in tort and contract. The 'problem' of concurrency as between contract and tort turns out, on closer examination, to be a very little one. Much more serious and important questions are raised, for example, by the concurrency of a cause of action which gives a purely personal remedy and one which gives a proprietary remedy and priority in bankruptcy and insolvency.

Relevant Contract Silent about the Tort

Here we are dealing with cases in which the parties to a tort action are parties to a contract which deals with some aspects of their relationship but not with the circumstances which gave rise to the tort dispute. These are cases in which the contract does not deal expressly with the subject matter of the tort dispute and the court is not prepared to imply a relevant term into it. The law governing such cases now seems quite clear: if a person is under no

---

[184] See 145–7 above. The justification for this latter proviso is to encourage disclosure of information relevant to the pricing of the goods or services provided under the contract and to the purchase of liability insurance. In cases where there is no disparity of knowledge between the parties, it is said that the rule of remoteness in a contract action should be less generous to P than that in a tort action because P could have stipulated in the contract for a more favourable rule. This is an instance of the argument that P could and should have protected himself or herself by contract, which we will consider further below. It fails, of course, to take account of tort cases (in particular, cases of concurrent liability in contract and tort) in which the parties were in a pre-tort relationship such that in theory at least, P could have stipulated for the extent of recovery.

contractual duty, then that person can be under no tortious duty either.[185] In other words, if P cannot persuade the court to imply a term according to contractual principles, P cannot argue that a duty ought to be recognized according to tortious principles. At bottom, this rule (like the case against concurrency of tort and contract liabilities) seems to be based on the preference for contract argument.[186] In this light, the House of Lords' recent reaffirmation of concurrency is, to say the least, surprising. If a person who ought reasonably to have secured (express) contractual protection but has failed to do so should not be allowed to rely on tort law, surely a person who has secured contractual protection should not be allowed so to rely.[187]

Be that as it may, the principle which denies tort liability in the absence of contractual liability implicitly assumes that tortious principles may sometimes, in theory at least, justify the imposition of a duty in circumstances in which contractual principles would not. How might this come about? The ultimate basis of the imposition of tort duties in novel cases is social policy as encapsulated in the notions of foreseeability, proximity, justice, and reasonableness. According to traditional contract theory, there are three main grounds for implying a term into a contract:[188] that the term is necessary to give the contract business efficacy; that a reasonable person ('officious bystander') would have said that the parties must have intended such a term; and that social policy requires it. The first two tests for implying a term are identifiably different and distinct from that for deciding whether to impose a tortious duty of care in a novel case; one can imagine implied terms which these tests would not justify but which arguments of social policy could justify: the implied term to perform contractual services with reasonable care is probably an example.[189] But the third test is, to all intents and purposes, the same as the duty of care test. Both tests depend on social policy; and it is difficult to understand how arguments which would justify imposing a duty in tort on one party to another would not also justify implying a relevant term into their contract.

It would seem, therefore, that the basic rule in this area of 'no liability in tort if no liability in contract' only really makes sense if the tests for implying terms into contracts are less generous to plaintiffs than those for imposing tort duties. More particularly, if the necessity and reasonable bystander tests were the only criteria for the implication of contractual terms, then the rule that tort law could not be used to make good perceived gaps in contracts

---

[185] *Greater Nottingham Co-operative Society Ltd* v. *Cementation Piling and Foundations Ltd* [1989] QB 71 (this case illustrates one danger in the use of collateral warranties; for another see J. Cartwright [1990] *Construction LJ* 14); *National Bank of Greece SA* v. *Pinios Shipping Co. (No 1)* [1990] 1 AC 637 (reversed on a different point by the HL); *Reid* v. *Rush and Tompkins Group PLC* [1990] 1 WLR 212; *Bank of Nova Scotia* v. *Hellenic Mutual War Risks Association (Bermuda) Ltd (The Good Luck)* [1990] 1 QB 818.

[186] See 311 above.   [187] But see J. Stapleton (1995) 111 *LQR* 301, 338–9.

[188] Treitel, 185–95. Custom or trade usage is a further ground.

[189] This term existed as an implied term long before it was given statutory force by s. 13 of the Supply of Goods and Services Act 1982.

would be a logical application of the preference for contract argument. In fact the relevant law is in a very confused state. On the one hand, in *Bank of Nova Scotia* v. *Hellenic Mutual War Risks Association (Bermuda) Ltd*[190] the Court of Appeal refused to impose liability in tort, or to imply a contractual term as a matter of law, having decided that neither the business efficacy nor the bystander test justified the implication of the term. This approach might lead one to conclude that the rules about the implication of terms into contracts were in the process of being narrowed to reflect increased judicial unwillingness to restrict contractual freedom in the name of social policy, with the result that unless the implication of a term could be justified under either the business efficacy or the bystander test no term would be implied. But this conclusion is made difficult by the approach of the House of Lords in *Scally* v. *Southern Health and Social Services Board*.[191] The issue here was whether an employer was under either a duty of care in tort or an implied contractual duty to take reasonable steps to inform an employee of the details of a contractual superannuation scheme. It was held that the employer had no such duty in tort but that a term imposing such a duty should be implied into the contract of employment as a matter of law. In so holding, the House affirmed the existence of the category of 'terms implied in law' in addition to the categories of terms implied in accordance with the 'business efficacy' and 'officious bystander' tests. The test for the implication of terms as a matter of law was said to be 'necessity' not 'reasonableness'; but since the term implied by law into the contract was said not to satisfy the business efficacy test, 'necessity' clearly has a different meaning in the two contexts. This decision seems to suggest that the rules governing the implication by law of terms into contracts are more favourable to plaintiffs than duty of care rules in tort.

Scally and the *Bank of Nova Scotia* case are easily distinguishable on their facts,[192] but they do make it very difficult to work out the theoretical relationship between tort duties and implied contractual terms. On the one hand, as between contracting parties the two devices perform essentially the same function of supplementing the express terms of the contract. On the other hand, the preference for contract argument embodied in the principle of 'no tort liability if no contract liability' seems to require that terms should only be implied if they can be said in some sense to represent the unexpressed will of the parties. On this basis, if the express terms of contracts are to be supplemented in the name of social policy, this should be done honestly via the law of tort (for example), not surreptitiously by the implication of terms; and a belief that express terms should not be supplemented in the name of social policy would justify the approach of denying tort liability between contracting parties in the absence of express terms giving rise to contractual liability. What is distinctly odd is to allow a term imposing a duty on a contracting party to be implied into the contract in the name of law or social policy (as

---

[190] [1990] 1 QB 818.   [191] [1992] 1 AC 294.
[192] For a general discussion see H. Collins (1992) 55 *MLR* 556.

the House of Lords did in *Scally*) but at the same time to deny that an equivalent duty exists as a matter tort law.

The underlying problem is that the many English judges have not faced up to the fact that the law of contract is a set of rules generated by the organs of the State which parties can adopt and which (like the law of tort) they can to some extent modify by agreement between themselves.[193] There is quite a bright line between express contractual obligations and 'tortious obligations', but the line between implied contractual obligations and tortious obligations is more or less blurred. Although they rest on very different views about the proper relationship between tort and contract, both the principle of concurrency and that of 'no tort liability if no contract liability' assume a bright line between contractual and tortious obligations; and for that reason neither principle rests on very sure foundations.

The Protection of Contractual Expectancies

Here we are concerned with actions by one contracting party (P) against the other (D) based on the fact that, as a result of some conduct of D, P was led to enter a contract with D under which P's rights were not as valuable as P had expected or desired. The basic contractual remedy in this situation is avoidance (rescission) of the contract, together with restitution (*restitutio in integrum*) of property or benefits already transferred under the contract, and compensation for money paid to third parties in fulfilment of obligations under the contract. Some of the grounds on which contracts can be avoided do not, in themselves, give rise to tort liability: duress and undue influence are examples. But misrepresentation which induces a person to enter a contract may be tortious provided the representation was either fraudulent or negligent.

The fact that the remedy of rescission is available does not preclude liability in tort. Moreover, P may both rescind the contract and sue for damages in tort; and if the misrepresentation has become incorporated into the contract as a term, P may sue concurrently for damages for breach of contract and in tort (assuming that the misrepresentation is fraudulent or negligent; and subject to any effective provision in the contract excluding or restricting tort liability for misrepresentation);[194] or terminate the contract for breach (if the breach is such as to justify termination) and sue for damages in tort; or, since the enactment of section 1(a) of the Misrepresentation Act 1967, rescind the contract (for misrepresentation) and sue for damages in tort. In other words, there is complete concurrency of actions in contract and tort for misrepresentation. In New Zealand, by contrast, actions in tort in respect of misrepresentations made by contracting parties have been abolished.[195]

---

[193] Cf. *Rowlands* v. *Collow* [1992] 1 NZLR 178, 190–1.

[194] Cf. *BG Checo International Ltd* v. *British Columbia Hydro and Power Authority* (1993) 99 DLR(4th) 577.

[195] See 174, n. 156 above.

Parties not in a Contractual Relationship which 'Covers the Tort'

Where P and D were not in a pre-tort contractual relationship at all, or where their contract is not relevant to their dispute, two issues arise: first, could P have protected his or her economic interests by entering into a contract with D or with some third party, or by suing on a contract which P has with some third party;[196] and, if so, should P have done this? Secondly, if P could not have protected his or her interest contractually and or could have but is not required to have done so, ought P be allowed to make good the lack of contractual rights by suing in tort. A negative answer to this last question would mean that protection of the plaintiff's interest would fall outside the province of the law of tort.

Plaintiff has a Contract with a Third Party which 'Covers the Tort'

Where P has contractual rights against a third party (C) in respect of the subject matter of the action, a form of the concurrent liability issue arises: should P be allowed to choose between suing D in tort and C in contract? This question arises in a variety of contexts; for example, where the ultimate purchaser of goods wishes to sue some party other than the immediate supplier (such as a wholesaler or the manufacturer); where the owner of a building wishes to sue a subcontractor or a local authority rather than the main contractor with whom the owner had the building contract; where a purchaser of land wishes to sue the vendor's solicitor rather than the vendor in respect of misrepresentations;[197] where a cargo owner wishes to sue a classification society (a ship surveyor) rather than the shipowner is respect of loss of the goods;[198] where Lloyd's names wish to sue managing agents rather than member's agents.[199] In many, but not all, such cases P, C, and D are parties to a chain of sequential contracts under which D is to supply goods or services to P through the intermediation of C.

Grant v. *Australian Knitting Mills Ltd*[200] is authority for answering the question posed in the last paragraph positively in relation to economic (and other) loss consequential upon personal injury; and *D. & F. Estates Ltd* v. *Church Commissioners*[201] is authority for a positive answer in relation economic (and other) loss consequential upon physical damage to 'other property'.[202]

---

[196] At this stage it is important not to prejudge the question of whether such a contract action against a third party would be successful.

[197] *Gran Gelato Ltd* v. *Richcliff (Group) Ltd* [1992] Ch. 560; Cane (1992) 108 *LQR* 539..

[198] *Marc Rich & Co. AG* v. *Bishop Rock Marine Co. Ltd* [1995] 3 WLR 227.

[199] *Henderson* v. *Merrett Syndicates* [1994] 3 WLR 761.

[200] [1936] AC 85.   [201] [1989] AC 177.

[202] (1) But in this case itself there was no damage to 'other property'. Furthermore, I assume that P's lease gave it no right to sue the landlord in contract in respect of latent defects in the demised premises; in other words, the contract did not cover the alleged tort. (2) I am ignoring Pt. I of the Consumer Protection Act 1987 here; it is not immediately relevant.

The position in relation to purely economic loss is complicated. First, it should be noted that where P sues D for (intentional) interference with a contract between P and C, P may alternatively be able to sue C in contract if the action of C which D induced was an actionable breach of contract. This raises policy issues which are considered elsewhere and need not be examined here.[203] Our present concern is with cases in which there is no nexus of intentional inducement or disablement between D's conduct and C's breach of contract; or, in other words, where the tortiousness of D's conduct does not consist in precipitating C's breach of contract.

The reasoning in cases of this latter type operates largely at a conceptual level. There are three distinct approaches: the first looks to the relationship between P and D and asks whether it was sufficiently proximate;[204] the second looks to the nature of the plaintiff's injury (personal injury, property damage, or purely economic loss) and allocates certain types of injury (crudely, the first two of those just mentioned) to the law of tort;[205] and the third asks whether D 'assumed responsibility' to P.[206] In historical terms, the first approach is a response to the argument that there should be no liability in tort for purely economic loss because the conceptual mechanisms available in tort law are not restrictive enough to prevent the imposition of very heavy liability. The imposition of very heavy liability for personal injury is not regarded as problematic (witness mass drug and disaster litigation, for example), and liability for physical damage to property is rarely enormous in financial terms;[207] but economic interests are less deserving of protection, and so liability for interference with them ought to be limited. The first approach accepts this argument, and responds to it by inventing a strict control device of 'close proximity between the parties'. The second simply adopts the supposed historical bias of the law of tort in favour of physical interests on the basis that it is important to draw a demarcation line between contract and tort and that the distinction between physical and non-physical interests is clear and easily applied. The third approach looks for a relevant (non-contractual) transaction between the two parties as a basis for imposing tort liability for economic loss. The cases contain very little discussion of the reasons why plaintiffs forego contractual claims, and of whether the reason for wishing to sue in tort should affect the availability of such an action.

I shall mention seven relevant possible reasons why P may want to sue D

---

[203] See 124–5 above and 460 below.

[204] The leading case which adopts this approach is *Junior Books Ltd* v. *Veitchi Co. Ltd* [1983] 1 AC 520; its status is a matter of uncertainty (see Cane (1989) 52 *MLR* 200, 201–3, *Henderson* v. *Merrett Syndicates* [1994] 3 WLR 761, 790–1 and 213 above), but the approach adopted in it is of theoretical importance.

[205] The leading case adopting this approach is *D. & F. Estates Ltd* v. *Church Commissioners* [1989] AC 177.

[206] *Henderson* v. *Merrett Syndicates* [1994] 3 WLR 761.

[207] But it might be: suppose that a North Sea oil rig is sunk as a result of negligent navigation.

rather than C.[208] First, P may do so in tort rather than C in contract because some relevant rule of tort law (dealing with limitation of actions or assessment of damages for example) is, in the circumstances of the case, more advantageous to P than the corresponding rule of contract law.[209] Let us assume for the moment that the contract contains no provision dealing with the possibility of a tort action. If P were able and wanted to sue D in tort rather than contract, the principle of concurrency would allow this even if the result was that D's liability in contract would be greater than D's liability in tort. Should the rule be any different where there are two possible defendants, one potentially liable in tort and the other in contract? It is hard to see why, unless we give some juridical preference to contractual liabilities over tortious liabilities; but acceptance of the principle of concurrency seems inconsistent with doing this.

Secondly, let us change the assumption just made and suppose that P wishes to sue D in tort rather than C in contract because some provision of the contract (an exclusion or limitation of liability clause, for example) would cause P's claim to fail or P's recovery to be reduced.[210] Should P be allowed to evade a restrictive contractual provision in a contract between P and C by suing D in tort? In the first place, it should be noted that, if the exclusion clause in the contract between P and C purports to be for the benefit of D as well as C, D will be able to plead it in answer to P's claim in tort (subject to the provisions of the Unfair Contract Terms Act 1977[211] and the Unfair Terms in Consumer Contracts Regulations 1994, and provided, as a matter of interpretation, that it covers the tort). At first, D's right to plead such a clause depended on C having acted as D's agent in having the clause included in the contract with P; or, perhaps, on C being a bailee, and D a sub-bailee, of P's goods.[212] But now it seems clear that the courts will enforce such a clause simply on the basis that in the face of such a clause it would not be 'just and reasonable' to impose a duty of care in tort on D.[213]

Suppose, however, that the exclusion clause only purports to protect C. If

[208] There are others. F. M. B. Reynolds [1986] *LMCLQ* 97, 100, mentions three: D may be more amenable than C to the jurisdiction or to service out of it; D may have a ship which can be arrested (see 279 above); it may not be clear who can be sued in contract, thus making an alternative claim against D in tort prudent.

[209] In one important respect, P may sometimes be worse off suing D in tort rather than C in contract, in that C's liability in contract may be stricter than D's in tort: see N. E. Palmer and J. R. Murdoch (1983) 46 *MLR* 213, 223.

[210] Another possibility is that P could not sue C in contract because the contract is void for illegality. Whether a court would allow this fact to bar a tort action against D for negligence would probably depend on whether, in the view of the court, the policy of the relevant rule about illegality would be furthered by denying such an action.

[211] *Smith* v. *Bush* [1990] 1 AC 831.   [212] Reynolds [1986] *LMCLQ* 97, 104–7.

[213] *Norwich CC* v. *Harvey* [1989] 1 WLR 828; *Pacific Associates Ltd* v. *Baxter* [1990] 1 QB 993; *Junior Books Ltd* v. *Veitchi Co. Ltd* [1983] 1 AC 520, 546 (Lord Roskill; on the proper interpretation of this dictum, see G. H. Treitel [1986] *LMCLQ* 294, 302, n. 49 and B. Markesinis (1987) 103 *LQR* 354, 395); *Southern Water Authority* v. *Carey* [1985] 2 All ER 1077 (but see Markesinis (1987) 103 *LQR* 354, 392–5).

C and D were the same person, there could be no evasion of an effective exclusion clause; and it might be argued that unless, as a result of something said or done by D, P had some good reason to think that P would be able to recover against D even if P could not recover against C, then P should be no better off suing D in tort than suing C in contract. From D's point of view, it might be argued that, unless D said or did something which led P reasonably to think that D would answer to P without limitation if something went wrong, D should be entitled to insist that his or her legal exposure be limited to that arising out of D's dealings with C. These arguments assume, however, that there was some sort of pre-tort relationship between P and D. There was no such relationship in *Marc Rich* v. *Bishop Rock Marine*[214] in which a cargo owner sued a classification society for alleged negligence in certifying that repairs to the ship in which the cargo was being carried were seaworthy. The liability of the shipowner for loss of the cargo was limited by contract. There was no technical basis on which the benefit of that limitation could be said to extend to D and there had been no commercial contacts between P and D. Chiefly for these reasons the House of Lords held that D owed no duty of care in tort to P. Although this decision arguably makes good commercial sense, it might be thought problematic in terms of fairness and the desirability of giving classification societies incentives to take care.[215]

There is another important factor besides actual dealings between the parties, which is sometimes referred to as 'the commercial expectations of the parties'. Expectations in this context are (usually) unspoken assumptions about the way complex commercial relationships will operate in practice and, in particular, about the rights and liabilities of the parties *inter se*. The commercial relevance of such expectations is that they influence decisions about the purchase of insurance (whether it be liability insurance or loss insurance) and about the level of the prices, fees, or charges set by the various parties. It is often said that the law should attempt to fulfil and not to frustrate the 'commercial expectations of reasonable people'. This was an important strand of the reasoning of the Supreme Court of Canada in *London Drugs Ltd* v. *Kuehne & Nagel International Ltd*.[216] C contracted to warehouse P's transformer. The contract limited C's liability to $40. C's employee, D, damaged the transformer; P sued D in tort in order to evade the contractual limitation of liability. A majority of the Court[217] held that D could plead the contractual limitation in answer to P's claim.

It is important to realize, however, that the commercial expectations of the parties are a function, at least in part, of the legal rules governing their relationships with each other. Therefore, it is not possible for the law simply to

---

[214] [1995] 3 WLR 227.

[215] For further discussion see Cane [1994] *LMCLQ* 363; [1995] *LMCLQ* 000.

[216] [1992] 3 SCR 299.

[217] La Forest J thought that employees should be immune from tort liability in respect of accidents caused by them in the course of their employment.

mirror such expectations because they are in turn based on the law; the degree of accuracy depends on how clear and settled the law is and on how well the parties understand it. Furthermore, the notion of commercial expectations is not itself unproblematic. Apart from difficulties of proof, it may simply be unrealistic to think that the parties (let alone all the people involved in a particular commercial activity) share a common set of expectations. In fact, since the parties are in dispute it is quite likely that they had different expectations, even assuming that they had thought about the relevant matters at all.

Indeed, there is reason to believe that the appeal to expectations often has little empirical basis and is simply a way of legitimizing the result which the court thinks to be desirable for other reasons. For example, in *Junior Books* v. *Veitchi*[218] Lord Fraser asserted that ordinary consumers rely on retailers rather than manufacturers in respect of the quality (as opposed to the safety!) of mass-produced goods; but while it is clear that most people would complain to the retailer in the first instance about substandard goods, it would probably surprise many people to learn that this fact precluded further recourse against the manufacturer (guarantees aside). On the other hand, despite the expectations of many consumers, there may be a good argument for precluding such recourse in some cases.

More generally, the courts often seem to assume, without requiring proof, that where parties were joined by a vertical chain of sequential contracts for the supply of goods or services, the intention of all of them was that the contractual rights of each against adjacent members of the chain should constitute the sum total of their rights against members of the chain. But it is not clear that this assumption is always justified. For example, a distinction is drawn in the construction industry between nominated contractors and suppliers on the one hand and domestic contractors and suppliers on the other. The latter are engaged by the main building contractor ('the general') without reference to the client,[219] whereas the former are nominated by the client. 'The general usually has limited . . . rights to refuse to contract with the specialist chosen by the client, but otherwise does not participate in decisions about selection, terms or price'.[220] In this light, *Junior Books* v. *Veitchi*[221] (which allowed the building owner to sue a nominated subcontractor in tort) makes sense, as does the decision in *Simaan General Contracting* v. *Pilkington Glass*[222] that no action in tort lay against a nominated supplier at the suit of the general. So the scope of the tort liability of a nominated subcontractor to the owner could justifiably be held to depend, primarily at least, on the dealings between the subcontractor and the owner rather than on the contract

---

[218] [1983] 1 AC 520, 533D.
[219] And 'all decisions about the sub-contract are for the general and the sub-contractor alone': A. Williams [1987] *CLP* 233, 237.
[220] *Ibid.*
[221] [1983] 1 AC 520.
[222] [1988] QB 758.

between the subcontractor and the general, which would then govern just the subcontractor's relations with the general.

But even if there is reason to think, in a particular case, that people generally act on the assumption that their respective rights and obligations are such and such rather than so and so, and that the parties to the litigation shared this general assumption, it is still necessary to ask whether the proper role of the law is simply to give effect to such expectations. If one assumes that people tend, other things being equal, to organize their commercial affairs in a mutually advantageous and economically efficient way, and that the role of the law is to promote such mutually advantageous and economically efficient conduct, then the commercial expectations of the parties provide a suitable benchmark for the law. But to the extent that the law performs other functions and has other aims, there may be an argument for saying that it should seek to mould expectations to further those aims, rather than simply to reflect expectations formed with different aims in view. For example, the main traditional function of the law of tort is to compensate victims of faulty conduct; if, according to the law's criteria of fault, D has acted tortiously towards P, then there is *an* (although clearly not a conclusive) argument for saying that D should be liable in tort to P whether D 'expected' to be or not.

In this context it is worth noting the decision of the House of Lords in *Henderson* v. *Merrett Syndicates*[223] regarding the tort liability of Lloyd's managing agents to 'indirect Names'. The managing agents and the indirect Names were remote parties in a chain of sequential contracts, but the two groups clearly had quite different expectations about liability. Since their Lordships held in favour of the Names, they must have thought that there were good reasons to hold the agents liable. But the decision was supported by a bare assertion, which the agents no doubt vigorously rejected, that they had voluntarily undertaken responsibility to the Names. Moreover, while the House noted the need to reconcile its decision with the apparently contradictory approach in most building cases involving sequential contracts (with the awkward exception of *Junior Books* v. *Veitchi*), no convincing attempt was made to meet the need.

A third consideration relevant to the availability of tort actions against third parties is well illustrated by actions against local authorities by the owners or purchasers of defective buildings. The basis of such claims is usually that the local authority, by negligence in the exercise of some regulatory function, failed to prevent loss or damage being caused by the negligence of some other party such as a builder or architect. Local authorities present attractive targets because they rarely cease to exist (if they do, their liabilities will be assumed by some other body), and their liabilities are ultimately underwritten by public funds. Because they offer such attractive targets, there may be

---

[223] [1994] 3 WLR 761.

a temptation for plaintiffs to sue the authority alone and leave it to pursue any contribution rights it may have against the person primarily responsible for the loss. It is at least arguable that one of the reasons for the recent unwillingness of the courts to impose liability on regulatory authorities is because they think that, as between the public purse and the members of the insurance category to which the person primarily responsible belongs, the latter should normally bear such losses.[224] The logical conclusion of this approach, which has not yet been adopted, would be to say that regulatory authorities could never be liable in tort in respect of the performance of their regulatory functions unless a relevant statute expressly so provided.

Of course, it is by no means always the case that the person liable in contract is primarily responsible whereas the person liable in tort is only secondarily responsible: the reverse is true as between the manufacturer and the retailer of goods, for example.[225] But in some cases at least, judgments of relative fault may lead a court not just to apportion liability but entirely to relieve the less responsible of liability. Once again, this may be inconsistent with traditional notions of liability for faulty conduct, but it may be justified by other social goals of the law such as channelling liability to one particular faulty party.[226]

Fourthly, what should the law's attitude be if the reason why P wishes to sue D in tort rather than C in contract is that P has settled the contract claim out of court for less than the amount likely to be awarded in a tort action against D? One's immediate reaction might be to say that P should not be allowed 'two bites at the cherry'. On the other hand, if the law is prepared to allow people to make concurrent tort and contract claims against one and the same individual, it is hard to see on what basis it can object to a person making a contract claim against one person and a tort claim against the other, settling the former and pursuing the latter to judgment; provided, of course, that P does not recover in total more than the amount of the (greater) tort liability. Concurrency of causes of action does not require election: the plaintiff may sue on one or the other or both causes of action, subject only to the ban on 'double recovery'.

More difficult, perhaps, is the case, fifthly, where P sues D rather than C because P wants to preserve good relations with C and not sour them by

---

[224] In *Anns* v. *Merton LBC* [1978] AC 728 the House of Lords said that if a local authority could be held liable in tort for failure to enforce compliance by builders with building regulations, fairness dictated that builders should also be subject to tort liability for failure to comply. In *Murphy* v. *Brentwood DC* [1991] 1 AC 398 this linkage of local authorities' and builders' liability was reaffirmed in a negative form: if the builder could not be held liable in tort, fairness dictated that the local authority should not be liable in tort either. Unfortunately, neither case canvassed the desirable possibility that the builder but not the local authority should be subject to tort liability because in both cases the issue of liability or no was tied to the nature of the loss suffered by P rather than to the role of D in causing the loss.

[225] And as between the vendor and the vendor's solicitor in *Gran Gelato* v. *Richcliff (Group)* [1992] Ch. 560.

[226] See generally J. Stapleton (1995) 111 *LQR* 301.

litigation, whereas P has no such interest in keeping D on side. If this is P's only reason for suing D rather than C, it might seem flimsy. On the other hand, it could be argued that provided P has a good case against both D and C then if concurrency is acceptable in general, the fact that P's motive in taking advantage of it is collateral (in the sense of not based on any difference between the rules governing the two causes of action) is irrelevant. After all, D may well be able to claim contribution from C.

Sixthly, suppose P wishes to sue D in tort because C cannot be identified or traced. There is a dictum in *Lambert* v. *Lewis*[227] which supports a claim in such circumstances. This possibility appears, on reflection, to be a variant of the last: P chooses tort for a reason other than any feature of tort or contract liability as such. But this case is stronger than the last because here, if P cannot sue D, P cannot sue anyone. So, if one accepts (and, perhaps, even if one does not accept) that P should be entitled to choose tort in order not to offend C, P should be allowed to choose tort in this stronger case.[228]

Finally, we must consider the case where P sues D rather than C because C is bankrupt or insolvent. If P sued C's liquidator or trustee in bankruptcy for damages, then any award made would rank as an unsecured judgment debt; and if the trustee or liquidator were able in turn to sue D for contribution or a contractual indemnity, any damages recovered would go into the bankrupt estate to be distributed according to the ordinary rules of bankruptcy. By contrast, if P were allowed to sue D direct, P might recover more than P could ever have obtained as an unsecured creditor of C's estate. Whether this is undesirable or not depends on whether allowing P to sue D direct will give P an unfair advantage over C's other unsecured creditors. In the case where C's representative is able to claim contribution or an indemnity from D, it is not clear why C's other creditors should benefit from funds which are a part of C's estate only because D committed a tort against P.[229] If C's representative cannot claim contribution or an indemnity from D, then allowing P to sue D directly will not disadvantage C's other creditors at all. So the fact that C is bankrupt or insolvent seems no reason to refuse P the right to sue D in tort.[230] This conclusion is perhaps reinforced by the fact that if C is insured, P may be able to sue C's insurer direct under the Third Parties (Rights Against Insurers) Act 1930.[231]

But even apart from the question of the relevance of P's motivation in suing D in tort rather than C in contract, another issue arises particularly in cases where P, C, and D are parties in a chain of sequential contracts: suppose that P successfully sued C in contract for a breach caused by D's conduct, but that C could not sue D successfully in contract for an indemnity because of the presence of an exclusion clause in the contract between C and D, or because

---

[227] [1982] AC 225, 278.   [228] Cf. S. Stoljar (1959) 32 *ALJ* 307.   [229] *Ibid.*
[230] But see *Gran Gelato* v. *Richcliff* [1992] Ch. 560, 571 *per* Nicholls V-C.
[231] For a complicated variant which discusses the issues and holds that the only right of action is the liquidator's see *Macmillan* v. *A. W. Knott Becker Scott Ltd* [1990] 1 Lloyd's Rep. 98.

the contract was void for illegality, or because it had been terminated by D on account of a repudiatory breach by C, or for some other reason. Should the fact that D could not be sued successfully by C prevent P suing D? So far as an exclusion clause is concerned, in many cases, no doubt, C would gain protection by inserting an equivalent exclusion clause in the contract with P; in such a case there would seem to be a strong argument for allowing D to 'enforce' the exclusion clause against P. But if C was not so protected, P would be in a stronger position to argue against being saddled with an exclusion clause in a contract to which P was not a party, especially if P had no knowledge of the terms on which D contracted with C. This matter is discussed further below.[232]

In the case of illegality, the question whether P should be able to sue D in respect of performance of D's contract with C would, no doubt, turn on whether the court thought that the policy of the relevant statute required D to be protected from such suit. Finally, the fact that C had committed a repudiatory breach would in itself provide no reason why P should be denied recourse against D. One thing is clear: the question whether P should be able to sue D when C could not sue D cannot be answered in the abstract. Much will turn on the reason why C could not sue D.

Plaintiff has no Contract with a Third Party which 'Covers the Tort'

In cases where it is not open to P to sue anyone in contract, P is less likely to be met with an alternative remedies argument along the lines that even if P cannot sue in tort he or she will not be left remediless. If it can be argued that if P cannot sue in tort P will not be able to sue at all and that, as a result, a wrong will be left without legal redress, P is in a good position to persuade the court to hold D liable in tort.[233]

However, even a tort plaintiff who has no cause of action in contract against anyone may be met with the argument that he or she should have secured protection by contract.[234] The argument may not be as explicit as this: the court may simply say that the loss which P has suffered is not within the province of the law of tort but is properly the business of the law of contract. But both forms of the argument rest, at bottom, on the same case for preferring contract over tort which was examined in the section on concurrency. An example of use of the explicit argument is provided by *Leigh & Sillavan Ltd* v. *Aliakmon Shipping Co. Ltd (The Aliakmon)*:[235] P was the consignee of a shipment of steel coils, part of which was damaged during shipment by the negligence of the carrier. Because of a difficulty with payment,

---

[232] See 329.   [233] e.g., *White* v. *Jones* [1995] 2 WLR 187.

[234] Insurance can be seen as a form of protection by contract, and it will be considered later. Here we are concerned with contracts imposing on D duties to act, or providing for subrogation, indemnity, assignment of rights of action, and so on.

[235] [1986] AC 785.

the terms of the contract between P and the consignor were varied so that instead of property in the coils passing to P, the bill of lading was to be held by P to the seller's order and the goods resold to its account. The damaged coils had to be sold at a reduced price, and P sought to recover its loss on resale from the defendant carrier. Unfortunately for P, although property in the goods had not passed to it, the risk of their being damaged lay, as between it and the seller, on P; furthermore, and because property had not passed to P, it could not (by virtue of the wording of section 1 of the Bills of Lading Act 1855) sue the seller in contract for delivering substandard goods.[236] Furthermore, the House of Lords held that since P had no proprietary interest in the goods at the time they were damaged,[237] it could not recover in tort for economic loss resulting from the damage. Lord Brandon said:

the buyers, if properly advised, should have made it a further term of the variation [of their contract with the sellers] that the sellers should exercise [the right to sue the carriers] for their account[238] . . . or assign such right to them to exercise for themselves.[239] If either of these precautions had been taken, the law would have provided the buyers with a fair and adequate remedy for their loss.[240]

This decision has been much criticised on the basis that it is unfair that P should have had no remedy either in contract or in tort.[241] Several writers have given support to the 'transferred loss principle' enunciated by Goff LJ in the Court of Appeal:

Where [D] owes a duty of care in tort not to cause physical damage to [C's] property, and commits a breach of that duty in circumstances in which the loss of or physical damage to the property will ordinarily fall on [C] but (as is reasonably foreseeable by [D]) such loss or damage,[242] by reason of a contractual relationship between [C] and [P] falls upon [P], then [P] will be entitled, subject to the terms of any contract restrict-

---

[236] This problem would not now arise: under the Carriage of Goods by Sea Act 1992 the right to sue the carrier in contract now passes to the lawful holder of a bill of lading whether or not the holder has title to the goods.

[237] The 1992 Act has no impact on this rule.

[238] Before the 1992 Act, the seller in a situation such as that in *The Aliakmon* could have sued the carrier for damage to the goods (*The Albazero* [1977] AC 774); if the action was successful, the seller would have been accountable to the buyer for the proceeds of the action subject to a set-off for the price or any unpaid part of it. Under the 1992 Act, where the person who has suffered damage does not have the right to sue, the person with the right to sue can exercise it on behalf of the person suffering loss. The problem from P's point of view is that the person with the right to sue will often have no incentive to do so.

[239] e.g. *Kaukomarkkinat O/Y v. 'Elbe' Transport-Union GmbH (The Kelo)* [1985] 2 Lloyd's Rep. 85. The possibility of implying such terms was not considered in *The Aliakmon*.

[240] [1986] AC 785, 819.

[241] M. Clarke [1986] *CLJ* 382; B. S. Markesinis [1986] *CLJ* 384 and (1987) 103 *LQR* 354, 385–90; J. Adams and R. Brownsword [1990] *JBL* 23. The decision is supported by F. M. B. Reynolds (1993) 5 *Canterbury LR* 280, 297–8 and J. Stapleton (1995) 111 *LQR* 301, 333–4.

[242] This is elliptical: what falls upon C is not the physical damage to the property, but economic loss resulting from the physical damage.

ing [D's] liability to [C], to bring an action in tort against [D] in respect of such loss or damage to the extent that it falls upon him, [P].[243]

Six points should be made about this principle: first, read narrowly, it only applies in cases where a loss is 'transferred' from one party to another; so it would not apply in a case, such as that of the disappointed beneficiary in *White* v. *Jones*,[244] in which the loss suffered by P is different from that suffered by C, or where P suffers a loss which could never have been suffered by C. Secondly, read literally, the principle only applies to economic loss consequential upon physical damage to the tangible property of a third party. It could not, therefore, be used to justify recovery in cases such as *Ross* v. *Caunters*[245] or *Junior Books* v. *Veitchi*.[246]

Thirdly, the principle operates in cases where D owes a duty of care in tort to C, whether standing alone[247] or concurrently with a contractual duty of care. In this respect it should be contrasted with the German concepts of *Drittschadensliquidation* and 'contracts protective of third parties' which only operate where D and C are in a contractual relationship. In other respects, however, these German concepts are wider than Goff LJ's principle. Under the concept of *Drittschadensliquidation*, if D generates a loss by conduct which is a breach of a contract between D and C, but the loss falls on P because of some arrangement between P and C, P can recover damages from D for that loss. C must have expressly or impliedly assigned to P the right to sue D, but German courts are very willing to find an implied assignment. A related concept is that of the 'contract protective of third parties'. A contract may be held to protect a third party, even if it was not the aim of the contracting parties to benefit that party, in order to entitle the third party to recover damages for the injury suffered as a result of breach of the contract. The supposed advantage of such contractual techniques over allowing the injured party to sue in tort is that they make it conceptually easier to justify subjecting P to limitations of liability contained in the contract between D and C and to other features of contractual liability unfavourable to P (although they give no clear guidance about which features of contractual liability P should have to accept). But even under the contractual techniques it is necessary to define which third parties may sue; and at the end of the day, the criterion is bound to turn on the degree of knowledge which D has of P and the relationship between C and P.[248]

Fourthly, Goff LJ's principle only applies where the owner of the damaged property and the plaintiff were in a contractual relationship; the function of

---

[243] [1985] QB 350, 399; the principle was explicitly rejected by Lord Brandon in the House of Lords.

[244] [1995] 2 WLR 187.   [245] [1980] Ch. 297.   [246] [1983] 1 AC 520.

[247] So it covers the facts of *Candlewood Navigation Corporation Ltd* v. *Mitsui OSK Lines Ltd (The Mineral Transporter)* [1986] AC 1, for example.

[248] This point also applies to the rule that the measure of damages for breach of certain contracts is unrelated to the loss suffered by P as a result of the breach: see 331 below.

the principle is to plug a 'gap' in the contract between C and P (namely, the lack of a provision assigning C's rights against D to P), and to relieve P of the need to take the precautions suggested by Lord Brandon. It would not, read literally, give an action to a person who suffered loss by reason of having a contractual relationship with P (such as a subsequent purchaser of damaged goods, or a sub-time charterer of a damaged vessel).

The fifth point to note about Goff LJ's principle is that it contains the notion of reasonable foreseeability: prior to the enactment of the Carriage of Goods by Sea Act 1992 it was not uncommon for goods in shipment to be at the risk of a person who did not have any proprietary interest in them, particularly where the goods were part of a bulk shipment.[249] Because it was a common situation, it was possible to say that a carrier ought reasonably to have foreseen that P, not C, would bear any loss caused by the carrier's negligence.[250] But Lord Brandon was not prepared to accept the injection of the concept of reasonable foreseeability into this part of the law: the principle that a person with no proprietary interest in goods could not sue in tort for damage to them was, he said, an old and well-established one which provided a 'bright line' between liability and no liability. The certainty provided by clear and simple rules of liability was, his Lordship said, 'of the utmost importance, especially but by no means only, in commercial matters'.[251]

This argument contains two quite distinct elements. The first is that well-established rules ought to be left undisturbed; this is an unsatisfactory argument (which no judge would or should accept in an unqualified form)[252] because, applied across the board, it would completely stultify the common law. The second element is that certainty in the law is a good thing; if people know where they stand they can organize their commercial affairs, their contractual and insurance arrangements, in such a way as to minimize the impact of potential legal liabilities on their activities. This is undoubtedly true but, once again, cannot be accepted without qualification: the main burden of much of the criticism of *The Aliakmon* is that it unduly sacrificed justice to certainty in the circumstances of that case—Lord Brandon was too unwilling to create an exception to the general rule.[253] The strength of this criticism

---

[249] See now Carriage of Goods by Sea Act 1992, s. 5(4). See also Sale of Goods (Amendment) Act 1995.

[250] It is not clear why Goff LJ required that the transfer of the risk of loss without the transfer of property rights should be foreseeable by D. In traditional terms, foreseeability of injury to P creates a duty of care to P; whereas the transferred loss principle does not rest on a duty owed to P: P's right to recover is, according to Goff LJ's account, derived from C's right to recover. It is not unfair to D to have to compensate P even if D could not reasonably have foreseen P's existence, given that P's loss is the result of D's negligence towards C and it was foreseeable that C might suffer loss. Economic analysis seems to support this: W. Bishop and J. Sutton (1986) 15 *JLS* 347.

[251] [1986] AC 785, 817.   [252] The 1966 Practice Statement was a watershed.

[253] It is sometimes argued that bright line rules are undesirable because they may operate arbitrarily and fortuitously. But all legal rules are, in one sense and to a greater or lesser extent, arbitrary, because they are invented. The relevant questions are whether the rule deals with most cases satisfactorily and whether it can be displaced in the cases where it operates unsatisfactorily, either by agreement of the parties or by the creation of an exception by the courts.

depends on the reasonableness on the facts of the case of requiring the plaintiff to secure protection by contract; and this is a matter about which opinions can and do differ.

The sixth point to note about the 'transferred loss' principle is that it requires that D's liability to P in tort should be limited by any relevant exclusion or limitation clauses in the contract between D and C. We have already seen that, if P sues D in tort instead of C in contract, the law may limit D's liability in accordance with any exclusion clause in the contract between P and C. This is relatively unproblematic because, even if D was not aware of the exclusion clause, P certainly was; and the courts may not give D the benefit of any such clause unless it can be said that not to do so would be unfair because the clause was clearly meant to protect D as well as C,[254] and because P was in a position to adjust the contract price to take account of the fact that D, as well as C, might benefit from the clause. But where D seeks to enforce against P an exclusion clause in the contract between D and C for which P may have received no 'payment' and of which P might not even have been aware, greater problems arise.[255] In *The Aliakmon* the bill of lading between the seller and the defendant contained, by express incorporation, limitations of liability contained in the Hague Rules governing carriage of goods by sea. Lord Brandon in the House of Lords and Sir John Donaldson in the Court of Appeal took the somewhat feeble line that the provisions of the rules were so complicated that they could not be satisfactorily applied to a tort action.[256] Furthermore, in this case, P could fairly have been treated as cognizant of the provisions of the Rules, and could have taken them into account in bargaining with the seller about the price of the goods. But where P is not aware of the terms of the contract between D and C it seems harder to justify burdening P with provisions contained in that contract.

However, it might also be argued that it is unfair, even in cases where P is unaware of the terms of the contract between D and C, to deny D the benefit of such clauses[257] on the basis that D's liability was limited by the only contract to which D was a party. This argument seems especially strong in cases where D had no control over, and may not even have been aware of, the terms of the contract between P and C.[258] Goff LJ in *The Aliakmon* certainly contemplated that D's liability to P would be limited in accordance with the provisions of the contract between D and C even if P was unaware of the

---

[254] Failure to observe this proviso is one of the weaknesses in the reasoning of the Court of Appeal in *Marc Rich* v. *Bishop Rock Marine* [1994] 1 WLR 1071.

[255] Cf. *Ministry of Housing and Local Government* v. *Sharp* [1970] 2 QB 223, 243G: disclaimer attached to reply to inquiry did not bind P. Ironically, in *The Aliakmon* itself it was P who argued that the contractual exclusions should qualify its rights in tort: Treitel [1986] *LMCLQ* 294, 301–2. But normally it is the other way around, and so the text is couched as it is.

[256] See Clarke [1986] *CLJ* 382, 383–4 for a convincing rebuttal of this argument.

[257] Provided the clause in question would not be rendered ineffective by the Unfair Contract Terms Act 1977 or the Unfair Terms in Consumer Contracts Regulations 1994 if it were contained in a contract between P and D.

[258] *The Aliakmon* [1985] QB 350, 371 *per* OLiver LJ.

provisions of that contract.[259] Oliver LJ on the other hand seems to have been of the view that it would be unfair to hold P bound by exclusions of which P was not aware.[260]

In *The Pioneer Container*[261] the Privy Council held that where P is a bailor, C a bailee, and D a voluntary sub-bailee, P will be bound by terms of the sub-bailment if, but only if, P expressly or impliedly consented to them. Consent could be implied on the basis, *inter alia*, that C ostensibly had authority to sub-bail P's goods to D. This rule was said to be derived from principles of the law of bailment and not to depend on the existence of privity of contract or consideration between P and D. But it may be possible to argue that where P expressly or impliedly consents[262] to 'sub-contracting'[263] of work by C, then P should be bound by the terms of any sub-contract even if P was in fact unaware of them.[264] Where sub-contracting is standard practice, such a rule would reflect that practice.[265] This might, however, be unfair to P because P's interests in the sub-contracting may well not be the same as C's, and P may be in no position to protect itself in respect of the negotiations between C and D.[266] At all events, the difficulties involved in working out the relationship between tort liability and exclusion clauses in contracts between one of the litigants and a third party are ultimately questions of policy rather than technical issues.

The Aliakmon, then, provides an example of the courts denying liability in tort explicitly on the ground that P should have protected itself by contract. An example of the implicit form of the argument ('the plaintiff's loss is outside the province of the law of tort') is provided by *D. & F. Estates Ltd* v. *Church Commissioners*.[267] In that case a lessee of a flat sued a subcontracting plasterer in respect of faulty plasterwork. The House of Lords held that since P had suffered no physical damage to 'other property', it could not

---

[259] Cf. *White* v. *Jones* [1995] 2 WLR 187, 207 *per* Lord Goff: disappointed beneficiary/plaintiff would be bound by any exclusion clause in the contract between the solicitor/defendant and the testator even if the beneficiary was, at the time of the alleged negligence, unaware of the existence of the testator or the will.

[260] [1985] QB 350, 381–2. Oliver LJ thought that however desirable it might be for D to be liable to P subject to limitations of liability contained in his contract with C, this result could be achieved only by legislation. See also *Simaan General Contracting Co* v. *Pilkington Glass Ltd (No. 2)* [1988] QB 758, 782–3 *per* Bingham LJ; and Cane in Miller (ed.), *Comparative Product Liability* (London, 1986), 57.

[261] [1994] 3 WLR 1.

[262] Consent is obviously present where the sub-contractor was nominated by P; and by utilizing the notion of consent, one of the objections to the decision in *Junior Books* v. *Veitchi* ([1983] 1 AC 520), namely thay D might not be protected by limitations of liability in the contract with C, would be overcome. But see 321 above: the distinction between domestic and nominated sub-contractors might pull in the opposite direction.

[263] This term is here used broadly to include, e.g., the provision of goods or the entering into a contract of carriage by a seller of goods, as in *The Aliakmon*.

[264] A. Phang (1989) 9 *OJLS* 418.   [265] Treitel [1986] *LMCLQ* 294, 302–3.

[266] As in the case of employment of a domestic sub-contractor by a main building contractor: see 321 above.

[267] [1989] AC 177.

recover the cost of repairing the plasterwork or consequential economic loss. The practical effect of this decision is similar to that of *The Aliakmon*: a lessee in this situation should seek protection by avoiding the inclusion in the lease of repairing covenants extending to mere defects of quality which do not cause damage to other property, or by securing inclusion in the lease of an assignment of the lessor's right of action against building contractors and subcontractors[268] or a promise by the lessor to sue on the tenant's behalf.

The practical importance of a party injured by a breach of contract being able to require the third party to sue in its name on behalf of the injured party has been considerably increased by the recent decision of the House of Lords in the *St Martins' Property Corporation* case.[269] The basic facts of the case were that P contracted with D for the construction of buildings which D knew were likely to be occupied or purchased by a third party. When P sold the buildings to A for full value it purported to assign to A the benefit of the building contract with D; but the assignment was held ineffective because D's consent was neither sought nor given (as required by the contract between D and P). Some time after the sale the buildings were found to be defective. As it happened, P and A were both wholly-owned subsidiaries of the same parent; and when P sued D for breach of contract the House of Lords held that although P had suffered no loss as a result of the breach, P could recover damages representing the loss suffered by A as a result of the breach.[270]

The scope of the rule enunciated in the *St Martin's Property Corporation* case (that the basic measure of damages for breach of contract is not the loss suffered by P as a result of the breach but rather the difference in value between the performance as promised and the performance as rendered) is unclear. The majority rejected Lord Griffith's view that it applied to any and every contract for work, labour, or the supply of materials. It seems that the rule will apply only if D knew or ought to have foreseen that loss caused by breach of the contract might fall on a third party; in which case, it could be said that the contract was for the benefit of all parties who might acquire an interest in its subject-matter.

It is difficult to understand why the House of Lords was prepared to allow the vendor in the *St Martin's Property Corporation* case to recover damages representing the purchaser's loss when it would not have allowed the purchaser to sue the builder directly in tort to recover damages for that loss. From D's point of view, the contractual liability is potentially more onerous than tort liability would be because it may not require P to prove fault, and the quantum of damages may be greater than it would be in a tort action. Furthermore, the basis of the contractual liability is simple foreseeability and

---

[268] It is apparently common practice in Germany for contractors to assign their contractual rights against sub-contractors to the building owner: Markesinis (1987) 103 LQ 354, 359.

[269] *St Martin's Property Corporation Ltd v. Sir Robert McAlpine Ltd (sub nom Linden Gardens Ltd v. Lenesta Sludge Disposals Ltd* [1994] 1 AC 85.

[270] Such damages would be held on trust for A: *Darlington BC v. Wiltshier Northern Ltd* [1995] 1 WLR 68 *per* Dillon and Waite LJJ.

not some stricter requirement of proximity as would probably be the test in tort. The only advantage to D of the contract solution is surely undeserved: why should D's liability depend on whether the third party can persuade or force P, who has suffered no loss, to sue on its behalf? Other difficulties from the third party's point of view are that it is not clear whether D can plead defences arising out performance of the building contract for P; and whether the contract between P and D could validly prohibit P from suing on behalf of the injured party.[271]

The idea that people ought to protect their financial interests by contract also seems to underpin the rule that the time charterer of a vessel which is damaged by the tort of a third party may not recover in tort for economic loss flowing from damage to the vessel (in which the charterer has only a contractual interest). The charterer could, for example, bargain for inclusion in the charterparty of a clause providing for a reduction or cessation of the chartering charges in the event of incapacitation of the ship.[272] Again, cases such as *Yuen Kun Yeu* v. *Attorney General of Hong Kong*,[273] which refuse to impose liability on regulatory authorities for loss suffered by third parties as a result of alleged failure of regulation, may be seen as partly justified by the idea that persons with financial interests in regulated activities and institutions ought to protect those interests by securing their own financial advice rather than by relying on the regulator to protect them.

There are, however, two important difficulties with this preference for contract as a means of protecting financial interests. First, the idea that a person *should* have secured contractual protection presumably assumes that the person *could* have secured such protection. Does this assumption refer to theoretical possibility or practical possibility? Sometimes it will not have been possible for P to secure contractual protection even in theory: an example would be the inability of an intended beneficiary under a will, the existence of which the beneficiary knows nothing about, to secure contractual protection from effects of negligence by the testator's solicitor. Another example is provided by the lessee or purchaser of an already completed building: once the building is complete, it is too late for the lessee to bargain with *the builder* (although not with the lessor or vendor) for protection.

More commonly, perhaps, any barriers to contractual protection will be practical: a person may not be able to afford independent financial advice; inequality of bargaining power may make it difficult or impossible for a person to negotiate protective provisions (for example, a shortage of rented accommodation may enable landlords to impose full repairing covenants on lessees), even if the person knows of the desirability of such provisions and is in a position to pay a lawyer to draft them. Furthermore, the insertion of

---

[271] A. G. J. Berg [1994] *JBL* 129, 137–9.

[272] As, e.g., did the time-charterer in *Candlewood Navigation Corporation Ltd* v. *Mitsui OSK Lines Ltd (The Mineral Transporter)* [1986] AC 1 to the extent of about 75%.

[273] [1988] AC 175.

one-off protective provisions into standard form contracts in common commercial transactions may be difficult to negotiate and commercially undesirable.[274] In relation to the sale of real property in particular, the doctrine of *caveat emptor* reduces the protective potential of contract to an enormous extent: although in theory it can be bargained around, in practice this is not normally possible. Again, assignment of contractual rights by C to P may be forbidden by C's contract with D, at least without the D's consent.[275] Where the number of potential victims of economic loss resulting from damage to the property of a third party is large, the costs of negotiation may be quite out of proportion to the benefits to be obtained thereby.

The courts do sometimes recognize practical barriers to contractual protection. In *Smith* v. *Bush*[276] the House of Lords acknowledged that purchasers of modest houses are less likely to be able to afford an independent survey than purchasers of more expensive houses. But often when the courts require recourse to contract, they seem to assume that such practical problems can be overcome; or they ignore them entirely, presumably on the basis that they are not the courts' concern. But if such problems exist and cannot easily be overcome, the argument for bypassing the market and imposing tort liability is that much greater. On the other hand, the reluctance of the courts to consider practical barriers to contractual solutions is understandable: defining the degree of poverty, ignorance, or powerlessness needed to justify bypassing the market would be extremely difficult. One response to this difficulty may be to impose tort liability generally and to allow parties to bargain around it; the trouble with this is that the effects of market imperfections would not be eliminated but would operate at the later stage of bargaining around the liability. There is no obvious solution to this impasse so long as the courts take the view that, in relation to economic loss and except in extreme cases, it is not part of their function, but is the role of the legislature, to neutralize the effects of market imperfections.[277] If the courts were to abandon this approach they might feel able to adopt a principle such as that people should take reasonable steps to protect their financial interests by contract; or, more specifically, that persons 'dealing as consumers'[278] should not normally be expected to protect themselves by contract but that

---

[274] Markesinis (1987) 103 *LQR* 354, 386, n.92 and accompanying text.

[275] As in the *St Martin's Property Corporation* case. On the other hand, this fact does not mean that P should not have bargained with C for protection, thus giving C an incentive to sue D.

[276] [1990] 1 AC 831. Cf. *James McNaughton Paper Group Ltd* v. *Hicks Anderson & Co.* [1991] 2 QB 113.

[277] In some cases a more viable practical approach for potential plaintiffs is to bypass both bargaining with potential defendants and the tort system, and instead purchase loss insurance. This course of action has many potential advantages, but is not always easy to pursue. For example, latent damage insurance such as the plaintiff in *D. & F. Estates* [1989] AC 177 might have purchased is difficult to obtain in Britain.

[278] In the sense used in the Unfair Contract Terms Act 1977, s. 12.

other participants in the market should.[279] Some such principle could explain the results in such diverse cases as *The Aliakmon*, *Smith* v. *Bush* and *White* v. *Jones*.[280]

The second problem with the law's preference for contract is just as puzzling: the law does sometimes impose tort liability for purely economic loss even when P could reasonably have been expected to secure contractual protection. This is so in the context of liability for negligent misstatements and for the negligent performance of professional services of a financial nature (that is, services not associated with the provision of tangible property). The plaintiff in *Hedley Byrne* v. *Heller*[281] could have protected itself by contract by paying for the advice it received. Ironically, this fact was recognized by the House of Lords when it gave effect to the defendant's disclaimer of responsibility, but it did not go further and require P to pay for the advice if it wanted to be able to sue in case the advice was wrong. Nor did the House seek to justify its ruling on duty of care in terms of any practical difficulty facing plaintiff in bargaining for contractual protection; and, indeed, there was apparently no such difficulty. In other words, the imposition of tort liability in this context cannot be seen as a direct response to the shortcomings of contract as a protective device. A similar willingness to abandon the preference for contract in cases concerned with the performance of financial services is seen in the decision of the House of Lords in *Henderson* v. *Merrett Syndicates*.[282]

8. DEFENDANT'S INTEREST IN MINIMIZING LIABILITY

As we noted earlier, the defendant's interest in minimizing his or her liability in tort is an economic interest about which the law has much to say. Contract is an important means by which a potential defendant can protect that interest; and now we must look in a little more detail at ways in which contract can be used to this end.

Contract Terms and Notices

Much has already been said about the applicability of contractual exclusion clauses in tort actions. It is clear that many judges and writers consider that a party who negotiates a contractual exclusion clause ought, as a matter of general principle, to be allowed to take advantage of that clause in a tort action arising out of performance of the contract, whether brought at the suit of the other contracting party or of a third party. Furthermore, where the

---

[279] Cf. J. A. Hayes (1992) 12 *OJLS* 112.
[280] See generally J. Stapleton (1995) 111 *LQR* 301.   [281] [1964] AC 465.
[282] [1994] 3 WLR 761.

plaintiff in a tort action was in a pre-tort non-contractual relationship with the defendant, the courts have taken the view that as a matter of general principle non-contractual disclaimers of tort liability for economic loss (these are called 'notices' in the Unfair Contract Terms Act 1977 (UCTA)) should be given the effect intended by the defendant.[283]

However, the effectiveness of exclusion clauses and disclaimers[284] is limited by legislation. This is important not only because the legislation directly affects the possibility of excluding tort liability,[285] but also because of its impact on the argument that the plaintiff should have protected him- or herself by contract: if it is legally possible for D to exclude liability by contractual provision then it may not be reasonably possible for P to protect his or her interests by means of contract law. Even more indirectly, the fact that the undertakings of quality implied by statute into contracts for the sale of goods cannot be excluded as against a person dealing as a consumer makes it less important in those cases that the consumers should be given tort remedies against the producer than it is in the case of real property, in relation to which contracts of sale give almost no protection in respect of quality.

Under UCTA, exclusion clauses and disclaimers are either rendered entirely ineffective or are subjected to one of several requirements of reasonableness. Given that we are concerned solely with liability for damage other than personal injury, the only relevant case of complete ineffectiveness relates to attempts to exclude, as against a consumer, the undertakings of quality and title implied by statute into contracts for the sale and hire-purchase of goods;[286] or liability in respect of the quality of or title to goods transferred under the terms of a contract of bailment (other than a hire-purchase contract).[287] Except in the case of contracts for the sale and hire-purchase of goods,[288] the Act only applies in relation to the attempted exclusion of 'business liabilities', that is, liabilities for breach of obligations or duties arising from things done or to be done by a person in the course of a business (whether the defendant's or another's).[289] In other words, in these cases the Act is only relevant in actions against commercial defendants. Where, as will usually be the case in a tort action involving a contractual exclusion or a disclaimer, the plaintiff is suing for breach of a duty of reasonable care, the requirement of reasonableness applies regardless of whether the plaintiff was dealing as a consumer.[290]

In relation to contract terms, the basic test of reasonableness is whether the term was a fair and reasonable one to have included in the contract having regard to the circumstances which were, or ought reasonably to have been,

---

[283] This was, of course, first established in *Hedley Byrne & Co. Ltd* v. *Heller & Partners Ltd* [1964] AC 465.

[284] Note that UCTA, s. 13 gives a very extended interpretation to the phrase 'exclusion clause or notice'.

[285] e.g. *Smith* v. *Bush* [1990] 1 AC 831.   [286] UCTA, s. 6.   [287] S. 7.

[288] See further Treitel, 230.   [289] S. 1(3).   [290] S. 2(2).

known to or in contemplation of the parties when the contract was made.[291] In relation to non-contractual notices, the basic test is whether it would be fair and reasonable to allow reliance on the notice having regard to all the circumstances obtaining when the liability arose or (but for the notice) would have arisen.[292] In relation to terms in contracts under which property in goods passes, Schedule 2 to the Act specifies a number of factors to be taken into account in judging reasonableness. Although these factors strictly apply only to contracts under which property in goods passes, it is generally agreed that they are relevant, by analogy, to other types of contract as well. The factors include the bargaining positions of the parties relative to each other; whether the plaintiff could have contracted with someone else without having to accept the term in question; and whether the plaintiff knew or ought reasonably to have known of the existence and 'extent' of the term. In *Smith* v. *Bush*[293] it was held that, while it was unreasonable for a surveyor to disclaim responsibility for the accuracy of a survey report on a house at the lower price end of the housing market, such a disclaimer might not be unreasonable in relation to a report on commercial premises or an unusually expensive house: in such cases the purchaser might be expected to take independent advice in the face of such a disclaimer or to bargain around it.

Where the contract term or notice purports to restrict liability to a specified sum of money, it is also relevant to ask whether the defendant could have expected to have resources available for the purpose of meeting 'the liability',[294] and whether D could have secured protection by (liability) insurance.[295] One would expect these factors to be relevant in other cases, too. It is clear from *Photo Production Ltd* v. *Securicor Transport Ltd*[296] that in commercial cases not covered by UCTA, one of the reasons exclusion clauses will not normally be subject to challenge is that in such cases, parties are presumed usually to insure against the risks allocated to them by the terms of the contract, including any exclusion clauses. Where UCTA applies, the fact that the defendant could have insured against liability would be relevant to the reasonableness of any clause purporting to exclude (rather than just limit) that liability.[297]

It has been argued that in cases involving two commercial parties and where UCTA applies (that is, where the plaintiff did not deal as a consumer) the courts should hold clauses and notices to be unreasonable only in extreme cases, and that appeal courts should rarely reverse the decisions of trial judges on this issue.[298] The basis for this argument is that UCTA is essentially a consumer protection measure, and that where neither party deals as a consumer

---

[291] S. 11(1).   [292] S. 11(3).   [293] [1990] 1 AC 831.

[294] This term must mean the liability as it would be if the limitation did not exist.

[295] *George Mitchell (Chesterhall) Ltd* v. *Finney Lock Seeds Ltd* [1983] 2 AC 803.

[296] [1980] AC 827.

[297] See *George Mitchell (Chesterhall) Ltd* v. *Finney Lock Seeds Ltd* [1983] 1 QB 284, 307 *per* Oliver LJ (CA).

[298] J. Adams and R. Brownsword (1988) 104 *LQR* 94.

the courts should assume rough equality of bargaining power. This approach receives support from *Smith* v. *Bush*;[299] it is also consistent with the absence from English law of any general doctrine of inequality of bargaining power. The legislative definition of consumer can be used to draw a rough line between cases of equality of bargaining power and cases of inequality; and the obvious pro-consumer bias in the legislation can be used to justify a cautious approach to the invalidation of exclusion clauses and notices in other situations.

The Unfair Terms in Consumer Contracts Regulations 1994 (UTCCR) (which implement an EC Directive) may also have an impact on standard exclusion and limitation clauses in contracts between business suppliers of goods and services and consumers.[300] Under the regulations, a term which is unfair in the sense that, by virtue of being contrary to the requirement of good faith, it 'causes a significant imbalance in the parties' rights and obligations under the contract to the detriment of the consumer' is not binding on the consumer.

The common law rules of tort liability do not, on the whole, draw a distinction between 'consumers' (that is, persons acting in a personal capacity and not for commercial profit) and businesses: a consumer who commits a tort against another consumer, or even against a business, is just as liable as a business which commits a tort against another business or a consumer. It is for some such reason that the legislature had to come to the rescue of unions which organized strikes (in contemplation or furtherance of a trade dispute) by workers in breach of their contracts of employment: the unions were seen as protecting their members' personal interests against the employers' business interests. The main context in which the law of tort does distinguish between private defendants and business defendants is that of liability for negligent misstatement: as a general rule, a defendant will only be liable for statements made in the course of a business.[301] Even here, however, no distinction is drawn between the business plaintiff and the personal plaintiff.[302] In practice, of course, businesses are more likely than others to be sued for interference with economic interests because they are more likely to be insured against liability or, if they are not, to be able to meet any judgment given against them; and businesses are more likely than others to sue for interference with their economic interests because they are more likely to be able to afford the costs of litigating and to put up with the hassle it involves.

---

[299] [1990] 1 AC 831.

[300] See esp. Sch. 3, paras. 1(a), (b), and (q).

[301] *Esso Petroleum Co. Ltd* v. *Mardon* [1976] QB 801; *Howard Marine and Dredging Co. Ltd* v. *A. Ogden & Sons (Excavations) Ltd* [1978] QB 574. Contrast *Chaudhry* v. *Prabhakar* [198] 1 WLR 29; but the decision is premised on an arguably incorrect concession: *per* May LJ at 38–9.

[302] Nor is this distinction always relevant under UCTA; but only consumers can take advantage of UTCCR.

Professional Liability[303]

Statutory limitations on the effectiveness of exclusion clauses and notices are primarily directed at their use in the context of the supply of goods and services in commercial contexts. In this country (and in most others) a distinction is usually drawn between commercial services and professional services.[304] Professional groups such as lawyers and accountants have traditionally claimed special social status and freedom from governmental control on the basis that professional firms are not ordinary businesses concerned only, or at least primarily, with their own profitability; rather, it is said, they offer a service to the community the honesty and quality of which is guaranteed abstractly by the existence of a strong professional ethos of service, and concretely by codes of professional ethics enforced by self-regulatory bodies, such as discipline and complaints committees of professional governing bodies.[305]

It has usually been thought inconsistent with this ethos of service that professionals should seek to limit or exclude their legal liability for incompetent[306] work: one of the bases of the trust which has traditionally been seen as central to the relationship between professional and client is that the professional will act in the best interests of the client both in dealings with third parties and *vis-à-vis* the client personally. Because professionals claim special status on account of their special knowledge and skill, it is incumbent on them not to seek to take advantage of their clients either in exercising that skill or in seeking to avoid the consequences of failure to exercise it properly.

It is clear that this professional ethos is now breaking down. The policy of the Conservative government towards the professions since 1979 has been that they should be subject to a combination of market forces (leading, for example, to price competition) and legal regulation. But even independently of this, lawyers and accountants, especially those involved in the world of international business and high finance, have begun to see the services they offer as similar to those offered by other groups which have never claimed or been accorded the title and status of professional. A number of factors have, no doubt, contributed to this shift of perception, but two seem partiularly noteworthy in the present context. First, the change has to some extent been forced on professional groups by their commercial clients, in particular,[307] who have (probably as a result of hard economic conditions in the late 1970s

---

[303] There is much useful material in the Likierman Report on *Professional Liability* (HMSO, 1989).

[304] It is beyond the scope of this book to analyse this distinction or to examine the desirability of or justification for drawing it.

[305] See further 366 below.

[306] Liability for dishonesty cannot be excluded by contract: Treitel, 224.

[307] But by no means exclusively. The Director of the Solicitors Complaints Bureau recently said: 'We are working in the age of the empowered consumer. The public is making higher demands of its professional advisers, as it does with all service providers': *The Times*, 12 Oct.1994, 8.

and early 1980s), become much more willing to sue or to threaten to sue their professional advisors for negligence when things go wrong. Secondly, the amounts of money at stake in large financial deals has become enormous in recent years. As a result, professionals often now find themselves facing claims (sometimes very large ones) for financial loss allegedly caused by their negligence. Partly as a consequence of this, professional indemnity insurance premiums have risen dramatically in the last fifteen years or so. This has forced professionals involved in high-value deals to think much more carefully about techniques for improving and controlling the quality of the services they provide, and about ways of limiting their financial exposure when things go wrong.

Incorporation

The relevance of such developments in the present context lies in some of the responses to them by professional groups, such as lawyers and accountants.[308] First, there was pressure to allow firms of professionals to incorporate,[309] and thus to gain the advantages of limited liability. Why, it was asked, should a company whose shareholders cannot be sued personally if the company cannot meet its obligations, be able to bankrupt a self-employed professional or firm of professionals?[310] The traditional justification for the unlimited personal liability of professionals is that it is part of the price for freedom from external scrutiny and control which professionals enjoy but which companies do not. It is not clear that all professionals would welcome having their activities subjected to the accounting and other obligations which rest on companies. Furthermore, the traditional argument for limited

[308] See e.g. T. Holland [1992] *New LJ* 1129. For an economic perspective, see C. G. Veljanovski and C. J. Whelan (1983) 46 *MLR* 700, 709–11.

[309] Groups of professionals traditionally operate as partnerships, with each partner being fully liable for the debts of the others. S. 9 of the Administration of Justice Act 1985 authorizes the Council of the Law Society to make rules for the incorporation of solicitors' practices. Rules came into effect in 1992, but very few firms have taken advantage of them. Auditors also may incorporate, but few have done so. Tax disadvantages partly explain this reluctance. It was recently reported that one of the largest accountancy firms is considering incorporating its audit practice: *Financial Times*, 23 Aug. 1995. Incorporation has been more popular amongst chartered surveyors. The major attraction of incorporation is the opportunity it provides to raise capital and to improve internal management structures.

[310] Another notable instance of unlimited personal liability is that of private investors ('Names') who fund underwriting at Lloyd's. Names are equivalent to shareholders but are subject to unlimited personal liability. In recent years Names belonging to certain insurance syndicates have received large calls to meet huge claims on certain types of insurance. Much litigation has been generated. Insurance (called 'stop loss' insurance) is available to cover the liability of Names. Lloyd's operates a compensation scheme for the benefit of Names who suffer through the fraud or insolvency of their underwriting agents; but the maximum amount payable to any individual is £48,000. A special fund operated for some time to assist Names most heavily hit by the losses of the late 1980s. It will be recalled that company directors can incur personal liability for the company's trading debts incurred when the directors knew or ought to have known that the company was insolvent: see 205 above.

liability is that it encourages the taking of commercial risks which are justified in terms of the financial benefits which will accrue if things go as planned. It is no part of the business of a professional to take risks of this sort unless on the instructions of the client; in which case there would be no liability for taking the risk. Furthermore, incorporation would not shield individual professionals in the company from actions for negligence.

At all events, the logic of the argument in favour of incorporation is faulty because it only applies to corporate clients, not personal clients.[311] Moreover, given the wide-spread practice (which is compulsory in the case of some professions) of taking out liability insurance, incorporation is really only of relevance in relation to uninsured liability. In fact, if one assumes that incorporated professionals would insure at least as much of their potential liabilities as unincorporated professionals, the relevance of the incorporation proposal is further restricted to uninsurable liability. In practice, this means that it is relevant only in relation to work involving very large amounts of money, which tends to be done by large or very large firms of professionals. If one further assumes (as seems reasonable) that exposure to such uninsurable liability is unlikely to lead to improvements in the quality of the services provided by such firms, and that the more likely result is that relevant services will not be available, then it may well be in the interests of commercial clients to accept the risk of uninsurable losses themselves.

Statutory 'Caps' on Liability

Secondly, there have been calls for statutory limits (or 'caps') on liability.[312] Such proposals would shift part of the cost of professional negligence onto clients (and other claimants) who must then protect themselves, if they can, by taking out insurance (for example). It is worth recalling that here we are only discussing financial loss. The proposal is not that awards for non-pecuniary loss should be limited; indeed, except in the case of health-care professionals, compensation for such loss is of little importance in claims against professionals. In other words, in the present context proposals for limits on the quantum of liability do not raise issues about the assessment of damages for losses which are not subject to market valuation; they only raise issues about the allocation of losses on which market mechanisms can place a value.

Proposals for statutory limits on liability assume that professionals will not incorporate, and usually contemplate compulsory insurance up to the statutory limit of liability. The best thought-out proposals pitch the limit high enough to cover work done for the vast majority[313] of individual (that is, non-

---

[311] See also B. Walsh [1988] *PN* 80.

[312] Walsh [1988] *PN* 80. But the Chartered Association of Certified Accountants opposes caps: *Financial Times*, 25 Apr. 1994. See also A. Jack, *Financial Times*, 11 Oct. 1993, 12.

[313] The limit could be waived by agreement in particular cases. For the protection of clients, the limit would have to apply to each individual claim rather than to each particular act of negligence.

commercial) clients.[314] The avowed aim is to protect professionals, who are subject to unlimited personal liability, from being bankrupted by incorporated clients the members of which enjoy the protection of limited liability. In this way, the proponents of statutory caps attempt to tip the balance of fairness in favour of professionals and away from their (corporate) clients. Such proposals are also designed to restrain increases in liability insurance premiums.[315] However, since it is not clear that cases of very large liabilities (as opposed to an increased number of claims of all sizes) have made a major contribution to such increases, it is unclear whether the proposals would have this effect. Indeed, they might encourage claims within the statutory limit, and this could itself put upward pressure on premiums. Also, it is often argued that the top slices of very large liabilities are uninsurable or, at least, frequently uninsured. Furthermore, it is difficult to assess the acceptability of such proposals in the abstract without information about whether it would be any easier or cheaper for clients[316] to insure themselves.

Exclusion Clauses Again

Thirdly, it has been proposed that professional groups should make more use[317] of exclusion and limitation clauses in their contracts with their clients with a view to reducing their exposure to the burden of financial loss.[318] In relation to individual ('private') clients, the impact of UCTA and UTCCR would make such clauses of limited efficacy: the notions of 'reasonableness' in UCTA and 'good faith' in UTCCR would, no doubt, be interpreted in the light of traditional assumptions about the nature of the professional–client

---

[314] What about claimants who are not clients?

[315] According to one report, professional indemnity insurance premiums paid by auditors have increased 37·5 times since the mid-1980s: *Financial Times*, 25 Feb. 1994. According to another, the average deductible borne by the six largest auditing firms has increased from £0.4m in 1983 to £28.8m in 1993 while average cover available in excess of deductible has dropped from £120.7m to £38.5m in the same period. For these firms litigation costs as a percentage of fee income have risen from 2·6% to 8% in the decade since 1983: *Independent on Sunday*, 22 May 1994.

[316] The chance of potential third party claimants being in a position to insure against risks of which they may not even be aware, is slight.

[317] Risk-sharing arrangements between professionals and clients are by no means unknown. The Law Society takes the view that, subject to suitable safeguards, there is no objection to solicitors seeking to limit their liability by contract: Law Society's Discussion Paper, 'Multi-Disciplinary Partnerships and Allied Topics' (Apr. 1987), para. 3.1.1. But s. 60(5) of the Solicitors Act 1974 renders exclusion clauses in contentious business agreements void. Concerning the exemption of auditors from liability to the company see Companies Act 1985 ss. 310 and 727; see also A. T. Craswell (1981) 9 *ABLR* 224; D. Gwilliam [1987] *PN* 167. S. 310(3) of the 1985 Act (as substituted by Companies Act 1989, s. 137) allows companies to take out insurance to indemnify auditors from liability in certain circumstances (contrast TULRCA, s. 15). The Likierman Report on Professional Liability (HMSO, 1989) recommended that auditors should be allowed to negotiate contractual caps to their liability to the company; but an attempt to include provisions for negotiated caps in the Companies Bill 1989 failed just a week before the report was published. The report also recommended that the law of joint and several liability be reviewed.

[318] M. Gill (1987) 61 *ALJ* 552.

relationship.[319] In other cases the use of such clauses would be open to negotiation and would, no doubt, be more or less directly related to the availability of liability insurance. So, once again, the focus of attention becomes uninsurable liability for economic loss. Indeed, the whole question of the limitation of professional liability comes down to this. Compulsory liability insurance is a suitable technique for dealing with the great majority of potential claims, provided the level of cover required is realistic: say £2 million for solicitors, for example (instead of the present £1 million). Above that level, it seems reasonable to leave professionals and their clients to bargain about the allocation of the risk of economic loss resulting from professional negligence.[320] This does not seem inconsistent with traditional notions of professional service because at this financial level, the traditional picture of the professional as a servant of the community rather than a purveyor of a particular service for a stated price seems irrelevant. The relationship between a professional and a multi-national corporate client is surely quite different from the former's relationship with Average Citizen.

If it be accepted that a combination of compulsory liability insurance up to a fixed level and free market bargaining above that level is a suitable way of dealing with professional liability for financial (and other) losses, a couple of other issues need to be considered. First, there might be an argument for simply rendering exclusion clauses inoperative in relation to the compulsorily insured component of every claim;[321] this would reduce disputes about the efficacy of such clauses and save costs. Secondly, there is the problem of third-party claims. As we have seen, there are circumstances in which professionals can be liable for economic loss suffered by parties other than their clients. This liability can be disclaimed according to principles similar to those which govern the excludability of contractual liability to clients. But there may be cases in which the professional is held liable to parties who were not, in practice, amenable to a disclaimer. If disclaimers were rendered inoperative up to the compulsorily insured amount, this would not be a problem in most cases. Furthermore, the number of cases in which a professional could be held liable to third parties to whom the professional was not in a position to issue a disclaimer is perhaps so small that the problem is marginal.

9. CONCLUSION

We have seen in this Chapter that the law of tort is not an island unto itself but part of a large continent. Its borders and its relationships with its neigh-

---

[319] M. F. James [1987] *JBL* 286.

[320] The more competitive the market for professional services, the less easy will it be for professionals to secure advantageous arrangements. From their point of view, therefore, statutory caps are preferable.

[321] I assume here that the compulsory insurance scheme would not impose a limit on annual aggregate liability.

bours are complex: there is considerable cross-border trade, but the law of tort still retains many distinctive national characteristics. Some of these are no more than accidents of history which cry out for rationalization: several of the differences between torts and equitable wrongs provide a good example. Other features of tort are, however, a function of its nature; through these, tort can provide types of protection for economic interests which are distinctively different from the protections offered by other bodies of law. If we are fully to understand the present operation and future potential of tort law as a means of protecting economic interests we must pay attention to the 'geopolitics' of the region tort law inhabits as well as its domestic arrangements.

7

Methods of Resolving Tort Disputes

An important aspect of the practical impact of any body of legal rules is the way disputes are settled according to those rules. The aim of this Chapter is to examine (in a fairly theoretical way) a range of more or less formal processes for dealing with civil legal disputes in general and tort disputes in particular. Underlying the discussion in this book so far has been an assumption that adjudication by a formal, state-run court is the paradigm method for resolving legal disputes. As is well-known, however, very few legal disputes are resolved by formal court adjudication. In this Chapter we examine procedural alternatives to court adjudication. These alternatives also represent, in a sense, substantive alternatives to tort law because the substantive outcome of each of these alternatives need not and may not result from a strict application of relevant rules of tort law. On the other hand, courts which decide tort disputes are, of course, normally under an obligation to resolve the dispute according to relevant rules of tort law and only those rules.

Procedural alternatives to litigation are all designed to avoid, to a greater or lesser extent, what are usually identified as the three main evils of court adjudication, namely formality (court proceedings are often frightening and incomprehensible to the uninitiated), delay, and expense.

1. SETTLEMENT OF CLAIMS[1]

Perhaps the most important alternative to formal litigation is out-of-court settlement. Settlement is significantly different from litigation in that it involves only the parties in dispute and, perhaps, their (partisan) advisors: no independent 'outsider' is involved in assisting the parties to reach an agreement or, *ex hypothesi* in imposing a solution on them. A formal settlement out-of-court involves a written contract under which (for example) one party agrees not to pursue, or not to pursue further, legal claims asserted against the other

[1] Harris, 12–14, 342–3; O. M. Fiss (1984) 93 *Yale LJ* 1073; J. K. Lieberman and J. F. Henry (1986) 53 *U Chi. LR* 424.

party and which are the subject of the agreement; and under which the latter agrees to pay to the former a sum of money, or to take some other action, typically without admission of liability, in full and final satisfaction of the former's claims. But many disputes are, no doubt, settled informally without consulting lawyers and without the execution of formal documents. Settlement out-of-court is made attractive partly by uncertainty:[2] neither party is usually in a position to assess the strength of the other party's case fully and accurately; and even if both parties had all the information relevant to assessing the outcome of a trial of the claim, it would often not be possible to predict with absolute certainty what that outcome would be, not only because judging involves the exercise of a greater or lesser amount of personal judgement and discretion but also because the law itself is often uncertain. Such uncertainty in the law is sometimes the result of the very content of the rules (for example, the requirement of reasonable foreseeability, or the element of discretion in the decision whether or not to award an injunction), and sometimes because it is unclear what the relevant legal rules are.

The typical settlement involves compromise.[3] From the claimant's point of view, it might be worthwhile to accept something less than would be awarded by a court if the claim succeeded in full so as to be free of the uncertainty about the fate of the claim. And, of course, 'a bird in the hand is worth two in the bush': the time taken by litigation may involve the risk of financial disaster for the claimant; and if the other party knows this that party can often exploit and prolong the delays inherent in litigation. Conversely, it might be in the best interests of the party claimed against to offer more to the claimant than a court would award if the defence succeeded in full in order to be free of the claim and its attendant uncertainty, including the risk of having to bear two sets of costs greatly increased by the litigation itself.[4] Litigation is expensive of time,[5] money, and human resources, and is only worth pursuing to the

---

[2] There are several ironies here: uncertainty in the law itself tends to generate disputes. Once a dispute has arisen, this uncertainty renders settlement attractive as a way of resolving the uncertainty quickly, but also tends to make settlement more difficult because it creates room for disagreement and exploitation of the weaker by the stronger party. On the importance of designing legal rules so as to facilitate settlements see D. R. Harris and C. G. Veljanovski (1983) 5 *Law & Policy Q* 97.

[3] But see S. Wheeler, *Reservation of Title Clauses* (Oxford, 1991), 100.

[4] Settlement is, thus, a contractual technique by which a party can minimize total financial exposure to litigation: the amount the party pays in compensation may be greater than if the claim were pursued to judgment, but the *total* costs of resisting the claim (including legal fees and administrative costs) may be less as a result of settlement than they would be if the claim were successfully defended in court. Under s. 13 of the Legal Aid Act 1988 a defendant who does not have legal aid may be awarded costs out of the Legal Aid Fund if the proceedings were brought by a legally aided plaintiff, and they are 'finally decided in favour of the unassisted party'. However, if the real or nominal defendant is a corporation, and especially if it is an insurance company, its costs are very unlikely to be paid by the Fund. This is why insurance companies pay out each year many relatively small sums in order to settle doubtful claims: the cost of defeating the claim would exceed the cost of paying out. Furthermore, s. 13 does not apply to claims which are settled before judgment.

[5] But settlement is often very slow too: T. Swanson (1991) 11 *OJLS* 193, 199–200.

end if the potential benefits (whether pecuniary or not), discounted according to the estimated chance of securing those benefits, outweigh that cost. The fact that most claims are settled out of court is a reflection of just how expensive litigation is.[6]

Settlement out-of-court also brings important social benefits:[7] if only a small proportion of settled cases were litigated either court lists would become even longer than they are now, thus increasing the delay involved in litigation, which itself militates in favour of settlement; or more money would have to be spent by the government on providing additional court facilities. Since it is government policy to make the English civil court system self-financing, any unwillingness to increase the number of courts and judges would appear to derive from social as much as financial concerns. The main thrust of the government's financial policy in respect of the civil justice system is to contain expenditure on legal aid by discouraging recourse to the court system and encouraging the use of voluntary non-curial modes of dispute resolution which do not qualify for legal aid.

Another important feature of settlements is that they are private affairs between the parties. Indeed, it is commonly made a condition of settlement that the claimant will not publicize its terms; and a claimant can sometimes use the other party's desire for secrecy to increase the financial payout. Settlement may not only enable the party claimed against to avoid publicity (which may damage that party's commercial reputation and alert other potential claimants to the possibility of success), but it may also prevent the creation of a legal precedent which might be used against that party[8] by others in the future.

From our point of view, the crucial thing to note about the settlement process is that it is a bargaining process; its outcome is determined not just by the legal rules relevant to the dispute between the parties,[9] but also by the interests of the parties involved in the process[10] and by their relative bargaining strengths. It follows from this that the legal rules governing tort liability which we have examined provide, in the majority of disputes, little more than a starting point for negotiations. The final outcome of settlement

---

[6] However, this argument should not be taken too far. How much cheaper it is to settle a claim than to litigate it to judgment depends on when it is settled: the earlier it is settled, the lower the costs. The costs of a settlement at the door of the court are unlikely to be much less than the costs of litigation to judgment, because preparation for trial tends to be much more expensive than the trial itself. And, of course, the interests of the parties are different: the claimant is likely to benefit by holding out for as long as possible.

[7] But in certain contexts, settlement out of court is perceived to be socially problematic; criminal plea bargaining is the clearest example, but there may be others: see e.g. J. C. Alexander (1991) 43 *Stanford LR* 497, 568ff.

[8] If the party is insured, the insurer will also be concerned to avoid a precedent which might be used against other insureds in the same risk pool.

[9] This is particularly true when the relevant law is unclear: Wheeler, *Reservation of Title Clauses*, esp. 198–9. Uncertain law is not a rigidly fixed constraint on settlements but a resource which can be interpreted and manipulated to achieve desired outcomes: *ibid.*, 35.

[10] See Alexander (1991) 43 *Stanford LR* 497 discussing securities class actions in the US.

negotiations may reflect a range of factors—pragmatic, commercial, moral, and so on—which are not reflected in the relevant legal rules. Indeed, it may not be worth the while of the parties' legal advisors to research the relevant law in great detail. However, this point should not be exaggerated: a 'settlement', in the sense in which the term is being used here, is an agreement to resolve a conflict about legal liability; if the parties do not perceive their disagreement as a legal dispute, then any agreement they reach to resolve the dispute is not a settlement in the relevant sense. *A fortiori*, if their agreement is not seen by them as the resolution of a conflict but as, for instance, a co-operative venture for their mutual benefit, then it is not a settlement in the relevant sense.

Claims for Compensation for Past Loss

Although reliable supporting statistics are available only in respect of claims for personal injury, we can confidently assume that a large proportion of tort claims for damages for interference with financial interests are settled out of court;[11] and in very many cases, even without the issue of a writ. The importance of extra-legal factors in the process of settling personal injury claims has been the subject of detailed empirical research.[12] Claims of this type have several important features. First, for most people, making a personal injury claim is a once-in-a-lifetime event; so the claimant is likely to be ignorant of how such claims are made and resolved and to be frightened of an adverse outcome. Secondly, many personal injury claimants are represented by solicitors who are not specialists in making such claims; thirdly, and conversely, respondents to personal injury claims are nearly always represented by a solicitor engaged by an insurance company who has a great deal of experience in handling the type of claim in question. Fourthly, the small average size of personal injury claims, the operation of the legal aid rules, and the fact that the plaintiff's solicitor–own client costs are normally[13] included in the settlement figure,[14] all seem to combine to discourage solicitors from pursuing claims very vigorously. The result may be a conflict between the interests

---

[11] Cf. S. Macauley (1963) 25 *Am. Soc. Rev.* 55; H. Beale and A. Dugdale (1975) 2 *Brit. J Law & Soc.* 45; Wheeler, *Reservation of Title Clauses*, 5. A significant number of large commercial disputes are arbitrated; but these are more likely to involve contract claims than tort claims.

[12] The most thorough study is H. Genn, *Hard Bargaining* (Oxford, 1987).

[13] But on small claims see 359 below.

[14] The issue of costs, and the impact of legal aid, are crucial to the settlement process: see Genn, *Hard Bargaining*, ch. 5. Of particular theoretical importance in personal injury claims is the role of payments into court: P. Cane, *Atiyah's Accidents, Compensation and the Law* 5th edn. (London, 1993), 231–3; but it is unclear how often the procedure is used in practice: Genn, *Hard Bargaining*, 111–3. This procedure is also available in the case of non-personal injury claims, but its impact on the settlement of such claims is impossible to assess. Matters will be even more complicated in cases where a contingent fee arrangement operates: see R. C. A. White (1978) 41 *MLR* 286, 295–6; C. Boxer, *Professional Liability Today*, July 1989, 2.

of the claimant, who may be best served by tenacious pursuit of the claim, and those of his or her solicitor, who may be better off settling the claim quickly and with a minimum of resistance.[15] Where P does not qualify for legal aid, the interest in a quick settlement will be shared by solicitor and client: most personal injury claimants cannot themselves afford to pay their solicitors to investigate and prepare their claims adequately and to pursue them at length. On the other hand, the respondent's insurer normally has considerable resources available for investigating and preparing the case. A claimant who has legal expenses insurance may be in a better bargaining position; but such insurance is, as yet, relatively very uncommon.[16]

Fifthly, the individual personal injury victim, particularly one who has suffered serious injuries with permanent effects, has much more at stake than any individual involved on the injurer's side: the injurer is normally insured and the interests of the insurer are commercial, not personal. As a result, the respondent has much less to lose by delay, by taking risks, and by fighting the claim hard than the claimant has to lose by corresponding aggressiveness. Genn's conclusion is that the cards are stacked heavily against the seriously injured[17] personal injury claimant in the settlement process. From our point of view, this conclusion shows that settling out-of-court is, in such cases, a very effective way of protecting the respondent's economic interest in limiting legal liability to pay damages.

To what extent is this conclusion likely to be relevant to claims arising out of interference with financial interests?[18] The first and obvious point is that, *ex hypothesi*, all personal injury claimants are individuals seeking to protect their personal, as opposed to, or at least in addition to, their business or purely financial interests; by contrast, the claimant in a financial loss case is, in practice, probably more likely to be a business than a private individual.[19] *Prima facie*, one would expect Genn's account of the settlement process to fit financial loss claims by individuals better than such claims by businesses:[20] for the individual financial loss claimant, *this* claim is likely to be the only such claim he or she has ever made, or ever will make. The claimant may well be represented by a solicitor in general practice rather than a specialist in the relevant type of litigation; whereas the respondent will very often be insured and represented by a solicitor experienced in defending claims of this type. Similar financial pressures apply here as in personal injury cases: the

---

[15] Swanson argues that the incentives are the reverse of this: (1991) 11 *OJL* 193, 204–17.

[16] See further 418 below.

[17] Small claims which are a 'nuisance' to insurers are often settled quickly and for more than they are worth: Cane, *Atiyah's Accidents, Compensation and the Law*, 5th edn. (London, 1993), 236–7.

[18] See also Wheeler, *Reservation of Title Clauses*, 157–9.

[19] e.g. the majority of small claims in the County Court are debt collection actions brought by traders against consumers.

[20] Indeed, it is probably the case that the vast majority of financial loss claims by individuals are incidental to personal injury claims arising out of road accidents, which represent about half of all personal injury claims.

claim is likely to be relatively small, the levels of legal aid payments are relatively low, and the claimant, especially one who does not qualify for legal aid, may be unable, out of his or her own resources, to pay a lawyer enough to enable the lawyer to investigate and prepare the case adequately.[21] The lawyer's interests may be best served by a quick (even if low) settlement which frees him or her to take on other more remunerative, non-contentious work. Finally, the individual claimant is likely to have a lot of emotional capital tied up in the claim, and much more than the respondent.

On the other hand, Genn's picture is less likely to fit claims by commercial claimants so well. Businesses are more likely than individuals to have been involved in other (similar) legal disputes, whether as claimant or respondent;[22] and some, such as owners of valuable intellectual property rights, finance houses, or landlords, may have frequent recourse to law. They are much more likely than private individuals to employ solicitors who specialize in commercial litigation generally or disputes of the relevant type in particular; and so, although the respondent may be represented by specialist lawyers, there is less likely to be a great disparity of skill and experience than in the case of the private claimant. The value of any particular claim may well be much greater than in the typical case brought by an individual; but even if it is not, the commercial claimant is more likely to be willing and able to pay the solicitor at a sufficiently attractive rate to enable the latter to give the case adequate attention. Finally, while much is often at stake in commercial litigation, the individuals directly involved in it are normally not as personally interested in the outcome, either financially or emotionally, as is the individual litigant.

Of course, these assertions are unsupported by empirical evidence, and they are generalizations. Generalizations may be more misleading in relation to business plaintiffs than in relation to individuals because businesses probably vary much more in relevant respects than do individuals, at least individuals involved in personal injury litigation. For instance, there is evidence that many small businesses hesitate to consult a lawyer for fear of the cost and delay.[23] Delay may be just as effective a bargaining weapon against a business as against an individual.[24] It is no doubt true that many business

---

[21] An important feature of the American legal process is the conduct of litigation on a '*pro bono*' (that is, free) basis. In the absence of state-funded legal aid, there is a strong ethical obligation on lawyers to do some free work every year. There is no such obligation on English lawyers, but some lawyers do a certain amount of free work. Furthermore, there are several privately-funded groups of lawyers, including the Bar's Free Representation Unit (a registered charity funded largely by the Bar and the Inns of Court which provides representation before tribunals: see General Council of the Bar, *Quality of Justice, The Bar's Response* (London, 1989), 72–6), the Women's Legal Defence Fund (which handles sex discrimination and equal pay cases), and the Centre for International Environmental Law (concerned with the use of international law to protect the environment), which provide free legal advice, assistance, and representation.

[22] Cf Wheeler, *Reservation of Title Clauses*, 64–5.

[23] C. Batchelor, *Financial Times*, 8 Sept. 1992.

[24] Wheeler, *Reservation of Title Clauses*, 142–3.

claimants are represented by lawyers who are less competent, less experienced, and less vigorous than their opponents and their advisers.[25] It is also probably true that smaller businesses are at a disadvantage when negotiating a settlement with a larger business, especially if they are financially dependent on their opponent: commercial self-interest may demand a willingness to settle for a sum less than might be accepted by a claimant of roughly similar bargaining strength to the respondent. Research has shown that an important factor in the settlement of contractual claims in commercial contexts is that where one party (who may be the claimant or the respondent) has a financial interest in the continuance of its relationship with the other after the resolution of the dispute, that party has an incentive not to be too aggressive in settlement negotiations.[26] If both parties have such an interest, the dispute may never be raised. But even where neither party is concerned to preserve a commercial relationship with the other, one side may be in a stronger bargaining position than the other and be able effectively to control the claim negotiation process.[27]

There is another very important structural difference between the normal personal injury claim and at least some financial loss claims. The real respondent to a personal injury claim is typically an institution: normally an insurance company. By contrast, the real respondent to a financial loss claim may be an individual facing a business claimant (for example, an individual tenant *vis-à-vis* a commercial landlord). If so, there may well be gross inequality of bargaining power, but in the claimant's favour. In such a case, settlement may be much less attractive for the respondent than trial, and may not represent an effective technique for protecting the financial interest in limiting legal liability to pay damages. A threat of litigation[28] made by a wealthy and powerful individual or institution against a party who is, for whatever reason, in a position of weakness, can be a very effective weapon.

Genn argues convincingly that measures ought to be taken to redress some of the imbalances in the personal injury settlement process. Among the most important developments in this context are the emergence of a larger number of specialist personal injury lawyers, the tendency for law firms to join together in national or regional consortia, and the partial removal of restrictions on advertising by lawyers. One of the most significant remaining sources of the weakness of the position of the typical personal injury claimant is the difficulty of financing litigation: the legal aid system leaves much to be desired, and it remains to be seen whether the introduction of conditional fee

---

[25] Cf. Wheeler, *Reservation of Title Clauses*, 103–5 and 162–72. Wheeler also found that 'relatively few claimants use lawyers': *ibid*. 160.

[26] Beale and Dugdale (1975) 2 *Brit. J Law and Soc.* 45, esp. 47–8.

[27] Wheeler found that the process of settling claims under reservation of title clauses was largely controlled by insolvency practitioners: *Reservation of Title Clauses*. But some claimants are in a stronger position than others: *ibid*. 102.

[28] Assuming the threat is not, itself, unlawful: see 266 above.

arrangements as permitted by section 58 of the Courts and Legal Services Act 1990 will help significantly.[29]

In relation to financial loss claims, the case for action may not be so great, if only because financial interests do not rank as high in our social scale of values as bodily interests. Furthermore, the law only gives limited protection against the effects of inequality of bargaining power on the financial interests of 'consumers', and it might be argued there is no obvious reason why settlement contracts should receive special attention. On the other hand, it might be contended that settlement contracts do deserve special treatment because they concern the resolution of legal disputes: society has an interest that the outcome of the settlement process should be just to the parties involved. In our society, justice is not seen as a commodity to be distributed by market forces operating freely. So we might be prepared to countenance greater inequality in the distribution by contract of goods and services than we are prepared to allow in the administration of justice; certainly, the weaker party to litigation is, potentially at least, much better protected in court than out of it.

Furthermore, whereas in other contractual contexts a person very often has some choice of contracting partner, in this context there never is any. This generates the possibility of strategic behaviour and exploitation of the inequalities between the parties. As we have seen, the law contains an array of provisions designed to prevent the formation and exploitation of monopoly economic power, and this general policy of the law might be thought to justify some control over the settlement process. In some cases settlements are subject to court approval,[30] but the sheer volume of settled cases obviously rules this out as a general approach.

Disputes about Future Conduct

The previous section concerned the settlement of claims for compensation arising out of conduct which inflicted loss in the past, in cases where the claimant makes no attempt to control loss-causing conduct by the respondent in the future. Claims in negligence, for example, are always of this type.[31] But claims in respect of continuing interference with property (and other legal) rights often involve attempts to prevent (further) interference in the future by means of an injunction. Where the rights which the plaintiff is seeking to protect are property rights, the basic rule of English law is that once the the likelihood of interference in the future has been established, P is *prima facie* entitled to an injunction. This rule gives P a tactical advantage which does not exist in cases where the only possible remedy is an award of damages, or

---

[29] The section allows 'no win-no fee' agreements. See Conditional Fee Agreements Order and Regulations 1995 (SIs 1674, 1675).

[30] RSC Ord. 80, rr. 10, 11.

[31] But see 95 above.

where an injunction might be available but there is no presumption in favour of its award.[32]

The Protection of 'Diffuse Interests': 'Mass Claims'

The implicit assumption in the preceding discussion of the settlement process has been that a single claimant is in dispute with a single respondent. But what about cases in which there are many claimants or many alleged tort-feasors?[33] Such cases can involve personal injuries or injury to financial interests. The claims arising out of use of the drugs Thalidomide and Opren and of the Dalkon shield intra-uterine device provide examples of the former; while cases involving widespread environmental pollution,[34] investor or shareholder claims arising out of the collapse of businesses, the thousands of actions brought by Lloyd's names, and actions for damages in competition law, provide examples of the latter. English court procedure is ill-equipped to deal with cases involving large numbers of plaintiffs;[35] in particular, it is usually said that representative (that is, class) actions cannot be brought to recover damages (although it may be possible to obtain a declaration that all the individual members of a represented group are entitled to damages). Fewer procedural problems arise in suing multiple defendants,[36] but such actions are obviously complex and cumbersome, and the substantive rules of causation may render such actions pointless.[37]

What is the likely impact on the settlement process of the fact that there are many parties involved in the case? Obviously, the conduct of settlement negotiations involving many interested parties will require more organiza-

---

[32] Harris, 342–3.   [33] P. H. Lindbolm and G. D. Watson (1993) 12 *CJQ* 33.

[34] Such cases may also, of course, involve claims in respect of personal injuries.

[35] e.g., orders for discovery of documents are only available against the party sued in a representative capacity and not against the parties represented: *Ventouris* v. *Mountain* [1990] New LJ 666. Concerning the amenability of represented parties to costs orders see D. Kell (1994) 13 *CJQ* 233. Trial of selected cases can, by agreement, be used in establishing guidelines for the settlement of others: *S.* v. *Distillers Co. (Biochemicals) Ltd* [1970] 1 WLR 114; *Thompson* v. *Smiths Shiprepairers (North Shields) Ltd* [1984] QB 405. In the United States, the procedural device of consolidation of actions at the pre-trial stage (English law is very underdeveloped in this respect, too: witness *Davies* v. *Eli Lilley & Co.* [1987] 1 WLR 428; but see *Horrocks* v. *Ford Motor Co. Ltd, The Times*, 15 Feb. 1990 (CA); *Chapman* v. *Chief Constable of South Yorks, The Times*, 20 Mar. 1990 (Steyn J); and *Chrzanowska* v. *Glaxo Laboratories Ltd, Independent*, 13 Mar. 1990 (Steyn J): the court, rather than the parties, should manage multi-party litigation) and class actions have played an important part in facilitating mass claims in several areas of the law: race relations, antitrust, personal injuries. For further discussion of class actions see 409 below.

[36] The number of defendants will normally be relatively small, and the standard mechanisms for joinder of parties will often be adequate. The fact that different defendants may have different grounds for resisting a claim does not necessarily mean that they do not have the same interest such that they may be sued in a representative action: *Irish Shipping Ltd* v. *Commercial Union Assurance Co. PLC (The Irish Rowan)* [1991] 2 QB 206.

[37] If, e.g., P can prove that the loss was caused by the conduct of one of the defendants but cannot prove which one was responsible.

tional effort and skill. This probably means that in practice such cases will be handled by large, specialist firms of lawyers on both sides, so that we can assume rough equality of technical and bargaining skill (but not, necessarily, of bargaining *power*). It is increasingly common for financial loss claimants and their lawyers to form action and support groups. Such pooling of resources and expertise presents defendants with much stronger opposition than any individual claimant could hope to mount. As in the personal injury field, permanent claimants' pressure groups, such as the Subsidence Claims Association,[38] have begun to spring up. On the other hand, cases involving many parties may take even longer to settle than cases involving only a few parties,[39] if only because of the complexity generated by large numbers; this may work to the disadvantage of either or both sides, but will often bear very harshly on groups of individual claimants who have lost significant amounts of money. Where negotiations are being conducted by or on behalf of a large number of people, they may well be complicated by the fact that the interested parties do not have identical interests and may not desire the same result from the settlement; such internal conflicts may make it difficult or even impossible to reach an agreement, especially if one or more claimants hold out for an unrealistic result. In the more common case where there are many claimants but only one respondent, these factors obviously work in the latter's favour. Furthermore, where the claimants are individuals, there may be problems in funding the legal services required.[40] In particular, where the claimants want the respondent to behave differently in the future, any

[38] M. Scott, *The Independent*, 4 July 1992.

[39] But an impressive example of the speed with which mass claims can be settled is provided by a case in 1989 in which a solicitor negotiated a settlement on behalf of 150 shareholders in the newly incorporated Abbey National Building Society who, allegedly as a result of negligence on the part of the Society, failed to receive their share certificates by flotation day, and so were unable to sell their shares at the high opening price. The claim was settled in a matter of weeks, and included compensation for legal costs, out-of-pocket expenses, and interest charges on amounts borrowed to buy the shares, but *not* compensation for loss of the opportunity to sell at the high opening price: *Independent*, 26 Aug. 1989.

[40] For an example of the problems which may arise see Cane, *Atiyah's Accidents, Compensation and the Law*, 5th edn., 221–2. S. 34(3) of the Legal Aid Act 1988 gives the Legal Aid Board power to modify by regulation provisions of the Act relating, e.g., to the means test, the merits test, provisions for costs and the statutory charge 'for the purposes of [the Act's] application to prescribed descriptions of persons or in prescribed circumstances'. This provision could be used to overcome problems in financing group actions. (For the current rules about representative actions, see Civil Legal Aid (General) Regulations 1989, reg. 32). The new conditional fee arrangements may help some mass claims (but not those in which the relief sought is not damages); but such claims are often risky in legal terms, and the more risky the case, the less likely it is that any lawyer would accept it on a conditional fee basis. Also, a lawyer is likely to take on such a case on a conditional fee basis only if he or she is representing a fairly large number of claimants. The Legal Aid Board has made certain proposals for facilitating multi-party actions (in a Consultation Paper of May 1989), but at the moment they are confined to personal injury actions. Legal expenses insurance is becoming increasingly common, but the chance that a significant number of plaintiffs will have such insurance is slim. Furthermore, insurers, like the legal aid authorities, are less likely to fund a claim the more risky it is. Under s. 51 Supreme Court Act 1981 costs may be awarded against a person who has supported proceedings (whether financially or not) and against a person interested in the outcome of proceedings.

agreement by the latter to do so will benefit all affected parties whether or not they contributed to the cost of negotiating the agreement.[41] The defendant's position may also be bolstered by the fact that even if recourse to litigation is open in theory, it may not be a practical option for the claimants because of restrictive procedural rules.

However, cases involving many claimants also present problems for respondents. Such claims often attract a great deal of publicity, which puts considerable pressure on institutional respondents to settle quickly and on 'fair' terms even if there are doubts about the exact extent of the respondent's liability and even if litigation is not a practical option for the claimants. The amounts of money involved may be so great that it is in the long-term financial interests of respondents to take a co-operative rather than an agressive approach to the negotiations. A different sort of problem resides in the fact that because a settlement is a contract it is not binding on potential claimants who are not parties to it even if it approved by a court;[42] the fear of being confronted with additional claims even after settlement has been reached with a large number gives the respondent a very strong incentive to co-operate with the claimants' lawyers (and, perhaps even to assist them financially) in seeking to identify and bring into the settlement process as many potential claimants as possible.[43] In other words, the respondent in cases such as these has an interest in maximizing the payout so as to gain protection from further exposure in the future.

Bargaining around Judicial Remedies

The fact that a defendant has failed to negotiate a pre-judgment settlement and that judgment is entered against D does not necessarily mean that D has no further chances to minimize the financial liability by bargaining.[44] If the judgment requires the payment of a specified sum of money, it might seem that there would be little room for further negotiation, except as to the manner of payment. But even in such a case if, for example, D is in financial

[41] Economists call this the 'free-rider' problem.

[42] In the United States, courts sometimes play an active role in the process of settling mass claims: P. H. Schuck (1986) 53 *U of Chi. LR* 337. A British example of court involvement is provided by the Opren litigation: under the settlement agreement, persons refused compensation by the defendant, or those dissatisfied with the amount offered could have their claims arbitrated by a High Court judge according to principles and procedures laid down by him (*Randall* v. *Eli Lilley & Co., Independent*, 4 Feb. 1988). If a representative action is brought under RSC Ord. 15, r. 12, the judgment binds 'all the persons as representing whom the plaintiff sues', and there is no mechanism for individual members of the class to opt out.

[43] Worldwide media advertising was used to alert potential claimants to the Dalkon shield litigation. A 1987 decision of the Takeover Panel required Guinness PLC to pay compensation to certain (unidentified) shareholders, and this led to press advertising to alert such shareholders to their rights (decisions of the Panel are not, in strict legal terms, binding).

[44] Regarding the possibility that a plaintiff may bargain around a refusal of financial relief, see Harris, 317; clearly, the refusal of relief would give D a powerful bargaining counter.

difficulties, it might be in P's best interest to forego enforcing the judgment in full so as to avoid forcing D into bankruptcy or liquidation. The plaintiff is not required to enforce the judgment, and this fact may give D some room for manoeuvre even at this late stage.

More important, however, is the possibility that D may bargain around a specific remedy such as an injunction or an order for the possession of real property. The basic rule of English law is that a person who can establish that his or her property rights are likely to be interfered with in the future is *prima facie* entitled to an injunction to restrain that interference; and an order for possession is the normal remedy for the wrongful taking of possession of land.[45] Of course, the injunction is a discretionary remedy; and if the order sought would require D to take positive steps rather than just refrain from action, the court will need to be convinced that the cost of complying with the order is not disproportionate to the loss likely to be suffered by P before it will exercise its discretion in favour of the latter.[46] In some cases, too, the court may lessen the financial burden imposed on D by the award of an injunction by suspending its operation to give D time to devise ways of complying with it.[47] But in other cases, a plaintiff may well be awarded an injunction even if P's real motive in bringing the action was not to have D's interference stopped, and even if the cost to D of complying with the injunction is likely to be greater than any loss which the interference will cause to P. Put crudely, D may be ordered to cease an interference even if P does not actually want it to stop and even if the financial cost of doing so is likely to outweigh any consequential economic benefit to P.

Of course, in some cases the liability rules which determine *prima facie* entitlement to an injunction may contain notions of cost-benefit analysis: an interference with the use and enjoyment of land will constitute a nuisance only if it is unreasonable; and one, but only one, factor relevant to judging reasonableness is the cost of preventing the nuisance relative to the loss likely to be suffered by the plaintiff. But a defendant can be liable in nuisance even if D took all reasonable precautions to reduce the interference to a minimum. Furthermore, in some torts such as trespass, liability is strict: notions of reasonableness do not enter in at all.

It is clear, then, that there may well be room for the defendant to bargain around an injunction (or other specific order). A good illustration of this point is provided by the cases about crane jibs on construction sites which overfly adjoining property: the adjoining landowner is unlikely to want to prevent the overflight, and so a landowner who is awarded an injunction is likely to be prepared to accept a licence fee in return for not enforcing it.

[45] By contrast, an order for the return of specific goods is not the normal remedy for misappropriation of goods: P will only be awarded such a remedy if P can convince the court, in effect, that damages would not be an adequate remedy. So the present analysis does not apply to this situation, nor to cases where an injunction will be awarded only if damages would be an inadequate remedy.

[46] *Redland Bricks Ltd* v. *Morris* [1970] AC 652.   [47] Harris, 325–7.

Thus, the practical effect of the grant of an injunction (especially a mandatory injunction) may well be to provide P with a powerful bargaining weapon which can be used to secure the maximum monetary compensation which D is prepared to pay in return for being able to continue the activity.[48] Indeed, the strength of P's position may enable P to secure a monetary payment in excess of any financial loss suffered or likely to be suffered by P. An award of monetary compensation imposes on the parties a monetary valuation of the right to interfere with P's property rights, whereas an injunction may enable them to arrive at such a valuation for themselves.

Apart from awarding damages in lieu of an injunction, the court may render post-judgement bargaining less likely by suspending the operation of the injunction for the likely duration of the interference.[49] The effect of such suspension is to grant D the right to interfere; whether P pays for the privilege will depend on whether the court imposes, as a condition of the suspension, a condition that D compensate P for loss inflicted during the suspension. By suspending the injunction the court can signal the fact that although D is in the wrong as a matter of technical law, the merits of the case rest, at least partly, with D. There is another course of action open in theory, but never adopted by an English court, namely to award an injunction but to require P to pay or to contribute to the costs of complying with the injunction, or to compensate D for having to comply with it. This solution is particularly appropriate in cases where P has 'come to the nuisance' or has been in some way at fault and where the merits of the case rest, in part at least, with D. It requires P to compensate D out of the financial benefits which the cessation of the tortious conduct will bring.

In commercial terms then, the notion of property rights which the law of tort uses is unrealistic: it does not recognize that typically property is essentially a financial asset which, in a business context, has no intrinsic value but is just a means to economic gain. From one point of view, this approach of the law puts it out of touch with commercial reality. But from another point of view it might be said that, by refusing to treat property simply as a commercial asset even though the parties involved treat it in this way, the law is stating a preference for allowing the parties to bargain between themselves and for not imposing on them external valuations of their assets or, in effect, forcing property owners to sell their property to interferers for what the court thinks it is worth.[50] This, however, is an analysis of questionable validity

---

[48] There is a large literature, mostly American, which discusses the theory relevant to answering the question when a court should award an injunction (with or without conditions), and when a monetary remedy would be more appropriate. The rule of *prima facie* entitlement to an injunction makes this literature of limited practical importance in the English context. On post-judgment bargaining see B. H. Thompson (1975) 27 *Stanford LR* 1563. For English discussions see A. I. Ogus and G. M. Richardson [1977] *CLJ* 284; S. Tromans [1982] *CLJ* 87; Harris, 333–42.

[49] Suspension for a shorter time still leaves room for bargaining about what is to happen when the period of suspension expires.

[50] Harris, 318.

because we are here talking about post-judgment bargaining: parties normally litigate only because they have not been able to settle their dispute by bargaining. By recourse to litigation parties seek to obtain from an authoritative third party what they have been unable to obtain by exercising their own bargaining strength. Only if the law consistently refused to assist plaintiffs could it be seen as deferring to the result of the parties' own bargaining. Sometimes the remedy which the law gives can be seen as an attempt to impose on the parties the result which they would have arrived at through bargaining if conditions for bargaining had been ideal: the notion of reasonableness in the torts of negligence and nuisance, if interpreted in terms of economic cost-benefit analysis, may be viewed in this way. But as we have seen, sometimes the law is based on notions, such as property, the logic of which yields results which the parties may then seek to bargain around; and the granting of a remedy may well alter the dynamics of the bargaining process.

Some judges, at least, recognize that the award of an injunction will furnish a plaintiff with a powerful bargaining weapon,[51] and this realization may cause a judge to be wary about awarding an injunction. We cannot, however, conclude from this that when a judge does award an injunction, this is done in order to encourage the parties to bargain around it. This may be the outcome of the granting of the remedy but it cannot convincingly be seen as the purpose of it. Indeed, such a conclusion would run counter to the notion, deeply embedded in the common law, of the sanctity of property. Witness, for example, the general rule that a person who commits a nuisance can normally be restrained from continuing it no matter how great the abatement costs.[52] It is more convincing to see the 'sanctity of property' approach of the common law as out of step with the idea of property as a commercial asset or as consciously espousing a countervailing concept of property than to see it as effectively adopting the view that a property right is a right *either* not to be interfered with *or* to be paid for interference, whichever makes the more commercial sense.[53]

Several writers have argued that the courts should abandon the rule of *prima facie* entitlement to an injunction and award, in any particular case, either an injunction (whether absolute, suspended, or subject to conditions) or damages according to the court's assessment of the costs and benefits of the activities of the two parties and of abating the nuisance.[54] English courts are, perhaps, unlikely to follow this advice; whether one thinks they ought to depends ultimately on the view one takes on two issues: first, is the role of tort law, so far as it protects property rights, to play a part in ensuring that property is used in an economically efficient and socially acceptable way? Or is it to vindicate the right of property owners to decide how their property

---

[51] See 54, n. 90 above.   [52] Harris, *Remedies in Contract and Tort*, 324ff.
[53] Cf. *ibid*. 324, 339–42.
[54] Ogus and Richardson [1977] *CLJ* 284; Tromans [1982] *CLJ* 87; Harris, *Remedies in Contract and Tort*, 333–42.

will be used and to enable them to prevent, or to obtain compensation for, interferences with it? Secondly, if the former is thought to be part of the proper role of tort law, the question arises of how effective tort law is likely to be in securing the efficient use of property.[55]

2. ARBITRATION

Arbitration is very difficult to define[56] and the word is often used rather loosely. One important feature of arbitration, which it shares with court adjudication, is that the arbitrator[57] decides how the dispute between the parties is to be resolved; and this decision binds the parties either because they have contractually agreed in advance to be bound or because the submission of the dispute to an arbitrator is required by statute. The arbitrator is often chosen by the parties themselves, but if they cannot agree on a particular person the choice may be given to a neutral third party. Another important feature of arbitration is that the procedure followed by the arbitrator is often more flexible and informal than that followed by a court, and strict rules of evidence are usually not applied. This procedural flexibility affords the possibility of considerable savings of time and money especially in the preparation of cases, which is the most expensive part of the court adjudication process. Arbitration of disputes arising out of commercial activity is most commonly used to resolve contractual disputes; but it may also be used to resolve tort disputes, even where the parties were not in a pre-tort relationship, by means of an agreement to arbitrate made after the dispute arises.

For our purposes, there are two important distinctions to be made: the first is between court-annexed and private arbitrations; and the second is between commercial and consumer arbitrations.

Court-Annexed and Private Arbitration

The chief example of court-annexed arbitration is found in the County Court:[58] here, defended claims[59] worth up to £3,000 ('small claims') are auto-

---

[55] For the view that the courts are unlikely to be able to use the law of nuisance to prevent inefficient pollution see P. Burrows in P. Burrows and C. G. Veljanovski, *The Economic Approach to Law* (London, 1981), ch. 6.

[56] Sir M. J. Mustill and S. C. Boyd, *Commercial Arbitration*, 2nd edn. (London, 1989), ch. 2.

[57] Arbitrators, like judges, are immune from liability in tort arising out of the performance of their functions as arbitrators: see 232 above. Many arbitrators are not lawyers, and this may create tensions in the arbitration process: J. Flood and A. Craiger (1993) 56 *MLR* 412.

[58] R. Walker and R. Ward, *Walkers and Walker's The English Legal System*, 7th edn. (London, 1994), 402–3.

[59] The procedure does nothing to encourage people to defend claims, and a very large proportion of County Court judgments are given in default of an appearance by the defendant.

matically referred to arbitration before a District Judge,[60] who also has a discretion to rescind the referral in certain cases;[61] cases worth more than £3,000 may be referred if the parties agree. Arbitration of small claims is designed to facilitate the presentation of cases by the litigants themselves without legal representation;[62] and to save costs.[63] The decision of the District Judge is an ordinary judgment of the court, but the procedure of arbitrations is flexible and informal: the County Court rules leave it to the District Judge to adopt the procedure best suited to affording each party a fair and equal opportunity to present their case, and the District Judge may take a more active role in the proceedings than would an ordinary County Court judge. Strict rules of evidence do not apply, and rights of appeal are very limited.[64]

Cases brought before the Commercial Court (which is part of the High Court) are decided by a High Court judge assigned to the Commercial Court, and the judge's decision is an ordinary judgment of the High Court.[65] But proceedings before the Commercial Court bear some of the marks of arbitration: judges of the Commercial Court, like many arbitrators, are specialists in commercial law; they are available at relatively short notice to deal with disputes; procedure in the court is streamlined and strict rules of evidence can be relaxed by consent. The aim of these measures is the saving of time and expense (full trials are relatively rare in the Commercial Court).[66] Mention should also be made of what is known as 'official referees business';[67] these cases are heard by nominated Circuit judges, and in practice most of them are building disputes. Once again, the reason for recognizing this special category of cases is so that they can be referred to specialist judges who have developed procedures well adapted to dealing with technically

---

[60] The District Judge is the arbitrator unless the Court orders otherwise.

[61] See *Afzal* v. *Ford Motor Co. Ltd* [1994] 4 All ER 720; *Joyce* v. *Liverpool City Council*, [1995] 3 WLR 439. It has been recommended that the power to transfer cases out of the small claims jurisdiction should be broadened: Woolf Report on *Access to Justice* (1995).

[62] Legal representation is not forbidden, but legal aid is not available for arbitrations. Concerning lay representation see Lay Representatives (Rights of Audience) Order 1992; G. A. (1992) 11 *CJQ* 343.

[63] With minor exceptions, the arbitrator has no power to award costs. This has led to the use of tactics by litigants which have generated a considerable amount of litigation about the proper criteria for recission of referral of cases to arbitration. See esp. *Afzal* v. *Ford Motor Co. Ltd* [1994] 4 All ER 720.

[64] For suggested reforms of the small claims procedure see National Consumer Council, *Ordinary Justice* (London, 1989), ch. 10. For a radical approach see T. G. Ison (1972) 35 *MLR* 18. For a proposal for court-annexed arbitration of High Court actions, see R. Bernstein [1988] *New LJ* 720.

[65] The sorts of cases which may be dealt with by the Commercial Court are defined in RSC Ord. 72, r. 1(2).

[66] See generally *Walker and Walker's English Legal System*, n. 58 above 364–5; J. R. Spencer *Jackson's Machinery of Justice*, 8th edn. (Cambridge, 1989), 44–6.

[67] As defined in RSC Ord. 36, r. 1(2); *Walker and Walker's English Legal System*, 365–7; Spencer, *Jackson's Machinery of Justice*, 76.

complex disputes involving large numbers of documents, with a view to saving time and money.[68]

Another alternative to court adjudication which bears some of the marks
of arbitration is adjudication by a tribunal. For our purposes, the most important tribunals are Industrial Tribunals, which hear cases involving allegations
of race and sex discrimination in matters of employment, and the
Employment Appeal Tribunal, which hears appeals in such cases.[69] Procedure
is relatively informal in these tribunals, and parties may be represented by
whomever they choose. Orders for costs are not normally made, but legal aid
is not available for claims before Industrial Tribunals (although it is for
claims before the Employment Appeals Tribunals). In practice this means that
these tribunals are out of the reach of many complainants unless assisted by
some body such as the Equal Opportunities Commission or the Commission
for Racial Equality.[70] There is also evidence that parties without legal representation do not do as well before Industrial Tribunals as those with it.[71]
Tribunals are often seen as cheaper, more 'user-friendly' and faster than
courts; but this view is not universally held.[72] Some think that these tribunals
should operate in a more arbitrative way than they currently do, and that
their members should take a more interventionist approach in dealing with
cases;[73] others favour greater use of private arbitration.[74] As of January 1995
the government has been considering proposals to 'streamline' the procedure
of Industrial Tribunals in an attempt to reduce backlogs and delays, especially in respect of sexual harasssment and discrimination claims.

The most basic distinction between court-annexed and private arbitration[75]

---

[68] There is also a separate Patents Court which deals with intellectual property litigation; its
raison d'être is to ensure that such cases are heard by judges with relevant specialist knowledge.
Edmonton County Court in North London was established as the first 'patents county court' as
an attempt to provide facilities for parties discouraged by the cost of High Court litigation:
Chaplin Patents Holdings Co. PLC v. *Group Lotus PLC, The Times*, 1 Dec. 1994. Cases dealt with
by the Copyright Licensing Tribunal (see 396 below) are normally between commercial parties.
The Admiralty Court deals mainly with shipping cases, and it has one feature worth noting in
this context: whereas in ordinary actions the court is informed about matters beyond its expertise by the calling of (competing) expert witnesses by the parties, in the Admiralty Court expert
'assessors' can sit with the judge and give assistance in deciding technical issues. Similarly, a
District Judge conducting a County Court arbitration can consult an expert or commission a
report from an expert or ask an expert to attend the hearing. Private arbitrators are often themselves experts in the technical (as opposed to the legal) subject matter of the dispute they are
arbitrating.
[69] *Walker and Walker's English Legal System*, 160–2 and 176–7.
[70] On the powers of the Commissions to assist complainants see Race Relations Act 1976,
s. 66 and Sex Discrimination Act 1975, s. 75.
[71] H. Genn and Y. Genn, *The Effectiveness of Representation at Tribunals* (Report to the Lord
Chancellor, 1989).
[72] *Ibid.*; J. Gregory (for the EOC), *Trial by Ordeal* (HMSO, 1989).
[73] L. Dickens, M. Jones, B. Weekes, and M. Hart, *Dismissed* (Oxford, 1985).
[74] R. Lewis and J. Clark, *Employment Rights, Industrial Tribunals and Arbitration: The Case
for Alternative Dispute Resolution* (Institute of Employment Rights, London, 1993).
[75] For a brief account, see Spencer, *Jackson's Machinery of Justice*, ch. 12; for detail, see
Mustill and Boyd, *Commercial Arbitrations*. The Supreme Court Procedure Committee's

is that in the latter case the choice of the arbitrator is made by or with the agreement of the parties; and so the arbitrator's decision binds the parties because of their agreement to be bound and not because of the office or authority of the arbitrator. Private arbitrations pursuant to an arbitration agreement are subject to the provisions of the Arbitration Acts 1950 (Part I) and 1979 and to a large body of common law rules. The current legal policy towards private arbitration[76] is that it should be autonomous and as free as possible from control and interference by the ordinary courts; this policy is a response to the wishes of the main users of private arbitration, namely large commercial entities. Thus, the grounds on which arbitration awards can be challenged in the courts are narrow (see below); and while an arbitration agreement cannot lawfully prevent either party bringing court proceedings in respect of the dispute, if the agreement requires that the dispute be referred to arbitration (or to some other non-curial forum of dispute resolution)[77] before being litigated, a court will normally stay any legal proceedings until the dispute has been submitted to arbitration (or other forum).[78]

An arbitrator's award can be set aside by a court for excess of jurisdiction or for breach of the rules of natural justice; and, in certain very limited circumstances,[79] an appeal may be brought to the High Court on any question of law arising out of the award. But such appeals are rare: awards of arbitrators are much less likely to be challenged than decisions of courts. While the arbitration is in progress, recourse may be had to the courts for a variety of reasons including obtaining a determination of a preliminary point of law or securing a *Mareva* injunction to prevent the disposal of assets pending the conclusion of the arbitration. The award of an arbitrator can, with the leave of the High Court, be enforced in the same way as a judgment or order of the court; and an award of damages made by an arbitrator is a contractual debt on which action may be brought in the normal way.

The main advantage of private arbitration over adjudication by a court is that the parties can exercise much more control over the course of arbitration proceedings than over court proceedings. They can choose their own arbitrator; they can agree that the dispute is to be resolved according to rules other than the applicable rules of English law; they can agree to waive or modify the application to the proceedings of the rules of procedure or evidence which govern court proceedings, and in this way reduce the formality,

Working Group on defamation law chaired by Neill LJ (1991) recommended that a voluntary arbitration system for defamation complaints should be 'encouraged'. The Government has proposed the introduction of a summary procedure for certain defamation cases: Lord Chancellor's Department, *Reforming Defamation Law and Procedure* (July, 1995), 12–14.

[76] And other non-curial forms of dispute resolution: J. Kendall (1993) 109 *LQR* 385.

[77] *Channel Tunnel Group Ltd* v. *Balfour Beatty Construction Ltd* [1993] AC 334.

[78] Arbitration Act 1975, s. 1(1); *Scott* v. *Avery* (1856) 5 HL Cas. 811.

[79] *Pioneer Shipping Ltd* v. *BTP Tioxide Ltd (The Nema)* [1982] AC 724; *Antaios Compania Naviera SA* v. *Salen Rederierna AB (The Antaios)* [1985] AC 191. But see *Ipswich BC* v. *Fisons PLC* [1990] Ch. 709. The Arbitration Act 1979 contains provision for agreements to exclude appeals in some cases.

length, and cost of the proceedings as compared with litigation. On the other hand, whether arbitration is cheaper than court proceedings will depend very much on the complexity of the dispute, on whether it is to be decided according to the applicable rules of law, and on the conduct of the parties. If the matters in dispute are complex, it will inevitably take time to sort them out; and if the arbitrator is to apply ordinary rules of law, the parties will have to prepare their cases more or less as extensively as they would if their dispute were being heard by a court. Arbitrations may be just as liable to be obstructed by delaying tactics as are court proceedings.[80] Furthermore, legal aid is not available for private arbitrations (although this is of little concern to many businesses), and whereas it is the state which pays judges,[81] it is the parties which pay the arbitrator. However, arbitration is very popular, especially amongst large businesses; and many private arbitrations are quick and relatively cheap because many are completed without a hearing: the parties simply submit papers to the arbitrator for consideration.

Commercial and Consumer Arbitrations

This distinction cuts across that between court-annexed and private arbitrations. In a consumer arbitration (in the sense I am using this term) one of the parties is an individual, not a business; a commercial arbitration (in my sense) is one in which both parties are traders, merchants, or other commercial entities. Most small claim arbitrations in the County Court are consumer arbitrations while most cases which come before the Commercial Court or an Official Referee are between businesses. Many private arbitrations are commercial in this sense, but there is also an important private consumer arbitration sector. Under section 124 of the Fair Trading Act 1973 the Director General of Fair Trading has a duty to encourage trade associations to prepare codes of good business practice for their members, and many of these codes contain provision for disputes between traders and consumers to be settled by conciliation[82] in the first instance, and failing that, arbitration.[83]

We have already noted the advantages of County Court arbitration; and private consumer arbitration is designed to share the advantages of informality, cheapness, and speed. This partly explains the success in the 1970s of the London and Manchester Voluntary Arbitration Schemes which were privately organized and funded schemes for handling small claims which would otherwise have been initiated in the County Court. These schemes:

---

[80] Like court proceedings, arbitrations can, unless the arbitration agreement provides to the contrary, be struck out for want of prosecution: Courts and Legal Services Act 1990, s. 72; D. R.Thomas [1990] *JBL* 110.

[81] But it is government policy to make the civil courts self-financing in the near future. But it has been estimated that even after planned increases, court fees will cover only a third of the costs of providing civil courts: *Guardian*, 17 Feb. 1995.

[82] See 364 below.   [83] R. Thomas [1988] *CJQ* 206, 208–9.

broke new ground by attempting to combine oral hearings with fast, cheap, informal and interventionist procedures. In particular the administrators of the schemes helped litigants to prepare their cases.[84]

Both schemes advertised their services and were inundated with cases; but both ceased to operate in 1979–80 for lack of secure funding. Their voluntary nature also meant that they were of little use against unco-operative defendants.

Furthermore, the advantages of arbitration may only accrue to one of the parties: an agreement to arbitrate is a contract, and if one party is in a stronger bargaining position than the other, that party may be able to organize the arbitration in such a way that the other's interests are less well protected than they would be in court proceedings. In particular, since legal aid is not available for private arbitrations, poor parties may be less able to protect themselves in an arbitration than they would be in litigation.[85] If a consumer complainant has to share with a trader the cost of hiring an arbitrator, the complainant may well not be able to afford to go to arbitration, and as a result may accept any offer the trader makes, however inadequate.

Many private consumer arbitration schemes overcome this last problem by making the services of an arbitrator available to the complainant for a nominal registration fee (the real cost being met by the trade association's members), but not all private schemes operate in this way. This, coupled with the fact that the existence of an expensive private scheme will usually preclude recourse to the cheap County Court arbitration system, led to the enactment of the Consumer Arbitration Agreements Act 1988 which, in certain circumstances, renders unenforceable an agreement to submit to arbitration a dispute which falls within the jurisdiction of the County Court in cases where one of the parties makes the agreement as a consumer[86] and the other does not. However, the Act only applies to agreements to arbitrate 'future differences arising between the parties', and it does not apply if the consumer consents to arbitration in writing after the differences have arisen. Thus, it is unlikely to apply to arbitrations of tort disputes. Nor does it apply to agreements to arbitrate disputes arising out of contracts which do not fall within the Unfair Contract Terms Act 1977: notably, insurance contracts.

Another disadvantage of arbitration from the complainant's point of view is that there may be even greater difficulties in arbitrating mass claims than in litigating them.[87]

---

[84] *Ibid.* 207; see also R. Egerton [1980] *New LJ* 488.

[85] From one point of view the unavailability of legal aid is a good thing because it discourages excessive formality and legality. But from another point of view it puts individuals, especially less well-educated ones, at a great disadvantage in presenting their case unless they can find an articulate friend, social worker, or other helper who will act as a representative for nothing.

[86] This phrase is defined in similar terms to those used in the Unfair Contract Terms Act 1977.

[87] Sir J. Donaldson [1983] *CLP* 1, 9–10; P. Naughton [1995] *New LJ* 383.

3. CONCILIATION AND MEDIATION

Apart from arbitration, there are two other important alternatives to adjudication by a court for the resolution of legal disputes: conciliation and mediation.[88] Both of these alternatives involve a third party. However, the conciliator or mediator, unlike the arbitrator, does not make a decision to resolve the dispute for the parties but helps them to reach an agreement between themselves. In other words, conciliation and mediation are forms of assisted settlement. The terms 'conciliation' and 'mediation' are not used with any great precision;[89] the important point about both of these modes of dispute settlement is that the third party provides the disputing parties with various facilities to assist them to resolve their dispute, such as a neutral venue; administrative services; research facilities; individuals to chair meetings between the parties and, perhaps, to suggest forms of compromise which may enable the dispute to be brought to an end. But the third party does not provide them with a decision. Furthermore, whereas the basic job of an arbitrator (as of a judge) is to resolve disputes according to law, the basic criterion relevant to conciliation and mediation is what the parties can mutually agree to accept: the outcome may bear little or no relation to the way in which a court or arbitrator would resolve the dispute.

Adjudication and arbitration (and, to a lesser extent, ordinary two-party settlement) are adversary processes which highlight differences and reinforce conflict; they separate the winners from the losers. Conciliation and mediation, on the other hand, are more concerned with enabling each party to perceive the weaknesses and the strengths of their own and the other party's position, and to identify an outcome which will benefit both parties: compromise, not conflict, is the key concept. The third party, by helping to defuse conflict and aggression, may enable the parties to reach a settlement faster than they would have done without assistance, or to reach a settlement instead of litigating. Advantages of good conciliation and mediation are informality, speed, and relative cheapness; they may also help the parties to preserve their relationship in the future by defusing conflict. Conciliation and mediation are flexible: the third party's involvement can take a variety of forms, as can the dispute-settling process;[90] and parties can choose exactly the form and amount of representation they want. Since the aim of the process

[88] An important provider of mediation services to commerce is the London-based, CBI-sponsored Centre for Dispute Resolution (CEDR). Another is the City Disputes Panel. ADR Net is a regional network of law firms which offer mediation services. Mediation UK is a charitable umbrella organization for mediation services throughout the country; disputes between neighbours, especially relating to noise, figure largely in the activities of such services.

[89] 'Mediation' is often used to signify that the third party takes a more active role than would a conciliator, in particular by suggesting strategies and formulae for resolving the dispute.

[90] There are more and less formal ways of pursuing these modes: see e.g. D. A. Newton (1987) 61 *ALJ* 562; R. S. Banks, *ibid.* 569; N. Royce [1989] *Construction LJ* 34; R. A. Schiffer, *Professional Liability Today*, Sept. 1988, 6; B. Cheney (1989) 19 *VUWLR* 153.

is not to establish the rights and wrongs of the situation but to enable the parties to stand back from the dispute and to see it from both sides with a view to reaching a quick compromise solution, much of the expensive and time-consuming preparation required for litigation can be dispensed with.

However, conciliation and mediation can only be successful and will, indeed, only be used at all, if the parties are prepared to adopt a conciliatory rather than an adversarial attitude to the resolution of their dispute.[91] It may be thought that the fact that most legal disputes are settled out of court shows that most parties to such disputes are prepared to adopt such an attitude. But the fact that the parties to a dispute settle it out of court does not mean that they have done so in a spirit of co-operation or that either party is satisfied with the outcome. In fact, conciliation and mediation are, in the vast majority of relevant cases, an alternative to traditional settlement out-of-court, not to court adjudication (or arbitration). Parties will be prepared to use such methods only if they see them as having advantages over traditional settlement techniques. From this point of view, an important characteristic of conciliation and mediation is their potential for de-legalizing disputes so as to render unnecessary much of the expensive and time-consuming pre-trial work which accompanies both adjudication and the traditional settlement process (as well as much arbitration); and their potential for removing the adversarial element of litigation and traditional settlement. American experience has also shown the value, from the point of view of defusing conflict, of parties agreeing to conciliation and mediation in advance of disputes arising, as is commonly done in respect of arbitration;[92] but this point has more relevance to contract disputes than to tort disputes and so is not directly relevant in the context of this book.

On the other hand, because conciliation and mediation require for their success a spirit of compromise, they are unlikely to work to the mutual benefit of the parties unless they are of roughly equal bargaining strength. If, for some reason, one party is much more in need of a speedy resolution of the dispute than the other, the likelihood is that he or she will be much more willing to compromise than the other party; and, if the other party knows this, that party will be able to take advantage of it. For this reason, these forms of dispute settlement are unlikely to be appropriate to disputes between businesses and consumers. It is not within the remit of the third party to favour one side rather than the other in such a way as to redress any inequality of bargaining power because it is of the essence of these modes of dispute resolution that each party trust the third party to be impartial:[93] such trust is

---

[91] See e.g. The Grubb Institute, *Community Mediation of Disputes Between Neighbours* (London, 1990), paras. 2.4.11, 3.1.9.2., 7.3.5. For this reason, lawyers may not, by training or temperament, be the best people to act as third parties. But see Newton (1987) 61 *ALJ* 562, 567.

[92] Available mediation facilities are less likely to be used the less compulsion there is to use them: R. Young [1989] *CJQ* 319.

[93] *Community Mediation of Disputes Between Neighbours*, s. 6.3. This provides another reason for doubting whether lawyers are suitable as mediators: S. Roberts (1993) 56 *MLR* 452, 462–7.

essential because the third party may, for example, meet each party separately without the other being present.

Most facilities for conciliation and mediation are privately organized and funded. However, court-annexed mediation and conciliation facilities, which involve judicial officials in assisting settlement, are not unknown, especially in the family law context. Such schemes (which may take a variety of forms) are often criticised for blurring the line between imposed and negotiated resolution of disputes.[94] There is a statutory and publicly funded conciliation service concerned with the resolution of disputes between employers on the one side, and employees and unions on the other: the Advisory, Conciliation and Arbitration Service (ACAS). ACAS derives its powers and functions from the Employment Protection Act 1975. Its general purpose is to help improve industrial relations and to encourage collective bargaining in industry; so it has no coercive powers. Its specific functions include providing conciliation and mediation services, and arranging voluntary arbitration[95] to assist in the settlement of trade disputes; and attempting to conciliate in cases brought before Industrial Tribunals, including sex and race discrimination cases.[96]

4. INVESTIGATIVE TECHNIQUES[97]

In the case of all the dispute settling techniques we have discussed so far, any third party involved usually relies on the parties to supply an account of the relevant facts. Even if the third party takes an active role in deciding what procedure to adopt, in making suggestions as to how the dispute might be settled and even in eliciting relevant information from the parties it is not normally seen as the third party's function personally to investigate the source and nature of the dispute between the parties. This reliance on the parties for information is a central feature of the adversarial system of handling legal disputes. By contrast, one of the most important functions of an 'ombudsman' is personally to investigate complaints independently of either party in order to ascertain what happened and whether the complaint is justified in fact. Ombudsmen typically have extensive access to relevant documents in the respondent's possession and are sometimes free to interview officers and employees of the respondent. The dispute-settling powers of ombudsmen

---

[94] S. Roberts (1993) 56 *MLR* 452, 458–62.

[95] ACAS does not itself arbitrate: this is often done by the Central Arbitration Committee. Arbitration is seen as a last resort; and conciliation is seen as preferable to mediation. See generally ACAS Annual Report 1978, 51–72.

[96] I. T. Smith and J. C. Wood, *Industrial Law*, 5th edn. (London, 1993), 32–4; L. Dickens in R. Baldwin and C. McCrudden, *Regulation and Public Law* (London, 1987), 114–24. For an account of the conciliation work of ACAS in unfair dismissal claims before Indutrial Tribunals, see Dickens, Jones, Weekes, and Hart, *Dismissed* (Oxford, 1985), ch. 6.

[97] R. Thomas [1988] *CJQ* 206, 209–11.

vary,[98] and they may choose between the various dispute settling techniques already discussed; but the investigative (or 'inquisitorial') mode of operation is one of the hallmarks of the office of ombudsman. Another crucial feature of the ombudsman technique is that it is free to the complainant; this sets it apart from every other dispute solving mechanism we have considered so far.

The ombudsman technique was first applied to central government, and spread from there to local government and the National Health Service. The technique is now widely used in the private sector, especially in the financial services industry. For instance, Self Regulating Organizations and Recognized Professional Bodies registered under the Financial Services Act 1986 are required to have effective complaints (investigation) procedures. There are also ombudsman schemes covering banks,[99] building societies, and corporate estate agents.[100] The Commission for Racial Equality and the Equal Opportunities Commission have the power to investigate complaints of discrimination against named persons, in addition to the power to undertake more general investigations to ascertain whether discriminatory practices are being engaged in. Membership of many non-governmental ombudsman schemes is voluntary, but the building societies and financial services industries ombudsman schemes have a statutory basis.[101] Not all complaints mechanisms which follow the ombudsman pattern bear the name. In particular, complaints of substandard work against solicitors are dealt with in the first instance by the Solicitors Complaints Bureau.

The system for dealing with complaints against solicitors is perhaps the most highly developed of all those dealing with financial services professions;[102] and for this reason, it is worth considering in a little detail. A distinction has to be drawn between complaints of professional *misconduct*,

[98] e.g., in respect of the bindingness of the decision on the respondent. The power to make awards binding on the respondent is a noteworthy feature of non-governmental ombudsman schemes which is not shared by governmental schemes. But it is, perhaps, unlikely that the power will often be used in practice: P. E. Morris [1987] *JBL* 199, 205. The most common forms of redress are an apology, the reversal or reconsideration of a decision and compensation.

[99] P. E. Morris [1992] *LMCLQ* 227; M. Seneviratne, R. James, and C. Graham (1994) 13 *CJQ* 253. Typically, financial services ombudsmen only deal with complaints by customers of banks, insurance companies, and so on. So, for instance, the insurance ombudsman does not deal with complaints by third parties, such as an accident victim dissatisfied with the way a liability insurer has handled its customer's claim on the liability policy.

[100] M. Clarke, D. Smith, and M. McConville, *Slippery Customers: Estate Agents, the Public and Regulation* (London, 1994), 257–60.

[101] Building Societies Act 1986, Pt. IX; Financial Services Act 1986, s. 48(2)(j) and Sch. 7, para. 4 (J Birds and C. Graham [1988] *CJQ* 313, 324–6).

[102] A. L. Newbold and G. Zellick [1987] *CJQ* 25; B. Walsh [1987] *PN* 114; [1989] *PN* 22; M. Zander, *A Matter of Justice* (Oxford, 1989), 90–102; R. Abel, *The Legal Profession in England and Wales* (Oxford, 1988), 248–58; C. Staughton and G. Whalley (1989) 105 *LQR* 661, 664–5. Concerning barristers see also Abel, *The Legal Profession*, 133–6. The Bar's complaints mechanism is concerned primarily with *discipline*, not with making good the results of 'shoddy work'. In Dec. 1994 the Chairman of the Bar announced that a new complaints system would be in place by Jan., 1996. The investigation of complaints will be under the control of a lay commissioner. Compensation of up to £2,000 will be payable in cases of misconduct or inadequate service.

complaints of bad or inadequate service ('shoddy work'),[103] and complaints of overcharging. In relation to the first, the Council of the Law Society has the power to reprimand or fine a solicitor, or bar him or her from practising; but it cannot award compensation to an aggrieved person. In relation to the second, the Council of the Law Society has the power to deal with complaints that the professional services provided by a solicitor were not of the quality that could reasonably have been expected. Such complaints may be made by a client or a third party (such as the other party to litigation or a beneficiary under a will) or another solicitor. A solicitor who is the subject of a successful complaint may be ordered to refund, remit, or waive some or all of the charges for the services; to pay the client compensation of up to £1,000;[104] to rectify any error, omission, or deficiency resulting from the 'shoddy work'; or to take other action 'in the interests of the client'.[105] Complaints of overcharging can be dealt with as cases of professional misconduct if they are serious enough; otherwise, the client can ask the Law Society to check the bill and issue a 'Remuneration Certificate' (in respect of non-litigious work), or have the bill taxed by a court.[106]

The powers of the Council in respect of complaints of shoddy work (which are our main concern here) are exercised by the Solicitors Complaints Bureau. In the first instance, complaints are screened by the SCB's Primary Investigation Unit.[107] In appropriate cases, the complainant will be told first to utilize the solicitor's internal complaints procedure (which all firms are now required to operate).[108] Allegations involving more than £1,000 may be referred to the Solicitors Indemnity Fund.[109] The majority of complaints are passed to the Conciliation Unit. If conciliation fails, the complaint may be dealt with more formally with written reports. If the complaint is not resolved to the satisfaction of the complainant, there is a right of appeal to the Adjudication and Appeals Committee which operates in sub-committees of two solicitors and one lay member each. In deciding whether to exercise its powers in relation to shoddy work, the Council is directed by statute to con-

[103] The term 'shoddy work' is misleading: delay can be a cause for complaint even if the work was meticulously done. Of course, delay, incompetence, or bad service may, if serious enough, give rise to complaints of misconduct. Such serious cases could also be dealt with as shoddy work cases.

[104] The Legal Services Ombudsman thinks that this should certainly be increased to £2,000 and probably to £5,000: *Fourth Annual Report* (London, 1995), para. 3.22.

[105] Solicitors Act 1974, s. 37A (inserted by Courts and Legal Services Act 1990, s. 93).

[106] But the time linmit for applications is treacherously short: 12 months in the case of taxation (*Harrison* v. *Tew* [1990] 2 AC 523); and in the case of a remuneration certificate, one month after being informed by one's solicitor of the right to apply (Solicitors Remuneration Order 1972). A Remuneration Certificate is not available if the bill has been paid. Taxing is considered again below at 384.

[107] The Unit (which used to be called the Diagnostic Unit) has been heavily criticized by the Legal Services Ombudsman: *Second Annual Report* (1992), paras. 4.14–17; *Third Annual Report* (1993), paras. 3.14–22.

[108] Solicitors Practice Rules, r. 15; R. James and M. Seneviratne (1995) 58 *MLR* 187, 198–9; [1995] *New LJ* 1119.

[109] See 384 below.

sider whether the complainant could be reasonably expected to bring a civil action against the solicitor; but the existence of a cause of action for negligence, for example, does not, either in theory or in the practice of the Bureau, preclude an investigation by the Bureau or by the Solicitors Indemnity Fund. Under section 44B of the Solicitors Act 1974, the Council (in practice, the Adjudication Committee) has power to order the production of documents by the solicitor complained against.

If a complainant is dissatisfied with the way the Bureau handles a complaint, he or she can make a complaint in writing to the Legal Services Ombudsman (LSO), who is appointed by the Lord Chancellor and is not a practising lawyer.[110] The LSO can (but usually does not) investigate the original complaint against the solicitor as well as the Bureau's handling of it. The LSO can recommend that the complaint be considered or reconsidered; or that the solicitor or the Bureau pay compensation for loss, inconvenience, or distress caused, or reimburse (part of) the cost of making the complaint.[111] The LSO has no powers of coercion, but if a recommendation is not complied with, this fact and the reasons for it have to be publicized in such manner as the LSO specifies.[112] The LSO also has an advisory role in respect of the complaints-handling arrangements of the Bureau and can make recommendations in this regard which the Bureau is under a duty to consider. In practice, the LSO is engaged in continuing dialogue with the Bureau about general procedures as well as particular complaints.

If a complainant fails to obtain satisfaction from any of these bodies it is, finally,[113] possible to sue the solicitor in respect of the shoddy work. But it may not be easy for a dissatisfied client to find another solicitor prepared to act; this fact puts solicitors in an even stronger position than other professionals in evading law suits for negligence. Moreover, it has been held that the Law Society owes no duty to take care in investigating complaints made to the Solicitors Complaints Bureau.[114]

---

[110] Courts and Legal Services Act 1990, s. 21. The Ombudsman can also investigate the handling of complaints against barristers and licensed conveyancers. See generally James and Seneviratne (1995) 58 *MLR* 187.

[111] Courts and Legal Services Act 1990, s. 23(2). There is no limit to the amount which may be recommended. In 1994 the LSO made 109 recommendations for the payment of compensation, 60 of these against individual lawyers. In a majority of cases the amount of compensation was less than £500; in 10 cases the amount was over £1,000; and the largest amount was £59,809. The LSO takes the view that his office lacks the resources to deal with difficult or complex cases of alleged professional negligence in which large awards of compensation might be appropriate: *Fourth Annual Report* (1995), paras. 4.13–14, 4.18–19.

[112] In 1993 there was only one case of failure to comply with a recommendation.

[113] The LSO cannot investigate a matter which is being determined or has been determined by a court or the Solicitors Disciplinary Tribunal; but the LSO can investigate a matter even though it could form the subject of court proceedings.

[114] *Wood* v. *Law Society* [1993] *New LJ* 1475. Miss Wood failed to obtain legal aid for an appeal against this decision: [1994] *New LJ* 523. The appeal was heard and Miss Wood lost: *Independent*, 1 Mar. 1995. She applied unsuccessfully for leave to appeal to the House of Lords; and according to latest reports, she intends to seek redress in the European Court: [1995] *New LJ* 1119.

The Law Society provides a number of services ancillary to this formal complaints mechanism: it offers a free interview with a solicitor to anyone considering making a complaint, and with a panel of solicitors to anyone who thinks they may have a cause of action for negligence against a solicitor. There is also a voluntary arbitration scheme run and financed jointly with the Chartered Institute of Arbitrators; it offers documents-only arbitration for a modest flat fee payable by each party. A conciliation scheme also operates within the Solicitors Complaints Bureau to deal with minor complaints which do not require deep investigation.

Despite the variety of these arrangements for dealing with complaints against solicitors, there is still dissatisfaction with the system.[115] Apart from complaints about the complexity of the system and of delay and administrative inefficiency, much of the criticism centres around the fact that the majority of the members of the Adjudication Committee are solicitors, and half are members of the Council of the Law Society; and the fact that the existence and role of the Investigation Committee is not widely publicized by the Law Society. Thus the independence of the complaints mechanism is open to doubt. Indeed, the Investigation Committee itself, one of the functions of which is to oversee the complaints mechanism, recommended, in its response to the Lord Chancellor's Green Paper on Legal Services, that a complaints board independent of the Law Society be set up and given the power to award compensation of up to £2,000 for misconduct, incompetence, or shoddy work.

There is no doubt that the proliferation of private ombudsman schemes has increased consumer choice of complaints mechanisms;[116] but membership of such schemes is typically voluntary, and it seems clear that there is a large element of commercial and professional self-interest in the development. As one writer puts it, 'the creation of a specialist ombudsman by a private industry or professional organization can be justified in hard commercial terms and as a sound tactical ploy in a campaign to stave off anticipated statutory controls'.[117] Recourse to a private ombudsman is usually allowed only as a last resort, to be pursued after complaints to the respondent itself have failed to

---

[115] There is trenchant criticism in the *14th Annual Report* of the Lay Observer (London, 1988), paras. 68–70 (on the Adjudication Committee) and paras. 90–99 (on the shoddy work powers). The Bureau also has attracted criticism from the LSO (*Second Annual Report* (1992), paras. 4.11–18; *Third Annual Report* (1993), paras. 3.14–22; but note the qualified praise in *Fourth Annual Report* (1995), paras. 3.2, 3.18–21, 6.2), from the National Consumer Council (*Ordinary Justice* (London, 1989), 213–18 and *The Solicitors Complaints Bureau: A Consumer View* (London, 1994)), and from one of its own lay members: [1995] *New LJ* 1250. Some practitioners have also been less than happy: see e.g. [1992] *New LJ* 722, 742, 797. At the time of writing, the Bureau is engaged in a consultation exercise about its future: [1995] *New LJ* 298, 334, 406, 841, 843, 861.

[116] Most private ombudsmen deal only with complaints from individuals, not businesses. For claims of widespread consumer dissatisfaction with two such ombudsmen schemes see National Consumer Council, *Ombudsmen Services: Consumers' Views of the Office of the Building Societies Ombudsman and the Insurance Ombudsman Bureau* (London, 1993).

[117] P. E. Morris [1987] *JBL* 131, 133.

produce an acceptable response. Viewed positively, this proviso signifies a laudable intention to improve in-house complaints procedures; from a negative point of view it may be seen as a way of limiting the impact of the ombudsman on the affairs of the industry. If the arrangements for complaints against solicitors are anything to go by, complaints mechanisms run by the trade or profession in question may generate significant dissatisfaction. Even if such measures of self-regulation in fact inject an element of independence into the handling of complaints, this may not create an appearance of independence sufficient to make such mechanisms a fully adequate alternative to the courts.

Like the Solicitors Complaints Bureau, ombudsmen generally are not limited to dealing with complaints which could be pursued in a court.[118] Because ombudsmen may consider non-legal complaints, the norms which they can apply in settling disputes are not limited to legal rules and principles.[119] For example, ombudsmen can have regard to, and indeed develop, principles of good business practice relevant to the business in question. However, the emphasis in the work of most ombudsmen is on the resolution of individual complaints rather than on establishing general standards of conduct for the relevant trade or profession. By statute, the Building Societies ombudsman may decline to investigate a complaint on the ground that it has been or is being adjudicated upon by a court.[120] However, no consensual ombudsman scheme could lawfully prevent a complainant pursuing any judicial remedy in respect of the complaint: the complainant is free not to accept the ombudsman's decision. If the complainant accepts the decision, it is normally binding on the institution; except that under the building societies scheme a society can refuse to comply provided it publicizes its reasons for so doing. The ombudsmen in the financial services industries all have the power to award compensation of up to £100,000 to a complainant.

The activities of governmental ombudsmen are also of some relevance here. For example, in 1989 the Parliamentary Commissioner for Administration (PCA) investigated the role of the Department of Trade and Industry in the collapse of the Barlow Clowes investment group;[121] and several other similar

---

[118] Note that the power of the Building Societies Ombudsman to investigate 'maladministration' includes power to deal with negligent valuations by employees of societies: *Halifax Building Society* v. *Edell* [1992] Ch. 436.

[119] But they may develop principles which amount to principles of law. E.g., the Insurance Ombudsman developed a set of rules dealing with failure by claimants under travel insurance policies to take reasonable care of their possessions: *1988 Annual Report of the Insurance Ombudsman* (London), 20–2. However, the CA later adopted an approach more favourable to the insured: *1989 Annual Report of the Insurance Ombudsman* (London), 3–5.

[120] Building Societies Act 1986, Sch. 12, para. 2(b).

[121] See *First Report of the PCA for 1989–90* (HC 76). The PCA found that the DTI had committed acts of maladministration. Although the Government disagreed with several of the findings, substantial compensation was paid to investors on an an *ex gratia* basis in return for assignment to the Secretary of State of the rights of investors in the liquidation and against third parties. These rights were subsequently exercised and judgment was obtained by the DTI against Clowes: *Financial Times*, 19 Mar. 1992.

investigations have been conducted.[122] Allegations of negligence which might, in theory at least, form the basis of tort actions, were made against the Department in these cases. The PCA is required by statute not to investigate a complaint which could form or could have formed the basis of a court action unless it would, in his view, be unreasonable to expect such action to be taken.[123] As in the Barlow Clowes case, the PCA is sometimes able to secure for a complainant (*ex gratia*) monetary compensation in respect of action, such as the giving of incorrect or misleading advice, which might have given rise to tort claims.

5. CRITERIA FOR CHOOSING A DISPUTE SETTLING MECHANISM

Are there any criteria according to which we could judge the appropriateness or otherwise of particular dispute-settling mechanisms for resolving particular disputes? This question can be asked at two levels: at a practical level, since the choice of mechanism is usually for the parties themselves, the question for them concerns which mechanism will suit their dispute best. At a more theoretical level it might be possible to say that a particular mechanism is better suited to one type of dispute than to others and that this provides a policy justification for channelling disputes of that type towards a particular mechanism. A number of criteria of choice may be suggested.[124] First, how private is the dispute? A dispute may be private either in the sense that the parties (one or both) wish to keep it out of the public eye, or in the sense that it is a dispute which has no significant implications for third parties or for society as a whole. Adjudication by a court is public in both senses: it usually takes place in public; it resolves disputes by applying rules of law of general appplication; and it establishes binding general rules for the avoidance and settlement of similar disputes in the future. So if a party wishes to influence the future conduct of the other party, or of third parties,[125] court adjudication is the most appropriate mechanism. Traditional settlement, by contrast, normally takes place in private, and the terms of any settlement (which may be only loosely based on legal rules) are typically kept private. Ombudsmen tend to investigate in private, but usually publish the results of at least some of their investigations; they may also seek to establish (non-legal) principles of good conduct in the course of resolving individual complaints. Arbitration, conciliation, and mediation usually take place in private

---

[122] In one, concerning the collapse of Selective Investment Brokers Ltd, the PCA found in favour of the DTI.

[123] Parliamentary Commissioner Act 1967, s. 5(2).

[124] J. Effron (1989) 52 *MLR* 483; R. Thomas [1988] *CJQ* 206, 212–6.

[125] See the suggestion of P. Cockburn ('Litigation puts Lloyd's reputation at risk', *Financial Times*, 26 Feb. 1990) that mass litigation against members of Lloyd's was designed in part to put pressure on Lloyd's to 'launch a reinsurance lifeboat' to rescue suffering names.

and the outcome is often kept private;[126] but arbitration awards are usually based on ordinary rules of law, whereas the results of conciliation and mediation may bear no relationship to the legal rights and obligations of the parties.

A second criterion concerns whether parties to a dispute who had a (good) relationship before the dispute arose wish that relationship to continue after the dispute is resolved. This criterion is most relevant to contract disputes, but it is by no means true that all tort disputes arise between strangers: disputes between neighbouring landowners and between businesses arising out of misstatements are obvious counter-examples. As a general principle, the more adversarial the dispute-solving mechanism the more likely it is to destroy, or at least to injure, the parties' relationship. If the parties wish to preserve their relationship, they are much more likely to choose a more co-operative form of dispute resolution and thereby maximize the chances that their relationship will survive intact or even be strengthened. On the other hand, if one party has a much greater interest in the continuance of the relationship, then it may be very difficult to persuade the other to agree to co-operate, especially if the other knows of the dependence; in which case, the best mechanism for the dependent party may be the most formal (adversarial court adjudication), because it offers most protection from inequality of bargaining power.

A third criterion concerns the nature of the dispute. This is a complex issue,[127] but for our purposes the only relevant question is whether the dispute is a legal one or not. In other words, are the parties arguing about their legal rights and obligations or does their dispute have some other basis? Adjudication is the mechanism most suited to resolving legal disputes on points of law: courts must decide cases according to law and judges are experts in the law. Arbitrators may be lawyers, but are not always so: they may be experts in the technical subject matter of the dispute. Furthermore, arbitrations are not always based on rules of English law or even on rules of law at all: the parties can decide for themselves the basis on which their dispute is to be resolved.[128] If the basis is legal, then this would give the parties a reason to choose as arbitrator a person with appropriate legal qualifications

---

[126] There is an implied term in arbitration agreements that the award and the reasons of the arbitrator will not be disclosed to third parties unless this is necessary to establish legal rights against a third party: *Hassneh Insurance Co. of Israel* v. *Mew* [1993] 2 Lloyd's Rep. 243; *Insurance Co.* v. *Lloyd's Syndicate, Independent*, 8 Nov. 1994.

[127] See J. Effron (1989) 52 *MLR* 483, 486–90.

[128] Thus arbitration, as well as conciliation and mediation, is a mechanism which allow the parties to avoid the operation of unwanted legal rules. This can create special problems where the relevant legal rules require the court explicitly to take the public interest into account in reaching its decision. E.g., in deciding whether to grant an interlocutory injunction to restrain strike action the court must consider the probable impact of the strike on the public; if the parties to the dispute could, by avoiding litigation, avoid consideration of the public interest, serious conflicts might arise between government on the one hand and employers and unions on the other: Effron (1989) 52 *MLR* 480, 495–7.

and experience; but other factors may favour appointment of a non-lawyer. In this context, it should be recalled that rights of appeal from arbitration awards on points of law are very limited. Many of the complaints dealt with by ombudsmen could not give rise to a cause of action in law; but even if a particular complaint could be pursued in a court or tribunal, the ombudsman may not (and probably will not) resolve it strictly according to legal rules. Conciliation and mediation are designed not to give effect to the legal rights and obligations of the parties (if any), but to find a mutually acceptable and advantageous result on any basis. The more at stake financially, the more likely is it that the parties will insist on their strict legal rights.

A fourth criterion is the value of the complainant's claim. There is no financial limit to the jurisdiction of the High Court; and private commercial arbitrators are usually unlimited in this respect. Private ombudsmen, for example, can often award compensation only up to a relatively low ceiling. Large claims are seen as the province of the courts and of arbitration.

A fifth criterion is the relative resources (both financial and human) and the relative bargaining strength of the parties. The more unequal they are, the better it is for the weaker party to have an independent third party involved; the better it is for that party to have a mechanism which operates according to procedures decided by a third party and enforceable against an unco-operative defendant; and the better it is for the third party to have a mechanism the substantive outcome of which does not depend on co-operation and compromise but on rights and obligations (whether legal or not). On these criteria, court adjudication seems most appropriate in such cases. Of all the dispute-resolving mechanisms in our society courts are, and appear to be, the most independent, whereas 'domestic' complaints mechanisms and private ombudsman may find it difficult to be, and to appear, completely independent of the group subject to complaint and investigation. Also, the procedures of courts are backed up by the coercive power of the state whereas private dispute settlement relies, to a greater or lesser extent, on the co-operation of the respondent. On this scale, private arbitration falls between the two extremes.

Despite its advantages for weaker parties, court adjudication has three relevant major defects: if the parties differ in their ability to cope with delay, adjudication may be less appropriate than some other faster mechanism; secondly, if the parties differ in their ability to finance the litigation, some other cheaper mechanism may be more appropriate; thirdly, since most court actions are settled, the weaker party will usually not, in practice, secure the theoretical protection which courts offer to the weak against the strong.

Sixthly, a relevant criterion of choice for the claimant concerns the ease with which any decision or settlement in the claimant's favour can be enforced. If the outcome is that one party is to make a monetary payment to the other, then a court order to this effect is, in theory at least, more easily enforced than a contractual agreement that one party pay the other. Except in the case of an arbitral award (which can, with the leave of the court, be enforced as if it were a court order), the beneficiary of a contractual agreement to pay money would have to bring an action on the contract before enlisting the state's machinery of enforcement. Where the outcome is that a party is to take some action other than payment of money to the other, if this outcome is embodied in a court order, failure to comply will be punishable as a contempt; but if it is embodied in a contract, its enforceability would depend, in theory at least, on the availability of a decree of specific performance. In practice, whether a party actually does what is required will often depend on how much (non-legal) pressure can be brought to bear by the other; and this, in turn, will depend on the relative resources and persuasive strength of the parties. Formal enforcement will usually be a last resort. Where the dispute-resolving mechanism has been organized by a trade association or other commercial body, then members may be sufficiently committed to the scheme to ensure that they will comply: in such cases, peer pressure is important. On the other hand, non-members of the relevant group who are unco-operative may be beyond the reach of anything but court proceedings.

Seventhly, it is worth comparing the various dispute-resolving mechanisms according to how they are funded. There are three important questions for the claimant: how much does it cost to make a complaint? How important is it to be represented and how much will representation cost? And who, at the end of the day, will bear the costs of the complaint? Of course, these questions are also of concern to the respondent. As regards the first question, industry-based complaints, arbitration, and conciliation mechanisms are most attractive: they are often free (or, at least, very cheap) to the complainant, and the respondent will probably have paid a levy unrelated to the incidence of complaints against it. Initiating proceedings in a tribunal tends to be cheaper than doing so in a court, whereas the costs of one-off private arbitrations are borne by the parties as agreed between them.

So far as representation is concerned, as a general rule legal aid is available for court proceedings, but not for most tribunal proceedings or for private arbitrations, conciliation, or mediation.[129] So far as tribunals are concerned, the denial of legal aid is justified in terms of a desire to prevent excessive technicality, formality, legalism, and complexity; but there is evidence that (legally) represented applicants do better before at least some tribunals than do litigants in person. Even where proceedings are flexible and informal and are conducted by a third party who can take an active role in ensuring that the proceedings are conducted fairly to both parties, if there is a disparity of knowledge, resources, skill, or experience between the parties, representation may be the most effective way of redressing the balance. The mechanism which least requires assistance or representation is the ombudsman technique;

---

[129] The Woolf Report on *Access to Justice* (1995) recommends that in a review of legal aid, the funding of mediation services 'should be considered'.

this is because of its investigatory nature: the ombudsman's staff take the place of the parties' representatives.

So far as concerns the ultimate bearing of costs, court proceedings are very risky because of the basic rule that costs follow the event. No other mechanism (not even traditional settlement) is as risky as this: either each party bears its own costs or they agree in advance that the costs are to be borne in some other way or the costs are met from a fund to which one or other of the parties (usually the respondent) may have made a contribution.

Finally, there are some relevant differences between court adjudication (which is state-run) and privately organized mechanisms.[130] First, because a respondent will normally be amenable to a private mechanism only by agreement, the respondent is more likely to be prepared to comply with the outcome than when forced to submit to the jurisdiction of a court or tribunal. Secondly, private mechanisms can be more flexible than courts and tribunals. They may be more accessible in terms of physical location and hours of operation. They can adopt and develop a wider range of procedural and remedial options,[131] and they can draw on a wider range of information and expertise than can courts and tribunals. Thirdly, industry-based schemes are in a better position to 'observe and systematially draw attention to trends and practices revealed by individual disputes'.[132]

On the other hand, the state court system is much more geographically decentralized and much better known to the public than most private mechanisms. Secondly, a complainant is more likely to be able to secure an oral hearing in court proceedings than before a private body. Thirdly, the courts can provide redress against respondents who would not willingly submit to any consensual mechanism. Fourthly, the funding of courts, tribunals, and public ombudsmen is much more stable than the funding of private schemes, which depend on the continued support of potential respondents as a group or of private benefactors. Fifthly, state-run mechanisms are more likely to be

---

[130] R. Thomas [1988] *CJQ* 208, 212–6.

[131] This remedial flexibility is well illustrated by the City Panel on Takeovers and Mergers, which operates in an arbitral mode in dealing with claims of breach of the Takeover Code. E.g., in 1987 the Panel held that Guinness had influenced the price of the shares in the Distillers Company, for which it was making a takeover bid, in contravention of the Code. It ordered Guinness to pay compensation to former Distillers shareholders even though the relevant shareholders had not been parties to the 'action' before the Panel and were, indeed, unidentified. Guinness used newspaper advertising to locate the shareholders entitled; it has been estimated that the total amount of compensation payable may have been as high as £100 million. Another example is an order made by the Panel in 1989 requiring Plessey, which was the target of a takeover bid by GEC and Siemens of West Germany, to modify a statement made in a circular to its shareholders to the effect that the bidders were seeking to buy Plessey shares at less than their market value. There is no reason why courts should not be given powers to make such orders, but the important point is that the Takeover Panel has felt free to make such orders without being given the power to do so by any other body, and unconstrained by historical constraints which limit the remedial options of the courts.

[132] Thomas [1988] *CJQ* 206, 213. In this respect, state ombudsmen are similar to private ombudsmen.

(and to be seen to be) independent of the respondent than are privately run schemes (except, in some cases at least, one-off arbitrations).

6. CONCLUSION

At the beginning of this Chapter I said that non-adjudicatory methods of resolving tort disputes represented not just procedural alternatives to adjudication but also, in a sense, substantive alternatives to tort law because the rules and principles of tort law may be less determinative of the outcome of such alternatives to adjudication than of adjudication. It does not follow from this that the rules of tort law are a sham because processes which operate in the shadow of the law can only do so effectively if the contours of the shadow are sharp. However, it does mean that in order to extend our understanding of tort law beyond its purely doctrinal content to its social impact we need to improve our knowledge and appreciation of (*inter alia* the processes by which tort disputes are commonly resolved.

8

Administrative Methods of Protection

INTRODUCTION

In the last Chapter we considered various procedures for dealing retrospectively with bilateral disputes[1] concerning the civil law rights and obligations *inter se* of a person who alleges that some economic interest of that person has been interfered with and of the person who allegedly interfered with that interest; and those procedures are ones in which both the interferer and the 'victim' play a part. By contrast, this Chapter focusses on various mechanisms which can play a part in protecting economic interests but which lack one or more of these characteristics. I use the word 'administrative' simply as an umbrella term to cover a disparate collection of techniques for protecting economic interests of the sort also protected by the law of tort. This Chapter continues the task of locating the law of tort in the larger jigsaw of legal techniques for protecting economic interests which operate beside and interact with tort law.

1. COMPENSATION SCHEMES

All of the dispute-settling mechanisms which we considered in the last chapter have, as one of their possible outcomes, a payment of monetary compensation to the complainant. Such compensation would be paid either by the respondent personally[2] or by an insurance company under the terms of an insurance contract between the respondent and the insurer. A respondent who pays personally might, in turn, pass the cost of that payment on to others, such as consumers (by charging more for goods or services provided), or shareholders (by paying smaller dividends), or employees (by awarding lower wage and salary increases), or a combination of these. However the compensation is funded, the essence of all of these mechanisms is the making of a complaint against an individual and the resolution of that complaint by the making of a payment (or the doing of some other action) by or on behalf of

---

[1] In this respect, mass claims consist of a large number of bilateral disputes arising out of the same set of circumstances.

[2] But not necessarily out of his or her own resources.

the respondent. By contrast, the essence of an administrative compensation scheme is that the applicant makes a claim on a compensation fund and not against any individual whose conduct may have led to the making of the claim. That individual may have contributed to the fund, as may other persons who are or may potentially have been or may in the future be, respondents to similar complaints about their conduct; but compensation payments under administrative schemes are not the result of such a complaint against an individual but of a decision that the applicant satisfies the criteria for the award of compensation from the fund.

In a sense, the whole social security system is an administrative compensation fund which compensates victims of various vicissitudes and misfortunes, some of which may be more or less directly attributable to particular acts of particular individuals. But here we are more specifically concerned with compensation funds which are designed, in part at least, to compensate victims of acts of the sort with which the law of tort deals. The most prominent of such schemes deal with personal injuries—the Industrial Injuries Scheme[3] and the Criminal Injuries Compensation Scheme,[4] for instance. The Industrial Injuries Scheme is a 'no-fault' scheme in the sense that it is not a precondition of entitlement to compensation payments under the scheme that the applicant prove that his or her physical condition was the result of anyone's fault. By contrast, the Criminal Injuries Compensation Scheme compensates for personal injuries 'attributable to a crime of violence', so that it is necessary for the applicant to trace a causal connection between the injuries and a criminal act. Benefits payable under both schemes[5] are calculated on the basis of fairly rigid formulae as the result of an administrative (not a judicial) process designed to determine whether the applicant meets the criteria for the award of a monetary payment.

An important adjunct to the Criminal Injuries Compensation Scheme is the power of criminal courts to make compensation orders.[6] Although such orders are made against an indvidual, not a fund, it is convenient to consider

---

[3] Cane, *Atiyah's Accidents, Compensation and the Law,* 5th edn. (London, 1993), 279ff.

[4] *Ibid.,* ch. 12.

[5] At the time of writing, the introduction of tariffs under the Criminal Injuries Compensation Scheme had been held unlawful by the House of Lords; but it is assumed that the Government will re-introduce tariffs legislatively.

[6] Powers of Criminal Courts Act 1973, s. 35 (as amended by s. 104 of the Criminal Justice Act 1988; see also ss. 105 and 106). Note should also be taken of s. 43A of the 1973 Act (inserted by s. 107 of the 1988 Act): under it the court can order that the proceeds (or part thereof) of the sale of property, the subject of a forfeiture order (under s. 43 of the 1973 Act, as amended by s. 69 of the 1988 Act) shall be paid to a person who suffered personal injury, loss, or damage as a result of the offence for which the offender was convicted. This power is useful in cases where the forfeited property does not belong to the victim (and so cannot be reclaimed from the police), but it is the main asset out of which any compensation order might have been satisfied. Indeed, an order can be made under this s. only if, but for the inadequacy of the offender's means, the court would have made a compensation order. Of course, compensation orders can only be made where the criminal is identified and successfully prosecuted. In many cases, victims of property crimes may suffer considerable hardship, and social security payments may be their only source of relief.

them here. A criminal compensation order requires a convicted offender to pay compensation 'for any personal injury, loss or damage resulting from that offence'. Orders are made only in simple cases where, for example, the issue of causation is straightforward.[7] If a court does not make a compensation order in a case where it is empowered to do so, it must give reasons. The court may award such compensation as it thinks appropriate in the light of all the circumstances, including the means of the offender.[8] Where the court wishes to impose a fine and make a compensation order but the offender has insufficient means to pay both, the compensation order is given preference. In the case of an offence under the Theft Act 1968, damage done to property while it was out of the owner's possession is treated as resulting from the offence however it was caused and whoever caused it.[9]

If the victim of the crime brings a civil action against the offender after a compensation order has been made and the civil court holds that the injury, loss, or damage resulting from the offence was less than the criminal court took it to be, the compensation order may be discharged or the amount payable under it reduced. Also, if the order related to property which has since been recovered, the order may be discharged or reduced in amount.[10] Damages in any subsequent civil action are assessed without regard to the compensation order, but there are provisions to prevent the defendant paying more than the greater of the compensation order and the damages award.[11]

Compensation orders can be made in respect of road accidents, but only in cases where the offender was uninsured in relation to use of the vehicle and where the Motor Insurers Bureau (MIB) will not pay.[12] In cases covered by the MIB scheme, the Bureau will pay compensation for property damage up to £250,000, but not the first £175. A compensation order can include an amount representing a lost no-claims bonus. If a compensation order was made and the MIB subsequently accepted liability, the amount of the order would be set off against the Bureau's payment.

Criminal compensation orders are important for our purposes for two reasons: first, they can provide compensation for property damage and purely economic loss resulting from criminal offences (which may also amount to

---

[7] R. v. *Kneeshaw* [1975] QB 57, 60; R. v. *Daly* [1974] 1 WLR 133; R. v. *Vivian* [1979] 1 WLR 291.

[8] There is no upper limit on the amount which an offender can be ordered to pay by a Crown Court; magistrates are limited to £5,000. Most awards are modest for the simple reason that the means of most offenders are modest. It has also been said, for instance, that the proper way to make a substantial claim for personal injuries is by civil suit, not by way of an application for a compensation order: *Herbert* v. *Lambeth LBC* [1991] 90 LGR 310. On the other hand, in one case a company director who was convicted of recklessly making false VAT returns on behalf of the company was ordered to pay the substantial sum of £9,635 to the Customs authorities: R. v. *Chappel* (1984) Cr. App. R 31.

[9] For some empirical research on the use of compensation orders in cases of property offences see R. Tarling and P. Softley [1976] *Crim. LR* 422.

[10] Powers of Criminal Courts Act 1973, s. 37.   [11] S. 38.

[12] On the MIB see *Atiyah's Accidents, Compensation and the Law*, 5th edn., 212–6.

torts). Secondly, they can be made in respect of any offence which causes loss.[13] Whereas a tort action for breach of statutory duty will only lie in cases where the court interprets the statute as meant to give rise to such an action, a compensation order can be made regardless of whether the statute which created the offence aimed to protect individuals or not.[14]

Compensation schemes dealing with property damage and purely economic loss are less common than schemes dealing with personal injuries; this is, no doubt, simply a function of our hierarchy of social values. But there are some noteworthy financial loss compensation schemes. Some of them deal with loss suffered as a result of government activity, and others with loss suffered as a result of the actions of private individuals. Into the first category falls the statutory scheme for the payment of compensation to people who have suffered miscarriages of justice.[15] Such compensation may include an amount for pecuniary losses, such as loss of wages. Another important scheme of the first type is that established by the Land Compensation Act 1973. There is, of course, a general common law principle, which has elaborate statutory backing,[16] that if the government takes private land for some public purpose, it must pay compensation to the owner. Under this Act, property owners can be compensated for the effects on the value of their property of noise, vibration, smell, fumes, smoke, artificial lighting, and discharge of substances, resulting from the use of public works, such as motorways, which would,[17] but for the operation of the defence of statutory authorization, constitute a nuisance.[18] Compensation is not payable in respect of claims worth less than £50.[19]

Under Part XVI of the Housing Act 1985, grants are payable to people who have purchased council houses[20] to enable them to remedy certain defects in their houses. The provisions are designed to deal with defects in system-built houses and flats constructed since 1945 which render the affected dwelling virtually unsaleable or unmortgageable. The Secretary of State decides which

[13] They are often made, e.g., in the case of successful prosecutions under the Trade Descriptions Act 1968: Harvey and Parry, 226–8, 370–1. See also *Herbert* v. *Lambeth LBC* [1991] 90 LGR 310 (failure to comply with order to abate statutory nuisance).

[14] e.g. in *R.* v. *Bokhari* (1974) 59 Cr. App. R 303 a landlord who was convicted under s. 30 of the Rent Act 1965 of harassing a tenant was ordered to pay compensation totalling £550; but in *McCall* v. *Abalesz* [1976] QB 585, s. 30 was held not to give rise to a civil cause of action.

[15] See 00 above.

[16] For an account see K. Davies, *Law of Compulsory Purchase and Compensation*, 5th edn. (Croydon, 1994).

[17] The Act only applies in cases where the authority responsible for the works is immune from liability in nuisance: s. 6(1); see also s. 17.

[18] See generally Davies, *Law of Compulsory Purchase and Compensation*, 189–97. For an argument to the effect that there is no meaningful distinction between a claim for statutory no-fault compensation and a tort claim see G. L. Williams and B. A. Hepple, *Foundations of the Law of Tort*, 2nd edn. (London, 1984), 24–6.

[19] Land Compensation Act 1973, s. 7.

[20] But not privately-owned houses. The compensation scheme was introduced to restore confidence in the Government's right-to-buy scheme for council tenants. It has been estimated that the total cost may exceed £900 million.

defects qualify under the scheme. The scheme is not primarily concerned with removing dangers to health or safety: a defect can be designated if, as a result of its existence becoming known, the value of some or all of the affected dwellings has been substantially reduced. Such a defect may, of course, threaten health or safety, but it need not. In certain circumstances (for example, where the cost of repair is unreasonably high, or where a scheme for repair has not yet been approved for the type of defect in question[21]), the house may be repurchased from the owner; and if this is done, the local authority is under a duty to grant the former owner a protected tenancy of council housing (this will often be the acquired house or flat).

Into the category of schemes concerned with the actions of private individuals falls, for example, the Home Office scheme for compensation for property damage or loss caused by absconders from Borstals and open prisons.[22] Under this scheme, compensation is only payable in relation to property in the neighbourhood of the institution from which the escape was made, and which was uninsured.[23] Compensation is assessed on ordinary insurance principles. This scheme, like the Criminal Injuries Compensation Scheme, is an informal one not backed by statute; payments made under it are *ex gratia*, not a legal entitlement. Mention should also be made of the Riot (Damages) Act 1886 under which compensation can be claimed for damage to or destruction or loss of buildings and their contents resulting from riots. If the damage or loss is covered by insurance, the insurer can recover the amount paid out under the policy. A person aggrieved by failure by the compensation authority to award compensation, or by the amount awarded, can sue the authority.

Another important statutory compensation scheme is that under section 54 of the Financial Services Act.[24] Under this section, the Securities and Investments Board may make rules to 'establish a scheme for compensating investors in cases where persons who are or have been authorized persons[25] are unable, or likely to be unable, to satisfy claims in respect of any description of civil liability incurred by them in connection with their investment business'. Membership of the scheme is a condition of membership of the self-regulating organizations (SROs) set up under the Act. The scheme is funded partly by levies on members of SROs and partly by insurance; and the max-

---

[21] R. v. *Thamesdown BC, ex parte Pritchard, Independent*, 29 Dec. 1988.

[22] C. Harlow, *Compensation and Government Torts* (London, 1982), 154–6.

[23] Although if it was insured, and as a result of the claim the insured lost a no-claims bonus, compensation in respect of this loss might be paid. The claim in *Dorset Yacht Co. Ltd* v. *Home Office* [1970] AC 1004 did not fall within the scheme because the property was insured.

[24] Financial Services (Compensation of Investors) Rules 1994. For a general evaluation of compensation schemes in the financial services industry see A. C. Page and R. B. Ferguson, *Investor Protection* (London, 1992), 71–4; and concerning the scheme under the Financial Services Act see *ibid.*, 262–4.

[25] That is, authorized under the provisions of the Act to carry on investment business.

imum compensation payable to any one investor is £48,000.[26] Only private (that is, not business or professional) investors may claim under the scheme.[27] There is a limit of £100 million on the maximum amount payable to meet defaults occurring in any one year;[28] this limit might cause difficulties if there were a large default late in an accounting year because the excess of one year cannot be carried over into the next.

The compensation scheme is triggered when an investment firm defaults or is unlikely to be able to meet all of its liabilities (which may include tort liabilities). Claims in respect of property of the claimant held by the firm in default and those arising out of uncompleted transactions are automatically compensatable, while other types of claim are compensatable only if and to the extent that[29] the fund manager 'considers that this is essential in order to provde fair compensation to the investor'.[30] Claims based solely on 'failure of investment performance to match a guarantee given or a representation made' are not compensatable.[31] It is clear, therefore, that the scheme does not cover all claims which might be actionable in tort.

Claims must be made within six months of the date when the investor became aware, or ought reasonably to have been aware, of the default. The scheme manager assesses the claims against the firm (which must, to be compensatable, relate to a liability established before a court of competent jurisdiction or one which the managers of the fund believe could be so established), and the assets available to pay them, and then pays compensation for any shortfall not recoverable from the firm to all eligible investors. The scheme is designed to prevent those with legal claims against a firm from suffering by its bankruptcy: instead of recovering a proportionate part of the assets available for distribution to creditors, investors protected by the scheme will recover in full, up to the limit of £48,000.[32] Beyond that, they are relegated to the position of unsecured creditors. There is no appeals mechanism from decisions of the manager of the fund.

The compensation payable will normally cover investment funds lost and investment gains not realized; but the fund manager has a discretion not to pay in full where this would 'provide benefits to. the investor which are disproportionate either to the return which he might reasonably have expected or to actual returns made on similar investments with other firms'.[33] The fund manager can make payments to investors even before the assets and

---

[26] The formula is that the investor can recover 100% of the first £30,000 lost, and 90% of the next £20,000. Compensation paid out in the year to the end of Mar. 1995 totalled more than £16.6 million (£17.5 million in 1993–4). The largest payouts have been in respect of the 'home income plan' and 'personal pensions misselling' scandals.

[27] Financial Services (Compensation of Investors) Rules 1994 r.2.02.2.a.

[28] R. 2.07.2.

[29] R. v. *Investors Compensation Fund, ex parte Bowden* [1995] 3 WLR 289.

[30] R. 2.04.1.   [31] R. 2.04.3a.

[32] There is a similar, but more generous, scheme which protects the holders of insurance policies against insolvency of the insurer, established under the Policyholders Protection Act 1975.

[33] Financial Services (Compensation of Investors) Rules 1994, r. 2.06.2.

liabilities of the firm have been fully ascertained. The fund is subrogated to the compensated investors' claims against the firm.

It should also be remembered that the SIB can apply to the court for an order for the payment into court of amounts representing profits made or losses inflicted by contravention of a range of provisions of, and rules made under, the Financial Services Act.[34] Such an order in effect generates a compensation fund out of which investors who entered into unlawful transactions are paid. In the 1980s a very large number of people were unlawfully sold personal pensions which were less valuable than pensions available to them under occupational schemes. The Personal Investment Authority (the relevant SRO) required the offending insurance companies to set up a compensation fund, and it is estimated that the total compensation bill may be as high as £3 billion.

The Law Society runs two compensation funds: the Compensation Fund (CF) and the Solicitors Indemnity Fund (SIF). The latter is a mutual insurance scheme to which all solicitors must belong and which provides compulsory cover up to £1 million, basically for losses resulting from negligence. Being a form of liability insurance, it will be considered in more detail in the next chapter. The Compensation Fund, on the other hand, is not an insurance scheme, but is funded by levies on solicitors' firms.[35] Payments from it are discretionary.[36] The CF operates as a last resort from which payment will be made only when there is no other available source of compensation. It covers fraudulent and dishonest conduct by solicitors (which may, of course, be tortious).

The compensation schemes we have examined can usefully be divided into two groups. The first is represented by the Land Compensation Act scheme: it provides compensation for conduct which would not be actionable in tort because authorized by statute; so it has the obvious advantage over tort liability that it may provide compensation where the tort system would not. The same is true of the compensation scheme in respect of system-built houses considered above. But most of the compensation schemes which we have reviewed pay out on the basis of legal liability (which may, in some cases, mean tort liability).[37] What advantages do such 'liability-based' schemes have over the tort system of obtaining compensation?

The three main criticisms of the tort system are that adversarial court procedure is highly formal, and so intimidating to those not accustomed to it, and that litigation is costly and slow. How do liability-based compensation schemes score on these points? In the first place, they are not adversarial in the way that court adjudication is: although the issue of liability has to be decided by the scheme's administrators, this is typically done as a result of

---

[34] See 181 above.   [35] It operates on a pay-as-you-go basis.
[36] R. v. *Law Society, ex parte Reigate Projects Ltd* [1993] 1 WLR 1531. See also A. E. Hoffman [1994] *New LJ* 333.
[37] For this reason, lawyers need to be heavily involved in the administration of such schemes.

investigation and not of an adversarial contest between the applicant and the alleged wrongdoer; so an element of conflict is removed. In this respect, such schemes are superior to traditional settlement as well as to court adjudication. Secondly, such schemes normally operate, at first instance anyway, on the basis of documents only without oral hearings or interviews. So one of the most intimidating elements of the court process is absent.

However, it should be remembered that most tort actions are settled out-of-court without any personal contact between the parties themselves; and the price for this, in many cases, is that one or other of the parties is at a bargaining disadvantage *vis-à-vis* the other, against which formal court hearings would give a (large) degree of protection. Administrative determination of claims on compensation funds eliminates the effect of such disparities by eliminating the bargaining process. As a result, it is much more feasible for a claimant on such a fund than for a tort claimant to dispense with legal representation in making the claim. On the other hand, it may be difficult for a lay person who has no legal assistance to present his or her case fully and accurately in writing and without the aid of a face-to-face meeting with the administrator; and it may be difficult for the administrator to assess the claim properly without interviewing one or both of the parties.

Thirdly, an administrative scheme is likely to be much cheaper to run than the tort system. For example, the Pearson Commission found that, whereas it cost about 85 pence to deliver £1 of tort compensation for personal injuries, it cost only about 11 pence, on average, to deliver £1 of social security benefit. The administrative costs of the (non-tariff version of the) Criminal Injuries Compensation scheme (which is essentially a liability-based scheme[38]) are about 10 pence for every £1 of compensation paid out. But we need to exercise some caution with these figures. Those for the tort system include the costs of raising the compensation (that is, the brokerage and associated administrative costs, and the advertising costs, of liability insurers), as well as the legal costs of plaintiffs and defendants; whereas the costs of raising the taxes by which social security and criminal injuries compensation are funded are not included in the costs of these schemes, and neither are the legal costs (if any) of applicants. Even taking this into account, however, we can safely assert that even liability-based compensation schemes are likely to be significantly cheaper overall than the tort system. One would expect particularly significant cost savings in cases involving large numbers of claimants: as we have seen, court procedures do not facilitate the consolidation of large numbers of claims for damages whereas, under an administrative scheme, a

---

[38] Both the cost and speed of a compensation system are affected by the simplicity or complexity, the clarity or vagueness, and the certainty or uncertainty of the rules of entitlement. Much of the cost and delay of the tort system is a function of the complexity, vagueness, and uncertainty of many of the rules of tort law. Since liability-based schemes may also suffer from these features of tort law, this will affect the cost and speed of such schemes. On the other hand, 'no-fault' schemes are not necessarily based on simple, clear, and certain rules: witness the Industrial Injuries Scheme.

single investigation (albeit longer and more complex than one involving one or only a few claimants) may enable a large number of claims to be met. Most importantly, perhaps, compensation schemes are usually free to claimants who need not incur legal costs in presenting their claims.

Fourthly, speed: one would expect that the investigative, non-adversarial nature of liability-based compensation schemes would make them faster than the tort system: the person under investigation will be less able to cause delay than in ordinary litigation. Furthermore, rules of evidence applicable to court proceedings would not apply to an administrative investigation, and the delays caused by the need to prepare for an oral trial would not occur. Of course, this is not to say that administrative schemes will necessarily produce quick results. The compensation scheme established under the Financial Services Act deals with the possibility of delay by allowing for the making of interim compensation payments pending full investigation of the defaulter's financial position.[39]

Despite the potential advantages of liability-based compensation funds, recourse to such a compensation scheme may be less attractive than making a claim against the wrongdoer,[40] if only because the compensation available under such a scheme will typically be less than the hypothetical legal liability of the wrongdoer. A fund claimant could not, in the absence of statutory provision to this effect, be required to accept compensation from the fund as a substitute for litigating the claim. But it will usually be in the best interests of a claimant to accept what is on offer from the fund; and such sums would, no doubt, be set off against common law damages if the claimant subsequently brought an action against the wrongdoer.

What if the claimant is dissatisfied with the decision of the administrators of a liability-based compensation scheme? Such a scheme may provide an internal appeals mechanism (but the Financial Services Act scheme does not). The Legal Services Ombudsman deals with complaints against the Law Society and the Bar relating to the investigation of complaints against solicitors and barristers. Another possibility might be an application for judicial review on the ground, for example, that the administrator made an error of law or exercised a discretion unreasonably or followed an unfair procedure.[41] It is very likely that such an application could be made even if the compensation scheme in question was non-statutory, and even if there was no contract between the claimant and the administrators of the fund.[42] However,

---

[39] Financial Services (Compensation of Investors) Rules 1994, r. 2.09.

[40] It has been reported that a mass court action is being planned on behalf of alleged victims of the 'pensions transfer scandal' who are dissatisfied with the way their claims are being dealt with under the Investors Compensation Scheme.

[41] E.g. *R. v. Investors Compensation Scheme, ex parte Weyell* [1994] 3 WLR 1045; *R. v. Investors Compensation Scheme, ex parte Bowden* [1995] 3 WLR 289. Judicial review might also be available in respect of non-liabiltiy based schemes such as that for victims of miscarriages of justice: e.g. *R. v. Secretary of State for the Home Department, ex parte Howse, The Times*, 1 July 1994.

[42] *R. v. Panel on Takeovers and Mergers, ex parte Datafin PLC* [1987] QB 815.

the courts will probably adopt a cautious attitude to such applications on the ground that if the decisions of the administrators could be easily upset some, at least, of the advantages of such schemes would be threatened.[43] Such an approach would be in line with the *laissez faire* attitude of the law to private arbitrations.

Another possibility for a claimant dissatisfied with a decision of the administrators of a compensation fund may be to sue them for negligence in handling the claim. However, the prospects of such a claim succeeding are slim in the light of the decision in *Wood* v. *Law Society*[44] that the Solicitors' Complaints Bureau owes no duty of care in the investigation of complaints against solicitors. The crux of the decision seems to have been that complainants should look primarily to the lawyer complained about for monetary compensation (as Miss Wood had done in this case) and to the Legal Services Ombudsman to deal with complaints about the investigation process. The judge also thought that the SCB was performing a quasi-judicial function. Such immunization of compensation fund managers from the discipline of the law of tort seems hard to justify despite the fact that they are not the party primarily responsible for the applicant's loss.

One important feature of administrative compensation funds is that the issue of funding can be separated from the issue of entitlement to compensation: under the tort system, the plaintiff's entitlement to compensation and the defendant's liability to compensate are decided according to one and the same set of rules. Of course, the defendant is free to pass on and spread the liability by means of insurance, by charging higher prices, or by paying lower wages or dividends; and, in some cases, potential defendants are required, either by statute or by some non-statutory rule, to insure against liability. But the defendant's legal liability to pay is a mirror image of the plaintiff's right to be compensated. There is no such necessary link between entitlement and funding in the case of administrative schemes. Even in the case of liability-based schemes under which the claimant's entitlement to be compensated is based on a finding of legal liability in the alleged wrongdoer, the compensation may not be funded on a liability-related basis. Indeed, one of the main functions of such schemes is to provide compensation in circumstances where the wrongdoer has disappeared and so cannot be sued; or where a judgment against the alleged wrongdoer would be unenforceable because of the wrongdoer's lack of means. It is one of the major advantages of administrative compensation schemes over the tort-cum-liability-insurance system that the claimant may recover even if the wrongdoer cannot, for one reason or another, be sued or lacks the means to satisfy any judgment.

On the other hand, if the compensation fund is not financed on a risk-related (or 'insurance') basis, then it may be inferior to the tort system in terms of deterrence,[45] even if entitlement to compensation is liability-based.

---

[43] Cf. R. v. *Investors Compensation Scheme, ex parte Bowden* [1994] 1 All ER 525, 533e–f.
[44] [1993] *New LJ* 1475.   [45] See 474–5 below.

If potential wrongdoers do not contribute to the fund proportionally to the risk that their activities will generate successful claims on the fund, their liability to contribute will not give them the 'correct' incentives to avoid claim-generating conduct. It may, therefore, be important for such schemes to be supported by regulatory and policing mechanisms in order to minimize the incidence of claims-generating incidents.

2. REGULATION[46]

The common law in general and the law of tort in particular are primarily concerned with the past; in the context of this book, they provide remedies (usually damages) for past interferences with economic interests, and they do this at the suit of individual 'owners' of such interests who activate the legal process by commencing (or threatening to commence) a court action or by making a claim against another based on legal rights and obligations. But the law of tort is not wholly concerned with the past: first, injunctions are sometimes available to restrain anticipated future interferences with economic (and other) interests; secondly, the granting of remedies for past interferences on the basis of the rules of tort law may have an effect on the future conduct of the particular person against whom a remedy is granted and also of others who know of the rules and who wish to avoid incurring legal liability in similar circumstances. In other words, the law of tort may have deterrent effects; and to the extent that it does, it may be said to regulate human conduct. However, the prime function of the English law of tort is the correction of past wrongs; the deterrence of future wrongful conduct is a secondary, although not unimportant, aim.

An injunction is a measure of (what may be called) 'targeted deterrence': it instructs the person to whom it is addressed to cease or not to commence a particular interference with another's interests. An award of damages, on the other hand, is a measure of (what may be called) 'flexible deterrence' in the sense that, although it instructs D to pay P a sum of money, it does not instruct D not to interfere further in the future with P's interest for interference with which the damages were awarded. In this sense,[47] it is for D to decide how to react to the judgment. Economic theory says that D will take measures to avoid future interferences with P's (and others' similar) economic interests if the cost of avoiding future interferences is less than the cost of paying damages (discounted by the risk of being held liable); otherwise D will not take such precautions but will, if possible, pool the cost of possible future liability by insurance or pass on the cost of past and possible future liability by increasing the price of goods or services or by paying lower wages or div-

---

[46] Sir G. Borrie [1990] *PL* 552.

[47] But in this sense only because, as we have seen, a defendant is free to, and may be able to, bargain around an injunction: see 354–8 above.

idends. In the latter case the market, rather than the defendant, will decide the 'proper' level of interference with economic interests by reacting to the economic impact of the cost of liability.

But both specific remedies (such as injunctions) and monetary remedies (such as damages) can have (what might be called) 'general deterrent' effects in that if the award of these remedies is based on publicly known[48] rules of law (as tort remedies always are), it may influence the conduct of parties other than the particular individuals against whom such remedies are granted. In this way (as we have said), the law of tort can have (what we might call) a 'regulatory effect' on human conduct in that the rules of tort law, being general and prospective in form, may influence the way people behave even though these rules are normally applied retrospectively after some interference with economic (or other) interests has taken place.

It is impossible to assess the regulatory effect of the rules of tort law concerned with economic interests for the simple reason that there is no relevant empirical evidence. Such evidence as there is in the context of liability for personal injuries suggests that tort law is a relatively inefficient regulator of human conduct and that the criminal law, for example, is more effective.[49] This issue will be discussed in more detail Chapter 10. The important point to be made here is that on the whole tort law provides flexible rather than targeted deterrence because damages are the most common remedy for torts. The theory of flexible deterrence requires, for its success in practice, that the market operate freely and without imperfections arising from deficiencies of knowledge, high contracting costs, or distortions arising, for example, from the existence of monopolies. To the extent that the market does not operate freely then one would, in theory, expect that the flexible-deterrent and regulatory effects of tort law would not be fully realized. Indeed, imperfections in the market may even hinder the targeted-deterrent effects of tort law because, as we saw in an earlier chapter, tort remedies can be bargained around.

One view of tort law is that it is a technique for correcting certain imperfections in the operation of the market; and because the basic legal form of market activity is contract, tort law is, from this point of view, an adjunct to contract law. But in this role tort law is, as we have just observed, itself the victim of market imperfections because defendants can very often decide for themselves how they will react to tort judgments against them and can give effect to this decision in the market. So tort law itself[50] may in theory, and does in practice, need 'assistance' from other forms of law, notably

---

[48] Or perhaps we should say, more realistically, 'publicly knowable'.

[49] For general discussion see Cane, *Atiyah's Accidents, Compensation and the Law*, 5th edn., 361ff.

[50] And, indeed, the whole of the common law, which operates similarly to tort law so far as its regulatory effects are concerned.

regulatory laws backed up by criminal sanctions[51] which cannot, at the end of the day, be bargained around.

Another important feature of tort law which serves to weaken its regulatory power is that it normally has to be activated by individuals who have suffered (or are likely in the near future to suffer) some harm or injury which is recognized by the law of tort as a proper subject of its attention, as the result of some tortious conduct on the part of an identifiable individual who is amenable to legal process. Not only is the legal system inaccessible to many would-be litigants, but individuals may lack the knowledge and information required for them to realize that they may have a legally recognized grievance.[52] Furthermore, a distinction is often drawn between courts and regulatory agencies on the basis that the latter can be much more expert in the subject matter of their activities than can judges. But this is a difficult argument. It is true that judges are trained as lawyers rather than as scientists or economists, for example; but they can draw on experts for information and they can themselves acquire knowledge. Also, it has often been pointed out that it is a mistake to assume that problems such as pollution, to which regulation is directed, can be solved in purely technical terms. Normative decisions are a crucial part of the regulatory process; and law is one form of normative enterprise.

Nevertheless, there are several features of tort law which make it a relatively inefficient regulator of human conduct: it is sporadic in its operation; it is dependent on the initiative, energy, and resources of individual litigants; it does not recognize all relevant forms of harm or injury as compensatable; it typically operates only after injury or harm has been suffered; it recognizes only certain types of conduct as wrongful; and it only operates when the perpetrator of the harm can be made to submit to the jurisdiction of the court. The settlement of legal disputes out-of-court is not subject to all these limitations, or not to the same extent as the legal process itself; but it lacks the features of publicity and bindingness (both in respect of third parties and the future conduct of the parties themselves) which form the basis of the regulatory effect of court-enforced tort law. Furthermore, it is even more susceptible to distortion by bargaining inequalities than is tort law.

It should be noted that investigation, conciliation, mediation, and private arbitration also lack the publicity and bindingness of decisions of the courts; that they are all, to a greater or lesser extent, susceptible to distortion by inequalities of power; that they all need to be activated by individuals who have some recognized cause of complaint; and that none of them will oper-

---

[51] An important point of contact between regulatory criminal law and tort law is the possibility, in some cases, of an action for breach of statutory duty in respect of a statutory offence: see 219–20 above.

[52] This problem of knowledge and information is shared by all victim-initiated systems, including regulation to the extent that it is reactive. The point is that the courts cannot operate proactively, whereas other institutions may have such power.

ate to full effect (or at all) in the absence of the person against whom the complaint is made.

From our point of view, therefore, the important features of regulatory law are, first, that regulation can be much more systematic than tort law; secondly, bodies which administer regulatory law often do not need to be activated by individual complainants; thirdly, regulatory steps can be taken (and are ideally intended to be taken) before any individual has suffered injury or harm and before the person regulated has done any proscribed act; fourthly, the existence and application of regulatory law is highly public (and often well publicized); and fifthly, it is often backed up by enforcement procedures and penalties which cannot be bargained around once they have been successfully invoked.[53] In general terms, it may be useful to think of tort law as primarily curative or corrective and of regulatory law as primarily preventive or prophylactic.

It is beyond the scope of this book to examine in detail all bodies of regulatory law which are relevant to the protection of economic interests which also fall within the province of tort law. The most that can be done is to survey briefly some important and relevant regulatory regimes and to explore their relationship with relevant rules of tort law.

Property Interests

Real Property

Two bodies of regulatory law deserve mention here: the law governing the development of land (planning law);[54] and laws designed to control environmental pollution. Both these bodies of law are relevant to the tort of nuisance, which protects the right of 'landowners' to use and enjoy their land without unreasonable interference and to be free from material damage to their real property. An important function of planning law is to prevent incompatible uses of land being carried on in close proximity to one another. Outline plans for the development of particular areas (which set out general policies) are laid down in advance and (with some exceptions) particular developments are subject to the grant of planning permission by local planning authorities. If development which needs permission is carried on without it or in breach of any permission given, criminal sanctions and demolition orders are available

[53] The criminal law is not, as such, regulatory law: criminal law normally only penalizes criminal behaviour after it has occurred; indeed, it is a basic feature of English criminal law (its so-called 'golden thread') that a person is presumed innocent until proven guilty both in respect of acts and of state of mind. Preventive justice (in the form, for example, of injunctions to restrain breaches of the criminal law or of binding-over orders or of arrest for apprehended breach of the peace) are exceptional. Criminal sanctions are an important adjunct to regulatory law but they are not its heart.

[54] For a discussion of development control with special reference to commercial development, see J. Alder, *Development Control*, 2nd edn. (London, 1989).

to enforce the law. The exercise of their powers by planning authorities is subject to the law of judicial review. There is also a system of appeals to the Secretary of State for the Environment, whose decision may be preceded by a local inquiry.[55]

The fact that planning permission has been given for a development does not mean that the development itself or the way it is used may not constitute a nuisance.[56] The planning system is not designed to prevent nuisances, as such, and the mere fact that land is being used in a permitted way does not provide a defence to an action in nuisance. In this respect, a statute is a preferable basis for development[57] because statutory authorization is a defence to a nuisance action, and authorizing statutes are interpreted generously to the developer.[58] Also, planning authorities can make mistakes, as seems to have happened in *Miller* v. *Jackson*[59] in which houses were built so close to the boundary of a playing field that cricket balls were not infrequently hit into the adjoining properties.

The tort of nuisance is not, therefore, irrelevant here. Although it cannot overturn the work of the planning system, it can be used to control the detailed use of permitted developments which the planning system does not, on the whole, regulate; and it may provide some remedy for the results of planning mistakes. The fact that adjoining landowners and objectors at local inquiries may be able to challenge development proposals in the High Court by means of an application for judicial review does not render tort law entirely superfluous because judicial review is only of benefit to those who are aware of the proposals as they are being considered. Furthermore, the tort of negligence may have some part to play in providing landowners with a remedy against planning authorities in respect of planning 'mistakes'.[60] On the other hand, the law of tort will normally only assist those whose land is in close proximity to the development because it is only they who are likely to suffer physical damage to their property or interference with the use of their property as a result of the development. At all events, it is clear that the system of development control relegates the law of tort to a supporting role in this context.

So far as the control of environmental pollution is concerned, both public nuisance and private nuisance (including the rule in *Rylands* v. *Fletcher*) have a part to play. In economic terms, pollution is a cost generated by an enterprise which is not borne by that enterprise but is forced onto third parties: it

---

[55] In most cases, in practice, appeals are decided by inspectors of the DoE on the basis of documents.

[56] But a grant of planning permission may so change the nature of a neighbourhood that what would have been a nuisance before the development took place will no longer be: *Gillingham BC* v. *Medway (Chatham) Dock Ltd* [1993] QB 343; *Wheeler* v. *J. J. Saunders Ltd* [1995] 2 All ER 697.

[57] A statute may be needed where, for example, private land has to be acquired—for instance, to build a railway. But private Acts can only be promoted where the ordinary planning system cannot authorize the development.

[58] See 248 above.   [59] See 87 above.   [60] See 87 above.

is an 'externality'. The role of tort law in this context is to internalize the costs of socially unacceptable externalities either by requiring the polluter to put an end to the pollution or to pay damages to victims of pollution. The role of regulatory law is to set standards for the conduct of particular activities which reflect society's judgement about the acceptable level of pollution and to enforce those standards, ultimately by the use of criminal sanctions.[61] So, for example, the National Rivers Authority is charged with control of river pollution; and local authorities are charged with control, for example, of noise and environmental health hazards.[62] These authorities work within a statutory framework which lays down fairly broad guidelines for pollution control but leaves the enforcement agencies with considerable discretion in the detailed work of day-to-day enforcement. Such authorities as these often act on the basis of complaints ('reactive regulation'), but they also have a programme of self-initiated work ('proactive regulation').

Tort law is of very little importance in the control of environmental pollution. It is not entirely clear why this is so.[63] It is true that the effects of environmental pollution tend to be widespread; and, as we have seen, English law has not developed effective mechanisms for class actions, especially where the relief claimed is damages. But, as we have also seen, the *prima facie* remedy for nuisance in English law is an injunction. If one litigant is awarded an injunction against a polluter, this will benefit all victims; and there is nothing to stop all the victims contributing to the costs of the action. Furthermore, the Attorney-General may be asked support a relator action to restrain a public nuisance even in cases where no particular individual has been affected more than members of the public generally. Thus, difficulties of proof which might bedevil a claim which depended on showing that a particular plaintiff had suffered particular damage as a result of a nuisance can, in theory, be evaded because, in cases where 'particular' or 'special' damage does not have to be shown, the mere fact of pollution is enough to justify the award of a remedy provided the court is prepared to say that the pollution is at an 'unreasonable' level.

So what explains the dearth of nuisance actions in respect of environmental pollution? One possible explanation is simply the cost, time, formality, and hassle involved in litigation. Another is that the legal aid system is not very well adapted to mass claims; a third is that it is, no doubt, quite difficult to co-ordinate the institution and funding of mass claims. Fourthly, it may be difficult to enforce a court judgment even if obtained. Perhaps most

---

[61] A. I. Ogus in G. M. Richardson, A. I. Ogus, and P. Burrows, *Policing Pollution* (Oxford, 1982), ch. 3.

[62] On statutory nuisance procedures see R. A. Buckley, *The Law of Nuisance* (London, 1981), chs. 10 and 11.

[63] In some cases tort liability is excluded by statute: e.g., Civil Aviation Act 1982, s. 76(1), which was held not to infringe Art. 8 of the European Convention on Human Rights in *Powell and Rayner* v. *UK* (1990) 12 EHRR 355.

importantly of all, in Britain we tend to prefer regulatory techniques[64] which are decided on by the Government to judicial techniques. Pollution control requires social engineering on a large scale, and we do not see private litigation as constitutionally the proper method or as economically the most efficient method[65] of performing this social function.

Goodwill

Exploitation of goodwill and damage to goodwill are often the result of advertising. Advertising in Britain is, to some extent, regulated by the advertising industry itself through the Advertising Standards Authority which administers the voluntary British Code of Advertising Practice. The basic principle underlying the Code is that advertisements must be legal, decent, honest, and truthful, framed with a sense of responsibility to the consumer, and in conformity with principles of fair competition. As we will see below, there are also various statutory provisions which regulate advertising, but most of them are not relevant in this context.

Confidential Information and Reputation

Regulation of the written word in the form of restraint prior to publication ('censorship') is generally thought to be undesirable in a free society. Thus, injunctions to restrain the publication of defamatory statements are not freely granted and, as a general rule, not at all in cases where the defendant claims that the allegedly defamatory statements are true. Nor is there any public regulatory mechanism for preventing the publication of defamatory material.

Injunctions to restrain the publication of confidential information are more readily available because such information is often seen as a form of property and because equity regards breach of confidence as unconscionable conduct. But, once again, there are no public regulatory mechanisms for controlling the publication of confidential information. The only exception is the so-called 'D-notice' system by which the Ministry of Defence attempts to exercise some control over the publication of information which it considers detrimental to national security and through which approval for the publication of particular material can be obtained. However, the D-notice system is purely voluntary and does not have the force of law. Contravention of a D-notice does not make prosecution (or proceedings for breach of confidence) inevitable, nor does clearance by the Committee provide any immunity from legal proceedings.[66] Newspapers may feel, with some justification, that they

---

[64] For a brief account see A. I. Ogus, *Regulation: Legal Form and Economic Theory* (Oxford, 1994), 204–13.

[65] P. Burrows in P. Burrows and C. G. Veljanovski (eds.), *The Economic Approach to Law* (London, 1981), ch. 6.

[66] See generally G. Robertson, *Freedom, the Individual and the Law*, 7th edn. (London, 1993), 189–92; D. Fairley (1990) 10 *OJLS* 430.

are vulnerable to legal proceedings; and unless clearance by the Secretary of the D-notice Committee were held to give some protection in such proceedings (for example, under s. 5 of the Official Secrets Act 1989), editors might think that the advice of their lawyers was more useful than that of the Secretary. If so, the D-notice system might become an irrelevance. At all events, the notices only cover part of the ground dealt with by the 1989 Act and of the area in which actions for breach of confidence may be brought.[67]

Contractual Interests

Of relevance here are (for instance) the making of Codes of Practice by the Advisory, Conciliation and Arbitration Service (ACAS) in the field of industrial relations; and schemes for the regulation of professional and other services. The first is also relevant to the protection of contractual expectancies, and is discussed below; the second, which are also relevant to the protection of non-contractual expectancies and monetary wealth, are discussed below, too.

Contractual Expectancies

The main topics dealt with under this head in Chapter 4 were industrial relations law, competition law, anti-discrimination law, and the law relating to misstatements inducing contracts. There are a number of regulatory regimes relevant here. First, in the field of industrial relations, one of the functions of ACAS[68] is to draft Codes of Practice for consideration and promulgation by the Secretary of State with the aim of improving industrial relations. ACAS is also consulted before draft codes are issued under section 203 of TULRCA.[69] ACAS codes are the result of consensus between employers and unions and so tend to be less controversial than codes drafted by the government under this provision. The contentious Code on Picketing,[70] for example, was made under the predecessor of section 203 of TULRCA. Section 207 of TULRCA provides that failure to comply with a code of practice does not itself attract legal liability but that the provisions of a code can be taken into account by a court in determining any question to which, in the opinion of the court, it is relevant. One of the basic functions of codes of practice is to influence the conduct of those to whom they are addressed with a view to minimizing recourse to legal sanctions.

Regulation forms the heart of EC and British competition law. The prime

---

[67] See 75 above.   [68] TULRCA, s. 199.
[69] L. Dickens in R. Baldwin and C. McCrudden, *Regulation and Public Law* (London, 1987), 119–21.
[70] See 129 above.

organ charged with ensuring free competition within the European Community is the European Commission,[71] and actions for damages for breach of Articles 85 and 86 of the Treaty of Rome are seen as an adjunct to the enforcement work of the Commission.[72] Similarly, in domestic law, the main vehicle of control over restrictive trade practices is a registration system, while the main vehicle of control over monopolies is an administrative regime involving the Director General of Fair Trading, the Monopolies and Mergers Commission, and the Secretary of State. Once again, while civil actions are available (including applications for injunctions by the Director General) in several situations, these are subsidiary to the regulatory regime.[73] The same is true of actions for damages under recent legislation privatizing essential services: the basic techniques of control are regulation and licensing.[74]

In relation to intellectual property rights, mention should be made of the provisions for the granting of compulsory patent and design right licences,[75] and of the Copyright Licensing Tribunal, which exercises control over schemes for the granting of copyright licences to ensure that they do not impose unreasonable conditions.[76] The Tribunal's jurisdiction is of considerable importance given the increasing use of collective enforcement techniques by copyright owners.[77]

Civil actions for damages play a more prominent role in anti-discrimination law but they are, nevertheless, subsidiary to the regulatory activities of the Commission for Racial Equality and the Equal Opportunities Commission.[78] Both these bodies are charged with responsibility for eliminating discrimination and promoting equality of opportunity in their respective fields of operation, and to this end they are empowered, for example, to engage in research and educational activities, to issue codes of practice,[79] and to conduct formal investigations.[80]

Both the Commissions can carry out formal investigations for purposes connected with any of their statutory functions, and they must carry out an investigation if requested to do so by the Secretary of State. Such investigations can either arise out of complaints of discrimination on the part of particular individuals or institutions ('named-person' investigations), or they may be made even when there have been no specific complaints of discrimination ('general investigations'). General investigations can be exploratory and designed to see whether discriminatory activities are being engaged in; a named person may be investigated only if the Commission believes that

---

[71] See Whish, ch. 9.   [72] See 160 above.   [73] See 161 above.

[74] See 164–5 above.   [75] Cornish, 205–10, 388.   [76] Cornish, 328–32.

[77] Cornish, 261–3, 343–50.

[78] See 157 above. On the limits of private law techniques as a means of eliminating discrimination see L. Lustgarten (1986) 49 *MLR* 68.

[79] But the SDA contains no power to issue codes. Under RRA, s. 47(10) failure to comply with a code is relevant in proceedings before a tribunal but is not in itself unlawful.

[80] On formal investigations by the EOC in the field of employment see R. Townshend-Smith, *Sex Discrimination in Employment* (London, 1989), 215–9.

discrimination has taken place. If an investigation shows that there has been discrimination the Commission may issue a non-discrimination notice requiring a person not to commit specified acts of discrimination and to inform the Commission of steps taken to eliminate unlawful practices. The ultimate sanction for non-compliance with a non-discrimination notice is the award of an injunction on application to a County Court by the Commission within five years from the issue of the notice.[81] However, the Equal Opportunities Commission has never made such an application.[82] The Commissions also have the power (in certain cases, including that of discriminatory advertisements) to make a complaint to an Industrial Tribunal or County Court, and may be awarded a declaration or an injunction.

The investigatory powers of the Commissions are, in theory at least, of considerable importance. They go some way to making good the lack in English law of effective procedures for class actions,[83] which have played a crucial role in dealing with discrimination (especially race discrimination) in the United States. However, the powers have been relatively little used, and when they have, they have often been the subject of challenge in the courts which have, on the whole, interpreted the relevant statutory provisions in such a way as to make formal investigations difficult.[84] This, no doubt, is one reason why the Commissions have directed more of their energies to assisting victims of discrimination to bring actions before Industrial Tribunals,[85] and why such actions have become relatively more important in this area than in the regulation of competition.

So far as misstatements inducing contracts are concerned, we have already noted that the Advertising Standards Authority administers the (voluntary) British Code of Advertising Practice. Television and radio advertisements are subject to statutory schemes of regulation administered by the Independent Television Commission and the Cable Authority. Under the Control of Misleading Advertisements Regulations 1988 (as amended by the Broadcasting Act 1990), complaints about misleading[86] advertisements (other than television and radio advertisements[87] and advertisements issued by persons authorized to carry on investment business under the Financial Services Act 1986) can be made to the Director General of Fair Trading who must

---

[81] Sex Discrimination Act 1965, s. 71; Race Relations Act 1965, s. 62.

[82] Townshend-Smith, *Sex Discrimination in Employment*, 222.

[83] But see D. Pannick, *Sex Discrimination Law* (Oxford, 1985), ch. 10.

[84] C. McCrudden in R. Baldwin and C. McCrudden, *Regulation and Public Law*, ch. 11; V. Sacks (1986) 49 *MLR* 560, 578–86; (1984) 47 *MLR* 334.

[85] Sacks (1986) 49 *MLR* 560, 572–7.

[86] An advertisement is misleading 'if in any way, including its presentation, it deceives or is likely to deceive the persons to whom it is addressed or whom it reaches and if, by reason of its deceptive nature, it is likely to affect their economic behaviour or, for those reasons, injures or is likely to injure a competitor of the person whose interests the advertisement seeks to promote.' Thus, the regulations protect only economic interests.

[87] Complaints about TV and radio advertisements must be made to the Independent Television Commission or the Radio Authority.

investigate them unless they are frivolous or vexatious, provided other avenues of redress (including self-regulatory ones) have been exhausted. The Director General has power to seek an injunction from the court against any person concerned with the publication of the advertisement. The Director General in deciding whether or not to apply for, and the court in deciding whether to award, an injunction must take into account, 'in particular', the public interest.[88] An injunction can be granted even without proof of actual loss or damage, and without proof of intention or negligence on the advertiser's part.

There is an elaborate statutory regime for regulating the making of consumer credit agreements, but considerations of space preclude any consideration of it. Nor is there room to discuss the work of the Office of Fair Trading under the Fair Trading Act 1973, or the law of trade descriptions under the Trade Descriptions Act 1968[89] and the Property Misdescriptions Act 1991,[90] or the elaborate law about the safety, quality, and quantity of food and drugs.[91] All we can do is to note that these bodies of regulatory law are concerned with the inducement of persons generally, and individual consumers in particular, to enter contracts. They may, therefore, cover ground also covered by the law of tort concerning liability for inducing contracts; but, of course, their scope is much wider than this. Their prime aim is to make good consumers' lack of the information and expertise needed for the making of sound market decisions.

It should also be noted that under Part III of the Fair Trading Act 1973 the Director General of Fair Trading has powers which can be used against persons who persist in conduct which is detrimental to the interests of consumers and which, *inter alia*, involves the breach of duties enforceable by civil proceedings, whether or not proceedings have actually been brought.[92] The first step is for the Director General to seek an assurance from the person that he or she will cease the conduct in question. If no such assurance is forthcoming, or if such an assurance is given but not honoured, the Director may either bring proceedings in the Restrictive Practices Court or, in smaller cases, the County Court. The court may obtain an undertaking to desist or may order the person to desist from the course of conduct; and breach of such an undertaking or order is punishable as a contempt of court. Court action is taken in only a few cases a year.[93] The Director General also has a statutory obligation to encourage the drafting and adoption of codes of practice by trade associations.[94] Such codes often contain provisions dealing with techniques

---

[88] *Director General of Fair Trading* v. *Tobyward Ltd* [1989] 1 WLR 517.

[89] Note, in particular, s. 14 of the Trade Descriptions Act 1968 which creates an offence of knowingly or recklessly making a false statement about services; Harvey and Parry, 357–61.

[90] Harvey and Parry, 361–2.

[91] Harvey and Parry, *Law of Consumer Protection and Fair Trading*, ch. 13.

[92] Fair Trading Act 1973, s. 34(2) and (3).   [93] Harvey and Parry, 315–9.

[94] Fair Trading Act 1973, s. 124(3); Harvey and Parry, *Law of Consumer Protection and Fair Trading*, 319–23; I. Ramsay in Baldwin and McCrudden, *Regulation and Public Law*, 190–2.

for inducing consumers to contract with traders. Finally, the Office of Fair Trading plays an active part in disseminating information to the public at large, in examining commercial practices affecting consumers, and in proposing new measures of consumer protection.

Another elaborate statutory scheme for regulating the inducement of contracts is contained in the Financial Services Act 1986, various provisions of which were mentioned earlier.[95] This Act establishes an extremely complex regime of what might be called 'controlled self-regulation'; it involves the use of a variety of legal techniques: licensing, inspection, rule-making, criminal sanctions, and civil actions; and it regulates advertising,[96] among many other things. The SIB can appply to the court for an injunction to restrain breach of rules contained in and made under the Act. There is a similar power to apply for an injunction contained in section 93 of the Banking Act 1987.[97] Mention should also be made here of the City Panel on Takeovers and Mergers which regulates company takeovers (that is, the making contracts for the purchase of shares) by a combination of rule-making, advising, and arbitration. The corporate insurance industry is controlled (in respect of its non-investment business) under the Insurance Companies Act 1982 which (*inter alia*) establishes a licensing system, and regulates insurance advertising.[98] The Lloyd's insurance market runs a system of self-regulation of the making of insurance contracts, amongst other things.

All these regulatory regimes are wider in their operation than the law of tort in that they regulate (*inter alia*) practices which would not necessarily be actionable in tort as misstatements; but they also attempt to prevent practices which might give rise to actions in tort at the suit of a contracting party.

Non-contractual Expectancies and Monetary Wealth

Our main concern here is with the quality of buildings, goods, and services which may, if they are substandard, cause injury or loss to a person who was not in contractual privity with the 'builder' of premises, the manufacturer of goods, or the provider of services. So far as goods are concerned, although there is legislation designed to secure that goods are safe,[99] there is no statutory control of the quality of goods which are not unsafe. Regulation of product safety has some relevance to the subject of this book in that goods which are unsafe to people (for example, inflammable furniture or unsafe cars) may also threaten damage to property. The most common technique for controlling safety is by means of regulations backed up by criminal sanctions.

---

[95] See 179–80 above.   [96] Financial Services Act 1986, ss. 48(2)(e), 57.

[97] On the regulation of advertising by banks see ss. 32–5 of the 1987 Act. Under s. 33 the Bank of England can direct a bank to alter or withdraw offending advertisements.

[98] On advertisements see Insurance Companies Act 1982, ss. 72 and 73.

[99] Harvey and Parry, 231–44.

Quality of goods is dealt with by the law of contract and, to a very limited extent, by the law of tort, rather than by controls over the production process. There are, no doubt, several reasons for this: safety is more important than quality; monitoring and enforcing regulation of quality would be difficult and expensive; and the concept of quality is more relative to price than is the concept of safety.

So far as buildings are concerned, building regulations, which are monitored and enforced by local authorities, deal primarily with health and safety. On the other hand, buildings of substandard quality are perhaps more likely also to affect the health and safety of occupants than are goods of substandard quality likely to affect the health and safety of users; so many (although by no means all) aspects of the quality of buildings may fall under the head of health and safety. The National House Building Council, which runs insurance schemes in respect of latent defects in new and newly-converted houses, performs a role in setting and monitoring compliance with standards for construction work. However, the insurance offered by the Council only covers 'major damage' resulting from structural defects, or (in the case of new houses only) from subsidence, settlement, or heave; and in certain cases, failure to comply with building regulations which results in danger to the health or safety of occupiers. So the Council's interest in quality is limited.

The quality of financial services is the subject of considerable regulation, such as that under the Financial Services Act 1986; such regulation enures chiefly to the benefit of clients of the service provider and of persons who make contracts with the provider as a result of regulated activities. Apart from building-related services (which the law of tort deals with according to principles relevant to the safety and quality of buildings),[100] the services which are most likely to affect third parties who are not in a contractual relationship with the service provider and who do not subsequently make a contract with the provider are those of auditors and solicitors. Regulation of the quality of such services has traditionally been left to the relevant professional bodies, such as the Law Society and the Institute of Chartered Accountants. For example, section 25 of the Companies Act 1989 lays down the qualifications of company auditors basically in terms of membership of one of several professional organizations of accountants. Solicitors must belong to the Law Society and (unlike barristers) must have a current practising certificate.

Such professional bodies promulgate codes of professional practice, but such codes normally do not have the force of law. A report a few years ago by the Consultative Committee of Accountancy Bodies recommended that accounting standards should be given the force of law, but the leading

---

[100] The same applies, *mutatis mutandis*, to services related to the production of goods; but it is very rare for a person to sue anyone other than a supplier or manufacturer in respect of the quality or safety of goods, whereas actions against architects or surveyors, for example, are much more likely in respect of buildings.

accountants' professional bodies which belong to the committee rejected the recommendation chiefly on the basis that it would result in a rigid and legalistic system. The Law Society also objected strongly to government suggestions that the services of solicitors should be made the subject of externally imposed codes of conduct and practice even though these would not have had direct legal force.[101] The ethos of professional self-regulation is very strong, but its acceptability is weakened by deficiencies in mechanisms for monitoring and enforcing compliance with codes of practice and for dealing with complaints. Even worse, there are some groups of purveyors of financial services which are more or less unregulated, whether from without or within: surveyors are a notable example.[102]

There is another major defect with regimes of (self-) regulation, such as that affecting solicitors, which are based on licensing.[103] This is that while the initial grant of a licence often requires the licensee to demonstrate a minimum level of ability and competence, renewal and continued holding of a licence rarely does. For example, solicitors can be denied a practising certificate or even struck off the roll of solicitors for misconduct, but not for incompetence which does not amount to misconduct. Furthermore, a solicitor does not have to demonstrate continuing competence in order to have his or her practising certificate renewed. In other words, bodies which license the providers of financial services rarely make any serious attempt to ensure that licence-holders continue to be competent and reasonably skilled.[104] Thus the burden of maintaining quality falls significantly on market forces, and on complaints mechanisms and the civil law.

In the case of solicitors, we have seen that, although there is an elaborate set of complaints procedures, their operation in practice leaves something to be desired. As for competition,[105] there are very considerable barriers to the exercise of consumer choice as an effective means of weeding out incompetent solicitors. For example, the distribution of solicitors' practices means that many people have little effective choice; the average consumer lacks the

---

[101] Law Society, *Striking the Balance* (London, 1989), sect. 1. Under provisions of the Courts and Legal Services Act 1990 qualification regulations and codes of conduct governing advocacy and the conduct of litigation made by the Law Society and the Bar require the concurrence of the Lord Chancellor who is advised by the Lord Chancellor's Advisory Committee on Legal Education and Conduct. For an economic analysis of regulation of legal services see W. Bishop (1989) 52 *MLR* 326.

[102] K. Richards (1995) 5 *Consumer Policy Review* 2. Regulatory controls over real estate agents are also weak: M. Clarke, D. Smith and M. McConville, *Slippery Customers* (London, 1994), ch. 11.

[103] For a brief general account of licensing of professionals see Ogus, *Regulation*, 216–25.

[104] F. R. Marks and D. Cathcart [1974] *U Ill. Law Forum* 193. Solicitors must engage regularly in a continuing education programme. Failure to comply with training regulations may lead to non-renewal of a solicitor's practising certificate if it amounts to 'professional misconduct'. Effective monitoring of this continuing education scheme is not likely to be easy. The Bar operates no continuing education programme.

[105] The Courts and Legal Services Act 1990 contains elaborate provisions designed to introduce more competition into the provision of conveyancing and probate services.

knowledge required to discriminate between good and bad legal services; and not only is advertising by solicitors restricted by Law Society rules, but also lawyers have not shown great eagerness to exercise such freedom to advertise as they have.[106]

In the case of lawyers, however, there is an element of external regulation which is lacking in the case of other professional groups. Solicitors are 'officers of the Supreme Court', and this fact forms the basis of the exercise of what is called the 'inherent jurisdiction' of the court over them.[107] In exercise of this inherent jurisdiction, the court can strike a solicitor off the roll of solicitors for misconduct or suspend a solicitor from practising.[108] The inherent jurisdiction of the court can also be exercised in cases where a solicitor fails to honour an undertaking made to the court. In such a case, the court may order the solicitor to perform the undertaking (if this is still possible) and also to compensate any person who has suffered loss as a result of failure to perform the undertaking.[109] A solicitor can be ordered to perform an undertaking even if no consideration was given for it by the person seeking to enforce it.[110]

The court exercises control over the fees charged by solicitors by means of the procedure of 'taxation' of bills;[111] and the court can order a solicitor or barrister personally to pay (or repay) the costs of his or her own client (or the Legal Aid Board) or of another party to litigation.[112] Improper, unreasonable, or negligent[113] acts or omissions may attract a 'wasted costs

---

[106] The rules for barristers are similar; but the position of barristers is very different from that of solicitors because, with a few exceptions, they cannot have direct dealings with lay clients. So the main impact of their advertising will be on solicitors (and other professionals, such as accountants, architects, and surveyors) who may brief them and who may be more often able than their clients to supplement the bare details provided in the advertising with 'inside' information from other professionals about the competence of particular barristers.

[107] Barristers can only be disciplined by an Inn of Court or the Senate of the Inns of Court and the Bar.

[108] S. 50(2) of the Solicitors Act 1974 preserves this inherent jurisdiction. In addition, the court has certain statutory jurisdiction to strike off under s. 39(2) of the 1974 Act. The Solicitors Disciplinary Tribunal, too, has the power to suspend and strike off; it can also impose fines. It has been said that the prime function of the Tribunal is not to punish defaulting solicitors but to maintain the reputation of and public confidence in the legal profession, so that the Tribunal may properly impose penalties greater than the fault of the individual by itself would justify: *Bolton* v. *Law Society* [1994] 1 WLR 512.

[109] *Udall* v. *Capri Lighting Ltd* [1988] QB 907.

[110] *John Fox* v. *Bannister, King & Rigbeys* [1988] QB 925, 931 *per* Sir John Donaldson MR.

[111] R. Walker and R. Ward, *Walker and Walker's The English Legal System*, 7th edn., 383–5; for a trenchant criticism of the system see H. Hawkins (1988) 132 *Sol. J* 1199. The present rule is that a client who has his or her own solicitor's costs taxed must prove that costs were both unauthorized and unreasonably incurred or unreasonable in amount in order to have the bill reduced.

[112] Supreme Court Act 1981, s. 51(6)–(7), 52(2A); Prosecution of Offences Act 1985, s. 19A; Magistrates' Courts Act 1980, s. 145A.

[113] It is arguable that 'negligence' in this context refers to acts or omission which no reasonable lawyer would commit (i.e. the *Bolam* test): *Ridehalgh* v. *Horsefield* [1994] Ch. 205, 233.

order'.[114] The 'wasted costs jurisdiction' has a number of advantages over an action in contract or tort: it is typically quicker and cheaper, application normally being made by an originating summons; it bypasses the immunity of advocates from liability in contract and tort; and it is particularly useful in cases where a party without legal aid is successful against an assisted party, because the former will not usually be awarded costs against the Legal Aid Fund.[115] On the other hand, it only covers cases in which costs have been wasted and not where, for instance, costs have not been incurred because the lawyer has failed to act.

General Issues Concerning Regulation

It may be useful to draw together this short consideration of regulatory regimes by drawing attention to some general issues relevant to assessing the relative contribution of regulation and tort law to the protection of economic interests of the kind with which we are concerned in this book.

Techniques of Regulation

Rule-making

First, let us briefly enumerate the main regulatory techniques. Perhaps the most important is rule-making. The main difference between 'regulatory' rule-making and judicial rule-making by the courts is that the former can be much more systematic and thorough than the latter. Furthermore, because of the unwillingness of the higher courts to admit the policy-making aspects of their adjudicatory activities, let alone to develop in any coherent way the policies which underlie the common law, regulatory rule-making can be a much more potent tool for establishing and achieving policy goals. As we have seen, it is common for regulatory rule-making to take the form of codes of practice which are not legally binding. Such codes emphasize the educational and admonitory function of rules at the expense of their coercive function. They play a central role in self-regulation, which is discussed in a little more detail below.

Criminal Sanctions

Externally imposed rules are often, although certainly not always, enforced with the help of criminal sanctions.[116] But even where criminal sanctions are

---

[114] Under certain circumstances, magistrates can be ordered to pay the costs of a party if they have been guilty of flagrantly acting improperly or perversely or in disregard of some elementary principle of law: *R.* v. *Lincoln JJ, ex parte Count, Independent*, 2 Aug. 1995.

[115] For extensive guidelines on the proper exercise of the jurisdiction see *Ridehalgh* v. *Horsefield* [1994] Ch. 205. See also *Sampson* v. *John Boddy Timber Ltd* [1995] New LJ 851; P. Jones and N. Armstrong (1994) 13 *CJQ* 210.

[116] Richardson, Ogus, and Burrows, *Policing Pollution*, 14–19, 55–62; J. Rowan-Robinson, P. Watchman, and C. Barker, *Crime and Regulation* (Edinburgh, 1990).

available, there is much evidence to suggest that regulators are very unwilling to use them except as a last resort. We will return to this point below. When the criminal law is used, it is normally activated by an official regulatory agency, whereas civil law is usually, although not always, invoked by some individual who has suffered injury, harm or loss as a result of the breach of a regulatory rule. As we saw, especially in Chapter 4, there has been a growing tendency in recent years for statutes to provide that breaches of their provisions shall be actionable in tort as breaches of statutory duty. This increasing recourse to civil law as a means of enforcing regulatory rules can be explained in a number of ways: it is part of a wider process of attempting to reduce the involvement of the state in the economic activity; it provides a way of relieving pressure on state enforcement agencies (although only at the cost of putting more pressure on the courts), and gives the government an excuse for funding enforcement agencies less generously; and it is based on a belief, held by some, that the civil law can play an important part in strengthening the deterrent impact of the law.[117] In this last respect, American experience is drawn upon to show that well-organized and large-scale consumer, antitrust, and anti-discrimination litigation can play an important part in achieving social goals without the involvement of administrative agencies.[118] On the other hand, cultural, constitutional, and political differences between Britain and the USA, coupled with differences in court procedure and the way litigation is funded in the two countries, perhaps make it unlikely that private litigation will ever play more than a marginal role in regulating the quality and supply of goods and services in Britain.

An alternative to large-scale private civil litigation is invocation of the civil law by administrative agencies. We have seen that the Securities and Investments Board and the Director General of Fair Trading, for example, have powers which enable them to seek injunctions and sometimes even monetary compensation on behalf of groups of victims of breaches of regulatory law.[119] Usually such action is the result of individual complaints against the defendant, but there is clearly scope for much wider use of this device which, because of the absence of criminal overtones, may be more acceptable to various groups than the use of criminal sanctions.

Licensing

A feature of many regulatory regimes is licensing. As we have seen, licensing as a technique of control of the provision of goods and services suffers from a number of serious problems: the criteria which need to be met to obtain a licence may not do much to guarantee that the goods or services produced are of high quality; often little or no attempt is made to ensure that those

---

[117] B. A. K. Rider [1988] *CLP* 47, 58–60.

[118] US courts often have to become much more heavily involved in the process of enforcing the outcome of such litigation than English courts would be prepared to do.

[119] R. Cranston *Consumers and the Law*, 2nd edn. (London, 1984), 100–1.

who hold licences continue to satisfy the criteria for the granting of a licence in the first place; and there is very little legal recourse against inferior performance by licensing agencies of their regulatory functions.

Enforcement

The ultimate test of any regulatory regime is how effective it is in preventing breaches of its rules and injury, loss, or harm to those whom it is designed to protect; and how effective it is in enforcing its rules against offenders. Unfortunately, lack of statistically reliable and significant empirical evidence makes it very difficult accurately to assess most regulatory regimes in either of these respects. An important failing of many regulatory regimes is that insufficient time and money is devoted to regular inspection and monitoring of the conduct of regulated persons and to research and educational activities.[120] Such activities might help the regulated to improve the quality of their performance; they could play a part in informing consumers of what they have a right to expect from the providers of goods and services, and in assisting them to evaluate the quality of what they receive, as well as the relative quality of the goods and services offered by different producers; and they may contribute to improving the performance of regulatory agencies themselves. The Director General of Fair Trading and the Commissions concerned with sex and race discrimination both see research and education as important aspects of their role.

Taxation

Finally, we should mention a regulatory technique which we have not discussed at all so far, namely taxation (including 'negative taxation' or 'subsidies'[121]). While the law of tort is primarily concerned with compensation, it is also concerned with providing financial incentives to potential defendants to avoid liability. In economic terms, the law of tort helps to internalize certain injury costs to the enterprises which generate them. In this respect, the civil law is a better designed tool than the criminal law, because criminal sanctions usually do not represent the costs which the offender's activity has inflicted on the victim.[122] But the sporadic and unsystematic nature of the civil law, coupled with defects in the operation of market forces which may enable potential defendants to ignore the deterrent signals given by the civil law, make it a relatively inefficient tool for the internalization of costs. Taxation can, in theory at least, be much more efficient. So, for example, many have urged the introduction of 'green taxes' to discourage particular environmentally harmful activities (lead-free petrol is already taxed less than leaded); another proposal is that motorists who drive into central London should be charged for the privilege. On the other hand, taxation shares one disadvantage with civil law claims for damages, namely that its financial

[120] M. Zander (1978) 128 *New LJ* 576. [121] Ogus, *Regulation*, 246–54.
[122] Cf. Rider [1988] CLP 47, 58–60.

impact can often be passed on and spread through increased prices and so on; and this fact seriously undermines its overall efficiency as a tool for internalizing costs.

Taxation lies somewhere between civil liability and criminal liability as a technique for discouraging particular activities: like the civil law, it leaves individuals with a considerable amount of freedom to decide how they will react to the deterrent signals they receive; whereas the criminal law is designed to remove freedom to choose particular courses of conduct (although, to the extent that penalties for offending are purely financial, its impact may be similar to that of a tax unless enforcement levels are very high). On the other hand, because taxes can be levied much more systematically and thoroughly than can civil law damages awards, then provided the tax is not too easily evaded, the deterrent signals given by a tax system will be much louder than those given by the civil law. Of course, the deterrent efficiency of a tax system, like that of the civil law, depends heavily on how well it assesses the amount to be levied having regard to the level at which those subject to it engage in the activity to be discouraged.

Taxation is flexible in another respect as well: tort law can only apply the stick; it cannot offer a carrot. The tax system, by offering tax breaks, for example to manufacturers who install 'environment-friendly' equipment or produce 'environment-friendly' products, can give positive incentives for desirable behaviour which are financially justifiable in that the behaviour induced inflicts less harm on third parties than the behaviour which is discouraged.[123]

Styles of Regulation[124]

As we saw when we discussed dispute-settling techniques, an important constraint on the effectiveness of the common law, both as a compensatory mechanism and as a deterrent to further unlawful conduct is the fact that most legal disputes are settled by some sort of consensual arrangement between the parties. One result of this is that the dynamics of the bargaining process and the relative bargaining strengths of the parties, rather than the law itself, are often the main determinants of the outcome. One of the arguments for regulation is that it facilitates the elimination of the effects of bargaining between the regulated and their clients on enforcement of the law. However, it is clear that regulatory law, like civil law, is often not applied and enforced according to its terms. Much research has been done which

---

[123] But the question of which activities to tax or subsidize with a view to minimizing environmental pollution, for example, is an extremely complex one.

[124] Richardson, Ogus, and Burrows, *Policing Pollution*; K. Hawkins, *Environment and Enforcement* (Oxford, 1984); B. M. Hutter, *The Reasonable Arm of the Law?* (Oxford, 1988); R. A. Kagan [1989] *Law and Policy* 89.

shows that where regulators have discretion[125] as to how they will achieve the goals of the regulatory regime, they will often choose non-coercive in preference to coercive methods. So, for example, even if criminal sanctions are available for use against those who do not comply with regulatory rules, the use of such sanctions is often seen as a last resort. Criminal prosecution is more important as a threat to encourage co-operation than as a tool for directly securing compliance with regulatory requirements.

The explanations for this state of affairs are complex, but four points deserve mention. First, regulatory criminal offences are often offences of strict liability, whereas regulators tend to the view that the criminal law should only be used against offenders who are morally culpable in a fairly strong sense. Secondly, many regulators believe that, human nature being what it is, an aggressive policy of enforcement is less likely to promote the goals of the regulatory programme than a more co-operative and friendly approach to the regulated. Thirdly, regulators may be more likely to use their full legal powers in the face of public complaints about the conduct of regulated persons than they would be in cases where their regulatory activities were not in public view. Regulatory authorities are not immune to political pressure, and general community attitudes to enforcement (whether for or against) may be influential in particular cases. Fourthly, regulators typically take account of the financial means of the regulated in deciding what measures to require them to take: regulators are unwilling to demand action which is beyond the financial means of the regulated and which might cause them to go out of business, even if it would be better in broad social terms that the activity being engaged in did cease unless the action was taken. Like courts applying flexible standards such as 'reasonable care', regulators often calculate the costs and benefits of alternative courses of conduct in very narrow terms.

At all events, the basic point to be made is that, just as we can only fully understand the use of civil law to protect economic interests if we pay attention to its application in practice, so we can only understand regulation properly if we pay attention to the way regulators actually use (or do not use) the powers they have. Formal legal rules and processes may be of no more relevance to the practical operation of regulatory law than they are, in the majority of cases, to the practical operation of civil law. Another apposite example of the same point is provided by the relative unwillingness of the Equal

---

[125] Discretion is pervasive in regulatory regimes in Britain. Wide discretion is much more accepted when exercised by a regulatory agency than when exercised by a court. Courts are meant to apply rules, and discretion is seen as having a relatively marginal role in judicial reasoning. Discretion tends to be identified with politics; and courts, unlike regulatory agencies, are meant to be independent of politics. An interesting example is provided by the contrast between the role of the Restrictive Practices Court in regulating restrictive trade practices and the role of the Office of Fair Trading and the Monopolies and Mergers Commission in regulating monopolies: P. P. Craig in Baldwin and McCrudden, *Regulation and Public Law*, 222–3.

Opportunities Commission to launch formal investigations: the Commission prefers to avoid confrontation and to work for voluntary change.[126]

Regulation and Self-Regulation

Self-regulation[127] is important to the subject matter of this book because of our concern, *inter alia*, with liability for loss resulting from the performance of professional services: one of the identifying features of a profession is that professional groups generally claim the right to formulate and enforce their own rules of conduct.[128] In Britain, self-regulation is also important in the financial services industry,[129] although the regime established under the Financial Services Act 1986 is, in many ways, a very attenuated form of self-regulation, chiefly because the Act lays down many requirements for the content of the rules made by the Securities and Investments Board and the Self Regulating Organizations set up under the Act. In this context, the law of tort can be seen as a form of external regulation. Although external regulation and self-regulation can be viewed as alternatives, there are important differences between them, at least in theory.

A prime example of a self-regulating profession is the Bar: at common law, advocates[130] are immune from tort liability in respect of their work as advocates; and now that there is no rule that barristers cannot make contracts with their clients,[131] this immunity extends to liability in contract.[132] The mechanism set up by the Bar for handling complaints against barristers deals mainly with allegations of misconduct, and not with complaints of incompetent work;[133] and a large proportion of the members of the complaints-handling and disciplinary bodies at all levels are barristers.[134] Finally, whereas the Supreme Court exercises an inherent jurisdiction over solicitors, it exercises no such jurisdiction over barristers: the Bar and the Inns of Court have sole jurisdiction.[135] No matter how independent the Bar's self-regulatory

---

[126] Townshend-Smith, *Sex Discrimination in Employment*, 219.

[127] Ogus, *Regulation: Legal Form and Economic Theory*, 107–11.

[128] R. Dingwall and P. Fenn (1987) 7 *Int. Rev. Law and Econ.* 51.

[129] P. Cane [1987] *CJQ* 324, 324–33.

[130] As defined in Courts and Legal Services Act 1990, s. 62(1).   [131] *Ibid.*, s. 61.

[132] *Ibid.*, s. 61(2).

[133] The Professional Conduct Committee of the Bar Council can investigate complaints of 'professional misconduct' and 'breach of proper professional standards'; but the function of the complaints mechanism is disciplinary, not compensatory. 'Breach of proper professional standards' is a lesser form of misconduct, not a synonym for shoddy work. The Bar Standards Review Body chaired by Lord Alexander of Weedon recommended in 1994 that a simplified complaints procedure should be set up which would allow for the awarding of compensation of up to £2,000 for shoddy work.

[134] But the Legal Services Ombudsman can investigate complaints about the operation of the Bar's complaints procedures and the initial complaint itself. See e.g. *Third Annual Report of the Legal Services Ombudsman 1993* (London), paras. 3.2–13. The new arrangements mentioned in the previous paragraph will be supervised by a lay person.

[135] R. v. *Visitors to the Inns of Court, ex parte Calder* [1994] QB 1.

process is in fact, it is impossible for such a set-up to have the appearance of independence. Few regimes of self-regulation are so extremely internal as this, but all such regimes have difficulty in answering the suggestion that self-regulation is anything other than self-protection.[136] By contrast, the civil law represents, in theory at least, an important, if residual, independent check on the quality of professional services.

Regulation Versus Civil Liability[137]

Because of the differences between regulation and civil law as techniques for protecting economic (and other) interests, there is not really a choice between them: there is no way that civil law could ever perform the same functions as regulation even if class actions were easier to bring than they are, and even if much more public money was made available to fund such litigation. English judges are unlikely to be willing to tackle the sort of political issues raised by class actions in areas such as competition and discrimination law, or to become actively involved in the management of the litigation in the way that is necessary if class actions are to be efficiently tried.[138] Conversely,

[136] There has been continuing criticism of the lack of independence and 'democratic mandate' of the Auditing Practices Board set up by the major UK professional accountancy bodies which sets audit standards: *Financial Times*, 16 Dec. 1994. It is Labour Party policy to impose external regulation on the auditing industry and to reverse the decision in *Caparo* v. *Dickman* (see 00 above): letter from Austin Mitchell, *The Times*, 24 Mar. 1992; *Financial Times*, 8 Apr. 1992, 10. Many believe that there is an unacceptably wide gap between public perceptions of the proper role of auditors and the narrowness of their legal liabilities: D. Glynn and D. Ridyard, *Financial Times* 9 Apr. 1992, 12; R. Trapp, *Financial Times*, 24 Nov. 1992, 23; A. Jack, *Financial Times*, 1 Oct. 1992; J. Freedman and M. Power (1991) 54 *MLR* 769, 777–83. For the views of US auditors about this debate see the papers in (1993) 2 *J of Economics and Management Strategy*.

[137] M. J. Trebilcock, 'Regulating Service Quality in Professional Markets' in D. N. Dewees (ed.), *The Regulation of Quality* (Toronto, 1983). On the relative advantages and disadvantages of land development control on the one hand and the civil law of nuisance on the other, see B. J. Pearce (1981) 52 *Town Planning Review* 47; J. Alder, *Development Control*, 2nd edn. (London, 1989), 5–6.

[138] It is, however, important to distinguish between two different types of class actions. Class actions for damages (which are not currently available in English law) are primarily designed to secure compensation; they may also have a regulatory effect especially if, as is sometimes the case in US law, large awards of exemplary damages can be made. The chief advantage of a class action for damages is that it allows a large number of small claims, which would not individually be worth pursuing in the courts, to be aggregated so that the total amount claimed justifies the cost of mounting the action. Such actions are even more useful if they can be brought by a pressure group or a public body or official of its own motion (e.g. an action for restitution brought by the Securities and Investments Board under the Financial Services Act 1986, s. 61): this option offers much more protection to the poor and ignorant than a mechanism which individual complainants have to activate, and it overcomes the problem that private representative plaintiffs can often be bought off. Class actions for damages may present difficult issues which are, in some sense, beyond the competence of the courts: product liability claims in respect of design defects are a classic example. But some class actions for damages, although administratively complex, present no such conceptual difficulties and no problems of judicial competence. See generally R. Tur (1982) 2 *OJLS* 135. By contrast, class actions for a specific remedy such as an injunction are designed not to compensate for past loss but to regulate the defendant's conduct in the future. This type of class action may require judges to decide issues of policy which

because civil law concentrates on the individual's rights and obligations, and because court adjudication is based on the notions of independence, adversariness, and publicity, civil law and the courts which administer it may offer some benefits which regulation does not. The fact is that both regulation and civil law have a role to play in protecting economic interests, and neither is sufficiently effective that it leaves no room for the other. Perhaps ironically, the best stategy may be that which is presently pursued, namely to provide a range of legal techniques for achieving regulatory goals.

A factor which is obviously relevant to the assessment of the relative advantages and disadvantages of different methods of protecting economic interests is their cost. It is certainly possible to make rough estimates of the cost of regulatory schemes,[139] and of the costs of litigation.[140] Unfortunately, however, because regulation and civil law are complementary rather than alternative to one another, and because the law of tort plays such a marginal role in protecting many of the economic interests which regulatory schemes cover, meaningful cost comparisons between regulatory and civil law techniques are impossible to make.

Quis Custodiet Ipsos Custodes?[141]

When it comes to regulating the regulators, the relevant choice is between legal accountability and political accountability in the case of governmental regulatory bodies; and between legal accountability and no formal accountability in the case of non-governmental (self-regulatory) bodies. Legal accountability effectively means either amenability to judicial review,[142] or liability in contract or tort. The courts have been much more prepared to expand the limits of judicial review (to bodies such as the Takeover Panel[143] and the Advertising Standards Authority[144]), than to allow tort actions[145] against regulatory bodies. However, we should not, perhaps, read too much into this: the limits of judicial review have been extended in response to the realization that there was no real alternative method of legal control of regulators, whereas the judgments in the leading cases which have all but closed the door to tort actions against regulatory bodies have stressed the impor-

---

English courts are unaccustomed to confront and to take an active and 'administrative' role in fashioning the remedy and policing its enforcement. The classic discussion of such 'regulatory litigation' is A. Chayes (1976) 89 *Harvard LR* 1281.

[139] It has been estimated, e.g., that in 1994 it cost over £300 million to run the regime set up under the Financial Services Act 1986: *Financial Times*, 18 Aug. 1995. On the cost of consumer protection legislation see Harvey and Parry, 23–7.

[140] J. R. Spencer, *Jackson's Machinery of Justice* (London, 1989), 456.

[141] Ogus, *Regulation*, 111–17.

[142] Baldwin and McCrudden, *Regulation and Public Law.*

[143] *R. v. Panel on Takeovers and Mergers, ex parte Datafin PLC* [1987] QB 815.

[144] *R. v. Advertising Standards Authority, ex parte The Insurance Service PLC* (1990) 2 Admin. LR 77.

[145] D. Feldman [1987] *PN* 23; H. McLean (1988) 8 *OJLS* 442, 449–56.

tance of the availability of alternative (and often non-judicial) remedies. Furthermore, the tort cases have been complicated in a way that the judicial review cases have not been by questions about liability for pure omissions; and the judicial review cases have stressed that judicial intervention will only be appropriate in fairly extreme cases of legal error or procedural inadequacy. In other words, the case law concerning the legal control of regulatory bodies is all underpinned by a passive and non-interventionist philosophy of the judicial role, by a deference to the value of self-regulation, and by a preference for non-judicial forms of control of regulatory bodies.

One of the main arguments against judicial control, in whatever form, is that regulators must be left free to perform their duties and fulfil their functions without having constantly to look over their shoulders for fear of being brought before a court. But this is a deeply unsatisfactory and unappealing argument because it applies to all forms of external scrutiny and control. It is clear, for example, that government departments do not welcome the investigations of the Ombudsman or scrutiny by a Parliamentary Select Committee any more than they like being the defendant or respondent to a court action. Arguments such as that regulation is an activity which requires considerable technical expertise and that its conduct can only be judged by experts militate against any form of external scrutiny, whether political or legal; and they should be seen for what they are, namely part of a bid by technocrats for unchallengeable supremacy. It is obvious that judicial control of regulatory bodies is unsatisfactory and inadequate in a number of ways; but it does not follow from this that it is necessarily worthless or positively harmful. Just as civil law and regulation should not be seen as alternatives but as complementary, so the courts should attempt to analyse the strengths and weaknesses of judicial control of regulators and to fashion the relevant rules of law in the light of such an analysis.

3. RISK MANAGEMENT

In Chapter 6 we discussed at some length the interest of defendants in minimizing their legal liability and how this could be done by means of contractual arrangements between service providers and actual or potential plaintiffs dealing with the way legal disputes are to be resolved. Just as regulation is a technique, *inter alia*, for preventing legal disputes occurring, so 'risk management'[146] refers to attempts by potential defendants to prevent themselves getting into legal disputes. Risk management is a form of self-regulation, although the latter tends to be used to refer to industry- or profession-wide schemes rather than to steps taken by individual members of the industry or profession. Risk management is 'loss prevention', or 'quality control'; it is a

---

[146] Another term used with similar meaning is 'contingency planning'.

management or 'administrative' technique for minimizing legal liability.[147] It is the response which, viewing tort law as having a deterrent function, the imposition of tort liability is designed to encourage in the defendant and in others who are aware of the impact of tort law on their activities.

It deserves a mention here because of the impact of liability insurance on the operation of tort law. Liability insurance weakens any deterrent effect tort law might have had in its absence[148] in two ways: by spreading the financial impact of liability among a number of potential defendants it reduces very significantly the amount which any individual will have to pay to meet any court judgment; secondly, it is usually the case that the liability insurance premiums payable by any particular insured are imperfectly correlated with the risk that the insured will be held liable,[149] and this fact further distorts and muffles any deterrent signal which the premium might otherwise have conveyed. One way in which this weakening of deterrent signals may be counteracted is by the insured, either at the behest of the insurer or independently, taking positive steps to reduce the chance of an insured event occurring. Indeed, the insurer's liability to pay out under the policy may be conditional on such steps being taken. However, such requirements may have only a limited impact in preventing insured events unless the insurer also monitors compliance: a risk that the policy will be avoided by the insurer if the precaution is not taken operates similarly, in incentive terms, to the risk that the insured will incur liability in the first place, and an insured may calculate that the increase of the risk of liability which failure to take the specified precautions produces, does not justify the outlay required to put the precautions in place.

4. CONCLUSION

Tort law is part of what is sometimes called the law of obligations. The law of obligations involves organizing social interactions in terms of bilateral relationships between individuals. Tort law protects economic (and other) interests by creating bilateral rights and obligations between individuals. In this Chapter I have sought to show how legal techniques which do not organize social interactions bilaterally can be used as alternatives to or in order to bolster tort law. Essential to a full understanding of the social impact of tort doctrine is an appreciation of the fact that the bilateralness integral to tort law is only one of the legal techniques available for protecting economic (and other) interests.

---

[147] Some law firms, for instance, have been awarded a 'kitemark' for compliance with the British Standards Institute's standard BS 5750 which covers maintenance of quality control systems. See further S. Fennell (1992) 8 *PN* 115, 117–9.

[148] Of course, this hypothetical is unrealistic because uninsured persons are rarely sued: the least deterred are the uninsured.

[149] See 479–81 below.

9

Insurance and Tort Law

It is impossible to understand the practical impact of tort law without taking account of insurance, both liability (third party) and loss (first party) insurance. Without widespread liability insurance, many fewer tort claims would be made than actually are; and very many tort claims are, no doubt, forestalled because the injured party has loss insurance. However, this Chapter is not concerned with issues about the tort claims process but rather with the impact of the social practice of insurance on the rules and principles of tort law and vice versa. I will also examine the relationship between an important aspect of insurance law—the doctrine of subrogation—and the law of tort.

1. THE IMPACT OF INSURANCE ON THE LAW

It is now accepted wisdom that the practical operation of the law of tort cannot be understood without paying attention to the fact and extent of insurance, whether it be liability (that is, third party) insurance, loss (that is, first party) insurance, or legal expenses insurance (which covers the cost of making or defending legal claims). At the most general level, in many cases it is only the fact that a person is insured against liability which makes that person financially worth suing. This is most obviously true in the case of individual defendants; but it is also clear that many businesses and institutions take out liability insurance partly out of fear that they may be confronted with a claim which they could not meet out of their own resources. We have seen, too, that the fact that one or both of the parties is insured is of great importance to the settlement of tort claims. Furthermore, if the plaintiff is insured against the loss suffered as a result of the defendant's tort, the incentive P has to sue D will normally be greatly reduced and the more important practical question for D will be whether D's insurer will choose to exercise its subrogation rights, if any.

Nor can it be doubted that the existence and wide availability of insurance has had an effect on the content of the law. Here are some examples.[1]

---

[1] These examples concern economic interests in particular. For a general discussion, and for detailed consideration of the law of personal injuries see P. Cane, *Atiyah's Accidents, Compensation and the Law*, 5th edn. (London, 1993), chs. 9 and 11.

Direct Actions Against Insurers

Because an insurance policy is a contract, the basic common law rule is that it creates rights and obligations only between the parties to it: the insurer and the insured. Suppose that P's property, which is insured by C against 'accidental' damage, is damaged as a result of D's negligence. If C pays out to P according to the terms of the policy, C is 'subrogated' to P's right to sue D in tort;[2] but this only means that if P sues D and recovers, P holds the amount recovered as trustee for C. It does not mean that C can sue D in tort:[3] the contract of insurance between P and C is an entirely separate matter from and is collateral to the rights of P against D. Conversely, suppose P suffers injury or loss as a result of the tort of D, who has insured against the risk of being held liable in tort by taking out a liability insurance policy with C. Suppose, further, that D has disappeared and cannot be traced but that P knows about the policy with C. P cannot sue C directly because the liability policy is matter between D and C, collateral to P's rights in tort against D.[4]

The logic of this latter application of the basic rule is that liability insurance is a means by which a potential defendant can gain protection against financial ruin as a result of suffering judgment for a large amount of money; and this is the way liability insurance was originally viewed. But as it became more widely available, and as personal injuries suffered on the road came to be seen as a major social problem, liability insurance came to be seen at least as much as a protection for injured plaintiffs against the possibility that the defendant might be unable to satisfy judgment. As a result, it is now compulsory for users of cars to take out liability insurance in respect of personal injuries arising out of the use of the car; and for employers to take out liability insurance in respect of injuries to their employees arising out of their work.[5]

This compensatory view of liability insurance also produced other legislation to supplement the first statute requiring liability insurance for road accidents. Suppose that a defendant who has liability insurance goes bankrupt either before or after being held liable to the plaintiff. If P is reduced to proving the judgment debt in D's bankruptcy, P will rank only as an unsecured

---

[2] Subrogation is discussed in greater detail below: 435.

[3] *Simpson & Co.* v. *Thomson* (1877) LR 3 App. Cas. 279; criticized by P. S. James (1971) 34 MLR 149. The decision in this case can be supported by arguments against subrogation: see 000–000 below and *Leigh & Sillavan* v. *Aliakmon Shipping Co.* [1985] QB 350, 380 (Oliver LJ), 398 (Robert Goff LJ).

[4] But P could bankrupt D and then sue C directly under the Third Parties (Rights Against Insurers) Act 1930.

[5] An insured car owner who allows a person not specified in the policy to use the car is not only guilty of an offence but also may be sued for damages for breach of statutory duty by anyone injured or damaged by negligence of the uninsured driver: *Monk* v. *Warbey* [1935] 1 KB 75. But failure by an insurer to take out insurance to cover liability to employees, although (or because it is) an offence, is not actionable in tort at the suit of an injured employee: *Richardson* v. *Pitt-Stanley* [1995] 1 All ER 460.

creditor and will be entitled to no more than the same dividend as is payable to other such creditors. The Third Parties (Rights against Insurers) Act 1930 (which is not restricted to compulsory insurance, nor to insurance against liability for personal injuries) provides that in this situation the rights of the bankrupt defendant under the liability insurance policy are vested in the plaintiff who can recover under the policy directly from the insurer. The effect of this provision is to elevate the plaintiff to the position of a secured creditor.[6]

The right to sue the insurer direct only arises once the liability of the defendant has been decided by the judgment of a court or the decision of an arbitrator or an agreement between P and D.[7] In *Bradley* v. *Eagle Star Insurance Co. Ltd*[8] the defendant company was defunct and had been removed from the companies register for longer than the two years during which a company can be restored to the register for the purpose of being sued.[9] The House of Lords held that since the company no longer existed and so could not be sued in tort its liability could not be established; and so P had no direct right to indemnity against the insurer. This case illustrates a basic rule about insurance; and it also reveals one of the basic characteristics of the tort system of providing compensation, namely that P has to be able to find a 'guilty' party; the fact that P can find a liability insurer is irrelevant because the obligations of the liability insurer only arise once liability has been established; and this can only be done by proceedings against or by an agreement with the tortfeasor.

The effects of this rule are particularly unfortunate in the field of personal injury claims where compensating relevant injured persons is seen as by far the most important function of the law of tort and of liability insurance. But it is not clear that we view liability insurance in quite the same light in all cases of economic loss. For example, one of the reactions to large rises in premiums payable by professionals, such as accountants, for liability insurance in the 1980s were calls for statutory limitations on the liability of professionals to a level which would protect most personal clients but which would require large institutional clients themselves to share the burden of losses arising from professional negligence. Those who make such calls seem to view liability insurance as basically a protection for individual clients and for professionals, but not for corporate clients.

Thus, the question of the role of liability insurance appears to be part of a

---

[6] See also K. Michel [1987] *LMCLQ* 228; A. McGee (1988) 9 *Company Lawyer* 183; A. Quick [1995] *New LJ* 918.

[7] *Post Office* v. *Norwich Union Fire Insurance Society Ltd* [1967] 2 QB 363. If the insurance funds available are inadequate to meet all the claims made, the funds are distributed on a chronological basis: *Cox* v. *Bankside Members Agency Ltd*, *The Times*, 16 May 1995.

[8] [1989] AC 957.

[9] Companies Act 1985, s. 651. But for the purposes of suing a dissolved company for personal injuries or under the Fatal Accidents Act 1976, there is now no time limit on making an application for revival of the company: Companies Act 1989, s. 141.

larger question about the role of tort law. Where parties are in a position to enter into a pre-tort risk-sharing agreement and the parties are sufficiently equal in bargaining power to ensure that the agreement is not too one-sided, liability insurance taken out by the defendant can, like loss insurance taken out by the plaintiff, be viewed simply as a means by which the insured can spread the risk of an insured event occurring. But in cases where pre-tort risk-sharing agreements are not, for one reason or another, possible or desirable, then we are much more inclined to view liability insurance primarily as a protection for the injured party rather than for the tortfeasor.[10]

Under section 3 of the 1930 Act no agreement between the insured and the insurer made *after* the defendant goes bankrupt and concerning the rights of the insured under the liability policy is enforceable against the plaintiff by the insurer. This provision is designed to prevent a bankrupt defendant from settling a claim under the policy for a sum less than the amount of D's potential liability to P. In *Normid Housing Association* v. *Ralphs*[11] P sought an injunction to restrain D from settling its claim against its insurer *before* it went bankrupt; this case is clearly not covered by the wording of the 1930 Act, and the Court of Appeal held that there was no other basis on which P could prevent D exercising his contractual rights in whatever way he wanted. This latter holding treats liability insurance as purely a matter between the insured and the insurer, which is, as we have seen, the traditional common law approach.

Compulsory Insurance

As we have already noted, insurance against the risk of being held liable for personal injuries is, in some cases, required by statute. Compulsory insurance against liability for economic loss is less common. Until 1987 compulsory road accident liability insurance related only to personal injuries. Now, as a result of an EC Directive, regulations have been made requiring motor liability insurance to cover property damage up to £250,000.[12] The first £175 does not have to be covered. The Motor Insurers Bureau has entered into an agreement with the Government[13] under which it will meet such liability in

---

[10] But consider s. 137 of the Companies Act 1989 (s. 310(3) of the Companies Act 1985) which allows companies to take out insurance to indemnify directors and officers against liability, exclusion of which is prohibited by s. 310 of the 1985 Act. Such insurance is viewed by those who promote it primarily as a protection for directors and officers because s. 310 itself was designed to ensure that directors and officers are exposed to liability. But, of course, it also operates to protect plaintiffs and, somewhat ironically, makes directors and officers more attractive targets for litigation.

[11] [1989] 1 Lloyd's Rep. 265.

[12] Motor Vehicle (Compulsory Insurance) Regulations 1987 (SI 2171/1987).

[13] On this and other such agreements see Lewis (1985) 48 *MLR* 275.

cases where the driver of the vehicle responsible for the damage was uninsured, but not in cases where the driver cannot be traced.[14]

Liability insurance in respect of economic loss is often a requirement of membership of a professional body such as the Law Society or the Bar. Such requirements are contained in the rules of such bodies, and not in statute; but if the body in question has monopoly licensing powers, the requirement is equivalent to a statutory one. Solicitors must take out £1 million worth of cover, and barristers £250,000 worth. Beyond the compulsory limit it is for each individual to decide whether to take out further cover or, for example, seek to limit their liability by agreement with individual clients. For instance, the Model Terms of Engagement issued by the Association of Consulting Engineers provide for agreements between the engineer and the client concerning the level of liability insurance the engineer will take out in respect of the particular project and for the client to contribute to the premiums; the idea is that the parties will also agree that the liability of the engineer will be limited to the level of the insurance cover agreed.[15]

Exclusion of Liability, Insurance, and Risk-shifting

From the insured's point of view an insurance contract is a risk-shifting contract, and it operates similarly to a contract clause or a non-contractual notice which excludes or limits liability:[16] if, by means of such a clause or notice, a party shifts a risk on to another individual rather than on to an insurer, the other may then shift the risk again on to an insurer or some other third party or group of third parties. And if the two original parties are in a contractual relationship, the party who benefits from the exclusion clause may well have to pay a 'premium' to the other in return for the shifting of the risk on to the other.

Because insurance and exclusion clauses and notices are alternative ways of shifting risks, it may be relevant to ask which method is to be preferred. So, for example, the test of reasonableness under section 11(4) of the Unfair Contract Terms Act 1977 applicable to clauses and notices which limit liability to a specified amount, refers to whether it was open to the person seeking to rely on the clause or notice to gain protection by insurance.[17] The other tests of reasonableness under the Act do not refer to insurance, but there is

[14] The latter type of case is covered by the Bureau's agreement in relation to personal injury. It is not covered in relation to property damage because of what insurers call 'moral hazard' or, in other words, the risk that a person will invent or engineer a claim by damaging his or her own car, and then claim that it was the result of the tort of a hit-and-run driver.

[15] *Professional Liability Today*, Nov. 1986, 5.

[16] Or like a contract term which explicitly allocates a particular risk to one party or the other. Such a term may well fall within s. 13 of UCTA. It is also common for commercial contracts to require one party to take out and maintain insurance to cover specified risks.

[17] On this insurability consideration see J. Hellner (1981) 1 *OJLS* 13, esp. 44–8; and 423–9 below.

no reason to think that it would not be relevant in relation to them. Furthermore, it is clear that in cases which do not fall under the Act, the question of insurance is relevant to the scope of exclusion clauses.[18]

Legal Costs and Insurance

We have seen that the interaction of liability insurance and the legal aid system has an important impact on the settlement of tort claims: the fact that the plaintiff's solicitor's costs are normally included in the amount of any settlement and that such costs are likely to be at a higher level than legal aid payments gives solicitors an incentive to settle early even when this may not be in the best interests of the client. If the client does not qualify for legal aid, both the client and the solicitor have a strong incentive to settle rather than to issue proceedings with all the risks which that entails. It is possible to buy insurance to cover the costs of bringing or defending claims although such insurance is not, as yet, very common.[19] One reason for this is that such insurance tends to be most attractive to high-risk insureds; so most legal expenses policies concentrate on claims, such as those arising from car accidents and home ownership, which are less affected by moral hazard than, for example, debt claims. For this reason, however, legal expenses insurance may be more significant in respect of tort claims than in respect of contract claims. There are also on the market commercial legal fees policies for businesses.

Legal fees policies typically offer access to a free telephone advice service. Individual policies vary considerably in respect of the sort of claims covered. Such policies operate similarly to legal aid in the sense that the insurer, like the legal aid authorities, decides whether the case is worth pursuing. Furthermore, just as solicitors are often discouraged from advising their clients to apply for legal aid because of the complications introduced by having to deal with the legal aid authorities, the fact that the legal expenses insurer will wish to exercise some control over the conduct of the proceedings may set up conflicts between the interests of the three parties involved (client, solicitor, and legal expenses insurer[20]), the result of which may be that some of the bargaining advantage which accrues from having the insurance in the first place may be lost. Nevertheless, a person who does not qualify for legal aid but has such insurance is likely to be in a stronger bargaining position than they would otherwise be.

In *Russell* v. *Wilson*[21] it was held that the fact that a plaintiff bringing a small claim in a County Court had legal expenses insurance and that the

[18] See 336 above.

[19] For a proposal for compulsory legal expenses insurance to be taken out by potential defendants for the benefit of potential plaintiffs see A. Tunkel [1991] *New LJ* 264.

[20] Especially if the legal expenses insurer also carries on liability business; on which see Insurance Companies (Legal Expenses Insurance) Regulations 1990 (SI 1159/1990).

[21] *The Times*, 26 May 1989.

defendant was also insured with the result that they could both afford representation did not provide a reason for rescinding automatic reference of the claim to arbitration because compulsory arbitration of small claims was designed to discourage representation. The reference was challenged by the legal expenses insurer because costs are not recoverable in small claims arbitration proceedings. The fact that one party to a small claims arbitration had insurance covering legal expenses but the other did not would not justify rescission of an automatic reference either, because it has been held that inequality of representation is a factor to be taken into account by the arbitrator in deciding what procedure to adopt for the arbitration and not on the question of referral.[22] In cases where legal aid is available,[23] those eligible for it may be disqualified if they have legal expenses insurance; and such insurance is likely to be particularly attractive to the poor, who are also most likely to be eligible for legal aid.

Another example of the interaction of County Court costs rules and insurance is *Hobbs* v. *Marlowe*.[24] This case involved property damage resulting from a road accident caused by the defendant's negligence. The plaintiff had a comprehensive insurance policy under which he received £227; but he had to pay a £10 excess (or 'deductible'), and the policy did not cover the cost (£63) of hiring a substitute car. P wanted to recover the £73 of uninsured loss from the defendant.[25] However, if he had sued for £73 he would not have been entitled to an award of costs; so his solicitor sued for the full £300 of P's loss.[26] The House of Lords held that although P was entitled to sue for £300 the County Court judge was entitled to refuse P costs on the ground that he had no good reason to make a claim for more than £73 given that his insurer apparently did not wish to exercise its subrogation rights.[27] In this type of situation, it would be much cheaper in financial terms for the insured to take out more comprehensive insurance than to seek to recover uninsured losses from the defendant. Indeed, there is a public policy argument for abolishing the basic rule that recovery under a policy of loss insurance does not bar an action against the tortfeasor.[28]

Defective Premises

Section 1 of the Defective Premises Act 1972 imposes a duty on persons who take on work for or in connection with the provision of a dwelling to use

---

[22] *Afzal* v. *Ford Motor Co. Ltd* [1994] 4 All ER 720, 734–5.
[23] It is not normally available for County Court arbitrations.   [24] [1978] AC 16.
[25] Uninsured losses are recoverable as tort damages: *Ironfield* v. *Eastern Gas Board* [1964] 1 WLR 1125.
[26] The fact that P had received £227 of this from his insurer did not prevent him suing for the whole £300 because, as we have noted above, the insurer is subrogated to the plaintiff's rights against the defendant and the plaintiff would be under a obligation to repay the £227 to the insurer out of the proceeds of the action.
[27] Contrast *Smith* v. *Springer* [1987] 3 All ER 252.   [28] See 336 below.

proper materials and to do the work in a workmanlike or professional manner so that the dwelling, when completed, will be fit for human habitation. This duty is owed to the person to whose order the work is done and to anyone who acquires a legal or equitable interest in the dwelling. The limitation period under the Act begins to run when the work is completed. Section 2 of the Act provides that section 1 does not apply where the dwelling is covered by an 'approved scheme'. Until sometime in the 1980s[29] the approved scheme was the National House Building Council Scheme which is an insurance scheme applying to all new dwellings and which gives limited but significant protection to house owners against defects in the dwelling.[30] The scheme covers a dwelling for ten years after completion; in respect of the first two years, the Council underwrites a contractual warranty given by the builder which is in the terms of the duty imposed by section 1 of the Act and which also guarantees that NHBC building standards have been complied with; whereas in respect of the other eight years the Council assumes a primary responsibility for 'major damage' resulting from failure to comply with its requirements. The main advantages of the scheme over the Defective Premises Act regime are that it protects house purchasers from builders who abscond or go bankrupt and, in respect of the eight-year period, obviates the need to claim against the builder. In addition, it shares with the Act a number of advantages over the common law.[31] On the other hand, the NHBC scheme only covers the cost of repair, and not consequential losses which are recoverable at common law.[32] It has been described as 'extremely complicated, with many difficulties and procedural pitfalls'.[33]

The NHBC scheme only applies to dwellings. In a 1988 report[34] the Insurance Feasibility Steering Committee of the National Economic Development Council examined the law relating to liability for defective buildings in the context of commercial building and found it seriously wanting: the outcome of civil claims is chancy; the cost of making such claims is high; settlement may take years and the amount recovered may fall far short of the loss suffered; in the meantime, all parties involved live in a state of uncertainty, while the building which is the subject of the claim may be dete-

---

[29] There is now apparently no approved scheme: I. N. Duncan Wallace (1991) 107 *LQR* 228, 242–3. In 1992 a report of the Monopolies and Mergers Commission which concluded that the scheme was anti-competitive and against the public interest was unsuccessfully challenged: *R. v. Monopolies and Mergers Commission, ex parte National House Building Council*, *The Times*, 7 Oct. 1992.

[30] For details, see A. M. Dugdale and K. M. Stanton, *Professional Negligence*, 2nd edn. (London, 1987), 187–90. The Council also runs a 6-year voluntary scheme covering newly-converted houses along the same lines as the compulsory scheme for new houses.

[31] See 217 above.

[32] One writer has also suggested the possibility of a scheme, along the lines of the NHBC scheme, to cover house surveys: M. Harwood (1987) 50 *MLR* 588, 602.

[33] Duncan Wallace (1991) 107 *LQR* 228, 243.

[34] *BUILD: Building Users' Insurance against Latent Defects* (1988); see also report of the Construction Professionals Study Team in the *Likierman Report on Professional Liability* (HMSO, 1989), paras. 5.4.4. and 10.5.

riorating; and the process of making and settling such claims does not encourage the achievement of building quality, but rather leads to attempts on the part of the parties involved to limit their personal liability. The Committee suggested that greater use should be made of first party, no-fault insurance (provided by private insurers) to cover material damage caused by specified latent defects for a period of ten years from completion. Such insurance, purchased by the developer or builder, would be transferable to successive owners and tenants of whole buildings. Insurers would agree to waive their rights of subrogation against any person liable in law for the defect, except in respect of the period during which the builder's contractual warranty operated.[35]

The committee's proposals were chiefly a response to the defects of the common law in bringing home liability to those legally responsible for building defects. Such schemes may also be important in providing cover for defects for which the common law does not provide compensation. The desirability of first party insurance[36] is clear in the light, for example, of the decision in *D. & F. Estates Ltd* v. *Church Commissioners*[37] in which the House of Lords held that liability in tort for defective building work only extended to personal injury or damage to property other than the defective building itself (or the defective part of a complex structure).

Judicial Reasoning in the Law of Tort

The Insurance Position of the Parties

All the examples we have considered so far have involved statutory provisions or some equivalent rule. More difficult to work out is the relationship between insurance and the outcome of particular cases in the courts. The traditional approach is encapsulated by Viscount Simonds in *Lister* v. *Romford Ice and Cold Storage Co Ltd*:[38] 'in determining the rights *inter se* of A and B, the fact that one of them is insured is to be disregarded'. The justification for this approach is straightforward: the basis for imposing liability in tort is that

---

[35] For trenchant criticism of these proposals see I. N. Duncan-Wallace [1990] *Construction LJ* 87. The Committee also suggested that such policies incorporate deductibles as an incentive to maintain quality. But it is not easy to see how this fits with the notion of a first-party loss insurance policy taken out for the benefit of the building owner or lessee, since under such a policy the 'insured' is the owner or lessee, not the builder. Of course, the owner or lessee might be subject to a deductible, but this would do nothing to maintain the quality of building work. In Apr. 1995 the DoE issued a Consultation Paper ('Latent Defects Liability and "Build" Insurance') rejecting compulsory first-party insurance but giving cautious support to the idea of a voluntary scheme: paras. 44–57.

[36] Which is not very widely available: B. Gloyn (1987) 84 *Law Soc. Gaz.* 2034.

[37] [1989] AC 177.

[38] [1957] AC 555, 576–7. Cf. *Davie* v. *New Merton Board Mills Ltd* [1959] AC 604, 626–7. See also *Launchbury* v. *Morgans* [1971] 2 QB 245, 263 *per* Megaw LJ; *Hunt* v. *Severs* [1994] 2 AC 350, 363 *per* Lord Bridge.

D ought to be held responsible for the injury, loss, or harm suffered by P: the fact that D is or is not insured helps to answer the question whether D could meet any damages award, but it is irrelevant to answering the question whether D ought to be ordered to pay damages. *A fortiori*, whether or not P is insured is irrelevant to answering this question. A central question in any and every tort action is whether D's conduct *caused*[39] P's loss. If it did, D may or may not be liable depending on what other conditions for the imposition of liability the law lays down; but if it did not, then even if all other conditions which the law lays down for the imposition of liability are satisfied, D cannot be liable in tort. Taking out insurance against the risk of suffering or being held liable for causing loss cannot prevent loss occurring; and failing to take out insurance against suffering, or being held liable for causing, loss cannot cause loss.[40]

It is, therefore, easy to understand why there is so little mention of the insurance position of litigants in the law reports; and why it is often impossible to tell, simply by reading the reports, whether an action is being brought on behalf of an insurer who has already paid out to the plaintiff and is exercising its right of subrogation or whether the defendant is backed by a liability insurer. Furthermore, even when the court knows the facts about the insurance position, it will often deny that they are relevant. Of course, the fact that the court does not mention insurance or even denies that it is relevant to the outcome of the case does not mean that the judges deciding the case were uninfluenced by the insurance position: it may only mean that they do not consider that the facts about insurance are relevant to the reasons which they give for their decision. A judge may be encouraged to reach a particular decision because of the fact that one or other or both of the parties is or is not insured, but the judge may also feel compelled to rationalize and justify that decision in terms of the traditional categories of the law. A judge is bound to feel more confident about a decision if the result which seems sensible in insurance terms can also be justified in traditional tort terms.

This is not to say that existing patterns of insurance are always ignored by the courts. For instance, it seems likely that one of the reasons why the House of Lords refused to impose liability on the carrier in *Leigh and Sillavan* v. *Aliakmon Shipping Co.*[41] was that the parties and others involved in international carriage of goods by sea would have arranged their insurance and fixed their charges on the basis of the law as it was understood to be before the case was decided. Insurance practice may be good evidence of commercial practice and commercial practice is, in matters of commercial law, seen as an

---

[39] In whatever sense the law gives to this term.

[40] In a number of decisions (see 202 above) it has been argued that D ought to have advised P to take out insurance or that D ought to have taken it out on P's behalf; and that this failure has caused P financial loss. In these cases, no question arose of P being insured against the economic loss which formed the subject matter of the action (that is, loss resulting from lack of insurance), or of D being insured against liability for such loss.

[41] [1986] AC 785.

important factor in deciding what the law ought to be because certainty and predictability is furthered if the law reflects accepted practice.[42] In other words, facts about insurance are not important in themselves but they are relevant as evidence of patterns of commercial practice. The law is justified in reflecting commercial practice, so the argument goes, because it is reasonable to assume that commercial parties are of roughly equal bargaining strength, and if the current arrangements were not mutually advantageous they would have be changed by mutual agreement. The law should be such as to promote mutually advantageous commercial activity, not to thwart it. Of course, this argument is weakened (if not entirely vitiated) by the fact that commercial practice in general and insurance practice in particular tend to reflect the law and would change if the law changed.

Nevertheless, the simple fact that the defendant to a tort claim is covered by liability insurance in respect of that claim, or that the plaintiff has insurance covering the loss allegedy caused by, D is irrelevant to the question of whether D is or ought to be held liable in tort to P.

The Insurability Argument

In *Lister* v. *Romford Ice* Viscount Simonds did not say that it was irrelevant to the legal rights *inter se* of A and B to ask whether one or the other of them, even if not insured, could have taken out insurance. At a general level, it is difficult to believe that the widespread availability of insurance against tort liability has not had an expansionary effect on the development of the law.[43] Weir, for example, seems to be in no doubt that the decision in *Hedley Byrne* v. *Heller*[44] was motivated, in part at least, by the 'economic view that investment and extension of credit should be encouraged to the extent of imposing some of their risks on liability insurers'.[45] Nor is it easy to believe that Lord Wilberforce put forward his (now rejected) idea of the *prima facie* duty of care in *Anns* v. *Merton LBC*[46] without being aware that new legal liabilities usually evoke an appropriate response from liability insurers, who are always keen to write new business. It is undoubtedly true that many professional groups attribute at least part of recent steep rises in their liability insurance premiums to new heads of tort liability, and proposals for statutory caps on damages and for greater use of limitation clauses are a response to such views about the relationship between liability rules and liability insurance premiums. These views are now beginning to be addressed explicitly by some

---

[42] [1986] AC 785, 817A–B.

[43] Of course, we are here concerned only with liability for unintentional interference with economic interests. Insurance is not available against liability for interferences which are typically the result of deliberate conduct because of what insurers call 'moral hazard', that is, the danger that the insured will be encouraged to bring about an insured event in order to collect the insurance or will, at least, have less incentive to avoid insured events.

[44] [1964] AC 465.   [45] [1963] *CLJ* 216, 218.   [46] [1978] AC 728.

judges. For example, in *Caparo* v. *Dickman* both Bingham and Taylor LJJ[47] expressed the view that their decision[48] to impose liability for negligence on company auditors in favour of existing shareholders should not make liability insurance for auditors unduly expensive. In *Smith* v. *Bush* Lord Griffiths thought that the general availability of adequate insurance cover was relevant to the question whether the valuer should be liable in tort to the purchaser.[49]

However, the only judge in recent times who has regularly and explicitly given weight to insurance considerations is Lord Denning. In the context of personal injuries, for example, he justified holding the learner driver to the same standard of care as the experienced driver partly on the basis that the driver would be insured, whether experienced or not.[50] Conversely, he was in favour of limiting the damages payable to 'human vegetables', partly on the basis that otherwise liability insurance premiums might become 'dangerously high'[51] (whatever that means). So far as economic loss is concerned, his guiding principle seems to have been that first-party loss insurance was preferable to third-party liability insurance. So, in *Lamb* v. *Camden LBC*[52] he justified not imposing liability on the Council partly on the basis that damage to real property is normally covered by insurance; similarly, in *Spartan Steel* v. *Martin*[53] he justified not allowing recovery for purely economic loss resulting from the cutting off of electricity supplies partly on the basis that commercial parties could insure against the risk of such loss. However, in cases where loss insurance was not a realistic option, Lord Denning was not averse to pointing to the possibility of liability insurance to justify imposing liability: for example, on the auctioneer in *R. H. Willis and Son* v. *British Car Auctions Ltd.*[54]

On the other hand, Lord Denning's commitment to considering the impact of insurance did not lead to consistent results. For example, although his Lordship clearly took account of the fact that the yacht owner in *Dorset Yacht Co. Ltd* v. *Home Office* was insured against damage to the yacht,[55] nevertheless he held that the Home Office could, as a matter of law, owe a duty of care to a person whose property was damaged by escaping prisoners. In *Spartan Steel* v. *Martin* his Lordship held that P could recover for physical damage to its property resulting from the cutting off of the electricity supply even though, if P had had insurance against interruption of the supply it would surely have covered physical damage as well as purely economic loss.

---

[47] [1989] QB 653, 688–9 and 703 respectively.
[48] Reversed by the House of Lords [1990] 2 AC 605.   [49] [1990] 1 AC 831, 858–9.
[50] *Nettleship* v. *Weston* [1971] 2 QB 691, 699–700.
[51] *Lim Poh Choo* v. *Camden AHA* [1979] QB 196, 217: Lord Denning dissented. Cf. *Fletcher* v. *Autocar and Transporters Ltd* [1968] 2 QB 322, 363 *per* Salmon LJ.
[52] [1981] QB 625.
[53] [1973] QB 27, 38; contrast the approach of Lawton LJ (at 47) who acknowledged that contractors frequently insure against the risk of liability arising out of the cutting off of essential services, but then ignored this fact in discussing the law governing the contractor's liability.
[54] [1978] 2 All ER 392, 395.   [55] [1969] 2 QB 412, 424.

This leads one to suspect that even Lord Denning saw insurance as a secondary consideration: if adverting to it helped him to bolster a conclusion he wanted to reach on other (and usually 'legal') grounds, he would mention it; otherwise, he would ignore it. More generally, although it seems unlikely that judges generally are unaware of and completely uninfluenced by insurance considerations, it is probably true that most judges do not analyse the issue of insurance as it bears on the case before them in any detail; and to the extent that insurance is influential it only serves to bolster conclusions reached by more traditional legal routes.

It is frequently argued that, although the actual insurance positions of the parties ought to be ignored in deciding whether to impose on one person legal liability for injury, loss, or harm suffered by another the law, the law ought to take account of whether one or other or both of the parties could have insured against the liability or the loss, as the case may be.[56] The argument for taking account of insurability is not without difficulty. In the first place, while the distinction between actual insurance and hypothetical insurability is clear in theory, it may not be so clear in practice because, in some cases at least, the fact that a party has not insured may be the best evidence that insurance was not available, at least at an economic cost (which means, in theory, at a cost less than the expected loss, multiplied by the estimated chance of the loss occurring, or of the insured being held liable for the loss, as the case may be).[57]

Secondly, a criterion of insurability will give clear guidance only where one party could insure but the other could not. Where both could insure, the criterion must be different: which party could insure more cheaply, perhaps. As we saw above in relation to liability insurance, many factors affect the price of insurance; but in the present context, four are important. The first is the cover provided by the policy. To the extent that the cover provided by each of the policies available to the two parties differs, it may be very difficult to compare their relative cost and decide which is best value for money. The second factor is the relative ability of the parties to define the insured event; the more precisely and narrowly the risk insured against can be specified, the narrower the scope of the policy and the less likely that it will cover events against which the insured does not want insurance. The narrower the coverage of the policy the lower the premium, other things being equal. Also, the more precisely the risk can be defined the more accurate can be the insurer's actuarial assessment of the risk. Thirdly, one party may have an advantage over the other in terms of the insurer's administrative costs. For example, from this point of view it is cheaper for an employer to take out one policy to cover the liability of all his employees to third parties than for each and every employee to take out a separate policy to cover the employee's own

---

[56] R. Stevens (1964) 27 *MLR* 121, 145, 153, n. 37; J. A. Smillie (1982) 32 *U Tor. LJ* 231; F. James (1972) 12 *JSPTL* 105 (reprinted from (1972) 25 *Vanderbilt LR* 43).

[57] J. Hellner (1981) 1 *OJLS* 13, 45.

liability. Fourthly, it is usually assumed that the administrative and legal costs associated with first-party loss insurance are lower than those associated with third-party liability insurance.[58] This is because there are fewer issues involved in settling claims under first party policies, and so fewer grounds for dispute; and there are only two parties involved, not three. First-party insurance is also less likely to generate litigation than third-party insurance because the issue of liability in tort, for example (on which the insurer's liability under the policy depends), is much more complex and difficult than the sort of questions of interpretation on which the insurer's liability under a first-party policy typically depends. For these reasons, it is usually assumed that, other things being equal, loss insurance taken out by the plaintiff is to be preferred to liability insurance taken out by the defendant.[59]

However, in cases where neither the insurability criterion nor the 'cheaper insurer' criterion yields a reasonably clear result, insurability will not help to resolve the dispute. If the criterion of liability is to be based on insurance, the question at this stage must become a normative one: who ought to insure, given that either party could insure? This question can only be answered by paying attention to what insurance does. The effect of insurance is to spread the risk of specified events among a group of insureds, all of whom face the risk. From the insured's point of view, insurance evens out the financial impact of the risk: instead of having to absorb the full impact of the risk if and when it materializes, the insured pays a relatively small premium each year; and if the risk materializes the cost is borne by the insurer. In the case of liability insurance, the insured benefits in the way just described; but the plaintiff also benefits because the defendant's insurance removes the risk that the defendant will not be able to bear the cost of liability when it occurs. Insurance is a means by which the financial disruption resulting from adverse events can be lessened; and since financial disruption often produces poverty and because, in a humane society, poverty needs to be relieved by community action, insurance relieves society as a whole from the burden of helping the victims of insurable adverse events.

Looked at in this way, the answer to the question of which party should insure would appear to be: either, so long as someone does. But although insurance is a good thing, its benefits to society as a whole are reduced if the same risk is insured more than once. So even if it is a matter of indifference which of two parties insures, it is important to develop rules which discourage multiple insurance of the same risk. It is this insight which underlies much of the objection to the doctrine of subrogation. But abolition of the right of subrogation would only go part of the way in avoiding multiple insurance. Take comprehensive motor insurance: subrogation rights are very rarely exer-

---

[58] Some insurers suppport the assumption: A. V. Alexander (1972) 12 *JSPTL* 173, 174; but others do not: E. W. Hitcham in M. Furmston (ed.), *The Law of Tort* (London, 1986), 199.

[59] e.g., J. A. Weir [1965] *CLJ* 186, 188; James (1972) 12 *JSPTL* 105, 112–6; Note (1966) 66 *Col. LR* 917.

cised in this context even though much physical damage to motor vehicles is the result of actionable negligence. Comprehensive policies cover actionable as well as non-actionable damage. And yet liability insurance against physical damage to third party property is now compulsory.

Liability insurance, of course, benefits motorists who do not buy first party loss insurance, but it duplicates the cover provided by such insurance to those who buy it. Since all motorists now have to buy liability insurance in respect of third-party property damage, it would have been less wasteful and no more onerous on individuals to make first-party property loss insurance compulsory and to abolish tort liability for damage to vehicles caused in road accidents.[60] The reason for preferring compulsory liability insurance to compulsory loss insurance must, at bottom, lie in some notion of personal responsibility and corrective justice: why should I have to insure myself against damage which is someone else's responsibility? In other words, the answer to the question who ought to insure may be seen as the same as the answer to the question who ought to bear the loss as a matter of fairness or corrective justice.

If this is right, then in cases where both parties could insure with more or less equal ease, insurance is seen just as an adjunct to the tort system; the fact that the person on whom the law imposes the loss can insure against it may provide an additional justification for the result, but the fact that one or other of the parties could insure has no independent force. Indeed, there is reason to think that the courts always view insurance in this way. A distinction should be made between saying, on the one hand, that a person ought to insure against a loss which the law places on that person (or allows to stay on that person); and on the other, that a person ought, by law, to be required to bear a loss because that person could insure against it. The latter argument is one based on paternalism and notions of distributive justice which are alien to the common law of obligations, while the former is not an argument about where the law ought to place the loss but rather about how the financial impact of the loss can be best dealt with either by the plaintiff or the defendant. The insurability argument purports to be an argument about where the law ought to place the loss; but it is quite inconsistent with the notions of personal responsibility and corrective justice which underlie the common law of obligations.[61] To take an extreme case, it is not possible to insure against liability for intentional wrongdoing, but this fact provides no good argument for not imposing liability for such wrongdoing; nor, conversely, does the fact that property can easily be protected from theft by loss insurance provide a good reason for not imposing tort liability on thieves. The real weakness of

---

[60] Whether some compensation scheme for uninsured motorists would be desirable is a different issue, on which see 449 below.

[61] See *Caltex Oil (Australia) Pty Ltd* v. *Dredge 'Willemstad'* (1976) 136 CLR 529, 580 *per* Stephen J; discussed in E. J. Weinrib (1985) 14 *JLS* 681, who says (at 683) that 'if the likelihood of insurance becomes a factor in the process of assigning liability . . . [t]he presence of insurance is transformed into a means for creating the liability to which it is supposed to respond'.

the insurance argument is that insurance is essentially a group or social phenomenon, whereas the common law of obligations is concerned with individuals. Disputes between individuals do not provide a good medium through
which to decide what is the best pattern of insurance in a particular area. If
it is thought that a particular type of loss should be allocated not according
to corrective justice criteria but according to insurance criteria, that loss
would be best removed from the province of the civil law of obligations and
dealt with by legislation concerning insurance against that type of loss. As
Weinrib says, the invocation of insurance in tort disputes undermines the conception of tort law as concerned with the immediate personal interaction of
the doer and the sufferer of harm.[62]

There is another problem with the notion of insurability: does it mean that
insurance of the relevant type is actually available, or that insurance might
be available if there were a market for it? Insurers, of course, react to the law,
and if the law creates a new liability, insurers will make policies available to
cover the new liability.[63] Similarly, if the law does not impose liability for
particular losses, insurers may see the chance to develop an appropriate loss
insurance policy. This interrelationship between the law and the insurance
market undermines the insurance argument in a serious way because it threatens it with circularity. It may be possible to say that some losses and some
liabilities are, in practical terms, uninsurable because, for example, they are
subject to extreme moral hazard. But many liabilities would be insurable if
they existed; and many losses against which people do not insure would be
insurable and insured if they were not the subject of liability rules. If a particular type of insurance is currently difficult or impossible to obtain, should
the law reflect this or should it place losses in such a way as to encourage
development of the market in that type of insurance? At the end of the day,
this question might turn on the relative merits, in terms of administrative and
legal costs, of liability insurance on the one hand and loss insurance on the
other. But it would make no sense to decide a case simply on the basis that
liability insurance or loss insurance was unavailable, because the availability
of insurance tends to reflect the state of the law.

Finally, it should be noted that, while it is easy to discover the actual insurance positions of the parties, insurability is much more difficult to ascertain.
In order to decide, with any degree of accuracy, whether a particular loss or
liability was insurable, the court would have to call expert evidence about the
current state and future prospects of the insurance market. But even if this

---

[62] (1985) 14 *JLS* 681, 683.

[63] A pertinent example is the growth in Directors and Officers (D & O) insurance in the wake
of the introduction, *inter alia*, of the new wrongful trading provisions (see 000 above) and the
amendment to the Companies Act allowing companies to take out such insurance. It is said that
between 1989 and 1992 the number of firms taking out such insurance more than doubled:
R. Lapper, 'Boost seen for liability insurance', *Financial Times*, 17 Feb. 1992. For a general discussion of the market in Directors' and Officers' (D & O) liability insurance see V. Finch (1994)
57 *MLR* 880, 892ff.

were done, judgments of insurability would inevitably be more or less speculative.

2. THE IMPACT OF THE LAW ON INSURANCE

So far as the incidence of insurance is concerned, it is no doubt true to say that there is a direct but crude relationship between the incidence of legal liability and the availability of insurance. So if the law imposes liability in particular circumstances, insurers are likely to offer greater or lesser cover against the risk of incurring such liability. Conversely, if the law imposes no liability in respect of certain losses, insurers are likely to offer greater or lesser cover against the risk of suffering such losses. The relationship between legal liability and the incidence of insurance is bound to be crude because the state of the law is only one of the factors which determines the availability of insurance; and because, for a variety of reasons, people often insure against losses in respect of which another may, in principle at least, be legally liable.

It is more difficult to work out (even crudely) the impact of the law on the cost of insurance. As a matter of theory, one would expect the law's impact on the cost of liability insurance to be much greater than its impact on the cost of loss insurance. Take insurance against fire damage to property: some fires are caused in circumstances where someone might be liable in law for causing them, but very many are not the result of legally wrongful conduct. Only a small fraction of the premium payable for a fire policy is likely to be referable to damage for which someone could, in theory, be held legally liable. So even if tort liability for damage to property were abolished, the impact of this reform on the cost of fire insurance would probably be negligible. In fact, the impact would be even less than this argument suggests because it is probably the case that, even when a fire is the result of legally wrongful conduct, the fire insurer may well not exercise its right of subrogation against the culprit; and, to the extent that rights of subrogation are not exercised, the abolition of liability would have no impact at all on insurance premiums.

In the case of property damage caused in road accidents, it is well known that rights of subrogation are rarely exercised, mainly because the expense of doing so is not justified by the amounts typically at stake. Instead, insurers used to enter into knock-for-knock agreements with other motor insurers under which they agreed not to exercise rights of subrogation against each other's insureds when they caused accidents. Because the implementation of such agreements involved subsidization of liability-only policy holders by comprehensive policy holders, as a result of premium competition from insurers who write very few liability-only policies, they have now been largely replaced by negotiated formulae for the apportionment of responsibility. Although these new arrangments technically involve the exercise of subrogation rights, in reality they constitute an administrative alternative to the costly process of pursuing such rights in individual cases. Indeed, the ending of knock-for-knock agreements is said to have led to premium reductions of about 10 per cent for comprehensive motor policies. Furthermore, we know that the vast majority of motor accidents are never made the subject of a tort claim, a particularly significant fact given that the majority of motor accidents cause only property damage and that the majority of tort claims in respect of property damage arise out of motor accidents.

By contrast to loss insurance, liability insurance is a direct response to the risk of being held liable in law; so one would expect there to be a much more direct relationship between rules of legal liability and the cost of liability insurance. So, for example, the premium (as a percentage of gross fee income) for barristers specializing in criminal work is less than half that for those specializing in civil work because much more of the work of the former than of the latter is covered by the advocate's immunity from liability in tort.

However, although it is obvious that there is a relationship between liability rules and liability insurance premiums, on closer analysis it appears that the relationship is far from simple. In the first place, the great majority of contract and tort claims are settled out of court; and, as we have seen, the settlement reached may, in many cases, be only very loosely based on the relevant legal rules. The most important factor in determining insurance premiums is the number and size of claims paid; and a settlement has the same effect on the insurer's accounts whether or not the insured was liable in law. Secondly, commercial insurers (as opposed to mutual insurers)[64] need to make a profit; and to ensure continued profitability, they need to advertise. The insurer's profit margin plus its administrative and advertising costs add significantly to the cost of liability insurance; so does the cost of the legal services needed either to resist or to settle claims, and so does the cost of reinsurance. Furthermore, the amount of investment income which the insurer can generate out of its premium income affects premiums.

Thirdly, while legal rules obviously provide the framework within which liability insurance operates, the practical operation of those rules is crucially affected by such factors as the type and quality of the goods and services being provided by particular insureds, and by the willingness of people to litigate. There is reason to think, for example, that one of the main reasons why the cost of professional indemnity insurance rose very greatly in the 1980s was that commercial clients (in particular) became much more prepared to sue their professional advisers when things went wrong.[65] The increasingly commercial approach of professionals, such as lawyers and accountants, to their work has encouraged this greater willingness to sue.

[64] See 432 below.

[65] According to one report, the number of open claims against accountants in respect of their auditing activities rose from fewer than 10 in 1982/3 to over 600 in 1992/3: *Independent on Sunday, Business*, 6 Mar. 1994, 7.

In Britain, the most dramatic rises in the cost of liability insurance in recent years have been in the case of professional financial advisers such as lawyers, surveyors, architects, and accountants, especially in the mid-1980s.[66] Despite the complexity of the issues involved, it is not uncommonly asserted that changes in the law of tort from the late 1970s onwards played a significant part in precipitating such increases.[67] The changes pointed to included a generally expansionary attitude to tort liability on the part of the courts (both as to questions of duty and the issue of standard of care) which is traced to Lord Wilberforce's judgment in *Anns* v. *Merton LBC*;[68] the extension of concurrent liability in tort and contract to financial advisors (the main importance of this change is usually said to be that the limitation period in tort is more generous to plaintiffs than that in contract); the introduction of tort liability for purely economic loss suffered by plaintiffs not in contractual privity with the defendant; and, in the context of liability for defective buildings, the advent of liability for the cost of repair.

However, on closer examination, it seems unlikely that any of these changes could explain the large increases during the 1980s in professional indemnity premiums. The effects of Lord Wilberforce's approach were not limited to professional liability claims as normally understood.[69] Nor is there any evidence that the courts have raised the standards of care required of professionals in recent years. So far as concurrent liability and limitation periods are concerned, the law is so unclear about when the limitation period in a tort action for purely economic loss begins to run that it very difficult to say, in general, whether a plaintiff will be better off suing in tort than in contract. Thirdly, some professsional groups (such as accountants and surveyors) are much more vulnerable to third-party claims than others (such as lawyers), and yet all of the financial professions experienced greatly increased premiums. Much the same point can be made about liability for the cost of repairing defective buildings and chattels (which became a recoverable head of damage following the decision in *Anns* v. *Merton LBC*[70] in 1978): it is irrelevant to some professional groups (such as lawyers) which experienced large increases in insurance costs. It cannot be denied that the decision in *Hedley Byrne* v. *Heller* greatly increased the potential liability of financial advisers and probably led to many more claims being made than would otherwise have been the case. However, since that case was decided in 1963 it cannot, by itself, explain increases in premiums in the 1980s.

[66] For more detailed discussion, see P. Cane (1989) 14 *Geneva Papers on Risk and Insurance* 347; D. C. Davies [1985] *PN* 169; G. N. Reid [1986] *PN* 10; D. C. M. Blackburn [1987] *PN* 11; N. Kohn [1991] *PN* 32.

[67] See, e.g., Lord Hacking, HL Debs., Vol. 485, cols. 1463–7; Lord Oliver of Aylmerton, 'Developments in Professional Liability' (The Chartered Insurance Institute, London, 1988).

[68] [1978] AC 728.

[69] *Leigh and Sillavan* v. *Aliakmon Shipping* Co. [1986] AC 785, an important example of reaction against Lord Wilberforce's approach, concerned liability for physical damage to property caused by bad stowage.

[70] [1978] AC 728.

So it is difficult to trace a clear link between such changes in tort law and increases in the 1980s in professional liability insurance premiums. Indeed, it is probably the case that many insurers responsible for fixing premiums have little detailed knowledge of the relevant law. Another problem in working out the relationship between law and premiums is that the insurance market, like the stock market, is very sensitive to uncertainty. The law of tort as it relates to the liability of professionals for economic loss has been in a state of flux and uncertainty for the past fifteen years or so;[71] and this, much more than the substance of the law itself, may explain changes in the level of premiums: if insurers are uncertain and anxious about the future, they will increase premiums to the highest level the market will bear. It is at this point that it becomes important to note that there has been a long-term chronic lack of capacity, and hence of competition, in the professional indemnity sector of the insurance market; if there had been more competition, premiums might not have risen as high as they did. Ironically, at the same time the large premium increases of the mid-1980s are usually seen as having been, in part, a reaction to very low rates produced by short-term excessive competition in the early 1980s followed by large underwriting losses and the withdrawal of a significant number of underwriters from the professional indemnity market.

In short, we can say that the case of professional indemnity insurance alerts us to the complexity of the question of the impact of the law on the cost of liability insurance.

3. MUTUAL INSURANCE

One reaction of some professional groups[72] to the rising cost of indemnity insurance has been to set up mutual (that is, co-operative) insurance schemes: both the Law Society[73] and the Bar, for example, run such schemes.[74] The Law Society's Solicitors Indemnity Fund, which provides the compulsory cover of £1 million, is supplemented by a privately managed and voluntary top-up fund called the Solicitors Indemnity Mutual Insurance Association. Unlike commercial insurance, which involves an insurer pooling and underwriting risks in return for a premium, a mutual is a risk-sharing arrangement in which all the members of the scheme are both insurers and insureds. The advantages which mutual schemes are said to have over the commercial insurance market are that a mutual does not need to make a profit or to spend much on advertising; and, by virtue of specialization, there is the expectation

---

[71] Case law developments are more productive of uncertainty than statutory developments because there is often very little warning that they are coming; and because the narrowness of the reasoning in many cases makes it very difficult to predict the future direction of the law.

[72] But not only professional groups: London Transport has set up an insurance company in which the 10 London bus companies own shares. The main motivation was cost-cutting: *Financial Times*, 23 June 1994.

[73] Solicitors Act 1974, s. 37.   [74] See also *Professional Liability Today*, Nov. 1989, 8.

that claims will be handled more quickly and cheaply.[75] Furthermore, mutuals typically do not build up large reserves to meet possible future claims but operate on an annual pay-as-you-go basis. Mutuals play an important role in cases where it is compulsory for professionals to take out a certain amount of liability cover: it may be very expensive, or even impossible, for some high risk practitioners to obtain the compulsory cover on the open market. A mutual can set premiums in such a way as to subsidize some practitioners at the expense of others so as to ensure that all qualified practitioners have the compulsory cover. This mode of operation is particularly important in the case of solicitors, for example, who are very rarely prohibited from practising merely on grounds of negligence.[76]

Another context in which mutual insurance is of importance to the subject matter of this book is that of liability for oil pollution.[77] Mutual insurance of marine risks through what are known as 'Protection and Indemnity (P & I) Clubs has a long history. These clubs provide ship owners, charterers, and operators with insurance against liability to third parties from a wide variety of causes, including oil pollution. Apart from the common law, liability for oil pollution damage is governed by Chapter III of the Merchant Shipping Act 1995 which, in its original form, was enacted (in 1971) to give effect to the International Convention on Civil Liability for Oil Pollution Damage 1969 (the 'Liability Convention'). The Act imposes strict liability on shipowners for the discharge or escape from ships of 'persistent hydrocarbon mineral oil' in respect of damage caused outside the ship by the escape or discharge of oil (whether part of the cargo or of the ship's fuel), and in respect of the cost of cleaning up and of any damage caused by the cleaning-up process. The Act also imposes liability for the cost of preventing or minimizing damage outside the ship in cases where there is a 'grave and imminent threat of damage by contamination resulting from an escape or discharge of oil'. In relation to oil being carried as cargo, the Act applies to oil pollution in the area of the United Kingdom and of other Convention countries; but in relation to bunker (i.e. fuel) oil it only applies to spills in UK waters. Despite the fact that the liability is strict, contributory negligence is available as a defence (s. 153(8)); and certain other defences are provided by section 155 of the Act where the escape or discharge, or the relevant threat of contamination, is the result of events beyond the shipowner's control. In cases to which the Act applies, a

---

[75] But the Lay Observer repeatedly criticized the Solicitors Indemnity Fund managers for using similar delaying tactics to those common amongst commercial insurers: *13th Annual Report* (1987), para. 40; *14th Annual Report* (1988), paras. 56–65. The SIF is run day-to-day by a broking firm—London Insurance Brokers. Administrative costs are low: about 6% of 'premium' income.

[76] There is no economic argument for subsidization of higher risk practitioners at the expense of lower risk ones. If high risk practitioners were faced with the full cost of the risks they created they would have stronger incentives to improve their performance or change occupation. For an airing of this and other criticisms of the Solicitors Indemnity Fund see S. Wallach, 'A Safety Net Sprouting Holes', *The Independent*, 5 June 1992.

[77] D. Wilkinson (1993) 5 *J Env. L* 71; P. Wetterstein [1994] *LMCLQ* 230.

shipowner is not liable for oil pollution damage other than under the provisions of the Act (s. 156). Certain other persons (such as employees of the shipowner or charterer) can be held liable, but only if they acted intentionally or recklessly. Liability for 'impairment of the environment' is limited to financial loss (s. 156(3)). The shipowner can limit its liability to a certain sum in cases where the damage is not the result of intentional or reckless conduct on the shipowner's part (s. 157).[78]

Where the ship's cargo of oil is more than 2,000 tons it cannot enter or leave the UK nor, if it is a ship registered in the UK, any other Convention country, unless it is covered by insurance against liability under the Act (s. 163). Furthermore, the insurer can be sued directly unless the escape or discharge was the result of the wilful misconduct of the insured (s. 165). The insurer can limit its liability to the same extent as the shipowner. Such insurance is largely provided by P & I Clubs.

Chapter IV of the 1995 Act in its original form was enacted in 1974 to give effect to the International Convention on the Establishment of an International Fund for Compensation for Oil Pollution Damage 1971 (the 'Fund Convention'). The Fund Convention created a compensation fund financed by levies on imports of oil. It provides compensation in cases not covered by Chapter III of the 1995 Act or where claims exceed the limits of liability under that chapter. There are also voluntary compensation agreements[79] between oil tanker owners and oil cargo owners which operate in certain cases where the Liability Convention does not; they provide for the payment of compensation to governments and to private individuals who suffer damage as a result of oil spills.[80] The voluntary agreements were a response to the danger that governments would impose safety precautions and other restrictions on the movement of oil which oil companies would find commercially disadvantageous. Once again, liability under the voluntary agreements is largely insured through P & I Clubs.

The insurance facilities provided by P & I Clubs play a central role in providing compensation for damage caused by oil spills.[81] On the other hand,

---

[78] On limitation of liability in respect of other shipping claims see Merchant Shipping Act 1995, s. 185; *The Bowbelle* [1990] 1 WLR 1330.

[79] The Tanker Owners Voluntary Agreement Concerning Liability for Oil Pollution (TOVALOP), supplemented by the Contract Regarding an Interim Supplement to Tanker Liability for Oil Pollution (CRISTAL).

[80] Under TOVALOP any right of the pollution victim to sue in tort or use other domestic remedies is unaffected by the existence of a claim under it; whereas under the CLC, if a spill occurs in the territory or territorial waters of a country which is party to the Convention, no claim may be made against the assest of the shipowner except under the CLC.

[81] C. Hill, B. Robertson, and S. J. Hazelwood, *An Introduction to P & I* (London, 1988); C. Springall (1988) 6 *J of Energy and Natural Resources Law* 25. The rules of P & I Clubs commonly provide that the Club does not become liable to pay until the member becomes liable and *has paid*: *Firma C-Trade SA* v. *Newcastle Protection and Indemnity Association* [1991] 2 AC 1. In such cases the Club provides an indemnity, rather than insurance in the true sense. This case arose out of claims under the Third Parties (Rights Against Inusrers) Act 1930, under which the injured person who sues the insurer has only the same rights against the insurer as the bankrupt

liability under the 1971 and 1974 Acts and the various agreements is limited both in its scope and in monetary terms, and liability outside the scope of operation of these arrangements may not be adequately insured against. Furthermore, it has been suggested that the financial limits on liability have had the effect of making oil companies complacent, and of discouraging them from taking proper measures to deal with very large spills.[82]

4. SUBROGATION AND CONTRIBUTION

Arguments For and Against

In the law of insurance a distinction is drawn between insurance contracts which are contracts of indemnity and those which are not. The basic idea behind this distinction is that under a non-indemnity contract the insured is entitled to payment of a fixed sum or of a sum calculated according to a fixed scale, whereas under an indemnity contract the insured is entitled to be fully indemnified, but no more than fully indemnified, for loss suffered which falls under any of the heads of loss specified in the policy. The distinction has, however, become mechanical (and, as a result, difficult to rationalise): fire, property, and liability policies are indemnity contracts but life policies and personal accident policies generally are not.[83] The courts do not examine individual contracts to see whether or not they provide for an indemnity.[84] The present relevance of the distinction is that the insurer under an indemnity contract is subrogated to any legal rights of the insured against any person who has caused the loss insured against; but this right of subrogation does not apply to non-indemnity contracts. The right of subrogation entitles to insurer to enforce the legal rights of the insured in the name of the insured, not in the insurer's own name. Related to the right of subrogation is the rule that if an indemnity insurer pays the insured under the policy in respect of

insured; in each case it was held that the injured party's claim against the Club could not succeed because, until the member had paid the injured party, the Club came under no liability to the member. This rule is clearly extremely unsatisfactory for claimants against bankrupt or defaulting members of P & I Clubs; but a spokesman for one Club has strongly expressed the view that the Clubs operate solely for the benefit of their members 'and not for third parties to whom no contractual liability has been assumed': Howe *Professional Liability Today*, June 1988, 8. S. 165 of the Merchant Shipping Act 1995 simply says that proceedings may be brought against the insurer 'in respect of' alleged liability under the Act. S. 165(2) allows the insurer to plead wilful misconduct on the part of the insured 'in addition to any defence affecting the owner's liability'. S. 165(3) allows the insurer to limit its liability in monetary terms. On the basis of these provisions, it might be arguable that the insurer could not take advantage of a 'pay first' provision in a case falling under the Act.

[82] See 'The well protected oil operators', *Financial Times*, 20 Apr. 1989, 11.

[83] J. Birds, *Modern Insurance Law*, 3rd edn. (London, 1993), 272–3; R. Hasson (1985) 5 *OJLS* 416, 418–9. According to S. A. Rea, 'Non-indemnity contracts are most likely to arise when the pecuniary value of the loss is not easy to measure': (1993) 13 *Int. R of Law and Econ.* 145, 152.

[84] S. L. Kimball and D. A. Davis (1962) 60 *Mich. LR* 841.

the insured loss and in addition the insured receives a payment from a third party in respect of the insured loss, the insurer is entitled to recover its payment to the extent that, as a result of having received two payments in respect of the insured loss, the insured has been more than indemnified (has been 'unjustly enriched').[85] The term 'subrogation' is most accurately applied only to the former of these rights. The latter is best described as a right to restitution.

The juridical basis of the right of subrogation so defined is not clear. If the distinction between indemnity and non-indemnity policies had not become mechanical, the right of subrogation could be seen as arising expressly or impliedly from the terms of contracts of indemnity insurance. As things are, however, the right of subrogation attaching to indemnity insurance is not necessarily based on the terms of the contract but may be seen as arising 'by operation of law' as a function of the classification of the insurance contract as one of indemnity. This uncertainty about the legal basis of subrogation is important because if subrogation is a contractual right, it can be justified simply in terms of giving effect to the agreement of the parties (assuming that there is no good reason why such agreements should be banned); whereas if the right of subrogation is not based on agreement, it will have to be justified in other ways. In fact, discussions of subrogation usually ignore the agreement of the parties as a source of justification and focus on 'public policy' arguments.

Two such public policy arguments are commonly used to justify subrogation.[86] First, if the insurer was not subrogated to the rights of the insured, there would be nothing to prevent the insured recovering twice, once from the insurer and once from the person liable in law for the loss.[87] If the insurer has agreed to indemnify the insured but no more and the insured is compensated by the defendant, the insurer should be allowed to recover any amount paid out to the insured under the policy which, under these circumstances, can be said to represent an unfair profit (an 'unjust enrichment'). On the other hand, if the insurer has agreed to pay the insured a fixed sum or according to a fixed scale, it cannot argue that the insured has recovered twice over if the insured receives compensation from the defendant in addition to payment under the policy. The problem with this argument is that it confuses the insurer's right to be subrogated to the insured's legal rights and the insurer's right to recover from the insured any amount by which the insured has been

---

[85] See generally C. Mitchell, *The Law of Subrogation* (Oxford, 1994), 67–80. The insurer has a proprietary interest in the proceeds of any action brought by the insured against the responsible third party which can be enforced by a lien: *Lord Napier and Ettrick* v. *Hunter* [1993] AC 713.

[86] See also M. Clarke, *The Law of Insurance Contracts*, 2nd edn. (London, 1994), 832–5.

[87] But what if the insured's loss is greater than the amount payable under the policy? See A. A. Tarr (1987) 11 *Adelaide LR* 232. It is a curiosity of the notion of indemnity insurance that the amount of the indemnity can be limited to a specified sum; that is, the insured is entitled to have losses met up to a certain sum. This in itself blurs the distinction between indemnity and non-indemnity policies.

'unjustly enriched'. It does not follow from the fact that an indemnity insurer should be able to recover any such amount from the insured that the insurer should be entitled to exercise a legal right which the insured has not exercised. Conversely, it does not follow from the fact that an insured under a non-indemnity policy would not be unjustly enriched by receiving a payment in respect of the insured loss from a legally liable party that the insurer should not be subrogated to the insured's (unexercised) rights against that party.

Secondly, it is argued that unless the insurer can sue in the name of the insured those legally responsible for inflicting losses may go scot free because, once the insured has recovered under the policy, the insured has much less incentive to sue the defendant. In other words, subrogation furthers the deterrent aim of the law: the costs of negligent conduct (for example) should fall ultimately on the activity which generated them and not on a first-party insurer. It is only if activities 'pay their way' that they will be conducted in an economically efficient way and to an economically efficient extent. There is a danger of circularity in this argument: how much incentive there is for a person who has been paid by an insurer to sue a tortfeasor responsible for the insured loss may depend partly on whether the insured will have to account to the insurer for any proceeds of the action; and this, in turn, depends on whether or not the insurer is subrogated to the insured's rights against the tortfeasor.

A number of arguments are commonly made against allowing subrogation. First, it is argued that the insurer should not be able to take a premium for bearing a risk and then, by exercising a right of subrogation, offload the risk onto someone else when it occurs. To the extent that subrogation rights are based on the agreement between insurer and insured, there may be two answers to this argument. It may be conceded that the argument has some force, but that its force is met by the rule that an insurer may not exercise subrogation rights against a person covered by the relevant policy.[88] Alternatively, it may be denied that the insurer has accepted a premium for the risk of an insured loss resulting from conduct for which a third party is legally liable: on the contrary, the agreement of the parties in respect of such losses was that the insurer should have a right of subrogation. To the extent that subrogation rights are non-contractual, the force of the argument may depend on whether, in practice, premiums rates accurately reflect subrogation opportunities. It would seem unfair for insurers to calculate premiums on the basis that subrogation rights would not be exercised, but also to reserve the right to exercise them when they chose. In fact, it seems that subrogation rights are relatively rarely exercised, and they probably have a minimal effect on premiums.[89]

---

[88] *Simpson* v. *Thomson* (1877) 3 App. Cas. 279; *Stone Vickers Ltd* v. *Appledore Ferguson Shipbuilders Ltd*, *The Times*, 30 Jan. 1991.

[89] Hasson (1985) 5 *OJLS* 416, 422–3; S. R. Derham, *Subrogation in Insurance Law* (Sydney, 1985), 152–4.

Secondly, it is argued that to the extent that subrogation rests on deterrence arguments, it suffers from the weaknesses of the deterrent view of civil liability, which we shall discuss in the next chapter.[90] It is sometimes suggested that subrogation should be abolished except in cases where the defendant acted deliberately and so might be amenable to being deterred.[91] This compromise is not attractive: if the defendant is insured against the liability, the case of deliberate wrongdoing is, for all practical purposes, indistinguishable from that of unintentional wrongdoing. If D is not insured, it will usually not be worthwhile for P's insurer to sue: if the amount involved is small, the cost of recovering it would not be justified; and if it is big, an uninsured defendant is unlikely to be able to pay it.

Thirdly, the argument that without subrogation losses would not fall where they should has force (it is said) where the plaintiff and the defendant are engaged in quite different activities but not where they are engaged in the same activity. Take the case of motor accidents: if a comprehensive motor insurer recoups loss from a liability motor insurer in respect of damage to a vehicle, the loss is shifted from one group of motorists to another group of motorists. No matter which insurer ultimately bears the loss, motoring bears the loss; and because all motorists are at risk both of causing and suffering loss in road accidents, it is really to no one's benefit (except that of insurance companies and lawyers) to spend money shifting losses from one insurer to another.[92] Hence knock-for-knock agreements and formulae for the apportionment of losses between insurers.[93]

Fourthly, like all civil law rights, subrogation rights are expensive to enforce; and in practice they are only worth enforcing in the case of very large claims and when the defendant is insured against liability. For this reason, it is argued, subrogation is wasteful because it encourages[94] multiple insurance of the same risk: potential plaintiffs insure in case they suffer loss for which they cannot successfully sue a third party, and potential defendants insure against liability for such loss in case they are held legally liable for causing it. On the assumption that most people would rather not insure against the same loss twice, it is undesirable that the law should generate this situation.

Arguments analogous to these can be used to justify or to oppose the right of contribution between persons legally responsible for infliction of loss or damage, primarily under the Civil Liability (Contribution) Act 1978, and also rights of indemnity as between wrongdoers. Indeed, in the case of liability insurance, the liability insurer's right of subrogation consists of a right to enforce contribution or indemnity rights against other wrongdoers.

---

[90] Hasson (1985) 5 *OJLS* 416, 423–5; Derham, *Subrogation in Insurance Law*, 154–7.

[91] Birds, *Modern Insurance Law*, 299; Hasson (1985) 5 *OJLS* 416, 437; C. G. King (1951) 30 *Texas LR* 62, 65.

[92] Hasson (1985) 5 *OJLS* 416, 425–7.   [93] See 429 above.

[94] Hasson (1985) 5 *OJLS* 416, 425 goes further and sees subrogation as designed to increase the demand for insurance.

In terms of the law of tort, rights of subrogation, indemnity, and contribution are economic interests, and the enforcement of such rights allows
recovery for purely economic loss. We have seen that the law of tort does not
allow the insurer to sue the tortfeasor directly in its own name,[95] although,
of course, the insurer's right of subrogation achieves a similar effect as does
a direct right of action. Rights of contribution were never developed by the
common law and exist solely by statute. The only context in which the law
of tort recognizes a right of indemnity as such is between employer or principal and an employee, agent, or independent contractor for whose tort the
employer or principal is held vicariously liable.[96] This right is most likely to
be exercised in the 'employer's' name by its liability insurer,[97] but only if
some other insurer is obliged to pay in respect of the 'employee's' tort. The
negative effect of such actions on industrial relations has been recognized by
insurers, who have agreed amongst themselves not to exercise their subrogation rights in master–servant cases unless there was evidence of wilful misconduct or collusion. In *Morris* v. *Ford Motor Co. Ltd*[98] the Court of Appeal
held that the right of indemnity was unacceptable in an industrial setting and
that it was impliedly excluded by the terms of the contract in that case
between the employer and its employee. This reasoning is rather artificial and
lacking in clear principle,[99] but the decision is a sensible one in practical
terms.[100]

In *Lambert* v. *Lewis*[101] one of the issues was whether the supplier of a
defective automotive coupling could sue the manufacturer in tort in respect
of its contractual liability to pay compensation for personal injuries resulting
from the failure of the coupling. The supplier could not claim contribution
from the manufacturer because, at the relevant time, the contribution legislation did not extend to liability in contract; nor could it claim in contract
against the manufacturer because it had bought the coupling from an intermediate supplier who could not be identified. In the end, this issue did not
have to be decided because the supplier was held not liable in contract. But
the House of Lords suggested that a tort action might lie in such circumstances on ordinary principles: ought the (negligent) manufacturer have foreseen that if it did not take care in manufacturing the coupling, an
intermediate supplier might suffer (economic) loss consisting of liability to
pay damages? This decision has been criticized on the ground that questions

[95] *Simpson* v. *Thomson* (1877) LR 3 App. Cas. 279.
[96] *Lister* v. *Romford Ice and Cold Storage Co. Ltd* [1957] AC 555.
[97] But sometimes the employer may sue the employee. For instance, it is not unknown for
solicitors to sue allegedly negligent employees to recover the amount of any excess under a professional indemnity policy: S. Wallach, 'Taking liability to excess', *The Independent*, 18 Feb.
1994.
[98] [1973] 1 QB 792.
[99] Hasson (1985) 5 *OJLS* 416, 435. Lord Denning also argued that the right of indemnity was
an equitable right which had to be exercised equitably.
[100] Birds [1979] *JBL* 124; ironically, in this case the employer was not insured.
[101] [1982] AC 225, esp. 277–8.

of indemnity should be decided according to contractual and restitutionary principles and not according to principles similar to those which govern liability in tort for physical damage.[102] Since such actions are likely to be brought by one insurer against another, they are subject to similar objections as apply to subrogation actions generally.

A different criticism of contribution actions by liability insurers has been made in the context of liability of regulatory authorities for the exercise of their regulatory powers.[103] Suppose an architect employed by a building owner to supervise building work negligently fails to notice that the builder has not complied with building regulations in some respect. Or suppose that an accountant employed by a prospective investor negligently fails to notice warning signs in the published accounts of a company which is licensed by a public authority to carry on a particular type of business. Suppose further that the building owner successfully sues the architect or the investor successfully sues the accountant in respect of financial loss suffered as a result of the negligence of the adviser; and that the adviser then sues the local council responsible for enforcing building regulations or the regulator responsible for issuing licences to do business for a contribution. If, as will usually be the case, the adviser is insured against liability in tort, then to allow the liability insurer to exercise a right of subrogation (by way of contribution proceedings) against the regulator would be to shift the cost of the negligence from the activity primarily responsible for it on to the taxpayer. However, this is not really an argument against allowing subrogation via contribution proceedings but rather against imposing tort liability on statutory regulators; and the courts have dealt with it in this way by generally refusing to impose duties of care on statutory regulators in favour of the beneficiaries of regulation.[104]

Should Subrogation Rights be Abolished?

This question needs to be answered in two stages. First, should the parties to an insurance policy be allowed to agree that the insurer is to be subrogated to any legal rights of the insured against third parties in respect of the occurrence of the insured loss? My view is that, however strong the arguments against subrogation may be, they are not strong enough to justify a generally negative answer to this first question. However, there is a problem about how we are to determine whether the parties have agreed that the insurer should have subrogation rights. The law's current criterion is that an indemnity insurer has subrogation rights but a non-indemnity insurer does not. As noted above, this criterion is unsatisfactory because it is applied mechanically in terms of the category of insurance into which any particular contract of insurance falls (fire, life, liability, and so on) and not according to the express or

---

[102] G. Samuel [1982] *New LJ* 833.   [103] Tony Weir [1989] *PL* 40.
[104] See 241 above.

implied intention of the parties to the contract. In other words, there is nothing wrong with allowing contractual rights of subrogation, but we need a better test for deciding when such rights arise; that is, a test which requires an analysis of the terms of individual contracts of insurance. There is also, in my view, nothing wrong with allowing an insurer and an insured to agree that if, as a result of receiving payments both from the insurer and from a third party in respect of an insured loss, the insured ends up with more than the insurance contract stipulated, the insurer should be allowed to recover the excess.

The second question is whether the law should ever give insurers subrogation rights regardless of whether they were bargained for between insurer and insured. In my view, the balance of the arguments for and against subrogation favours a negative answer to this question, at least in relation to fire, property, and liability insurance.[105] There is no good reason why the law should give an insurer a right of subrogation when the insurer has not bargained for the inclusion of such a right in the insurance contract; and there are good reasons why it should not. Such a reform of the law would reduce the waste involved in multiple insurance of the same risk and would save the costs involved in loss shifting by one insurer to another.

If non-contractual subrogation rights were abolished to the extent suggested, what would be the proper attitude for the law to take in cases where an insured party received payments in respect of an insured loss both under a first-party insurance policy and from a party legally liable for that loss? In such situations would it be right for the law, as at present, to allow the insurer to recover its payment from the insured regardless of whether the insurer had stipulated for such recovery in the insurance contract? The answer to this question might depend, in legal terms, on whether it could be said that in such a situation the insured had been unjustly enriched at the expense of the insurer. In the absence of any contractual agreement between the insurer and the insured requiring repayment by the insured, it is very difficult to see why the insured should be required to reimburse the insurer;[106] and in my view, reimbursement should not be available to the insurer as a matter of law (as opposed to agreement between insurer and insured).

Subrogation in the Courts

There is very little sign that English courts are worried about the doctrine of subrogation. For example, in *Metal Box Co. Ltd* v. *Curry's Ltd*[107] goods

---

[105] Hasson (1981) 5 *Can. Bus. LJ* 498. Rights of subrogation have been limited in Australia: Insurance Contracts Act 1984 (Cth), ss. 65, 66.

[106] For an attempt to find a good ground for restitution see Burrows, *The Law of Restitution* (London, 1993), 80–1.

[107] [1988] 1 WLR 175.

owned by P were damaged; the goods were insured, and the court acknowledged that the action was one by way of subrogation except to the extent of the deductible under the policy. P claimed compensation only for loss of value of the goods resulting from the damage; it claimed no damages for loss of profits. D argued that P (that is, the insurer) should not be awarded interest on the sum claimed on the ground that, since the goods were non-profit-earning and P claimed no damages for loss consequential upon the damage, an award of interest would make P better off than it would have been had the tort not occurred. The court rejected this contention. One can see the force of D's argument so far as P's interest in the goods was concerned, but from the insurer's point of view its claim was simply to be reimbursed for a sum paid out to P. From the date when it made the payment and its right of subrogation arose, it was being kept out of its money; and since an award of interest is designed to compensate for being kept out of money, such an award seems, from the insurer's point of view, quite justified. On the other hand, the interest awarded was for the period between the date when the cause of action arose and the date of judgment; whereas the insurer was not kept out of its money for this period but for the shorter period between the date of its payment to the plaintiff and the judgment. This case takes the insurer's right to subrogation very seriously,[108] while at the same time illustrating the fact that the insurer is not seen as the plaintiff in subrogation proceedings.

This last point is reinforced by the decision of the House of Lords in *Esso Petroleum Co. Ltd* v. *Hall Russell & Co. Ltd*.[109] The plaintiffs owned a tanker from which oil escaped, allegedly as a result of a defect in a coupling on a pipe which was attributable to negligence on the part of the builder of the ship; the plaintiffs, *inter alia*, made compensation payments in respect of oil pollution damage to crofters under the terms of one of the voluntary compensation schemes mentioned earlier.[110] They then sought to recover the amounts paid out from the shipbuilders, arguing that they were subrogated to the rights of the crofters against the shipbuilders in respect of the damage caused to the crofters. The House of Lords applied the rule in *Simpson* v. *Thomson*,[111] and held that P had no direct right of action against D; but it was made clear that under certain circumstances Esso could have acquired the right to sue in the name of the crofters. It was also held that since the payments to the crofters were voluntary they could not be said to be a loss resulting from the negligence of D but were the result of Esso's decision to

---

[108] In *The Sanix Ace* [1987] 1 Lloyd's Rep. 465, 470, Hobhouse J said that part of the rationale for the rule that a seller of goods can recover for damage to the goods sustained while they were in its ownership even though it has been paid in full for them by the buyer was that the loss would, in reality, be borne by the seller's insurer and not by the buyer. On this basis, the fact that a plaintiff could obtain loss insurance would not constitute a reason to deny liability for the loss but a reason to impose liability for the sake of the insurer. This is an extremely unattractive approach.

[109] [1989] AC 643.   [110] See 434 above.   [111] (1877) LR 3 App. Cas. 279.

enter the voluntary scheme. If Esso had been liable in law to make payments to the crofters,[112] they could have recovered those sums in tort as being consequential on the damage to the pipe which resulted from the accident. The argument for allowing Esso to offload its (insured) payments to the crofters on to the shipbuilder is not obvious, especially since both were commercial parties. But their legal inability to do this is seen, in this case, not as a result of any dissatisfaction with the concept of subrogation but as a function of technical limitations on its operation.

One case which does put some limitation on the operation of the doctrine of subrogation is *Mark Rowlands Ltd* v. *Berni Inns Ltd*.[113] In this case, demised premises were damaged by a fire which was admittedly the result of negligence on the part of employees of the defendant lessee. The premises were insured by the plaintiff lessor against fire, but under the terms of the lease the lessee paid about a quarter of the premium and was relieved of the obligation to repair in respect of insured damage. The Court of Appeal held, as a matter of interpretation of the lease, that it was the intention of the parties that the lessor should recoup losses resulting from fire damage from the insurer and not by action against the lessee. The lessor could not, therefore, sue the lessee in respect of the damage, and as a consequence, there was no right of action to which the insurer could be subrogated. While this is an eminently reasonable decision, the reasoning does not attack the doctrine of subrogation head-on. It is based on interpretation of the terms of the particular lease; so a case in which the plaintiff had not covenanted to insure or in which the defendant had not contributed to the premium might be distinguishable. Furthermore, the decision is primarily based on an analysis of the rights of the lessor against the lessee: the rights of the insurer are subsidiary to the rights of the lessor. So, for example, the lessor would not have been able to sue the lessee even if, for some reason, the insurer had been entitled to avoid the insurance contract. It seems right to conclude that English courts are unlikely to adopt reasoning which would justify direct modification of the doctrine of subrogation.[114]

5. CONCLUSIONS

In this Chapter I have made four main arguments. First, the question whether or not the defendant in a tort action should be held liable does not and ought not to depend on whether or not D was insured against liability or on whether or not P was insured against the loss suffered. Secondly, the question whether or not the defendant in a tort action should be held liable does not and ought not to depend on whether D could have obtained insurance

---

[112] The Merchant Shipping (Oil Pollution) Act 1971 did not apply.
[113] [1986] QB 211; J. Birds (1986) 6 *OJLS* 304. See also *Barras* v. *Hamilton* [1994] SCLR 700.
[114] Birds (1986) 6 *OJLS* 304, 309; see also Hasson (1985) 5 *OJLS* 416, 430–3.

against liability or on whether or not P could have obtained insurance against the loss suffered. Thirdly, the question whether or not an insurer has a right of subrogation should not turn on the distinction between indemnity and non-indemnity contracts of insurance. Fourthly, the insurer's non-contractual right of subrogation should be abolished, as should the right to recover from the insured payments as a result of which the insured recovers more in respect of an insured loss than was stipulated in the insurance contract.

PART IV

10

The Province and Aims of Tort Law

The common law of tort may be conceived of as a loose federation of causes of action sharing certain common aims. The preceding chapters have, I hope, convinced the reader that economic interests do not constitute a small foreign enclave within the territory of tort but that they figure largely in the concerns of many components of the tort federation. In this Chapter, I will attempt to draw together some of the loose ends left hanging in earlier discussions by examining the coastline of the province of tort law rather than its internal geography; and by discussing the aims which tort law seeks to achieve in protecting economic interests.

1. THE PROVINCE OF TORT

'Pushing Back the Frontiers of the (Tort) State'

As was noted in Chapter 1,[1] some would contend that the law of tort should not provide remedies for physical damage to[2] tangible property. Because abolishing the right to sue in tort for such damage would involve a significant redistribution of wealth (in the form of tort rights) away from property owners, it would require legislation. Perhaps the main argument used to support this position is that property insurance is freely available and is preferable to tort liability-cum-liability insurance as a device for protecting the property owner's interest in property. This issue was discussed to some extent in Chapter 9. There are a number of additional points worth making here. Several concern the argument that property damage insurance is freely available. First, the reformers' proposal is not, apparently, that tort law should adopt a criterion of insurability as a test of liability in relation to damage to property but that such damage ought to be removed from the common law of tort by legislation. So, difficulties attaching to insurability as a test of tort liability need not be considered in this context.

Secondly, the proposal cannot be fully understood without paying some

---

[1] See 13 above.
[2] 'Physical damage to' includes 'destruction of' and, presumably, 'loss of'.

attention to the notion of 'insurable interest'.[3] In general, a person may insure against damage to property only if that person has an insurable interest in the property; the aim of this requirement is often said to be to prevent insurance contracts being used merely as a form of speculation or gambling.[4] The basic rule is that a person has an insurable interest in property only if that person has some proprietary or possessory interest in it. A person with an equitable proprietary interest has an insurable interest in the property even if the interest would not found a right to sue in tort in respect of damage to the property.[5] However, a person who has only a contractual interest in property or who simply stands to lose financially if the property is damaged has no insurable interest in it (and cannot sue in tort in respect of damage to it). Furthermore, the insured must have the relevant interest at the time the loss insured against occurs. A particularly apposite illustration of the rule is provided by an old American case in which a turnpike company insured a bridge over a stream; the bridge connected two sections of the company's road, but the company had no legal or equitable interest in the bridge. It was held that the company had no insurable interest in the bridge.[6] There is, however, one important exception to the basic rule, namely that a party to a contract for the sale of goods who bears the risk of their loss under the terms of the contract has an insurable interest in the goods.[7] An insurable interest in property may be only a limited interest. Because property insurances are contracts of indemnity, the insured is entitled only to recover to the extent of his or her interest in the property even if the property has been insured for its full value.

It is unclear whether the requirement of insurable interest in relation to real property is statutory and so not waivable.[8] The requirement as it applies to goods is to some extent based on the statutory prohibition of gaming contracts in section 18 of the Gaming Act 1845. But to the extent that the concept of 'insurable interest' imposes a more stringent requirement than the statute, that requirement is based on contract only, and so could be waived by a suitable term in the insurance policy. This creates the possibility that a person might insure goods for the benefit of a third party.[9] A person who insures goods in which that person has no or only a limited insurable interest and in which a third party has an insurable interest may recover under the policy to an extent greater than his or her interest in the property; but the proceeds would be held on trust for the third party to the extent that they

[3] J. Birds, *Modern Insurance Law*, 3rd edn. (London, 1993), 45–65; N. Palmer and E. McKendrick (eds.), *Interests in Goods* (London, 1993), ch. 24.

[4] But see S. A. Rea (1993) 13 *Int. R of Law and Econ.* 145, 146–9; M. Clarke, *The Law of Insurance Contracts*, 2nd edn. (London, 1994), 100–2.

[5] *Leigh & Sillavan* v. *Aliakmon Shipping* [1986] 1 AC 785, 812 *per* Lord Brandon.

[6] *Farmers' Mutual Insurance Co.* v. *New Holland Turnpike Road Co.* (1888) 122 Pa 37.

[7] *Inglis* v. *Stock* (1885) 10 App. Cas. 263; Clarke, *The Law of Insurance Contracts*, 122. Such a person cannot sue in tort for damage to goods until property, and not just risk, passes to that person: see 90, 326 above.

[8] Birds, *Modern Insurance Law*, 45–9.

[9] e.g. *Petrofina (UK) Ltd* v. *Magnaload Ltd* [1984] 1 QB 127.

did represented the third party's and not the insured's interest in the property. Whether a party may insure for the benefit of another depends on the terms of the policy. There are, as we have seen, circumstances in which a party can recover tort damages representing more than that party's interest in property.[10]

The point of stating these rules is to show that certain issues about sufficient interest to sue in tort in respect of property damage have their counterparts in insurance law, and would have to be settled if the proposal to remove property damage from tort law were accepted. There is a view that the definition of insurable interest in relation to property is unnecessarily narrow in that it prevents people insuring interests in property which are by no means speculative.[11] In Australia, section 17 of the Insurance Contracts Act 1984 (Cth) provides that a person may insure property provided only that the person stands to benefit from its existence or would suffer loss by its destruction. It is worth bearing this in mind when we consider below the considerations which have led the courts to insist on a proprietary or possessory interest in property as the basis for entitlement to sue in tort.

Thirdly, it is worthwhile giving some thought, in broad terms, to the purpose of insurance, which is to spread losses both over time and among a large group of people so that insureds do not suffer undue financial disruption or dislocation when an insured event occurs. On the other hand, in relation to damage to tangible property the main aims of tort law are to compensate the victims of such damage and to reduce its incidence. Neither of these aims of tort law would be sacrificed if tort liability for physical damage to property were abolished. Insured property owners would still be compensated; although, of course, the cost of the compensation would be very differently allocated. The liability of the insurer to pay out under the policy could (and would, as is often the case at present) be made subject to the taking of appropriate measures to minimize the risk of insured event;[12] although, of course, by the insured rather than, as under the law of tort, by potential defendants. Property insurance is subject to what insurers call 'moral hazard' which is, crudely, the risk that the insured will 'engineer' an insured event. Requirements that the insured take precautions against loss reduce moral hazard, as do deductibles and the requirement of an insurable interest. Another way of reducing moral hazard is to exclude intentionally caused loss from the scope of the policy.

One of the most serious problems with the proposal that damage to property should be removed from the law of tort concerns uninsured and uninsurable losses. A solution to the problem of uninsured losses is compulsory insurance. Mortgagees, for instance, typically require the mortgagor to take

---

[10] See 93, n. 427 above.

[11] J. Birds in N. Palmer and E. McKendrick (eds.), *Interests in Goods*, 621–6.

[12] Although it may not be a matter of indifference whether the burden of reducing the incidence of property damage is placed on property owners or on potential causers of damage.

out loss insurance in respect of the mortgaged property. But the mortgagee's main concern is to protect its own interest in the property, not the mortgagor's; and it may be thought that statutory compulsion designed to protect property owners against their own improvidence is inappropriate in respect of property loss. The argument for some form of compulsory 'social insurance' in respect of uninsurable losses may be thought even weaker. Thus, Ison gives four arguments against any such scheme: property loss, unlike personal injuries, is often only a capital and not an income loss; and even if it reduces a person's earnings, it rarely reduces them to zero; besides, property is usually replaceable, and much property loss is suffered by businesses and corporations, not individuals.[13] On the other hand, if uninsurability is the result of social or demographic factors, such as levels of crime in particular geographical areas, it might be thought that the State ought to intervene at least to protect private individuals.

A fourth point to make about the 'first party insurance argument' for abolition of tort liability for damage to property is that its logic is not restricted to physical damage to tangible property. To the extent that other economic losses can also be insured against, the argument could also be used in support of excluding them from the province of tort law. Take, first, economic loss consequential upon physical damage to property. It is certainly possible to insure against loss of use of the damaged property and against loss of profits,[14] although such cover is not nearly as common as basic cover for the cost of repair or replacement of damaged property. If property damage were removed from the law of tort, such consequential loss would surely also fall outside its scope.

The case of economic loss not consequential upon physical damage to property is more difficult. As we have seen, such loss is recoverable in tort in a wide variety of circumstances. In many cases, insurance against economic loss would simply be unavailable: it is not possible to insure against the risk of unlawful exploitation of intellectual property rights or against loss resulting from unlawful industrial action or of loss resulting from negligent professional advice (except, on a very limited scale, in cases where it causes latent damage to buildings). So, even if it is arguable that some such losses ought to fall outside the province of tort law, the ready availability of insurance is unlikely to provide support for such an argument.

The ready availability of insurance is not the only argument used to justify exclusion of property damage from tort law. Abel has two others.[15] The first is that the relevant rules of tort law are 'hopelessly ambiguous and arbitrary'. Abel's basic point is that, since the courts are not prepared to allow recovery

[13] T. Ison, *The Forensic Lottery* (London, 1967), 97.

[14] D. C. Jess, *The Insurance of Commercial Risks*, 2nd edn. (London, 1993), ch. 14; D. Cloughton (ed.), *Riley on Business Interruption and Consequential Loss Insurances and Claims*, 7th edn. (London, 1991).

[15] M. Furmston (ed.), *The Law of Tort* (London, 1986), ch. 8.

for all property damage which causes a person foreseeable loss (for example, loss is recoverable only if the plaintiff has a proprietary interest in the property), decisions on whether loss is recoverable or not rest on expediency, not principle. In fact, Abel applies this argument to all forms of economic loss and not just to property damage. Ison also argues that the incidence of liability for property damage is fortuitous, and that the key notion of 'negligence' is nebulous.[16]

There seem to be two points underlying these arguments: first, that the notion of 'fault', which forms the basis of most of the law of tort as it relates to property damage (etc.), is unclear in theory and inconsistent in application; and secondly, that the courts qualify the operation of the fault principle in this area in the name of a variety of poorly articulated policy considerations (such as the desirability of certainty and predictability). It is by no means obvious that this area of the law is more incoherent or more qualified by policy-based exceptions than many other areas. Indeed, it is arguable that the common law as a whole is inherently unstable, partly because of the need to strike a balance between flexibility and fairness on the one hand and certainty and predictability on the other; and partly because of the need to give effect to policies through the medium of rules and principles. As a decision-making technique, adjudication concentrates on the interests of the parties before the court; but the legitimacy of the courts as decision-makers rests, in part at least, on the imperative to formulate rules and to deal with like cases alike; and these two factors tend to pull in different directions. Furthermore, the courts cannot totally ignore the wider consequences of their decisions, so that they may not be able to preserve the logical or analytical integrity of legal rules in the face of strong policy-based pressures to carve out an exception or qualification.

In other words, any area of the common law could be criticised more or less convincingly for being ambiguous and arbitrary; and there is no reason to think that the law of tort as it relates to liability for property damage and economic loss is much more ambiguous and arbitrary than many other areas of the law of tort or of other legal categories. One response to the realization that the law is inherently contradictory and unstable is that of some members of the Critical Legal Studies movement: to look to the abolition of law in favour of some utopian ideal of community and co-operation.[17] Such a response is understandable, even if unrealistic. It seems a much weaker response to suggest that one particular area of the law, which is no more contradictory or unstable than many others, should alone be signalled out for abolition.

Abel's other argument for excluding property damage (and other economic loss[18]) from the province of tort is threefold: dominion over financial assets

---

[16] *The Forensic Lottery*, 98.   [17] For a lucid account see D. A. Price [1989] *CLJ* 271.
[18] Abel includes loss of wages as a result of personal injury in his definition of economic loss, but this part of his argument is beyond the scope of this book.

is not 'integral to one's being in the same way as physical and emotional integrity are'; financial assets are unequally distributed throughout society, and the law ought not to reinforce such inequality by protecting financial assets; and the protection of financial assets is not as high a priority in our society as the protection of personal health and safety (protection of financial assets undermines our sense of community). If taken seriously, such arguments would exclude civil (and, query, criminal) liability for all financial loss, no matter what its source and no matter how it was caused. In other words, they would entirely rule out private property rights and any right to accumulate wealth. In their place would be an obligation on the part of the State 'to guarantee a minimum entitlement to income and other necessities (housing, car)'.[19] However attractive (or unattractive) such an approach may be to the reader, it is clearly far too abstract and general to deal with the myriad complex arguments on which tort liability for economic loss is based, and which have been canvassed in this book.

In my view, the arguments put forward for abolishing the right to sue in tort for physical damage to tangible property are not sufficiently strong to justify such a change in the law. Except in the context of road accidents, tort claims for physical damage to tangible property are relatively rare. In other words, tort law is of only marginal importance as a remedy for physical damage to tangible property. Although this state of affairs apparently causes no serious hardship to property owners, there seems to be no positive reason to focus on physical damage to tangible property and to recommend that it should be excluded from the province of tort law while other invasions of economic interests remain within it.

Boundary Disputes

Property

Despite the fact that tort law plays an important role in protecting a variety of economic interests, the assertion is not uncommonly made in a number of contexts that the protection of economic interests is properly left to some other branch of the law, and that tort law should concern itself with economic harm only in marginal cases. It is very important to analyse this assertion carefully. In the first place, those who make it do not normally mean to suggest that tort law should not continue to play a central role in protecting the owners of proprietary rights in tangible and intangible assets from misappropriation, exploitation, or interference with use. The law of tort has, historically, provided this protection, and there is no obvious reason why it should not continue to do so. Nor does it seem to be questioned that tort law

---

[19] Abel in Furmston, *The Law of Tort*, 181, n. 32.

is an appropriate vehicle for protecting intangible property, such as goodwill, from damage. Tort law, in this context, is an adjunct of property law. Because property law never developed rules of its own which compete with the rules of tort law in this area, there is very little reason to object to the fact that the relevant rules are seen as part of tort law rather than property law. If tort law and property law adopted conflicting or mutually inconsistent approaches to the same issues, the matter would be different. But they are, in the area of their mutual interest, imbued with much the same philosophy: both recognize certain assets (which we call 'property') as being of such social importance that they deserve, *prima facie*, to be protected from all interferences except those to which the owner of the property (or of some relevant right in it) consents.

Furthermore, even if first party insurance is freely available and widely bought to protect particular property interests against particular invasions (for example, insurance against theft of chattels), the ideological force of classifying an asset as property tends to be seen as outweighing any argument to the effect that such insurance is the appropriate means of protecting the asset to the exclusion of tort liability: tort liability, in respect of property interests declares the importance of property and gives deterrent signals to would-be interferers.

The position in tort law of physical damage to tangible property is more problematic, as we saw in the previous section. However, the inclusion in tort of physical damage to (or destruction of but not, perhaps, loss of) tangible property has been recently reaffirmed by the House of Lords in *D. & F. Estates* v. *Church Commissioners*.[20] Tort law protects property, including tangible property. If tangible property suffers traumatic physical damage (or destruction) by fire or collision, for example, then it is widely accepted that in appropriate circumstances it is part of the proper role of tort law to provide the owner with compensation. But what about the case where a person loses the tangible property of another without meaning to misappropriate or exploit it or to interfere with the owner's use or enjoyment of it. The law of tort traditionally treats inadvertent loss similarly to damage: if it is the result of tortious conduct, then it is actionable. If loss is less often actionable than damage, this is not because of any relevant difference between loss and damage but because loss is more often the result of inaction than of action.[21] But some see *loss of* as intrinsically different from *damage to*. Loss of tangible property is, they say, purely economic loss which ought to be compensated for, if at all, only according to the principles of the law of contract. But from the owner's point of view, 'loss of' is indistinguishable from 'damage to'; it is from the defendant's point of view that the former often looks different from the latter because the former is often the result merely of inaction. As a basic rule applicable to many, but not all, cases it is, no doubt, salutary that

[20] [1989] AC 177.   [21] See 89 above.

people should be expected to pay so that another will take positive care of their property. However, if the loss is the result of positive carelessness it is difficult to see why the lack of payment should be any more crucial here than in other contexts.

Relational Interests

Also problematic are so-called 'relational interests'. If a person will suffer economic loss if someone else's physical property is damaged, destroyed, or lost, that person has a relational interest in that property. Relational interests in property may be either contractual or non-contractual: a time charterer has a contractual interest in the vessel whereas a cargo owner has no interest in the vessel but only a financial interest in its continued safety. Tort law protects neither type of relational interest against negligent interference.[22] A number of justifications are given for this stance.[23] The first champions certainty and efficiency: the rule has stood for a long time, it is widely known and well-understood, and it reflects commercial practice. Because the distinction between proprietary and non-proprietary interests is a relatively straightforward one, it establishes a bright line between liability and no-liability and this, in turn, reduces the volume of litigation generated by the rule and encourages settlement of disputes out of court. None of this adds up to much: the fact that a rule is old does not mean that it should be allowed to grow even older. The courts exist to do justice, and this may not coincide with the business community's understanding of fairness. Nor is it the case that any alternative rule would be intolerably uncertain (for example, a rule that buyers of goods to whom risk, but not property, has passed could recover in tort for damage to the goods, would be as clear as the rule that they cannot).

A second justification relates only to contractual relational interests:[24] if the plaintiff's contract with the goods owner does not protect P, P should not be allowed to make good that deficiency by suing a third party in tort. Such an approach can be based on the sort of arguments for the primacy of contract law (including those concerned with the applicability of contractual exclusion clauses in tort actions) which were examined in Chapter 6; and such an approach is the main basis of the decision in *The Aliakmon*.[25] It can also be supported on economic grounds: Rizzo argues that the rule of no-liability is justified because it encourages people to 'channel' their economic losses through the property owner, and thus reduces litigation (costs).[26] However,

---

[22] But it gives some protection against intentional interference.

[23] For a judicial discussion of several of these see *State of Louisiana* v. *MV Testbank* (1985) 725 F 2d 1019.

[24] This casts doubt on the validity of a single rule covering all relational interests.

[25] See 326 above.

[26] M. J. Rizzo (1982) 11 *JLS* 281; cf. P. S. Atiyah (1967) 83 *LQR* 248, esp. 276, n. 66.

Rizzo's theory has been vigorously criticized.[27] One important shortcoming of the theory is that it seems to assume that it will always be relatively easy and cheap to negotiate a channelling provision in a contract with the property owner.[28] Rizzo, like many English judges,[29] seems to equate the theoretical possibility of contractual protection with practical posssibility. By contrast, some economic analysts of law argue that the difference between owning (property) and hiring (contract) is purely a matter of economic convenience on which a defendant who negligently causes damage to physical property ought not to be allowed to rely: whoever suffers the loss, potential injurers should be given an incentive to avoid causing such loss.[30] A middle way between these two positions would be to argue that tort law should protect relational interests but only in cases where it would not be reasonable to expect the plaintiff to protect him- or herself by contract in such a way as would bring the libaility ultimately to rest on the defendant.[31] According to this approach there would be no blanket ban on tort liability for injury to relational interests; but liability would arise only in cases where there was some significant barrier to self-protection by the plaintiff.

A third justification for excluding relational interests from tort law is the so-called floodgates argument.[32] This argument rests primarily on the fear that, because purely economic loss is not, by definition, physically restricted in its incidence, a single act of negligence may give rise to a number of claims which is undesirable *either* because it is very large *or* because it is indeterminate. The floodgates argument applies more obviously to non-contractual than to contractual relational interests.[33] Suppose that the supply of some essential service to a large area is cut off by tortious damage to the service provider's property; or suppose that a public bridge is put out of action by a tort. Any such incident could generate a large and indeterminate number of tort claims. The floodgates argument may also be relevant in cases which do not involve relational interests in the sense I have defined them, but which involve analogous circumstances: suppose, for example, that a large number of shareholders and investors in a company suffer loss as the result of negligence on the part of the company's auditor in certifying the company's accounts; or that a negligent oil spill damages fish stocks on which fishermen

[27] e.g. W. Bishop in Furmston, *The Law of Tort*, ch. 4; D. R. Harris and C. G. Veljanovski, *ibid.*, 70, n. 37.

[28] Or, to put it in economic terms, that the 'transaction costs' of contracting will be relatively low. If they are not, then the law may be justified, according to economic ideas, in imposing liability which achieves the effect which would have been achieved by contract if the costs of contracting had not been so high as to discourage the making of a contract. The crucial practical question is how high transaction costs must be before legal intervention is justified. Economic analysts of law have not answered this question.

[29] See 332 above.

[30] Harris and Veljanovski in Furmston, *The Law of Tort*, 65; W. Bishop and J. Sutton (1986) 15 *JLS* 347: this is an economic version of the transferred loss idea discussed at 326–30 above.

[31] J. Stapleton (1995) 111 *LQR* 301. [32] P. S. James [1987] *Denning LJ* 97.

[33] This throws doubt on any rule which deals with all relational interests in the same way.

456 Tort Law and Economic Interests

and others rely for their livelihood.[34] A slightly different version of the floodgates argument is the 'where-will-it-all-end' argument:[35] in a complex society of interdependent economic actors, purely economic loss to one person can have knock-on effects for many others, such as relatives, customers, creditors, suppliers. If the one person were allowed to recover, it might not be easy to justify refusing recovery to all the others as well.

Those who espouse the version of the floodgates argument which is couched in terms of the potentially large volume of claims are concerned that the court system should not be unduly overburdened with cases. There are two possible answers to this concern. One is that the mere fact that many claims arise out of a single tort does not make each one individually any less strong or any less deserving of the attention of the legal system. This is accepted in the case of personal injury and property damage where the fact that many suffer as a result of a single act of negligence is not seen as weakening any individual victim's legal claim to compensation. On the contrary, the larger the number of victims, the more just it seems that the plaintiffs should have access to the legal process and that the tortfeasor should pay. In this light, the concern is not that tortfeasors will be held liable for large damages, but rather that the law ought to be less willing to make large damages awards in economic loss cases than in physical damages cases. A better response to the concern about imposing undue strain on judicial resources might be to make it easier to bring class actions. The other answer to the volume-related version of the floodgates argument is that the fear is unrealistic: most claims are settled out of court, and the time, expense, and hassle involved in litigating is quite sufficient to discourage all but the most determined claimants with substantial claims.

Those who espouse the indeterminacy version of the floodgates argument[36] seem to be concerned that if potential defendants do not know in advance what their likely liabilities are they will be unable to take appropriate measures to prevent causing actionable loss and unable to buy appropriate insurance cover. But once again, the indeterminacy problem is not unique to economic loss cases as a class (although it may be more common and acute in that class of case); and so, at bottom, the crux of the argument seems to be that economic interests are less worthy of the law's protection than physical interests.

A fourth justification for the exclusionary rule for relational interests is sometimes put in terms of fairness: because a single act of negligence could injure the relational interests of a very large number of people, and because economic loss can have a domino effect in the affairs of individuals thus

---

[34] e.g. *Union Oil Co.* v. *Oppen* (1974) 501 F 2d 558. These are, incidentally, all cases in which it seems unlikely that a channelling clause of the type envisaged by Rizzo could be easily negotiated.

[35] Vividly stated by Morgan J in *Stevenson* v. *East Ohio Gas Co.* (1946) 73 NE 2d 200.

[36] e.g. J. Stapleton (1991) 107 *LQR* 249, 254–5.

swelling the size of individual claims, the total amount of damages payable by a defendant as the result of a single act of negligence may turn out to be very large indeed, and quite out of proportion to the culpability of the tortious conduct. It is, however, difficult to take this argument seriously, at least in this form. In the first place, it is a basic principle of the English law of tort that there are no degrees of legal fault; so there is no criterion for judging whether any particular award of damages is out of proportion to the defendant's conduct. Secondly, very large amounts of damages can be payable for personal injuries and property damage as a result of disasters such as explosions in chemical factories or on marine oil platforms; but no one suggests that the damages payable should be limited because they may be out of proportion to the degree of fault involved. On the contrary, the degree of (moral) fault seems to be judged according to the size of the injury inflicted, regardless of the nature of the tortious conduct. Thirdly, although financial advisers, such as accountants, may complain about the potential size of damages awards against them in respect of purely financial loss, it is not normally suggested that even very large awards are somehow disproportionate to fault. Fourthly, rules about remoteness of damage serve to limit the amount recoverable by any individual plaintiff. In fact, the argument based on the potential amount of the defendant's liability seems to have no independent force: at most, it can bolster a conclusion against liability reached on some other ground.

A more sophisticated argument based on the amount of injury inflicted relates to cases in which a large number of potential plaintiffs each suffer quite small losses which, in aggregate, may be very large indeed. If a commercial defendant is held liable for such losses, it will very likely spread them in some way. If this happens, the result of litigation will be that loss which is initially spread relatively widely and thinly will be aggregated, only to be spread again, possibly among a group containing many of the original loss sufferers; and the whole process will have been enormously expensive of time and money. In other words, mass claims for damages are very expensive to process, but the net effect of processing them in terms of the distribution of losses may be insignificant. Only if it were clear that the group which would end up bearing the loss was quite different from or considerably larger or smaller than the group which originally suffered it,[37] would the cost of shifting the loss be at all worthwhile; only if that were so would the loss-shifting exercise achieve anything significant either in terms of compensation or in terms of deterrence.

A fifth ground for excluding relational interests from the scope of tort law is based on insurance: it may be reasonable to expect a person with a relational interest in property to insure against economic loss consequential upon

---

[37] As, perhaps, in *Union Oil* v. *Oppen* (1974) 501 F 2d 558; B. Feldthusen, *Economic Negligence*, 3rd edn. (Toronto, 1994), 259–64.

physical damage to the property,[38] and this may provide a reason not to impose liability on a person who negligently damages the property at the suit of a third party who suffers economic loss as a result. Even if we accept (as I do not) that insurance considerations of this sort provide an acceptable basis for determining the scope of tort liability (a matter discussed above in Chapter 9), the argument is weak in this context because it has no direct relationship to the distinction between proprietary and relational interests in property. If it is reasonable to expect a person to insure against economic loss resulting from damage to property in which they have only a relational interest and to exclude tort recovery on this basis, it is arguably also reasonable to adopt a similar approach to tort claims for economic loss consequential upon damage to the plaintiff's own property. But the law does not do this. Moreover, individuals are much less likely than businesses to have or to be able to obtain insurance against economic loss consequential upon damage to the property of another; but the exclusionary rule applies indiscriminately to all claimants.

Money

When the law of tort classifies an asset as 'property', those with contractual or non-contractual (financial) interests in it receive short shrift: they are told to look elsewhere for protection, most notably to contract or insurance.[39] But the attitude of the law of tort to assets which it does not classify as 'property' is quite different. To understand the difference, we need to remind ourselves of the bedrocks of contractual liability: undertaking, intention to be bound, privity, and consideration (that is, value given in exchange for undertakings). The core (but by no means the only) function of the law of contract is the making good of disappointed expectations of financial gain.

When we turn to that part of the law of tort which protects monetary wealth we find that the law of contract is not alone in the field. In the first place, the law of tort will give damages for disappointed financial expectations, although almost always calculated on an opportunity cost basis which is, in principle, less generous than the normal measure of expectation damages in contract. Secondly, the implication of *Hedley Byrne* v. *Heller*[40] is that tort damages may be awarded to persons who could have protected themselves by paying for financial advice but did not do so. This relationship between the parties in that case was 'equivalent to contract' in that P requested information which D supplied in circumstances in which D ought to have foreseen that P would detrimentally rely on its accuracy for some such

---

[38] Or to take other steps to reduce or eliminate the economic effects of damage to another's property by making back-up arrangements. The clearest statement of this argument in the English cases is by Lord Denning MR in *Spartan Steel* v. *Martin* [1973] QB 27.

[39] As noted above, economic analysis supports this approach where transaction costs are low.

[40] [1964] AC 465; I am treating it as a two-party case for present purposes.

purpose as that for which P did rely on it, and in which it was reasonable for P so to rely. What the transaction between P and D needed to turn it into a contract was consideration; that is, value given in exchange for the statement.

Thirdly, the implication of *Smith* v. *Bush*[41] is that tort damages may be awarded to persons who could (in theory at least) have protected themselves by contract (in that case, most simply by buying an independent survey), but (reasonably) chose not to. In this case the relationship between P and D was 'equivalent to contract' in the sense that D gave advice for which P effectively paid in circumstances in which D ought to have foreseen that P would rely on the accuracy of the advice for the purpose for which it was relied upon, and in which it was reasonable for P so to rely. What the relationship between P and D lacked to make it contractual was privity.

The crucial question is that of why the law in these instances is prepared to impose tort liability for economic loss in favour of parties who could have protected themselves by contract. An answer, which was popular for some time after the decision in *Hedley Byrne*, was that reasonable reliance by the plaintiff on the defendant's negligent conduct made good the lack of consideration or privity, as the case might be. But it now seems to be accepted that reliance goes to causation, not to liability.[42] The decision in *Smith* v. *Bush* rests ultimately on the unreasonableness of requiring purchasers of modest houses in the lower end of the housing market (as opposed to purchasers of expensive houses or of commercial premises) to spend the extra money required to get an independent survey. From this we might generalize and say that the courts may impose tort liability in favour of parties who could have protected themselves from the loss in question by contract but failed to do so, provided that it would not be reasonable to expect them to have availed themselves of that opportunity.[43]

The general principle just enunciated faces at least two difficulties. First, it is not easy to see why it would have been unreasonable to expect the plaintiff in *Hedley Byrne* to pay for the advice. Secondly, it might be argued that a principle couched in terms of 'reasonableness' is too vague to be of any real use. If thought desirable, a possible way of meeting this objection would be to utilize the distinction between consumers and others. If this were done, the role of tort law in relation to interference with non-proprietary assets would be to protect consumers but to leave others to protect themselves in whatever way they could. Moreover, this distinction could also be used in cases in which the plaintiff's economic interest was relational.

It should be noted that such an approach is not underpinned by the economic argument that the proper role of the law of tort is to provide a remedy when the plaintiff could not, because of the high ('transaction') costs of

---

[41] [1990] 1 AC 831.

[42] See 184 above; and Cane in P. Cane and J. Stapleton (eds.), *Essays for Patrick Atiyah* (Oxford, 1991), 357–63.

[43] J. Stapleton (1995) 111 *LQR* 301.

contracting, have protected him- or herself. For instance, in *Smith* v. *Bush* the reason the plaintiff did not buy an independent survey was not that the transaction costs of doing so were prohibitively high but simply that P did not want to pay or was not able to afford the fee for such a survey. High transaction costs may provide a reason for not requiring a person to contract; but so may a desire to allocate risks to one social group rather than another, as *Smith* v. *Bush* shows. The effect of *Smith* v. *Bush* was that the surveyor ended up bearing a risk which it would have voluntarily accepted only in return for a larger fee than the plaintiff paid.

As a general rule, the idea that tort law should protect only consumers against interference with economic interests would be unacceptable. For instance, it seems perfectly legitimate for the law of tort to protect commercial property from improper exploitation. But in the narrower context of negligent interference with non-proprietary economic interests, it may be more attractive.

Alliances

The relations between tort and contract are complex: in some areas they co-exist uneasily whereas in others they are engaged in active partnership and co-operation. Thus, English law allows concurrent actions in tort and contract. This is inconsistent with the contemporary preference for contract over tort: if tort liability can be ruled out because P should have protected him- or herself by contract, then why should P be allowed to sue in tort if P has protected him- or herself by contract? So some would argue that English law should abandon concurrent liability in tort and contract. There are, as we have seen, other areas of possible concurrence of causes of action: between tort and equity or tort and restitution, for example. But in these instances the issue is not whether the claimant should have taken steps for self-protection but simply whether the law should allow a person to gain advantages by opting for one cause of action rather than another.

Tort reinforces the protection which contract gives to contractual interests by allowing actions for interference with contract by third parties. Once again, this form of tort liability can be attacked on the ground that people ought to be restricted to enforcing their contractual rights against the other contracting party. But this leaves open the question of what to do if a person has no enforceable contract rights against the co-contractor. The law of tort makes good the lack of such enforceable rights in two ways: first, it may allow a person to recover damages in respect of action which makes the performance of contractual obligations more expensive;[44] and, secondly, it may allow an action even if what the other contracting party has done as a result

[44] J. Danforth (1981) 81 *Col. LR* 1491, 1519–20; American Law Institute, *Restatement (Second) of Torts*, s. 766A.

of the defendant's actions does not amount to an actionable breach, provided it amounts to a failure to comply with the terms of the contract.

It might be argued that the law of tort is more justified in coming to a person's aid in cases where that person has no enforceable contractual rights than in those where the person does have such rights. But this puts the conceptual cart before the horse because the cases which do not involve actionable breaches of contract are seen as an extension of the basic protection afforded to contractual rights. The best justification for the basic protection (and, perhaps, its extensions as well),[45] is that it protects and stabilizes the operation of the market: contract is the chief legal form of market transaction, and the smooth operation of the market is of such fundamental economic importance that it needs to be protected from interference by third parties as much as (but, query, no more than) from interference by contractual parties.[46] Interference with contracts is a form of unfair competition; and the requirement of intention or recklessness serves to weaken the force of the argument that the plaintiff should be restricted to his or her contractual rights.

Much more surprising than tort's willingness to reinforce contractual obligations is its protection for contractual expectancies. Tort law protects the expectation of making an advantageous contract in at least three ways: first, it sometimes imposes liability for intentional interference with contract-making by use of independently unlawful means; secondly, it provides remedies against third parties and against the other contracting party for misstatements which induce disadvantageous contracts. Thirdly, in cases of unauthorized exploitation of or interference with property, the law of tort protects what has been called the 'opportunity to bargain'. Thus, damages for exploitation of property calculated on the basis of the value to the defendant of the use of the property can be seen as an award to the plaintiff of the reasonable value of the opportunity to sell the right to exploit the property.[47] Again, when damages are awarded in lieu of an injunction to restrain exploitation of property or interference with property in the form of trespass or nuisance, the defendant is effectively allowed to purchase the right to interfere or exploit. The second instance of liability is problematic because it seems to ignore the problems which concurrence of causes of action in contract and tort is seen to produce in other contexts. The first and third forms of tort liability are problematic because in different ways they both fly in the face of a fundamental tenet of the common law of contract, namely that no one has an enforceable right to make a contract with anyone else. This principle has

---

[45] Danforth (1981) 81 *Col. LR* 1491, 1517–9. Here Danforth discusses unenforceable contracts but the basic reasoning would also apply to cases where the induced non-performance was not a breach: the contract contemplated performance despite the clause excluding liability for non-performance.

[46] *Ibid.*.

[47] R. J. Sharpe and S. M. Waddams (1982) 2 *OJLS* 290; for criticism see J. Beatson, *The Use and Abuse of Unjust Enrichment* (Oxford, 1991), 233.

been selectively modified by statute and there are certain rules of the common law of contract which can be seen as inconsistent with it;[48] but in general, it still holds good.

The third form of tort liability can be justified in terms of the protection of property rights: the law of tort is, in effect, creating a contract for the parties not simply to force them into contractual relations but to redress an interference with property rights. It is not unfair to require a person to make a contract which the person should, by rights, have made in the first place. The law does not require people to make contracts *simpliciter*, but it does require them to buy other people's property rights and not just seize them. The economic logic of this argument is clear: the existence of some property rights is a precondition of market exchanges; if the law (of tort) did not give strong protection to property rights, the market would degenerate into a mere battle of strength in which goods were distributed according to each individual's ability to secure and retain whatever was available for acquisition.

The first form of tort liability (intentional interference with contract-making by independently unlawful means) is harder to justify in the light of the doctrine of freedom of contract. At a conceptual level, writers differ in their approach to the protection of contractual expectancies. At one extreme is the traditional view that contractual expectancies should not be protected because the function of the law is to promote the stability of existing contractual arrangements but not to hinder competition in the formation of contracts.[49] At the other extreme is the view that contractual expectancies deserve better protection by tort than existing contractual interests because a contract action will usually lie to vindicate existing contractual interests but will not to protect contractual expectations.[50] But such conceptual arguments do not get us very far; what we need to decide is whether the protection provided by the law of contract is adequate in social, moral,[51] and economic[52] terms.

[48] P. S. Atiyah, *Rise and Fall of Freedom of Contract* (Oxford, 1979), 742–54.

[49] Danforth (1981) 81 *Col. LR* 1491.

[50] D. C. Dowling (1987) 40 *U of Miami LR* 487. See also *Restatement (Second) of Torts*, s. 766B, which puts liability for interference with contractual expectancies on the same basis as liability for interference with existing contractual rights ('intentionally and improperly').

[51] D.B. Dobbs (1980) 34 *Ark. LR* 335 argues against liability for interference with contract by intrinsically lawful means on such grounds.

[52] For an economic argument against liability for interference with contract by intrinsically lawful means see H. S. Perlman (1982) 49 *U of Chi. LR* 61. The basic thrust of economic analysis in respect of liability for inducing actionable breaches of contract is that tort law should be consistent with the doctrine of efficient breach: just as a contracting party should not be forced to perform a contract if breaching it and compensating the injured party would be more 'efficient' (that is, generate more wealth), so third parties should be liable in tort for inducing efficient breaches only to the same extent as the breaching party would be liable in contract. Thus damages in tort for inducing breach should be no greater than the damages payable by the breaching party in contract. Perlman adds, however, that liability for inducement of breach itself generates certain transaction costs over and above those created by liability for breach of contract, and this argues against the imposition of such liability, at least in the absence of unlawful means. Where the induced action constitutes non-performance of a contractual obligation but is

From this point of view, the most important issue in this area concerns the extent to which the common law should get involved in regulating competition. Without free competition a market economy cannot operate properly; and a precondition of fair competition between economic actors is (rough) equality of economic power. An important role of the law in general (both common law and statute) is to preserve (or create) a reasonable degree of equality between competing economic actors (to create 'a level (economic) playing field' as it is sometimes put). But it is far from clear how this task should be distributed between the common law and statute.

A distinction is often drawn between two types of undesirable competitive activity: 'excessive or unfair competition' on the one hand, and various sorts of anti-competitive behaviour on the other. This is not, however, a sharp distinction because the aim of excessive competition is often to drive one's competitors out of business. The law of tort contains a number of devices for dealing with both types of 'unfair competition'. Excessive competition, in the form of exploitation of a competitor's 'trade values'[53] is the concern of the intellectual property legislation, the tort of passing off, and the law of breach of confidence. We also considered in Chapter 4 whether the common law ought to develop wider liability for wrongful exploitation of trade values. Excessive competition in the form of false advertising or false trade descriptions is dealt with by the tort of passing off (which involves a misrepresentation that the defendant's product is connected in some way with the plaintiff's) and the tort of injurious falsehood. However, there are many forms of unfair or misleading advertising which do not fall within either of these torts as currently defined. For example, a trader may have a window display which suggests that it stocks the plaintiff's products in order to lure customers, even though it only stocks its own products and makes this quite clear to customers when they enter the shop and make inquiries (this practice is called 'switch selling');[54] or a trader may make truthful but misleading (because, for example, incomplete) comparisons[55] between its product and the plaintiff's,[56] in order to promote sales of its own (cheaper) product.

The question whether the common law of tort ought to be extended to protect traders against forms of excessive competition against which they are not

not an actionable breach, economic analysis would suggest no tort liability for inducement in cases where the contractual exclusion of liability for breach represents an efficient allocation of the risk of non-performance. So far as contractual expectancies are concerned, economic analysis would recommend no liability for interference unless the interference had the effect of reducing competition to an inefficient extent. Perlman argues, in effect, that 'unlawful means' should be interpreted to mean 'inefficiently anti-competitive action'.

[53] For a definition of this term, see 186 above.

[54] Held not to amount to passing off in *Rima Electric Ltd* v. *Rolls Razor Ltd* [1965] *RPC* 4; G. Dworkin thinks that switch-selling would be actionable as passing off: [1979] *EIPR* 241, 245.

[55] Without suggesting that its product is in any way connected with the plaintiff's.

[56] Or, indeed, untrue statements about its own products—such statements are not caught by the tort of injurious falsehood which only applies to false statements about the plaintiff's products.

currently protected is a vexed one. The courts are held back from developing the law through unwillingness to become involved in deciding which forms of excessive competition are unfair. However, given that the common law does castigate some forms of competition as unacceptable, this unwillingness comes down to a refusal to develop the common law any further, probably on the ground that regulation of competition is now primarily a task for the legislature. Another important consideration is that the interests of competitors do not always coincide with those of consumers. When competitors make false statements, both competitors and consumers suffer; but this is not necessarily so in other cases of strong competition. The courts are understandably more prepared to intervene when the two sets of interests coincide than when they do not.

Typical anti-competitive practices involve 'horizontal agreements' between traders to engage, for example, in boycotts and cartels, or to fix prices so as to force competitors out of the market; and the development of concentrations of market power (monopolies) by, for instance, the acquisition of competitors or of patents, or by making agreements (often by use of coercion) with potential competitors to restrict their competitive activities or with customers to restrict their dealings with competitors. The common law's attempt to deal with practices of the last two sorts is contained in the doctrine of restraint of trade.[57] The law of tort is relatively impotent to deal with anti-competitive behaviour because of its insistence that liability cannot be imposed in the absence of independently unlawful conduct or combination or false statements;[58] and on its willingness to allow concerted action to be justified by pleading that the predominant purpose in injuring another was to further one's own commercial interests. Ironically, the common law historically proved most effective against workers and trade unions rather than competitors because their attempts to further their interests by injuring their employers often involve interference with existing contracts as opposed to interference with contractual expectancies; and this effective use of tort law led to early legislative intervention on behalf of workers, the proper scope of which has frequently been the subject of deep political dispute.

Accidents of History

In some respects, the borders of the province of tort law can be seen as accidents of history. The relevant historical facts concern jurisdiction: both the Admiralty courts and the Chancery courts developed separately from the common law courts, and all three sets of courts developed their own peculiar bodies of substantive law. But there are wrongs actionable in Admiralty and

[57] Treitel, 401–24.
[58] Even some proponents of a more general tort of unfair competition see it as confined to misappropriation and misrepresentation: e.g. P. Burns [1981] 11 *EIPR* 311.

according to rules of equity which share many similarities with torts; and a study of these wrongs can throw interesting light on tort law. The historical distinction which has had most impact on tort law is that between legal and equitable property rights. There is no intrinsic reason why the law of tort should not protect equitable property rights at least against some interferences; and the protection from interference which such rights receive under equitable rules, while different in detail, is not alien to the conceptual set-up of the law of tort.

2. AIMS OF TORT LAW

It should be clear by now that the part of the law of tort concerned with the protection of economic interests performs a variety of different and sometimes conflicting functions and purposes. We should distinguish in the discussion of aims between the common law of tort and statutory causes of action. A statute is typically the culmination of a policy-formation process which is quite open and public; the terms of the statute are designed to give effect to policy aims already identified, and the legislature is under no constitutional obligation to ensure that either the policy embodied in the statute or the concepts and words in which it is embodied are consistent or coherent with any existing or past statute or body of common law. Although it may not be easy to be sure about the policy aims which motivated the enactment of any particular statutory provision, it is usually relatively easy to discern, in general terms, the policy objectives of the statute and of its main provisions even without recourse, which the courts largely deny themselves, to *travaux préparatoires*.

The position in respect of the common law is quite different. For supposedly constitutional reasons, British courts do not see it as their prime function to develop, enunciate, and give effect to social policies. Of course, when a superior court is confronted with a completely novel case it will be difficult for it to pretend that non-legal considerations do not form the main foundation of its decision. But in all other cases the court will seek to apply an existing rule or to develop an existing rule in what we might call a conceptual way; that is, by discerning the internal conceptual 'logic' of the cases in which the rule was developed and in which it has since been applied and by extrapolating from the decided cases to the case at hand. Some judges are prepared to recognize that even this operation frequently requires policy choices to be made, but the perceived constitutional requirement that judges decide cases in ways which are consistent with the past so as to create a coherent body of legal rules and principles provides a convenient facade.[59]

[59] See generally N. McCormick, *Legal Reasoning and Legal Theory*, revised edn. (Oxford, 1995). There is, of course, an enormous literature on the topic of judicial reasoning; and the text here is distinguished only by being simplistic and naïve. But it will (or if it will not, it must) suffice for present purposes.

For present purposes, there are two important consequences of this state of affairs: the first is that judges do not often or much discuss or articulate the social, economic, ethical, and other 'policy' considerations which influence them, whether consciously or unconsiously, in reaching decisions which do not involve, even by their own admission, simple rule-following. The second is that it is often very difficult to be confident about the policies which any particular court or judge was pursuing in reaching any particular decision. So it is even more difficult to do what commentators on the common law often seek to do, namely to discern the policies underlying whole lines of cases or even whole areas of the law. It is, however, necessary to attempt to do this exactly because British courts labour under an obligation to pursue consistency and coherence; and once beyond the pull of binding precedents, this must mean consistency and coherence in policy choices. Conceptual or logical consistency and coherence are not enough: the logic of the concepts may well lead the court down paths it thinks it ought not to tread. Furthermore, as we have seen throughout this book, the concepts of the law of tort cover such a heterogeneous variety of situations that the mere fact that two situations can be analysed in terms of one and the same legal concept or principle does not mean that they should be treated on the same way.

Direct Aims

Direct aims I shall define as those immediate ends which the law seeks to achieve by means of the remedy awarded in any particular case. The distinction between common law and statute does not seem of much importance here.

Compensation

Compensation is usually seen as the basic direct aim of the law of tort. We should distinguish between issues of liability and issues about remedies. In relation to the former, the aim of compensation is always qualified by rules about the nature of the defendant's conduct and often by rules about the nature of the interest the invasion of which has given rise to the claim for compensation. The law does not compensate for all damage or for all losses or for every invasion of interest.

In relation to remedies, there are two important things to bear in mind. The first is that, although damages (that is, monetary compensation) are the most usual remedy available in a tort action, mandatory remedies (most notably, the injunction) are by no means unknown, especially in the context of interference with property rights. Secondly, we should avoid the equation of monetary compensation with compensation for loss, in the sense of diminution of existing resources. Damages may be awarded in a tort action in lieu of an injunction, and such damages look to the future rather than to the past. Furthermore, as we have seen, damages are not infrequently available in tort for loss of expected future income calculated on an opportunity cost basis. This is so not only in cases involving interference with property rights (where such damages may be in lieu of an injunction) but also in cases arising out of the negligent performance of professional services where the purpose of the service was to secure some benefit for the plaintiff. It is misleading to say that the law of tort is concerned to compensate only for actual loss suffered as opposed to benefits not received.

Disgorgement

The law of tort is prepared not only to compensate for gains which the plaintiff would have realized if the defendant had not acted tortiously but also, in some cases, for gains which the defendant made by the tort but which the plaintiff could not or simply would not have made personally. This result is achieved by means of damages awarded under the 'user principle', or by the equitable remedy of account of profits (in cases of infringement of intellectual property rights and of breach of confidence), or by means of exemplary damages. The user principle and the remedy of account are limited to cases involving interference with property and related rights, but awards of exemplary damages are not so limited. It was argued earlier that the disgorgement element of exemplary damages ought to be kept separate from the punitive element: disgorgement damages ought not to be viewed as punitive because a gain made by committing a wrong against another is, in an important sense, unjust, as the user principle recognizes. In relation to property rights, disgorgement remedies protect a person's right to decide whether, how and by whom the property will be exploited.

Punishment[60]

With this clarification, it is easier to see in what sense and to what extent the law of tort punishes: it only does this in cases where it is prepared to award damages greater in amount than the sum of any loss suffered by P and any gain made by D as a result of the tort. Of course, where a gain is made by a combination of tortious conduct and D's non-tortious effort, it may be difficult to work out how much of D's gain resulted from the tort in any other than a 'but-for' sense; but this does not vitiate the principle. The law blurs this issue by lumping disgorgement and punitive damages together; and also by recognizing a category of aggravated damages which are supposedly compensatory but which are difficult to distinguish from punitive damages. They

[60] Another way of stating this aim is in terms of expression of the court's (or society's) disapproval of D's conduct.

are kept distinct in theory by saying that aggravated damages compensate for non-pecuniary loss.

Vindication or Satisfaction

Another way of looking at aggravated damages, and perhaps punitive damages as well,[61] is in terms that they provide the plaintiff with a sense of satisfaction or vindication. Punishment and vindication are really the same thing looked at from different points of view.

More broadly, it is often said that one of the aims of the law of tort is to satisfy the plaintiff's feelings of resentment that his or her rights have been interfered with, or that the defendant has inflicted injury on P or secured some benefit at P's expense. Such resentment has been said to generate 'demoralization costs'. It has been argued that in determining whether liability to 'compensate' ought to be imposed (whether by common law or statute), it should be recognized that if compensation is not awarded such resentment, which is a real cost of tortious behaviour, may remain unrequited.[62] Such an approach could explain why, for example, damages may be awarded for unauthorized exploitation of property even if P could not or would not have exploited the property personally: if such damages were not awarded, P would suffer unrequited resentment at the fact that D had exploited the property without permission.

Control of Future Conduct

Monetary compensation may be concerned only with the past: with some loss already suffered or some gain the chance of which has already passed or which, although yet to arise, will never now do so because of tortious conduct. Such awards may affect the way the defendant and others similarly placed behave in the future; but this is not their chief aim. The law of tort does, however, concern itself directly with regulating future conduct by the award of remedies. The most obvious example is the injunction, which may operate so as to put an end to tortious loss-causing or gain-producing conduct. Conversely, by awarding damages in lieu of an injunction the court may license future loss-causing or gain-producing conduct so that it ceases to be tortious.

There is one other way in which the law of tort can look to the future: it may award damages to enable a person to remove a source of loss. In the law of nuisance such damages take the form of the reasonable costs of abating the nuisance. They are usually awarded after some loss has already occurred in order to prevent further loss. A real likelihood of imminent damage may also be actionable in nuisance, so that the cost of abating a nuisance could

---

[61] *Lamb* v. *Cotogno* (1987) 74 ALR 188, 192.   [62] A. I. Ogus [1984] *CLP* 29.

be awarded before any loss had actually been suffered. In the law of negligence, such damages take the form of 'preventive damages'; they were first held recoverable in *Anns* v. *Merton LBC*[63] as a means of forestalling illness or personal injury (and, perhaps, property damage) resulting from defects in buildings. As a general rule, such damages are no longer recoverable. The reason for this is that at common law such preventive damages are treated as damages for purely economic loss; and such loss is not normally recoverable in actions arising out of the acquisition of defective premises. On the other hand, we have seen that purely economic loss is recoverable in nuisance; and there is no conceptual reason why the costs of abating a nuisance which threatens economic loss should not also be recoverable. If this is so, the law is on a confused state indeed.

An important reason for the unwillingness to allow preventive damages appears to be a fear of encouraging speculative actions. This fear does not seem to have operated in the past in relation to nuisance; rather, the requirement that the plaintiff prove a real risk of imminent damage seems to have sufficed. Furthermore, some writers favour defining the province of tort in terms of personal injury *and the risk of* personal injury; in other words, although preventive damages are damages for economic loss, some people see them as taking their colour from the loss they are designed to prevent. If the loss which is threatened would be compensatable if it occurred, there is surely good reason to allow damages to forestall it, subject to safeguards to prevent highly speculative actions. Both justice and economic good sense ('prevention is better than cure') seem to combine in favour of such a result.

Deterrence of Tortious Conduct[64]

We noted in the last section that loss prevention is not the main aim of tort damages for past injuries. If it were, the law would not, for example, allow a defendant who negligently caused damage to property owned by C to escape liability on the basis that P had only a contractual interest in the property; nor would it, for instance, immunize builders from liability to subsequent purchasers or auditors from liability for share purchasers. But loss prevention is one of the aims of tort law. This is most explicit in cases in which exemplary damages can be awarded. It is also implicit in the fear, expressed by some judges, that the imposition of liability in particular cases may lead to 'defensive' practices on the part of groups of potential defendants, such as doctors; in other words, the fear of 'over-deterrence'. But the idea that being held liable in tort for having inflicted a particular injury will

---

[63] [1978] AC 728.

[64] Or, more positively, the encouragement of non-tortious conduct. For example, liability of professionals in tort can be seen as a way of maintaining a minimum level of care and competence on the part of practitioners: J. R. S. Prichard in L. Klar (ed.), *Studies in Canadian Tort Law* (Toronto, 1977), 377ff; see also C. G. Veljanovski and C. J. Whelan (1983) 46 *MLR* 700.

have a significant effect on a person's future conduct and, in particular, that it will cause that person (and others) to cause fewer injuries in the future, is highly questionable. Apart from the impact of insurance on tort liability, which we will return to below, its major defect is that it assumes that tortious conduct is calculated in the sense that its economic pros and cons are weighed up in advance; and that the cost of possible liability is one of the economic cons which is taken into account. To the extent that tort liability is liability for inadvertent conduct, the picture of the calculating tortfeasor is clearly irrelevant; the same is true in relation to liability for conduct which the actor could not have known in advance to be wrongful. Much of the law of tort is so unclear, either intrinsically (for example, the concept of negligence) or because it is in a state of development, that it would not be easy to be sure in advance, even if one thought about it, what were the chances of being held liable for any particular conduct. Furthermore, in relation to torts which can be committed by entirely innocent conduct which, by definition, one would believe to be innocent at the time it was done, the idea of calculation to avoid such conduct seems logically incoherent.

Nevertheless, much tort liability for economic loss is liability for calculated behaviour (for example, where liability is based on intention); and the defendant in many tort actions for purely economic loss will be a business (including in this term self-employed professionals) which might be expected to take the risk of legal liability into account in deciding how to act. For example, newspaper editors no doubt sometimes think about the law of defamation before they decide to publish; and a great deal of calculation undoubtedly goes into much behaviour which ends up being challenged as infringement of intellectual property rights. But businesses vary enormously and some are, no doubt, much more aware of the law as a constraint on their activities than others. Without empirical evidence it is very difficult to be other than tentative; but as a generalization it is probably true to say that the deterrent theory of tort liability is most likely to be relevant to torts involving liability for calculated conduct, and to businesses as defendants.

The deterrent theory of liability is also relevant to judging the relative value of tort liability and alternatives to it. For example, non-tort compensation schemes will probably be even less successful as deterrents than tort law unless they are funded by potential causers of compensatable events and unless the contribution of each is more or less proportional to the risk that each will cause such an event. Again, it is often assumed that the regulatory and criminal law is likely to be superior to the civil law as a deterrent. But this depends crucially on the level of enforcement of the law and of the severity of the penalties imposed. The fact, if it be so, that tort law is a relatively inefficient deterrent of a particular type of injury does not mean that any alternative will necessarily be any better. Lack of relevant empirical evidence prevents statements more definite than these.

Modern economic theories of tort law elevate deterrence of tortious con-

duct into the main aim of the common law of tort.[65] The basic idea underlying all such theories is that the decision whether to impose liability and the
choice of remedy once liability has been imposed should rest on a calculation
of the financial (that is, the monetary) pros and cons (or costs and benefits)
of imposing the liability and awarding the remedy. If the economic injury[66]
done to the plaintiff[67] is greater than the sum of the cost to the defendant of
avoiding that injury *plus* the cost of securing and executing judgment against
the defendant, then liability ought to be imposed.[68] In this way, people will
be encouraged to avoid actions which inflict greater costs than benefits. In
other words, legal liability for injury ought to be imposed if,[69] but only if,
doing so would encourage economically 'efficient' behaviour on the part of
both the injurer and the injured and discourage economically inefficient
behaviour.[70]

Whether, in a case involving a continuing course of conduct on the part of
the defendant (as opposed to a 'one-off accident'), the remedy ought to be an
injunction on the one hand or a monetary award on the other depends, once
again, on weighing the economic pros and cons of the different remedies. The
basic question is whether it would be financially better that the defendant

---

[65] The very tip of an enormous iceberg of literature is R. Posner *Economic Analysis of Law*
3rd edn. (Boston, 1992).

[66] But see Ogus [1984] *CLP* 29 and 468 above. Ogus's argument rests on the fundamental point
that monetary wealth and utility (or 'pleasure' or 'happiness' or 'satisfaction') are not synonymous.

[67] There is an important complication lurking here. Economic analysis is concerned with maximizing the sum of financial benefits in society as a whole. So if P's loss represents an equivalent
gain to some other member of society (and so is a purely private, and not a social, loss), there
is no economic reason to seek to deter the type of conduct which caused it. This is one explanation of why the law does not impose liability for losses inflicted by ordinary competition: one
competitor's loss is another's gain. Economists disagree about which private losses are also social
losses and which are just wealth transfers. It should be noted, too, that the law often reverses
wealth transfers on the basis that the defendant has been 'unjustly enriched' thereby.

[68] There is another problem here: economic analysis of the common law, like the common
law litigation it analyses, is limited in its focus. It considers only three options for maximizing
wealth namely, holding the defendant liable, not holding the defendant liable, and holding the
defendant partly liable. It cannot consider options which involve third parties. For example, it
might be better, all things considered, to deal with road accidents by a combination of social
welfare payments and criminal sanctions than through the tort system.

[69] The positive limb of the statement should not be ignored. For example, one argument for
protecting contractual relational interests in tangible property is that if P was not in a position
to protect him- or herself by contract from loss resulting from physical damage to the property,
then unless the law of tort comes to P's aid the injurer will be given no incentive to avoid such
loss in the future: see 455 above. Again, an argument for imposing tort liability in a case such
as *Smith* v. *Bush* [1990] 1 AC 831 is that since P probably lacked the resources to buy an independent survey, and since the building society had no incentive to sue the surveyor, the only way
of giving the surveyor an incentive to take care in the future was to impose tort liability: see 333
above. But the law does not consistently adopt this approach: in *D. & F. Estates Ltd* v. *Church
Commissioners* [1989] AC 177 the tenant plaintiff may well not have been in a position to protect itself by contract, and the owner of the freehold probably had no incentive to sue. So the
decision not to impose liability arguably left D with inadequate incentive to take care.

[70] If the court is unable to perform the relevant cost-benefit analysis, it should let the loss rest
on the party in the better position to negotiate a post-judgment agreeement with the other party
to shift the loss in case the court placed it on the wrong party.

should stop conduct which gave rise to the plaintiff's action; or, on the other hand, whether greater aggregate benefit would accrue from D being allowed to buy the right to inflict financial injury on P by paying P the economic 'value' of that injury.

In other words, according to the economic view of tort law, a defendant ought only to be liable to a plaintiff when the imposition of liability will produce greater economic benefit overall than refusal to impose liability. This general principle applies regardless of whether liability is strict or is based on negligence. The only relevant question is: would it be better, in economic terms, that injury of the type inflicted on P by D should not occur? If the answer is yes, and liability is strict, then if D could not have avoided inflicting loss by the taking of cost-justified precautions, D will cease or reduce the level of the activity which caused the injury; and this will, in turn reduce or prevent occurrence of injury of the type in question. Alternatively, D will invest in research and development in order to discover a cost-justified method of preventing the injury in question. If D could have avoided the injury by cost-justified precautions then, whether liability is strict or not, D will be encouraged, by being held liable, to take those precautions; and in this way, injury of the type in question will be avoided. So, the distinction between strict liability and liability based on negligence is of relatively little economic significance. Its main impact may be on litigation (and settlement) costs: it may be cheaper to apply a rule of strict liability than to apply one based on fault.[71]

So far as liability for injury caused intentionally or recklessly is concerned, a distinction needs to be drawn. In some cases, liability for intentional or reckless acts is an *a fortiori* case of liability for inadvertent acts: particular loss may be actionable whether inflicted intentionally, recklessly, or inadvertently. In such cases, cost-benefit analysis would, as a generalization, be more likely to justify the imposition of liability for loss inflicted intentionally or recklessly than for loss inflicted inadvertently because the cost of avoiding the former is likely to be very low. In other cases, however, loss is actionable only if intentionally or recklessly inflicted. This is chiefly so of economic competition between businesses and in the context of industrial relations between employers and employees.[72] This, too, can be justified in economic terms: economic analysis of law is based on the microeconomic theory of supply and demand, that is on the idea of a free competitive market. The very idea of

[71] This discussion ignores the impact of insurance, on which see 479 below. Indeed, it may sometimes be seen as a function of strict liability to encourage insurance. Generally, if the cost of insurance is less than the loss inflicted and of cost-justified precautions against such loss, the potential injurer's most sensible course of action is simply to insure against the risk of liability for such loss.

[72] Industrial action designed to improve wages and conditions is a form of competitive activity in the sense that the aim of the action is to achieve a redistribution of wealth from the employer to the employees, just as traders seek to divert wealth from their competitors to themselves.

competition involves the infliction of foreseeable (private, not social) economic loss on others; so economic theory could not countenance legal liability for such behaviour because law exists to support the market. Indeed, competition often involves the intentional infliction of economic loss on one's competitors, and so economic theory (along with the law) does not disapprove of all intentional infliction of economic loss in competitive contexts. But the aim of every capitalist is to eliminate competitors, and in this way competition contains within itself the seeds of its own destruction. So both economic theory and the law impose limits on intentional infliction of economic loss on one's competitors. The law does this by defining 'unlawful competition' whereas economic theory, as one would expect, recommends that degree of competition which maximizes social wealth.

Some Applications of Economic Analysis of Law

Economic theories of law have two aspects, one normative and the other descriptive. The descriptive aspect of such theories involves the assertion that the basic (or even the only) aim of the common law is, in fact, to discourage economically inefficient behaviour. Such an assertion seems difficult to maintain in the light of rules such as that a person whose property rights have been, or are likely to be, interfered with is *prima facie* entitled to an injunction to restrain future interference regardless of whether such interference will cause the person any economic harm. The user principle, which allows damages to be awarded in respect of gains made by exploiting property of another even in circumstances where P could not and would not have exploited the property personally, is also difficult to reconcile with the descriptive aspect of economic theories. Problematic, too, in this regard, is the distinction which is drawn by the courts between defective buildings and products which cause personal injury or damage to other property and those which do not. Producing shoddy buildings or products may be economically inefficient and so as worthy a subject of the law's concern as producing products which cause personal injury or property damage. Indeed, the distinction between physical damage and purely economic loss makes no sense in economic terms.

The normative aspect of such theories, which asserts that the law ought to seek to maximize economic efficiency and to encourage activity which generates a surplus of economic gains over economic costs, is more important for our purposes. This aspect is the subject of an enormous economic and philosophical literature, much of it of a very technical nature. The idea that economic efficiency as defined by economic theorists and the deterrence of inefficient injury-causing conduct are acceptable goals for the law, either on their own or in conjunction with others, has been attacked on a variety of grounds. Detailed discussion of the literature is beyond the scope of this book and of the competence of its author. But there are certain insights contained in such theories which can assist our understanding of tort law. Most of these have already been discussed in some form, but they deserve to be made explicit here.

Deterrence and Compensation

The basic idea of deterrence which underlies economic theories of law does not (at least according to one version of the notion of 'efficiency') require that the victim of 'inefficient injury' be given monetary compensation for that injury. It requires only that the person responsible for the injury be given some incentive not to cause such injury in the future (whether or not that incentive is in the form of an obligation to pay money to someone, not necessarily the plaintiff).[73] This is not to say that paying compensation to injured people is necessarily inefficient,[74] but only that the idea of economic efficiency does not demand it. Even so, since delivering compensation is costly, it may be that some cheaper way of providing the injury-causer with an incentive to stop causing injury might be better, provided that the benefits of the alternative method were at least as great as those of a system of giving compensation.

This basic insight about compensation, namely that it is only one way of providing incentives for the modification of conduct which causes 'inefficient injury', provides the foundation for discussions of alternatives to the common law as techniques for influencing behaviour. Recall the discussion in Chapter 8 of regulation. Recall, also, the discussion in that chapter of alternatives to the tort system for delivering compensation: the foundation for this discussion was the idea that it may be possible to deliver compensation more cheaply than the tort system does, but at the same time to give incentives for the reduction of injury-causing conduct as great as, or even greater than, those which tort law gives.

Of course, even if, at the end of the day, we decided that compensating individuals, whether through the tort system or otherwise, was an unnecessarily costly way of deterring inefficient injury-causing conduct and that some other method of deterring such conduct which did not involve compensation would be more efficient in money terms, we might still want to compensate individuals for some reason other than deterrence. Furthermore, we might want to require compensation to be paid even in some cases where the defendant's action was efficient in some sense. For example, a defendant might be required to pay damages for interference with contract even if the gain made by interfering was greater than the loss suffered by the victim. This could be justified by viewing the case in a wider economic perspective: a free market based on executory contracts will operate properly only if contracts are secure

---

[73] However, if compensation is not given, the victim may be encouraged to take (inefficient) precautions to avoid suffering injury in the future: Harris and Veljanovski in Furmston (ed.), *The Law of Tort*, 50–1. Given that the enforcement of tort law depends on private litigation, the actual payment of compensation is also necessary in order to provide injured parties with an incentive to sue.

[74] S. Holtermann (1976) 43 *Economica* 1.

from outside interference. Economic analysis of law is based on the idea of a properly operating free market, and this justifies the preservation of the basics of a free market even if, in the particular case, greater short-term gains could be reaped by undermining it: in the long term, and practised on a large scale, such conduct could destroy the market.

Litigation Costs

Providing incentives through the medium of litigation (as through any other medium) costs money. These costs must be added to that of reacting to the incentive in an appropriate way in order to arrive at the true cost of the incentive. It is this insight which underlies the idea, discussed above, that the aim of the law about tort liability for injury to relational interests ought to be to encourage the making of channelling contracts with the property owner: such action would reduce the amount of litigation. If many people suffer small amounts of injury as a result of a single tortious act, the cost of shifting and aggregating those injuries by means of tort litigation may add so significantly to the cost of providing an incentive to avoid such loss that some alternative medium for providing an incentive may be preferable. It is less likely that the litigation costs, when added to the cost of reacting to the incentive, will be greater than the cost of the injury inflicted because, *ex hypothesi*, the result of the litigation will be to aggregate a large number of small losses which, in total, may be very significant.

Another insight based on the costliness of litigation is that legal rules which encourage settlement of disputes out of court, or which can be used as the basis of agreements which prevent disputes arising, are highly desirable. Rules which are clearly formulated, which are couched in terms of easily ascertained facts, and which do not contain vague concepts such as reasonableness are preferable in this respect. When courts opt for so-called 'bright-line' rules they are, arguably, seeking to use tort law as a means of reducing litigation and encouraging bargaining and settlement of disputes.[75]

Cost-Internalization and Injury Avoidance

This last point is sometimes used as the basis for a different argument. In theory, in order to provide a person with an incentive to take precautions to avoid causing injury, it is only necessary to place on that person injury costs which just exceed the cost of taking precautions. So it is sometimes argued that there is nothing to be gained, in economic terms, in shifting larger amounts of injury costs on to the defendant because such additional costs will have no additional deterrent effects. Such an argument assumes that economic theory requires only that economically avoidable injury be avoided. However, the logic of cost-benefit analysis also requires that even if injury cannot be avoided economically the activity which caused it should bear its

---

[75] For economic discussion see T. W. Merrill (1985) 14 *JLS* 13; R. A. Epstein (1988) 48 *Ohio State LJ* 469.

cost so that the price of that activity to its consumers will accurately reflect the costs of carrying on the activity. These costs consist not only of the inputs required to conduct the activity but also of any costs inflicted by the activity on third parties ('externalities'). If the costs of externalities are not reflected in the price of an activity to its consumers, that price will be too low and the activity will be carried on at an uneconomically high level.

In economic theory, each and every social activity should bear all its costs; but in practice, there may be great difficulties in achieving this desideratum. In the first place, much depends on how widely or narrowly any particular activity is defined: other things being equal, the narrower the definition of an activity the larger the externalities it produces and vice versa. Secondly, it may be hard to decide which costs ought to be attributed to which activities[76] and to quantify these costs. Thirdly, it may be difficult to predict what will happen if costs are laid upon a particular activity—this may, for example, simply cause one activity to be abandoned in favour of another activity which generates, but does not bear, external costs. Nevertheless, the basic point is valid: the notion of economic efficiency requires that activities bear their costs, even if (or, perhaps, especially if) the activity will be economically non-viable as a result.[77]

The Cost of Information

One of the fundamental requirements for the operation of a free market is that the participants in the market have enough information to enable them to choose the commodity which represents the best value for money. Of course, information may itself be one of the commodities for sale in the market; but it is also a prerequisite of the efficient operation of the market. If information were treated only as a commodity, those who could not afford it would have no access to it. But if this were so, market forces could not operate properly to ensure that only the most efficient producers survived.

These facts about information have generated a number of insights about tort law.[78] One concerns rules of remoteness of damage: in cases where the victim of injury knows facts about the likelihood of that injury occurring as

---

[76] This is essentially a question of causation.

[77] A slightly different argument against awarding damages greater than necessary for efficient deterrence is that the risk of incurring liability to pay very large damages may encourage potential defendants to make themselves 'judgment-proof' by under-insuring or not insuring at all ('going bare'): Harris and Veljanovski in Furmston (ed.), *The Law of Tort*, 53. This argument deserves to be treated with some caution. First, most individuals could not afford to pay even quite modest damages awards but many would, nevertheless, take avoidance measures or buy insurance out of a sense of moral obligation. Secondly, corporations which under-insure often do so with the intention of paying out if they are held liable rather than with the intention of avoiding payment. Thirdly, the fact that the defendant is un- or under-insured will not necessarily discourage litigation: the plaintiff may be happy to get what can be got by bankrupting the defendant—witness the US asbestos litigation (J. Fleming, *The American Tort Process* (Oxford, 1988), 250–1), which also shows that even corporations are not all indifferent to the prospect of insolvency.

[78] W. Bishop (1983) 12 *JLS* 241.

the result of a particular activity carried on by another, and the other does not know those facts, then if the parties have had relevant dealings about the conduct of the activity before the injury occurs, the injury causer should be held liable for that injury only if the victim conveyed to the former the relevant facts about its likely occurrence. In such a situation, the victim should be encouraged to reveal relevant information known only to him or her. Hence the rule in *Hadley* v. *Baxendale* about remoteness of damage in contract: the two limbs of the rule distinguish between cases in which there is a disparity of knowledge between the parties and those in which there is not. The tort rules about remoteness of damage are not so discriminating in that they make no distinction, as such, between cases where one party could have told the other of relevant facts before the tort occurred and those in which this was not possible (although they do, of course, distinguish between cases according to whether D actually knew the relevant facts).

The law of tort does sometimes pay attention to the degree of the defendant's knowledge of special circumstances, although it does this under the rubric of liability rather than remoteness of damage. For example, a professional person will be made liable in tort for gains not realized only if the professional knew (or ought to have known) that the plaintiff would not realize a particular gain if the professional did not take care.[79] Also, one aspect of the concept of proximity which is particularly relevant in negligence actions concerning economic loss is how much D knew about P in particular and about the particular transaction in which P was involved. The law in this respect is uncertain, but it seems clear enough that the sort of accident between complete strangers (such as a road accident) which can give rise to tort liability for personal injury and property damage will not give rise to an action for purely economic loss.[80] This may be seen as an attempt to encourage efficient information exchange so that service providers can decide whether to act, how much to charge for acting, and how to protect themselves against potential liability for acting.[81]

Another important insight about information concerns information as a commodity.[82] Those who can afford it may be able to make good a lack of the information relevant to the making of sound market choices by buying information from persons who can collect it more efficiently than they can themselves. If a person pays another (that is, enters into a contract with the other) to provide information, it may be economically efficient to hold that other liable for failure to provide accurate information. Even if the recipient does not pay for the information in a form which the law recognizes as consideration, it may still be efficient to impose liability if the plaintiff has, in

[79] See 142 and 172 above.

[80] In personal injury cases knowledge of special circumstances can raise the standard of care: *Paris* v. *Stepney BC* [1951] AC 367.

[81] D. Cohen (1984) 18 *UBCLR* 289.

[82] Bishop (1980) 96 *LQR* 360; cf. *Caparo* v. *Dickman* [1990] AC 605, 621C–D *per* Lord Bridge.

effect, paid for the information.[83] The nature of information is such that it may be difficult for the provider of it to restrict its use to persons who have paid for it in some sense. Third parties who have not paid may be able to take the benefit of information when it is accurate and they may suffer loss when it is inaccurate. Just as economic theory requires that activities (here, information providing) should bear the costs they generate, it also requires that they reap the benefits they generate; otherwise, imposing costs will give the wrong incentives.[84] If people who do not pay for (sound) information are allowed to sue for loss suffered by acting on unsound information, information providing will be unduly discouraged. This may have been the point Lord Reid was aiming at in *Hedley Byrne* v. *Heller*[85] when he said that words needed to be treated differently from acts because they 'travel far and fast'. It may also serve to justify judicial caution in imposing liability in tort for negligent misstatement. On the other hand, it would explain why the law feels no qualms about imposing tort liability on top of contract liability for misrepresentations which induce contracts: in such cases, by entering the contract with the defendant, the plaintiff pays for the information.

The Primacy of Contract

The fact that information is costly provides just one example of a wider point. The cost of acquiring information is what economic analysts of law call a 'transaction cost'. In pure economic theory, a market only works properly when transactions in the market generate no transaction costs. The rules about remoteness of damage (etc.) which we have just looked at are designed to minimize the cost of acquiring information by encouraging openness on the part of those who have it. But if the cost of acquiring information is too high, it may be beyond the reach of many actors in the market; and the law may be justified in stepping in to ensure that enough information is made available to enable the market to work reasonably efficiently. This can be generalized: if some defect in the operation of the market (such as lack of information, or undue concentration of market power) makes it too expensive[86] for a significant number of people to make efficient exchanges of money for commodities (or vice versa) in the market, the law may be justified in stepping in to reduce or remove the barriers to free market transactions.

If we particularize this general proposition with special reference to the law of tort we can say that if a person could not, for some reason, protect him- or herself from inefficient financial injury by making a contract (a market transaction: contract is the basic legal form of the market), then the law of tort may be justified in stepping in and protecting the person from that injury or compensating the person after it has occurred. A similar proposition could

---

[83] *Hedley Byrne* v. *Heller* [1964] AC 465; *Smith* v. *Bush* [1990] 1 AC 831.

[84] W. Bishop and J. Sutton (1986) 15 *JLS* 347.   [85] [1964] AC 465, 483.

[86] How expensive is too expensive is an evaluative question to which economic theory, as such, gives no answer.

be made in relation to the implication of terms into contracts: the purpose of such implication is often to give a person the benefit of a contractual clause which, for some reason, the person could not have secured for him- or her-self. In some cases we go even further than this and allow tort law to step in even if the plaintiff could have protected him- or herself by contract: in relation to personal injury, we do not require people to protect themselves by contract even if they could have; nor do we allow a contract which deprives a person of compensation for personal injuries to stand in the way of imposing liability. But in relation to purely economic loss and also, to some extent at least, tangible damage to physical property,[87] the law of tort is relatively unwilling to step in if P could have protected him- or herself by contract or if P has entered a contract which deprives him or her of such protection.

We have discussed this preference for contract over tort in detail already. A couple of further points need to be made here. The first is that the preference has become identified with a particular brand of economic theorizing about law. But it does not follow inexorably from the idea that the law should further economic efficiency, because that idea allows as much intervention in the operation of the market as is necessary to ensure that it allocates resources to their most efficient use and that inefficient injury does not occur. However, economic analysis sees all legal forms other than contract (and property) as remedial: contract is the prime legal form of the free market and other legal forms should only be utilized to the minimum extent needed to ensure that inefficient injury is not inflicted. This point of view rigorously excludes any function for the law other than supporting the market and enabling it properly to do its job of efficient resource allocation.

Secondly, we have seen that the primacy of contract is a very important strand in modern English tort law and theory. English judges do not see it as concerned primarily with economic efficiency but more with notions of individual autonomy and personal responsibility and with the role of payment in justifying the imposition of legal liabilities. We shall return to it yet again below.

Deterrence and Insurance

If we assume that one of the aims of tort law is to provide incentives for the avoidance of inefficient injury, and if we assume further that the outcome of a particular case can be justified in terms of that aim, then to the extent that either party can modify the outcome so as to reduce the incentive which it gives that party, the aim of the law is frustrated. The main technique available to alter the incentives provided by the law of tort is insurance.[88] If we

---

[87] *Norwich CC* v. *Harvey* [1989] 1 WLR 828: if the owner had wanted the subcontractor to bear responsibility for fire damage, the owner should have contracted with the subcontractor to that effect.

[88] (1) Of course, the decision in any particular case may also give deterrent signals to (uninsured) third parties. (2) The High Court of Australia has even held that exemplary damages may appropriately be awarded in cases where the defendant's liability to pay such damages is covered by complsory insurance: *Lamb* v. *Cotogno* (1987) 74 ALR 188.

assume that the insurance market is itself operating properly, insurance should cost an amount equal to the anticipated loss insured against multiplied by the chance of its occurring during the currency of the policy (plus a share of the insurer's total administrative costs associated with that insurance line and of its profit margin). If the cost of preventing the loss insured against were known to be less than that of insuring against its occurrence, the insured would have no incentive to buy insurance. In this sense, insurance is based on the same idea as the deterrence theory of tort law. Insurance distorts deterrence incentives because it allows the cost of the loss insured against to be spread over persons and over time in a way that the cost of precautions may not be spreadable; in other words, it prevents the financial dislocation which would be caused by having to meet the cost of the insured loss in one instalment. The psychological effect of this is that people tend to view the cost of the insured loss as being that of the insurance for the policy period in which the loss occurs. This ignores the fact that many other people have contributed to meeting the loss in that period; and also that premiums are payable even in periods when no loss is suffered.

This problem of reduced incentives to avoid insured events (what insurers call 'moral hazard') arising from the very existence of the insurance itself, plagues loss insurance as much as liability insurance.[89] There are a number measures which insurers can take to reduce this moral hazard:[90] the insurance cover may be subject to an upper limit or ceiling (unless such limits are prohibited by law) or to a lower threshhold (an 'excess' or 'deductible'); or it may be a condition of insurance cover or of lower premiums that the insured take specified precautions against the insured event occurring;[91] or, more drastically, the insurer may simply refuse to insure against particular events.

Another technique is to ensure that the premium paid by any particular insured matches as closely as possible the risk of injury or loss being insured against (that is, risk classification). This statement may seem too obvious to deserve enunciation. But a number of factors stand in the way of the full utilization of the technique.[92] First, it costs money to gather the information relevant to assessing the risk presented by any particular insured and to sort all insureds into narrow risk bands, let alone to calculate a unique premium for each individually. The more accurate the fit between the premium and the risk, the greater the cost of achieving it; and there comes a point before very

[89] Loss insurance is relevant here because if the loss causer is held not liable, this gives the victim an incentive to take steps to avoid the injury suffered.

[90] P. Fenn in A. Harrison and J. Gretton (eds.), *Crime UK 1986* (London); C. G. Holderness (1990) 10 *Int. R of Law and Econ.* 115.

[91] Property insurers utilize this technique much more than liability insurers. The insurer's incentive to monitor and survey risks is much reduced by the insured's obligation of material disclosure and the insurer's right to avoid the contract for material non-disclosure.

[92] Risk classification will only have the intended effect if purchasers of insurance properly understand and react to the signals it gives: W. P. J. Wils (1994) 14 *OJLS* 449, 454–5.

long when the reduction in moral hazard to be expected from increased accuracy is perceived to be less than the cost of achieving it. Secondly, provided the insurer's total income is sufficient to cover claims and administrative costs plus a profit, the insurer's only incentive for reducing the level of claims is to gain an advantage over competitors—reducing the level of claims may enable an insurer to set its premiums lower than those of its competitors. Thus, the competitiveness of the insurance market is an important factor in determining the level of risk differentiation: the more competitive the market the greater the incentive to differentiate between risks. But other ways of reducing premiums (including cutting administrative costs and increasing investment income) may be cheaper and easier than greater differentiation between risks.

Thirdly, while commercial insurers may have an incentive to reduce the degree of subsidization of poor risks by good ones (which is the result of inadequate risk differentiation), mutual insurers, particularly those set up by professional bodies, are not under the same pressure. Thus it is common for contributions to mutual insurance funds to be very imperfectly related to risk in order, for example, to subsidize younger practitioners or to provide a minimum level of cover within the financial reach of all practitioners.[93] This is particularly so where membership of the mutual is compulsory for all practitioners or where there is no real commercial alternative to the mutual. In other words, risk differentiation on certain grounds and in certain contexts may be socially unacceptable.[94]

Indirect Aims

By indirect aims I mean intermediate or long-term social or economic aims which are pursued in particular cases but which transcend the details of any one case. In this context, the distinction between the aims of the common law and the aims of statute is important, as we shall see.

Protection of Property

We need only note here that the law of tort gives wide and deep protection to all the powers and privileges which collectively constitute property rights.

---

[93] e.g. in 1988 16·3% of the amounts paid out by the Solicitors Indemnity Fund were attributable to sole practitioners but only 9% of the contributions to the Fund came from such practitioners. Firms with over 25 partners contributed 14·3% of the income of the fund but accounted for only 7·9% of claims paid: [1989] *New LJ* 818. It is estimated that the contributions payable by sole practitioners would need to increase by 80% to eliminate the imbalance. This might put some practitioners out of business and this would, in turn, have an impact on the availability of legal services, because sole practices are more common outside cities than are large practices. Contributions to the SIF are calculated primarily on the basis of the gross fee income of firms. See further [1995] *New LJ* 841.

[94] Wils (1994) 14 *OJLS* 449, 458–60.

Both the common law and the statutory law of tort have the protection of property as perhaps its major aim. In economic terms, the explanation and justification for this is that property rights are the very stuff of market transactions: without some property rights (understood broadly to include rights, such as a person's right to dispose of his or her own labour, which are analogous to property rights) there could be no market. This is not to say that property is the only subject of market transactions: contractual rights can also be bought and sold. But in economic terms, contract is parasitic on property: contract is, basically, a means of exchanging property. In other words, the law of tort, by protecting property, provides the bedrock on which the capitalist market economy rests.

Deterrence

I mention this here only in order to point out that deterrence can be seen as both a direct and an indirect aim: particular cases give deterrent signals to the parties to it, but they may also give signals to others similarly placed. Indeed, the doctrine of precedent makes little sense except on the basis that non-parties to a particular case may decide how to act on the basis of it.

There is considerable evidence for the view that the courts are increasingly adopting a sophisticated theory of deterrence which distinguishes between parties (primarily) responsible for causing losses and parties (secondarily) responsible for preventing losses occurring. Thus, the courts are unwilling to impose tort liability on regulatory bodies for failures of regulation or to impose tort liability for failure to warn another of impending economic loss or to take steps to prevent such loss being suffered. This trend may be attributable to dissatisfaction with the doctrine of joint and several liability. To impose full liability on a party whose responsibility for the loss suffered was small may be seen as creating a risk of over-deterrence if, for some reason, other responsible parties will end up not bearing their fair share of the liability.[95]

Preserving the Primacy of Contract

Tort a Last Resort

It seems clear that current judicial policy favours minimizing the role of the law of tort in protecting non-proprietary economic interests. There is much evidence for a general principle (subject to certain exceptions) that a contracting party may not have recourse to the law of tort to make good some perceived deficiency in the protection afforded by the contract to his or her economic interests. We have also seen that the courts, as a general rule, now expect people to protect their economic interests in property belonging to

[95] See generally J. Stapleton (1995) 111 *LQR* 301.

others and their economic interest in acquiring non-defective property by contractual arrangements and not by recourse to the law of tort. In other words, people are to be encouraged to protect their non-proprietary economic interests by means of market transactions rather than by recourse to tort law.

It is tempting to see such recent developments in the law as a reflection of the ideological shift in British social and economic life which took place in the 1980s largely as a result of the efforts of Margaret Thatcher. Tort law, it might be said, represents paternalism and external constraint on economic activity; the legal form of the 1980s is contract, which represents free enterprise, personal autonomy, and individual responsibility. But we must set against this judicial policy of treating the law of tort as a last resort a clear legislative and governmental policy, manifestations of which we noted in Chapter 4, in favour of the use of tort law to protect the interests of economic actors in maintaining a strongly competitive economic environment. The Thatcher government apparently believed in the efficacy of the civil law as a means of attacking anti-competitive behaviour of various sorts. In one way, this is consistent with the judicial policy noted above because tort law, in this context, is contrasted with regulation: tort law represents individual initiative while regulation represents external state intervention. But in an important way, the increasing statutory provision of tort actions for breach of statutory duty in economic contexts recognizes the defects and shortcomings of the market, left to its own devices, in achieving the goals even of its proponents.

It is also important to notice that many of the statutory actions for breach of statutory duty with which we are concerned are designed primarily for use by businesses: these are not devices designed to protect individual consumers. Rather, they are designed to protect the less powerful business against more powerful competitors and even against what is seen as the abuse of governmental power. In this way, they seem to recognize that inequality, concentration, and abuse of market power are dangers intrinsic to the very existence and operation of the market. By contrast, although the common law draws no distinction between consumers and businesses, it is often expressed or implied in cases which marginalize tort that businesses can be expected to look after themselves; conversely, the interpretation given to the requirement of reasonableness in *Smith* v. *Bush*[96] suggests that the courts may now see the role of tort law at least partly in terms of consumer protection. Of course, the distinction between consumers and others is itself statutory; but the increasing provision of actions for breach of statutory duty in respect of market activities suggests that the government sees a role for the law of tort in protecting businesses as well as consumers. In this light, the tendency of the courts to relegate tort to a marginal role in protecting non-proprietary economic interests may be seen as too crude a reaction to the ideological shift of the last decade.

---

[96] [1990] 1 AC 831.

Furthermore, the common law approach has at its heart, as we have seen,[97] an extremely puzzling distinction between financial services and services associated with the manufacture, construction, and provision of tangible property. The courts seem to be giving the law of tort a larger role to play in respect of the former than the latter in a way which does not appear, on the surface at least, to be consistent with the policy of marginalizing tort. It is difficult to find any satisfactory explanation for this distinction. The judgments in the relevant cases do not give much help. The line of cases which allows recovery for loss suffered as a result of negligent financial services seems to be based implicitly on the desirability of giving incentives to take care; and explicitly on notions of purpose, reliance, proximity of relationship, and, particularly, assumption of responsibility. Imposition of liability could be justified on the basis of such notions in some cases at least involving manufacturing and construction services.

On the other side, the reasons adduced in *D. & F. Estates* for excluding recovery for economic loss add up to very little. There are assertions that the law of tort is concerned only with personal health and safety and with property damage (which is patently false), and that the spheres of tort and contract need to be kept distinct (for unstated reasons). Objection is also taken to the idea of imposing 'tortious warranties of quality'. Two ideas seem to underlie the objection: one is just that the law of tort is not concerned with quality; and the other is that, unless the plaintiff paid the defendant for the property, there would be no way of determining what the appropriate standard of quality was. But the law of tort is concerned with quality so far as financial services are concerned; and in that context, courts seem to feel able to decide appropriate levels of quality even in cases in which the plaintiff did not pay the defendant for the service. We might think that the refusal of tort law to concern itself with the quality of tangible property is simply a reflection of the contractual rule of *caveat emptor*. But *caveat emptor* has not applied to goods in anything like its full rigour for a very long time; and, in relation to real property, the force of the principle is surely satisfied by the rule that the vendor, as such, is immune from liability in tort in respect of the quality of the premises.

The Preservation of Competition

Contract is the prime legal form of market transactions. The perfect market is perfectly competitive. The real market is imperfectly competitive. Measures designed to control anti-competitive or excessively competitive behaviour seek to make the market as near to perfectly competitive as is consistent with other public policy goals. By seeking to prevent excessive concentration of market power or unfair elimination of competitors, such measures can be seen as preserving the conditions necessary for justifying a legal policy of min-

---

[97] See 207 above.

imum interference with the making of individual contracts. In this sense, they can be seen as furthering a policy of preserving the primacy of free and voluntary transactions over legally regulated transactions.

Both the statutory and the common law of tort play a part in preventing distortions in competition. The common law concerns itself mainly with excessive competition in the form of passing off, injurious falsehood, defamation, and interference with contracts and contractual expectancies. Intellectual property legislation is concerned with excessive competition; and the statutory law of tort plays a significant part, in theory at least, in controlling anti-competitive behaviour, as we saw in Chapter 4. Anti-discrimination legislation, as it applies to employment, can also be seen as concerned with preserving competition in the job market.

Both the courts and the legislature need to draw a line between fair and unfair competition. The common law does this in terms of the nature of the defendant's conduct by means of concepts such as intention and recklessness, unlawfulness, misrepresentation, and combination. Intellectual property legislation establishes monopoly rights designed to encourage research, innovation, and invention, and qualifies these in an attempt to prevent the right-holder freezing out competitors to an unacceptable extent. Competition and discrimination legislation adopts open-textured tests of uncompetitive behaviour and leaves it to various bodies to apply these tests in disputed cases. Whatever the technique used, the ultimate aim is the same.

Regulation of Industrial Relations

Common law and statute are inextricably intertwined in this context. The common law of tort, to the extent that it affects industrial action by workers, operates in the space left by the statutory immunities from tort liability. This space varies from time to time according to current government policy towards workers and unions. Although, in one sense, the common law is the basic law and the statutory provisions are laid on top of it, the attitude of the courts towards the development of the law in areas outside the statutory immunities is heavily influenced by statutory policy at any given time. Unfortunately, however, judges are not agreed about the appropriate reaction to the legislation. One view is that the common law ought to follow the legislation, so that if the statutory immunities are wide the common law outside the immunities ought to be pro-union also; and if the immunities are narrow, the common law ought to take an anti-union stance. But a different approach is possible: if statute gives unions a large area of immunity then perhaps they should be treated ungenerously outside that area; conversely, if the area of immunity is small then perhaps the courts should not strain to make life outside the areas of immunity any more difficult than necessary. In the absence of explicit statutory guidance, either approach could be painted as a possible legislative intention. So one should not expect to find any consistent judicial policy in this respect.

Reinforcement of Contract

Because contract is the prime legal form of market transactions, and because many market transactions involve the making of executory contracts, it is important that the law of contract provide remedies for parties to executory contracts whose contract-based expectations have been disappointed and whose commercial planning has been upset by failure to perform executory undertakings. The same need for stability and predictability as a basis for future planning also justifies the willingness of the law of tort to protect contractual rights against third party interference. The argument for the protection of contractual expectancies is not so strong, and so the law of tort is more willing to protect contractual rights from interference by conduct which is not itself unlawful or actionable.

It is sometimes said that the law of tort is more justified in protecting contractual expectancies than contractual rights because the latter are, but the former are not, also protected by contract law. The extension of the tort of interference with contract to failures of contract compliance which do not amount to actionable breaches of contract spoils the symmetry of this argument. The real issue is not whether the law of contract is prepared to protect one contracting party against the other; rather, it is whether the freedom of action of third parties ought to be constrained. The fact that the plaintiff could or could not sue a contracting party does not decide the question whether third parties ought to be discouraged from interfering with other people's business transactions to further their own ends. Nor can the nature of those ends be ignored: the common law defence of justification not only applies to interference with both rights and expectancies but also requires a delicate balancing of interests. Whether the distinctions between actionable breaches and non-actionable breaches and contractual expectancies is important must depend, to a large extent, on the facts of individual cases.

Regulating Commercial Transactions

The law about competition is, as it were, 'supply-side' law. Here we are concerned with the 'demand side'.

Consumer Protection

The common law's attempt to protect consumers as such[98] is largely embodied in the concept of misrepresentation. Passing off and injurious falsehood are based on misrepresentation, but these torts are designed primarily to protect competitors; it just so happens that in this context the interests of competitors and consumers coincide. More important is the fact that the law of tort tries to encourage honesty and care for truth in the contracting process.

---

[98] Rules designed to maintain healthy competition protect consumers indirectly; here our concern is with more direct regulation of individual transactions.

But the concern of the law of tort is not for truth as such (it provides no remedy for innocent misrepresentation), but only to discourage fraud and negligence. Furthermore, even within that field its interest in encouraging high standards of care in business dealings is limited: it will not, for example, give a remedy for negligent (or, probably, even fraudulent) failure to warn another that a fraud is being perpetrated on the other.[99]

The law of tort also provides protection from fraud and carelessness in utterance outside the contractual context. Further, it protects the consumers of financial services from shoddy work; this protection is most often, but not exclusively, afforded to parties in a contractual relationship with the service provider. We should note that the common law's definition of 'consumer' is different from the legislative one: the common law protects everyone from fraudulent or careless untruths, not just individuals acting in their own private interests. So the common law of tort is not concerned to protect against inequality of bargaining power:[100] this is seen as the function of the legislature.

The common law has apparently set its face against protecting purchasers of sub-standard goods or premises in the absence of misrepresentation, personal injury, or damage to 'other property'. There is even a dictum in *Junior Books* v. *Veitchi*[101] to the effect that consumers who have direct dealings only with a retailer could not recover from the manufacturer for defects of quality. This dictum is of great importance because *Junior Books* represents the high-water mark of the courts' willingness to compensate in tort for defects of quality.[102] Furthermore, except possibly in a few circumstances, damages are not recoverable in tort to forestall personal injury or property damage threatened by unsafe products or premises.[103]

As we saw in Chapter 4, tort techniques are little used in statutes concerned with trade descriptions; this is in marked contrast to recent statutory policy in respect of competition law. But this may mean no more than that the Thatcher government did not turn its attention to the question of civil actions for the enforcement of consumer protection legislation. On the other hand, consumers of gas, water, and electricity (after privatization of these industries), among others, are given actions for breach of statutory duty as a last resort to enforce compliance by suppliers with their obligations towards their customers.[104] We have also seen that there are a variety of statutory provisions which could be seen as consumer protection devices which impose

---

[99] See 202 above.

[100] I am here concerned with economic interests. The eclipse in this century of the defence of *volenti non fit injuria* in master–servant cases seems to provide a clear example of tort law protecting the weaker party.

[101] [1983] 1 AC 520, 533D *per* Lord Fraser.

[102] For academic views see J. A. Smillie (1978) 8 *NZULR* 109; C.J. Tobin (1970) 4 *NZULR* 36; P. Cane in C. J. Miller (ed.), *Comparative Product Liability* (London, 1986), 55; S. Whittaker (1986) 49 *MLR* 369.

[103] See 208 and 210 above.   [104] See 164 above.

liability for misrepresentations which induce contracts.[105] But none of these applies exclusively to consumers in the narrow sense of persons acting in a private capacity and solely with a view to personal gain: large corporations can use the provisions as freely as private individuals.

From our point of view, perhaps the most important statutory measure of consumer protection (in the narrow statutory sense of consumer) is the Unfair Contract Terms Act 1977. Through it consumer protection values are beginning to seep into the common law of tort: *Smith* v. *Bush*[106] supports the proposition that businesses (and individuals in a strong bargaining position) may be expected to protect themselves by contract in circumstances where individuals in a weak bargaining position would not be. In one way, this displays a more subtle approach than UCTA in that it acknowledges that not all consumers have equal bargaining strength.

Dealings with Property

The main issue here is whether the law of tort ought to protect contractual interests in property against purchasers. From a purchaser's point of view, the two most important desiderata are that the purchase should be capable of being concluded quickly and that the purchaser should be able to know exactly what he or she is buying. Similarly, it is important to institutions which finance the purchase of property to know exactly what they are being asked to finance. From this point of view, the best rule would be that contractual interests in goods should not be enforceable, or protected by the law of tort, against a purchaser of the property; this is particularly true in relation to unregistrable interests in property title to which is registered. However, such a rule may be too one-sided. The law of tort has apparently opted for the rule that the purchaser will be liable in tort for interference with contract only if the purchaser knew of the interest or was reckless as to its existence. Some argue that a purchaser should only be bound by interests of which the purchaser actually knew. The choice between the alternatives is a matter for fine value-judgement.

Commercial Expectations

Another way in which the courts seek to prevent the law of tort interfering unduly with commercial activity is by seeking to fashion rules which reflect what are called 'commercial expectations'. This was discussed in Chapter 6;[107] the deference to existing commercial practice which underlies it is of questionable value, but the ideological shift of the last decade has, no doubt, reinforced it.

Certainty in the Law

Commerce of certain sorts thrives on certainty and predictability. Thus, courts often justify particular decisions in cases dealing with commercial

---

[105] See 179 above.   [106] [1990] 1 AC 381.   [107] See 320 above.

transactions by pointing to precedents. In this context, too, so-called 'bright-line' rules are highly prized. Such rules are easy to apply because they turn on easily ascertained facts and not on difficult, fact-specific, value judgements. Bright line rules also minimize litigation and encourage settlement of disputes.[108] In this way, the courts can prevent judicial resources being used to decide cases which they consider to be of relatively little social importance.

Controlling the Quality of 'Goods' and Services

It is worth noting again that the common law of tort plays a much larger role in regulating the quality of financial services than of services associated with the manufacture of goods and the construction of premises; and hence, it plays a relatively small role in regulating the quality of goods and premises. So far as goods are concerned, Part I of the Consumer Protection Act 1987 embodies a similar unwillingness to control quality as such; and in relation to dwellings, the Defective Premises Act 1972 is concerned only with fitness for human habitation.

Loss-Spreading

Losses can be spread in a number of ways: insurance, increased charges for the goods or services which gave rise to the loss, reduced wages or dividends. Loss-spreading[109] is desirable because it reduces the impact of losses on particular individuals and so reduces financial disruption in the affairs of individuals. For present purposes, the most important means of loss-spreading is insurance. The prevalence of insurance, both first-party and third-party, means that economic losses may be spread whether or not they are compensatable in a tort (or other) action. But, of course, neither loss insurance nor liability insurance is universal; nor, in respect of any particular loss, is it necessarily the case that loss insurance will be as readily or cheaply available as liability insurance, or vice versa; nor, of course, will any particular loss be spread in the same way by both types of insurance. In the light of these facts, it is difficult to see loss-spreading as an aim (as opposed to a consequence) of loss allocation by means of tort law. At best, we may view insurability as one, but only one, criterion of loss allocation.

We discussed the insurability criterion at some length in Chapter 9. Here we need only ask whether there is any evidence that the law does seek to promote loss-spreading via insurance. The common law could hardly be seen as promoting liability insurance: it may be true that some heads of tort liability exist only because they can be insured against. But it is unlikely that a judge would ever refuse to impose liability simply on the ground that it could not

---

[108] Harris and Veljanovski (1983) 5 *Law & Policy Q* 97.
[109] P. Cane, *Atiyah's Accidents, Compensation and the Law*, 5th edn. (London, 1987), 354–7; J. A. Jolowicz (1972) 12 *JSPTL* 91 (loss 'absorption').

be insured against if other grounds for imposing liability existed. Statutory provisions for compulsory liability insurance (or compulsory industry-wide compensation schemes) can be seen as designed to promote loss-spreading, although they are more convincingly viewed as designed to protect plaintiffs than to reduce the impact of liability on the defendant. Provisions requiring or encouraging loss insurance are the best evidence of a policy of seeking to reduce the impact of losses by spreading them. Outside the area of personal injuries, such provisions are virtually non-existent.

So far as the common law is concerned, the only cases which can at all convincingly be seen as based on a policy of encouraging loss insurance are those which refuse to impose liability for relational loss or for failure to prevent loss being caused to the plaintiff by the acts of a third party. Lord Denning made explicit reference to the possibility of loss insurance in several such cases. On the other hand, these cases are also replete with arguments based on traditional tort ideas of foreseeability and control. There are also cases in which the courts have refused to impose liability for failure to purchase loss insurance on another's behalf or to advise another of the wisdom of purchasing such insurance.[110] These cases are equivocal because a decision either way could be seen as encouraging the purchase of loss insurance by the defendant on the plaintiff's behalf if the duty contended for was held to exist; or by the plaintiff, if it was not. The reasoning actually employed does not advert to the issue. In *Reid* v. *Rush & Tompkins Group*[111] there is much discussion of the employer's statutory duty to insure against liability for injuries to employees caused by fellow employees; but since the insurance in question is liability insurance, it does not tell us anything directly about the court's attitude to the desirability of loss insurance. On the other hand, there are many situations in which tort liability can arise despite the the fact that the injured party was covered by loss insurance: cases of physical damage to tangible property provide the most obvious example.

Furthering Particular Public Interests

In Chapter 5 we saw that the courts promote a variety of public interests against the private interests which it is the main function of the law of tort to protect. There is no point in reiterating the discussion.

3. CONCLUSIONS

It will be clear that I do not belong to that school of thought which thinks it important to search for some unitary over-arching theory of the aims or rationale of tort law. Tort law is a human artifact which is infected by the

---

[110] See 203 above.   [111] [1990] 1 WLR 212.

confusion and potential mutual inconsistency of the many aims which society seeks to achieve through law in general and through tort law in particular. For this reason, I have not sought to rank the functions surveyed in this Chapter in any sort of priority. The view which has informed this Chapter and the whole of this book is that tort law plays an important part in protecting economic interests, that it does this in a complex and inconclusive way, and that its aims and effects are multifarious and often not mutually-reinforcing. In this respect, tort law is no different from any other area of law.

Nevertheless, I believe that the examination in this book of the way tort law protects economic interests has yielded some important insights which provide useful signposts in exploring the complex world of tort law and which deserve reiteration here. First, tort law involves the use of a set of techniques for protecting economic (and other) interests which are identifiably different from those which are used by other bodies of 'private law' such as the law of property, trusts, and contract. By attempting to describe the techniques used by these different bodies of law, we gain a better understanding of the borders between them and of the way they interact with one another. This emphasis on juridical techniques is, I believe, a valuable side-effect of the organization of this book in terms of protected interests, because this approach leads us to ask *how* these interests are protected.

Secondly, the interactions between different bodies of law which protect economic interests are of three quite different kinds. In some ways they reinforce one another; for example, tort law plays an important part in protecting rights created in accordance with the rules of property and contract law. In other respects, bodies of law interlock; for example, in recent years the courts have made many attempts to work out when the law of tort should help people who have not protected their economic interests by contract—in other words, to work out where the protection offered by tort law should end and that provided by contract law begin. Thirdly, bodies of law may overlap: one and the same set of facts may give rise to more than one cause of action—in tort and contract, for example.

A third important insight generated by the discussion in this book is that in order properly to understand the techniques of tort law we must break down some of the barriers between common law and statute. If we identify tort law in terms of a particular set of juridical techniques, there is no reason why statutory provisions which utilize those techniques should not be treated as an integral part of it, and every reason why they should be so treated. This is why I have considered statutory intellectual property rights in some detail in this book and why, in Chapter 4, I discussed aspects of discrimination and competition law (for instance). Furthermore, the significance and potential of common law causes of action can sometimes only be fully understood in the light of their interaction with statutory causes of action: the relationship between passing off and infringement of a trade mark, and between the common law and statutory remedies available to evicted tenants, provide good examples of this point.

Fourthly, it is important to our understanding of tort law not to be satisfied with an account of the rules and principles (the doctrine) of tort law, but also to consider the social impact of this doctrine. A full examination of the social impact of tort law would require a mass of empirical research data which does not and never will exist. However, this does not prevent us from seeking to identify the sorts of issues and questions which would need to be considered and answered in order properly to assess the social impact of tort law. I tried to identify some of these issues and questions in Chapters 7, 8, and 9. Once again, approaching tort law in terms of the techniques it uses for protecting interests leads naturally on to a consideration of how those techniques operate in practice and of alternatives to them, such as regulation.

Finally, I think that the discussion in this book shows that focussing on economic interests as I defined them in Chapter 1 yields valuable insights about the structure and purposes of tort law. For instance, it leads us to consider the similarities, differences, and interactions between tort law and bodies of law, such as those dealing intellectual property, restitution, and trusts, which are solely concerned with economic interests but which are usually considered more or less in isolation from tort law. I also believe that the recognition that the only interest people often have in their tangible property is economic leads us to ask important questions about the way the law of tort deals with physical damage to such property. Economic interests are impersonal in the sense that they can be exchanged for other things of precisely equivalent value. Non-economic (such as dignitary) interests derive their personal nature from the fact that each individual is unique. If and to the extent that the law of tort is or ought to be more concerned to protect non-economic interests than to protect economic interests, it is important to recognize that tangible property does not, merely by virtue of being tangible, have non-economic value.

Index